THE OLD TESTAMENT

THE OLD TESTAMENT

A Historical and Literary Introduction
to the Hebrew Scriptures

MICHAEL D. COOGAN

New York   Oxford
OXFORD UNIVERSITY PRESS
2006

To Pam, with love

Oxford University Press, Inc., publishes works that further Oxford University's
objective of excellence in research, scholarship, and education.

Oxford   New York
Auckland   Cape Town   Dar es Salaam   Hong Kong   Karachi
Kuala Lumpur   Madrid   Melbourne   Mexico City   Nairobi
New Delhi   Shanghai   Taipei   Toronto

With offices in
Argentina   Austria   Brazil   Chile   Czech Republic   France   Greece
Guatemala   Hungary   Italy   Japan   Poland   Portugal   Singapore
South Korea   Switzerland   Thailand   Turkey   Ukraine   Vietnam

Published by Oxford University Press, Inc.
198 Madison Avenue, New York, New York 10016
http://www.oup.com

Oxford is a registered trademark of Oxford University Press

Library of Congress Cataloging-in-Publication Data

Coogan, Michael David.
The Old Testament : a historical and literary introduction to the Hebrew scriptures / Michael D. Coogan. p. cm.
Includes bibliographical references and index.
ISBN-13: 978-0-19-513911-2 (pbk.)

ISBN-13: 978-0-19-513910-5 (hardcover)

1. Bible. O.T.-History of Biblical events. 2. Bible.
   O.T.-Criticism, interpretation, etc. 3. Bible. O.T.-Language, style.
   I. Title.
   BS1197.C56 2006
   221.6'1—dc22
   2005027222

The editor and publisher gratefully acknowledge permission to quote from the New Revised Standard Version
of the Bible, copyright © 1989 by the Division of Christian Education of the National Council of Churches
of Christ in the U.S.A. Used by permission. All rights reserved.

Printing number: 9 8 7 6 5 4 3

Printed in the United States of America
on acid-free paper

BRIEF CONTENTS

Contents

PREFACE

The title of this text indicates its scope: It covers all of the books that form the Bible for Jews and the Old Testament for Christians. Recognizing that differences exist both between these religious communities and among Christians about precisely which books belong in these categories, my coverage here is maximal. In traditional terms, this book covers the entire Hebrew Bible, as well as those books included in Christian canons known as the apocryphal or deuterocanonical books.

The principle of arrangement is chronological. I follow the narrative chronology of the first third of the Bible, from Genesis to 2 Kings; for the sixth century BCE and later I adhere to a historical chronology. Within this chronological framework I discuss books as they are dated by internal evidence or by scholarly consensus regarding the period being discussed; thus, Amos and Hosea are covered in the chapter dealing with the northern kingdom of Israel in the eighth century BCE, Jeremiah in the chapter dealing with Judah in the late seventh and early sixth centuries BCE, and so forth.

Rather than begin with introductory material about canon, history, geography, and the like, I introduce students immediately to the biblical text. I also begin where the Bible does, with the opening chapters of Genesis, although of course this is not the oldest biblical material. I intersperse the chapters dealing with the early part of Genesis with background material. Those who prefer to give students an initial overview before turning to the Bible may choose to begin with Chapters 2 and 4, as well as the Appendix.

I begin with a close look at a relatively small amount of material in Genesis 1–11 to introduce students inductively to new ways of interpreting what for many is familiar material. Beginning with Genesis 12, however, I have followed a general principle of proportionality; that is, for the most part I have attempted to give the various books discussion roughly proportionate to their length, so as not to privilege any one biblical book or period.

Each chapter begins with a short introduction connecting the chapter with what has gone before and providing a preview of the material to be covered in the chapter. Each chapter closes with a "retrospect and prospect," summarizing the chapter as well as linking it with what has preceded and what will follow. At the end of each chapter is a list of important terms that have been highlighted in the chapter; these terms are defined in the glossary at the end of the book. There is also a short list of questions for review.

Each chapter is followed by a brief bibliography, with suggestions for further reading and research on the material covered in the chapter. The items have been selected to introduce students to major tools of biblical research and to provide recent expositions of views expressed in the chapter as well as of other approaches. I have not attempted to provide a comprehensive history of interpretation because that level of detail is not appropriate for an introductory text, and I have generally refrained from discussing the views of individual scholars except for the most important. A more general bibliography is found at the back of the book, and the works listed give ample references to fuller treatments.

One of the problems with using a text in introductory courses, I have found, is that students tend to read it rather than the Bible itself. For the most part, therefore, I have refrained from detailed paraphrase of the biblical sources. Often, however, to introduce students to different interpretive strategies and to the problems of interpretation, I have provided more detailed analyses of relatively small units.

The primary translation used is the New Revised Standard Version (NRSV), although I have occasionally modified it when a more literal, or in my view a more correct, translation is important for the discussion. I also have followed the numbering of chapters and verses in the NRSV. I have used a simplified transliteration system for Hebrew that will be apparent to those familiar with the language.

ACKNOWLEDGMENTS

In working on this book I have had the support and assistance of a large number of people, and I gladly acknowledge them here.

First, I am grateful to the superb editorial and production staff at Oxford University Press, and in particular to my editor, Robert Miller. No author could wish for a more professional and collegial publisher. I am also grateful to several readers of the manuscript at various stages for Oxford, and in particular to Marc Brettler, whose detailed and constructive criticism improved this book in many ways.

Versions of this book were used in manuscript form by students at Stonehill College, Harvard Divinity School, and Oberlin College, and I very much appreciate their comments and corrections. Among them I especially thank Larry Spears, who read the entire manuscript and made innumerable valuable suggestions about style and content. In a broader sense, this book was formed over many years of teaching, and my students at Harvard University, Wellesley College, The University of Waterloo, Boston College, and Stonehill College helped shape this book and clarify my thinking in ways that fellow teachers easily appreciate.

The administration of Stonehill College has been generous in providing support to enable this work to move forward, and I am grateful for it.

I also wish to thank the many colleagues and friends who assisted me with matters large and small, especially Frank Moore Cross, Nathaniel DesRosiers, Greg Schmidt Goering, Jo Ann Hackett, Paul Hanson, Elizabeth Hill, Robert Hopkins, John Huehnergard, Philip King, Mary Joan Leith, Peter Machinist, Kyle McCarter, and Lawrence Stager.

Finally, it is a pleasure to recognize the enormous contribution of my wife, Pamela Hill, who read every word—truly a labor of love!—and whose incisive comments and suggestions helped me find my voice and say what I intended. I dedicate this book to her.

ABBREVIATIONS

Acts	Acts of the Apostles		KJV	King James Version
Am	Amos		Lam	Lamentations
Bar	Baruch		Lev	Leviticus
BCE	Before the Common Era (used in dates instead of BC)		Lk	Luke
			Macc	Maccabees
CE	Common Era (used in dates instead of AD)		Mal	Malachi
			Mic	Micah
chap(s).	chapter(s)		Mk	Mark
Chr	Chronicles		Mt	Matthew
Cor	Corinthians		Nah	Nahum
Dan	Daniel		Neh	Nehemiah
Deut	Deuteronomy		NRSV	New Revised Standard Version
Eccl	Ecclesiastes		Num	Numbers
Esd	Esdras		Pet	Peter
Esth	Esther		Phil	Philippians
Ex	Exodus		Prov	Proverbs
Ezek	Ezekiel		Ps(s)	Psalm(s)
Gen	Genesis		Rev	Revelation
Hab	Habakkuk		Rom	Romans
Heb	(The Letter to the) Hebrews		Sam	Samuel
Hebr.	Hebrew		Sir	Sirach
Hos	Hosea		Song	Song of Solomon
Isa	Isaiah		Tim	Timothy
Jas	James		Tob	Tobit
Jdt	Judith		v(v).	verse(s)
Jer	Jeremiah		Wis	Wisdom of Solomon
Jn	John		Zech	Zechariah
Jon	Jonah		Zeph	Zephaniah
Josh	Joshua			
Judg	Judges			

CREDITS

PART ONE

COSMIC ORIGINS

CREATIONS

CHAPTER

1

Genesis 1–3

The Bible begins with the book of Genesis, which means "beginning," and, more literally, "birth." The book of Genesis is a narrative about beginnings: of the world as the ancients understood it, of the first humans, and especially of the ancestors of Israel. The entire narrative is tied together by a series of genealogies, or births, beginning with the "generations of the heavens and the earth" (Gen 2.4) and continuing through Abraham and Isaac to the descendants of Israel's ancestor Jacob (37.2; see also 46.7–27). We will start where the Bible does, with the very beginnings of the cosmos, in Genesis 1–3. In our examination of these opening chapters, we will see how the biblical writers adopted, adapted, and sometimes rejected myths from the rest of the ancient Near East.

THE BOOK OF GENESIS

Genesis can be divided by its content into two major sections. Chapters 1–11 are a series of accounts of cosmic origins, including accounts of the creation of the world, the garden of Eden, and the first humans until after the Flood. Linked to these chapters by genealogies, chapters 12–50 are the beginnings of the story of the Bible's principal focus, that of ancient Israel; in them we read of Israel's ancestors Abraham and Sarah; Isaac and Rebekah; and Jacob and Leah, Rachel, Zilpah, and Bilhah and their children.

Like most of the books of the Bible, Genesis is a complex work. It was compiled over many centuries by ancient writers who made use of all sorts of historical and literary materials; it was given its final form during the second half of the first millennium BCE, long after the occurrence of the events it narrates. A major accomplishment of modern biblical scholarship has been the identification of many stages of this development. Because of its importance and its complexity, Genesis will be treated in the next several chapters.

In this chapter we will examine two narratives (chaps. 1–3) about how the world as the ancients perceived it came to be, two distinct creation **myths** (see Box 1.4). Careful examination of these myths will show both their differences from one another and their similarities to other ancient Near Eastern texts.

GENESIS 1 AND THE SABBATH

The first account of creation, with which the Bible opens, is in Genesis 1.1–2.4a, that is, the first chapter and the first few verses of the second (see Box 1.1). It begins:

> When God began to create the heavens and the earth—the earth was a formless void, and darkness was on the face of Deep and a wind from God was swooping over the face of the waters—then God said, "Let there be light!" and there was light.

The more familiar translation of the opening words—"In the beginning God created"—is influenced by the beginning of the Fourth Gospel (Jn 1.1: "In the beginning was the word") but is incorrect according to a strict grammatical interpretation of the original Hebrew, which should be translated "When God began to create" or, more literally, "In the beginning of God's creat-

ing." The verse thus does not describe "creation out of nothing," a later theological notion, nor does it address more modern questions such as the ultimate origins of matter; rather, it deals with the formation of a cosmos, an ordered universe, out of preexisting but chaotic matter—an unformed earth and an unruly sea over which a wind from God (see Gen 8.1) swoops like a large bird (see Deut 32.11).

The process of creation begins with the divine command "Let there be light!", a command that is immediately fulfilled—"and there was light." God separates the light from the darkness and names them "Day" and "Night." Thus ends the first day. The process of creation continues, with a kind of liturgical rhythm, through six days in all.

Box 1.1 CHAPTER AND VERSE

Since ancient times the Bible has been separated into books. In the late Middle Ages each book was divided for easy reference into larger units, or chapters, and a few centuries later the chapters were further divided into smaller units, or verses. Modern printing convention usually puts a period or colon between the numbers designating the chapters and the verses, so that Genesis 1.2 (or 1:2) means the book of Genesis, the first chapter, the second verse. That is the system used in all Bibles, and the one we will use in this book.

The divisions do not always correspond either to the natural divisions of the text or to modern understandings of it. The opening chapters of Genesis actually consist of two separate accounts of creation. The first of these continues from the first chapter into the first few verses of the second, and the second begins in the middle of the fourth verse of the second chapter. Thus, in shorthand notation, the first account is found in Genesis 1.1–2.4a, and the second in Genesis 2.4b–3.24.

Different print editions also have some variation in numbering. The system used in this book is that of the New Revised Standard Version (NRSV), which follows the tradition of the ancient translation of the Hebrew Bible into Greek. Hebrew manuscripts sometimes have a different numbering. For example, in Genesis Hebrew manuscripts start chapter 32 after 31.54, while in Greek manuscripts, followed by the NRSV, chapter 32 ends with verse 55; there is thus a one-verse discrepancy between the two systems, so that NRSV 32.1 = Hebrew 32.2. Similar discrepancies are found throughout the Bible and are noted in the textual notes to the NRSV.

The sequence of events can be outlined as follows:

Day 1	light		*Day 4*	heavenly bodies
Day 2	dome		*Day 5*	aquatic creatures and birds
Day 3	land plants		*Day 6*	land animals humans

This arrangement is a literary one, with creations on each of the first three days paralleled by successive creations on each of the next three. Thus, corresponding to the creation on the first day of undifferentiated light is the creation on the fourth day of the heavenly bodies that produce light; corresponding to the creation on the second day of the dome that keeps back the waters is the creation on the fifth day of those creatures that inhabit the regions nearest the dome, the birds and sea creatures; and corresponding to the double creation on the third day of land and plants is the creation on the sixth of animals and humans, who live on the land and eat the plants.

Each act of creation is described by a formula: "God said . . . it was so (*or* God created) . . . God saw that it was good." As the repetition of the formula on the third and sixth days indicates, on each of them are two separate acts of creation. This may be a literary device, or it may indicate that an eight-act scheme has been fitted into a six-day chronology so that the seventh day may be highlighted (see Box 1.2).

The last act of creation is that of humans, made "in the image of God," whose role in the universe is to be its rulers—to "fill the earth and subdue it; and have dominion over . . . every living thing" (1.27–28). But that is not the conclusion of the narrative. Rather, it ends with the divine rest on the seventh day, and thus one of its purposes is to highlight the sabbath, the day of rest (see Box 1.3).

Enuma elish

Although at first reading Genesis 1 is apparently monotheistic, with a sole creator responsible for everything that exists, a number of ancient polytheistic texts have similarities to the Genesis ac-count. One of these is *Enuma elish*, a work in seven tablets that describes how the god **Marduk** became the king of the gods and the chief god of Babylon. Although often called "the Babylonian creation epic," in fact *Enuma elish* is a kind of epic in praise of Marduk, reflecting the rise to power of Babylon under Nebuchadrezzar I in the late second millennium BCE.

The poem opens with a description of the world before creation:

> When above the skies had not been named,
> Nor earth below pronounced by name.

The opening words are also the conventional title of the poem, for *enuma elish* means "when above." Then, we are told, two primeval realities, Apsu, the god of the fresh water, and **Tiamat**, the goddess of the salt waters, "mixed their waters together," and from their union the first generation of gods was born; among these were earth and sky. The myth thus explains how, in southern Mesopotamia, the land and hence the horizon, the sky, came into being where the fresh waters of the Tigris and Euphrates issue into the salt water of the Persian Gulf, and a delta was formed.

Subsequent generations of gods were born, and their noisy gatherings disturbed Apsu, who, despite Tiamat's objections, decided to kill the younger gods. They, however, learned of the plan and killed Apsu. Enraged, Tiamat then decided to kill the younger gods, and they were apparently powerless to stop her. Finally, one of the youngest of the gods, Marduk, the god of the storm, proposed that he would defeat Tiamat on condition that he be given supreme power among the gods. They agreed, and Marduk set out to battle Tiamat with his weapons—a bow, lightning bolts, a net, and various winds:

> Face to face they came, Tiamat and Marduk, sage of the gods,
> They engaged in combat, they closed for battle.
> The Lord spread his net and made it encircle her,
> To her face he dispatched the evil wind, which had been behind:
> Tiamat opened her mouth to swallow it,
> And he forced in the evil wind so that she could not close her lips.

Box 1.2 GENESIS AND SCIENCE

Ever since the Bible came to be considered authoritative, the account in the opening chapter of Genesis of creation in six days has often been taken as a scientifically accurate account of the beginnings of our universe. Using biblical chronology literally, it was calculated by some that the world was created in six days, from October 18 to 23 in 4004 BCE. As scientific understanding advanced, astronomers, geologists, paleontologists, and other scientists were frequently denounced because their discoveries were inconsistent with the biblical account.

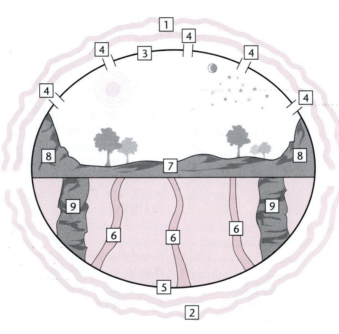

FIGURE 1.1. The ancient Israelite view of the world as described in Genesis 1. In this view, which was shared by many ancient Near Eastern and Mediterranean peoples, surrounding the world is water, shown here as the waters above the earth (1) and the waters below the earth (2). The waters are kept in place by a double "dome" or "firmament." In the upper dome (3), the sky, are "windows" (4) through which rain is released, and from the lower dome (5) springs and rivers (6) flow upward to the earth (7). Into the upper dome are set the heavenly bodies, which rise in the east and set in the west. According to other biblical passages, "pillars" or mountains (8) support the upper dome, and other pillars (9) support the earth.

Whatever the character of the inspiration of the Bible, however, it was written by men (and, probably, women) whose knowledge was that of their times, not ours. In their understanding, like that of their contemporaries, the earth was the center of the universe, and the heavenly bodies revolved around the earth (see Figure 1.1). But they were writing a religious rather than a scientific text. One of the religious messages of the first account of creation is the importance of the **sabbath**, whose observance is part of the very fabric of the universe. Since the sabbath lasts for one day, and also since the word "day" elsewhere in the Bible means what we would call a twenty-four-hour period, it is misguided to attempt to identify the first six days of Genesis 1 with geological eras, so that modern science and the narrative of creation are in harmony. Moreover, it is impossible to reconcile the account given here with that which follows in Genesis 2–3, which suggests that even for ancient readers the two accounts of creation were not taken as literally true.

Fierce winds distended her belly;
Her insides were constipated and she stretched her
   mouth wide,
He shot an arrow which pierced her belly,
Split her down the middle and extinguished her
   life.

The mythic battle also has a correlation in nature, in a dark thundercloud over the sea, roiling it and exposing its depths. (See Figure 1.2.)

Marduk then proceeded to take Tiamat's body and to form the cosmos from it:

He divided the monstrous shape and created mar-
   vels from it.
He sliced her in half like a fish for drying:
Half of her he put up to roof the sky,
Drew a bolt across and made a guard hold it.
Her waters he arranged so that they could not
   escape.

In the sky he established the constellations as "stands for the great gods," which would determine the calendar—the twelve months of the year and the phases of the moon. Then, having established Babylon as his own home, he rewarded the gods for their support by creating humans. With the consent of the divine assembly, Tiamat's ally Qingu was killed, and from his blood humans were created:

He created mankind from his blood,
Imposed the toil of the gods (on man) and released
   the gods from it.

The epic concludes with a divine banquet at which the gods celebrated Marduk's victory and acknowledged his supremacy by reciting a litany of his fifty epithets; this comprises about one-seventh of the epic, another indication of its character.

Enuma elish and Genesis

Like *Enuma elish* and other ancient Near Eastern texts that include accounts of creation, or **cosmologies**, Genesis begins with a temporal clause describing realties that existed before the process of creation began; the next account of creation in the Bible, which begins in Genesis 2.4b, also has the same syntax. Neither the biblical writers nor their counterparts elsewhere were interested in the abstract philosophical question of ultimate origins. Rather, both myths offer an explanation of the structure of the cosmos, an account of how the creator deity ordered already existing matter. "When God began to create," the earth was "a formless void," and there were also turbulent waters; creation was the process by which these already existing realities were transformed into an orderly cosmos.

The second verse of Genesis seems to allude to the battle between the storm-god and the primeval sea, found in *Enuma elish* and in other ancient Near Eastern sources: "[D]arkness was on the face of Deep and a wind from God was swoop-

Box 1.3 **THE SABBATH IN JEWISH AND CHRISTIAN TRADITION**

The word "sabbath" in Hebrew (*shabbat*) is related to the verb meaning "to rest," as in Genesis 2.2–3, which also makes it clear that it is to be the seventh day of the week. In the ancient system of reckoning, the seventh day of the week was Saturday (see, for example, Mt 28.1, where the first day of the week was the day after the sabbath). As in Genesis, the Decalogue (the Ten Commandments) in Exodus 20 connects the sabbath with creation:

> Remember the sabbath day, and keep it holy. Six days you shall labor and do all your work. But the seventh day is a sabbath to the LORD your God; you shall not do any work—you, your son or your daughter, your male or female slave, your livestock, or the alien resident in your towns. For in six days the LORD made heaven and earth, the sea, and all that is in them, but rested the seventh day; therefore the LORD blessed the sabbath day and consecrated it. (Ex 20.8–11)

Another version of the Decalogue, however, gives a different motivation:

> Observe the sabbath day and keep it holy, as the LORD your God commanded you. Six days you shall labor and do all your work. But the seventh day is a sabbath to the LORD your God; you shall not do any work—you, or your son or your daughter, or your male or female slave, or your ox or your donkey, or any of your livestock, or the resident alien in your towns, so that your male and female slave may rest as well as you. Remember that you were a slave in the land of Egypt, and the LORD your God brought you out from there with a mighty hand and an outstretched arm; therefore the LORD your God commanded you to keep the sabbath day. (Deut 5.12–15)

This humanitarian motivation is anticipated in one of the earliest biblical law codes: "Six days you shall do your work, but on the seventh day you shall rest, so that your ox and your donkey may have relief, and your homeborn slave and the resident alien may be refreshed" (Ex 23.12). These variants, however, share the notion that the Israelites are to imitate God—by resting as he did or by treating their slaves as he had treated them in Egypt.

The origins of the sabbath are obscure, and no convincing parallels in other ancient Near Eastern cultures exist. It is mentioned only infrequently in biblical narratives concerning Israel's earlier history, and the earliest reference in the Bible to the sabbath apart from the Decalogue is Amos 8.5. By the time of the exile to Babylon in the sixth century BCE, however, sabbath observance had become a hallmark of Jewish observance, as it is today. In Jewish tradition, the sabbath, like all days, begins at sundown, as Genesis suggests in its phrasing "There was evening and there was morning," and thus runs from Friday at sunset to Saturday at sunset.

The earliest Christians continued to observe Saturday as the sabbath, but soon also observed Sunday, the first day of the week, as a day of religious assembly (Acts 20.7; this day is called "the Lord's day" in Rev 1.10), and by the second century CE they had abandoned the seventh-day observance in favor of the first day, in part to distinguish themselves from Jews. Some Christian groups, however, such as the Seventh Day Adventists, continue to observe the seventh day, Saturday, as the day of rest, since there is no biblical authorization to change it to Sunday.

is found elsewhere in the Bible (Ps 33.6; see also Isa 55.10–11); in an Egyptian creation myth in which the god Ptah created other gods "through what the heart thought and the tongue commanded"; in a hymn to the Mesopotamian moon-god Nanna, whose creative and fruitful word is praised; and in *Enuma elish* itself, in which Marduk's command can both create and destroy (4.25).

In the last act of creation, the second on the sixth day, the formula by which God creates human beings varies significantly from that used for earlier creations: "God said: 'Let us make humans, in our image, according to our likeness'" (Gen 1.26). The use of the plural here, as elsewhere in the primeval history (Gen 3.22; 11.7), probably refers to the **divine council**, the assembly of the gods, which is invoked here for the last, climactic, and most significant act of creation. In *Enuma elish* the assembly of the gods also ratifies Marduk's decision to execute Qingu and from his blood to make humans. The biblical writers shared the widespread concept of a supreme deity presiding over the other gods, and the Bible contains frequent references to the divine council (for example, Job 1.6; Ps 82.1; Jer 23.18).

Finally, like *Enuma elish*, the Bible begins with a series of births. This first account of creation ends with the summary phrase: "These are the generations of the heavens and the earth" (2.4). The word translated "generations" means something like "genealogy," but etymologically it has to do with giving birth or begetting. The same word is used throughout Genesis to introduce the lists of descendants of various individuals, beginning in 5.1: "These are the generations of Adam" (see also 6.9; 11.10, 27; 25.19; 37.2). The begetting of the elemental aspects of the cosmos—the heavens and the earth—by the creator deity is also found in Egyptian myth.

The first account of creation in Genesis both employs and alludes to mythical concepts and phrasing, but at the same time it also adapts, transforms, and rejects them. Thus, while in *Enuma elish* and other ancient Near Eastern creation myths such realities as the sun, moon, constellations, and even the primeval sea are deities,

FIGURE 1.2. Marduk standing victorious on Tiamat, who is depicted as a dragon whose home is in the waters. This drawing is based on a mid-second-millennium BCE relief.

ing over the face of the waters." Moreover, the Hebrew word for "deep," *tehom*, is linguistically related to the name of the goddess Tiamat, and in the Bible *tehom* never occurs with the definite article; thus it should probably be translated "Deep" rather than "the deep" wherever it occurs. Genesis 1.2 thus seems to be setting the stage for a retelling of the battle, but instead we are told simply that God spoke.

The notion that the word of a deity was creative and powerful is not confined to Genesis; it in Genesis there is only one god, who creates what for other cultures are divine. To avoid even the hint that these other deities are present, the authors of Genesis 1 use circumlocution to designate the sun and moon—"the greater light to rule the day and the lesser light to rule the night" (1.16), although "sun" and "moon" are common words elsewhere in the Bible; and among the creatures created on the fifth day are "the great sea monsters" (1.21), the singular form of which elsewhere even in the Bible is a mythological being (the "dragon" of Isa 27.1; 51.9; Ps 74.13; Job 7.12).

Moreover, in *Enuma elish* and other ancient Near Eastern cosmologies human beings were created to do the work that the gods had previously been doing for themselves—it was now humans who would build the gods' houses (their temples) and grow and prepare their food (sacrifices), so that the gods would have a life of ease. In this understanding humans were essentially the slaves of the powers that control the cosmos, but in Genesis 1 human beings are its rulers, given dominion over every living thing (1.28; see also Ps 8.5–8).

Thus, while alluding to older mythic traditions, the first account of creation in Genesis also partially demythologizes them. This account, as we will see, is probably to be dated to the time of the exile in Babylon in the sixth century BCE. Its authors are in effect giving an alternative to the account found in *Enuma elish*, which other Babylonian texts, also of the sixth century, inform us was recited annually during the spring new year festival in Babylon. At the same time they stress the importance of the sabbath, which the exiles could continue to observe even in Babylon.

The Battle before Creation Elsewhere in the Bible

Although the first account of creation in Genesis 1, while alluding to the battle between the storm-god and the sea that preceded creation, also partially rejects that mythic motif, other biblical passages from different periods retain the mythological language. Psalm 74 is typical:

God my King is from of old,
   working salvation in the earth.
It was you who drove back Sea by your might;
   who broke the heads of the dragons in the waters.
It was you who crushed the heads of Leviathan;
   who gave him as food for the creatures of the wilderness.
It was you who cut openings for springs and torrents;
   it was you who dried up ever-flowing streams.
Yours is the day, yours also the night;
   it was you who established the luminaries and the sun.
It was you who fixed all the bounds of the earth;
   it was you who made summer and winter.
   (vv. 12–17)

Here the primeval chaotic sea—also called a multiheaded dragon and Leviathan (see Box 28.3)—is defeated by the creator before he begins his work of creation. Similar language is used in Job 38.8–11; Psalm 104; and Psalm 89.5–12, in which the primeval watery adversary of the deity is also given the name Rahab, as in Isaiah 51.9–10. (See further page 103.)

Thus, in other parts of the Bible not only is there often no reference to the six days of creation, but there is also a much more explicit mythology that the biblical writers shared with their ancient Near Eastern contemporaries (see Box 1.4). For the biblical writers, of course, the deity who was victorious over the primeval chaotic waters was the god of Israel:

By his power he stilled Sea,
   and by his skill he crushed Rahab,
by his wind the heavens were made clear,
   his hand pierced the fleeing serpent.
Lo, these are but glimpses of his power;
   what a faint whisper we hear of him:
   who can comprehend the thunder of his might.
   (Job 26.12–14)

THE SECOND ACCOUNT OF CREATION (GEN 2.4b–3.24)

Like Genesis 1, *Enuma elish*, and a number of other ancient Near Eastern accounts of creation,

Box 1.4 MYTH AND THE BIBLE

Ancient cultures were as intrigued as we are by beginnings, and they constructed elaborate myths—narratives in which the principal characters are gods—to explain their own prehistory. The establishment of the natural and social orders is typically presented in these myths as the work of a deity, usually the principal god or goddess of the city or region in which they were written. Like their ancient Near Eastern neighbors, biblical writers made use of myths to explain the origins of their world. For both groups, however, the narratives of origins were not just myth, but history too. The modern distinction between myth and history probably is drawn too sharply, since mythic conventions informed the interpretation of the past in ancient historical writing, and accounts of origins were the beginning of the record of a historical process that was guided divinely.

The early chapters of Genesis deal with prehistory and are largely mythical. In these Israelite expressions of the origins of the world, of society, and of civilization, the principal agent is the god of Israel. Although intended as a prologue to the larger historical narrative that follows in Genesis and beyond, these chapters are not historical in any modern sense: that is, they do not accurately represent what astrophysics, geology, paleontology, and other disciplines show took place, whether in terms of chronology or the origin of species. (See Box 1.3.)

---

the second account of creation begins with a temporal clause:

> On the day that the LORD God made the earth and the heavens—no wild shrub was yet on the earth, and no wild plant had yet sprouted, for the LORD God had not yet made it rain on the earth, and there was no human to work the ground . . . —then the LORD God formed the human, from the soil of the ground, and breathed into his nostrils the breath of life. (Gen 2.4–7)

But while the grammatical structure of this introduction is roughly parallel to that of the preceding creation account in Genesis 1, it is also significantly different, and those differences are more apparent as this narrative of creation and the events in the garden of Eden unfold (see Box 1.5).

First, the style is different. Whereas the first account is formally structured and somewhat abstract, the second is less repetitious, is more dramatic and spontaneous, and employs frequent plays on words. The vocabulary used is also different: Instead of "the heavens and the earth," we now have "the earth and the heavens"; instead of "male and female," we now have "the man and his wife"; instead of the verb "to create" we now have "to make" and "to form."

Most significantly, as we will see, the deity is called "the LORD God" instead of "God" (see Box 1.6), and the character of this deity and the ways he is described are also not the same in the two accounts. In the first, God is somewhat remote, even transcendent, and he creates effortlessly, by his word alone. In the second, by contrast, the LORD God is down to earth, immanent, and described in vividly **anthropomorphic** language, as if he were human. He is depicted as a potter who shapes the lifeless figure of the first human from

Box 1.5 THE GARDEN OF EDEN

The garden of Eden appears to be precisely located in the Bible: It is at the source of four great rivers (Gen 2.10–14). Two, the Tigris and Euphrates, are well known as the major watercourses of Mesopotamia. A third, the Pishon, cannot be identified (one ancient suggestion is that it is the Ganges, although that seems far removed from the biblical writers' frame of reference). The fourth, the Gihon, has a name that means "gusher," and it is used in the Bible only of the intermittent spring that was the main water supply of ancient Jerusalem (2 Chr 32.30), which still produces as much as 300,000 gallons (over 1,000,000 liters) of water per day. But the Gihon in Genesis is further described as flowing around the land of Cush, which is either Nubia or Ethiopia in east Africa (Gen 10.6; 2 Kings 19.9) or Midian in northern Saudi Arabia (Hab 3.7), both a considerable distance from Jerusalem.

It is more likely that the geography of Eden is an ideal geography. It is the divine home, "the garden of God" (see Ezek 31.8–9), from which, as in many ancient mythologies, all of the major rivers of the world flow. There are probably four rivers named in Genesis because for many ancient peoples, as for us, the world could be divided into four quarters, as in the four points of the compass.

---

the clayey soil and then breathes life into him (2.7). He plants a garden in Eden (2.8) in which the man works (2.15), just as in *Enuma elish* and other texts humans do the work that the gods had formerly done, and in this garden the LORD God habitually takes a walk in the late afternoon, like a country gentleman on his estate (3.8). Later, he makes clothes for the man and his wife (3.21).

There are also important differences in content. For example, the first account of creation opens with a watery chaos; in the second, the world is a rainless landscape. In the first, animals are created before humans, and humans are created "male and female," apparently at the same time; in the second, the first human is made, then the animals, and finally the woman is formed from the human. Finally, in the second account no mention is made of seven days, heavenly bodies, or divine rest, just as in the first no mention is made of the garden of Eden, the tree of life, the tree of knowledge, disobedience, or divine punishment.

This second account of creation and its sequel in the garden thus seems to be from a different author. One of its purposes is to answer, in a somewhat folkloric way, some perennial human questions: Why are humans afraid of snakes? Why do they wear clothing? Why are the sexes attracted to each other? Why is life so difficult and childbirth so painful? Why do we have to die?

Thus, for example, the question of sexual attraction is explained by the story of the creation of the woman. In a remarkable clustering of anthropomorphisms, the LORD God, recognizing that the human is alone, by a kind of trial and error makes all the animals and birds as potential partners for him, but none is suitable. Finally, like an anesthesiologist, the LORD God casts the man into a deep sleep; like a surgeon, he removes one of his ribs and closes up the incision; and then, like a builder, he makes the rib into a woman. The man reacts jubilantly, yet with a touch of annoyance: "This one, this time, is bone of my bone

Box 1.6 "GOD" AND "THE LORD (GOD)"

Various titles are used for the god of Israel in the Bible. One of the most frequent is the Hebrew word **elohim**, which is used in Genesis 1. Although plural in form, when referring to the god of Israel it is treated as a singular, and correctly translated "God." In other contexts the word can be plural, as in the commandment "You shall have no other gods (*elohim*)" (Ex 20.3). Beginning in Genesis 2.4, the deity is called "the LORD God," and later simply "the LORD." The alternation between "God" and "the LORD" will continue throughout Genesis, and will be an important datum in analyzing different sources (see further pages 22–25).

The term "the LORD" is not really a translation. Rather, it is a pious substitution for the sacred and personal name of God, written *yhwh*. Although this name was used throughout much of ancient Israel's history and occurs thousands of times in the Bible, by late in the biblical period it came to be considered sacred, and eventually was not pronounced at all. Rather, for the sacred name various substitutions were made in reading, most commonly *adonay*, which means approximately "the Lord." The oldest translation of the Bible, that into Greek in the third century BCE (the Septuagint), followed this practice and used "the Lord" in place of the divine name, and most translations ever since have done the same. So far-reaching was this substitution that although the four consonants *yhwh*, also called the **Tetragrammaton** (see Figure 1.3), continued to be written in biblical manuscripts, their actual pronunciation was lost, and so the conventional vocalization of the divine name as "**Yahweh**" is likely but not absolutely certain.

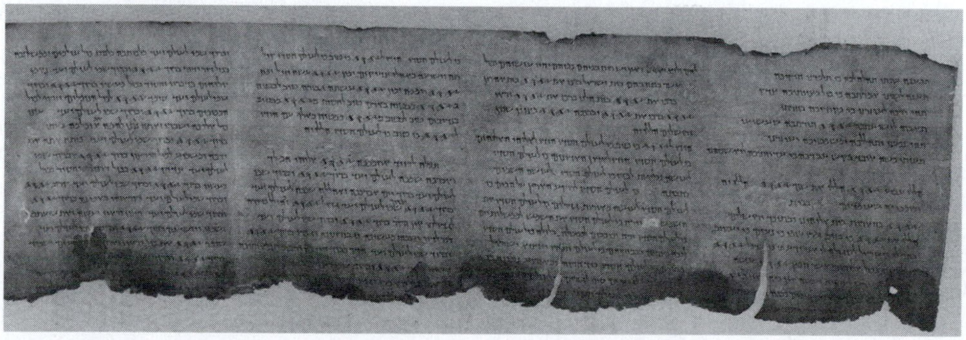

FIGURE 1.3. A section of a text of the book of Psalms among the Dead Sea Scrolls, dated to the mid-first century CE. The divine name *yhwh*, the Tetragrammaton, is written in an archaic script, indicating its sacred character.

and flesh of my flesh" (Gen 2.23). In one of the several examples of wordplay that are used in this second account, she is called "woman" (*ishshah*) because she came from "man" (*ish*). That is why, the narrator tells us, "a man leaves his father and mother and clings to his wife and they become one flesh." An apparent suggestion is made here that, as in Plato's *Symposium*, there was originally an androgynous being who was split into two parts, man and woman, and ever since their separation they have been trying to get back together. That is the explanation of the power of sexual attraction.

The first human is called *adam* because he is formed, as by a potter, from *adamah*, the reddish soil that characterizes the Levant. Generally in the Hebrew Bible the term *adam* means humankind, the human species in general; an individual male is called *ish*. Beginning in Genesis 4.25, and in the genealogy that follows in 5.1–5, but only once or twice elsewhere, *adam* is the personal name of the first human, hence Adam.

The fashioning of humans from the soil is a well-attested motif in the ancient Near East. In one Egyptian myth the god Khnum formed animals and humans from clay on a potter's wheel, and in the Mesopotamian myth of *Atrahasis*, which includes a variant of the flood story found also in *Gilgamesh*

(see pages 40–41), humans are made by the birth-goddess from a mixture of clay and the blood of a slain god, so that, as in *Enuma elish*, the gods will no longer have to work. The biblical narrative shares this widespread notion of the divine origin of all things and the related idea that humans have a divine component: Thus, the LORD God breathes life into the clay figure that he had formed.

Two trees are singled out as of special importance in the garden, the **tree of life** and the **tree of the knowledge of good and evil**. The tree of life is an example of a theme found in many cultures, something that will give immortality and even eternal youth. It is frequently depicted in art (see Figure 1.4), and the seven-branched candlestick of Jewish tradition, the menorah, is probably a stylized representation of the tree of life. We will return to the other tree in a moment, but first we will consider an ancient Near Eastern text that sheds some light on the narrative as a whole.

FIGURE 1.4.   Divine guardians of a stylized tree of life on an Assyrian relief of the early first millennium BCE.

Gilgamesh

Neither the questions implicitly asked in the second account of creation nor the language used for the answers given to them is unique to the Bible. A clustering of similar motifs is found in the epic of **Gilgamesh**, one of the oldest and most popular tales in the ancient Near East. The earliest surviving versions of the epic date as far back as the third millennium BCE, and a very late version comes from the second century BCE. The epic is also widespread, with copies found at many sites in Mesopotamia proper and also in Turkey, Syria, and Israel, where a fragment of the epic was found at the site of Megiddo. Its hero, named **Gilgamesh**, is mentioned in many other sources, including in one of the Dead Sea Scrolls, where he is included among the giants who existed before the Flood.

Gilgamesh was a legendary ruler of the central Mesopotamian city of Uruk. Whether or not he was a historical figure is debated, but if he was, his literary character has embellished the historical record greatly, much as in the case of King Arthur. As the epic opens, we are introduced to Gilgamesh as an unpopular king, one who forced his soldiers to participate in athletic contests and who also insisted that it was his right to sleep with brides on their wedding night. The citizens of Uruk complained to the gods, and their response was a complicated plan. The mother-goddess Aruru made a new creature out of clay, named **Enkidu**. Enkidu lived on the fringes of civilization, a kind of abominable snowman, a yeti or sasquatch, naked and with hair uncut:

> His locks of hair grew luxuriant like grain.
> He knew neither people nor country; he was
>   dressed as cattle are.
> With gazelles he eats vegetation,
> With cattle he quenches his thirst at the watering
>   place.
> With the wild beasts his heart delights in water.

As time passed, a hunter glimpsed the creature and discovered that he had been freeing the animals that the hunter had trapped. He went to Uruk for Gilgamesh's help, and Gilgamesh sent back with him a prostitute, Shamhat. Following instructions given, the prostitute seduced Enkidu:

> Shamhat spread open her garments, and he lay
>   upon her.
> She did for him, the primitive man, as women do.
> His love-making he lavished upon her
> For six days and seven nights. . . .
> When he was sated with her charms,
> He set his face toward the open country of his
>   beasts.
> The gazelles saw Enkidu and scattered,
> The beasts of the open country shied away from
>   him.

Enkidu returned to Shamhat, and she addressed him:

> You have become wise Enkidu, you have become
>   like a god.
> Why should you roam open country with wild
>   beasts?
> Come, let me take you to Uruk.

She then clothed him with part of her clothing and led him back toward Uruk, where they met Gilgamesh at a house where a marriage was about to be consummated, and he was about to exercise his royal prerogative of sleeping with the bride. Shocked, Enkidu blocked the door of the house, and he and Gilgamesh fought. The fight, which Gilgamesh won, apparently distracted him from his purpose, and he and Enkidu embraced and became friends.

Gilgamesh and Enkidu then set out on a series of adventures together. This section of the epic has parallels with the *Odyssey*, and in fact there are many connections between *Gilgamesh* and the Homeric epics. At one point in their journeys the goddess Ishtar attempted to seduce Gilgamesh, but he rudely rejected her advances, and in punishment it was decreed that Enkidu must perish. Afflicted with a terrible disease, Enkidu finally died, and Gilgamesh was grief-stricken.

Enkidu's death made Gilgamesh realize that he too was mortal, and so he set out on a quest for immortality. His journey eventually led him across the ocean and beyond the waters of death to the only humans whom the gods had made immortal, the hero Utnapishtim and his wife. Gilgamesh inquired how they achieved such status, and Utnapishtim replied with the long story of the Flood, which takes up the entire eleventh tablet of the epic's twelve tablets in its best known ancient edition. We will return to the close relationship between this account of the Flood and that found in Genesis 6–9 on pages 40–41. Here we will note by way of summary that although the gods had decided to destroy all humans by a flood, Utnapishtim survived with his family in a boat that he built according to the instructions of one of the gods, and after the Flood immediately offered a sacrifice of thanksgiving. The smell of the roasting meat reminded the gods why humans had been created in the first place, so that the gods would not have to perform such labor themselves, and in gratitude they made Utnapishtim and his wife immortal. Thus, explained Utnapishtim, his attainment of immorality was an unrepeatable event.

As Gilgamesh was leaving, Utnapishtim, at the urging of his wife, gave him directions about how to get a plant from the bottom of the sea, which would restore youthful vigor. Gilgamesh retrieved the plant, but on his journey home, as he was taking a refreshing swim, a snake carried off the plant. Gilgamesh lost the plant, but the serpent shed its skin, having restored its youth. Gilgamesh finally returned home to Uruk, a sadder but wiser ruler.

Gilgamesh and the Garden of Eden Narrative

This summary of the epic of *Gilgamesh* has highlighted a number of plot elements that are also found in the garden of Eden narrative in Genesis 2–3. These include the presence of a snake, its association with a plant that gives a kind of immortality, and a preoccupation with the inevitable fact of death. Perhaps most significant are the parallels between the account of the seduction of Enkidu and the changes in the situation of the man and the woman in the garden. Like Enkidu, at first the man and the woman are in harmony with nature. Enkidu loses his own closeness to nature through intercourse with the prostitute, but in doing so he also becomes humanized—wise, like a god—and thereafter is no

longer naked but clothed. Similarly, after having eaten the fruit of the tree of knowledge of good and evil, the man and the woman realize that they are naked, cover themselves up with fig leaves, and are eventually clothed by the LORD God. At the same time, however, they have become like God (see Gen 3.22), and among their punishments is that the soil from which they were formed becomes resistant to their efforts.

But what of the fruit of the tree of the knowledge of good and evil? The phrase "knowledge of good and evil" has been interpreted in a number of ways. It is probably a mistake to look for only one meaning, for literature allows for multiple interpretations. On one level, "knowledge of good and evil" may be a figure of speech known as merism, in which a totality is expressed by mentioning the opposite extremes (for example, "young and old," meaning everyone). Thus, in 2 Samuel 14, the king is described as "like a messenger of God, discerning good and evil" (v. 17), and this is paraphrased a few verses later as "wise like . . . a messenger of God knowing all things that are on the earth" (v. 20). In this sense, prohibiting the man and the woman from eating of the fruit of the tree of knowledge of good and evil would be equivalent to barring them from acquiring divine omniscience.

"Knowledge of good and evil" can also mean moral knowledge or intellectual maturity; thus, children are described as not knowing good and evil (Deut 1.39; Isa 7.15–16). While this meaning is possible, however, it is difficult to see why the humans should be prevented from acquiring such knowledge, except perhaps to say that they are still innocent, and that this innocence is somehow a better condition.

A third level of interpretation understands the phrase to have sexual connotations, as the parallels with Enkidu's seduction also suggest. In Hebrew, the verb "to know" can sometimes refer to that intimate knowledge that is a part of sexual intercourse (hence the phrase " 'to know' in the biblical sense"). In Genesis 4.1 we are told that "the man knew his wife Eve, and she became pregnant." And in at least one case, "to know good and evil" seems to have a sexual connotation (2 Sam 19.36; perhaps also Isa 7.15). Moreover, eating is a metaphor for sex in many cultures, including ancient Israel; note, for example:

> This is the way of an adulteress:
> she eats, and wipes her mouth,
>   and says, "I have done no wrong." (Prov 30.20;
>   see also 9.17)

Again, however, it is difficult to see how the narrator could have wanted to imply that the first couple was not sexually active; that is inconsistent with Genesis 2.24. Rather, taking into account other data, it is possible that the episode functions as a warning not to participate in forms of worship by which humans attempted to gain control of fertility, which was a divinely held prerogative. Among the common representations of goddesses in the Near East is that of a goddess who is nude, and thus presumably a fertility-goddess, and who is sometimes depicted holding one or more snakes. The snake has plausibly been interpreted as a phallic symbol. (See Figure 1.5.)

What then is the moral of the narrative? What precisely was the offense for which the man and the woman were punished? On one level, of course, it was simply disobedience to an explicit, if somewhat arbitrary, divine command. Yet on another level, the offense of the man and the woman had a sexual component. Eating the forbidden fruit of the tree of the knowledge of good and evil can be interpreted sexually, and by subtly associating serpents, divine knowledge, and nakedness, the authors of this episode may be giving a polemic against some types of ancient Near Eastern rituals by means of which humans attempted to participate in the divine prerogative of fertility, and also of eternal life. Thus, for their attempt to "become like God, knowing good and evil," the man and the woman are expelled from the garden of Eden and are barred access to the tree of life, which would give them immortality and make them fully divine. (See Box 1.7.)

RETROSPECT AND PROSPECT

The first three chapters of Genesis are a kind of prologue or overture, introducing themes that will

FIGURE 1.5. A gold pendant from Ras Shamra (ancient Ugarit), dating to the fourteenth or thirteenth century BCE. It depicts a nude fertility-goddess flanked by snakes, standing on a lion, and holding ibexes in her hands. The background probably represents a starry sky.

be developed as the narrative of Genesis and the rest of the Bible proceeds. Among these themes are the divinely established order of the cosmos, the observance of the sabbath, the importance of strict obedience to divine commands, and the experience of exile.

The interpretation of these chapters also provides a sample of some of the interpretive strategies or methodologies that will be used throughout this book. Two are especially im-

Box 1.7 ADAM AND EVE IN JEWISH AND CHRISTIAN TRADITION

The garden of Eden is occasionally referred to elsewhere in the Bible as a marvelously fertile kind of oasis (for example, Isa 51.3; Ezek 36.35). In very late biblical writings, once the concept of an afterlife has been developed (see page 495), Eden, also called "paradise" (originally a Persian word meaning "enclosed garden"), becomes a symbol of the eternal reward that awaits the elect in the world to come. Adam too is mentioned occasionally in the Bible as the first human (1 Chr 1.1). But despite its importance in later Jewish and Christian tradition, the narrative of human rebellion in the garden of Eden is alluded to rarely in the Hebrew Bible. We see a reference to a myth like that of Genesis 2–3 in Ezekiel 28, a prophetic attack on the king of Tyre, a city on the Mediterranean Sea just north of ancient Israel. Although he had once lived in Eden, the garden of God, this king's hubris led him to equate himself with God, and so he was expelled from the divine home. This parallel suggests that the story of rebellion in Eden was more widely known, but it is the only explicit reference to the story in the Hebrew Bible.

In subsequent tradition, however, the narrative becomes a kind of archetype to which later theological developments are attached. Thus, the serpent becomes identified with the devil or Satan, the "father of lies" (Jn 8.44), although in Genesis the serpent is not only clever (Gen 3.1) but also truthful: He tells the woman that eating from the forbidden fruit will make her and the man "like God," and that is precisely what happens (see Gen 3.22). Moreover, the disobedience of the man and the woman becomes the "original sin" responsible for the "fall" of the human species, whose punishment is a difficult life ending in death (see Rom 5.12).

The punishment includes subjection of the woman to the man because she was the first to eat of the forbidden fruit, and thus the episode is used in support of a patriarchal order in which women are inferior to men (see 1 Tim 2.11–14). In later references to the narrative, Eve is frequently singled out:

> From a woman sin had its beginning,
> and because of her we all die. (Sir 25.24)

This attribution of guilt to Eve is perhaps hinted at in the text. Adam names her (Gen 3.20), a sign of his rule over her (3.16), and the name he gives her, Eve, is related to the word for life. Yet while, as "the mother of all the living" (3.20) she is the mythical maternal ancestor of all humans, her name is also ironic, for she was the agent of death, much as in Greek myth, Pandora, whose name means "all gifts," was responsible for all human woes. This will become a frequent interpretation of early Christian writers, for whom "the serpent deceived Eve by his cunning" (2 Cor 11.3).

As familiar as many of these developments are, however, it is important to remember that none is explicitly stated in the text. The second creation story makes no mention of Satan, an afterlife, original sin, or even sin. All of these are later developments, as is the identification of the forbidden fruit as an apple, because in Latin the words for "evil" (*malus*) and "apple" (*malus*) are homonyms.

portant. First, to understand the meanings of a word or concept in a particular biblical passage, it is necessary to examine how it is used elsewhere in the Bible. Second, because the biblical authors did not live in a vacuum, it is essential to look at other writings from the ancient Near East, which will often provide parallels and sometimes contrasts with the biblical text.

The opening chapters of Genesis have also introduced us to the issues of repetition, inconsistency, and contradiction within the Bible, and in the next chapter we will begin to examine how modern scholars have explained these phenomena.

IMPORTANT TERMS

anthropomorphic

cosmology

divine council

elohim

Enkidu

Enuma elish

Gilgamesh

Marduk

myth

sabbath

Tetragrammaton

Tiamat

tree of life

tree of the knowledge of good and evil

Yahweh

QUESTIONS FOR REVIEW

1. What levels of meaning can be found in Genesis 1.1–2.4a?

2. What are the similarities and differences between the biblical and the Babylonian presentations of cosmic beginnings?

3. What levels of meaning can be found in Genesis 2.4b–3.24?

4. Compare the two accounts of creation in Genesis 1–3. What are the differences in order, style, and vocabulary?

5. How did the biblical writers make use of ancient Near Eastern mythology in their accounts of creation?

BIBLIOGRAPHY

An excellent short commentary on Genesis is John S. Kselman, "Genesis," pp. 83–188 in *The HarperCollins Bible Commentary* (ed. J. L. Mays; San Francisco: HarperSanFrancisco, 2000).

The most detailed modern commentary on Genesis in English is Claus Westermann, *Genesis* (trans. John J. Scullion; Minneapolis: Augsburg, 1984–86). There is also an abridged version of this three-volume work:

Genesis: A Practical Commentary (Grand Rapids: Eerdmans, 1987).

Among the many translations of ancient myths, including *Enuma elish* and *Gilgamesh*, the following are especially recommended: Stephanie Dalley, *Myths from Mesopotamia* (Oxford: Oxford University Press, 1989)—the translations in this chapter from *Enuma elish* ("The Epic of Creation") and Gilgamesh are adapted from this work; Andrew George, *The Epic of Gilgamesh* (New York: Penguin, 2003); and Benjamin Foster, *The Epic of Gilgamesh* (New York: Norton, 2001).

Comprehensive anthologies of ancient Near Eastern and Egyptian texts, including these myths, are William W. Hallo, ed., *The Context of Scripture* (3 vols.; Leiden: Brill, 1997–2002); James B. Pritchard, ed., *Ancient Near Eastern Texts Relating to the Old Testament* (3d ed.; Princeton, NJ: Princeton University Press, 1969)—there is also an abridged version, *The Ancient Near East: An Anthology of Texts and Pictures* (2 vols.; Princeton, NJ: Princeton University Press, 1958, 1975); and Bill T. Arnold and Brian E. Beyer, eds., *Readings from the Ancient Near East: Primary Sources for Old Testament Study* (Grand Rapids: Baker, 2002).

An insightful discussion of these various myths is Richard J. Clifford, *Creation Accounts in the Ancient Near East and in the Bible* (Washington, DC: Catholic Biblical Association, 1994).

THE FORMATION OF THE PENTATEUCH

Two different accounts of creation appear in the first three chapters of Genesis, each with a distinctive style, vocabulary, and content, and even a different way of naming the deity. Doublets, or passages that are variant treatments of the same general subject, occur throughout the Bible. Some are extensive. For example, the Hebrew Bible contains two major histories of the monarchy in ancient Israel, one in 1–2 Samuel and 1–2 Kings and another in 1–2 Chronicles. The New Testament has four gospels describing the life and teaching of Jesus. In both of these cases, although much of the material is the same, there are also significant differences.

Careful readers of the Bible will observe many such repetitions on both a large and a small scale, and comparison of parallel passages will also uncover many contradictions. In this chapter we will focus on the first five books of the Bible, known in Jewish tradition as the **Torah** and in scholarly discourse as **the Pentateuch** (from the Greek for five works or books). Since the seventeenth century, scholars have developed an important theoretical explanation for its doublets and inconsistencies.

THE TRADITIONAL VIEW

In premodern Jewish and Christian tradition Moses was considered the human author of the first five books of the Bible. His preeminence in the tradition gave these books a special authority within the Bible: They were the "torah," the teaching or the law of Moses. Thus, for example, rabbinic tradition often prefaced quotations from the first five books of the Bible with "Moses said," as did early Christian writers (such as Paul, in Rom 10.5). The Gospels also have Jesus doing the same (for example, Mk 7.10; Jn 7.22).

In the Middle Ages, a few Jewish and Christian scholars recognized that problems existed with the traditional notion of Mosaic authorship. Thus, for example, some argued that since the last few verses of the last book of the Torah describe Moses' death and burial (Deut 34.5–12), it was unlikely that he had written those verses himself; rather, their author was probably Joshua, Moses' divinely designated successor. Others countered, however, that since Moses was a prophet (Deut 34.10), he could have foreseen, by divine revelation, what would happen at the end of his life. Apart from this and a few similarly minor items, however, the doctrine of the Mosaic authorship of the Pentateuch remained unchallenged until the seventeenth century.

THE DEVELOPMENT OF MODERN INTERPRETATION

Beginning in the seventeenth century, with the rise of critical thought and, especially in Protestant circles, growing freedom from dogmatic presuppositions, such thinkers as Thomas Hobbes (1588–1679) in England and Baruch (Benedict) Spinoza (1632–77) in the Netherlands more directly challenged traditional views about the Bible. In his *Leviathan, or The Matter, Form, and Power of a Commonwealth Ecclesiastical and Civil* (1651), Hobbes argued briefly that although Moses was the author of much of the Pentateuch, he could not have written all of it because passages such as Genesis 12.6 and Deuteronomy 34.6 indicate that the writer was living some time later. Likewise, Spinoza, who had read Hobbes, argued at greater length in his *Theological and Political Treatise* (1670) that, because of the large number of anachronisms and evidence of later authorship, "the belief that Moses was the author of the Pentateuch is ungrounded and even irrational" (*Treatise*, chap. 8). Rather, he proposed that it had been composed by the fifth-century BCE Jewish leader Ezra, "a scribe skilled in the law of Moses" (Ezra 7.6), who, to be sure, did incorporate some laws that went back to Moses himself.

The earliest systematic treatment of the question was by a French Catholic priest, Richard Simon, who in 1678 wrote a book titled *Critical History of the Old Testament*. In it he reasoned that Moses could not have written the Pentateuch because it contains historical details and refers to events about which he could not have known. These include mention of the Philistines, who did not arrive on the coast of Palestine until at least a century after the latest plausible date for Moses (see further pages 98–99), and statements like "These are the kings who reigned in the land of Edom, before any king reigned over the Israelites" (Gen 36.31), which must have been written by an author who lived during or after the time when the Israelites themselves were ruled by kings, which was several centuries after Moses. Simon also pointed out geographical oddities. Moses died east of the Jordan River, never having entered the Promised Land, yet Deuteronomy begins: "These are the words that Moses spoke to all Israel across the Jordan" (Deut 1.1), words clearly written by an author situated on the west side of the Jordan River (see also Gen 50.10–11). Moreover, as the previous quotation shows, apart from the direct quotation of speeches attributed to him, the Pentateuch is not a first-person narrative by Moses himself, but is written by another author (or authors), often about Moses, and nowhere does the text suggest that Moses wrote the whole.

To this challenge to the traditional view that Moses himself was the author of the entire Pentateuch, Simon's ecclesiastical superior, the famous preacher Bishop Bossuet, responded by condemning his book. It was, however, soon translated into English, and it influenced such diverse thinkers as the writer John Dryden, in his *Religio Laici* (1682), and the philosopher John Locke (1632–1704).

The analysis that Simon had begun was carried further, but from a more traditional perspective, by another Frenchman, Jean Astruc (1684–1766), who was court physician to King Louis XV. Astruc recognized that in Genesis two different names were used for God (Yahweh [the LORD] and God [*elohim*]) and that the passages in which each occurred were generally distinct. Astruc concluded that while writing Genesis Moses must have had two sources in front of him, which he incorporated into his work. Astruc's book, *Conjecture on the Sources That Moses Apparently Used in Composing Genesis*, published in 1753, was in fact a nuanced defense of the doctrine of Mosaic authorship, but the method he used, based on the variation in the divine name, was a methodological breakthrough.

Using this method, further work was done, principally in Germany, resulting in the identification of other sources. In Genesis, it was observed, one source called God Yahweh; others used different names. On the basis of these differences, it was possible to describe the various sources and their characteristics in detail. Even though all of the sources generally used Yahweh after the revelation of the divine name to Moses in the early chapters of Exodus, other distinctive features still made it possible to separate them in the last four books of the Pentateuch.

The classic statement of what came to be known as the "Documentary Hypothesis" was that by Julius **Wellhausen**. Wellhausen (1844–1918) was a professor at the University of Greifswald in Germany; in 1878, two centuries after the appearance of Simon's book, he published *History of Israel* (later to be called *Prolegomena to the History of Ancient Israel*). In it he attempted to sketch the history of ancient Israel, especially its religious practices and beliefs, based on the sources available; for Wellhausen these sources were almost exclusively the biblical books, since nonbiblical documents were only beginning to be deciphered and translated. As a responsible historian Wellhausen recognized that the biblical narratives were not objective eyewitness accounts of what had taken place, but rather were later writings that reflected the views of their authors. It was those views, properly dated, that were the basis of a history of biblical times.

Summarizing the conclusions of his predecessors over the previous two centuries, Wellhausen articulated the **Documentary Hypothesis**. The Pentateuch, he argued, comprises four distinct and relatively intact sources, or "documents," labeled **J, E, D, and P**, which we will discuss in detail on pages 25–27. Wellhausen used these sources and other data to construct a kind of evolutionary model of the development of the religion of ancient Israel, which moved from a kind of pristine, if primitive, worship of one god among many, or monolatry, during and immediately after the time of Moses, through the centralization of worship during the time of the monarchy and the powerful ethical monotheism of the prophets, and finally to the dry legalism of the priests in the period after the exile to Babylon.

Wellhausen's evolutionary model is questionable on several counts, and in any case was very much a product of its times, including an implicit anti-Semitism in its characterization of early Judaism, as exemplified by the P source, as sterile and legalistic. Likewise, Wellhausen's assumption that Israel's prehistory as related in the books of the Pentateuch had no historical value can be criticized as overly skeptical. But although Wellhausen's conclusions have not remained influential, his formulation of the Documentary Hypothesis became a classic, and it continues to be an indispensable starting point for subsequent discussions of the formation of the Pentateuch, the processes by which the first five books of the Bible reached their present shape.

The analysis of the various sources, or documents, of the Pentateuch is often called "literary criticism," an unfortunate term since it is not the same as literary criticism used in other disciplines. Rather, it is more properly understood as source analysis. As such, it shares methods with those used for the study of, for example, the New Testament; in such studies scholars have explained the many verbal correspondences among the first three gospels with the theory that Mark, the earliest, was used independently as a source by both Matthew and Luke. The correspondences between Matthew and Luke, where there is no parallel in Mark, have been explained by positing the existence of a hypothetical source Q (from the German *Quelle*, meaning "source"), which consisted largely, if not entirely, of sayings of Jesus.

For the Pentateuchal sources J, E, D, and P, as for the Q source used by Matthew and Luke, the recovered documents are hypothetical—that is, none has ever been discovered. But the Documentary Hypothesis provides the best explanation of the data that careful analysis uncovers, data that include repetitions, similarities, inconsistencies, and contradictions. (See Figure 2.1.)

A SUMMARY OF THE DOCUMENTARY HYPOTHESIS

The original basis for separating various strands or documents in the Pentateuch was the different names used for God. In one source, J (or the Yahwist), the beginning of the worship of the god of

[5]And YHWH saw that human bad was multiplied in the earth, and every inclination of their heart's thoughts was only bad all the day. [6]And YHWH regretted that He had made humankind in the earth.

And He was grieved to His heart.

[7]And YHWH said, "I'll wipe out the human whom I've created from the face of the earth, from human to animal to creeping thing, and to the bird of the skies, because I regret that I made them." [8]But Noah found favor in YHWH's eyes.

[9]These are the records of Noah:

Noah was a virtuous man. He was unblemished in his generations. Noah walked with God. [10]And Noah fathered three sons: Shem, Ham, and Yaphet. [11]And the earth was corrupted before God, and the earth was filled with violence. [12]And God saw the earth; and, here, it was corrupted, because all flesh had corrupted its way on the earth. [13]And God said to Noah, "The end of all flesh has come before me, because the earth is filled with violence because of them. And here: I'm destroying them with the earth. [14]Make yourself an ark of gopher wood, make rooms with the ark, and pitch it outside and inside with pitch. [15]And this is how you shall make it: three hundred cubits the length of the ark, fifty cubits its width, and thirty cubits its height. [16]You shall make a window for the ark, and you shall finish it to a cubit from the top, and you shall make the ark's entrance in its side. You shall make lower, second, and third stories for it. [17]And I, here: I'm bringing the flood, water on the earth, to destroy all flesh in which is the breath of life from under the skies. Everything that is in the earth will expire. [18]And I shall establish my covenant with you. And you'll come to the ark, you and your sons and your wife and your sons' wives with you. [19]And of all the living, of all flesh, you shall bring two of each to the ark to keep alive with you. They shall be male and female. [20]Of the birds by their kind and of the domestic animals by their kind, of all the creeping things of the ground by their kind, two of each will come to you to keep alive. [21]And you, take some of every food that will be eaten and gather it to you, and it will be for you and for them for food." [22]And Noah did it. According to everything that God commanded him, he did so.

7 [1]And YHWH said to Noah, "Come, you and all your household, into an ark, for I've seen you as virtuous in front of me in this generation. [2]Of all the pure animals, take seven pairs, man and his woman; and of the animals that are not pure, two, man and his woman. [3]Also of the birds of the skies seven pairs, male and female, to keep seed alive on the face of the earth. [4]Because in seven more days I'll rain on the earth, forty days and forty nights, and I'll wipe out all the substance that I've made from on the face of the earth."

[5]And Noah did according to all that YHWH had commanded him. [6]And Noah was six hundred years old when the flood was, water on the earth. [7]And Noah and his sons and his wife and his sons' wives with him came to the ark from before the waters of the flood. [8]Of the animals that were pure and of the animals that were not pure, and of the birds and everyone that creeps on the ground, [9]they came by twos to Noah, to the ark, male and female, as God had commanded Noah. [10]And seven days later the waters of the flood were on the earth. [11]In the six hundredth year of Noah's life, in the second month, in the seventeenth day of the month, on this day all the fountains of the great deep were split open, and the apertures of the skies were opened. [12]And there was rain on the earth, forty days and forty nights. [13]In this very day Noah came, and Shem and Ham and Yaphet, Noah's sons, and Noah's wife and his sons' three wives with them to the ark, [14]they and all the wild animals by their kind and all the domestic animals by their kind and all the creeping animals that creep on the earth by their kind and all the birds by their kind, all fowl, all winged things. [15]And they came to Noah, to the ark, by twos of all flesh in which was the breath of life, [16]and those that came were male and female; some from all flesh came, as God had commanded him. And YHWH closed it for him. [17]And the flood was on the earth for forty days, and the waters multiplied and raised the ark, and it was lifted from the earth. [18]And the waters grew strong and multiplied very much on the earth, and the ark went on the face of the waters. [19]And the waters had grown very, very strong on the earth, so they covered all the high mountains that are under all the skies. [20]Fifteen cubits above, the waters grew stronger, and they covered the mountains. [21]And all flesh that creep on the earth—of the birds and of the domestic animals and of the wild animals and of all the swarming creatures that swarm on the earth, and all the humans—expired. [22]Everything that had the breathing spirit of life in its nostrils, everything that was on the ground, died. [23]And He wiped out all the substance that was on the face of the earth, from human to animal to creeping thing and to bird of the skies, and they were wiped out from the earth, and just Noah and those who were with him in the ark were left. [24]And the water grew strong on the earth a hundred fifty days.

Key: J E P RJE R *Other*

(a)

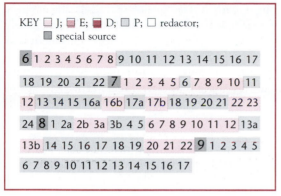

KEY ☐ J; ▨ E; ▧ D; ☐ P; ☐ redactor;
    ▨ special source

6 1 2 3 4 5 6 7 8 9 10 11 12 13 14 15 16 17

18 19 20 21 22 **7** 1 2 3 4 5 6 7 8 9 10 11

12 13 14 15 16a 16b 17a 17b 18 19 20 21 22 23

24 **8** 1 2a 2b 3a 3b 4 5 6 7 8 9 10 11 12 13a

13b 14 15 16 17 18 19 20 21 22 **9** 1 2 3 4 5

6 7 8 9 10 11 12 13 14 15 16 17

(b)

FIGURE 2.1. The results of source criticism (also called "literary criticism") can be represented schematically in a variety of ways. This figure gives three examples of how one section of the biblical text, in this case Genesis 6–9, can be visualized. In (a), the text is represented in its entirety, with the different sources (and later stages of their formation) indicated by different fonts. In (b), only the verse numbers are given. In (c), the various sources are arranged synoptically, in parallel columns.

	P	J
The Flood		
Prologue		6:5–8
Story	6:9–22	
		7:1–2
		[7:3a]
		7:3b–5
	7:6	7:7
	7:11	7:16b
		[7:8–9]
		7:10
		7:12
	7:13–16a	
	[7:17a]	7:17b
	7:18–21	7:22–23
	7:24	
	8:1, 2a	8:6a
		8:2b, 3a
	8:3b–5	8:6b
	8:7	8:8–12
	8:13a	8:13b
	8:14–19	
Epilogue		8:20–22
	9:1–17	

(c)

This is my name forever,
  and this is my title for all generations."
  (Ex 3.13–15)

Israel as Yahweh is placed back in the primeval age: "It was then that the name Yahweh was first invoked" (Gen 4.26). In this source in Genesis the deity is known as Yahweh by Noah (8.20), Abraham (12.8; 15.7; 24.6), Isaac (25.21), Jacob (27.20; 28.13), and others. But according to other sources, this was not the case. In P, throughout Genesis, God is known as God (*elohim*) or by titles such as God Almighty (*el shadday*; see further pages 81–82), but it was not until the time of Moses that the divine name Yahweh was revealed: "God [*elohim*] spoke to Moses and said to him: 'I am the LORD [*yahweh*]. I appeared to Abraham, Isaac, and Jacob as God Almighty [*el shadday*], but by my name "The LORD [*yahweh*]" I did not make myself known to them'" (Ex 6.2–3). In the E source as well, the revelation of God's personal name Yahweh is also set in the time of Moses:

Moses said to God, "If I come to the Israelites and say to them, 'The God of your ancestors has sent me to you,' and they ask me, 'What is his name?' what shall I say to them?" God [*elohim*] said to Moses . . . "Thus you shall say to the Israelites, 'The LORD [*yahweh*], the God of your ancestors, the God of Abraham, the God of Isaac, and the God of Jacob, has sent me to you':

This inconsistency about whether God was known as Yahweh before the time of Moses made it possible to isolate various sources in Genesis and, once this was done, to identify other characteristics that the sources had apart from the divine name, and so to differentiate them in the books of the Pentateuch after Genesis, where all sources regularly use Yahweh.

Here we will summarize some of the main characteristics of each source. More detailed discussion will be found in the appropriate chapters that follow.

J

The J, or Yahwist, source, is identified in Genesis first by its consistent use of the divine name Yahweh (spelled *Jahwe* in German; hence "J"). In the passages where that name is used, Yahweh is described with vivid anthropomorphisms, that is, in very humanlike ways. Thus, as we have seen, in the narrative of the garden of Eden (Gen 2.4b–3.24), he actually forms the first human from clay like a potter and breathes life into him; he walks in the garden; and he makes clothes for the man and the woman. In subsequent J passages he shuts the door of the ark after all have boarded (Gen 7.16); he smells the odor of the sacrifice that Noah offers after the Flood (8.21); he goes down to view the tower of Babel (11.5); he visits Abraham for a meal (18.1–8) and bargains directly with him (18.22–33); and he meets Moses and tries to kill him (Ex 4.24).

In J the geographical location of many of the narratives concerning the ancestors of Israel (Gen 12–50) is in the territory of Judah, which was the dominant southern tribe and later the name of the kingdom ruled by the dynasty founded by David. Jacob's son Judah, the ancestor of the tribe that bears his name, also features prominently in the ancestral narratives in J.

In J, the father-in-law of Moses is named Reuel (Ex 2.18), and the mountain on which Moses receives the law is called by its familiar name, Sinai (Ex 19.18).

The J source has a principal theme of a threefold promise to Abraham of land, descendants, and blessing. The boundaries of the Promised Land in J, "from the river of Egypt to the great river, the river Euphrates" (Gen 15.18), encompass the territory controlled by David and Solomon, kings of Israel in the tenth century BCE. This is one of the reasons that many scholars date J to the tenth century, although others opt for a ninth-century date (as did Wellhausen), and others prefer still later dates. In this book we will assume a tenth-century date.

The J source is the fullest of the four sources; when isolated from the others it can be read as a fairly continuous narrative.

E

The E, or Elohist, source gets its name from its consistent use of the divine title *elohim* ("God") in Genesis and until the revelation of the name Yahweh to Moses in Exodus 3. Because the original version of E was truncated when it was com-

bined with J (see page 28), E is fragmentary throughout the Pentateuch. It may begin as early as Genesis 15, and there is general agreement that it occurs from Genesis 20 onward.

In E, the deity is more remote than in J, typically revealing himself indirectly, through dreams (for example, Gen 20.3; 28.12), divine messengers ("angels"; Gen 21.17; 22.11; Ex 3.2), and prophets. The use of the term "prophet" is in fact characteristic of E; only in E is Abraham called a prophet (Gen 20.7), and the same is true of Miriam (Ex 15.20); see also Numbers 11.29; 12.6.

In E, the mountain of revelation to Moses is called Horeb (Ex 3.1; 33.6), and Moses' father-in-law is named Jethro (Ex 3.1; 18.1).

In Genesis 12–50, the geographical setting of E narratives is often in the northern part of Israel, which from the late tenth to the late eighth century BCE was a separate kingdom, somewhat confusingly also called Israel. In poetic texts this northern kingdom is often named for its dominant tribe, Ephraim, and so E is focused on Ephraim as J is focused on Judah (a coincidence that may serve as an additional mnemonic). This focus on the north, and also the emphasis on prophecy, suggests that E in fact originated in the northern kingdom, probably in the ninth century, but perhaps in the eighth (the date given by Wellhausen).

Because of its fragmentary nature, some scholars have questioned whether E actually existed as a separate source. Others prefer simply to speak of JE, recognizing that while there probably were originally distinct sources, they are largely indistinguishable.

D

The D, or Deuteronomic, source is found entirely, or almost entirely, in the book of Deuteronomy. According to a scholarly consensus developed in the nineteenth century by Wellhausen's predecessors, the core of Deuteronomy is the book that was discovered in the Temple during the reign of Josiah, the king of Judah, in the late seventh century BCE (see 2 Kings 22.8). As we will see, Deuteronomy has its own complicated history, and it certainly makes use of traditions that are older than the seventh century. There are some connections between D and E; like E, D uses Horeb (Deut 1.2; 5.2) as the name of the mountain of revelation rather than Sinai, and D also emphasizes prophecy (Deut 13.1–5; 18.15–22). Like E, it probably also originated in the northern kingdom of Israel. (For further discussion of the particulars of D, and the Deuteronomic school for which it was a primary text, see pages 173–83.)

P

The P, or Priestly, source is named because of its emphasis on matters of religious observance and ritual. Thus, in Genesis, the first account of creation, which is P, concludes with the account of divine rest and hence of the sabbath observance (Gen 2.2–3); later, the sabbath is identified as the sign of the covenant between God and Israel on Mount Sinai (Ex 31.15–17). P is also concerned with details of dietary law (for example, Gen 9.4–6), and, in the ancestral narratives, the command to Abraham to practice circumcision appears in P (Gen 17.9–14).

In P, as in E, the deity is often called *elohim* until the revelation of the divine name to Moses (Ex 6.2–3). Unlike E, however, P preserves other designations of the deity, such as *el shadday* and other combinations with *el*; we will discuss these further on pages 81–82. In P, the deity is even more remote and transcendent than in the other sources, never appearing directly, as in J, or even indirectly through dreams and messengers, as in E. For P, especially beginning in Exodus, the deity is typically manifest in his "glory." This is a concrete image that means a light-filled cloud that both indirectly reveals the divine presence and simultaneously conceals it, like the sun behind a cloud in the sky.

While J has a covenant with Abraham (Gen 15.18–21), and J and E also describe the covenant at Sinai/Horeb, in P a thematic series of covenants occurs. The first is the covenant with Noah and his descendants, whose sign is the bow in the sky (Gen 9.12–17). The second is the covenant with Abraham, whose sign is circumcision (Gen 17.11). The third is the covenant between God and Israel, whose sign is the sabbath

(Ex 31.12–17); this covenant is mediated by Moses on Mount Sinai, which is P's name for the mountain of revelation.

Because P was the final editor of the already existing sources, the first chapter of the Pentateuch (Gen 1) is P, and its last chapter (Deut 34) is also largely P; P has thus framed the Torah. In Genesis P connects the J and E narratives by an elaborate system of genealogies, beginning, as we have seen, with the "generations of the heavens and the earth" (Gen 2.4). While there are some narrative passages in P, the most important P sections are not narrative, however, but are the divinely given instructions concerning various matters of ritual and religious observance, especially in the books of Exodus, Leviticus, and Numbers. Much of this material was not original with the Priestly writers, but was derived from the traditions of the Temple in Jerusalem where the Priestly school had its origins. Thus P has, for example, lengthy descriptions of priestly vestments and sacred architecture and objects, as well as detailed regulations concerning ritual purity and the sacral calendar. The sacrificial system was especially important to P, and because Moses and his brother Aaron, the first priest, are central to P's schematic presentation of the early history of Israel, P contains no sacrifices before the time of Moses.

Characteristic P phrases include "male and female" (in the case of animals translated "the male and his mate," although the Hebrew makes no such distinction) and "be fruitful and multiply."

The date of P is debated, although at least one stage in its development was during the sixth century BCE, as part of an effort to preserve and consolidate traditions in the wake of the destruction of the Temple and the exile to Babylon. The position adopted in this book is that the substantial formation of P occurred in the sixth century BCE.

CHALLENGES TO THE DOCUMENTARY HYPOTHESIS

The Documentary Hypothesis was challenged from its inception, in part by conservatives for whom it was an attack on the authority of the

Torah as divinely revealed to Moses. Thus, Roman Catholics were prohibited by Vatican decree from teaching the Documentary Hypothesis, a ban not lifted until the mid-twentieth century. By then, however, it had been widely accepted by most Protestant scholars and also by many Jewish scholars.

Those scholars who accepted the broad outlines of the theory, however, continued to debate its details, and some scholars added a bewildering variety of other sources to the basic four. Thus each source or document was further divided, so that, for example, J was divided into J^1, J^2, J^R, and so forth. Other sources were hypothesized, such as K (for Kenite), L (for Lay), and S (for Seir, or south). Others proposed to find the Pentateuchal sources in subsequent books of the Bible, so that, with the inclusion of Joshua, the corpus to be analyzed became a Hexateuch, with Judges a Heptateuch, and so on. Many scholars also questioned whether E even existed.

There is no doubt that the Documentary Hypothesis does not provide a full explanation of the complicated processes by which the Pentateuch was formed. For example, some passages cannot easily be identified as belonging to one of the four sources. Other methodologies also need to be employed to explain the prehistory of the sources that comprise the Pentateuch, the stages of its development, and its final shape.

In the last quarter of the twentieth century more challenges to the classic formulation developed, especially concerning dating. Some scholars have argued that the J source was not a product of the early monarchy, but rather a kind of antiquarian, archaizing text written centuries later, during the sixth century BCE or even subsequently.

What these modifications of the basic hypothesis and continuing disagreements about such issues as dating show is that the data—the repetitions, the inconsistencies, and the contradictions—are extremely complex. But the data must be explained, and almost all scholars agree with the general principle that underlying the present text of the first five books of the Bible are distinct sources. A majority of scholars, if by no means all, continue to follow some version of the classic formulation of the Documentary Hypothesis summarized here.

THE FORMATION OF THE PENTATEUCH

A description of the process by which the separate sources or documents were combined is also hypothetical, but a possible scenario is as follows. Using some earlier traditions, and reflecting their own perspectives as well, J and E were independently written, the former in Judah, probably during the tenth century BCE, and the latter in the northern kingdom of Israel in the ninth, or perhaps a century or so later. When the northern kingdom fell to the Assyrians in 722 BCE, refugees from there brought with them to Jerusalem the E source, which was combined with J in Jerusalem, but in such a way that while J remained intact, E was used as a kind of supplement; this accounts for its fragmentary character. These hypothetical developments are summarized in Figure 2.2.

OTHER STRATEGIES FOR INTERPRETING THE PENTATEUCH

Subsequent work on the process of formation of the Pentateuch has developed other methodologies. Among these is form criticism, the study of the smaller units within each source. As this brief description indicates, form criticism and other methods used in connection with it recognize that the Pentateuchal sources were not constructed out of nothing, as it were; they used preexisting traditions. That raises questions about the form, function, and sources of those traditions, and also about their historical reliability—was Wellhausen's skepticism about them correct, or do the sources preserve in some way authentic historical memory? We will examine such issues in subsequent chapters.

In the other direction chronologically is the question of how the sources were combined. Formerly the tendency had been to see the redactors, or editors, as merely scissors-and-paste hacks.

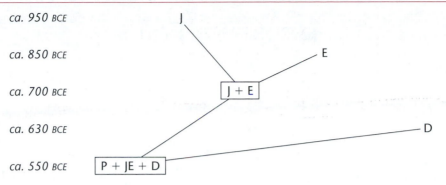

FIGURE 2.2. Hypothetical development of the formation of the Pentateuch.

Careful analysis of the editorial processes, however, has led many scholars to conclude that there was creative design at this stage as well, that the process was dynamic rather than mechanical. This type of analysis is called "redaction criticism," and it overlaps with another method, called "tradition history," which incorporates elements of both form criticism and redaction criticism into its analysis to study the entire process of the formation of the Pentateuch.

The complicated processes of formation for each source suggest that we might think of them not as produced at one point in time, but rather as an ongoing process, produced by a school whose existence and influence lasted for several centuries. As we will see, this understanding is especially well suited to D and to its ideological soul mate, the Deuteronomistic History (see further pages 191–93), and also to P, whose influence is found in books outside the Pentateuch, for example, in Ezekiel (see further pages 392–93).

Yet another approach is to focus on the final form not just of the Torah but of the Bible as a whole. This recognizes that the biblical traditions are in a kind of dialogue with each other, and thus in some ways the earliest interpretations of the Bible are to be found within the Bible itself. Since one goal of interpretation may be stated as to determine what the original text meant, in order, for some, to determine what it has continued to mean for subsequent and even for contemporary audiences, early "inner-biblical" interpretations give us a glimpse of how at least some ancient readers understood the texts in front of them. Closely related to this "inner-biblical exegesis" is what is called "canonical criticism," which likewise attempts to look at the entire Bible, the "canon" (see Appendix) of various communities of faith, as a complete text with its own inner unity.

RETROSPECT AND PROSPECT

The fact that two different accounts of creation occur in the opening chapters of Genesis has led us to consider how this might have come to be. In this chapter we have examined the dominant scholarly explanation, the Documentary Hypothesis. Although over the last century individual scholars have often modified, supplemented, and corrected the classic formulation given by Wellhausen, the Documentary Hypothesis has been the point from which scholars begin. For the next several chapters we will be using the Documentary Hypothesis alongside other methods to interpret the biblical text. We will continue in the next chapter with the rest of the primeval history in Genesis 4–11.

IMPORTANT TERMS

D

Documentary Hypothesis

E

J

P

Pentateuch

Torah

Wellhausen

QUESTIONS FOR REVIEW

1. What are the data that led scholars to arrive at the "Documentary Hypothesis"?

2. How does the Documentary Hypothesis explain these data?

3. What are the principal characteristics and themes of the four documents or sources?

BIBLIOGRAPHY

A useful introduction to the Documentary Hypothesis is Norman C. Habel, *Literary Criticism of the Old Testament* (Philadelphia: Fortress, 1971).

For more detailed discussion of the various documents or sources and their characteristics and themes according to the classic model, see Walter Brueggemann and Hans Walter Wolff, *The Vitality of Old Testament Traditions* (2d ed.; Louisville: Westminster John Knox, 1982); and Richard Elliott Friedman, *The Bible with Sources Revealed: A New View into the Five Books of Moses* (San Francisco: HarperSanFrancisco, 2003). Friedman has also provided a lively introduction to the Documentary Hypothesis and related issues in *Who Wrote the Bible?* (New York: Summit, 1987).

For one statement of alternate views, see as a start John Van Seters, *The Pentateuch: A Social-Science Commentary* (Sheffield: Sheffield Academic Press, 1999).

An excellent resource for investigating the history of scholarship on the Bible is John H. Hayes, ed., *Dictionary of Biblical Interpretation* (2 vols.; Nashville: Abingdon, 1999).

PRIMEVAL HISTORY

Genesis 4–11

We return now to the biblical text, the rest of the introductory chapters of Genesis, which contain a variety of mythic and other materials about early human history after creation and until the birth of Abraham. In this chapter we will also continue our investigation of the Documentary Hypothesis, looking at the two sources, J and P, that are found in Genesis 4–11. First we will consider episodes where the two sources are distinct; then we will look at the Flood narrative, where they are combined. As in the accounts of creation in Genesis 1–3, in the chapters that continue the primeval history both sources freely borrow and adapt material from the cultures and literatures of their neighbors, and our understanding of the biblical sources is greatly enhanced by examining parallel materials from the ancient Near East.

J (THE YAHWIST SOURCE)

As in its narrative of the garden of Eden (Gen 2.4b–3.24), the J source has a folkloric character. It includes familiar episodes, such as the stories of Cain and Abel and of the tower of Babel. In these, and in the other smaller J units in Genesis 4–11, three interrelated themes can be identified: the deteriorating relationship between humans and the soil, the divinely ordained separation of the divine from the human realms, and the progressive corruption of humanity.

Humans and the Soil

The close relationship between humans and the soil was established in the J account of creation (Gen 2.4b–3.24), in which the first human is called *adam* because he is taken from the soil (*adamah*). That originally harmonious relationship was broken by the disobedience of the man and the woman: One of the punishments that they were given was that "the soil (*adamah*) is cursed because of you, with toil you shall eat from it all the days of your life" (3.17). Nevertheless, at death, humans will return to the soil, in burial: "[F]or out of it you were taken; you are dust, and to dust you shall return" (3.19).

The relationship between humans and the soil further deteriorates with the pollution of the ground by the blood of Abel; his murderer, his brother Cain, is also "cursed from the ground" and is told that the ground will no longer produce for him. Hence he is to become a wanderer on the earth; his expulsion "east of Eden" (4.14, 16) parallels that of his parents (3.24) (see Box 3.1).

Box 3.1 **CAIN AND ABEL**

The short narrative of Cain and Abel raises a number of issues. One is why Yahweh preferred Abel's offering to Cain's. Although postbiblical tradition will attempt to fill in the blanks with a moralizing expansion, such as that Abel gave the best he had but Cain gave a lesser offering, the text itself is silent. In the Bible, God often chooses a younger son over his older brother; for example, Isaac is preferred to Ishmael (Gen 17.20–21[P]) and Jacob to Esau (Gen 25.23 [J]), and David, the divinely chosen king, is the youngest of seven brothers (1 Sam 16.6–13). The theme of rival brothers is common in world literature, including that of the ancient Near East. Both Egyptian and Mesopotamian texts tell of such sibling conflict, often with deadly consequences. The Bible contains a number of accounts of sibling rivalry. In Genesis, examples include Noah's sons (Gen 9.22–27; see Box 3.2 on page 33), Isaac's twin sons Jacob and Esau (see, for example, Gen 27), and among the sons of Jacob (for example, Gen 37). The narrative of David's court describes a struggle for succession among his sons: Absalom killed Amnon, only to be killed himself (2 Sam 13.28–29; 18.14–15), and Solomon succeeded to the throne instead of his older brother Adonijah, whom Solomon eventually had killed (1 Kings 1.1–2.25). Other themes found in many literatures include the exaction of divine vengeance on a murderer and the idea that the soil is rendered infertile by blood that has been shed violently.

Another explanation for the choice of Abel over Cain concerns their lifestyles. Abel was a shepherd, Cain a farmer. Throughout the Bible, God often shows a preference for the seminomadic lifestyle of the shepherd, and several leaders chosen by God are said to have been shepherds, including Moses (Ex 3.1) and David (1 Sam 16.11; 2 Sam 7.8). Moreover, after the Israelites had wandered in the wilderness with their flocks and herds, they eventually entered the land of Canaan, where the inhabitants lived in fortified cities (Num 13.28) and worshiped other gods. According to J, Cain's son Enoch was the builder of the first city. The narrative may thus also contain an implicit anti-urban polemic.

Another issue is who Cain's wife was. If the narrative is understood as continuous, then she must have been his sister because Adam and Eve were the only ones who could have been her parents. In this case, Cain and his wife would have committed incest. Again, however, this is not an issue that concerned the Yahwist; the building of the first city by Cain's son Enoch comes immediately after the narrative of Cain and Abel (Gen 4.17), implying that there was already a large population.

Finally, we may note that among Cain's descendants is the first metalsmith, Tubal-cain. Among the several puns on Cain's name in the text, one is the implicit connection with an identical word for "smith" (*qayin*); the same word is probably also the root of the name of the Kenites (*qenim*), a nomadic group whose activities probably included metallurgy and who often interacted with the Israelites. By implicitly connecting the Kenites with their murderous ancestor Cain, who was divinely cursed to be a wanderer, J both explains their itinerant lifestyle and expresses Israelite superiority over these neighbors. This kind of putdown of others by a pejorative account of their ancestor's reprehensible conduct is a motif often found in J.

An apparent restoration of the original harmony between humans and the soil seemed possible when Noah was born: "Out of the ground that the LORD has cursed this one shall bring us relief from our work and from the toil of our hands" (Gen 5.29). Noah was a "man of the soil" (*ish adamah*; Gen 9.20), but after the Flood Noah's agriculture led to trouble. He was the first to plant a vineyard and to make wine from its grapes. The wine made him drunk, and the events that followed eventually resulted in the cursing of his grandson (see further Box 3.2). Once again, J implies, the soil and human corruption are linked.

The Boundary between the Divine and the Human

J highlights the impassable boundary between the divine and the human realms, and any attempt to cross it is a violation of the divinely imposed order that Yahweh moves quickly to stop. Thus, in the garden of Eden story, by eating the forbidden fruit the man and the woman became like gods (Gen 3.22), and part of their punishment was banishment from the garden, so that they could no longer have access to the tree of life and become immortal and thus fully divine. Likewise, the sexual union of the sons of God with human women (Gen 6.1–4; see Box 3.3) violated the principle of separation, and Yahweh imposed a limit on the life span of their offspring. The same theme is also found in the story of the tower of Babel (Gen 11.1–9; see Box 3.4), which relates how humans literally tried to reach the divine home in the sky.

Progressive Human Corruption

A third theme of J in the primeval history is the increasing corruption of humans. The disobedience to a divine command by the man and the woman in the garden of Eden is followed by the first murder by Cain and the building of the first city by Cain's increasingly violent descendants.

Box 3.2 NOAH'S DRUNKENNESS

After the Flood, Noah planted a vineyard; harvested the grapes; made wine; drank it, apparently alone; and passed out, naked, in his tent. One of his three sons, Ham, "saw the nakedness of his father"; the other two "covered the nakedness of their father." When Noah learned what had happened, he cursed Ham's son Canaan. On the surface, Ham was guilty of not treating his father with appropriate respect, but there may be a sexual innuendo here, as is frequently the case in J. The idiom "to uncover [*or* to see] the nakedness" of someone means to have intercourse with them (Lev 18.6; 20.11, 17), and in a later story in J, drunkenness also leads to incest (Gen 19.30–38). Thus, J again attributes depravity to an ancestor of Israel's neighbors, in this case the Canaanites, descended from Ham.

A similarity of language and of theme thus occurs between this short episode and that in the Garden of Eden (Gen 3.1–24). Both have a disaster-causing plant, nakedness, and a curse. The sexual level of meaning in the story of the man and the woman in the garden is further supported by the innuendo in the story of Noah's drunkenness.

Box 3.3 THE SONS OF GOD

The brief passage in Genesis 6.1–4 seems to be a fragment of a fuller myth. Sexual intercourse between gods and humans was a common feature of ancient Near Eastern and Greek and Roman mythologies and was apparently familiar to the ancient Israelites as well. In these chapters in Genesis, where both the Yahwist and the Priestly sources drew heavily on ancient mythical themes, its presence is not entirely remarkable. The "sons of God" are mentioned occasionally elsewhere in the Bible, notably in Job 1.6 and Psalm 29.1, where they appear to be the members of the divine council that we have seen alluded to in Genesis 1.26 (see page 9). Mythology recounts a time when heroes of divine and human parentage existed; for J, these are the mysterious "Nephilim," the "heroes of old, the warriors of renown" (Gen 6.4). The only other biblical passage mentioning the Nephilim describes them as giants (Num 13.33).

The Yahwist uses this mythic tradition to advance the themes of boundary and corruption. Later these Nephilim are identified as fallen angels (the Hebrew word literally means "fallen ones"; 2 Pet 2.4; Jude 6), but of this there is no hint in Genesis.

This culminates in the summary that precedes the narrative of the Flood:

> The LORD saw that the wickedness of humankind was great in the earth, and that every inclination of the thoughts of their hearts was only evil continually. And the LORD was sorry that he had made humankind on the earth, and it grieved him to his heart. (Gen 6.5–6)

The Flood, however, does not solve the problem, for after the Flood Yahweh recognizes that "the inclination of the human heart is evil from youth" (Gen 8.21). The account of Noah's drunkenness after the Flood may also serve to illustrate the continuing problem of human wickedness (see Box 3.2).

The Genealogies in J

Most of the genealogies in Genesis belong to P (see pages 36–39). At intervals, however, a number of genealogies appear in J as well. These are mixed genealogies, which include fragments of narratives in addition to records of descendants. In the primeval history, they occur in Genesis 4 and 10.

In Genesis 4 we have a **genealogy** from Adam to Enosh, which is interrupted by a lengthy story about Cain and Abel and shorter stories about Cain's descendants, especially Lamech. The genealogy concludes with the statement that it was then that Yahweh was first worshiped. Most of the chapter is devoted to Cain, but at its end we find a shift to Seth, the child born to Eve as a replacement for Abel. This is what is called a "segmented" genealogy, which traces several different lines descended from a common ancestor, as opposed to a "linear" genealogy, which traces one line through several generations. The genealogy in Genesis 10, part of the "table of nations" (see Box 3.5), has a similar pattern.

J and P seem to be derived from different traditions. The names Lamech and Enoch occur in the line of Cain in J (Gen 4.17–18), but in that

Box 3.4 THE TOWER OF BABEL

In addition to continuing the theme of the separation of the divine and human realms, like several other J narratives in the primeval history the short narrative of the tower of Babel (Gen 11.1–9) is on one level an explanation or **etiology** of a phenomenon, in this case the multiplicity of languages. The phenomenon of different and mutually incomprehensible languages is yet another punishment from Yahweh, who was concerned about the ability of humans to do anything they wished; this expropriation of a divine prerogative could not be permitted, and so he confused a supposed original common language.

On another level, the narrative functions as a kind of satire on the pretension of the inhabitants of ancient Babylon, which was dominated by a large ziggurat or sacred platform on which a temple was built (see Figure 3.1). Babel, says the author, was named because there people began to "babble"; the pun (which is found in Hebrew as well as in English) is intentional, although not etymologically correct; such wordplay is another characteristic of J.

FIGURE 3.1.   Reconstruction of the Sumerian ziggurat at Ur in southern Mesopotamia, dating to the late third millennium BCE. The base of this ziggurat covered more than half an acre. A ziggurat was a stepped pyramid on which a temple was located. It was a standard form of sacred architecture in ancient Mesopotamia. In Babylon the ziggurat was called "the temple of the foundation of heaven and earth."

of Seth in P (5.18, 25). Although some of the names are the same, others have different forms, like that of the father of Lamech, Methushael in J (4.18), but Methuselah in P (5.21).

P (THE PRIESTLY SOURCE)

The Genealogies in P

The only two P narratives in Genesis 1–11 are the account of creation at the beginning (see pages 3–5) and that of the Flood in chapters 6–9 (see pages 39–40). The rest of the P material in these chapters consists of genealogies, which P uses as a way to connect human history from creation to Abraham.

Three principal P genealogies appear in this section of Genesis: from Adam to Noah in chapter 5, the sons of Noah in chapter 10 (vv. 1–7, 20, 22–23, 31–32), and from Seth to Abraham in chapter 11 (vv. 10–26). The first and third of these are linear genealogies; that is, they trace descendants in a direct line from father to firstborn son to his firstborn son and so on, and in a formulaic fashion they link the "generations" from Adam to Abraham; the second is the table of nations discussed in Box 3.5.

Endless speculation surrounds the genealogies, especially regarding the life spans of the individuals named in them. Some of the numbers are clearly symbolic. Enoch lived, we are told, 365 years; then, remarkably, he was no more, because God took him (Gen 5.23–24). Enoch "walked with God," and his life, a full circuit (the same number of years as there are days in the year), was complete (see further Box 3.6). Another transparently symbolic number is the 777 years of Lamech's life (5.31): This number is explained in

Box 3.5 THE TABLE OF NATIONS

In Genesis 10 we have a composite genealogy of the descendants of Noah by his three sons, arranged "by their families, their languages, their lands, and their nations" (Gen 10.32), constituting the entire world as the writers knew it, and thus providing a kind of map in prose, since in this list the names of descendants are usually place names (see Figure 3.2). The chapter has many inconsistencies and can relatively easily be divided into P (vv. 1–7, 20, 22–23, 31–32) and J (vv. 8–19, 21, 24–30); as in its earlier genealogy in chapter 4, J includes brief biographical details about some of the ancestral figures, notably Nimrod (vv. 8–11).

The descendants of Japheth are for the most part the lands to the north of ancient Israel in Asia Minor (modern Turkey), including the islands along the eastern coast of the Aegean Sea and Cyprus. The descendants of Ham are generally the lands to the south and southwest, along the Mediterranean coast and in Africa. The descendants of Shem (from whose name the term "Semitic" is derived) are to the northeast and southeast, mainly in Syria, Mesopotamia, and the Arabian peninsula.

As a whole, this table of nations reflects an ancient awareness of kinship and hence of cultural interconnectedness, although the details do not always agree with modern understandings of linguistic and historical links. P's mention of different languages for each group makes no reference to J's explanation of the same phenomenon in the story of the tower of Babel that immediately follows.

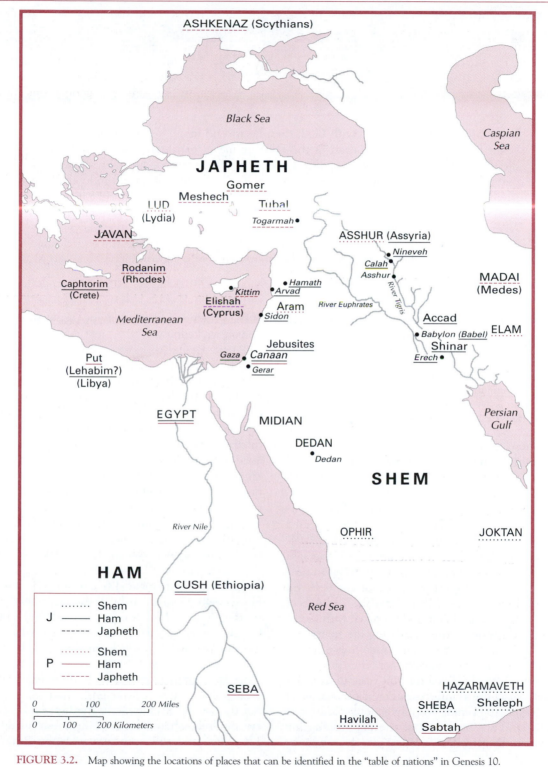

FIGURE 3.2. Map showing the locations of places that can be identified in the "table of nations" in Genesis 10.

Box 3.6 ENOCH

Enoch, we are told, "walked with God; then he was no more, because God took him" (Gen 5.24). The notice for each of the other primeval patriarchs ends with "and he died," but that formula is not given for Enoch. Because of his goodness, Enoch was apparently spared death, and ascended to heaven. He is the first of several individuals in the Bible who do so, either without dying or after death. Others are Elijah (2 Kings 2.11) and, in the New Testament, Jesus (Acts 1.9); in fact, the motif is widespread in ancient Near Eastern and Greek and Roman mythology. In postbiblical Jewish apocalyptic literature, Enoch returns to give detailed accounts of what will happen at the end of time; some of these revelations are preserved in the nonbiblical books of Enoch.

the fuller J account of Lamech, in which Lamech, who is a descendant of Cain, is even more violent than his ancestor; he vows:

> I have killed a man for wounding me,
> a young man for striking me.
> If Cain is avenged sevenfold,
> truly Lamech seventy-sevenfold. (Gen 4.23–24)

These genealogies show a general pattern of diminishing life spans. This reflects a widespread notion of a kind of golden age in the distant past, which was followed by successively worse eras; the same motif also underlies the garden of Eden narrative in J. As God became less and less pleased with humans, their lifespans diminished; it is almost a biblical cliché that a long life was a sign of divine favor and a premature death an indication of divine displeasure (see, for example, Ex 20.12; Deut 30.15–20; Ps 1; Prov 10.27; 22.4; Eccl 8.13). Noah, who like Enoch "walked with God," is an exception to the decreasing life spans—he lived, we are told, 950 years (Gen 9.29), longer than anyone else except for the proverbial Methuselah, who lived for 969 years (5.27). But after Noah the numbers quickly diminish, until we come to Terah, who lived only 205 years (11.32). Thus by means of the diminishing life spans in the genealogies, P provides the substance

of the J theme of growing divine displeasure with human wickedness.

Ancient parallels exist both to the extraordinary life spans of primeval humans and to the diminishing length of those life spans. One such parallel is the Sumerian King List, which in its present form dates to the early second millennium BCE. In it, a series of kings is described as having ruled in various cities. The list is divided into two eras, before and after the Flood. It begins: "When kingship was lowered from heaven, kingship was first in Eridu. In Eridu Alulim became king and ruled for 28,800 years. Alalgar ruled 36,000 years. Two kings thus ruled it for 64,800 years. Then . . . kingship was brought to Bad-tibira." The list continues with several other cities and kings, and then summarizes: "These are five cities; eight kings ruled them for 241,000 years. Then the Flood swept over the earth." It then resumes: "After the Flood had swept over the earth and when kingship was lowered again from heaven, kingship was first in Kish. In Kish, [name broken] became king, and ruled for 1,200 years." There follow some two dozen more rulers in their respective cities, all of whom have reigns of hundreds, but not thousands, of years. Near the list's end is the city of Uruk, where the hero Gilgamesh ruled for 126 years, and then the list suddenly shifts to more normal reigns of 30 years, 15, 9, 8, 36, 6, and so on.

The Sumerian King List and the biblical genealogies share a general pattern of enormously long life spans before the Flood and shorter life spans after it. Even though the numbers in Genesis are large by our standards, in comparison with those found in the Sumerian text they are almost realistic. In the King List, after Gilgamesh, born of a divine mother and a human father and the last of the antediluvian heroes in Mesopotamian literature, we move into actual history. In the biblical narrative this will not happen for some time, since the era of the ancestors as described in the succeeding chapters of Genesis was still distant from the perspective of the biblical writers; not until narratives concerning the first millennium BCE will people be reported to have lived to what we would consider a normal old age.

Although the figures given for life spans are clearly in the realm of myth, it should be noted that the time elapsed is relatively short, less than two thousand years, since the sons through whom the genealogy is traced were born relatively early in their fathers' lives. According to the figures given, Adam would still have been alive during the lifetime of Noah's father Lamech, and Noah would still have been alive when Abraham was born.

THE FLOOD

Generally in the Pentateuch J, E, and P are juxtaposed in fairly large units, so that a passage in one source is followed by a passage in another. We have observed this in the two accounts of creation, where the P account, Genesis 1.1–2.4a, is followed by the J account (2.4b–3.24). Occasionally, however, the sources are intertwined, as in the narrative of the plagues in Egypt (Ex 7–12), where J, E, and P are all found, and also in the narrative of the Flood (Gen 6.5–9.17), where, as in the rest of the first eleven chapters of Genesis, only J and P occur. The identification of the two sources in the narrative of the Flood is a classic example of how the Documentary Hypothesis works. (See Figure 2.1 on pages 24–25.)

The J Version

In J, generally easily identified because of the use of the divine name Yahweh ("the LORD"), the Flood is initiated by Yahweh because of his regret at human corruption (Gen 6.5–7). Only Noah found favor in the eyes of Yahweh, and he was instructed to bring into the ark seven pairs of the clean animals and birds and two pairs of the unclean. Noah did so, and "the LORD shut him in"; that is, in a typically vivid anthropomorphism, we are to visualize Yahweh closing the door of the ark after all had boarded. The Flood is caused by rain and lasts forty days and forty nights. After the Flood, Noah released three doves in succession; the first two returned to the ark, but when the third did not, Noah knew that it was safe to disembark. He immediately built an altar to Yahweh and sacrificed some of the clean animals and birds; when Yahweh, in another anthropomorphism, smelled the odor of the sacrifice burning, he said that he would never again curse the ground, despite human wickedness.

The P Version

Throughout the P account of the Flood, readers will easily identify much of the same terminology that was used in the P account of creation (Gen 1.1–2.4a). P gives the same basic reason for the Flood as J: the annoyance of God (*elohim*) at human corruption and violence. Noah, a blameless man who "walked with God" (Gen 6.9) like his ancestor Enoch (5.24), is given detailed instructions about the construction of the ark, almost a blueprint, and is told to bring into it his extended family and two of every kind of animal, male and female. In J, Noah offers a sacrifice after the Flood, and therefore needs extra pairs of the clean animals, those permissible for sacrificial use, so as not to cause their extinction. But in P no sacrifices occur before the time of Moses, so only a pair of each species of animals is required.

In J the Flood is caused by rain, but in P it results from an undoing of creation: "[A]ll the fountains of great deep burst forth, and the windows of the heavens were opened" (Gen 7.11). According to P's chronology, the Flood lasted for a full year. It ended in a kind of renewal of creation, when, as in the opening of the P creation account, "God made a wind blow over the earth" (8.1; compare 1.2). Then Noah released a raven, not a series of doves as in J; when it failed to return, he left the ark with all his family and the animals. God blessed Noah and his sons, the new ancestors of humankind, in language again suggesting a second creation: "Be fruitful and multiply, and fill the earth" (9.1; compare 1.28). In contrast to the vegetarian diet decreed in Genesis 1, now humans are permitted to eat meat, but they are commanded to refrain from eating blood or taking the life of another, "for in his own image God made humankind" (9.6; compare 1.26–30).

The Priestly source concludes its version of the Flood narrative with an account of the covenant between God and Noah, as representative of the human species and of all creation. In this covenant, God promises never again to destroy the world by a flood. This is the first of the three covenants that punctuate P's version of the Torah. Like the succeeding covenants with Abraham (Gen 17.11) and with Israel on Mount Sinai (Ex 30.16–17), this covenant too has a sign, "the bow in the clouds" (Gen 9.12–13).

Ancient Near Eastern Parallels

As we have seen, part of the *Gilgamesh* epic is an account of the Flood, as told by **Utnapishtim** to Gilgamesh in the eleventh tablet of the epic (see pages 15–16). This tablet was one of the first ancient Near Eastern texts to be deciphered, in 1872; it immediately attracted wide attention (see Figure 3.3). Some argued that the text proved that the Bible was true, for the Babylonians had simply copied the biblical account of the Flood. But subsequent discoveries made it clear that the Flood story was widespread in the ancient Near East, and although the Babylonian version deciphered by George Smith was contemporary with some biblical writers and therefore theoretically the Babylonians could have known of Genesis, other versions of the tale were written many centuries before biblical Israel existed.

FIGURE 3.3. Tablet XI of the standard version of the *Gilgamesh* epic. It contains the story of the Flood as told by its hero, Utnapishtim. Deciphered in 1872, it was one of the first modern discoveries to provide a close parallel to biblical traditions.

In any case, close connections are found between the biblical and the nonbiblical accounts. In both there is divine anger; the hero is warned by a god of a Flood about to occur; he is given detailed instructions about building and caulking a boat; and he is instructed to take on board his family and animals. After the Flood, the boat comes to rest on a mountain, and the hero releases three birds. Here is the version in *Gilgamesh*:

> When the seventh day arrived,
> I put out and released a dove.
> The dove went; it came back,
> For no perching place was visible to it, and it
>   turned round.
> I put out and released a swallow.
> The swallow went; it came back,
> For no perching place was visible to it, and it
>   turned round.
> I put out and released a raven.
> The raven went, and saw the waters receding.
> And it ate, preened, lifted its tail, and did not turn
>   round.
> Then I put everything out to the four winds, and I
>   made a sacrifice. . . .

The gods smelled the fragrance,
The gods smelt the pleasant fragrance,
The gods like flies gathered over the sacrifice.

The detailed parallels between this and the biblical account, especially J, are so close that there can be no doubt that the biblical writers made use of some preexisting Mesopotamian Flood story.

In other versions of the Flood in Mesopotamian literature, **Utnapishtim**, the hero saved by the gods who corresponds to the biblical Noah, is also named Ziusudra and Atrahasis. All of these names seem to be epithets: Utnapishtim means "He found life," referring to the immortality that was given to him, as does Ziusudra, which means "Life of long days"; Atrahasis means "Exceedingly wise." The story of the Flood in Gilgamesh in fact seems to be a later addition to the epic; for example, no motivation is given for the gods sending the deluge. A more complete version occurs in another epic, named for its hero—*Atrahasis*, the earliest known copy of which dates to about 1700 BCE, and the probable source of the Flood story found in *Gilgamesh*. It begins "when the gods were men," that is, when the gods had to do all the laborious digging and maintaining of the canals that irrigated the Mesopotamian plain. When they rebelled, the high god Enlil ordered the birth-goddess Belet-ili to create humans, which she did by mixing clay with the blood of a slain god; as in *Enuma elish* and in both creation accounts in Genesis, humans have a divine component. Within a few hundred years, however, the humans had reproduced and the earth became too noisy for the gods, so as a means of population control they inflicted the humans with disease, then drought, causing famine, and finally the Flood. Only Atrahasis, with the help of his patron god Enki, escaped in a boat built and caulked according to Enki's instructions. After the Flood he offered a sacrifice, and the gods decreed that humans could continue to exist, but their numbers would be limited by divinely caused birth control, including selective sterility and infant mortality.

Although *Atrahasis* is incompletely preserved, it does provide the motivation for the Flood: divine annoyance at excessive noise, reminiscent of Apsu's reason for wanting to kill the younger gods in *Enuma elish*—they too were making too much noise. This contrasts with the reason for the Flood in Genesis—not divine irritation, but rather the anger of an ethical deity at human wickedness and violence.

At the same time, in both *Atrahasis* and the Bible, creation and the Flood are linked in a continuous narrative. It seems clear that the biblical writers were drawing upon an ancient and widespread tradition when they included the Flood story in their account of primeval history.

Conclusion

As the parallels with other ancient Near Eastern texts make clear, the accounts of the Flood belong to the genre of myth, like the other narratives in Genesis 1–11. Although devastating floods have occurred in many parts of the world at various times, no geological evidence has been found for a worldwide deluge such as that described in Genesis and in *Gilgamesh* and *Atrahasis*. This mythic dimension continues in the conclusion to the Flood in P.

The sign of the covenant between God and Noah and every living creature is "the bow in the clouds" (Gen 9.13). This refers to the rainbow, which will remind God of his promise. But the bow also has mythological significance. The word for "bow" is same as the one used for the weapon that propels arrows. The storm-god, whose wind blew over the earth after the Flood as at the first creation, has set his terrible weapon in the clouds—he has permanently stored it there, so that it will not be used again. The conclusion of the Flood story thus reminds us of the beginning of Genesis 1, with its allusion to the battle between the storm-god and the primeval chaotic sea.

RETROSPECT AND PROSPECT

The opening chapters of Genesis are a kind of prologue, an overture as it were. Like other ancient Near Eastern peoples, the ancient Israelites developed myths of the origins of the cosmos and of the human condition. In retelling these myths the biblical writers introduce themes that will be developed as the narrative continues; among these are a mysterious deity who can be both unpredictable and generous, the phenomenon of sibling rivalry, and the experience of exile.

In P's schematic history, the genealogies link creation to Abraham. The primeval history ends with the genealogy of Terah, the father of Abraham, and thus provides a transition to the next section of Genesis, in which the focus of the biblical writers narrows to one branch of the human family, that of Abraham and his collateral relatives and descendants over four generations.

Before we turn to the narrative of Israel's ancestors, however, we will pause in the next chapter to consider one of the main concepts in the Bible as a whole, that of the Promised Land.

IMPORTANT TERMS

etiology   genealogy   Utnapishtim

QUESTIONS FOR REVIEW

1. What are the principal themes of the J and P sources in Genesis 4–11? How do they differ, and how are they similar?
2. How are these themes connected with the accounts of creation in Genesis 1–3?
3. Choose a small section of the Flood narrative, such as Genesis 7.1–16, and identify the parts of the passage that you would attribute to J and to P. What characteristic phrases of each source occur in the passage? How do they relate to Genesis 1.1–2.4a (P) and Genesis 2.4b–3.24 (J)?

BIBLIOGRAPHY

For commentaries on Genesis, see the bibliography to Chapter 1.

PART TWO

NATIONAL ORIGINS

THE PROMISED LAND: GEOGRAPHY, HISTORY, AND IDEOLOGY

Before turning to the next section of the biblical narrative, that concerning Israel's ancestors, it is appropriate to pause to consider the setting of that narrative, and of much of the entire Bible—the land of Israel. As we will see in the next chapter, one of the main themes of the ancestral narratives is that of the land, to which Abraham migrates from his original home, and which is promised to him and to his descendants forever. This "**Promised Land**" continues to be a central focus of the entire Bible, and remains so for Judaism as well.

GEOGRAPHY

Terminology

Since antiquity, a variety of terms have been used both for the larger region of which ancient Israel was a part and for ancient Israel itself. For the larger region, that is, the eastern Mediterranean and lands adjacent to it, scholarly convention uses the term "Near East." Like its older synonym "Orient" and similar terms like "Levant" and "Middle East," it is Eurocentric, that is, from the geographical perspective of one living in the West, but as there are no convenient alternatives

we will use it in this book. For the lands just east of the Mediterranean Sea, that is, the western part of the Near East between modern Turkey and Egypt, we will use "**Levant**."

Modern politics also complicates terminology for our primary focus, ancient Israel. In this book, unless explicitly stated, terms such as "Israel," "Syria," and "Palestine" refer to ancient entities rather than to the modern ones that have the same names. Also, following ordinary usage, the term "Israelites" means the ancient inhabitants of Israel ("Israelis" is generally used for the modern inhabitants).

For most of its history, the Promised Land was not called Israel. Prior to the emergence of a political entity that called itself Israel in the late second millennium BCE, this region formed part of what its frequent overlords, the Egyptians, called **Canaan**. That is how the Bible itself uses the term: The "land of Canaan" is the usual designation for the territory promised to Abraham, and it is used in the Bible almost exclusively for the period before Israel came into existence. Modern scholars often use the term "Canaanite" in a broader sense to designate the culture shared by the ancient inhabitants of modern Israel, Jordan, Palestine, Lebanon, and western Syria. Sometimes in the Bible Canaan is more precisely defined, as in Genesis 15.19–21: "the land of the Kenites, the Kenizzites, the Kadmonites, the Hittites, the Perizzites, the Rephaim, the Amorites, the Canaanites, the Girgashites, and the Jebusites." This list names at least some of the traditional pre-Israelite inhabitants of the land and makes it clear that the land had a history before the emergence of Israel.

The principal territory of the ancient Israelites extended from Dan in the far north to Beersheba in the south and from the Mediterranean Sea to the west and the Jordan River to the east. In some periods the Israelites controlled more territory, and in many far less. In this book, we will use the term "Israel" for this territory, as just defined. Modern scholars often also use the term "Palestine" as a general designation for the region to the south of Lebanon and Syria and to the northeast of Egypt, and we will use it occasionally also, especially to avoid confusion with the political entities that were called "Israel" in ancient times. The word "Palestine" is derived from the word for "Philistines," another group of ancient inhabitants of the land, especially on its southern Mediterranean coast, and is first attested in Greek historians of the fifth century BCE.

The term "**Israel**," however, is admittedly not always the most accurate, nor is it unambiguous. In the Bible, "land of Israel" (Hebr. *eretz yisrael*) in the sense of the entire territory is used half a dozen times. A related phrase, "the soil of Israel" (Hebr. *admat yisrael*; NRSV: "land of Israel"), is used only in Ezekiel. The term "Israel," however, while generally used of the entire nation, which regarded itself as descended from the patriarch Jacob, renamed Israel (Gen 32.28), also is used to refer to a distinct political entity, the larger northern half of the land of Israel, or the northern kingdom of Israel, which was in existence for about two centuries between the late tenth and the late eighth centuries BCE. Thus, "the land of Israel" can also mean just the northern kingdom (2 Kings 5.2, 4; 6.23; 2 Chr 30.25; Ezek 27.17). Readers of the Bible thus must be careful to determine what "Israel" means in a particular passage.

The southern counterpart of the northern kingdom of Israel was **Judah**, which was named after one of Jacob's sons and which became the dominant tribe in the south. For several centuries, beginning in the late tenth century BCE, this "kingdom of Judah" had an independent existence. After its conquest by the Babylonians in the early sixth century BCE, the name continued to be used. In the Persian empire, which succeeded that of the Babylonians in the late fifth century BCE, Judah (Yehud) was a Persian province and then, as Judea, a Greek and Roman province.

It is from the name "Judah" that the words "Judaism" and "Jew" come. Most scholars make a historical distinction between ancient Israel and Judaism, considering the latter as beginning no earlier than the sixth century BCE, after the end of Israelite autonomy and the dispersion of Judeans outside their land; that is the terminology we will use in this book. Others, however, correctly remind us that such a distinction fails to recognize the many continuities between ancient Israel and later Judaism, continuities that are a central facet of Judaism itself.

Other terms that we will use are "**Mesopotamia**," the Greek designation of the land "in the middle of the rivers," the fertile floodplain of the Tigris and Euphrates rivers comprising modern Iraq and northwestern Syria; "Transjordan," the region to the east of the Jordan River valley, in modern Jordan; and "Asia Minor," for the land mass roughly the same as that now forming Turkey, in western Asia.

The Larger Setting

The lands of the Bible include the regions bordering the eastern Mediterranean Sea and to their east, comprising the modern countries of Turkey, Syria, Lebanon, Israel, the Palestinian Authority, Jordan, Saudi Arabia, Egypt, Iraq, and Iran. In the late biblical periods Greece and Italy also came into play, and other lands, such as Arabia, Ethiopia, and Libya, are occasionally mentioned in the Bible. (See Figures 4.1 and 4.2.)

In the Near East, a wide band of arable land extended from the Persian Gulf northward

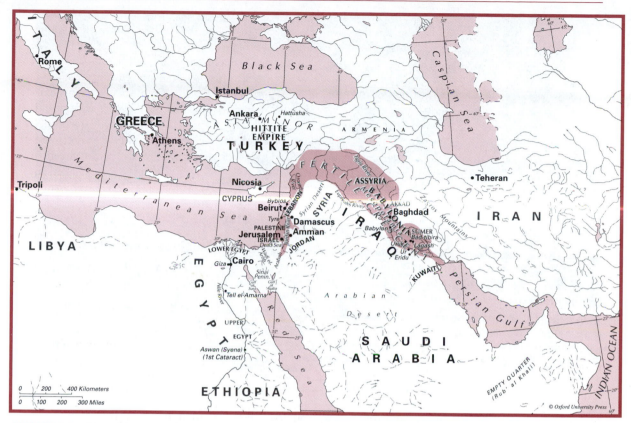

FIGURE 4.1. Map of the ancient Near East.

through Mesopotamia, then westward, bordering the Syrian desert, and southward into Palestine. This region, known as the **Fertile Crescent**, was linked by shared culture, by related languages, and, in some periods, especially from the first millennium BCE onward, by imperial control by various powers. Immediately south of the western arm of the Fertile Crescent was Egypt, which in many periods exercised considerable influence beyond its borders. To the east of Mesopotamia proper was Persia, also a major power from the sixth century BCE onward.

Knowledge of the shared culture of these regions, especially since the nineteenth century CE, has been extremely important in understanding the Bible, which after all did not come into existence in a vacuum. Rather, the biblical writers and their neighbors shared myths, legal traditions, literary genres, and similar understandings of various institutions, such as prophecy and kingship, and of divinity as well.

Topography

The area occupied by ancient Israel even at its greatest extent was relatively small, about 9,000 mi^2 (23,000 km^2), roughly the size of Belgium or the state of Vermont. Despite its size, however, it includes a number of dramatically distinct geographical regions. (See Figure 4.3.)

The Coastal Plain

The eastern coast of the Mediterranean is relatively straight, and in Israel has few natural harbors. Broadest to the south, the coastal plain narrows

FIGURE 4.2.   Satellite photo of the Levant, looking west, with the Mediterranean Sea at the top.

as one moves north, and then is interrupted by the Carmel range. The coastal plain then resumes briefly but completely disappears as one approaches Lebanon. Although much of the coastal plain today is sandy, in antiquity it was generally marshy. As a result, the principal north-south road in antiquity (the "way of the sea"; see page 52) was at the eastern edge of the coastal plain, where it meets the Shephelah.

The Shephelah

This region, whose name means "the lower part," consists of foothills that form the transition between the coastal plain and the central hill country to the east. The Shephelah contains many important archaeological sites, especially along its western side, where cities once guarded the main coastal road.

The Hill Country

Running through the land like a spine is the hill country, subdivided by the biblical writers into various districts, including the hill country of Ephraim and the hill country of Judah. The elevations within the hill country vary and are highest in the north. Thus, Jerusalem, in the hill country of Judah, is about 2,500 ft (760 m) above sea level, while in the hill country of Ephraim and the hill country of Naphtali (the Galilee) many elevations are over 3,000 ft (900 m), and the highest peak in the region, Mount Hermon, is over 9,000 ft (2,800 m) high. The hill country is relatively narrow, averaging about 20 miles (32 km) from west to east.

The Rift Valley

Immediately to the east of the hill country is a dramatic drop in elevation into the Rift Valley, a geological feature that extends from southern Turkey into Africa. This deep gouge in the earth's surface is in fact a fault between two tectonic plates. It forms a natural boundary between Israel and the regions to the east, especially because it contains several major bodies of water. From

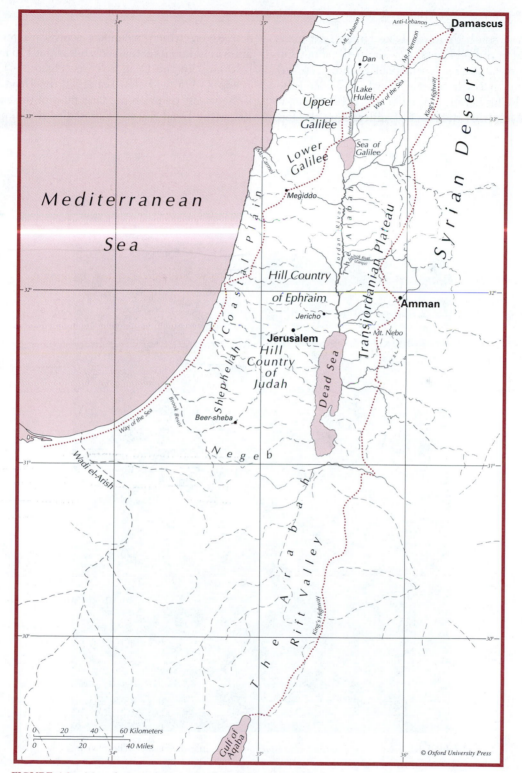

FIGURE 4.3. Map of principal geographical divisions and road systems of ancient Palestine.

north to south these are Lake Huleh (not mentioned in the Bible, and now drained), about 230 ft (70 m) above sea level; about 10 miles (16 km) south of it is the Sea (or Lake) of Galilee (also called Chinnereth), about 700 ft (210 m) below sea level; from the Sea of Galilee flows the Jordan River, which meanders southward for 70 miles (110 km; its actual length is about 135 miles [220 km]) to the Dead Sea (see Figure 4.4). At 1,300 ft (395 m) below sea level, the **Dead Sea** is the lowest point on the land mass of the earth. Below the Dead Sea the Rift Valley rises until it

FIGURE 4.4.   A view of the Jordan River as it flows into the Sea of Galilee, looking south.

meets the Red Sea, which is part of the same geological feature. Because of its low elevation, temperatures in the Dead Sea basin are extraordinarily high, resulting in continuous evaporation and increased salinity; its name in the Bible is the Salt Sea (Num 34.3, 12; NRSV "Dead Sea"). For this reason, little life can survive in the waters of the Dead Sea, and the desolate region that surrounds it is the setting for the story of Sodom and Gomorrah (Gen 19). The Rift Valley as a whole, and also parts of it, especially the Jordan Valley and the area from the Dead Sea southward, are often called the Arabah in the Bible.

The Transjordanian Plateau

East of the Rift Valley is another steep climb to a fairly level plateau, which is cut by a number of major streams: two tributaries of the Jordan, the Yarmuk (not mentioned in the Bible) and the Jabbok (modern Wadi Zerqa); the Arnon (Wadi Mujib), which flows into the Dead Sea; and the Zered (Wadi Hasa), just south of the Dead Sea. Elevations on this plateau are fairly constant, with modern Amman (ancient Rabbah, later Philadelphia) at an elevation of 3,200 ft (975 m) being typical.

The Negeb and Sinai

South of the hill country of Judah, beginning at Beersheba and extending southward to the Sinai Peninsula, is a semidesert region, not as arid as a true desert. This region is known as the Negeb (Negev) and is a marginal agricultural zone because of limited rainfall; hence in most periods it was sparsely populated.

Climate and Rainfall

For the last ten thousand years or so, the region's climate has been relatively stable. It is a temperate climate, without extremes of cold or heat except for high temperatures in the lower Rift Valley and the Sinai. Jerusalem is representative, with a mean low temperature in the winter of about 40°F (5°C) and a mean high temperature in the summer of 86°F (30°C). In the winter it rarely goes below freezing or snows,

except in the higher elevations. Summer temperatures can reach as high as 105°F (40°C), but this is infrequent.

As in much of the Mediterranean basin, there are essentially two seasons, a rainy one, extending from late fall to early spring, and a dry one, from late spring to early fall. The rain in the winter months is abundant; in Jerusalem, for example, rainfall averages about 22 in (550 mm) per year, about the same as in San Francisco, California, and London, England.

Because of the topography described earlier, the rainfall diminishes to the east. As the moisture-filled clouds proceed eastward from the Mediterranean, the elevation of the hill country forces them upward, causing much of the Rift Valley to be in a rain shadow, so that, for example, Jericho, just north of the Dead Sea, averages less than 6 in (150 mm) of rain annually. The moisture that remains in the clouds is deposited on the western part of the Transjordanian plateau; to its east, as the rainfall diminishes, begins the great desert that extends from northern Syria into the Arabian peninsula, the desert framed by the Fertile Crescent.

For some biblical writers, this was an ideal climate, providentially given:

> For the land that you are about to enter to occupy is not like the land of Egypt, from which you have come, where you sow your seed and irrigate by foot like a vegetable garden. But the land that you are crossing over to occupy is a land of hills and valleys, watered by rain from the sky, a land that the LORD your God looks after. (Deut 11.10–12)

From the perspective of the Israelites, the climate of Egypt was labor intensive. The Egyptians, of course, had a different view. From their perspective, the annual flooding of the Nile in summer regularly provided both water and also fresh topsoil in a generally rainless terrain; for those of other lands, who depended on rain—in the Egyptian view, whose Nile was in the sky—life was more difficult:

> As for the wretched Asiatic, unpleasant is the place where he is (with) trouble from water, difficulty from many trees, and the roads thereof awkward by reason

of mountains. (Translation by R. O. Faulkner, pp. 187–88 in W. K. Simpson, ed., *The Literature of Ancient Egypt* [New Haven: Yale University Press, 1972.])

But even for some biblical writers, Egypt was paradisiacal—like Eden, the garden of the LORD (Gen 13.10), where cucumbers, melons, leeks, onions, and garlic, as well as fish, were abundant (Num 11.5).

Road Systems

The topography affected the location of major roads. There were two major north-south routes. One, the "way of the sea" (Isa 9.1), was along the eastern edge of the coastal plain from Egypt northward; the southern part of this route is also called "the way of the land of the Philistines" (Ex 13.7). Just south of the Carmel promontory it moved to the interior through the great Valley of Jezreel (Judg 6.33; later called the Esdraelon Valley, as in Jdt 1.8), and then up the Rift Valley to Hazor and Damascus. The other major international route was the "King's Highway" (Num 20.17), just east of the Rift Valley on the Transjordanian plateau, connecting Arabia with Damascus; a subsidiary route across the northern Sinai Peninsula connected the King's Highway with Egypt. These two international routes were used by troops, traders, and travelers, and hence were guarded by major cities and forts along their lengths.

Subsidiary north-south roads went through the central hill country and through the Jordan Valley. Many smaller roads also connected various places in the hill country.

Produce

Like many of the lands that border the Mediterranean, ancient Israel had a fairly rugged terrain, but its soil was eminently suitable for growing grain, olives, and grapes and for raising sheep and goats. At many periods in its history it not only grew enough food for its own population, but also exported commodities to other regions, notably wine and olive oil to Egypt, where the climate is less suitable for growing grapes and olives (see Figure 4.5). Ezekiel 27.17 lists wheat, honey, oil, and balm as products exported by Judah and Israel.

The pattern of agriculture was that in the late fall the "early rain" (see Joel 2.23) softened the soil that had baked in the summer sun, enabling it to be plowed and the first crop of wheat or barley to be planted. This was harvested in the spring, and the soil was still moist enough (from the "later rain") to be planted with a second crop, which was harvested in the fall. Grapes, olives,

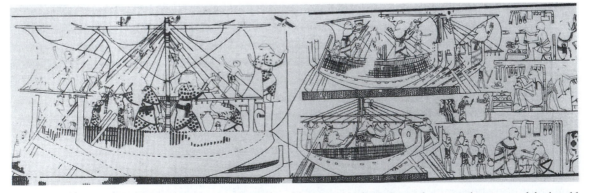

FIGURE 4.5. Canaanite traders unloading jars of wine or oil being imported into Egypt, from a tomb painting of the late fifteenth century BCE.

and other fruits and vegetables also were harvested in the late summer.

For the biblical writers, Israel was "a land flowing with milk and honey" (Ex 3.8). The "milk" was usually from sheep or goats rather than cows, since much of the land is not ideal for raising larger cattle, and was generally eaten as yogurt or cheese. The honey was probably not bees' honey, for although wild bees were known (see Judg 14.8), domesticated bees were not introduced until late in the first millennium BCE. Rather, it was a thick molasseslike syrup, made by boiling and straining grapes or dates. The phrase "flowing with milk and honey" thus indicates both a kind of utopian productivity and accurately names several of the principal products of the land.

The phrase also has mythological overtones. In ancient Canaanite myth, the high god El had a dream about how the land would be restored when the storm-god Baal was released from the power of Death:

the heavens will rain down oil,
the streambeds run with honey. (Compare Job 20.17.)

A similar image occurs in the description of the restoration of primeval abundance at the end time in Joel 3.18:

In that day
the mountains shall drip sweet wine,
the hills shall flow with milk,
and all the stream beds of Judah
shall flow with water. (See also Am 9.13.)

As in other ancient religions, the prosperity of the nation was inextricably linked to its patron deity. For Israel, this was Yahweh:

For the LORD your God is bringing you into a good land, a land with flowing streams, with springs and underground waters welling up in valleys and hills, a land of wheat and barley, of vines and fig trees and pomegranates, a land of olive trees and honey, a land where you may eat bread without scarcity, where you will lack nothing, a land whose stones are iron and from whose hills you may mine copper. You shall eat your fill and bless the LORD your God for the good land that he has given you. (Deut 8.7–10)

The Boundaries of the Land

Different biblical sources give different boundaries for the land of Israel. The maximum boundaries are given in detail in a number of texts, of which the following passage is typical: "Your territory shall extend from the wilderness to the Lebanon and from the River, the river Euphrates, to the Western Sea" (Deut 11.24). This summarizes a highly idealized view of the extent of Israel's territory. It encompasses the entire Levant, from the Euphrates River in northern Syria to the "wilderness" (the Negeb) in the far south. Paralleling the Euphrates as the northern boundary, some texts give as the corresponding southern boundary the "river of Egypt" or the "wadi of Egypt." This is probably not the Nile but one of the major watercourses (wadis) near Egypt that, like the arroyos of the American southwest, have water only in the rainy season; possible identifications are the Wadi el-Arish or the Brook Besor. These maximal limits are found mainly in J (Gen 15.18) and in texts from the Deuteronomic school, both of which can plausibly be dated to periods of strong monarchic control over an extended region, the tenth and the late seventh centuries BCE, respectively, that is, during the reigns of the kings David, Solomon, and Josiah. A narrower and in most periods more realistic definition is "from Dan to Beersheba" (for example, Judg 20.1), a phrase that is used half a dozen times, but only in narratives set in the late eleventh and tenth centuries BCE.

An example of the shifting boundaries of the land, reflecting degrees of actual control, is the status of Transjordan. In brief periods in their history, the Israelites seem to have controlled some territory in Transjordan north of the Arnon. This is the location of the tribes of Reuben, Gad, and eastern Manasseh; according to such passages as Numbers 34.14–15, their inheritance is "beyond the Jordan at Jericho eastward, toward the sunrise." Likewise, the ancient tribal catalogue found in the Song of Deborah notes that another component of Israel, Gilead, perhaps a subdivision of the tribe of Manasseh, "stayed beyond the Jordan" (Judg 5.17) rather than joining the tribes in the battle that the Song relates.

The first tribe to lose its territory was apparently Reuben. It is mentioned in the Song of Deborah (Judg 5.15–16) just before Gilead, but by the eleventh century BCE, as the Israelites were attempting to consolidate their territorial base west of the Jordan, their territory in Transjordan was under pressure from groups developing states there: the Moabites (see Judg 3.12–14), the Ammonites (1 Sam 10.27 addition), and, to the north, the Arameans (Judg 3.8; see also 1 Kings 22.3). Thus, in Genesis, where the stories about the twelve sons of Jacob reflect the history of the tribes named for them, Jacob's son Reuben loses his rights of firstborn (see Gen 49.3), just as the tribe for which he is named loses its territory; by the time of a later tribal catalogue "his numbers are few" (Deut 33.6), and in the census taken by David the tribe of Reuben is not even mentioned, apparently having been absorbed into Gad (see 2 Sam 24.5). Later texts give the Rift Valley as the eastern border of the territory controlled by Israel: "[Y]our eastern . . . boundary shall go down, and reach the eastern slope of the sea of Chinnereth; and the boundary shall go down to the Jordan, and its end shall be at the Salt Sea" (Num 34.10–12). Likewise, in the boundaries given by Ezekiel for the restored Israel after the Babylonian exile, all of the tribes are west of the Jordan, with their traditional tribal allotments rearranged to create a kind of ideal plan (Ezek 47.13–48.29).

HISTORY

Because the Bible is an anthology whose contents were written over the course of more than a thousand years, analysis of any part of the Bible requires knowledge of the historical context in which it was written. Moreover, many parts of the Bible are explicitly historiographic: They present themselves as an account of what happened to the people of Israel and to groups and individuals within it at various times. Thus, before returning to the biblical narrative, it is important to be familiar with the broad outlines of the history of ancient Israel. As we continue examining the biblical traditions, we will return to this history in more detail.

For the first ten or so books of the Bible it is difficult to speak of history in any verifiable sense, since there are no records apart from the Bible itself of the individuals and events that those books contain. But as we move further into the Bible, as the narrative deals with events described as taking place in the first millennium BCE, we find more and more correlations between the Bible and nonbiblical ancient sources. (See Box 4.1.)

Archaeologists have traced how culture developed from prehistoric hunter-gatherer societies to urban centers, a process that took many thousands of years. By the end of the fourth millennium BCE cities had emerged in the great river valleys of Egypt and Mesopotamia, and, in part at least to deal with the complexity of life in those cities, writing had also been invented. Many ancient texts have survived, especially in the media of baked clay tablets from Mesopotamia and papyri from Egypt. Using these texts, along with other archaeological evidence and the writings of ancient historians, it is possible to establish a chronology of the ancient Near East and to reconstruct in considerable detail the lives both of kings and queens and of ordinary men and women who lived there.

Following the rise of urban centers in Egypt and Mesopotamia is the period known in the Levant as the Bronze Age, subdivided into three eras: the Early Bronze Age, ca. 3300–2000 BCE, the Middle Bronze Age, ca. 2000–1550, and the Late Bronze Age, ca. 1550–1200. In Egypt, relatively stable rule over the entire Nile Valley had been established by the beginning of the third millennium BCE, inaugurating the Early Dynastic Period. Not long thereafter, the region immediately to the northeast of Egypt, Canaan, became part of the Egyptian ambit and was often under its direct control. In the Early Bronze Age this international contact included not only trade, but at times also some Egyptian colonization of the region, in the form of trading outposts, military garrisons, and administrative centers.

In Mesopotamia likewise, urban civilization had been established by about 3000 BCE, and

Box 4.1 TIMELINE

	Egypt	Canaan	Syria	Mesopotamia
ca. 3300–2000 BCE	Early Dynastic Period and Old Kingdom		Early Bronze Age	Sumerian city-states
ca. 2300–2000	First Intermediate Period	Under Egyptian influence and control	Under Mesopotamian influence and control	
ca. 2000–1550	Middle Kingdom		Middle Bronze Age	Rise of Babylon
ca. 1650–1550	Second Intermediate (Hyksos) Period			Rise of Hittites
ca. 1550–1200	New Kingdom		Late Bronze Age — Hittite control of northern Levant, Egyptian control of southern Levant	
ca. 1200–539	Collapse of power	Rise of smaller nation-states in Palestine and Syria	Iron Age	Collapse of power / Rise of Assyrians
ca. 1005–928		Rule of David and Solomon in Israel		
ca. 928		Separate kingdoms of Israel and Judah		
ca. 722		Fall of Israel to Assyria		
ca. 727–687		Rule of Hezekiah in Judah		
ca. 640–609		Rule of Josiah in Judah		
ca. 600–539		Neo-Babylonian Period		Rise of Babylon
ca. 586		Fall of Judah to Babylon and destruction of the First Temple		
ca. 539–332		Persian Period		Rise of Persia
ca. 332–63 BCE		Hellenistic Period		
ca. 63 BCE–330 CE		Roman Period		
ca. 70 CE		Fall of Jerusalem and destruction of the Second Temple		

Note: More detailed chronologies can be found in individual chapters and at the back of the book.

55

southern Mesopotamia was dominated by the Sumerians, from their southern city-states. Around 2300 the Sumerians were overtaken by Semitic-speaking Akkadians, but they regained control for the last century of the millennium under the leadership of the cities of Ur and later Isin.

At the end of the third millennium a period of instability reigned for several centuries in both Egypt and Mesopotamia. In Egypt this "First Intermediate Period" was followed by the Middle Kingdom, which lasted until the mid-second millennium, a time for the most part of prosperity and international influence. In Mesopotamia the history is more complicated, but eventually in the eighteenth century BCE the Babylonians from the south succeeded in controlling much of Mesopotamia and northern Syria for several centuries, including the homeland of the Assyrians to the north of Babylonia proper. In Palestine this was the Middle Bronze Age, a period of prosperity and wealth, enhanced by trade with Egypt.

(1550 BC) By the mid-second millennium the stability of the previous centuries was breaking down. In Egypt, a "Second Intermediate Period" of about a century was followed by rule by dynasties of foreign origin (the Hyksos), which lasted from 1650 to 1550 BCE. In Mesopotamia Babylon itself was captured in 1595 by the Hittites, an Indo-European people from Asia Minor (modern Turkey) who would become a major force in the Near East for several centuries; although the Hittites withdrew from Mesopotamia, no centralized control existed in Mesopotamia itself for several centuries. The balance of power in the northern Levant shifted to the Hittites, who from their homeland vied with Egypt for control of the coastal region between them, and with another new power, Mitanni, for control of northern Mesopotamia.

The expulsion of the Hyksos from Egypt in the mid-sixteenth century provides a convenient date for the beginning of the Late Bronze Age, a period of renascence that would culminate in Egyptian imperial control over much of the Levant. This "New Kingdom" was the apex of Egypt's power in antiquity. Egypt's rival for control of the Levant was the kingdom of Hatti, the home of

the Hittites, but after a series of costly battles in northern Syria in the early thirteenth century BCE, the two superpowers made peace and both flourished for another century.

No direct connections have been found between the abundant documentary evidence from the ancient Near East for the second millennium and the biblical narrative of Israel's ancestors and origins found in the first seven books of the Bible. As a result, it is impossible to determine with any certainty whether or not the individuals and events described in the Bible in fact existed, and, if they did, when they should be dated. Among scholars who find a historical kernel to the narratives, proposed dates for Israel's ancestors span the entire second millennium BCE. A convergence of possibilities makes a date in the first half of the millennium, during the Middle Bronze Age, not unreasonable. This hypothesis then connects the migration of Jacob and his family to Egypt, described at the end of Genesis, with the Hyksos period. Scholars are also divided on the historicity of the Exodus from Egypt. Many but by no means all scholars would date it to the reign of the Egyptian pharaoh Rameses II in the mid-thirteenth century BCE. This is based in part on the first occurrence of a biblical entity in a non-biblical source, the mention of Israel in a list of defeated foes in a victory hymn of Rameses II's successor Merneptah at the end of that century.

At the end of the Late Bronze Age and the beginning of the succeeding Iron Age, in the late thirteenth and early twelfth centuries BCE, major political and socioeconomic upheaval occurred throughout most lands bordering the eastern Mediterranean, and as part of this both the Egyptian and Hittite empires collapsed. In the power vacuum that resulted, several groups rose to prominence in Palestine. The Philistines were part of a group of Sea Peoples who had unsuccessfully attacked Egypt and had settled on the southeast coast of the Mediterranean. There they flourished and began to extend their territory to the north and east, coming into conflict with Israel, which was slowly increasing its own territory. Eventually what had been a loose confederation of tribes in Israel became a monarchy, under

Saul in the late eleventh century BCE and then David and Solomon in the tenth. These rulers were able to defeat the Philistines and to exercise some control over other neighboring states. Although the Bible remains our primary documentation for most of these events, archaeological data provide important supplementary evidence.

At Solomon's death what had been a united monarchy split into two separate kingdoms, the northern kingdom of Israel and the southern kingdom of Judah. In the northern kingdom, whose capital for the most part was at the newly established city of Samaria, a series of dynasties enjoyed prosperity for some time. In the less prosperous southern kingdom of Judah, the dynasty descended from King David continued to rule from its capital in Jerusalem. But by the late tenth century BCE, the Egyptians to the southwest and also the Assyrians in northern Mesopotamia had begun to recover some power and to extend their control beyond their own borders. Under the pharaoh Shishak, Egypt invaded Palestine about 924 BCE, destroying a number of cities. This campaign is mentioned in the Bible and in Egyptian sources and has left traces in the archaeological record. From this point on, more and more direct correlations of various bodies of data have been found.

Meanwhile, the Assyrians had begun to expand into the Levant, and their arrival in the region affected the smaller states. In a famous battle in 853 BCE, at Qarqar in northwest Syria, a regional coalition that included Ahab, the king of Israel, was able to check the Assyrians' advance, but by the late eighth century their march toward imperial domination of the entire region had resumed. They captured and destroyed Samaria in 722, making the former northern kingdom of Israel an Assyrian province, and they subdued the southern kingdom of Judah, laying siege to Jerusalem in 701 and forcing King Hezekiah's submission. With no more obstacles in their path, they proceeded to move toward Egypt, eventually capturing its capital of Memphis in 671 BCE.

Assyrian control of Egypt, however, was tenuous, and the Assyrian empire was overextended. By the mid-seventh century BCE the Babylonians in southern Mesopotamia had begun to assert themselves, and by the end of that century they had replaced the Assyrians as rulers of the Near East, having captured and destroyed the Assyrian capital of Nineveh in 612 BCE. Judah was caught up in these events and, despite moments of autonomy, succumbed to the Babylonians as well. Jerusalem was besieged in 597 by the army of the Babylonian king Nebuchadrezzar (also spelled Nebuchadnezzar), who forced its surrender and deported the king and some of the ruling class. The new king he installed, however, proved disloyal, and so in 586, after a long siege, the Babylonians destroyed the city of Jerusalem, including the Temple that Solomon had built, and brought to an end the dynasty founded by Solomon's father David in the tenth century BCE. A significant part of the population was deported to Babylon, and others fled to Egypt and elsewhere; this was the beginning of the Diaspora, or dispersion, of the Jewish people.

Babylonian control of the Near East was relatively short-lived. By the mid-sixth century BCE Babylon was threatened by the Persians to the east, who under Cyrus the Great captured Babylon itself in 539 BCE. Cyrus also allowed various groups of deportees to return to their native lands, among whom were the Judeans, or Jews, in Babylonia. Some did return, and they rebuilt the Temple in Jerusalem in the late sixth century. Persian control lasted for some two centuries. For Judah, now the Persian province of Yehud, it was a relatively peaceful time.

As the Persians expanded to the west, they came into conflict with the Greek city-state and were eventually defeated by them in the latter part of the fourth century BCE. Under Alexander the Great, the Greeks took over the Persian empire, including the Levant and Egypt. When Alexander died prematurely in 323, his generals divided his vast territories into three parts: Greece proper, taken by Antigonus; Egypt, taken by Ptolemy; and Syria and Mesopotamia, taken by Seleucus. The latter two were rivals for control of Palestine, but eventually the successors of Seleucus prevailed. For some time the Jews in Jerusalem were left relatively free to practice their religion, but in the early second century one of the Seleucids, Antiochus IV Epiphanes, tried to restrict the practice of Judaism and to impose Greek religion and culture on the Jews. Under the Maccabees a successful revolt was launched, and a semiautonomous kingdom was established in the region now called Judea.

Meanwhile, farther to the west, the Roman republic was expanding its control into the eastern Mediterranean and captured Jerusalem in 63 BCE. By the end of the first century BCE the Roman republic had become an empire, and it exercised unparalleled control over much of Europe, north Africa including Egypt, and western Asia. Under Roman rule Judea at first flourished, but internal dissent among the Jews exacerbated by inept administration by Roman provincial governors led the Romans to destroy the Temple and Jerusalem in 70 CE.

That year marks the end of any form of Jewish autonomy in the Promised Land in antiquity and is a suitable concluding point for this survey of the historical contexts in which the Hebrew Bible and the Christian Old Testament were formed.

Archaeology and the Bible

Since the nineteenth century CE, discoveries of texts and of artifacts have greatly enhanced our understanding of the historical and cultural contexts in which the Bible was written. Serious exploration of the Levant began with extensive mapping and with the identification of places mentioned in the Bible with actual sites. By the early twentieth century, European and American archaeologists were excavating major sites throughout the Near East and Egypt. In Palestine, attention focused on the major cites of ancient Israel, as Jerusalem, Samaria, Megiddo, Shechem, Jericho, Taanach, and Gezer were all partially uncovered. A preoccupation of many of these early excavators was historical, even apologetic: to identify, by independent data, the factual accuracy of biblical traditions.

In the 1920s and 1930s many more projects were begun, and excavation techniques improved. Greater accuracy in dating excavated remains was made possible through the refinement of ceramic typology. Using this method, archaeologists could date the ubiquitous pottery fragments and, more important, the layers or strata that contained them. But very little of the vast amount of material that was excavated and published could be related directly to the Bible, and debates often ensued about how to synthesize biblical and archaeological data.

When work resumed after World War II, new projects were undertaken and many sites that had been excavated earlier (and fortunately only partially) were redug with more sophisticated methods. In part because of the flood of material from periods long before and after biblical times or with little direct relevance to the Bible, archaeology began to develop as an independent discipline, as had already happened with the study of ancient Greece and Rome. More attention was given to the material culture of the region in various periods, and in some circles a theoretical tension developed between archaeology and biblical studies. Many earlier archaeologists were also biblical scholars. Now, more and more archaeologists were acquiring interest and expertise in periods and regions not directly pertinent to biblical history. The result, by the late twentieth century, was a vast amount of excavated material that is still being interpreted and synthesized, causing at times some antagonism between those in the fields of archaeology and biblical studies. Many archaeologists lacked sufficient expertise to connect what they excavated with written sources, especially the Bible, and many biblical scholars simply ignored the potential contributions of archaeology to the interpretation of the Bible.

Among the most important discoveries of the last century and a half are ancient texts from the entire ancient Near East, including Egypt. From a historical perspective, the repeated references, especially from the Iron Age onward, to individuals and events mentioned in the Bible made it possible to construct a detailed and accurate chronology. But for the most part, connections between ancient texts and the Bible are indirect. Moreover, like the Bible, other ancient texts also need to be interpreted, and also like the Bible, they cannot be taken at face value. For example, a ruler may claim a victory in a battle that other sources make clear ended in a stalemate or even a defeat. The nontextual discoveries, the material culture of the ancient inhabitants, are even more in need of interpretation, not just in terms of date, but also in terms of function and significance.

Yet despite undeniable chronological and geographical discontinuities, the literary, religious, and institutional traditions of the Levant, including ancient Israel, are best understood as part of a cultural continuum that, allowing for local particularities, was remarkably consistent and pervasive. It is thus impossible to interpret the Bible without taking into account both archaeological remains and ancient nonbiblical texts, and that is why we will refer frequently to them throughout this book. Reading the Bible without reference to all of the data that has been recovered is like reading the text of a play: Nonbiblical evidence, both archaeological and textual, often supplies the setting, the staging, and the costumes, as it were, enabling a much richer understanding and appreciation.

IDEOLOGY

Because the Bible is an anthology, its writers have different views of the land and of Yahweh's and Israel's relationship to it. One view, found in a number of biblical passages from various periods, is that the land belongs to Yahweh, who has given it to the Israelites; similar views of divine grants of territory by gods to their worshipers are found in other ancient Near Eastern religions. In the Bible this notion is expressed explicitly in Leviticus 25.23: "The land is mine, and you are resident aliens under my authority." Because of its connection with Yahweh, the land also has a sacred character; it is a "holy land" (Zech 2.12; Wis 12.3; 2 Macc 1.7), and by contrast other lands are "unclean" (Am 7.17). In the land, the capital city Jerusalem, also called Zion, has a special status. It is Yahweh's home, in which he has chosen to dwell (Ex 15.17; Ps 132.13–14), and it is called "the navel of the world" (Ezek 38.12), "the center of the nations" (Ezek 5.5), and "the joy of all the earth" (Ps 48.2).

Yahweh is not just the owner of the land, however; he is also its lover. The land and the people are thus identified. The fullest elaboration of this metaphor is found in Isaiah 62.4–5:

> You shall no more be termed Forsaken,
>   and your land shall no more be termed Desolate;
> but you shall be called My Delight Is in Her,
>   and your land Married;
> for the LORD delights in you,
>   and your land shall be married.
> For as a young man marries a young woman,
>   so shall your builder marry you,
> and as the bridegroom rejoices over the bride,
>   so shall your God rejoice over you.

This "land of Yahweh" (Hos 9.3) has been given to the Israelites as their possession. In the J and P traditions, the promise of the land is made without conditions. Yahweh promises that the land will belong to Abraham and his descendants forever (Gen 13.15; 17.8); it is an outright gift, not explicitly subject to being revoked.

In other traditions, since the Israelites are resident aliens in the land, having come from another place, their control of it is dependent on their observance of its owner's requirements: "Honor your father and your mother, so that your days may be long in the land that the LORD your God is giving you" (Ex 20.12; Deut 5.16). In this view, if the Israelites break the commands of Yahweh, they will be punished by being exiled from the land (Deut 28.63–65), and then the land will enjoy the sabbaths that they had failed to give to it (Lev 26.34–35). (See Box 4.2.) In this theory of retributive justice, the Israelites' successes and failures in the Promised Land are directly related to their relationship with Yahweh:

> If you will only heed his every commandment that I am commanding you today—loving the LORD your God, and serving him with all your heart and with all your soul—then he will give the rain for your land in its season, the early rain and the later rain, and you will gather in your grain, your wine, and your oil; and he will give grass in your fields for your livestock, and you will eat your fill. Take care, or you will be

Box 4.2 THE LAND OF ISRAEL IN JEWISH AND CHRISTIAN TRADITION

Although for most of Jewish history the Promised Land has been under the control of foreigners, attachment to the land of Israel has remained a central component of Jewish hope and aspiration, as the following examples illustrate.

Since at least the early Common Era, synagogues generally have been constructed with an orientation toward Jerusalem, the principal capital of ancient Israel and Judea. Thus, throughout the Diaspora, as well as in Palestine itself, Jerusalem has been a geographical focus. A similar and even more literal attachment to the land is the custom of Jews from the Diaspora being buried in the land of Israel, and especially in Jerusalem. The western slopes of the Mount of Olives contain tens of thousands of graves from more than two millennia, many of which contain the remains of Jews who had not lived in the land itself but whose remains were transported there from all over the world, just as Jacob's and Joseph's bodies were transported from Egypt for burial in the Promised Land (Gen 50; Josh 24.32). Likewise it became a custom for pilgrims to Jerusalem to bring back with them some of the soil of the land, so that when they died it might be thrown into their graves and they would rest in the land, or at least its soil. Finally, the Passover service includes the words "Next year in Jerusalem"; for centuries Jewish families everywhere in the world have spoken that wish annually, expressing their attachment to Jerusalem and the land surrounding it.

Although expelled from Jerusalem by the Romans early in the Common Era, Jews returned there fairly soon. They have lived there ever since, alongside many others, without interruption except because of occasional expulsion by Christian (and, much less frequently, Muslim) rulers. In the late nineteenth century, motivated in part by persecution of and discrimination against Jews throughout Europe, a movement called Zionism developed. The goal of Zionism was the establishment of a Jewish state in the ancient Promised Land, a goal that was achieved in 1948 when the modern country of Israel declared its independence.

Christianity's attitude toward the Promised Land has been ambivalent. Because it was the locale for many of the events described in the Bible, and especially those associated with Jesus, for Christians the land is the "Holy Land." As such, once Christianity became established in the Roman empire, by the fourth century CE, pilgrims often visited the Holy Land to view firsthand the context of the events described in the Gospels. Some also chose to live there, such as Jerome, the biblical scholar and translator, who took up residence in Bethlehem, the traditional birthplace of Jesus, in the late fourth century. Because of their view that Judaism had been superseded by Christianity, Christians felt a kind of entitlement to the land, a conviction that had its most violent consequences during the Crusades, when European Christians wrested control of the Holy Land from its generally benevolent Muslim rulers for a century.

Paradoxically, Christianity also spiritualized the idea of the land, hoping for "a better country . . . a heavenly one" (Heb 11.16) and for a "new Jerusalem coming down out of heaven" (Rev 21.2). This enabled Christians for the most part to distance themselves from the actual geographical space, and often to be indifferent to events there. It also made it possible for them to take the concept of a God-given territory and apply it to their own circumstances, as in the United States, where the idea of people divinely planted in a "New Canaan" has contributed to the conviction of a "manifest destiny."

---

seduced into turning away, serving other gods and worshiping them, for then the anger of the LORD will be kindled against you and he will shut up the heavens, so that there will be no rain and the land will yield no fruit; then you will perish quickly off the good land that the LORD is giving you. (Deut 11.13–17)

RETROSPECT AND PROSPECT

Israel's relationship to the land is a central theme of biblical literature, and that relationship was characterized as much by absence as by presence. The themes of exile and of return meet us at the very beginning of Genesis, when the man and the woman are expelled from the Garden of Eden in punishment for their disobedience to divine command; when Cain, "a fugitive and a wanderer on the earth" (Gen 4.12), as a punishment for having killed his brother Abel, also has to move "east of Eden" (4.16); and when the inhabitants of Babel are scattered by Yahweh over all the earth (11.9).

These episodes anticipate the narratives that follow, in which the geographical focus is the land of Canaan. There the ancestors of Israel lived, from there they journeyed to other lands, and there they ultimately returned. Their story is also the story of the nation as a whole, a story of presence and absence, of exile and return, of promise and fulfillment.

IMPORTANT TERMS

Canaan

Dead Sea

Fertile Crescent

Israel

Judah

Levant

Mesopotamia

Promised Land

BIBLIOGRAPHY

For a brief summary of the geography, history, and archaeology of ancient Israel, see *The New Oxford Annotated Bible*, (3d ed.; ed. M. D. Coogan; New York: Oxford University Press, 2001), pp. 494–97 and 505–19 ESSAYS, from which some of the material in this chapter is adapted; for the geography, see also M. D. Coogan, *The Oxford History of the Biblical World* (New York: Oxford University Press, 1998), Chap. 1, "In the Beginning." A fuller summary of the history and geography may be found in B. S. J. Isserlin, *The Israelites* (Minneapolis: Fortress, 2001 [1998]), pp. 21–92.

Summaries of archaeological discoveries as they relate to ancient Israel are found in John C. H. Laughlin, *Archaeology and the Bible* (New York: Routledge, 2000); and Walter E. Rast, *Through the Ages in Palestinian* *Archaeology: An Introductory Handbook* (Philadelphia: Trinity International, 1992).

For more detailed surveys, see Amnon Ben-Tor, ed., *The Archaeology of Ancient Israel* (New Haven: Yale University Press, 1991); and Amihai Mazar, *Archaeology of the Land of the Bible 10,000–586* B.C.E. (New York: Doubleday, 1990).

THE ANCESTORS OF ISRAEL

CHAPTER 5

Genesis 12–50

Following the mythic depiction of primeval times in Genesis 1–11, the story told by the narrators of Genesis continues with the introduction of Abraham and, then, in a series of episodes rather than in a continuous narrative, the lives of the ancestors of Israel: first Abraham and Sarah, then Isaac and Rebekah, and finally Jacob, his wives, and his children. Thus, Genesis 12–50 is essentially the story of four generations, and the books immediately following further narrow the focus to just one generation, that of the Exodus from Egypt.

This ancestral narrative includes repeated tales of rival wives and rival brothers, tales held together by a number of overarching themes, the most prominent of which is God's use of these rivalries to accomplish his purpose of establishing a new nation, Israel. The rivalries thus mirror tensions within Israel itself, and between Israel and its neighbor states in the late second and first millennia BCE. For the ancient biblical writers, then, the history of the nation's ancestors was a kind of prototype of that of the nation itself, a history in which divine testing and guidance mysteriously accomplished the deity's intent.

A subtheme in the narrative, already introduced in Genesis 1–11, is that of exile and return. This anticipates both the account of the Exodus from Egypt, which will be the principal narrative content of the books of the Pentateuch that follow Genesis, and also the return from exile in Babylon in the sixth century BCE. Thus the biblical writers, drawing on a variety of sources and traditions, some of which may well be very old, have shaped them so that they continue to have relevance for subsequent generations.

THE NATURE OF THE NARRATIVES

The narratives of the ancestors of Israel are essentially a series of interlocking family histories. The principal focus is on the line that leads from Abraham and Sarah through Isaac and Rebekah to Jacob and his four wives and their twelve sons, the ancestors of the twelve tribes of Israel. In the course of these narratives collateral lines also receive attention: that of Abraham's nephew Lot and his children, the ancestors of the Ammonites and the Moabites; that of Abraham's son by Hagar, Ishmael, and his twelve sons, the ancestors of north Arabian tribes; that of Abraham's six sons through his third wife, Keturah, also ancestors of north Arabian tribes; and that of Esau, Jacob's older brother, the ancestor of the Edomites.

The analysis of these interlocking narratives is a complicated task. First is the question of sources, or documents, as identified in the Documentary Hypothesis (see further pages 23–27). As in Genesis 1–11, this kind of analysis begins with passages that recount the same event. For example, on three different occasions, a patriarch in a foreign land claims that his wife is his sister (Gen 12.10–20; 20; 26.6–16); Hagar, Abraham's second wife, is twice forced to leave by Sarah (Gen 16; 21.8–21); and on two different occasions Jacob defrauds Esau of the inheritance that was his as the older son (Gen 25.29–34; 27). Many such repetitions can be attributed to the presence of different sources in the final form of the narrative.

Source criticism alone, however, does not fully explain either the prehistory of the narrative or its later stages of development. We must also look at the earlier units and traditions that the Pentateuchal sources adapted and incorporated into their narratives (this is called **form criticism**), as well as how the sources were combined into larger units (**tradition history**) and were shaped into their final form (**redaction criticism**).

As in much of the rest of the Pentateuch, the process of understanding these chapters in Genesis is like the excavation of a **tell**, an ancient mound consisting of the accumulated deposits of successive human occupations. Within it are fragments of very ancient tradition, sometimes misunderstood by the biblical writers themselves, sometimes too reused for purposes different from their original function, much as stones from an ancient wall might be reused in construction of a later period. As with excavation, also, it is difficult to reconstruct the earliest levels with any certainty. But the attempt to do so is a necessary one, which can often be illuminating, especially by using parallel data from other ancient texts.

SOURCE CRITICISM

The J Source in Genesis 12–50

With the exception of the extended story of Joseph (see pages 75–76), most of the narratives concerning the ancestors of Israel in Genesis 12–50 belong to the J (Yahwist) source, and they can be read as a group of linked episodes. They share a number of common themes, including a threefold promise of land, descendants, and blessing, announced at the beginning of the story of Abram, in Yahweh's command to him:

> Go from your country and your kindred and your father's house to the land that I will show you. I will make of you a great nation, and I will bless you, and make your name great, so that you will be a blessing. I will bless those who bless you, and the one who curses you I will curse; and by you all the families of the earth will bless themselves. (Gen 12.1–3)

Parts of this threefold promise, and sometimes the whole, are repeated with variations and expansions at intervals in the narrative, to Abraham (Gen 12.7; 13.14–17; 15.18–21; 18.18), Isaac (26.2–5, 24), and Jacob (28.13–15). (See Box 5.1.)

The promise of land is integral to the narrative. Abraham walks through the land, as if he were staking out a claim, and, according to J, its boundaries are extensive: "from the river of Egypt to the great river, the river Euphrates" (Gen 15.18), that is, from the border of Egypt to northern Syria. Yet throughout Genesis, and in fact throughout the Pentateuch, neither Abraham nor his descendants actually own any of the "Promised Land," except for the burial plot at Hebron (Gen 23), and before the end of Genesis, Jacob and his extended family have all migrated to Egypt. In fact, only in the tenth century BCE, during the reigns of David and Solomon, did Israel exercise control over that much territory. (See Figure 5.1.) (See further pages 256–57.)

It was in the tenth century BCE that Israel dominated most of its adjoining neighbors (see 2 Sam 8.12; 1 Kings 4.21). In its narrative J denigrates, often crudely, those nations by attributing to their ancestors questionable origin or dubious character. Thus, Ammon and Moab were the descendants of the incestuous union of Lot and his daughters (Gen 19.30–38), and the Edomites descendants of the hapless Esau (25.30). The second narrative of the expulsion of Ishmael, which

Box 5.1 ABRAM AND ABRAHAM, SARAI AND SARAH

Until Genesis 17, Abraham and Sarah are called by the less familiar names of Abram and Sarai. According to P, God changed their names, in Abraham's case to denote his new status as the "father of a multitude" (Gen 17.5), and since P is the final editor of the Pentateuch, the change is consistent in all sources from this point onward. The name change, made in connection with the divine promise that Abraham will be fruitful, is explained by a folk etymology derived from a similar sounding but unrelated Hebrew word; this etymology, like some others in Genesis and Exodus, is linguistically incorrect. Both Abram and Abraham (whose name in either form means "The father [the patron deity] is exalted") and Sarai and Sarah (both meaning "princess") are dialectal variants, reflecting different early traditions concerning these ancestors that were combined at a later stage.

some also have attributed to J, reflects the same kind of putdown: When Sarah sees Ishmael "making Isaac laugh," she persuades Abraham to send Hagar and Ishmael away (21.8–10). The same verb is used, with clearly sexual meaning, in Genesis 26.8, when Abimelech sees Isaac "making Rebekah laugh" and immediately knows that she is his wife, not his sister (see also Gen 39.14, 17; Ex 32.6). Like the Ammonites and the Moabites, then, the Ishmaelites too were descendants of an ancestor with questionable sexual proclivities (see also Gen 9.20–27, and Box 3.2 on page 33).

The second component of the threefold promise is that of descendants: "I will make of you a great nation," says Yahweh to Abraham in Genesis 12.2, and that is elaborated repeatedly: Abraham's descendants will be so many that they will be uncountable, like the dust of the earth (13.16; 28.14), the stars in the sky (15.5; 26.4), or the sand on the seashore (32.12). Yet, despite the promise of offspring, many of the ancestors have difficulty in having children except through divine initiative.

The third component of the promise is that of blessing: Abraham will be so fortunate that oth-

ers will ask to be as blessed as he. Yet despite this promise, Abraham and the other ancestors undergo great personal and collective suffering, from famine, from persecution, and even from divine caprice.

Thus, each part of the threefold promise is fulfilled in a complex and indirect way. As in the J narratives of Genesis 1–11, Yahweh is an unpredictable, even arbitrary deity. No motive is given for the divine choice of Abraham by Yahweh in the Bible, and he continues to act according to his own mysterious purposes, most notably by not following traditional inheritance customs in choosing a younger son as the heir of the promise, as in the choice of Isaac over his older brother Ishmael and Jacob over his older brother Esau.

Because J is our most extensive source, from it we also get a detailed look at the lifestyle of Israel's ancestors. With the notable exception of Genesis 14 (see page 80), they are depicted as seminomadic pastoralists, living for the most part in tents and moving about the land with their flocks, generally on the fringes of the more settled urban areas. For them, as for their ancient and modern counterparts, wells were essential

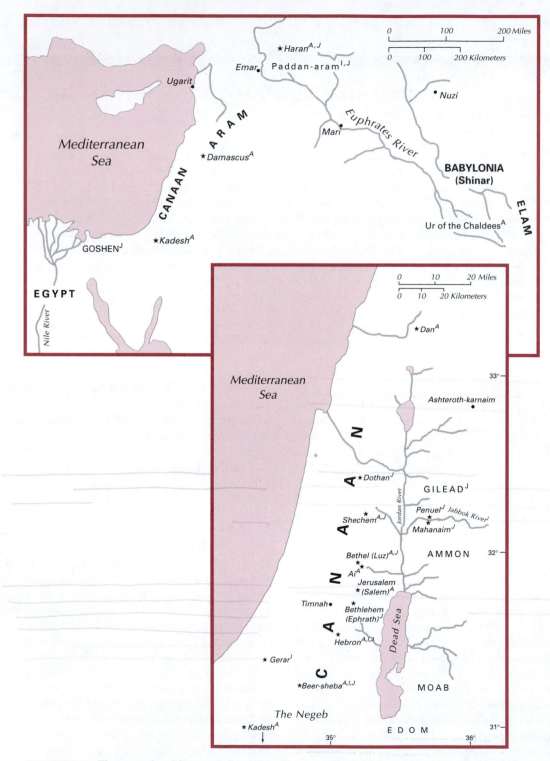

FIGURE 5.1. The geography of the ancestral traditions. Places associated with a particular ancestor are marked with a star, and the initial(s) of the ancestor(s) follows the place name: A(braham), I(saac), and J(acob).

(see, for example, Gen 26.15–33 and Figure 5.2) and hospitality was a primary virtue (18.1–5; 19.2–3).

The E Source in Genesis 12–50

Because E (the Elohist source) was joined with J as a supplement (see page 28), its narrative is fragmentary, and there are few passages in the narrative that can be securely identified as belonging to it. In them E features places of importance in the northern kingdom of Israel, especially its first capital, Shechem, and its second, Penuel (see 1 Kings 12.25). In E, Jacob acquires land near Shechem by purchase (Gen 33.18–19), rather than by violence, as in J (Gen 34), and E relates in detail the founding of the Transjordanian sanctuary of Penuel (Gen 32.30; see further pages 72–73). Bethel was another important sanctuary of the northern kingdom (see 1 Kings 12.29; Am 7.13), and the narratives of its founding (Gen 28.10–22) and of subsequent worship there by Jacob (Gen 35.1–8) are also principally E.

One of the clearest examples of E at work is its version of the wife-sister episode in Genesis 20. In contrast to the two J versions (Gen 12.10–20, of Abraham, and 26.6–16, of Isaac), in which the sexuality is more explicit, in E's version of what must have been a folktale told in several circles, the foreign ruler, Abimelech, never consummates his relationship with Sarah (contrast Gen 12.15). Rather, God (*elohim*, the characteristic designation of the deity in E) warns Abimelech in a dream that she was married to Abraham, who is identified by God as a prophet (20.7). Such indirect forms of revelation (by dreams and by prophets, rather than, as in J, by

FIGURE 5.2.   Wells are important elements of survival for seminomadic herders like the ancestors of Israel, as the frequent references to wells in Genesis 12-50 show. In this photograph, a modern herder is drawing water for his flock from a well in an arid region not far from the Dead Sea.

direct contact between Yahweh and humans, as in Gen 18) are also characteristic of E.

Another passage that many scholars attribute to E is the story of the "binding" (Hebr. *aqedah*) or sacrifice of Isaac in Genesis 22. This difficult passage has as one of its themes an **etiology**, or narrative explanation, of the place name of Mo-

riah, an unknown location somewhere in the Negeb, which a later writer identified with the Temple Mount in Jerusalem (2 Chr 3.1, the only other occurrence of Moriah in the Bible). The chapter shares with Genesis 20 the theme of "fear of God," which many scholars have identified as a characteristic E concept. (See further Box 5.2.)

Box 5.2 THE BINDING OF ISAAC

Although it can be read simply as another affirmation of Abraham's unwavering obedience to God, this episode has troubled both ancient and modern readers. Why at this stage in Abraham's life did God need to test him again? He had faithfully obeyed every divine command given to him, and in any case, should not an omniscient deity have known how obedient his servant was? We also see a somewhat sadistic tone in God's description of Isaac to Abraham as "your son, your only son, the one whom you love" (Gen 22.2). Thus, in some postbiblical retellings of the story, it is Satan rather than God himself who tests Abraham, a substitution influenced by Job 1–2.

In the final form of Genesis, Abraham's willingness to obey the horrible divine command stands in remarkable contrast to his daring insistence that God act justly and spare the innocent of Sodom (Gen 18.22–33). Yet when God orders him to kill Isaac, he agrees without objection. In *Fear and Trembling,* an extended essay prompted by Genesis 22, the nineteenth-century Danish philosopher Søren Kierkegaard asked whether a person was obligated to obey a divine command even if the person knew that the command was morally wrong. Kierkegaard concluded that one should, but others have questioned Abraham's compliant obedience.

Some interpreters have seen in this chapter an explanation of why the ancient Israelites did not usually practice child sacrifice (for examples to the contrary, see Judg 11.30–40; Jer 32.35; Mic 6.7). But this interpretation seems inconsistent with God's praise of Abraham for his willingness to do precisely that. It is more likely that the narrative served as a kind of explanation or etiology of the practice of substituting an animal for the firstborn son, who was believed to belong to the deity; see Exodus 13.13–15 and 34.19–20.

Modern readers have observed that after this episode, Abraham and Isaac never speak to each other again, and that immediately after it Sarah, who has been absent from the narrative, dies (23.1). Both have been interpreted as hints of how readers, like the characters themselves, may react to the implicit horror of the story. Thus, in its content, and in its larger context in Genesis, the narrative of the binding of Isaac raises profound questions.

The P Source in Genesis 12–50

For the most part, P (the Priestly source) in the rest of Genesis functions primarily as a compiler and editor, with few independent narratives of its own. As in Genesis 1–11, P shows the progress of history by means of genealogies. These genealogies began in Genesis 2.4a with the "generations of the heavens and the earth" and continued throughout the primeval history (Gen 5.1; 6.9; 10.1; 11.10, 27). Now P extends the series of "generations," or "births" (the Hebr. *toledot* means precisely that) with lists of the descendants of Abraham through Ishmael (Gen 25.12) and through Isaac (25.19) and lists of the descendants of Isaac's son Esau (36.1). The narrative of Jacob and his family includes the phrase "these are the generations of Jacob" (Gen 37.2), but the actual genealogy does not come until near the end of the narrative, in Genesis 46.8–27, an extended genealogy that begins with the phrase "these are the names," to be repeated in Exodus 1.1.

One of P's characteristic phrases is "be fruitful and multiply," as a divine command (Gen 1.22, 28; 9.1, 7; 35.11) and a divine promise (8.17; 17.2, 20; 28.3; 48.4), and also in narrative fulfillment (Gen 47.27; Ex 1.7). The genealogies are a kind of working out of this theme, as are accounts of marriages, births, and deaths. Thus, P recounts the union of Abraham and Hagar (Gen 16.3); the subsequent birth of their son Ishmael (16.15–16); the birth and circumcision of Isaac (21.1–5); the deaths of Sarah (23.2), Abraham (25.7–10), and Ishmael (25.17); the marriage of Isaac to Rebekah (25.20); the marriages of Esau (26.34–35; 28.8–9) and Jacob (27.46–28.9); the death of Isaac (35.29); and the death of Jacob (49.29–33) and his burial (50.12–13).

P has only a few sustained narratives, including the account of the covenant with Abraham (Gen 17), whose sign was **circumcision** (see Box 5.3), and that of the purchase of the family burial plot, a cave near Hebron (Gen 23; see Figure 5.3). These two narratives are also connected with birth and death, respectively.

FIGURE 5.3. The traditional site of the burial cave of Abraham and Sarah, Isaac and Rebekah, and Jacob and Leah (see Gen 23; 49.29–32). Shown here are the tombs of Isaac (on the right) and Rebekah (on the left). They are inside a mosque in the city of Hebron, whose Arabic name, Khalil, means "friend," a reference to Abraham, the "friend of God." Hebron was also King David's first capital.

FORM CRITICISM

Within the larger units of the ancestral narrative as defined by literary criticism, we can observe elements of earlier tradition. The identification of these smaller units is part of the method called "form criticism," developed by the German biblical scholar Hermann **Gunkel** in the early twentieth century, and especially worked out in his commentaries on Genesis and Psalms. Form criticism begins by trying to identify a form, or genre, and then to determine its function in its original context (or *Sitz im Leben*). One important "form"

Box 5.3 CIRCUMCISION

In Genesis 17, the practice of circumcision, the removal of the foreskin, is presented, in a repetitive legal style, as required of all the male descendants of Abraham on the eighth day after birth, and, implicitly, as a practice that originated with Abraham and was distinctive to his group. Thus, circumcision is characteristically practiced by Jews, and also by Muslims, who regard themselves as related to Abraham through Ishmael (see further Box 5.5).

But circumcision was not an exclusively Israelite procedure; in fact, it was widely performed in the ancient Near East. Many of the nations that bordered Israel practiced circumcision (see Jer 9.25–26, which mentions the Egyptians, the Edomites, the Moabites, and the Ammonites), with the notable exception of the Philistines, who are often called "uncircumcised," apparently a derogatory term (see, for example, Judg 14.3; 1 Sam 17.26). The Babylonians also were uncircumcised, and so the ritual is part of P's emphasis on observances that could be carried out anywhere, even in exile in Babylon. Other ancient and modern cultures have also practiced circumcision, probably going back to prehistoric times; the antiquity of the ritual is suggested by the use of stone knives in Exodus 4.25 and Joshua 5.2.

Comparative anthropological data, along with an actual Egyptian depiction of the procedure (see Figure 5.4), suggest that circumcision originated as a rite of passage at pu-

FIGURE 5.4.   An Egyptian relief from about 2200 BCE, showing the procedure of circumcision being performed on young men.

berty, when a boy became an adult and, in traditional societies, was allowed to marry. There are traces of this in the Bible. In the account of the rape of Jacob's daughter Dinah in Genesis 34, circumcision is insisted upon by her brothers as a precondition of marriage with their sister (Gen 34.14–17), and in the curious episode in which Yahweh attempts to kill Moses, the phrase "a bridegroom of blood by circumcision" (Ex 4.26) also associates marriage with circumcision (see further page 90). The only references to circumcision on the eighth day after birth elsewhere in the Bible are Genesis 21.4 and Leviticus 12.3, like Genesis 17 also P and therefore relatively late. But it is impossible to determine when, and why, the time when the procedure was performed was changed from puberty to the eighth day after birth.

According to Paul, since God approved of Abraham before he was given the command to practice circumcision, circumcision is not necessary for salvation and Christians are not obliged to be circumcised (Rom 4.1–12). This view was fiercely disputed in the early decades of Christianity, although it eventually prevailed. Nevertheless, many Christians, especially in North America, continue to have their infant sons circumcised, but for cultural rather than strictly religious reasons.

---

or genre is the etiological narrative, a tale whose function is to explain the origin of a name, a geographical feature, or a religious custom.

Thus, in Genesis, several narratives in both J and E are concerned with the establishment of shrines, and these narratives explain the origin of the shrine's name. Sometimes the founding of the shrine (for example, by the construction of an altar) is attributed to more than one of the patriarchs; thus, the shrine at Beersheba is connected with both Abraham (Gen 21.33) and Isaac (26.25), that at Shechem with both Abraham (Gen 12.6–7) and Jacob (33.20), and that at Bethel again with both Abraham (Gen 12.8) and Jacob (28.19; 35.7). Of these places that can be identified with certainty, only one, Shechem, has had responsible excavation. This revealed that at Shechem a major religious area in the city had been in use throughout much of the second millennium BCE. Because the name Bethel means "house of El" [NRSV "house of God"], it presumably had a permanent religious structure as well. What seems to have happened with these sites is that the myth of their founding stayed with them (Gunkel called this principle *Ortsgebundenheit*) and was appropriated by one or more groups

who frequented the site by attributing its founding to their ancestor.

This has historical implications. The repetition of so many of these narratives may indicate, as some scholars have suggested, that the tribal groups associated with Abraham, Isaac, and Jacob were originally distinct and united only later, a union expressed artificially in the overarching genealogy of Genesis, which makes Abraham the father of Isaac and Isaac the father of Jacob. This also indicates that the original narratives are earlier than the genealogies, and probably very old.

Etiological narratives are associated with personal names as well. The change of Abram's name to Abraham is explained in Genesis 17.5 (see further Box 5.1), and the meanings of the names of Ishmael, Isaac, Jacob, and Jacob's twelve sons are each explained by narratives associated with their conception or birth. In the case of Isaac several narratives play with the root meaning of his name, "to laugh." The original sense of the name was something like "(The deity) laughs," that is, rejoices at the birth of this child, but in these narratives wordplay is associated with the name: Abraham laughs (Gen 17.17), Sarah laughs (18.12–15; 21.6), Ishmael makes Isaac laugh

(21.9), and Isaac makes Rebekah laugh (26.8); the last two cases seem to have a sexual innuendo (see page 65).

Genesis 32

One of the shrines mentioned in the discussion on page 67 is Penuel, which is the setting of Genesis 32.22–32, the account of Jacob wrestling with a divine adversary. This short episode is an example of the multilayered density of the ancestral narratives; while often attributed to E, it also contains elements of older tradition.

As Jacob is preparing to return to Canaan after his twenty years of service to Laban, he sends his entourage ahead of him across the ford of the Jabbok River, one of the main eastern tributaries of the Jordan. Alone, and at night, he is attacked by a mysterious adversary, who is unable to defeat the patriarch, even with a low blow. Finally, at dawn the adversary asks Jacob:

> "Let me go, for the day is breaking." But Jacob said, "I will not let you go, unless you bless me." So he said to him, "What is your name?" And he said, "Jacob." Then the man said, "You shall no longer be called Jacob, but Israel, for you have striven with God and with humans, and have prevailed." Then Jacob asked him, "Please tell me your name?" But he said, "Why is it that you ask my name?" And there he blessed him. So Jacob called the place Peniel, saying, "For I have seen God face to face, and yet my life is preserved." (Gen 32.26–30)

Only at this point is the identity of Jacob's adversary disclosed: It is God (El) himself.

The narrative contains several etiologies:

- The name of the place, Penuel (also given as Peniel), which means "face of El" (or "face of God"); here, contrary to the dominant biblical view that no one can see God and live (see for example Ex 33.20; Judg 13.22), Jacob encountered the deity and survived.

- The explanation of an otherwise unattested dietary restriction: "Therefore to this day the Israelites do not eat the thigh muscle that is on the hip socket, because he struck Jacob on the hip socket at the thigh muscle" (32.32).

- An implicit explanation of the origin of the name of the river, based on the similar sounding Hebrew words *yabboq* (Jabbok), *ya'aqob* (Jacob), and *ye'abeq* ("he wrestled").

- The explanation of why Jacob's name was changed to Israel, based on his "wrestling" with God and with men. Jacob had also struggled with Esau before birth (Gen 25.22–26), and the two struggles are connected in a poetic summary of the Jacob story found in the eighth-century prophet Hosea:

> In the womb he tried to supplant his brother,
>   and in his manhood he wrestled with God.
> He wrestled with the angel and prevailed, he
>   wept and sought his favor. (Hos 12.3–4)

Behind these associations with Jacob and with Penuel, moreover, are widely attested folkloric elements. Originally, perhaps, this was a story about how a hero tamed the river, comparable to the tales in Germanic folklore of the trolls who guarded rivers and had to be defeated before the rivers could be crossed. The struggle of a river-deity or sea-deity with a hero is also attested in Greek mythology, as in the cases of the river Xanthus, who fought with Achilles outside the walls of Troy, and Proteus, "the old man of the sea," with whom Menelaus fought on his journey home from the Trojan War. Furthermore, like Grendel in the Anglo-Saxon epic *Beowulf* and various goblins, ghosts, and vampires of world culture who lose their power in daylight, Jacob's adversary apparently cannot be out after dawn. A similar, even briefer, narrative in Exodus 4.24–26 describes how Yahweh tried to kill Moses at night, as he was returning to Egypt, the place of his birth, at the divine command (see further page 90).

Another element that has folkloric background is the reluctance of Jacob's adversary to reveal his name. Divine or preternatural beings often show such reluctance, as with the divine messenger in Judges 13.17–18, and God himself in Exodus 3.13, because knowing the name could involve some form of control. Interestingly, the divine adversary does not know who Jacob is, and needs to ask his name so that he can give him a proper blessing; this is another indication that the original legend was unconnected with Jacob.

The change in the name of the patriarch from Jacob to Israel also marks a change in his character. Up to this point, Jacob has been a cheater, a liar, and a trickster. Yet here Jacob himself is tricked, as he had been in the substitution of Leah for Rachel, and from now on Jacob, renamed Israel, becomes a model character. From now on he is no longer a deceiver (except, perhaps, implicitly, in Gen 33.14), although he continues to be deceived, as when his other sons convince him that Joseph has been killed by a wild animal. His name is changed, by the divine adversary, and his essence is changed.

At the same time, even as the episode resumes the by now familiar themes of blessing and of return from exile, the final view of Jacob/Israel in this episode is poignant: the solitary hero, at sunrise, exhausted from his nocturnal struggle, limping as he crosses the river alone.

Repetitions

The Documentary Hypothesis explains only partially why some passages are similar. Another reason for repetition is that the compilers of the Bible wanted to preserve traditions that circulated, probably originally orally, in different groups. Examples include the birth of twin boys in which the younger somehow shows his superiority to his brother (Jacob and Esau, Perez and Zerah), the childless woman (Sarah, Rebekah, Rachel, Tamar), the matriarch in danger in a foreign land, the founding of a sanctuary or shrine, and the acquisition of rights to a well. Another is the use of clothing as a means of deception in the cycle of stories concerning Jacob. Jacob wears a disguise so that his blind and aged father Isaac will think that he is his older brother Esau and give him the inheritance. In ironic reversals, Jacob himself is deceived, by the substitution of Leah for Rachel at his wedding, possible because the bride was veiled (29.23; see 24.65; Song 4.1, 3), and by the presentation to him of Joseph's famous coat, stained with goat's blood so that Jacob will think that Joseph has been killed by a wild animal

(37.31–33). Similarly, Jacob's son Judah is deceived by his daughter-in-law Tamar, disguised as a prostitute (38.14–15), and Joseph's garment, left behind in his would-be seducer's hand, becomes the evidence that sends him to prison (39.12–20).

ANCIENT NEAR EASTERN PARALLELS

Many of the elements of the plot of Genesis 12–50 are found in other ancient literatures. Among these, perhaps the most significant is the epic of **Kirta** (also rendered Keret), partially preserved on three clay tablets found at Ugarit (see Box 5.4). The first of the surviving tablets opens midstory, and the last concludes abruptly; we have no way of determining how many more tablets came at either the beginning or the end. As the first tablet begins, we are introduced to Kirta, whose children have died and whose wife has left him. In a dream at night, the god **El** (see page 81) appears to him and gives him lengthy instructions for preparing an expedition to another city, where he will obtain a wife. When he awakes, Kirta carries out the instructions, in the repetition of command and execution common to ancient poetry and literature (for a biblical example, see Ex 25–31 and 35–40). In the course of his journey, he stops at a shrine, where he vows to the goddess Asherah that he will present her with substantial amounts of gold and silver if the journey is successful. It is, and Kirta returns to his home with a new wife. The marriage is blessed by the gods, and she soon produces sons and daughters.

The narrative continues with an account of how Asherah punished Kirta with a life-threatening illness for failing to fulfill his vow and how one of his sons rebelled against his ailing father (parallel in some ways to the revolt of Absalom against his father, King David, in 2 Sam 15–18). The end of the narrative is lost.

There are a number of similar plot elements to the ancestral narratives in Genesis. In both we have childless ancestors; divine promise of offspring, sometimes in a dream; a journey for a wife; in the course of the journey a stop at a shrine where a vow is made; and ultimately the birth of

Box 5.4 THE UGARITIC TEXTS

In 1928, a Syrian farmer plowing his field near the Mediterranean coast uncovered a tomb that contained ancient pottery. Further digging in the field uncovered more such tombs, and the French archaeological authorities in Damascus assigned a young archaeologist, Claude Schaeffer, to investigate the discovery. In his first season of excavation in 1929, Schaeffer excavated the cemetery and then began work at Ras Shamra ("Cape Fennel"), a large nearby tell or artificial mound composed of the layered remains of ancient occupation. Within weeks he had exposed the ruins of a once-flourishing city that had been destroyed in the late thirteenth century BCE; subsequent excavation would show that the city had been occupied, with interruptions, since about 6500 BCE during the Neolithic Period.

In the latest level of occupation, which is dated to the end of the Late Bronze Age about 1200 BCE, Schaeffer found many clay tablets, some inscribed with a previously unknown writing system. These tablets were quickly deciphered, and they revealed that the name of the site in antiquity was Ugarit; the language of the newly deciphered texts was thus dubbed **Ugaritic**. Eventually many thousands of texts were recovered in the ongoing excavations at Ras Shamra and in its vicinity. These were written in half a dozen languages, using a variety of writing systems, and included a large number of diplomatic and commercial texts. Several dozen tablets, written in Ugaritic and found in the vicinity of the city's temples, were myths, notably about the gods El and Baal, and epics, concerning the legendary founder of the royal house of Ugarit, Kirta, and another ancient hero, Danel (mentioned in Ezek 14.14); others were detailed descriptions of rituals, for which some of the myths may well have served as kinds of librettos, or performance pieces, as elsewhere in the ancient Near East.

This extraordinary discovery was probably the most important of the twentieth century for illuminating the larger context in which the Hebrew Bible was written. In these texts, the Canaanites speak for themselves, rather than through the often distorted vision of others, notably the Israelites, the classical writers, and the early Christian Church fathers. Knowledge of Canaanite religion and culture, of which the texts from Ugarit are an exemplar, was vastly enhanced, and the understanding of the religion of ancient Israel was transformed. The poetic diction of the myths and epics is very close to that of biblical poetry, especially in its use of parallel pairs, and also to that of the Homeric epics, in its use of stock epithets.

children. While the elements of plot found in the epic of Kirta do not occur in the same order in the ancestral narratives of Genesis, nor are all found in connection with every patriarch, a remarkable clustering of similar elements is found. It is likely that both the Canaanites of Ugarit and the ancient Israelites used a common set of motifs when telling the story of an ancestral founder, with different versions of the story varying in which motifs they included.

THE JOSEPH NARRATIVE

Some scholars have identified the cycle of inter-connected stories concerning Jacob's favorite son Joseph in Genesis 37–50 as belonging to the E source. As in E, dreams are a prominent feature of the Joseph narrative, and some of the action takes place near the important northern city of Shechem. Indeed, the tribes of Ephraim and Man-asseh, whose ancestors are the two sons of Joseph, form a central part of the northern kingdom; Ephraim is in fact a term often used in poetry for the northern kingdom of Israel as a whole.

An alternate view, held by most modern schol-ars, is that the Joseph narrative, especially Genesis 37.2–36 and 39.1–47.28, was an originally inde-pendent literary composition, a kind of novella (a term first applied to the Joseph story by Gunkel) or short work of historical fiction, not just a compos-ite of traditions like the preceding ancestral narra-tives. As such, it consists of an artfully constructed narrative about only one of the sons of Jacob, Joseph, and is not a complete account of his life but rather focuses on his fraternal relationships and his life in Egypt. Unlike the ancestral narratives that precede it, which are essentially family-centered, the Joseph story incorporates to a much fuller de-gree a plot from the Egyptian court, into which the story of Joseph's brothers is incorporated.

Although set in Egypt, little in the narrative has a distinctive Egyptian coloring, and few details can be correlated with Egyptian sources. Thus no in-ternal clues exist as to the original date of the Joseph story, and various times from the tenth century BCE onward have been proposed. Moreover, no men-tion of Joseph son of Jacob as an Egyptian official is found in any Egyptian records, as we might ex-pect there to be given his description as the most important official in Egypt after the pharaoh him-self (Gen 41.41–45). If there is some historical ker-nel underlying the narrative, then a plausible set-ting for the rise to power of a Semite in largely xenophobic and nationalistic Egypt is the period from the mid-seventeenth to the mid-sixteenth centuries BCE, called the "Hyksos Period," when for a brief time Egypt was ruled by dynasties originally of Semitic origin.

The hero of the narrative is Joseph, Jacob's fa-vorite son. Like fictional heroes of later biblical times, such as Daniel, Esther and Mordechai, and Tobit (see further Chapter 30), he manages to survive in exile in a foreign court, overcoming all sorts of obstacles with divine assistance, and even-tually saving his family as well.

In contrast to the earlier ancestral narratives, no direct divine revelation comes to Joseph, and women are for the most part absent from the Joseph story, except for the wife of Potiphar, who attempts to seduce Joseph, and a brief mention of his Egyptian wife Asenath. At the same time, the Joseph story has been integrated carefully into its larger narrative context. Most of the major char-acters in the Joseph story have been introduced already, especially Jacob and his many sons. Moreover, similarities of plot exist, especially the rivalry between brothers: As with Ishmael and Isaac and Jacob and Esau, Jacob's sons too are di-vided, according to their maternal lineage. Other themes familiar from previous chapters in Gene-sis include dreams, famine, danger to the hero, journey to Egypt, and deception. Clothing is es-pecially important: The "coat of many colors" shows his father Jacob's preference for Joseph, as the older son of Rachel, Jacob's favorite wife (Gen 37.3). He is stripped of this coat (37.23), and then it is stained with goat's blood by his brothers to deceive Jacob into thinking that Joseph has been killed (37.31–33). This distinctive garment was probably a special robe worn by royalty; it thus anticipates Joseph's rise to power in Egypt, where he became second only to the pharaoh himself; the exact phrase is used elsewhere only of the robe worn by King David's daughter Tamar (2 Sam 13.18–19). Joseph is stripped of his clothing again when he is accused falsely of rape (Gen 39.11–18). When he rises to power in Egypt, Joseph is clothed with appropriate Egyptian garb (41.42) and, in an ironic reversal, gives his broth-ers fine garments as a gift (45.22).

Thus, on the one hand, Joseph is somewhat in-cidental to the main narrative—the god of the ancestors is the God of Abraham, Isaac, and Ja-cob. Yet in terms of the larger plot of Genesis, he bridges the passage from Canaan to Egypt and then from Egypt back to Canaan; the return of his body, properly mummified in Egyptian manner, and its burial in Canaan (at Hebron) anticipates the eventual return of the entire family of Jacob to the Promised Land.

The story of Judah and Tamar (Gen 38) is a digression from the story of Joseph, and so most scholars do not consider it part of the original novella. It does, however, contain themes found both in the main narrative and the Joseph story, including deception by clothing, and especially the birth of twins, in which the younger supersedes the older, as in the case of Jacob and Esau (Gen 25.19–26).

THE ANCESTORS OF ISRAEL

The Patriarchs

The three patriarchs are presented in very different ways. Abraham is an ideal figure, unques-

tionably obeying every divine command. Although a modern reader might question his willingness to deceive, as when he tells Sarah to say that she is his sister (Gen 12.11–13) and when he conceals his intention of sacrificing Isaac both from his servants and from Isaac himself (22.5, 8), it is unlikely that ancient readers would have viewed such episodes negatively. Rather, Abraham seems to be a kind of model believer, which is how he is remembered by Jews, Christians, and Muslims (see Box 5.5).

Isaac is the least developed of the three male ancestors, appearing in only a few episodes as a major character, and even then often subordinate to his father or his wife Rebekah. All of these episodes are set in the south, and for this reason many scholars have proposed that Isaac was originally the ancestor of a relatively minor southern tribe that eventually joined Israel and was connected with the other tribes by a fictive ge-

Box 5.5 ABRAHAM, FATHER OF BELIEVERS

Abraham has a dominant role in the three monotheistic religions, Judaism, Christianity, and Islam—so much so that they are often called the "Abrahamic" religions. For all three, Abraham is both a progenitor and the "friend" of God (2 Chr 20.7; Isa 41.8; Jas 2.23; Quran 4.125).

For Jews, Abraham is their ancestor, through Isaac and Jacob. Postbiblical Jewish literature elaborates extensively on the often sparse biblical narratives, presenting Abraham as a model believer (see further page 82). Because Jesus was a Jew, he too was a descendant of Abraham (Mt 1.1; Lk 3.34). For Christians in general, Abraham is also a model of faith (Rom 4.16–22; see also Heb 11.8–19), whose righteousness was approved by God before he was commanded to practice circumcision (see Box 5.3). Muslims trace their connection to Abraham through Ishmael, Abraham's son by Hagar, and Ishmael's descendants include a number of tribes that can be identified as Arab. The prophet Muhammad, born in Arabia in the late sixth century CE, is considered a descendant of Abraham. Thus for Muslims too, Abraham is the father of believers, and he is considered the first Muslim, a word that literally means "one who surrenders" (to God): "Abraham in truth was not a Jew or a Christian; he was a muslim, and one pure of faith" (Quran 3.67).

nealogical link with Abraham and Jacob. This must have happened at a relatively early stage, however, since the material about Isaac includes J, E, and P, and throughout the Pentateuch the three patriarchs are frequently linked in formulas like "the god of your fathers, the god of Abraham, the god of Isaac, and the god of Jacob."

Jacob is the most complex of the three patriarchs. A trickster and a deceiver from birth, he himself is also ironically the victim of various treacheries and deceptions, as discussed on page 72. Unlike Abraham, he is not a paragon; rather, his descendants share his questionable character, as later prophetic tradition makes explicit:

> The LORD . . .
>> will punish Jacob according to his ways,
>> and repay him according to his deeds.
>> (Hos 12.2)

Despite Jacob's flaws of character, however, God works through him, and ultimately transforms him, when he sees God face to face and is renamed Israel (Gen 32.28–30).

The Matriarchs

Several generations ago, before feminist criticism existed, the great German biblical scholar Martin Noth asserted that each of "the female figures in the . . . 'patriarchal' history . . . appears not as an independent figure of tradition but always in relation only to this or that male figure." Feminist scholars, however, have correctly pointed out that the women in the narratives of Genesis 12–50 are often key characters in the plot, who can act independently of their husbands and fathers. They also have direct dealings with the deity, especially with regard to conception, for Sarah, Rebekah, Rachel, and Leah all at some stage are unable to conceive children.

Rebekah provides dramatic examples of how the matriarchs are active participants in the narratives. She apparently has some say about her marriage to Isaac (24.57–58), she receives a revelation from Yahweh (25.23; as does Hagar in 16.7–14), and she initiates the scheme to get the inheritance for her favorite son Jacob at the expense of his older

twin brother Esau. In fact, although the narrative traces the lineage from Abraham to Jacob through Isaac, Isaac himself is a less developed, more passive character than Rebekah.

Note also that Rachel, like Jacob, is a wrestler (Gen 30.8), one who, in the literal rendering of the Hebrew text, wrestled with God and prevailed over her sister. It was God who had closed her uterus and caused her older sister Leah to have children, even though Rachel was her husband Jacob's favorite. But Rachel had Jacob sleep with her maid Bilhah, who bore Jacob children, so she defeated both God and her sister, just as Jacob had defeated both God and his brother.

Still, the society depicted in the ancestral narratives is essentially patriarchal. A woman leaves her father's house to move to her husband's home (Gen 24.59–61; 31), meals are often depicted as participated in only by the men (see 18.8–9; 19.3), and descent is patrilineal.

The Sons of Jacob

The narratives about the various sons of Jacob are in many respects a kind of personalized history of the vicissitudes of the tribes whose supposed ancestors they are. In the end, the dominant tribes were Judah in the south and the Joseph tribe of Ephraim in the north (recall that Ephraim is a frequent poetic synonym for "Israel," the name of the northern kingdom), and the prominence of those two tribes is reflected both in the stories of their ancestors and in the extended positive poetic characterizations of them in the tribal catalogue in Genesis 49, an early Israelite poem.

Reuben, the firstborn of Jacob's sons, loses that status because he sleeps with Bilhah, his father's concubine (Gen 35.22; 49.4; see also 1 Chr 5.1–2). The next oldest, Simeon and Levi, are punished for their violence in the affair of the rape of Jacob's daughter Dinah (Gen 34; 49.5–7). Of the sons of Leah, that makes Judah the heir of Jacob (Gen 49.8–12), and Joseph, the older of the two sons of Rachel, is his counterpart (Gen 49.22–26).

The ancestors of the tribes that were geographically on the periphery, Dan and Naphtali, and Gad and Asher, are sons of the secondary wives of Jacob, Zilpah the maid of Leah and Bilhah the maid of Rachel. As such, they are given only perfunctory attention both in the narrative and in Genesis 49. (See further Figure 5.5.)

Genealogies

One social convention that recurs in the ancestral narratives is **endogamy**, marriage within one's ethnic, cultural, or religious community. For the survival of the community's identity, and for keeping its property within the group, endogamy was essential. In Genesis, as in much of the rest of the Bible, exogamy, or marriage outside the group, was undesirable.

Although he had moved some distance from his ancestral home in northern Mesopotamia, Abraham sent his servant back there to get a wife for his son Isaac from among his kin (Gen 24). Isaac urged Jacob to do the same, unlike his

brother Esau, who had married Canaanite women (28.1–5). In a poignant attempt to please his father, Esau then married one of his cousins in the family of Ishmael (28.6–9). Figure 5.5 shows the intricate network of relationships by marriage and descent in the extended family of Terah, Abraham's father.

Despite the cultural preference for endogamy, however, the patriarchs often married outside the group. Abraham fathered children through Hagar, an Egyptian, and through Keturah, probably also a foreigner (Gen 25.1–5); Esau "took his wives from among the Canaanites," both a Hittite woman and a Hivite woman (Gen 36.2), as well as Ishmael's daughter; Judah married Shua, also a Canaanite; Joseph married Asenath, also an Egyptian. The issue of intermarriage was one that continued to divide the Israelites and subsequently Judaism. Despite the recognition that marriage outside the group threatened the preservation of its identity, especially its religious identity (see, for example, Deut 7.3–4 and Neh

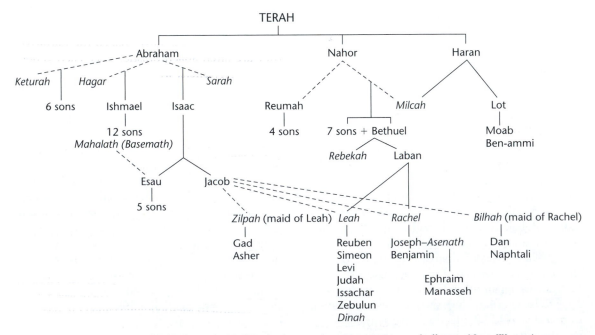

FIGURE 5.5.   The genealogy of the descendants of Terah, showing their intermarriages and offspring. Note: Women's names are in italics. Solid lines indicate descent; dotted lines indicate marriage.

13.23–27), individuals continued to do so, like Moses, whose wife Zipporah was the daughter of a priest of Midian. Other major biblical figures were acknowledged as born from such "mixed" marriages—most notably David, whose great-grandmother, Ruth, was a Moabite.

The genealogy in Figure 5.5 shows an ancient recognition of kinship among various groups. Thus, while the genealogies can exalt one group at the expense of another, they also reflect historical memory. This memory recognizes close connections among the various tribal and national entities in the Levant, as their related languages and shared cultural features illustrate. One of the latter is the organization of tribal groups by multiples of six or twelve: Nahor (Gen 22.20–24), Ishmael (17.20), and Jacob each had twelve sons, and Abraham had six by Keturah (25.2).

The narratives attached to the genealogies, and the poetic catalogue of tribes in Genesis 49, elaborate on the relationships. Thus, for example, the eventual loss of its land by the "tribe" of Levi (Num 18.23–24) is connected to its ancestor's role in the violent retaliation for the rape of Dinah (Gen 49.5–7), just as the tribe of Simeon, descended from the other brother in the story, was eventually absorbed by its more powerful neighbor Judah. With Levi removed from the list, in order to maintain the number twelve, another had to be added, and so the Joseph tribe was subdivided into Manasseh and Ephraim, who alone among his grandsons are blessed by Jacob. But Jacob reverses the birth order and gives the blessing to Ephraim, the younger son (Gen 48.14–20). Hence in the end we are left with two dominant tribes—Judah in the south and Ephraim in the north.

The genealogies thus are expressions of relationships between groups. They explain how one group became more powerful than another, but by attributing kinship to originally distinct groups, they support political and social interaction and even unity. In Genesis, for example, it has been suggested that originally several independent groups may have existed, an "Abraham" group, an "Isaac" group, and a "Jacob" group, and that these originally independent groups at some point united, with their union being expressed by making them all in the same genealogical line.

HISTORY AND THE ANCESTORS OF ISRAEL

The further removed biblical writers are from the events they describe, the less secure are modern scholars' attempts to determine their historicity, whether or not they actually happened. With regard to Abraham and Sarah, Isaac and Rebekah, and Jacob and his family, we are for the most part in the realm of legend, and it is extremely difficult to determine if any of the traditions concerning them in Genesis 12–50 have a historical basis. An analogy from British history is King Arthur, who may have been an actual historical figure, but the repeatedly retold legends about him are our only sources, making historical judgments difficult.

The quest for historicity is complicated by several factors. First, biblical chronology itself is essentially unreliable, given the ages attributed to the ancestors, and has its own internal inconsistencies. Second, because so many stages of composition and editing have shaped the narratives, they are often anachronistic, since each generation of storytellers, writers, and editors added elements from their own times. Third, because of the use of different sources in the final form of the narrative, many inconsistencies are found. (See further pages 22–23.)

For example, the ancestral homeland of the ancestors is northern Mesopotamia, in the vicinity of Haran. There Terah had lived (Gen 11.31) and Abraham was born (24.4); from there Abraham had left for the land of Canaan (12.4); and from the extended family in that region wives were arranged for Isaac (24.10) and Jacob (29.4). Only twice in Genesis (11.28–31; 15.7) is the place of origin of Terah and Abraham given as "Ur of the Chaldeans," a difficult phrase. There was a major city in southern Mesopotamia called Ur, occupied from the fifth to the mid-first millennium BCE. The term "Chaldeans" is often a synonym for Babylonians, but it is unattested in nonbiblical sources until the early first millennium. The identification of Abraham's original home as Ur may be an anachronism, perhaps to be connected with the exile in Babylon in the sixth century BCE. Details such as this, then, reflect the times of the writers and editors of the narratives and cannot be considered historical.

The ancestors of Israel are for the most part described as itinerant herders with flocks of small cattle, moving about the land but never settling in one place. They resemble the seminomads who have existed in the Middle East from earliest historical times to the present, interacting and sometimes in tension with the more settled agriculturalists, but primarily subsisting on the fringes of the latters' lands. As such, they would have been insignificant to the established societies of their day, extras, as it were, on the set of world history. Thus, it is not surprising that in the extensive but by no means complete written records we have from the entire second millennium BCE no mention is made of any of the characters in Genesis. This includes not only Abraham, Isaac, Jacob, and Joseph, but also Abimelech, the king of Gerar. In the one case where we have what appears to be a historiographic account, the story of the conflict between two groups of kings (Gen 14), none of the nine kings named in the narrative, nor Melchizedek, king of (Jeru)Salem (14.18), can be identified in nonbiblical sources. (That chapter is in many respects anomalous, and does not seem to be J, E, or P. For example, Abraham is depicted as the leader of a sizable private fighting force.) Conversely, no mention can be found in Genesis of any known historical figures. At times the writers of Genesis are tantalizingly vague, not naming, for example, the pharaohs who interacted with Abraham (Gen 12.15–20) and Joseph (Gen 41–50).

Given the lack of cross-references, it is not surprising that modern scholars have dated the period in which Israel's ancestors lived from as early as the mid-third millennium BCE to as late as the early first; some scholars are even more skeptical, proposing that the entire narrative is a historical fiction written late in the biblical period.

Other scholars have used indirect correlations, but the results have been inconclusive at best.

Among the materials that have been brought to bear on the problem of historicity are collections of texts from three northern Mesopotamian sites: Nuzi, east of the Tigris River in modern Iraq, and Emar and Mari, on the Euphrates in Syria. Tablets from Nuzi dating to the mid-second millennium BCE, and from Emar from slightly later, provide examples of marriage and family law that may be compared to those found in Genesis. Thus, in wills from both Nuzi and Emar, the inheritance included the family gods as part of the estate, and possession of these images may have been tantamount to control of the estate itself. These images apparently had some connection with the worship of deceased ancestors, implying an association with the inheritance passed down from one generation to the next. This may be the background of the story of Rachel's theft of the teraphim (Gen 31.19–35; NRSV: "family gods"); the use of teraphim, probably for a kind of divination, is attested elsewhere in the Bible. But for the biblical author the association has apparently been forgotten, or at least replaced by a derisory polemic against these foreign "gods," which can be sat upon by a menstruating woman. Evidence is also seen at Nuzi of various forms of adoption, including the adoption of a slave by a childless individual for reasons of inheritance, much as Abraham makes his slave Eliezer of Damascus his heir (Gen 15.2). But subsequent discoveries have made it clear that the Nuzi legal customs were more widespread both geographically and chronologically, and hence cannot be used conclusively for dating.

The texts from Mari relevant to this discussion date to the eighteenth century BCE. In them we find a clustering of names that are identical to or reminiscent of the names of some of Israel's ancestors in Genesis, including Benjamin, Laban, Zebulun, Ishmael, and Dan. Also found in sources contemporary with the Mari texts are other ancestral names, notably Jacob, which seems to have meant something like "May [the deity] protect [this child]." If the biblical writers were familiar with that meaning of the name, they deliberately ignored it, connecting it either with the noun for "heel" (Gen 25.26) or the verb "to supplant"

(27.36), in the punning type of folk etymology used repeatedly in the Bible. Most of the elements used in these names are common Semitic roots that occur in names from many periods, so the similarities in names cannot be used for purposes of dating. At least, or perhaps at best, they show that the names of the ancestors in Genesis could be relatively ancient.

Although parallels in other ancient texts have shed light on the Genesis narratives, they have not been able to provide conclusive evidence for dating of the earliest traditions within them. This much can be said: Many of the details of lifestyle and social custom embedded in the narrative are not inconsistent with a second-millennium BCE setting. At the same time, because the narratives were edited and reedited over the course of much of the first half of the first millennium BCE, they also contain many details that fit best in that period. But one additional body of data may be significant, concerning the deity worshiped by the ancestors, "the god of the fathers."

THE RELIGION OF THE ANCESTORS

As we have seen, in the J source, the name Yahweh is used from the time of Adam onward (see Gen 4.26; 12.8; 13.4; 21.33; 25.21–22; 28.13; etc.). But in both E and P, that name is not revealed until the time of Moses. Both of the latter sources use the Hebrew word *elohim* for the deity until that point, but P also uses other titles as well, especially ones compounded with El. The P account of the call of Moses summarizes its understanding as follows:

> God . . . spoke to Moses and said to him: "I am Yahweh. I appeared to Abraham, Isaac, and Jacob as El Shadday [NRSV: God Almighty], but by my name 'Yahweh' I did not make myself known to them." (Ex 6.2–3)

Not only does P here disagree with J, asserting that as Yahweh God was not known to the ancestors, but P uses an ancient title for the deity, "El Shadday." This title occurs five times in the P narrative in Genesis (17.1; 28.3; 35.11; 43.14; 48.3) and consists of two parts: the divine name

El and the epithet "Shadday," which probably means "the one of the mountain." The same divine name El is used in other combinations in Genesis, including "El Elyon" ("El the most high"), "El Olam" ("El the eternal"), "El Roi" ("El the one who appears" [or "the one who sees"]), "El Bethel" ("El of Bethel"), and especially in the phrase "El, the god of Abraham/my father/Isaac/etc."

The word "El" is a common Semitic word meaning "god." It can be used of any deity and occurs in a related form in Arabic, "Allah." It is also the name of the chief god of the Canaanite pantheon, known principally from the texts discovered at ancient Ugarit (see Box 5.4). In the "Kirta" epic referred to on pages 73–74, and in another epic called "Aqhat," the ruler of the gods is El, who presides over the council of the gods, in his tent, on his sacred mountain. His epithets characterize him: He is the king, the father of years, the eternal father, the creator of creatures, the bull, the kind and compassionate one. In "Kirta" and "Aqhat" he is the guider of ancestral destinies, who reveals himself in dreams, protects the protagonists in the epics, and guarantees that they will have progeny (see Figure 5.6).

This same El, the Canaanite high god, was the god of Abraham, Isaac, and Jacob. When Melchizedek, the king of Salem and high priest of its deity El Elyon, blesses Abram, Abraham accepts the blessing (Gen 14.18–20). Moreover, a number of proper names are formed with the element "el" (Ishmael, Israel, Bethel, Penuel), and no personal names in Genesis 12–50 include a form of the divine name Yahweh, which became the dominant pattern in Israel in the first millennium BCE.

Later, in the time of Moses according to biblical chronology, the ancestral deity El was identified as Yahweh. Yahweh retains many of the characteristics of El. El is called "the kind, the compassionate," and the same qualities are attributed to Yahweh, notably in the probably ancient formula in Exodus 34.6, which can be literally translated "Yahweh, Yahweh, [is] El the loving and merciful." Like El, he is a paternal and creator deity, as in Deuteronomy 32.6:

FIGURE 5.6. The Canaanite god El seated on his throne, blessing a worshiper or king standing to the left. This stone stela from ancient Ugarit dates to the thirteenth century BCE and is about 18 in (47 cm) high.

> Is not he your father, who created you,
>   who made you and established you?

Like El, he is also a king, and can be called "the bull" (Gen 49.24). And, remarkably, the latest source in Genesis, P, preserves a memory of a distant past, when the god of Abraham, Isaac, and Jacob was not Yahweh but El Shadday (see Ex 6.2–3).

A related question is whether or not the ancestors of Israel were monotheists. Postbiblical Jewish tradition gives a positive answer, elaborating as it often does on the silences in the biblical text. Why did Abraham have to leave Mesopotamia? Because in his zeal for the worship of the one true God he antagonized his neighbors, who threatened his life. But the au-

thors of Genesis make no such claim; for them, especially for P, the god of the ancestors is one among many. Note, for example, Jacob's instructions to his family:

> "Put away the foreign gods that are among you, and purify yourselves, and change your clothes; then come, let us go up to Bethel, that I may make an altar there to the God who answered me in the day of my distress and has been with me wherever I have gone." So they gave to Jacob all the foreign gods that they had. (Gen 35.2–4)

Unlike later reformers, Jacob does not destroy the images of the other gods; he simply orders them buried, so that when his family returns from worshiping the god whose temple is called "house of El" (for that is what "Bethel" means), they can retrieve them.

Genesis thus preserves very ancient memories of the time before Moses, when Israel's ancestors worshiped not Yahweh, but the Canaanite god El. As we shall see, however, sometime after about 1500 BCE, El was replaced as the principal deity of Ugarit by Baal. Thus, dating the ancestors to the first half of the second millennium, the Middle Bronze Age, is at least plausible. (See Figure 5.7.)

RETROSPECT AND PROSPECT

One of the principal themes of the ancestral narrative in Genesis is that of exile and return under divine guidance and protection. In Genesis 12.10–20, Abram goes down to Egypt, where Sarai is taken into the pharaoh's harem and Abram is enriched. In response, Yahweh afflicts the pharaoh with plagues, and the pharaoh orders Abram to leave. This is a kind of anticipatory summary of the account of the journey to Egypt by Jacob and his sons that dominates the end of Genesis (chaps. 37–50) and of the escape from Egypt that is the subject of Exodus 1–15.

Throughout Genesis 12–50, many of the major characters leave the Promised Land of Canaan and go to a foreign land, but they also

FIGURE 5.7. A caravan of Canaanite traders arriving in Egypt, depicted in an Egyptian tomb painting of the nineteenth century BCE.

return from it. In several cases the land to which they go is Egypt—Abraham (Gen 12.10); and, in the Joseph narrative, Joseph himself (39.1), then his ten brothers (42.3), then his ten brothers and Benjamin, his full brother (43.15), and finally Jacob himself along with his extended family (46.5–27). But the movement is often in the reverse direction as well—from Egypt back to Canaan, as in the cases of Abraham at the beginning of the ancestral narrative (13.1) and, at its end, Jacob himself, whose mummified body is brought back to Canaan for burial in the ancestral tomb at Hebron (50.13). But at the end of Genesis the rest of Jacob's family—"the sons of Israel"—are still in Egypt. The story of their emigration—their exodus—from Egypt back to Canaan is the subject of the books that follow. At his death Joseph's body has also been mummified in good Egyptian fashion (Gen 50.26), and it will be taken with the Israelites on their journey (Ex 13.19) and finally buried in Canaan (Josh 24.32).

One other character is also in Egypt. Accord-ing to E, God himself will accompany Jacob and his family into Egypt and out again: "I am God, the God of your father; do not be afraid to go down to Egypt, for I will make of you a great nation there. I myself will go down with you to Egypt, and I will also bring you up again" (Gen 46.4). The same idea is expressed in more litur-gical language in Deuteronomy:

> A fugitive Aramean was my father; he went down into Egypt and lived there as an alien, few in num-ber, and there he became a great nation, mighty and populous. When the Egyptians treated us harshly and afflicted us . . . the LORD heard our voice and . . . brought us out of Egypt . . . and gave us this land, a land flowing with milk and honey. (Deut 26.5–9)

This is the story of Jacob, anticipated in that of Abraham, of northern Mesopotamian origin, whose tenuous existence leads him from Canaan to Egypt. It is a good summary of the narrative of Genesis, which is ultimately a prologue to the story of the Exodus that follows.

IMPORTANT TERMS

circumcision	form criticism	tell
El	Gunkel	tradition history
endogamy	Kirta	Ugaritic
etiology	redaction criticism	

QUESTIONS FOR REVIEW

1. What are the principal themes of J, E, and P in Genesis 12–50?

2. Does the Documentary Hypothesis fully explain the existence of similar stories in Genesis 12–50? Why or why not?

3. What other kinds of analysis can be used to further understanding of these passages and their relationships to each other?

4. How do the passages contribute to the larger narrative of Genesis?

5. Discuss the importance of the Ugaritic texts for understanding both the ancestral narratives and the religion of the ancestors.

6. Discuss the theme of exile and return in the book of Genesis.

BIBLIOGRAPHY

For commentaries on Genesis, see the bibliography to Chapter 1.

Among the most important scholarly discussions of the history of the ancestral traditions is Martin Noth, *A History of Pentateuchal Traditions* (trans. B. W. Anderson; Englewood Cliffs, NJ: Prentice-Hall, 1972).

For an introduction to the discoveries from Ugarit and their significance, see Peter C. Craigie, *Ugarit and the Old Testament* (Grand Rapids: Eerdmans, 1983).

For translations of the Ugaritic texts into English, see especially Michael David Coogan, *Stories from Ancient Canaan* (Philadelphia: Westminster, 1978)—this volume, although dated, contains a helpful introduction to the translated texts as well as to the Canaanite material from Ugarit in general; Dennis Pardee and others, "West Semitic Canonical Compositions," pp. 237–375 in W. W. Hallo, ed., *The Context of Scripture*, Vol. 1: *Canonical Compositions from the Biblical World* (Leiden: Brill, 1997); and Simon B. Parker, ed., *Ugaritic Narrative Poetry* (Atlanta: Society of Biblical Literature, 1997).

For brief discussions of the problem of the historicity of the ancestral narratives, see B. J. Isserlin, *The Israelites* (Minneapolis: Fortress, 2001 [1998]) pp. 48–50; and R. J. Hendel, "Genesis, Book of: The Patriarchs and History," *ABD* 2.937–38.

ESCAPE FROM EGYPT

CHAPTER

6

Exodus 1–15

THE BOOK OF EXODUS

The birth of Moses at the beginning of the book of Exodus and his death at the end of the book of Deuteronomy define the chronological span and the narrative focus of the next four books of the Bible: Exodus, Leviticus, Numbers, and Deuteronomy. They recount the story of two generations, the one that experienced the Exodus and their immediate offspring, and, within the first generation, the life of one individual in particular, Moses. More space is given to this period and to Moses than to any other period or individual in the rest of the Hebrew Bible. That narrow focus indicates the importance the ancient Israelites placed on the time of Moses, a period they identified as formative, that is, when Israel itself came into existence, and as normative, one that set the patterns for Israel's beliefs and practices.

The word "exodus" comes from Greek and literally means "a going out," an appropriate title for the book that narrates how under the leadership of Moses the Israelites escaped from Egyptian persecution and began their journey back to the Promised Land. The book of Exodus, called "Names" (Hebr. *Shemot*) in Jewish tradition from its opening words ("These are the names," 1.1),

continues the narrative of Genesis, describing how the initial prosperity of the family of Jacob in Egypt was replaced by official persecution and even attempts at extermination. This is the context for the divine choice of Moses to lead the Israelites out of Egypt and back to the Promised Land. After the escape from Egypt, they arrive at the mountain of God (**Sinai**, or **Horeb**, depending upon the Pentateuchal tradition), where God gives them a series of laws, including the Ten Commandments, and instructions about religious rituals and ritual objects. These divine directives are set in a narrative context of repeated rebellion, including the episode of the golden calf. When the book concludes, the Israelites are still at Sinai, having constructed the ark of the covenant and the tabernacle following divine specifications. Because of the importance and the complexity of the material in the book of Exodus, we shall divide our treatment of it into three chapters, beginning with the escape from Egypt in Exodus 1–15.

As is the case for the rest of the Pentateuch/ Torah (see pages 21–22), Moses was traditionally viewed as the author of the book of Exodus. Modern critical scholarship, however, sees Exodus as a composite, shaped by Priestly writers from a variety of earlier sources, principally the earlier Pentateuchal traditions J and E, but also a number of others.

EXODUS 1–15

The Narrative

The book of Genesis ends with a paradox: The descendants of Abraham through Isaac and Jacob are not in the Promised Land of Canaan, but in Egypt, where they are called "Hebrews" (see Box 6.1). The first fifteen chapters of the book of Exodus describe their escape from Egypt and the beginning of their journey back to Canaan, both under Moses' leadership.

Packed into Exodus 1–15 are an extraordinarily large number of smaller units, in a variety of forms or genres, which have been combined into a relatively coherent narrative by the final Priestly editors. These include:

- The birth narrative of Moses (Ex 2.1–10)
- An extended **theophany**, in which God appears to Moses (3.1–4.17) and calls him to lead Israel out of Egypt
- Fragments of folklore, such as the account of a divine attack on Moses (4.24–26)
- Brief genealogies, of Moses and especially of Aaron (6.14–25)
- The contest narrative between Moses and the pharaoh (chaps. 7–11), into which the narrative of the plagues is set
- Legislation concerning the Passover ritual (chaps. 12–13)
- Fragments of the first stages of an itinerary from Egypt to Mount Sinai (12.37; 13.18, 20; 14.2; 15.22–23, 27)

Box 6.1 HEBREW AND HEBREWS

The language of the Hebrew Bible (and of modern Israel) is called **Hebrew**; the earliest use of the term "Hebrew" referring to language is in the prologue to the book of Sirach. In premodern English the term was also synonymous with "Jew." Neither was the ordinary usage of earlier antiquity, however. In the Hebrew Bible the language that the inhabitants of the kingdom of Judah spoke is called "Judahite" (Isa 36.11; Neh 13.24) and "Canaanite" (Isa 19.18; literally, "the lip of Canaan"). The term "Hebrew" is used only rarely, and in two principal contexts. First, it refers to Israelites or their ancestors living as resident aliens in another jurisdiction. Thus, it is used of Abram (Gen 14.13), Joseph (Gen 39.14), the descendants of Jacob in Egypt (Ex 1.15; etc.; compare Gen 43.32), David and his men (1 Sam 29.3), and Jonah (Jon 1.9), always in contexts where they are not in their homeland. The other context is for slaves, probably fellow Israelites (Ex 21.2; Deut 15.12; Jer 34.9).

In the New Testament, the term "Hebrew" is used somewhat differently. Sometimes (for example, Jn 19.13; Acts 21.40) it means Aramaic, the ordinary spoken language of Palestine in the first century CE. It is also used to distinguish Palestinian Jews—"the Hebrews," whose native language was Aramaic—from Greek-speaking Jews of the larger Hellenistic world—"the Hellenists" (Acts 6.1; compare 2 Cor 11.22; Phil 3.5).

- The hymn in Exodus 15.1–18, one of the oldest parts of the Bible, called "The Song of the Sea" or "The Song of Miriam"

The Early Life of Moses

Legendary material tends to accumulate around the early lives of important religious and political leaders. We have a number of such legends for Moses, beginning with the story of his rescue as a newborn.

The pharaoh, the king of Egypt, alarmed at the rapid growth of the population of the Hebrews, orders that all their male infants be killed. Moses' mother hides him as long as she can, but finally puts him in the hands of providence, setting him adrift in a papyrus boat on the Nile. His cries attract the attention of the pharaoh's daughter, who is bathing, and she rescues and adopts him.

This birth legend, which resembles other ancient traditions (see Box 6.2), serves several functions. It is an etiology, giving a folk etymology for Moses' name, erroneously connecting it with a similar sounding (but rare) Hebrew verb meaning to draw out (*mashah*). In fact, the name is a common Egyptian word, meaning "to be born," found in the names of pharaohs such as Thutmoses and Rameses. The legend also connects Moses with Noah, for the Hebrew word for the papyrus boat (*tēbâ* [NRSV: "basket"]) is used elsewhere in the Bible only for Noah's ark (Gen 6–9), and, like Noah's boat, the makeshift vessel into which Moses is placed is also smeared with pitch to make it waterproof (Gen 6.14; Ex 2.3; the Hebrew words are not the same). Moses' role as savior of his people thus is deliberately paralleled with that of Noah as the savior of the entire human species.

These observations, and the parallels in other traditions, suggest that the story of Moses' escape from death as an infant is not historical, a conclusion reinforced by details of the plot. The story makes no attempt to explain why Aaron and other males of Moses' generation who took part in the Exodus were not killed. Moreover, the narrative of Moses' call appears to contradict the story of Moses' being adopted by the pharaoh's daughter. When Yahweh appears to Moses and informs him of his mission, one of Moses' objections clearly shows his lack of status: "Who am I that I should go to Pharaoh and bring the Israelites out of Egypt?" (Ex 3.11): These are not the words of a pharaoh's adopted grandson!

Only one other event in Moses' life before his call is described, his murder of an Egyptian who was beating one of Moses' countrymen. As a result, Moses is forced to flee and settles down in Midian, where he marries the daughter of the local priest, and they have a son.

The Call of Moses

Each of the three primary Pentateuchal sources, J, E, and P, includes an account of the call of Moses to be the leader of the Hebrews in their exodus from Egypt. The account in Exodus 3–4 is a combination of J and E, with the E source providing the more complete account. In it, God appears to Moses at Mount Horeb in a burning bush, revealing himself as the god of his ancestors (3.6, 13).

In the first of a series of objections to the divine commission to secure the Israelites' release from the pharaoh, Moses asks this deity what his name is. God replies three times, with a slightly different answer in each response (Ex 3.13–15). In the first, "I am who I am" (NRSV), or perhaps better "I will be who [or "what"] I will be," God appears to be evasive, in effect refusing to tell Moses his name. Divine figures show reluctance to give their names elsewhere in the Bible (Gen 32.29; Judg 13.17–18) and in other literatures, for naming suggests control, and knowing a deity's name would allow the deity to be manipulated.

This is immediately followed by two further responses. The first of these abbreviates the sentence just given as "I am," and the second gives the deity's proper, personal name, Yahweh (see Box 6.3). From this point onward in E, Yahweh will be used frequently, and so E can no longer be distinguished from J using this criterion.

E's version of the call continues with further objections by Moses, each addressed by an increasingly impatient deity. Moses is given signs of his divinely

Box 6.2 LEGENDS OF RESCUE

The legend of the hero saved from apparently certain death as an infant is widespread in world cultures. Notable examples include Dionysus, Heracles, and Oedipus in Greece; Cyrus and Zarathustra in Persia; Romulus in Rome; and Jesus in Christianity (see below).

The closest parallel to the story of Moses' rescue is a first-millennium BCE autobiographical legend of the late third-millennium Mesopotamian king Sargon the Great, in which Sargon describes his origins as follows:

> I am Sargon, the great king, the king of Akkad.
> My mother was a priestess;
> my father I did not know. . . .
> My priestess mother conceived me,
> in secret she gave birth to me.
> She set me in a basket of reeds,
> she caulked its opening with bitumen.
> She cast me into the river, from which I could not rise.
> The river carried me off,
> it brought me to Akki, the drawer of water.
> Akki the drawer of water brought me up as he dipped his bucket;
> Akki the drawer of water raised me as his son.*

While many details are strikingly similar to the story of Moses' rescue, because of the chronological and geographical distances between the two texts it is unlikely that there is a direct literary connection between them. Rather, we have here an example of the tendency of rescue narratives to develop concerning important political and religious leaders. These legends show that the heroes who are their subjects are divinely protected from birth, and thus designated for a special role.

The rescue of the infant Moses from death at the pharaoh's hands is the principal source for the account of the infant Jesus' escape from Herod the Great's decree of death in Matthew 2 and forms part of that Gospel's thematic connection of Jesus with Moses. When Herod dies, it is revealed to Joseph that "those who were seeking the child's life are dead" (Mt 2.20), echoing Exodus 4.19.

---

*   Adapted from the translation of Benjamin R. Foster, p. 461 in *The Context of Scripture* (ed. W. W. Hallo; Leiden: Brill, 1997), Vol. 1.

bestowed authority, almost magical in form: He can change his staff into a snake, his hand from healthy to diseased, and the Nile's water into blood. But Moses is still unsatisfied, claiming his inability to speak will prevent him from being Yahweh's spokesperson, his prophet. Yahweh responds angrily, announcing that Aaron will serve as Moses' "mouth" (Ex 4.16), and Moses wisely stops objecting.

Box 6.3 THE DIVINE NAME YAHWEH

By the late biblical period the divine name was considered so sacred that it was rarely pronounced. A notable exception was its use by the high priest on the Day of Atonement, an exception that ended when the Temple was destroyed by the Romans in 70 CE. The actual pronunciation of the name, called the Tetragrammaton because it contained four letters (*yhwh*), is uncertain, although the form "Yahweh," based on a variety of ancient sources, is generally accepted.

The etymology of the name is also unclear, and the three different responses to Moses' question (Ex 3.14–15) probably reflect some uncertainty in ancient Israel itself about exactly what the divine name means. Most scholars identify it as a form of the verb "to be," meaning either "he who is" or "he who causes [something] to exist." The latter case is especially compelling, in part because of the frequent phrase *Yahweh seba'ot* (NRSV: "LORD of hosts"), which would identify the god of Israel as "(the one) who causes the heavenly armies to exist"; note also *Yahweh shalom* (NRSV: "The LORD is peace"; Judg 6.24). The name would thus originally have been a kind of title or epithet, identifying the deity as creator.

In Jewish tradition, various substitutes have been used for the divine name, including "heaven" and simply "the Name." In manuscripts of the Hebrew Bible, the most common was to read the word *adonay* (literally, "my Lord"). Originally Hebrew was written without vowels. In the rabbinic period, beginning around 500 CE, vowels were added to the text by means of a complicated system of dots and dashes ("points") that left the sacred consonantal text intact. To alert readers to the pious substitution for the divine name, the consonants YHWH were "pointed" with the vowels of *adonay*. Medieval Christians, not understanding the practice of writing the vowels of the substituted words with the consonants of the original, mistakenly read the divine name as *yehowah*, rendered into English as Jehovah. Most English translations, however, follow the ancient practice of substituting "LORD" for the divine name throughout the Hebrew Bible.

Moses' reluctance to accept the divine summons is itself part of the genre of the call of a prophet or leader. Like Moses, Jeremiah is a reluctant prophet who is given divine reassurances (Jer 1.6–10; see also Jon 1.2–3; 4.2); similarly, Gideon is a reluctant judge, who is given signs of divine presence and protection (Judg 6.15–24, 36–40).

P's account of the call of Moses, in Exodus 6.2–7.7, is set after Moses' return to Egypt and re-

peats much of the material found earlier in J and E, including the revelation of the divine name (6.2–3; compare 3.13–15), discussion of Moses' speech impediment (6.12, 30; see also 4.10), the appointment of Aaron as Moses' spokesperson (7.1; see also 4.14–16), and the announcement of the plagues (7.4–5; see also 3.19–20; 6.1). It also contains some characteristic P themes, especially the genealogy in 6.14–25 and a heightened role for Aaron. Aaron is important for P because he was the ancestor of the priests who officiated in the Temple in Jerusalem—they are called "the sons of Aaron" (Lev 1.7; etc.)—and who eventually produced the P source. Thus, beginning in Exodus 7.1, in P, Aaron's role is emphasized, sometimes even at the expense of Moses. It is Aaron, for example, who should "tell Pharaoh to let the Israelites go" (Ex 7.2; contrast 4.22), and it is Aaron's staff that turns into a snake (7.9–10; contrast 4.2–5).

We also find an important historical note in P: "I am Yahweh. I appeared to Abraham, Isaac, and Jacob as El Shadday, but by my name Yahweh I did not make myself known to them. I also established my covenant with them, to give them the land of Canaan" (Ex 6.2–4) This passage introduces a lengthy speech in which Yahweh reiterates his covenant promise to Abraham, Isaac, and Jacob to give the Israelites the land of Canaan (see Gen 15.18–21; 17.7–8, 19; 26.3; 28.13; 35.12), establishing continuity between the ancestral period and the time of Moses. At the same time, in a remarkable statement that preserves a very ancient tradition, P also stresses discontinuity: The ancestors did not know Yahweh by his personal name. This enhances the importance of Moses as the one through whom the full revelation of God is made to Israel, and at the same time recognizes that historically something new has happened. (See also pages 81–82 and 101–3.)

The Circumcision

Following the narrative of the call of Moses in chapters 3.1–4.17 is a short passage (4.24–26) that seems oddly inconsistent with the larger plot. Moses has finally acceded to the divine command to go back to Egypt and to secure the Hebrews' release from the pharaoh, yet one night, while Moses is on the way back, Yahweh tries to kill him. The scene is reminiscent of Genesis 32.22–32, in which a divine adversary attacks Jacob at night (see pages 72–73), and it anticipates the divine attack on the Egyptians, also at night (Ex 12.29–32).

The narrative, which has folkloric aspects and was probably originally more detailed, is compressed and therefore difficult to understand. What

is clear is that Moses' wife Zipporah averts the threat by circumcising her son and touching "his feet" with the bloody piece of skin. The term "feet," as often elsewhere in the Bible, is a euphemism for the genitals (see 2 Sam 11.8 [compare 11.11]; Isa 6.2; 7.20; Ruth 3.4, 7), but whose "feet" are being touched is unclear. The most probable explanation is that followed in the NRSV, which specifies the pronoun "his" by translating "Moses'." Thus, neither Moses' son nor Moses himself has been circumcised. Yahweh attacks Moses, perhaps because he is not circumcised. Zipporah takes action, circumcising her son and by touching the bloody skin to Moses' genitals makes it appear that Moses too has just been circumcised, thus tricking Yahweh into leaving Moses alone. (On circumcision, see Box 5.3 on page 70.)

The Plagues

In its present form the account of the plagues is a complex blending of the Pentateuchal sources J, E, and P. Each has its own themes and emphases, but they have been combined into a relatively smoothly flowing narrative. In this final form are ten plagues—the Nile turned to blood, frogs, gnats, flies, cattle disease, boils, hail, locusts, darkness, and death of the firstborn.

The analysis of the plague narrative according to the Documentary Hypothesis is difficult and often disputed in details. In general, however, if J, E, and P are viewed separately the familiar number of ten plagues no longer stands; rather, according to the standard identification of sources, we have something like eight plagues in J, only three at most in E, and five in P. We also find accounts of the plagues in Psalms 78.44–51 and 105.28–36. In these poetic treatments, synonymous parallelism links plagues that are separate in Exodus (for example, flies and gnats in Ps 105.31), and neither the order nor the number nor even the identification of the plagues is the same as in the final text of Exodus. Clearly the story of the plagues circulated widely in ancient Israel, with considerable variations in the retellings.

According to the generally accepted identification of J, E, and P, in the accounts of the first two plagues, blood and frogs, more than one source is found; the same is true for the last plague, the killing of the firstborn. Between them we have this division: Gnats and boils belong exclusively to P, and flies, cattle plague, hail, locusts, and darkness exclusively to J. There may be traces of E in the plagues of blood, hail, and locusts. If we look more closely at the sections identified as J and P, we see some important thematic differences. In the J sections, Moses is the principal Is-

raelite character; although Aaron is generally present, he has no significant role. The pharaoh's obstinacy is usually expressed by a word that literally means "heavy." In the P sections, on the other hand, Aaron is more prominent, and sometimes, for example in the plague of gnats, he is the principal character. The pharaoh's obstinacy is expressed by a word that literally means "harden" (see Box 6.4).

Box 6.4 THE HARDENING OF THE PHARAOH'S HEART

For modern readers (as also for Paul, in Rom 9.14–23), the repeated "hardening" of the pharaoh's heart is troublesome, especially when it is the Lord himself who is explicitly responsible for the hardening. Instead of a God who is supposed to "do what is right" (Gen 18.25), all sources depict God as deliberately making the pharaoh stubborn so that he will refuse to let the Hebrews go.

The poetic tradition states it bluntly:

> And Yahweh made his people very fruitful,
>   and made them stronger than their foes,
> whose hearts he then turned to hate his people,
>   to deal craftily with his servants. (Ps 105.24–25)

The result, of course, is enormous suffering for the Egyptians, culminating with the killing of their firstborn, "from the firstborn of Pharaoh who sits on his throne to the firstborn of the female slave who is behind the handmill, and all the firstborn of the livestock" (Ex 11.5; see also 12.29).

The same idiom is also used of the conquest of the land of Canaan: "It was Yahweh's doing to harden their hearts so that they would come against Israel in battle, in order that they might be utterly destroyed, and might receive no mercy, but be exterminated" (Josh 11.20).

In the case of both the plagues in Egypt and the conquest of Canaan, it is probably a mistake to look for subtle ethical distinctions. Rather, in a simplistic division, only two groups exist, the Israelites and their enemies. Yahweh is the god of Israel and is on the side of his people: Their enemies are his enemies, and whatever he and they do to these enemies is deserved.

At the same time, we may observe some discomfort in the text with the divinely caused stubbornness in the pharaoh that results in greater suffering. Alongside the most frequent expression that "Yahweh hardened Pharaoh's heart," we also find "Pharaoh hardened his own heart" and "Pharaoh's heart was hardened," both alternatives subtly suggesting that it was the pharaoh rather than Yahweh who was to blame.

P also introduces the characters of the Egyptian "magicians," properly "priests," like Moses and especially Aaron. The contest between the two sides, each representing their own deities (see Ex 12.12: "I will punish the gods of Egypt"; also P), has a comic dimension. In the prelude to the account of the plagues themselves, both Aaron and the Egyptian priests are able to turn a staff into a serpent—any good magician knows that trick! Likewise, the Egyptian priests are able to duplicate the first two plagues in P, those of the Nile being changed into blood and the frogs. When it comes to the third plague, the gnats (if that is the correct translation: fleas, lice, and mosquitoes are also possibilities), "the magicians tried to produce gnats by their secret arts, but they could not" (Ex 8.18). And the next plague in P, the boils, affects the magicians as well as the rest of the Egyptians. Aaron has clearly won the contest!

The initial ability of the Egyptian magicians to duplicate the feats of Aaron is one indication of genre: The account of the plagues is a contest narrative, like those found earlier in the story of Joseph (Gen 41) and, much later in the Bible, in the book of Daniel (chaps. 1–6). In all of these tales, the Israelite heroes prove themselves superior to their polytheistic rivals because God is on their side.

Throughout the ages, many suggestions have been made that relate the plagues to natural phenomena. Thus, it has been proposed that in its annual summer inundation the Nile carried in suspension particles of reddish soil, or perhaps algae, which made it look like blood; darkness has been supposed to refer to a solar eclipse or a sand storm; cattle plagues, hail, and locusts are frequent disasters in an agricultural economy; and so on. Although plausible, these rationalizations ignore the primary point of the plague narrative: The plagues are *not* natural phenomena but are caused by direct divine action; Deuteronomy calls them "great and awesome signs and wonders" (6.22; see also 4.34; 7.19; 11.3; etc.). While it is true that in ancient times even natural phenomena were perceived as the result of divine activity, the plagues are more than natural, as the immunity of the Israelites from the cattle plague, the

hail, and the darkness indicates. The last plague is clearly an extraordinary event caused by divine action: All the firstborn in Egypt die, but only the firstborn, and again not the Israelites' firstborn. The ability of the Egyptian magicians to replicate the first two plagues also shows that we should not take them literally: How could the Nile be changed into blood twice, or frogs cover the land of Egypt twice?

In the end, as Yahweh's representatives, Moses and Aaron have shown themselves to be superior to the pharaoh and his magicians, and, on the divine level, Yahweh has defeated the gods of Egypt.

Passover

The last plague is the killing of the firstborn of the Egyptians, in specific retaliation for the pharaoh's treatment of Israel, Yahweh's "firstborn son" (Ex 4.22). Closely associated with this terrible catastrophe is the celebration of the **Passover**. The legislation concerning this ancient ritual in Exodus 12.1–27 is primarily P; P has also incorporated another tradition (E, or perhaps D) in 13.1–16. As earlier in the P narrative with the legislation concerning the blood prohibition (Gen 9.4–6) and circumcision (Gen 17), the Passover is integrally related to the plot in which it is imbedded.

Underlying the Passover appear to be two distinct springtime rituals: one agricultural in origin, called the "festival of unleavened bread," and another probably pastoral in origin, of the sacrifice of the firstborn lamb. The most ancient law codes mention only the Festival of Unleavened Bread (Ex 23.15; 34.18), showing that it was originally a distinct ritual. It occurred at the time of the barley harvest, in the early spring; the alternate name for Nisan, the month in which the Passover occurs, is Abib, which means freshly ripened grain (see further Box 8.4 on page 135). In this ritual, farmers would offer to their deity bread made from the new harvest, with the flour unadulterated by "leaven," that is, sourdough from flour made from a previous harvest. The sacrifice of the newly born lamb, also occurring in the spring, would have been the shepherds' expression of gratitude to their deity for the fertility of their flocks, as well as a petition for continued fertility.

These separate spring rituals were joined as part of the process of Israel's emergence in Canaan, in which disparate groups, including farmers and shepherds, joined to form a new entity (see further pages 222–24). The rituals were also historicized, becoming linked with the commemoration of the defining experience of the Exodus. Thus, the eating of unleavened bread is explained by the haste with which the Israelites had to flee Egypt (Ex 12.34, 39; see also 12.11); Deuteronomy calls it "the bread of affliction" (16.3). Likewise, the eating of the lamb recalls the slaughter of the lambs whose blood was daubed on the doorposts of the houses of the Israelites in Egypt. As in the narrative of the sacrifice of Isaac, the lamb is a substitution for the firstborn (Gen 22.13). Finally, the "bitter herbs" (Ex 12.8), probably originally a type of lettuce, are associated with the bitterness of the oppression suffered by the Hebrews (Ex 1.14).

The Passover celebration is described as taking place in "the first month of the year" (Ex 12.2). The calendar of the ancient Israelites is only incompletely understood, and evidence exists both for a spring new year, as here, and a fall new year, as in later Jewish tradition, where Rosh Hashanah occurs in September or October (although there is scant evidence for the celebration of the New Year as such in biblical times). P's emphasis on the Passover as occurring at the beginning of the year is consistent with its portrayal of the entire Exodus complex as marking a new beginning, even a new creation. (On the Passover, see further Box 6.5.)

The Event at the Sea

As with other aspects of the Exodus traditions, as the event at the sea was told and retold, written and rewritten, it too was magnified. It should be remembered that these amplifications were motivated in part by the desire to praise Yahweh, who had brought Israel out of Egypt. Three versions of the event can be identified.

The P account of the event at the sea is the most familiar to modern readers, in part because it is the most detailed and the most dramatic, and also because it has repeatedly been presented in films, most notably perhaps in Cecil B. De Mille's *The Ten Commandments*. Found in Exodus 14 (vv. 1–4, 15–18, 22–23, 26–29, although other sources may also be present here), it features the sea divided as Moses lifted his staff: "The Israelites went into the sea on dry ground, the waters forming a wall for them on their right and on their left" (14.22). The Egyptians followed, and when the Israelites reached the other side, Moses lifted his staff again, and the returning waters engulfed the Egyptians.

At the same time, in its incorporation of other traditions into the final narrative, P implies that the event at the sea is a new creation: As in the accounts of creation (Gen 1.2, 9) and its renewal after the Flood (Gen 8.1, 14), the wind blew, the waters were divided, and the dry land appeared (Ex 14.21; probably J). What is being created here, however, is not the cosmos, but rather Israel itself, by Yahweh, the one who causes everything to exist.

Embedded in P's narrative is another version of the event at the sea:

> At the morning watch Yahweh in the pillar of fire and cloud looked down upon the Egyptian army, and threw the Egyptian army into panic. He clogged their chariot wheels so that they turned with difficulty. The Egyptians said, "Let us flee from the Israelites, for Yahweh is fighting for them against Egypt." (Ex 14.24–25)

According to this account, which is probably J, Yahweh caused the Egyptians to panic when their chariots got stuck in the mud.

Yet a third version of the event is found in Exodus 15, one of the oldest poems in the Bible. It relates how when Yahweh blew with his nostrils, the sea became churned up, and

> Pharaoh's chariots and his army he cast into the sea;
> his picked officers were sunk in the Reed Sea.
> The floods covered them;
> they went down into the depths like a stone.
> . . .

Box 6.5 THE DEVELOPMENT OF THE PASSOVER CELEBRATION

According to the earliest traditions (Ex 23.14–17; 34.18, 22–23; Deut 16.16), Passover was originally a pilgrimage festival, like the "festival of harvest" (also called "the festival of weeks" and "Pentecost," occurring in late spring) and the "festival of ingathering" (also called "the festival of Booths" and "Tabernacles," at the time of the fall harvest). The pilgrimage would presumably have been made to a local sanctuary. In the later Judean monarchy and subsequently, however, Passover became a national festival, during which all worshipers were required or at least urged to go to Jerusalem for the celebration. During the time of the monarchy, the insistence that the Passover be celebrated in Jerusalem is reflected in Deuteronomic legislation: "You are not permitted to offer the passover sacrifice within any of your towns that Yahweh your God is giving you. But at the place that Yahweh your God will choose as a dwelling for his name, only there shall you offer the passover sacrifice" (Deut 16.5–6).

According to the historical narratives, national celebration of the Passover was part of the religious reforms of two kings, Hezekiah in the late eighth century BCE (2 Chr 30) and Josiah in the late seventh (2 Kings 23.21–23; 2 Chr 35.1–19); according to Ezekiel's vision of the restored Temple, that national celebration would be reconstituted (Ezek 45.21–24). The Jerusalem-centered observance is also found in the book of Jubilees (second century BCE; chap. 49) and later sources, including the New Testament, in which Jesus goes to Jerusalem to celebrate the Passover (Lk 2.41; Jn 11.55), and the first-century CE historian Josephus, who reports that as many as three million people were in the city for the Passover celebrated in 65 CE (*War* 2.14.3; see also 6.9.3). The same Jerusalem orientation is retained in the prayer with which the Passover service concludes today: "Next year in Jerusalem."

Over the course of time, and in different cultural contexts, the "order" (*seder*) of the Passover changed. In P (Ex 12.3), because of the changed circumstances of the community after 586 BCE, with the Temple destroyed and many in exile in Babylon, the Passover became a family celebration, as it is in Judaism today. According to Deuteronomy 16.7, the Israelites are to boil (NRSV: "cook") the lamb, but P's recipe calls for broiling on a fire and forbids boiling (Ex 12.9); later, the Chronicler will harmonize this contradiction by describing the Passover offered by Josiah as "boiled . . . with fire" (2 Chr 35.13). By the second century BCE, wine was added to the celebration. The Last Supper of Jesus, incorporating the elements of unleavened bread and wine, seems to have been a Passover meal.

As the cultures of those who celebrate the Passover change, some elements need to be clarified:

> And when your children ask you, "What do you mean by this observance?" you shall say, "It is the passover sacrifice to Yahweh, for he passed over the houses of the Israelites in Egypt, when he struck down the Egyptians but spared our houses." (Ex 12.26–27)

Echoing this instruction, in the traditional Haggadah used in the family celebration of Passover, the youngest son asks, "Why is this night different from all other nights?" and the four questions that follow ask for an explanation of the differences between this commemorative celebration and ordinary meals:

> On any other night we eat both leavened and unleavened bread; why on this night do we eat only unleavened bread?
>
> On any other night we eat herbs of all kinds; why on this night do we eat only bitter herbs?
>
> On any other night we do not dip our herbs even once; why on this night do we dip them twice?
>
> On any other night we eat our meals either sitting upright, or reclining; why on this night do we all recline?

The answers to these questions provide a narrative of the Passover story.

Despite the cultural differences in the details of the celebration throughout the ages, however, what remains constant is the remembrance of the escape of the Hebrews from slavery in Egypt as the paradigm of divine action on their behalf, a divine action that is to be imitated in the Israelites' treatment of the most disadvantaged in their own society. As Yahweh remembered Israel when they were oppressed, so they are to remember what Yahweh did for them and to do the same to others in their situation: "I am Yahweh your God, who brought you out of the land of Egypt. . . . You shall not oppress a resident alien; you know the heart of an alien, for you were aliens in the land of Egypt" (Ex 20.2; 23.9).

> You blew with your wind, the sea covered them; they sank like lead in the mighty waters. (Ex 15.4–5, 10)

According to this account, the Egyptians, apparently in ships or barges, were swamped by a storm at sea and sank to the sea's bottom.

These three versions of the event are incompatible. If the Egyptians were already on the floor of the sea, as in P, then they could not sink like a stone or like lead. If they were on the sea's surface, as Exodus 15 suggests, their chariots are irrelevant. But here as elsewhere, the final Priestly editors of the Pentateuch were less concerned with a superficial consistency than with preservation of traditions, and one of those traditions, the account of the Egyptians' chariots getting stuck in the swamp, provides a clue to what may have occurred. A possible reconstruction is as fol-

lows. Under the leadership of Moses, a small group of Hebrew slaves (probably a few hundred at most; see page 99) escaped from their forced labor in the eastern Nile delta. They headed for one of the swamps or wetlands (the "Reed Sea"; see page 100) in the vicinity, pursued by their guards. Because they were on foot, the escapees were able to make their way through the swamp, but the Egyptians, in chariots, got bogged down and gave up the pursuit, so that the Hebrews got away. This event would have been relatively inconsequential to the Egyptians, but for those who escaped it was nothing short of a miracle.

Women in the Exodus Narrative

Throughout the narrative of the Exodus, women, both named and unnamed, are important characters. They are especially clustered in the stories associated with the early life of Moses, where they exercise initiative and are presented as liberators.

The first such women are the two midwives, Shiphrah and Puah (Ex 1.15–22), who serve as rescuers of Hebrews when the king of Egypt orders them to kill all newborn boys. Women characters are often unnamed in the Bible, and the naming of these heroic women suggests their importance. It is also likely that their story was one of those passed down by women, for, until modern times, midwifery and childbirth were principally women's concerns.

Next are Moses' mother and sister, in the narrative of his own rescue from the royal decree (Ex 2.1–10). Neither is named, nor for that matter is Moses' father; only later are we informed that his parents' names were Amram and Jochebed and that Moses' sister was Miriam (Ex 6.20; Num 26.59; 1 Chr 6.3). Both mother and sister are responsible for Moses' rescue. We have seen earlier that the use of the same word for "boat" connects Moses with Noah as savior. But Moses' mother is also a Noah-like figure; like Noah, she constructs the boat and waterproofs it (Gen 6.14; Ex 2.3). And Moses' sister serves as intermediary with the pharaoh's daughter, arranging for him to be nursed by his own mother until he is weaned.

Then there is the pharaoh's daughter herself, whose name also is not given. She is an exceptional Egyptian, the only one in fact presented positively. She too serves as a rescuer of Moses, drawing him from the waters of the Nile and adopting him; she also names him (often a mother's prerogative; see, for example, Gen 4.1, 25; 29.32–35; 30.6–24).

The final rescuer of Moses is his wife Zipporah, who, in the narrative of the divine attack at night (Ex 4.24–26), saves him from death by a surrogate circumcision (see page 90).

A different aspect of women's activities is found in the conclusion to the episode at the sea. In Exodus 15.20–21, Miriam, whose name is given here for the first time and who is identified both as a prophet and as Aaron's sister (but not Moses'; see Box 10.2 on page 162), leads the Israelite women in song and dance. Women generally led such victory celebrations, as did Jephthah's daughter after his defeat of the Ammonites (Judg 11.34). (See further "Excursus on Music in Ancient Israel" on pages 466–68.) As part of these celebrations, they composed victory hymns; such hymns are attributed both to the women of Israel welcoming Saul and David after their victories (1 Sam 18.6–7) and to Deborah (Judg 5.1), who like Miriam is also called a prophet (Judg 4.4). Miriam also sings a hymn:

> Sing to Yahweh, for he has triumphed gloriously;
>   horse and rider he has thrown into the sea.
>   (Ex 15.21)

This is also the beginning of the "Song of the Sea," which is attributed to "Moses and the Israelites" (Ex 15.1). It is at least possible Miriam should be credited as the author of the song. Later tradition transfers that credit to Moses, both because of the tendency to attribute so many traditions to him and also perhaps as a patriarchal suppression of the significant role that women had in the formation of the literature of ancient Israel. Nevertheless, the presentation of women in the Exodus narrative suggests that women had status in ancient Israelite society on a number of important levels.

THE EXODUS AND HISTORY

As is the case with the ancestral narratives in Genesis 12–50, no direct correlation exists between any person or event found in Exodus 1–15 and nonbiblical sources. Once again, the Bible is remarkably vague: Neither the pharaoh who begins the persecution of the Hebrews nor his successor, the pharaoh of the Exodus itself, is named, and their characters are devoid of particulars by which we might be able to identify them. If the biblical writers had given us the names of these pharaohs, we would know at least approximately when those writers thought the events took place. Moreover, the considerable documentation from ancient Egypt makes no mention of the Hebrews, Moses, Aaron, the plagues, or the defeat at the sea.

This lack of correlation has led some scholars to be skeptical that anything like the Exodus ever occurred. The view of a majority of scholars, however, is that the biblical traditions, although clearly containing anachronisms and signs of later editing, do preserve authentic historical memory.

First, the escape from slavery in Egypt under the leadership of Moses is a constant in biblical tradition, found in a variety of forms in all sources from the earliest to the latest. It is deeply imbedded in Israel's legal traditions, including the most ancient, such as the Ten Commandments, and in the earliest biblical poems, such as Exodus 15, Deuteronomy 33 (vv. 2–4), and Judges 5 (vv. 4–5). And the Exodus continues to be a major theme in Israel's literature, especially the historical books, the prophets, and the psalms.

Closely related to the pervasive importance of the Exodus in the Bible is the presence of indisputably Egyptian elements in the accounts of the Exodus. The names of Moses, Aaron, Phinehas, and others of the generation associated with the Exodus are clearly of Egyptian origin. The store cities of Pithom and Rameses (Ex 1.11) have tentatively been identified with specific sites in the Nile Delta (see Figure 6.1), and their construc-

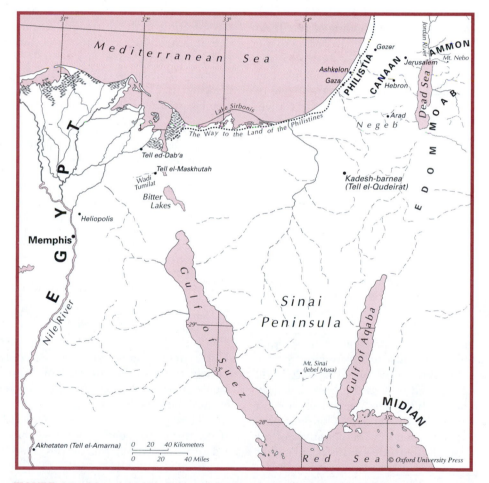

FIGURE 6.1. Map of the Nile Delta and the Sinai Peninsula. Tell el-Maskhutah and Tell ed-Dab'a have been identified as the biblical store cities of Pithom and Rameses (Ex 1.11). Jebel Musa in the southern Sinai Peninsula is the traditional identification of Mount Sinai, but that is questioned by most scholars.

tion is consistent with the most likely date for the Exodus (see below).

Although the Bible does lack specifics, nothing in the Exodus narrative is inconsistent with what is known about ancient Egypt. A convergence of evidence thus occurs, and the most parsimonious reconstruction based on that evidence is that an Exodus (or, according to some scholars, more than one) did take place. That is more reasonable than a hypothesis that the Exodus was a fictional conception.

The Date of the Exodus

Biblical tradition dates the Exodus in relation to other events. According to 1 Kings 6.1, it took place 480 years before the building of the Temple by Solomon. That occurred, according to the chronology used in this book, in about 965 BCE, which would mean that the Exodus took place in the mid-fifteenth century BCE. But the figure of 480 years is suspicious: It is the product of twelve, the number of the tribes, times forty, the typical length of a generation. The authors of the books of Kings understandably want to provide a symbolic link between Moses and the construction of the Temple under Solomon.

At least as far back as Josephus, the Exodus has been connected with the expulsion of the foreign Hyksos rulers from Egypt, which took place in the mid-sixteenth century BCE (see page 75). That event would have had repercussions for the Semitic populations of the Nile Delta, and a minority of modern scholars have followed Josephus in connecting the Exodus with the expulsion of the Hyksos.

There are, however, problems with such an early Exodus. It leaves a relatively long span of time, the entire Late Bronze Age (1550–1200 BCE) and beyond, covered only in the book of Judges. Moreover, although this was a period when Egypt controlled all of Canaan, no hint of Egyptian presence there can be found in the narratives of the book of Judges. Rather, the land is populated by groups whose existence is attested only at the end of the Late Bronze Age and especially at the beginning of the succeeding Iron Age, such as the Moabites, the Ammonites, and the Philistines. The Amarna Letters, an important collection of diplomatic correspondence with the Egyptian pharaoh Akhenaten dating from the fourteenth century BCE, give us a detailed view of Canaan in the Late Bronze Age. The correspondence includes letters from the kings of such city-states as Ashkelon, Shechem, Gezer, and Jerusalem, but there is no mention of any individual or group that could plausibly be identified with Israel, which would be expected if Israel had been a presence in the land for several centuries.

The principal alternative is to date the Exodus sometime in the thirteenth century BCE. This date is derived in part from the occurrence of Israel in a hymn on a victory stele erected by Pharaoh Merneptah (1213–1203 BCE) after a campaign in Syria and Palestine early in his reign (see Figure 6.2). It reads in part:

> The princes are prostrate, saying: "Mercy!"
> Not one raises his head among the Nine Bows.
> Desolation is for Tehenu; Hatti is pacified;
> Plundered is the Canaan with every evil;
> Carried off is Ashkelon; seized upon is Gezer;
> Yanoam is made as that which does not exist;
> Israel is laid waste; its seed is not;
> Hurru has become a widow for Egypt!
> All lands together, they are pacified;
> Everyone who was restless, he has been bound by the king of
> Upper and Lower Egypt: Ba-en-Re Meri-Amon; the son of Re:
> Merneptah Hotep-hir-Maat, given life like Re every day.*

This extremely important text—it contains the earliest reference in an ancient Near Eastern source of any person, entity, or event mentioned in the Bible—testifies to the presence of a group called Israel in the land of Canaan toward the end of the thirteenth century BCE, and thus provides a date before which the Exodus must have oc-

---

* Trans. J. A. Wilson, p. 378 in *Ancient Near Eastern Texts Relating to the Old Testament* (ed. J. B. Pritchard; Princeton: Princeton University Press, 1969).

FIGURE 6.2. The stela of Pharaoh Merneptah, which contains the first mention of Israel in a nonbiblical source.

curred. The other entities mentioned are geographical regions and cities; Israel is identified in the original hieroglyphic text as a people. According to the biblical chronology, it took some forty years for the escaped Hebrew slaves to enter the Promised Land. Accepting that figure as approximately accurate, then a mid-thirteenth century Exodus and an entry into the land by the Exodus group sometime thereafter, but before Merneptah's campaign, would allow for a group called Israel to become sufficiently established by the time of Merneptah so as to be mentioned in his victory hymn. This would make Merneptah's

father, Rameses II (1279–1213) (see Figure 6.3), the pharaoh of the Exodus, and his father, Seti I (1294–1279), the pharaoh who began the persecution of the Hebrews. This is the view held by most, but by no means all, biblical scholars.

The Embellishment of the Tradition

As the story of the Exodus was passed on, both orally and in writing, details were modified and often exaggerated. Remarkably, the final editors did not attempt to harmonize the traditions that they had received in order to create a consistent and seamless narrative. Rather, in part presumably because they considered the traditions themselves as sacred, preservation of those traditions was valued more than superficial consistency. This same impulse continues in the process of canonization, by which the Bible ends up being a remarkably diverse set of formulations, narratives, and above all witnesses to the beliefs of many different individuals over many generations.

Given the importance of the Exodus itself, it is unsurprising that the tendency to embellish what had originally occurred is evident in a number of ways in the various accounts we have of this central event. For example, how many people escaped from Egypt? Exodus 12.37–38 tells us that the number of the Israelites was "about six hundred thousand men on foot, besides children. A mixed crowd also went up with them, and livestock in great numbers, both flocks and herds." Allowing, conservatively, one wife for each man and two children for each couple, that adds up to a group of well over two million people, along with their sheep and goats ("flocks") and cattle ("herds"). This number is impossibly high, being greater than reasonable estimates of the entire population of ancient Egypt. Furthermore, that many people and animals would have left discernable traces in the landscape of the Sinai peninsula, but no evidence has been found of a substantial population living in that arid region at any time.

Significantly, another biblical tradition suggests a much smaller number of people. The nar-

FIGURE 6.3. Pharaoh Rameses II shown in his chariot in battle with his enemies the Hittites, in a copy of a relief from Karnak.

rative of the pious midwives, who "feared God" (Ex 1.17, 21) more than they did the king of Egypt, names them—Shiphrah and Puah. In a traditional culture, where women married soon after menarche and were repeatedly pregnant throughout their reproductive years, two midwives could serve only a relatively small number of women of reproductive age—no more than several hundred, and probably fewer. In any case, we have a population of an entirely different order of magnitude than that given in Exodus 12.37–38, and the number given there must be an exaggeration. If the number of the Hebrews was relatively small, the lack of mention in Egyptian sources of their escape from work-slavery is unsurprising.

A later example of the same tendency to aggrandize the tradition is the identification of the body of water crossed by the escapees with the Red Sea. The Hebrew term used throughout the Bible is *yam sûf*. Although this can oc-casionally refer to either of the two northern arms of the Red Sea, the Gulf of Suez (Num 33.11) and the Gulf of Aqaba/Eilat (Num 14.25; 1 Kings 9.26), it literally means "sea of reeds" (the word *sûf*, "reeds," is used in Ex 2.3, 5 of the "bulrushes" on the banks of the Nile), and the most likely geography of the Exodus lo-cates it just east of the region where the He-brews lived (see Figure 6.1). Several shallow bodies of water are possible identifications for this "**Reed Sea**," including the Bitter Lakes, Lake Timsah, and the Ballah Lakes, all lying between the Gulf of Suez and the Mediter-ranean, or Lake Sirbonis, on the Mediterranean coast just east of the Nile Delta. The ancient Greek translation of the Hebrew Bible (the Septuagint), dating to the third century BCE, translates *yam sûf* as "Red Sea," probably refer-ring to the entire body of water, making it a much more dramatic setting than a wetland for the miracle of the splitting of the sea.

THE EXODUS AND THE HISTORY OF RELIGIONS

Toward the end of the Late Bronze Age, about 1200 BCE, a remarkable shift occurs in the pantheons of much of the ancient world, in which rule over the gods passes from an older to a younger god. This transfer of power is evident in the myths of various groups. In Babylon, the epic *Enuma elish* recounts how Marduk, the god of the storm, is chosen as king of the gods when the older generation of gods, led by Anu ("sky"), is unable to counter the threat posed by the primeval goddess of the sea, Tiamat (see further pages 5–7). In Greek myth, the older god Cronus is supplanted as supreme deity by his son Zeus, perhaps originally a sky-god but better known as the "cloud gatherer" whose weapon is the thunderbolt. Reflexes of the same myth are also found in the Hittite pantheon, in which Kumarbi is supplanted by his son, the storm-god Teshub, and in the Aryan traditions of India, in which the sky-god Dyaus (a cognate of Zeus) is replaced as ruler of the gods by his son Indra, the storm-god.

The same shift in power is also found in Ugaritic myth (see Box 5.4 on page 74), in many respects the closest to the biblical traditions. In the Ugaritic Baal cycle, Prince Sea (also called by the parallel term Judge River) threatens the storm-god **Baal**, apparently with the support of the high god El, but Baal defeats Prince Sea and is acclaimed as king of the gods, who build him a suitable palace on Mount Zaphon, made of cedar as well as silver, gold, and precious stones. As his epithet "rider on the clouds" shows, Baal is the storm-god, providing the essential rains of winter, "the season of wadis in flood." When he "sounds his voice in the clouds, flashes his lightning to the earth . . . the earth's high places shake" (see Figure 6.4).

Reflexes of this widespread shift in power in the pantheon are also found in ancient Israel. At the time when the Exodus from Egypt most likely occurred, toward the end of the Late Bronze Age, both E and P describe a new revelation. As P reports in Exodus 6.2–3, during the ancestral period the god of Abraham, Isaac, and Jacob was El (see pages 81–82). Yahweh identifies himself as

FIGURE 6.4. A stela from ancient Ugarit depicting the Canaanite god Baal. He holds a lightning bolt in his left hand, illustrating his status as storm-god. The stela is about 4.7 ft (1.42 m) high and dates to the mid-second millennium BCE.

this deity, but in biblical literature Yahweh also has characteristics of a storm-god. Like Baal, he "rides upon the clouds" (Ps 68.4), and his voice is thunder:

The voice of Yahweh is over the waters;
  the God of glory thunders,
  Yahweh, over mighty waters.
The voice of Yahweh is powerful;
  the voice of Yahweh is full of majesty.
The voice of Yahweh breaks the cedars;
  Yahweh breaks the cedars of Lebanon. . . .
The voice of Yahweh flashes forth flames of fire.
The voice of Yahweh shakes the wilderness. . . .
    (Ps 29.3–8; compare Judg 5.4–5)

Like Baal, Yahweh reveals himself on a mountain in the midst of a storm (Ex 19.16–18), and, like Baal, he will eventually acquire a temple, "a house of cedar" (2 Sam 7.2; see also 1 Kings 6.14–18).

Often the storm-god is described as victorious over the forces of chaos, sometimes depicted in serpent form; this is the case in the myths of Marduk and Tiamat in Mesopotamia, and Indra and Vritra in India, and in both the creation of the world follows the victory. No detailed account of creation has been discovered at Ugarit, but the Bible provides numerous examples of the sequence in which the storm-god of Israel defeats the primeval waters and then creates the world. In addition to examples given on page 10, note especially Psalm 89:

Let the heavens praise your wonders, O Yahweh,
  your faithfulness in the assembly of the holy
    ones.
For who in the skies can be compared to Yahweh?
  Who among the gods is like Yahweh,
a god feared in the council of the holy ones,
  great and awesome above all those around him?
O Yahweh God of hosts,
  who is as mighty as you, O Yahweh?
  Your faithfulness surrounds you.
You rule the surging of the sea;
  when its waves rise, you still them.
You crushed Rahab* like a carcass;
  you scattered your enemies with your mighty
    arm.
The heavens are yours, the earth also is yours;
  the world and all that is in it—you have
    founded them. (Ps 89.5–11)

This mythic pattern is applied to the Exodus experience, especially in Exodus 15. As storm-god, Yahweh uses his wind, through his nostrils, and causes the sea to roil. But the myth is historicized: The enemy of the storm-god is not the sea itself, but the pharaoh and his army, and the sea is merely a divine weapon in the defeat of the Egyptian forces. Moreover, the event takes place in historical time. So in appropriating the myth of the storm-god and the sea, Exodus 15 partially demythologizes it. Yet some mythic elements remain, including the acclamation of Yahweh as the supreme deity and his enthronement in a new home:

Who is like you, O Yahweh, among the gods?
  Who is like you, majestic in holiness,
  awesome in splendor, doing wonders? . . .
You brought them in and planted them on the
    mountain of your own possession,
  the place, O Yahweh, that you made your abode,
  the sanctuary, O Yahweh, that your hands have
    established.
Yahweh will rule forever and ever. (Ex 15.11,
    17–18)

The same mythic motif is found in other biblical texts, as in Psalm 114:

When Israel went out from Egypt,
  the house of Jacob from a people of strange
    language,
Judah became God's sanctuary,
  Israel his dominion.
The sea looked and fled;
  Jordan turned back. (Ps 114.1–3)

Here the narrative chronology of the books of Exodus through Joshua is collapsed. Those books relate sequentially how the Israelites came out of Egypt, wandered in the wilderness for forty years, and then under the leadership of Joshua crossed the Jordan River and took possession of the Promised Land. The crossings of the bodies of water bracket this formative period, and the accounts of the crossing of the Sea of Reeds at the beginning (Ex 14–15) and of the Jordan River at the end (Josh 3) are deliberately paralleled: In both cases, the waters stand up in a heap (Ex 15.8; Josh 3.16), and the Israelites cross "on dry ground"

---

* Rahab is one of the names used in the Bible for the primeval sea.

(Ex 14.22; Josh 3.17; 4.22). But in Psalm 114, although the two bodies of water are again actual places—the (Reed) Sea and the Jordan (River)—they are personified and linked; this recalls the parallel titles of Baal's adversary, Prince Sea/Judge River.

Likewise, in the book of Isaiah's appeal to Yahweh to act as he has in the past, the defeat of the primeval waters is linked with the event at the Reed Sea:

> Awake, awake, put on strength,
>   O arm of Yahweh!
> Awake, as in days of old,
>   the generations of long ago!
> Was it not you who cut Rahab in pieces,
>   who pierced the dragon?
> Was it not you who dried up the sea,
>   the waters of great deep;
> who made the depths of the sea a way
>   for the redeemed to cross over? (Isa 51.9–10)

Just as elsewhere in the ancient world, then, toward the end of the Late Bronze Age Israel began to worship a new deity, or a new manifestation of the ancestral deity. From the perspective of the history of religions, Yahweh can be understood as the Israelite manifestation of the storm-god, who throughout the ancient Near East and elsewhere became the dominant deity toward the end of the Late Bonze Age.

The precise origins of the name and identity of Yahweh as a distinct deity are lost in the mists of history. Some nonbiblical texts locate the use of this name in the territory of Midian, east of the Red Sea, toward the end of the Late Bronze Age, precisely where the Bible has the name revealed to Moses, and it is at least possible that Moses adopted the worship of Yahweh from his father-in-law Jethro, the priest of Midian.

At the same time the Pentateuchal sources J, E, and P all emphasize continuity rather than discontinuity. In J, Yahweh has been worshiped since the time of Adam (Gen 4.26), and in E and P, the deity who reveals himself to Moses as Yahweh also identifies himself as the god of Israel's ancestors (Ex 3.15; 6.2–3). For the biblical writers, it is Yahweh who has been worshiped all along. Modern historians of religion correctly observe that change has occurred here, and they are able to do so, in part, because E and P recognize discontinuity, that is, that something new happened in the time of Moses and the Exodus, and thus there is, appropriately, a new revelation and an event of mythic dimensions.

RETROSPECT AND PROSPECT

The narrative of the escape from Egypt is the linchpin of the Pentateuch, the organizing principle that informs it from beginning to end. The many occurrences of the motif of exile and of return that recur throughout Genesis, from the narrative of the garden of Eden through the wanderings of Abraham and Sarah, of Hagar and Ishmael, of Isaac and Rebekah, and of Jacob and his extended family, have been in a sense preparation for the beginning of the narrative of the return of Israel to the Promised Land. That journey home—that exodus—is inextricably linked with Moses, and his character and his presence will continue to dominate the Pentateuch, which ends with his death in Deuteronomy 34, with the Israelites poised to reenter the land of Canaan.

As the interconnected stories of the Exodus and of Moses are retold, they continue to speak to new audiences and have relevance for their contexts. For example, Moses' encounters with the pharaoh anticipate and provide a literary model for later encounters between prophets and kings, and the celebration of the Passover continually recalls for Israel its origin as a people freed from slavery by a merciful and compassionate deity.

In the next several chapters we will also observe how in the rest of the Pentateuch legal and ritual traditions from many different periods are attached to Moses and the events associated with him, beginning with the Exodus and continuing with the revelation at Sinai.

IMPORTANT TERMS

Baal

Hebrew

Horeb

Passover

Reed Sea

Sinai

theophany

QUESTIONS FOR REVIEW

1. Choose a small section of the narrative of the plagues in Exodus 7–12, and identify the parts of the passage that you would attribute to J, E, and P. What characteristic phrases and themes of each source occur in the passage?

2. Compare the narrative of the plagues in Exodus with the hymnic summaries in Psalm 78.42–55 and Psalm 105.26–45. Be prepared to discuss the significance of the similarities and differences for understanding the history of traditions.

3. The description of the first Passover in Exodus 12 probably reflects the way the feast was celebrated during the monarchy. What earlier elements can be isolated in this chapter? How can the union of originally distinct agricultural and pastoral rituals be explained?

4. Compare Exodus 14 and 15. How do the prose and poetic accounts of the event at the Re(e)d Sea differ?

5. What are the issues involved in determining the historicity and the date of the Exodus?

6. How did the biblical writers make use of ancient Near Eastern mythology in their accounts of the Exodus?

BIBLIOGRAPHY

A good recent commentary on Exodus is Carol Meyers, *Exodus* (Cambridge: Cambridge University Press, 2005). For a shorter commentary, see P. K. McCarter, Jr., "Exodus," pp. 119–44 in *The HarperCollins Bible Commentary* (ed. J. L. Mays; San Francisco: HarperSanFrancisco, 2000). An important older commentary is B. S. Childs, *The Book of Exodus: A Critical, Theological Commentary* (Philadelphia: Westminster, 1974).

An excellent summary of the historical issues connected with the Exodus is C. A. Redmount, "Bitter Lives: Israel in and out of Egypt," Chap. 2 in *The Oxford History of the Biblical World* (ed. M. D. Coogan; New York: Oxford University Press, 1998).

For a summary of the use of the Exodus motif in biblical and later traditions, see M. D. Coogan, "Exodus, The," pp. 209–12 in *The Oxford Companion to the Bible* (New York: Oxford University Press, 1993).

For translations of the Ugaritic myths concerning Baal, see the bibliography to Chapter 5.

From Egypt to Sinai

Exodus 16–24

Once the Israelites have left Egypt, everything that follows in the Torah is set in the context of their journey to the Promised Land. That journey is interrupted, however, by a lengthy stay at Mount Sinai, where God gives Moses the Ten Commandments, along with many other laws and detailed instructions concerning religious ceremonies, the priesthood, sacred objects, and the like. The sojourn at Sinai begins in Exodus 19, and the Israelites do not leave Sinai until Numbers 10.12. This lengthy section contains both narrative and large sections of legal and ritual material and comprises about one-third of the entire Pentateuch, indicating its importance. We will cover this material in the next three chapters.

In this chapter we will examine the narrative of the first stage of the journey, from Egypt to Sinai, the making of the covenant at Sinai, and the first collection of laws embedded in the Sinai narrative, the Ten Commandments.

ITINERARIES

At intervals in the narrative from Egypt to Mount Sinai (Ex 12.37; 13.20; 14.2; 15.22–23, 27; 16.1; 17.1; 19.1–2), and then later from Mount Sinai

to Moab on the eastern border of Canaan (Num 10.12; 20.1; 22.1), the Priestly tradition (P) records the stages in the journey. These itineraries serve to organize the narrative and to move it along, as did the genealogies in Genesis. The itineraries are then brought together in Numbers 33 at the end of the journey, as a kind of summary, in a document that may in fact be the original from which various segments were inserted into the narrative at appropriate points. Few if any of the places named in the itineraries can be identified with certainty, as is the case with the entire geography of the Exodus.

INCIDENTS ON THE JOURNEY

Interspersed among the itineraries are narratives attached to particular places. Thus, on the journey from Egypt to Sinai in Exodus 16, a composite J and P narrative, we find an account of the divine provision of **manna** (see Box 7.1) and quails for the Israelites in the wilderness of Sin and, in Exodus 17.1–7, probably E, the miraculous production of water from a rock at Rephidim, renamed Massah ("test") and Meribah ("quarrel"). Variant traditions of these

Box 7.1 **MANNA**

The manna is ubiquitous in the traditions about Israel's wilderness wanderings; it is found in J (Ex 16.4–5, 35), E (Num 11), D (Deut 8.3, 16; see also Josh 5.12), and P (Ex 16.6–35), as well as in Psalms (78.24; 105.40). The descriptions of the manna vary and contain several rare words, suggesting that the traditions drew on independent and therefore presumably very ancient, probably oral, sources.

The manna was an unfamiliar substance to the Israelites, as its folk etymology explains: They called it *man* ("manna"; Ex 16.31) because when they first saw it they said *man hu* ("What is this?"; 16.15). Its physical attributes verge on the fantastic. In different sources and traditions, it was flaky, like frost, or shaped like coriander seed; was white, or, like gum resin, yellowish; tasted like honey-soaked wafers or cakes baked with oil; could be ground or pounded in a mortar, then baked or boiled; melted in the sun; and when stored it rotted or became worm-infested by the next day, unless that next day was the sabbath, except for a sample kept in a jar that was eventually placed in the ark of the covenant, where it lasted for many years. Even though individuals gathered different amounts, everyone had as much as they needed.

Various attempts have been made to identify the manna with some natural substance, such as the edible sweet excretions of a type of lice found in the Sinai Peninsula. Like the naturalistic explanations of the plagues (see page 92), this misses the point. The manna was not a natural phenomenon—rather, it was supernatural: It was "bread of heaven" (Ps 105.40; compare Ex 16.4), as its fuller description in another poetic version of the tradition also indicates:

> He commanded the clouds above,
>   and opened the doors of heaven;
> he rained down on them manna to eat,
>   and gave them the grain of heaven.
> Mortals ate of the bread of the mighty ones (NRSV: "angels");
>   he sent them food in abundance. (Ps 78.23–25)

An example of the divine care of the Israelites during their journey (see Deut 29.5), the manna continued to be provided from the time of the Exodus to when the Israelites had entered the land of Canaan (Ex 16.35; Josh 5.12).

events are reported on the journey from Sinai to Canaan, the manna and quails in Numbers 11, probably E, and the water from the rock in Numbers 20, which is P. The final editors of the Pentateuch have thus bracketed the stay at Sinai with parallel episodes.

A similar bracketing is found in narratives concerning the Amalekites. In Exodus 17.8–15 (E), under the leadership of Joshua, the Israelites defeat these traditional enemies, descended from Esau (Gen 36.12); in Numbers 14.45 (J), the Amalekites along with others defeat the Israelites in their first attempt to enter the Promised Land (see page 163).

Yet another example of bracketing occurs with the next episode, concerning the delegation of Moses' authority. In Exodus 18 Moses' father-in-law Jethro, the priest of Midian, visits the Israelite camp and observes that in acting as the sole judge, Moses has undertaken an impossible task; rather, he suggests, Moses should appoint judges at various levels and hear only the most difficult cases himself. The entire passage is E, and it is remarkable on several counts. One is that the establishment of a major institution, the judiciary, is attributed to a non-Israelite. In the Deuteronomic version of this event (Deut 1.9–18), the institution of the judiciary is presented as if it were Moses' idea, and Jethro is not mentioned, perhaps because of some discomfort with the attribution of the institution to Jethro. In the parallel passage after the departure from Sinai in Numbers 11.16–30 (also E), the story of the manna and the quail is interrupted by an account of how Moses' authority was delegated to seventy elders. In this variant, the initiative is entirely Yahweh's, who transfers some of Moses' "spirit" to them, the way charismatic authority was passed from one prophet to another (see 2 Kings 2.9, 15).

What is clear is the association of Moses with Midian, an association with which the biblical writers were somewhat uneasy. Nevertheless, they preserved what must have been very ancient traditions, attributing to Moses a controversial marriage with a non-Israelite (see Num 12.1) and to his Midianite father-in-law the institution of Israel's judicial system. (See further Box 7.2.)

AT SINAI

Three months after the Exodus, the Israelites arrived at Mount Sinai (see Figure 7.1), where they set up camp (Ex 19.1–2). Here begins the longest single stay at one location in the entire journey from Egypt to Canaan; according to P, they will be at Sinai for a nearly a year (compare Ex 19.1 and Num 10.11).

Upon their arrival, Moses made his first of several trips up the mountain; the number of trips is certainly increased because several sources are combined in the narrative. Yahweh announced that he was about to make a covenant with the Israelites. They are to be his "special possession," a "kingdom of priests and a holy nation" (Ex 19.5–6). This obscure phrasing, probably very ancient, declares Israel's special status, collectively set apart from other nations as priests are from ordinary persons. Following Moses' instructions, the people prepared for a divine revelation, in which Yahweh with all of the manifestations of the storm—cloud, thunder, lightning, earthquake—descended on the mountain. In Exodus 20 the giving of the Ten Commandments and other legal directives follows, to which we will return.

EXCURSUS ON COVENANT

The concept of **covenant** is central to the Bible. Its significance is indicated by its thematic importance in P, which is organized around three covenants, those between God and Noah, God and Abraham, and God and Israel. On a broader level, the two principal divisions of the Bible in Christianity are called the Old Covenant ("Testament") and the New Covenant. As the word "testament" implies, covenant is a legal term.

The Hebrew word for covenant, *berît*, has an uncertain etymology, perhaps meaning a bond or mutual agreement. In the Bible, *berît* means something like "contract," and it is used for various sorts of legal agreements, including marriage (Ezek 16.8; Mal 2.14; Prov 2.17), slavery (Job 41.4; compare Deut 15.17), solemn friendship (1 Sam 18.1–4), and especially a treaty. On several occasions in the Bible we are told of treaties between rulers. These are of two widely attested types: the parity treaty, in which the two parties are presumed equals, and the **suzerainty treaty**, in which one party, the suzerain, is superior to the other, the vassal, to use medieval terms. According to 1 Kings 5.12,

Box 7.2 **THE LOCATION OF SINAI**

The "mountain of God," called Sinai in J (Ex 19.20; etc.) and in P (Ex 19.1; 24.16) and Horeb in E (Ex 3.1; etc.) and in D (Deut 5.2; etc.) and related traditions (1 Kings 19.8), has traditionally been identified as Jebel Musa in the southern Sinai Peninsula. But there is no archaeological evidence of any significant activity at the site before Christian monks built a monastery there in the fourth century CE. As a result, scholars have proposed a number of other sites and locations, among which one good possibility is somewhere to the east of the northeastern arm of the Red Sea (the Gulf of Aqaba/Eilat), in the territory known in the Bible as **Midian**.

According to Exodus 3.1, after he fled Egypt, Moses was tending the flock of his father-in-law Jethro, the priest of Midian, which is where Horeb was located. Other biblical texts locate Midian in northwestern Arabia, where there is archaeological evidence of a distinctive culture dating to the end of the Late Bronze Age (thirteenth and twelfth centuries BCE). It was in this same region that according to Egyptian sources a deity called *yhw* was worshiped, and from this region, according to biblical poetry, Yahweh came forth (Hab 3.7; compare Judg 5.4).

The difficulty in identifying the mountain of God is compounded by the several names given to Moses' father-in-law in biblical tradition. J calls him Reuel (Ex 2.18; etc.) and also Hobab (Num 10.29; compare Judg 1.16; 4.11), while in E he is Jethro (Ex 3.1; etc.); in D and P he is not mentioned. Two mountains, two fathers-in-law, perhaps even two wives (one interpretation is that Moses' Midianite wife Zipporah and his Cushite wife mentioned in Num 12.1 are different women): One way to explain these inconsistencies is to assume that they are all true. God appeared to Moses both at Mount Horeb and at Mount Sinai; Moses had two wives, one Midianite and one Cushite, and thus more than one father-in-law. One set of traditions follows one appearance or marriage, another set follows the other. While this reconstruction is possible, it ignores the tendency of the Bible to preserve inconsistent traditions. As we have seen, such inconsistencies are found throughout the Bible, in both small and large units.

Some of the inconsistencies are resolved by closer analysis. That Moses' wife is called Midianite in some passages (Ex 2.15–22 [J]; 18.1 [E]) and Cushite in others (Num 12.1 [E]) need not mean that they were two different women. Although sometimes the term "Cush" refers to the region south of Egypt (ancient Nubia, modern Ethiopia, as in 2 Kings 19.9), Cush is also a poetic synonym for Midian (as in Hab 3.7, where an alternate form, "Cushan," is used), and is sometimes located in southern Arabia (as the genealogy in Gen 10.7 suggests).

In the end, while a location somewhere in northwestern Arabia, that is, in Midian, is likely, precise identification of the mountain (or mountains) in question is impossible.

FIGURE 7.1.   Jebel Musa, the traditional identification of Mount Sinai. As imposing as this mountain is (elevation 7,497 ft [2,285 m]), no ancient evidence connects it with the biblical mountain of revelation, and many scholars prefer another location, probably in southern Jordan or northern Saudi Arabia.

Solomon, the king of Israel, and Hiram, the king of Tyre, "cut a covenant"—that is, they made a treaty (see pages 113–14). This is an example of a parity treaty, for according to 1 Kings 9.13, Hiram calls Solomon his "brother," and later the prophet Amos will refer to this treaty as a "covenant of brothers" (Am 1.9); the same language is used in diplomatic correspondence between kings who consider themselves equals (see 1 Kings 20.32). In suzerainty treaties, or treaties between a superior and an inferior, like those between various kings of Assyria and Babylon and kings of Israel and Judah (see, for example, Hos 12.1; Ezek 17.13), several metaphors are used to describe the relationship of vassal to suzerain, including master-servant and father-son.

The Treaty Form

One of the most influential examples of the contribution of form criticism (see pages 69–71) to biblical interpretation is the elucidation of the structure of ancient Near Eastern treaties. The most important for the study of the concept of covenant is the suzerainty treaty, a pact between a superior power and an inferior one.

Many suzerainty treaties are now known from the ancient Near East, and two groups are especially important. The first is a series of treaties between the kings of Hatti, rulers of the Hittites in Asia Minor, Egypt's rivals for control of the Levant in the latter part of the second millennium BCE, and their vassals, smaller states that were subject to them, such as the kingdom of Ugarit in

Syria. Another group comes from the seventh century BCE and comprises treaties between the kings of Assyria and their vassals. We will look more closely at the Assyrian treaties on pages 181–83; here we will focus on the Hittite treaties.

The Hittite treaties, of which several dozen examples are known, have the following structure:

I. *Identification* of the suzerain

II. *History* of the relationship between the two groups, with emphasis on the benevolent actions of the suzerain toward the vassal

III. *Stipulations:* the obligations imposed upon the vassal, generally detailing the requirements of loyalty to the suzerain, including prohibition of relationships with other powers, prohibition of attacks on another vassal of the suzerain, requirement to respond to a call to assistance from the suzerain, requirement to submit disputes with another vassal to the suzerain, and payment of tribute

IV. *Provision for deposit of copies of the treaty in the temples of the principal gods of the two parties,* and often for its periodic public reading

V. *Divine witnesses to the treaty:* lengthy lists of the national deities of both parties who are summoned as witnesses to the treaty; these typically conclude with the invocation of the oldest generations of the gods, "the mountains, the rivers, the springs, the great Sea, heaven and earth, the winds (and) the clouds"

VI. *Blessings* for observance of the treaty and *curses* for violations of it, to be carried out by the gods who were its ultimate guarantors

While not all of the treaties contain all of the elements, their occurrence is sufficiently well attested to make this outline a kind of normative pattern (see Box 7.3).

Elements of the treaty form are found in the Bible in passages that concern covenant. We will examine in more detail on pages 115–16 the light that the form sheds on the Ten Commandments in particular; here are some examples from other texts:

- The identification of the suzerain (I) and the historical prologue (II) are found in the covenant renewal ceremony in Joshua 24.2–13.

- The "Book of the Covenant" (Ex 20.22–23.33; see further pages 122–25) may be understood as a lengthy list of stipulations (III).

- Corresponding to the placement of copies of the treaty in the temples of the two parties (IV) is the placement of the tablets of the law in the ark of the covenant (Deut 10.1–5), from which they are taken, as in the treaties, for periodic reading (Deut 31.10–13). The existence of two tablets of the text of the covenant (Ex 31.18; 34.29) may be derived from the practice of making copies of treaties and other contracts for each party.

- We also find allusions to the divine witnesses (V). In Deuteronomy heaven and earth are invoked as witnesses (Deut 4.26; 31.28), and in one instance these are associated as in the treaties with blessings and curses: "I call heaven and earth to witness against you today that I have set before you life and death, blessings and curses" (Deut 30.19).

In prophetic literature, one of the genres that the prophets use is that of the "covenant lawsuit," in which Yahweh as suzerain sues Israel for breach of contract. In a typical lawsuit passage, the most ancient divine witnesses to the treaties are also invoked:

> Hear what Yahweh says:
> Rise, plead your case before the mountains,
>   and let the hills hear your voice.
> Hear, you mountains, the lawsuit of Yahweh,
>   and you enduring foundations of the earth;
> for the Yahweh has a lawsuit with his people,
>   and he will contend with Israel.
> (Mic 6.1–2)

In some cases, the witnesses are demythologized. In the covenant renewal ceremony in Joshua, the people themselves serve as witnesses (Josh 24.22), and there is also another witness, a memorial stele (Josh 24.26–27), perhaps the very stone on which the text of the "law" had been written (Josh 8.32); this is reminiscent of the boundary stone that

Box 7.3 **EXCERPT FROM A HITTITE SUZERAINTY TREATY**

This treaty, between the Hittite king Mursilis II and his vassal, Duppi-Teshub, king of Amurru, dates to about 1300 BCE; the elements are numbered as on page 110.

I. These are the words of the Sun [*a title of the Hittite kings*] Mursilis, the great king, the king of the Hatti land, the valiant, the favorite of the Storm-god, the son of Suppiluliumas, the great king, the king of the Hatti land, the valiant.

II. Aziras [*the vassal*] was the grandfather of you, Duppi-Tessub. He rebelled against my father, but submitted again to my father. When the kings of Nuhassi land and the kings of Kinza rebelled against my father, Aziras did not rebel. As he was bound by treaty, he remained bound by treaty. As my father fought against his enemies, in the same manner fought Aziras. Aziras remained loyal toward my father [as his overlord] and did not incite my father's anger. My father was loyal toward Aziras and his country; he did not undertake any unjust action against him or incite his or his country's anger in any way. 300 (shekels of) refined and first-class gold, the tribute which my father had imposed upon your father, he brought year for year; he never refused it. When my father became god [*died*] and I seated myself on the throne of my father, Aziras behaved toward me just as he had behaved toward my father. . . . When your father died, in accordance with your father's word I did not drop you. Since your father had mentioned to me your name with great praise, I sought after you. To be sure, you were sick and ailing, but although you were ailing, I, the Sun, put you in the place of your father and took your brothers (and) sisters and the Amurru land in oath for you. When I, the Sun, sought after you in accordance with your father's word and put you in your father's place, I took you in oath for the king of the Hatti land, the Hatti land, and for my sons and grandsons. So honor the oath (of loyalty) to the king and the king's king. And I, the king, will be loyal toward you, Duppi-Tessub. When you take a wife, and when you beget an heir, he shall be king in the Amurru land likewise. And just as I shall be loyal toward you, even so shall I be loyal toward your son. But you, Duppi-Tessub, remain loyal toward the king of the Hatti land, the Hatti land, my sons (and) my grandsons forever! The tribute which was imposed upon your grandfather and your father—they presented 300 shekels of good, refined first-class gold weighed with standard weights—you shall present them likewise. Do not turn your eyes to anyone else! Your fathers presented tribute to Egypt; you [shall not do that!] . . .

III. With my friend you shall be friend, and with my enemy you shall be enemy. If the king of the Hatti land is either in the Hurri land, or in the land of Egypt, or in the country of Astata or in the country of Alse—any country contiguous to the territory of your country that is friendly with the king of the Hatti land—(or in) any country contiguous to the territory of your country that is friendly with the king of the Hatti land . . . —but turns around and becomes inimical toward the king of the Hatti land while the king of the Hatti land is on a marauding campaign—if then you, Duppi-Tessub, do not remain loyal together with your foot soldiers and your charioteers and if you do not fight wholeheartedly . . . you act in disregard of your oath. As I, the Sun, am loyal toward you, do you extend military help to the Sun and the Hatti land. If an evil rumor originates in the Hatti land that someone is to rise in revolt against the Sun and you hear it, leave with your foot soldiers and your charioteers and go immediately to the aid of the king of the Hatti land! But if you are not able to leave yourself, dispatch either your son or your brother together with your foot soldiers (and) your charioteers to the aid of the king of the Hatti land! If you do not dispatch your son (or) your brother with your foot soldiers (and) your charioteers to the aid of the king of the Hatti land, you act in disregard of the gods of the oath. . . . If a country or a fugitive takes to the road and while betaking themselves to the Hatti land pass through your territory, put them on the right way, show them the way to the Hatti land and speak friendly words to them! Do not send them to anyone else. If you do not put them on the right way, (if) you do not guide them on the right way to the Hatti land, but direct them into the mountains or speak unfriendly words before them, you act in disregard of the oath. . . .

[IV. *from another treaty*] A duplicate of this treaty has been deposited before the Sun-goddess of Arinna, because the Sun-goddess of Arinna regulates kingship and queenship. In the Mitanni land [*the vassal*] (a duplicate) has been deposited before Tessub. . . . At regular intervals they shall read it in the presence of the king of the Mitanni land . . .

V. [The Sun-god of Heaven, the Sun-goddess of Arinna, the Storm-god of Heaven, the Hattian Storm-god . . . Sin, lord of the oath, Ishara, queen of the oath, Hebat, queen of heaven, Ishtar, Ishtar of the battlefield, Ishtar of Nineveh, Ishtar of Hattarina, Ninatta (and)] Kulitta . . . Ereskigal, the gods and goddesses of the Hatti land, the gods and goddesses of Amurru land, all the olden gods, Naras, Napsaras, Minki, Tuhusi, Ammunki, Ammizadu, Allalu, Anu, Antu, Apantu, Ellil, Ninlil, the mountains, the rivers, the springs, the great Sea, heaven and earth, the winds (and) the clouds—let these be witnesses to this treaty and to the oath.

VI. The words of the treaty and the oath that are inscribed on this tablet—should Duppi-Tessub not honor these words of the treaty and the oath, may these gods of the oath destroy Duppi-Tessub together with his person, his wife, his son, his grandson, his house, his land and together with everything that he owns. But if Duppi-Tessub honors these words of the treaty and the oath that are inscribed on this tablet, may these gods of the oath protect him together with his person, his wife, his son, his grandson, his house (and) his country.[*]

---

[*]   Adapted from translation by Albrecht Goetze, pp. 203–5 in *Ancient Near Eastern Texts Relating to the Old Testament* (ed. J. B. Pritchard; Princeton: Princeton University Press, 1969).

Jacob and Laban erected when they made a covenant concerning their groups' boundaries (Gen 31.45–53).

• Finally, the Bible has repeated references to blessings and curses (VI) in covenant renewal contexts (for example, Josh 8.34; Deut 30.19) and lengthy lists of both (notably Lev 26; Deut 28) or of curses alone (Deut 27.15–26).

Although no biblical passage incorporates all of the elements of the treaty form, the cumulative evidence demonstrates that the biblical writers used the treaty analogue in their depiction of the covenant between Yahweh and Israel. It should also be noted that in the ancient Near East the Israelites are the only group known to have characterized their relationship with a deity using the language of contract or treaty.

Covenant Vocabulary

The treaty analogue also sheds light on some characteristic biblical phraseology used in covenant contexts. The relationship of the suzerain to the vassal is often expressed as a father-son relationship; a notable example is the declaration of loyalty by Ahaz, the king of Judah, to Tiglath-pileser, the king of Assyria: "I am your servant and your son" (2 Kings 16.7). The many references to Israel as Yahweh's son (for example, Ex 4.22; Deut 14.1; Jer 3.19; 31.9; Hos 11.1), and also to the reigning king as Yahweh's son (2 Sam 7.14; Pss 2.7; 89.26–27; see further pages 277–78), are illuminated by this characteristic idiom. The father-son metaphor also informs another idiom: In treaties and diplomatic correspondence, the relationship between the two parties is one of "love." The same language is also used in the Bible, for example, in 1 Kings 5.1, where we are told that Hiram, the king of Tyre, "loved" David, the king of Israel. In this relationship, the two parties also "know" each other; biblical examples include Deuteronomy 9.24 and 2 Samuel 7.20. Not surprisingly, the same language is used of the marital relationship, which as we have seen is also formalized by a *berît*, a contract or covenant: In a marriage, the wife and husband are to love each other, and also to know each other, in an intimate sexual sense. The marriage "covenant" was another analogue used by the biblical writers to describe the relationship between Yahweh, the husband, and Israel, the wife.

Thus, when the biblical writers term the relationship between Yahweh and Israel as *berît*, a "covenant," it has several levels of meaning, reflecting the varieties of such contracts. That multivalence also applies to "love" and "knowledge"; two examples from the prophets will serve as illustrations. First, in a context in Hosea where covenant is mentioned, Yahweh complains about Israel's failure to live up to its obligations:

> For I desire steadfast love and not sacrifice,
> the knowledge of God rather than burnt offerings. (Hos 6.6)

The word translated "steadfast love" is *hesed*, which is the mutual loyalty of the parties in a marriage or treaty relationship. As its husband (Hos 2.16), father (11.1), and covenant partner (6.7; 8.1), Yahweh expected from Israel love (*hesed*) and knowledge. Second, in Amos 3.1–2, concluding a condemnation of the Israelites for their repeated violations of covenant, the prophet passes judgment in the name of Yahweh:

> Hear this word that the LORD has spoken against you, O people of Israel, against the whole family that I brought up out of the land of Egypt:
>
> You only have I known
> of all the families of the earth;
> therefore I will punish you
> for all your iniquities.

Israel, who had been rescued from slavery in Egypt, was under special, even unique, obligation to Yahweh, and Yahweh's relationship to Israel was also unique: "You only have I known of all the nations of the earth"—Yahweh knew Israel, as covenant partner, as suzerain, as spouse. For this reason, Israel's obligation was, as repeatedly stated in Deuteronomy, a book profoundly influenced by the treaty form, to "love the LORD your God with all your heart, and with all your soul, and with all your might" (Deut 6.4).

The Hebrew idiom usually translated "to make a covenant" literally means "to cut a covenant." This is best explained as referring to ceremonies that were part of ancient treaty and covenant making, ceremonies that involved cutting an animal as a symbolic acceptance of the consequences of breaking the covenant. Evidence for such ceremonies can be found in both nonbiblical and biblical sources.

In eighth-century BCE treaties in which one of the parties was a North Syrian king named Matiel, we find references to various symbolic actions, including the dismemberment of a lamb:

> This head is not the head of a lamb, it is the head of Matiel, it is the head of his sons, his officials, and the people of his land, If Matiel sins against this treaty,

so may, just as the head of this spring lamb is torn off, and its knuckle placed in its mouth . . . the head of Matiel be torn off.[*]

In another treaty involving the same Matiel, the following imitative rituals are described:

> As this wax is consumed by fire, thus Matiel shall be consumed by fire. As this bow and these arrows are broken, thus [the gods] Ninurta and Hadad shall break the bow of Matiel and the bow of his nobles. As a man of wax is blinded, thus Matiel shall be blinded. As this calf is cut up, thus Matiel and his nobles shall be cut up.[†]

In the Bible, the prophet Jeremiah, referring the covenant obligation to free Hebrew slaves after six years of service, announces divine judgment with reference to the ceremony by which that covenant obligation was renewed:

> Those who transgressed my covenant and did not keep the terms of the covenant that they made before me, I will make like the calf when they cut it in two and passed between its parts: the officials of Judah, the officials of Jerusalem, the administrators, the priests, and all the people of the land who passed between the parts of the calf shall be handed over to their enemies and to those who seek their lives. Their corpses shall become food for the birds of the air and the wild animals of the earth. (Jer 34.18–20)

A similar ritual is found in Genesis 15, when Yahweh instructs Abram:

> "Bring me a heifer three years old, a female goat three years old, a ram three years old, a turtledove, and a young pigeon." He brought him all these and cut them in two, laying each half over against the other; but he did not cut the birds in two. And when birds of prey came down on the carcasses, Abram drove them away. . . . When the sun had gone down and it was dark, a smoking fire pot and a flaming torch passed between these pieces. On that day the LORD made a covenant with Abram, saying, "To your descendants I give this land, from the river of Egypt to the great river, the river Euphrates." (Gen 15.9–18)

Because this is a promissory covenant, in which the superior party makes a commitment to the in-

ferior without specifying a corresponding obligation in the opposite direction, it is only the deity, symbolized by the smoking firepot and the flaming torch (reminiscent of the pillar of cloud and of fire in Ex 13.21 and elsewhere) that passes between the parts of the cut animals.

Thus, the rituals implied by the idiom "to cut a covenant" are yet another connection between ancient Near Eastern treaties and the biblical concept of covenant. "Cutting a covenant" also often involved a sacrifice, as we will see on page 117.

THE TEN COMMANDMENTS

Immediately after the appearance of Yahweh on the mountain, accompanied by all of the manifestations of a theophany—thunder, lightning, fire, smoke, earthquake, trumpet blast, and cloud—he speaks to the Israelites, and the first set of his remarks is the familiar text of the **Ten Commandments** (Ex 20.2–17). The Bible actually calls them the "ten words" (Ex 34.28; Deut 4.13; 10.4), a literal translation of the Hebrew also preserved their alternate designation as the **Decalogue**.

It is important to note that the Bible itself contains three different versions of the Decalogue. The first is in Exodus 20.2–17; in its present form it has been edited by P; note especially the reference to Genesis 1's account of creation in six days (Ex 20.11). The version found in Deuteronomy 5.6–21 is largely the same as that found in Exodus 20, although there are some differences, most notably in the motivation given for the sabbath (Deut 5.15; compare Ex 20.11) and in the separation of the coveting of the neighbor's wife and property into two separate commandments.

But yet another version of the Decalogue is found in the Bible. In Exodus 34, in the context of the episode of the golden calf (see further pages 130–33), an angry Moses breaks the tablets that contained the text of the commandments, and so

---

[*]   Trans. E. Reiner, p. 532 in *Ancient Near Eastern Texts Relating to the Old Testament* (ed. J. B. Pritchard; Princeton: Princeton University Press, 1969).

[†]   Adapted from translation by F. Rosenthal, p. 660 in *Ancient Near Eastern Texts Relating to the Old Testament* (ed. J. B. Pritchard; Princeton: Princeton University Press, 1969).

he is instructed by Yahweh to go back up the mountain to get a replacement copy. That replacement copy is explicitly identified as "the words of the covenant, the ten words" (Ex 34.28), but the text that precedes this identification, Exodus 34.10–26, differs significantly from the more familiar versions in Exodus 20 and Deuteronomy 5. Unlike the other two versions, which combine rules about worship with rules about human conduct, this version is almost entirely concerned with worship; for this reason it has been called the "Ritual Decalogue." It is admittedly difficult to enumerate exactly ten "words" in this passage, but that is clearly what the authors intended. Since readers knew what was on the first set of tablets, there was no need to repeat their content. Instead, the editors of the Pentateuch took advantage of a twist in the plot to incorporate another Decalogue tradition. The presence of three different versions of the Ten Commandments suggests that although the general tradition about them was very ancient, variants clearly existed. For the editors of the Pentateuch, it was more important to preserve these variants than to harmonize them. (See further pages 133–34.)

Evidence of the antiquity of the Decalogue includes the references to it in the prophets Hosea in the eighth century BCE and Jeremiah in the late seventh. In a covenant lawsuit passage (see page 110), Hosea proclaims a divine indictment of Israel for breach of contract:

> Hear the word of the Yahweh, O people of Israel;
>   for Yahweh has a lawsuit against the inhabitants
>   of the land.
> There is no faithfulness or loyalty,
>   and no knowledge of God in the land.
> Swearing, lying, and murder,
>   and stealing and adultery break out;
>   bloodshed follows bloodshed. (Hos 4.1–2)

Likewise, when reminding the Israelites of their covenant obligations, Jeremiah catalogues their offenses: "[Y]ou steal, murder, commit adultery, swear falsely, make offerings to Baal, and go after other gods that you have not known" (Jer 7.9). In both cases, the words used are often the same as those found in the Decalogue, and it is reasonable to see in these prophetic passages allusions to it.

Another reason for assuming the antiquity of the Decalogue is the social setting presumed by its content. The society envisioned by the Decalogue is an agrarian one, with various animals and slaves, and also houses and towns, but it is apparently not a monarchy—there is no mention of a king, as there is in the later Deuteronomic Code (see page 179). Thus, although at least in its present form the Decalogue clearly is to be dated later than the time of the Exodus—many of the laws would have no immediate relevance for a group of runaway slaves huddled at the base of a mountain—it does seem to originate in the premonarchic period, that is, in the late second millennium BCE.

The Treaty Form and the Decalogue

On one level, the Ten Commandments can be interpreted as the text of the contract between Yahweh and Israel. Like the treaties, the Decalogue begins with an identification of the suzerain ("I am Yahweh your God") and a brief summary of what he had done for the Israelites ("who brought you out of the land of Egypt, out of the house of slavery"; Ex 20.2). The commandments that follow correspond to the stipulations of the treaty, with the first four concerning the relationship of Israel to Yahweh, as vassal to suzerain. They demand absolute loyalty ("You shall not have other gods apart from me") and specify the way Yahweh is to be worshiped. The remaining six commandments are comparable to the stipulations that concern relationships among vassals of the suzerain: Each individual Israelite is to respect his neighbor's (that is, his fellow Israelite's) life, person, marriage, legal reputation, and property, as well as to care for them when they are aged.

No witnesses are mentioned, although we have seen that they do occur in other passages concerning covenant renewal. Neither do explicit blessings and curses occur, although there may be echoes of this element in the expansion to the second commandment:

> [F]or I the LORD your God am a jealous God, punishing children for the iniquity of parents, to the third and the fourth generation of those who reject me,

but showing steadfast love to the thousandth generation of those who love me and keep my commandments (Ex 20.5–6)

Another possible use of the blessing element is the motivation given for observance of the command to honor father and mother, "so that your days may be long in the land that the LORD your God is giving to you" (Ex 20.12).

The Meaning of the Ten Commandments

It should be noted that the audience of the Decalogue is limited to the Israelites gathered at the base of Mount Sinai; this, then, is a covenant between Yahweh and Israel, narrower than that between Yahweh and all humanity, as was the case with Noah (Gen 9.8–17), or that between Yahweh and all the descendants of Abraham, as in Genesis 17. Moreover, the commandments themselves are phrased in the second person masculine singular; that is, they are specifically addressed to individual Israelite males, as the wording of the commandments about the sabbath ("you, your son or your daughter, your male or female slave") and about property ("your neighbor's wife") also makes clear. Like other law codes that we will consider (on pages 122–25, 145–49, and 175–80), the Decalogue codifies the values of the society that produced them. Among other things, that society was patriarchal, in which wives were considered property, and one in which slavery was an accepted institution.

Let us now look at the Ten Commandments in more detail; a critical step in determining what a law means is to determine what it meant. The first several commandments have to do with relationship between Yahweh and Israel. That relationship is an exclusive one, as the first commandment states: Israel is not to worship other gods. The commandment does not express monotheism, the belief that only one god exists, but rather presumes the existence of other gods. As in a marriage, one of the primary analogues for covenant, Israel is to be faithful, like a wife to her husband or, as in a treaty, like a vassal to his

suzerain. When the prophets condemn the Israelites for having worshiped other gods in violation of this commandment, the metaphors of marital and political fidelity are often invoked, sometimes graphically (as, for example, in Ezek 16.23–34; 23.5–21; Jer 2.23–25; 3.1–10). Yahweh is a jealous husband (see Ex 34.14, and compare Num 5.11–14, 30; Prov 6.34–35), and the worship of other gods, or making alliances with foreign powers, provokes his rage.

The worship of Yahweh is also to be qualitatively different from that of other gods. The second commandment prohibits the making of an image of Yahweh, or of any other divine, human, or animal form. Thus, the ark of the covenant, in addition to being a repository, a kind of safe deposit box, for the tablets of the covenant, was also the footstool of Yahweh's throne. That throne was empty: No statue of Yahweh was seated on the throne (see further pages 126–28). The third commandment concerns proper use of the sacred name of Yahweh, which he had been so reluctant to reveal (see Ex 3.13–15; compare Gen 32.29). It was not to be used wrongfully, that is, probably in magic, sorcery, or other types of rituals in which its invocation would somehow imply control of the deity. Finally, according to the fourth commandment, the Israelites are to observe the seventh day as a day of rest; P will identify the sabbath as the sign of the Sinai covenant (Ex 31.12–17); see further Box 1.3 on page 8.

The remaining six commandments have to do with intracommunity relationships: A man's life, his marriage, his person (stealing probably means kidnapping rather than theft), his reputation, and his property were to be inviolable by another Israelite (his "neighbor"). These are reminiscent of the stipulations in the treaties concerning relationships among vassals. Violations of these commandments unravel the fabric of the community of Israel, and are thus not just a violation of civil law but an offense against Yahweh, who had created that community.

Although eight of the Ten Commandments are negative prohibitions, the substance of the whole is a strong positive ethic, as later tradition recognized: The essence of the Decalogue is to love God and to love the neighbor (see Mic 6.8; Mk 12.28–33). As we will see, when Israel began to emerge in the Promised Land in the period after the Exodus, these two principles, exclusive worship of Yahweh and mutual support, were the essence of the contract or covenant that unified the Israelites. (See further Box 7.4.)

THE RATIFICATION OF THE COVENANT

The Decalogue is followed by another set of divinely given laws in Exodus 20.22–23.33. This very ancient collection is known as the "Covenant Code" and will be discussed in the next chapter with other legal and ritual material. Then in Exodus 24 the narrative resumes with a composite account of the ratification of the covenant. This apparently comes from two separate sources, but scholars disagree about how to identify them. In one (vv. 1–2, 9–11; possibly J), Moses and other representatives of the Israelites ascend the mountain, and there "they saw the God of Israel," under whose feet was a pavement of lapis lazuli (NRSV: "sapphire"), as clear as the sky itself. Although the usual penalty for seeing God was death (see Ex 33.20), we occasionally find exceptions (see Gen 16.13; 32.30; Judg 13.22; Isa 6.5), as in this case: "[H]e did not lay his hand on the chief men of the people of Israel" (vv. 10–11), and they shared a meal with God. The conclusion of a covenant with a meal between the two parties is attested in Genesis 31, where Jacob and Laban made a covenant (v. 44) to establish boundaries between their two groups, and then shared a meal (vv. 46, 54). On the basis of this parallel, we can interpret the eating and drinking on top of Mount Sinai as a meal in which the participants in the covenant, God and the representatives of Israel, ceremonially concluded their agreement.

Embedded in this fairly anthropomorphic account is another (vv. 3–8, probably E), in which a sacrifice is offered as a covenant ritual. A sacrifice is, on one level, a meal offered to a deity in a ritual context. Here, after the reading of "the book of the covenant" (v. 7), oxen were sacrificed and their blood sprinkled both on the newly constructed altar, representing the deity, and on the assembled people; this is "the blood of the covenant" (v. 8). The sacrifice concluding the covenant required the slaughter of animals, and this may be another level of meaning in the idiom "to cut a covenant," in addition to being a reminder of the consequences of failure to observe its provisions.

Finally, in Exodus 24.15–18, P resumes with Moses ascending the mountain alone and the cloud—the "glory of Yahweh"—descending on the mountain for six days; on the seventh, presumably the sabbath, Yahweh called to Moses, and Moses was in the cloud for forty days and forty nights.

RETROSPECT AND PROSPECT

Having arrived at Sinai, the Israelites remained there for some time. Into this sojourn the biblical writers inserted disparate materials concerning ancient Israel's laws and rituals. The first of these, and in many respects the primary revelation, is the Decalogue, which we have interpreted as the text of the contract or covenant between Yahweh and Israel, requiring worship of Yahweh alone and in the manner he specified and prohibiting offenses against a fellow Israelite.

As Exodus 24 ends, Moses has ascended the mountain once again, to be given a set of instructions concerning ritual. But his absence causes dismay among the Israelites left leaderless at the base of the mountain. This leads to the episode of the golden calf, which we will consider in the next chapter, along with Israel's ancient law code, the "Covenant Code," which follows the Decalogue, and the primarily Priestly material concerning the construction of the ark of the covenant and the tabernacle and other matters having to do with ritual.

Box 7.4 THE STATUS AND NUMBERING OF THE TEN COMMANDMENTS

In their original setting, the Ten Commandments were not intended to be universal, and they reflect the values of the society from which they came. In Christian tradition especially this historical particularity has been ignored or glossed over, and the Decalogue has generally been taken to be a universal code, a kind of "natural law." Thus, the prohibition of making of images of God and the requirement to rest on the seventh day of the week (not Sunday, which is the first day; see Mt 28.1) have generally been ignored in Christianity, and in modern times the values implied by a social system that included slavery and treated women as property have been rejected. Even so, at various times in the history of Christianity a more literal interpretation has been insisted upon by some, as is illustrated, for example, by the continuing divergence of practice on which day to observe as the sabbath and whether or not to use images in sacred settings.

Although the Ten Commandments have become a kind of icon, in religious education the biblical text is often abridged. Furthermore, different religious communities give them in somewhat different order. In Jewish tradition, the "ten words" begin with Exodus 20.2: "I am the LORD your God, who brought you out of the land of Egypt, out of the house of slavery." This is the first "word" or "utterance," and then follow the nine actual commandments, beginning with those about worship of Yahweh alone and images, which form one "word." In the Roman Catholic, Anglican, and Lutheran churches, the first commandment is Exodus 20.3–5, and the last two commandments follow the version in Deuteronomy 5, separating the "coveting" of the neighbor's wife and of his other property into two commandments. In most Protestant and Orthodox churches, the first commandment is "You shall have no other gods apart from me," followed by the remaining nine, following the text of Exodus 20. The following table shows the differences in numbering:

	Jewish	Eastern Orthodox, Most Protestant	Catholic, Anglican, Lutheran
Ex 20.2	1	(prologue)	1
20.3	2	1	1
20.4–6	2	2	1
20.7	3	3	2
20.8–11	4	4	3
20.12	5	5	4
20.13	6	6	5
20.14	7	7	6
20.15	8	8	7
20.16	9	9	8
20.17 (Deut 5.21)	10	10	9 & 10

IMPORTANT TERMS

covenant

Decalogue

manna

Midian

suzerainty treaty

Ten Commandments

QUESTIONS FOR REVIEW

1. What is the vocabulary connected with the concept of covenant in the Bible?

2. How does the suzerainty treaty form provide a useful model for understanding biblical traditions about covenant and covenant making?

What differences are there, and what is their significance?

3. Discuss the original audience and meaning of the Ten Commandments and the values that they incorporate.

BIBLIOGRAPHY

For commentaries on Exodus, see the bibliography to Chapter 6.

A good summary of the classic view of the relationship between treaty and covenant is George E. Mendenhall and Gary A Herion, "Covenant," pp. 1179–202 in *Anchor Bible Dictionary*, Vol. 1 (ed. D. N. Freedman; New York: Doubleday, 1992).

A selection of Hittite treaties is found in Gary Beckman, *Hittite Diplomatic Texts* (2d ed.; Atlanta: Scholars, 1999).

For a summary of scholarly views on the Ten Commandments, see Raymond F. Collins, "Ten Commandments," pp. 383–87 in *Anchor Bible Dictionary*, Vol. 6 (ed. D. N. Freedman; New York: Doubleday, 1992).

LAW AND RITUAL

CHAPTER

8

Exodus 20.22–23.33 and 25–40

As the book of Exodus continues, many more divine instructions are given to Moses, so much so that the narrative itself seems to be reduced to a framework for the materials that have been inserted into it. That in fact is the conclusion of critical scholarship: The final editors of the Pentateuch, the Priestly tradition, inserted into an older narrative legal and ritual traditions of different origins and dates, in part to provide them with a normative authority by associating them with Moses and the revelations at Sinai. In this chapter and the next we will examine several collections of laws, those known as the Covenant Code, the Ritual Decalogue, and the Holiness Code, as well as the material in which they are embedded in the books of Exodus and Leviticus, much of which is concerned with various aspects of worship. It is from collections such as these that the Pentateuch gets its reputation as a law book. Yet in it, as we have seen, law and narrative are intertwined, and in many respects law is a response to divine action, especially the Exodus. We will begin with a look at ancient Near Eastern law codes.

LAW IN THE ANCIENT NEAR EAST

The several collections of biblical laws, like many other genres found in the Bible, are paralleled elsewhere in the ancient Near East. About a dozen complete or virtually complete law codes are known, principally from ancient Mesopotamia and Asia Minor. The earliest are from ancient Sumer, dating to the late third millennium BCE, and the latest, from Babylonia, are from the seventh century BCE. In addition, literally hundreds of thousands of contracts and records of lawsuits and other court cases show how various legal principles functioned in ordinary life.

One of the very first of the ancient law codes to be discovered was the **Code of Hammurapi** (a more correct spelling than the traditional "Hammurabi"), engraved on a monumental basalt stela dating to the reign of the Babylonian king for which it is named, in the first half of the eighteenth century BCE. Because it is one of the most complete of the law codes that has survived, and because of its importance in the history of interpretation, we will take it as representative of the other codes (see Figure 8.1).

FIGURE 8.1. The Code of Hammurapi. Over 7 ft (2.2 m) high, carved of black volcanic rock, this stela was discovered in the ancient city of Susa in Persia in 1901–2. The top of the stela shows Hammurapi on the left, receiving from the sun-god Shamash (also the god of justice because he sees everything) the laws that the king is promulgating here.

In the Code of Hammurapi, the "code" proper is nearly three hundred laws, all in the form of particular cases and circumstances, dealing with such topics as perjury, theft, medical malpractice, real estate, banking, marriage (the longest section), and similar topics that are ubiquitous concerns of complex societies (see Box 8.1).

These laws are framed by a lengthy prologue and epilogue. This framework is written in the first person, as if by Hammurapi himself. The prologue describes how the gods exalted Marduk (see pages 5–7 for a mythic version of this in *Enuma elish*) and named Babylon, his city, as supreme. At that time they also named Hammurapi as shepherd, "to make justice prevail in the land, to abolish the wicked and the evil, to prevent the strong from oppressing the weak." As the prologue continues, Hammurapi describes himself with fulsome praise and concludes by introducing the laws themselves:

> When the god Marduk commanded me to provide just ways for the people of the land (in order to attain) appropriate behavior, I established truth and justice as the declaration of the land, I enhanced the well-being of the people. At that time [I decreed] . . .

In the epilogue Hammurapi calls on the gods and goddesses to curse any future ruler who breaks the laws or defaces the stela; this is reminiscent of the curses that occur in ancient treaties (see pages 110–12). The epilogue also suggests a purpose for the monument on which the laws are inscribed:

> Let any wronged man who has a lawsuit come before the statue of me, the king of justice, and let him have my inscribed stela read aloud to him, thus may he hear my precious pronouncements and let my stela reveal the lawsuit for him; may he examine his case, may he calm his (troubled) heart.

We can see several problems here. Few people could read the complicated cuneiform script used by the Babylonians, and ordinary people were not likely to be able to travel to wherever the stela was displayed. Moreover, the collection is obviously not comprehensive: Many crimes and situations are not addressed in it. We also find no evidence for the Code of Hammurapi (or any other collection) being cited in a specific legal action, as if it were a body of precedent or of principle. Rather, the principal purpose of the code and similar texts seems to be the glorification of royal power. At the same time, the Code did embody two key legal principles: These were laws that were binding throughout the kingdom, so that in

Box 8.1 EXCERPT FROM THE CODE OF HAMMURAPI

The following is a small sample of the more than three hundred laws included in the code:

195   If a child should strike his father, they shall cut off his hand.
196   If an *awilu* [a free person, the highest social class] should blind the eye of another *awilu*, they shall blind his eye.
197   If he should break the bone of another *awilu*, they shall break his bone.
198   If he should blind the eye of a commoner [the middle social class] or break the bone of a commoner, he shall weigh and deliver 60 shekels of silver.
199   If he should blind the eye of an *awilu*'s slave or break the bone of an *awilu*'s slave, he shall weigh and deliver one-half his value (in silver).
200   If an *awilu* should knock out the tooth of another *awilu* of his own rank, they shall knock out his tooth.
201   If he should knock out the tooth of a commoner, he shall weigh and deliver 20 shekels of silver.

Translated by Martha T. Roth, *Law Collections from Mesopotamia and Asia Minor*, pp. 120–21.

---

theory at least penalties for crimes were fixed and not subject to individual whim; and justice was to be proportionately retributive, that is, the punishment should more or less fit the crime.

Finally, we should note that the framing prologue and epilogue, like that of the picture of Shamash on the stela itself, implicitly set the Code into a religious context: Observance of the law promulgated by the king is required because the king's own authority is divinely given. In Babylon as elsewhere in the ancient Near East the sacred and the secular were linked.

THE COVENANT CODE (EX 20.22–23.33)

In addition to the Decalogue (see pages 114–17), the Pentateuch contains several other law codes or collections of legal material; among the most important are the Covenant Code (Ex 20.22–23.33), the Holiness Code (Lev 17–26), and the Deuteronomic Code (Deut 12–26). In this chapter we will examine the first of these, and the other two in later chapters (Chapters 9 and 11, respectively).

Each of these biblical codes is a complex document in its own right, with a literary history largely independent from that of the Pentateuch in which it has been included. The **Covenant Code** gets its name from the reference to the "book of covenant" in the narrative of the ratification ceremony that follows (Ex 24.7). Like the Code of Hammurapi and many other ancient Near Eastern codes, the Covenant Code consists largely of case or **casuistic law**. Since the early twentieth century, following the lead of the twentieth-century German biblical scholar Albrecht Alt, the genre of casuistic law has been distinguished from the more general apodictic laws found, for example, in the Decalogue. Casuistic laws deal with the particular: "If a man leaves a pit open, or digs a pit and does not cover it, and an ox or donkey falls into it, the one responsible for the pit shall make restitution, giving silver to the owner, but keeping the dead animal" (Ex 21.33–34). Sometimes a case becomes very complicated, or a number of alternate conditions are given, as in the case of the goring ox (Ex 21.28–32). **Apodictic laws**, on the other hand, are more general, and the Covenant Code contains some of these as well, for example, "Whoever curses his father or his mother shall be put to death" (Ex 21.17).

The Code of Hammurapi and similar nonbiblical collections consist of criminal and civil laws. The Covenant Code, like other biblical codes, differs from these by including among the laws dealing with criminal and civil matters various regulations concerning worship. In the Covenant Code, perhaps to emphasize the sacred character of the entire collection, these laws concerning worship frame the civil and criminal cases, as the following outline suggests:

Exodus 20.22–26	Regulations concerning the worship of Yahweh: It is to be exclusive and should not include gold and silver images of other gods; and the types of altars to be used in worship are specified.
21.1–22.17	The cases, arranged by topics: slavery (21.2–11); personal injury (21.12–32); property (21.33–22.17).
22.18–23.9	Miscellaneous religious and humanitarian laws, mostly apodictic in form.
23.10–19	Ritual calendar: the sabbatical year, the sabbath, and the annual festivals.
23.20–33	Divine promises and warnings, especially concerning exclusive worship of Yahweh.

The complex character of the Covenant Code is evident from the assortment of topics it addresses,

the various forms of laws that it includes, and the inconsistency in the way that it refers to the deity: Sometimes, especially in the opening and closing sections, the deity is speaking, but elsewhere he is generally spoken about.

The central section of the Covenant Code is the cases in Exodus 21.1–22.17. They are not comprehensive; rather, they deal with slaves, personal injuries, damages by and to animals, and loss of property. As is true of all laws, the Covenant Code gives us a kind of window into the organization and values of the society that produced it. Like the Ten Commandments, the Covenant Code reflects an agrarian society, one with grain fields, vineyards, and houses (see, for example, Ex 22.5–7). It was also a society in which slavery was an accepted institution and women were considered property. (For further discussion of the status of women in Israelite law and ritual, see pages 149–50.)

Because of its similarities to the Code of Hammurapi and other nonbiblical law codes, the collection of cases in Exodus 21.1–22.17 is probably derived from already existing Canaanite laws. Further evidence of a Canaanite origin is in the complicated law concerning disputed ownership:

> When a man gives his neighbor silver or goods for safekeeping, and it is stolen from his house, then the thief, if caught, shall pay double. If the thief is not caught, the owner of the house shall be brought before the *elohim*, to determine whether or not he had had laid hands on his neighbor's property. In any case of disputed ownership involving ox, donkey, sheep, clothing, or any other loss, of which one party says, "This is mine," the case of both parties shall come before the *elohim*; whomever the *elohim* condemn shall pay double to his neighbor. (Ex 22.7–9)

The word *elohim* is problematic. Although plural in form (-*im* is a masculine plural ending, as in seraph*im* and cherub*im*), in the Bible it often has a singular meaning and is correctly translated "God." Not infrequently, however, it can also mean "gods," as in the commandment "You shall not have other gods (*elohim*) apart from me" (Ex 20.3). In theory, in the first two occurrences in the law quoted here (as also in 21.6), *elohim* could mean "God," since there are no other grammatical indications about whether the word is singular or plural. But in the third occurrence there is a verb, which is also plural in form, and so the third occurrence must be translated as "gods." This plural was recognized by the translators of the King James Version (KJV; 1611), for example, who, however, rendered it as "judges," an otherwise unattested meaning, thereby bypassing the explicit polytheism of the Hebrew original.

What the law then proposes is that a dispute over property that cannot be resolved is to be taken to a sanctuary, where the truth will be determined. Other texts suggest a variety of means for such determination: by some self-imprecation or curse (as in Job 31.5–40); by oath (note the variant in the following law: "an oath before Yahweh" [Ex 22.11], and see also 1 Kings 8.31); by consultation of some oracular device (such as the Urim and Thummim; see page 130); or perhaps by some physical ordeal (as in Num 5.11–31). In other words, when truth or falsehood, innocence or guilt, were thought to be beyond ordinary judicial procedures, the decision was put in divine hands. What is significant is that in this case, as presumably in others that contain the same term, appeal was made to "the gods"; the original Canaanite substratum of the laws has survived.

Both the Code of Hammurapi and the Covenant Code set the laws in an explicitly religious context. In both, it is the deity who is ultimately the source of legal authority, and in both there is a human intermediary. Thus, as in most other aspects of life in the ancient world, the distinction between sacred and secular was not nearly as sharp as it is in much of the modern world. In both cases, violation of the law is ultimately an offense against the deity.

The laws that frame the case laws in the Covenant Code are more specifically religious and also more specifically Israelite (see Figure 8.2). As an example, we may cite the law concerning the sabbath: "Six days you shall do your work, but on the seventh day you shall rest, so that your ox and your donkey may have relief, and your homeborn slave and the resident alien may be refreshed" (Ex 23.12). Unlike the P version of the sabbath commandment (Ex 20.11),

the motivation for the sabbath observance here is a humanitarian one, a motive that extends even to one's animals. This same humanitarian motive is found in the version of the commandment found in the Decalogue in Deuteronomy (Deut 5.14–15), as well as in other laws in the Covenant Code.

Thus the Covenant Code reflects the values of the society that produced it. Some of these values are often different from our own, as the following two examples show. In the context of laws concerning property is the case of the seduced virgin: "When a man seduces a virgin who is not engaged to be married, and lies with her, he shall give the bride-price for her and make her his wife. But if her father refuses to give her to him, he shall pay an amount equal to the bride-price for virgins" (Ex 22.16–17). Because the wronged daughter is the father's property and her value has been diminished by her loss of virginity, the one who has seduced her must make restitution to the father by paying the full bride-price, even if he does not marry her.

A second example concerns the institution of slavery: "When a slaveowner strikes a male or female slave with a rod and the slave dies immediately, the owner shall be punished. But if the slave survives a day or two, there is no punishment; for the slave is the owner's property" (Ex 21.20–21; see further 21.2–11). The principle of retributive justice (see Box 8.2 on page 126) does not apply in the case of injury to a slave because the slave does not have the rights of an Israelite male.

At the same time, the Covenant Code also gives expression to principles that we might find more congenial. As in the Decalogue, the mother is put on the same level as the father (Ex 21.15, 17; compare 20.12). Moreover, members of at least some lesser social classes are to be the objects of special concern: "You shall not wrong or oppress a resident alien, for you were aliens in the land of Egypt. You shall not abuse any widow or orphan" (Ex 22.21–22; see also 23.9). In Deuteronomy, this same concern will be extended even to slaves (Deut 5.14–15). The appeal to the Exodus experience is significant, for it instructs the Israelites to remember what it was like to be

FIGURE 8.2.   Canaanite altar at Megiddo. A circular altar from the mid-third millennium BCE at Megiddo, about 30 ft (9 m) in diameter. Like the altar described in Exodus 20.25–26, it is made of unhewn stones, but it also has steps, which is forbidden in Exodus.

members of an underprivileged social class, and to treat the less powerful and less fortunate as God had treated them.

THE ARK, THE TABERNACLE, AND THE PRIESTLY VESTMENTS AND ORDINATION

In Yahweh's commands to Moses in Exodus 25–31, and Moses' carrying out of those commands in Exodus 35–40, the Priestly tradition (P) gives lovingly detailed descriptions of objects and institutions having to do with ritual. For all their detail, however, the descriptions are at least somewhat idealized. Many of the raw materials

specified for the construction of the various objects—including large quantities of gold, silver, and semi-precious stones—would not have been readily available to what was supposedly a group of runaway slaves in the wilderness.

The context in which P originated was the Temple in Jerusalem, constructed in the tenth century BCE and destroyed in the early sixth, and there can be no doubt that P's descriptions clearly are informed by the architecture, ritual objects, and practices of the Temple in Jerusalem. But are they simply idealized retrojections of the Temple and its rituals, with some modifications to suit the period of the Exodus and wandering in the wilderness, or do they have some historical basis in the period before the Temple was functioning? Some scholars

Box 8.2 *"AN EYE FOR AN EYE"*

The principle of "eye for eye, tooth for tooth," found in Exodus 21.24, known as the law of talion (Latin *lex talionis*) is also found, perhaps for the first time, in the Code of Hammurapi. It makes concrete an important legal principle, that the punishment should fit the crime. One of the functions of a code, at least in theory, was to prevent people from taking the law into their own hands and exacting disproportionate vengeance for offenses committed against them. In the Covenant Code, the principle of retributive justice occurs in the context of the case of a pregnant woman injured in a fight between two men. If there is no harm to the woman, then a fine is to be paid; but if there is harm, then the punishment corresponds to the harm done: "life for life, eye for eye, tooth for tooth, hand for hand, foot for foot, burn for burn, wound for wound, stripe for stripe" (Ex 21.23–25). The same principle is found, with slightly different wording, in the Deuteronomic Code (Deut 19.21).

In the Covenant Code, as in the Code of Hammurapi, this principle applied only to social equals; in the next law in Exodus, if it is a slave whose eye has been destroyed or whose tooth has been knocked out by his owner, the slave is to be freed, but the owner is apparently not to suffer any other damage (Ex 21.26–27). In the latest of the Pentateuchal codes, the Holiness Code, the "eye for eye" principle is immediately followed by the injunction: "You are to have one law for the alien and for the citizen" (Lev 24.19–22). The "alien" or stranger had a lower social status than the "citizen" or native-born Israelite, and by affirming that the same law applied to both, the Holiness Code provides an example of a broadening understanding of the law, to include at least some of those who were more marginal in the social structure.

In the Sermon on the Mount, Jesus is presented as broadening the understanding of this law even further, to nonviolent response to personal injury or property loss, and even to love of enemies (Mt 5.38–48). The latter principle is also implicit in the Covenant Code:

> When you come upon your enemy's ox or donkey going astray, you shall bring it back. When you see the donkey of one who hates you lying under its burden and you would hold back from setting it free, you must help to set it free. (Ex 23.4–5; compare Deut 22.1–4, where the same law concerns only the "brother")

have argued that the descriptions of the tabernacle (also called "the tent of meeting") in fact do preserve earlier traditions from the premonarchic period in the twelfth and eleventh centuries, when the **ark of the covenant** was a moveable sanctuary housed in a tent. Since the evidence is fragmentary, however, it is impossible to be certain.

The Ark of the Covenant

Among the detailed instructions given to Moses are those concerning the construction of the divine throne, which had two parts. First is the ark proper, 2.5 cubits (about 4 ft [1.1 m]) long and 1.5 cubits (about 2.5 ft [.7 m]) wide and high, made of acacia, a hard wood that is insect resistant and found throughout the desert regions. The ark was overlaid with gold and was carried by means of poles through rings attached to each side. The second part of the divine throne was a kind of covering for the ark, which included the **cherubim**, two gold statues of winged divine beings; the traditional translation for this cover, "mercy seat" (first occurring in Ex 25.17), is based on an ancient but disputed interpretation of the Hebrew word here.

Judging from parallels in ancient depictions of royal thrones, the cherubim themselves formed the throne of the deity, described as "enthroned" (literally "sitting on") the cherubim (2 Sam 6.2; Pss 80.1; 99.1), and the ark was his footstool (1 Chr 28.2; Ps 132.7) (see Figure 8.3). These two functions are summarized in the longest title of the ark: "The ark of the covenant (*berît*) of Yahweh of armies enthroned on the cherubim" (1 Sam 4.4).

In P, the ark is called "the ark of the testimony" (*aron ha-edut*, as in Ex 25.22), presumably because the covenant was sworn to in the presence of witnesses; in J and in D the ark is called "the ark of the covenant" (*aron ha-berît*); NRSV confusingly translates both Hebrew phrases in the same way, as "ark of the covenant." The ark also functioned as a container or safe-deposit box for the text of the covenant, the contract between Yahweh and Israel. In fact, in D's more austere presentation of Israel's ritual, this is all that the ark was, a container made of acacia wood (Deut 10.1–5), with no cherubim. In P, on the other

FIGURE 8.3. Part of the relief carved on the stone coffin of Ahiram, king of the Phoenician city of Byblos in the late second millennium BCE. It shows the king sitting on a throne whose sides are winged sphinxes, like the cherubim that formed part of Yahweh's throne. The king's feet rest on a footstool, recalling the designation of the ark of the covenant as the footstool of Yahweh. (See also Figure 13.3 on page 225.)

hand, not only were there the cherubim, no doubt based on those in the Solomonic Temple (see 1 Kings 6.23–28), but inside the ark in addition to the tablets were a jar of manna and Aaron's staff (see Heb 9.4; compare Ex 16.33; Num 17.10). For D's intellectual kinfolk, however, the Deuteronomistic Historians who wrote the books of Kings (see further pages 191–93), the ark contained nothing except the tablets (1 Kings 8.9).

As the visible sign of the invisible divine presence, the ark also served as what is called a palladium, a war emblem. When the ark participated in war, the divine presence was thought to be there (see 1 Sam 4.6–7), and so the war became a kind of "holy war" (see further pages 206–7). An ancient battle cry associated with the ark is preserved in Numbers:

> Arise, O LORD, let your enemies be scattered,
>   and your foes flee before you. (Num 10.35;
>   compare Ps 68.1)

Yahweh is the leader of the heavenly armies (the phrase "Lord of hosts" is an archaic translation, which means "Yahweh of armies"), who accompany him into battle (Deut 33.2–3; Ps 68.17; see also Judg 5.20). In the narratives of the crossing of the Jordan and the fall of Jericho (Josh 3–4; 6), the ark played a central role; another example of its use in battle is found in 1 Samuel 4.1–9. The ark's presence was thought to assure victory, and when the ark was absent, victory was unlikely. In Numbers, the people attempted to enter and conquer the land of Canaan from the south, but because the ark and Moses remained behind in the camp (Num 14.44) they were defeated. But the ark's presence did not always guarantee victory; in one battle between the Israelites and their enemies the Philistines, even though the ark had been brought to the battlefield, the Israelite army was defeated and the ark itself was captured (1 Sam 4.10–11).

The Tabernacle

The tabernacle (the Hebrew word literally means "dwelling") is the portable sanctuary envisioned by P for the wilderness period (see Figure 8.4). It is also called the "tent of meeting" because it was the place where Yahweh "met" with Moses and the Israelites (Ex 29.42–43). In the ideology of temples, sanctuaries, and similar ritual architecture, the earthly exemplar was a copy of the true divine home in the heavens; thus, later tradition observes, the tent that Moses constructs was "a sanctuary that is a sketch and shadow of the heavenly one" (Heb 8.5), "a copy of the holy tent that you prepared from the beginning" (Wis 9.8; see also Rev 15.5). That Yahweh's heavenly home was a tent is therefore presumed and is consistent with the relationship of Yahweh to the Canaanite high god El (see pages 81–82), who also lived in a tent. In fact, the same word for "dwelling" is also used for the heavenly homes of the gods in Ugaritic, which are also called tents. At the same time, P appropriately incorporates a tent-shrine into its description of the fully developed worship of Yahweh that began at Sinai, during the journey from Egypt to Canaan: a movable shrine for a people on the move.

Assessing the historical accuracy of P's details concerning the tabernacle is difficult. Clearly much of the detail is based on the plan and ornamentation of the Temple in Jerusalem, in which the priests who formed P served. At the same time, it is reasonable to assume that they also preserved at least in broad strokes authentic memories of Israel's earlier system of worship, probably from the period before the Temple was built, when the principal shrine of the Israelites was the ark of the covenant, housed in a tent or tabernacle.

The tabernacle was made of intricately woven curtains set on a frame of acacia wood. The entire structure was able to be disassembled and moved to another location. The plan of the tabernacle was bipartite, with a total enclosed area of 50 by 100 cubits (about 75 by 100 ft [22 by 45 m]). Within the tabernacle was an open courtyard, divided in half. On one side of this courtyard, which all the Israelites were permitted to enter, was a bronze basin used for purification rituals, and in the center of this half was the principal altar of sacrifice. The other half contained another enclosed area, "the holy place" (Ex

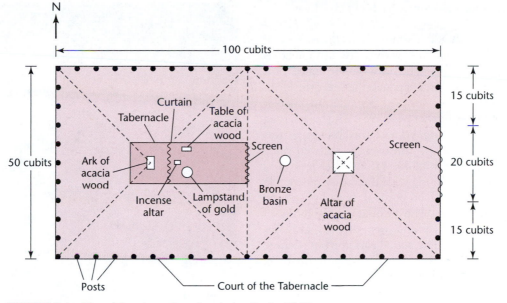

FIGURE 8.4.   Plan of the tabernacle as described in Exodus 25–27.

26.33), which only the priests were permitted to enter. Within it were situated an offering table, an incense altar, and an ornate, perpetually burning seven-branched lampstand. Part of this inner enclosure was a room, "the holy of holies" (Ex 26.34), the most sacred place, separated from the rest by an especially intricately woven curtain. Only the high priest (Aaron and his successors) could enter this space, and only on the Day of Atonement, for it contained the ark (see Lev 16.2–3).

The tabernacle, and the ark that it housed, was the sacred object at the center of worship. The ark was part of the divine throne, and thus the tabernacle was the place where the deity presented himself: "I will meet with the Israelites there, and it shall be sanctified by my glory" (Ex 29.43). The "glory" of Yahweh was, as we have seen (on page 27), the numinous light-filled cloud that both revealed and hid the deity. When the entire complex was dedicated, "the cloud covered the tent of meeting, and the glory of the LORD

filled the tabernacle" (Ex 40.34). It also served as a guide for the Israelites in their journey through the wilderness to the Promised Land: "Whenever the cloud was taken up from the tabernacle, the Israelites would set out on each stage of their journey; but if the cloud was not taken up, then they did not set out until the day that it was taken up" (Ex 40.36–37; see also Num 10.11).

The Priestly Vestments and Ordination

Exodus 28 gives detailed instructions for the priestly vestments, which, like the tabernacle curtains, were woven of multicolored yarns. The details are difficult to picture, although many are clearly deeply significant and symbolic. We may highlight as examples the ephod and the Urim and Thummim attached to it. The ephod, a kind of apron, was blue, with ornamental pomegranates and golden bells decorating its hem. Attached to the shoulder straps of the ephod were two semiprecious stones, each engraved with the names of six of the twelve tribes of Israel. Hanging from the shoulder straps was a "breastpiece of judgment," ornamented with twelve semiprecious stones, each also engraved with the name of a tribe. This was a kind of pouch that held the Urim and Thummim, stones used in rendering oracular judgments (see further page 298). The bells served as a kind of warning, because the chief priest was "Holy to the LORD," the words engraved on a rosette ornamenting the priestly headgear. As such, the priests along with the entire tabernacle complex needed to be purified, both by washing and by anointing. The ordination ceremony of the priests—Aaron and his sons—is also described in detail. The actual carrying out of these instructions, however, does not occur in the book of Exodus, but in Leviticus 8–9.

The instructions conclude with an elaboration of the commandment to observe the sabbath (see Ex 20.8–11). The Priestly writers, as we have seen, had three principal covenants, each of which had a sign: the covenant with Noah, whose sign was the bow in the sky (Gen 9.8–17); the covenant with Abraham, whose sign was circumcision (Gen 17); and the last, the covenant with all Israel at Sinai, whose sign was the sabbath (Ex 31.12–17).

FIGURE 8.5. A figurine of a male calf, cast in bronze and plated with silver, about 4 in (10 cm) high. With the calf was a ceramic shrine; both were found in a sanctuary at Ashkelon dating to the late seventeenth century BCE. Bull symbolism was used of the Canaanite gods El and Baal, as well as of Yahweh, the god of Israel.

THE GOLDEN CALF

Between the Priestly accounts of the divine blueprints for the ark, the tabernacle, and other ritual objects in Exodus 25–31 and of the manufacture of those items in Exodus 35–40 is an interruption: the episode of the **golden calf** and its sequel. The narrative of the golden calf (Ex 32) is extraordinarily complex and is another example of how different traditions have been intricately combined in the final form of the Pentateuch. (See Figure 8.5.)

At first reading, the narrative is straightforward. During Moses' absence of forty days and forty nights (see Box 8.3) on top of Mount Sinai, the Israelites at the base of the mountain became restive. They persuaded Aaron to make a gold statue of a young bull, which they worshiped; as Psalm 106 puts it:

> They made a calf at Horeb
>   and worshiped a cast image.
> They exchanged the glory of God
>   for the image of an ox that eats grass. (Ps 106.19–20)

Yahweh told Moses what had happened, and Moses descended from the top of the mountain, broke the tablets of the testimony in his anger, and punished the guilty parties.

Closer examination of the narrative in Exodus 32, however, reveals a number of complexities. First, despite the ancient interpretation found in Psalm 106, the calf is apparently not a symbol of another deity, a false god as it were. The people

Box 8.3 FORTY DAYS AND FORTY NIGHTS

In the history of biblical interpretation, the many numbers given in the Bible have often been interpreted symbolically. While such interpretations are often fanciful, in some cases numerical symbolism apparently is at work. We have seen some examples in the genealogy in Genesis 5 (see pages 36–38); another is the frequent use of the number forty in designation of time. Often the notice of a period of forty days (and nights) or forty years serves as a transitional marker, separating two distinct epochs in biblical narrative. Thus, the Flood (in J) lasts for forty days and forty nights (Gen 7.12), and it marks a new beginning. Likewise, in their journey from Egypt to Canaan, the Israelites spend forty years in the wilderness (Num 14.33; Deut 2.7; 29.5), and Moses twice spends forty days and forty nights on top of Mount Sinai (Ex 24.18; 34.28). Several of the judges have terms of forty years (Judg 3.11; 5.31; 8.28; 1 Sam 4.18), and that is also the span of the reigns of David (1 Kings 2.11) and Solomon (1 Kings 11.42). In some of the latter cases the numbers either may be accurate or may simply be round numbers.

This symbolism is picked up in the New Testament, where before his ministry begins, Jesus is in the wilderness for forty days (Mk 1.13), a period that in Luke is paralleled by the forty days between his being raised from the dead and taken up to heaven (Lk 4.2; Acts 1.3).

---

exclaim that it is the gods who brought Israel out of Egypt, but there is only one calf, and Aaron proclaims a "festival to Yahweh" (32.4–5), who was the god who did bring Israel out of Egypt. Moreover, while it is clear that for the final editors of the Pentateuch, and for other biblical writers (for example, Hos 8.4–5; 13.2), the making of the calf was a violation of the aniconic principle of the Second Commandment, the prohibition against making graven images, in the chronology of the narrative the Ten Commandments had not yet been delivered to the people.

An alternate to the interpretation of the calf as an image of Yahweh or of another god is that it was understood as a pedestal for a deity. Although the Egyptians often represented their deities in animal forms or with the head of an animal (for example, Re is often depicted as a falcon, Hathor as a cow, Anubis as a jackal, Sekhmet as a lioness, and Apis as a bull), their ancient Near Eastern contemporaries generally depicted their gods and goddesses in human form. In ancient Near Eastern literature, deities, like human rulers, may be given animal titles, such as ram, lion, bull, and gazelle. For example, the Canaanite god El, and probably Yahweh (Gen 49.24; Ps 132.2), are both called "the Bull," a title signifying strength and virility, but this does not mean that a statue of a bull or calf was used in their worship to represent them. Rather, the human form of the deity is often shown standing on an animal, an alternative to being seated on a throne (see Figure 8.6). The golden calf, then, may be interpreted as an alternative to the cherubim and ark, on which Yahweh was invisibly enthroned.

Underlying the text is a complicated series of polemics. One is a criticism of Aaron, whose leadership was found wanting. We will see another

FIGURE 8.6. Stela from the eighth century BCE depicting the storm-god Adad (who is also known as Hadad and Baal) standing on a bull and with lightning bolts in each hand. (See also Figure 1.5 on page 17.)

example of this in Numbers 12 (see page 161). It is possible, as some scholars have suggested, that the occasional conflicts between Moses and Aaron in the narrative are derived from rivalry between two priestly houses, each of which traced its ancestry back to one of the two founding fathers.

On another level the text is an attack on the northern kingdom of Israel, which split from the leadership of the dynasty founded by David in the late tenth century BCE. The first king of that kingdom, Jeroboam I, upon assuming power,

said to himself, "Now the kingdom may well revert to the house of David. If this people continues to go

up to offer sacrifices in the house of the LORD at Jerusalem, the heart of this people will turn again to their master, King Rehoboam of Judah; they will kill me and return to King Rehoboam of Judah." So the king took counsel, and made two calves of gold. He said to the people, "You have gone up to Jerusalem long enough. Here are your gods, O Israel, who brought you up out of the land of Egypt." He set one in Bethel, and the other he put in Dan. And this thing became a sin, for the people went to worship before the one at Bethel and before the other as far as Dan. (1 Kings 12.26–30)

This episode is found in the book of Kings, which forms part of a larger work, the Deuteronomistic History (see pages 191–93), written in Judah, the southern kingdom, after the split. The Deuteronomistic Historians routinely present the northern kingdom of Israel in a negative light. For them, the idolatry that was characteristic of the northern kingdom throughout its history began with its founder, Jeroboam I, when he had the golden calves made and installed in Bethel and Dan. But we must read behind the bias of the Deuteronomistic Historians. Jeroboam was probably not adopting a non-Yahwistic form of worship, but rather intended the calves as alternatives to the cherubim that had been installed in the Temple built by Solomon in Jerusalem. Jeroboam placed the calves at two of his royal sanctuaries, Bethel and Dan, strategically located at the southern and northern limits of his kingdom. Each was a kind of dais or throne for Yahweh, invisibly enthroned, as on the cherubim.

The Deuteronomistic Historians, however, interpret the calves pejoratively, as idols of false gods, whom Jeroboam is supposedly worshiping; a negative interpretation of the calves is also found in the prophet Hosea (8.5–6; 13.2). That interpretation has been inserted into the presumably altered text of Exodus 32, where the people say: "These are your gods, O Israel, who brought you out of the land of Egypt" (Ex 32.4), even though there is only one calf. The original would have been: "This is your God, O Israel, who brought you out of the land of Egypt," and would have referred to Yahweh. This hypothesis is confirmed by the retelling of this episode in the postexillic book of Nehemiah, where in the course of a long sermon cataloging Israel's disobediences, the scribe Ezra reminds the people of divine mercy: "Even when they had cast an image of a calf for themselves and said, 'This is your God who brought you up out of Egypt,' and had committed great blasphemies, you in your great mercies did not forsake them" (Neh 9.18–19). In this context of Israel's offenses, if the plural "gods," suggesting polytheism, had been present in the author's source, it would surely have been retained.

We can therefore reconstruct the following hypothetical stages in the formation of the story of the golden calf:

1. The earliest, preserved by E, originated in the northern kingdom and was a founding narrative for the worship of Yahweh enthroned on a golden calf, but, as on the cherubim, invisibly so. The founder was presented as Aaron.

2. When E and J were combined in the late eighth century BCE, the narrative was reworked to portray the northern kingdom in a negative light, as the Deuteronomistic Historians would also do a century or so later. The worship was presented as the worst kind of polytheism, with the suggestion of a sexual orgy. Exodus 32.6 describes the rituals:

[The people] rose early the next day, and offered burnt offerings and brought sacrifices of well-being; and the people sat down to eat and drink, and rose up to play.

The last word in the verse has a sexual innuendo; it is the same word used in the story of Abimilech's discovery that Rebekah was Isaac's wife (Gen 26.8; see page 165).

3. When P reedited the text, probably in the sixth century BCE, Aaron's guilt was minimized:

Moses said to Aaron, "What did this people do to you that you have brought so great a sin upon them?" And Aaron said, "Do not let the anger of my lord burn hot; you know the people, that they are bent on evil. They said to me, 'Make us gods, who shall go before us; as for this Moses, the man who brought us up out of the land of Egypt, we do not know what has become of him.' So I said to them, 'Whoever has gold, take it off'; so they gave it to me, and I threw it into the fire, and out came this calf!" (Ex 32.21–24)

In this version, what happened was ultimately the people's fault, not Aaron's, who was simply the unwitting agent in the process that produced the calf. Moreover, when the people were tried by ordeal and the guilty executed, Aaron was unpunished, as he also will be in the account of his and Miriam's rebellion against Moses in Numbers 12 (see page 161).

While a reconstruction such as this is only hypothetical, and scholars would not agree on all of its details or might assign the material to different sources, the narrative of the golden calf shows the many layers of tradition found in the Pentateuch, and also the difficulties in separating and identifying them.

Embedded in the narrative of the golden calf is an important theme that will recur often, the theme of Yahweh's anger at the Israelites that Moses manages to avert. In this case, while informing Moses what had happened at the base of the mountain, Yahweh suggests that he will destroy the Israelites, whom he calls "your people," and start again with Moses, making of him "a great nation" (Ex 32.7–10). Moses, however, reminds Yahweh that the Israelites are "your people, whom you brought out of the land of Egypt" (32.11), appeals to Yahweh's reputation, and quotes his promise to Israel's ancestors. "So Yahweh changed his mind about the disaster that he planned to bring on his people" (Ex 32.14). This portrayal of Moses as mediator, not just of the divinely given laws, but also between an angry deity and the rebellious Israelites, will be repeated in the narratives of the wandering in the wilderness (see, for example, Num 14).

Finally, following divine instructions, Moses ascends the mountain yet again, where he is to remain another forty days and forty nights (see Box 8.3).

THE RITUAL DECALOGUE

After the episode of the golden calf, following divine instructions, Moses returned to the top of Sinai, in order to get another set of the Ten Commandments to replace the tablets that he had broken. We would expect the text of the commandments to be the same, and, in fact, that is what the editors of Exodus want us to believe: "The LORD said to Moses, "Cut two tablets of stone like the former ones, and I will write on the tablets the words that were on the former tablets, which you broke" (Ex 34.1). But when the "ten words" (Ex 34.28) are presented, they are very different from the Decalogue that we have already encountered in Exodus 20 (see pages 114–17). Rather, this set of commandments, found in Exodus 34.10–26, while explicitly identified as the text of the covenant (34.10, 27), is entirely concerned with worship. For this reason scholars have named it the "Ritual Decalogue."

It is admittedly difficult to find ten commandments here. Also, although some of the commandments overlap with those found in Exodus 20, the wording is very different, as the following examples show:

You shall not make for yourself a graven image. (Ex 20.4)	You shall not make cast idols. (Ex 34.17)
Remember the sabbath day, and keep it holy. Six days you shall labor and do all your work, but the seventh day is a sabbath to the LORD your God; you shall not do any work. (Ex 20.8–10)	Six days you shall work, but on the seventh day you shall rest; even in plowing time and in harvest time you shall rest. (Ex 34.21)

We seem therefore to have a different Decalogue tradition, probably also very ancient. It has been inserted here because, as we have often seen, the editors of the Bible thought it important to incorporate diverse traditions even if they were inconsistent.

The Ritual Decalogue has two major emphases. One is that the worship of Yahweh is not to be corrupted by the practices of the Canaanites, and hence intermarriage is forbidden. The second is the establishment of regular holy days. In the Covenant Code, which is probably earlier than the Ritual Decalogue, three festivals are

mentioned. They are designated as pilgrimage festivals (Hebr. *hag*; compare Arabic *hajj*):

> Three times in the year you shall hold a festival for me. You shall observe the festival of unleavened bread; as I commanded you, you shall eat unleavened bread for seven days at the appointed time in the month of Abib, for in it you came out of Egypt. No one shall appear before me empty-handed. You shall observe the festival of harvest, of the first fruits of your labor, of what you sow in the field. You shall observe the festival of ingathering at the end of the year, when you gather in from the field the fruit of your labor. Three times in the year all your males shall appear before the Lord GOD. (Ex 23.14–17)

In the Ritual Decalogue, the same three pilgrimage festivals are prescribed:

> You shall keep the festival of unleavened bread. Seven days you shall eat unleavened bread, as I commanded you, at the time appointed in the month of Abib; for in the month of Abib you came out from Egypt. . . . You shall observe the festival of weeks, the first fruits of wheat harvest, and the festival of ingathering at the turn of the year. Three times in the year all your males shall appear before the LORD God, the God of Israel. . . . You shall not offer the blood of my sacrifice with leaven, and the sacrifice of the festival of the passover shall not be left until the morning. The best of the first fruits of your ground you shall bring to the house of the LORD your God. (Ex 34.18, 22–23, 25–26)

As in the Covenant Code, these three pilgrimage festivals were celebrated at a regional sanctuary and linked to the agricultural cycle (see Box 8.4): the harvest of the barley in the early spring, of the wheat in the late spring, and of fruits such as grapes and olives in the fall. Moreover, as is also the case with the Decalogue, this suggests a date of origin sometime after the Exodus, when the Israelites were already settled in the land with a primarily agricultural economy.

The early spring observance, connected with the barley harvest, is called the "festival of unleavened bread" in both the Covenant Code (Ex 23.15) and the Ritual Decalogue (34.18), and although it is linked with the Exodus, no mention is made of the Passover lamb. The late spring observance, called the "festival of harvest" and connected with the harvest of the winter wheat ("the first fruits"; Ex

Box 8.4 **AN ANCIENT HEBREW AGRICULTURAL CALENDAR**

An ancient Hebrew calendar excavated at Gezer in Palestine in 1908 (see Figure 8.7), divides the months of the year as follows:

Two months gathering	[September–October]
Two months planting	[November–December]
Two months late sowing	[January–February]
(One) month cutting flax	[March]
(One) month reaping barley	[April]
(One) month reaping and measuring (grain)	[May]
Two months pruning	[June–July]
(One) month summer fruit	[August]

The twelve-month calendar begins in the fall, perhaps indicating a fall new year festival, as in Judaism today, where the New Year (Rosh Hashanah) occurs in September or October. The dominant pattern in the Bible, however, is that the new year was celebrated in the spring; thus, the Passover is celebrated in the first month of the year (Abib or Nisan; for example, Ex 12.2; Lev 23.5; see also Esth 3.7). But evidence exists that a fall new year was also observed at some times in ancient Israel; for example, the festival of ingathering is said to take place at the "end of the year" (Ex 23.16; called "the turn of the year" in 34.22).

The three pilgrimage festivals in Exodus 34.22–23 correspond to the three principal harvests, which the Gezer calendar calls "reaping barley" (early April), "reaping and measuring grain" (late May), and "gathering" (September); the same Hebrew words for "reaping" and "gathering" occur with reference to the same times of year both in the Gezer calendar and in Exodus 34.22 (see also 23.16).

FIGURE 8.7. A limestone tablet from Gezer dating to the tenth century BCE, measuring about 3 by 4.5 in (8 by 11.5 cm). On it is an agricultural calendar written in an early form of the Hebrew alphabet.

23.16; Num 28.26), is also called the "festival of Weeks" because it occurs seven weeks and one day after the first (see Lev 23.15–16). This amounts to fifty days; hence the later term "Pentecost" (from Greek, meaning "fiftieth"; Tob 2.1; Acts 2.1). The fall observance, the "festival of ingathering," is later called the "festival of Booths" (as in another listing of the festivals in Deut 16.13). This probably recalls the practice of camping out in the fields during the labor-intensive fall harvest, but in later sources it is also linked with the Exodus: "You shall live in booths for seven days; all that are citizens in Israel shall live in booths, so that your generations may know that I made the people of Israel live in booths when I brought them out of the land of Egypt" (Lev 23.42–43).

Like many of the laws in the Covenant Code, which seem to have been non-Israelite in origin, it is likely that the three agricultural festivals were originally Canaanite and were adopted by the Israelites. Over time these festivals were, so to speak, Israelitized, especially by connecting them with the Exodus from Egypt, as in the case of the fall festival of Booths, and also the early spring festival of unleavened bread. The latter was also united with the spring ritual of the sacrifice of a newborn animal (see further pages 92–93). Thus, in the calendar in Deuteronomy, the Passover, the Exodus, the animal sacrifice, and the unleavened bread are combined:

> Observe the month of Abib by keeping the passover to the LORD your God, for in the month of Abib the LORD your God brought you out of Egypt by night. You shall offer the passover sacrifice to the LORD your God, from the flock and the herd, at the place that the LORD will choose as a dwelling for his name. You must not eat with it anything leavened. For seven days you shall eat unleavened bread with it—the bread of affliction—because you came out of the land of Egypt in great haste, so that all the days of your life you may remember the day of your departure from the land of Egypt. (Deut 16.1–3; see also Ex 12.1–20 [P])

SEQUEL

The purpose of Moses' return to the top of Mount Sinai was to receive a replacement set of the two tablets that he had broken; while there, talking with God (Ex 34.29), he fittingly experienced a special divine revelation:

> The LORD descended in the cloud and stood with him there, and proclaimed the name, "The LORD." The LORD passed before him, and proclaimed,
>
> "The LORD, the LORD,
> a God merciful and gracious,
> slow to anger,
> and abounding in steadfast love and faithfulness."
>   (Ex 34.5–7)

Then, at the end of Exodus 34, Moses came down from Mount Sinai. When he returned, he first gave the sabbath command (Ex 35.2–3), because, as we have seen for P, that is the sign of the covenant at Sinai. Then the instructions given to Moses in Exodus 25–31 are repeated virtually verbatim in the narrative account of their being carried out in Exodus 35–40. Such narrative repetition of command and execution is a technique often used in ancient poetry, as in the Homeric poems and also in Canaanite myths, both of which, like the Bible, were principally heard rather than read (see Neh 8.18). In oral performance, like the repeats in a sonata or symphony, these repetitions would allow the audience both to appreciate what the performer was doing and also in a sense to hear what they might have missed at the first occurrence.

So, following Moses' commands, the people contributed the materials and the artisans Bezalel and Oholiab made the tabernacle, the ark, and the vestments and Moses consecrated them. When all was complete, "the cloud covered the tent of meeting, and the glory of the LORD filled the tabernacle" (Ex 40.34). Even though the Israelites will be at Sinai until Numbers 10.11, Moses never ascends the mountain again. During the rest of the stay at Sinai (see Lev 1.1; Num 1.1) and thereafter (for example, Num 14.10–12; see also 12.5–9), Moses will usually receive divine instruction and guidance in the tabernacle, for that is where the deity manifests himself.

RETROSPECT AND PROSPECT

The final editors of the Pentateuch, P, have made the stay at Sinai the centerpiece of their narrative and have inserted into it legal and liturgical traditions from a variety of sources. In this chapter we have seen both some of the earliest, such as the Covenant Code, an early Israelite collection of laws that may have a non-Israelite origin, and some of the latest, such as the elaborate description of the equipment and personnel used in the worship of Yahweh. In the next chapter we will look at the book of Leviticus, which consists almost entirely of divine instructions to Moses concerning the forms of worship and the requirements for holiness, the prerequisite for participation in worship.

IMPORTANT TERMS

apodictic law	cherubim	golden calf
ark of the covenant	Code of Hammurapi	Ritual Decalogue
casuistic law	Covenant Code	tabernacle

QUESTIONS FOR REVIEW

1. What are some similarities and differences between ancient Near Eastern laws and Israelite laws? What is their significance?

2. What are the different types of laws found in the book of Exodus? What subjects do they deal with?

3. How are the laws related to their immediate and larger narrative contexts?

4. What were the functions of the ark of the covenant in various biblical sources?

5. What are the layers of tradition that are found in the narrative of the golden calf (Ex 32)?

6. What is the connection between the principal religious festivals in ancient Israel and the agricultural cycle?

BIBLIOGRAPHY

For commentaries on Exodus, see Bibliography to Chapter 6.

A good collection of law codes from the Ancient Near East is Martha T. Roth, *Law Collections from Mesopotamia and Asia Minor* (2d ed.; Atlanta: Scholars Press, 1997); some of this material is excerpted in Bill T. Arnold and Bryan E. Beyer, *Readings from the Ancient Near East* (Grand Rapids: Baker, 2002), pp. 104–17.

Many collections of laws are also found in James B. Pritchard, *Ancient Near Eastern Texts Relating to the Old Testament* (3d ed.; Princeton, NJ: Princeton University Press, 1969); and William W. Hallo, ed., *The Context of Scripture*, Vol. 2, *Monumental Inscriptions from the Biblical World* (Leiden: Brill, 2003).

A brief introduction to ancient Israelite law is C. S. Ehrlich, "Israelite Law," pp. 421–23 in *Oxford Companion to the Bible* (ed. B. M. Metzger and M. D. Coogan; New York: Oxford University Press, 1993).

On the ark of the covenant, see C. L. Seow, "Ark of the Covenant," pp. 386–93 in *Anchor Bible Dictionary*, Vol. 1 (ed. D. N. Freedman; New York: Doubleday, 1992).

RITUAL AND HOLINESS

CHAPTER
9

Leviticus

Following the construction of the tabernacle at the end of the book of Exodus, the next book, Leviticus, continues the narrative of the stay at Sinai with more divine instructions given to Moses. These instructions are concerned largely with ritual matters, and the entire book in its present form generally is thought to have been shaped by the Priestly writers. They included in their compilation detailed rubrics about types of sacrifices to be offered to Yahweh and regulations about ritual purity; they also incorporated into the final version of the book an independent source, the Holiness Code, which, as its name suggests, has as a central theme the separation between the sacred and the profane, the holy and the common.

THE BOOK OF LEVITICUS

The Hebrew name of the book of Leviticus is *(way)yiqra,* its first word, "(and) he [the LORD] called"; the conventional English name, derived from ancient Greek manuscripts, is inaccurate, since the focus of the book is not the Levites, who are mentioned only in 25.32–33. Rather, the book consists of further instructions given by God to

Moses (and also to Moses and Aaron), having mainly to do with ritual and holiness; it includes only a few chapters of narrative, which are connected closely with the ritual instructions. The outline of the book makes its contents clear:

Chapters 1–7   Instructions concerning sacrifices

8–10   Narratives describing the consecration of the tabernacle, the altar, and the priests, and the offering of illicit fire and its consequences

11–15   Instructions concerning purity and impurity

16   Instructions concerning the Day of Atonement

17–26   The Holiness Code: a separate collection of regulations concerning sacrifices, purity, ethical conduct, and sacred times, which includes one narrative section (24.10–23) concerning blasphemy and concludes with a catalogue of blessings and curses (chap. 26)

27   Additional instructions concerning vows and offerings

As this outline suggests, the book of Leviticus is a composite work. This is confirmed by the many editorial notes inserted throughout the text. The phrase "The LORD spoke to Moses" occurs over thirty times (and to Moses and Aaron another four times, in 11.1; 13.1; 14.33; 15.1; and once, in 10.8, to Aaron alone). This usage may indicate originally distinct sources, as does the presence of several apparent conclusions (see 7.37; 26.46; 27.34).

It was P who preserved and edited these disparate traditions. As is the case with the descriptions of the tabernacle and the ark in Exodus, P retrojects into the sojourn at Sinai the rituals and practices of later times. P thus both preserves traditions from the Temple liturgies and also in effect establishes a program for their restoration by the postexilic community in the late sixth century BCE and beyond. At the same time, however, Leviticus is not a consistent work, and it has been suggested plausibly that it preserves traditions not just from the Jerusalem Temple but also from other sanctuaries throughout the land, as does the book of Psalms (see page 457), even at the cost of some redundancy and inconsistency.

In its final form in the context of the entire Pentateuch, which was edited and shaped by P, Leviticus fits into its narrative context, as occasional references to Egypt as past and Canaan as future indicate—for example, "You shall not do as they do in the land of Egypt, where you lived, and you shall not do as they do in the land of Canaan, to which I am bringing you" (18.3).

SACRIFICES (LEV 1–7)

The Sacrificial System

For P, the sacrificial system was obviously of primary interest. **Sacrifice**, the offering of something of value to a deity, was an important part of the religious life of ancient Israel as of other ancient cultures; this is evident from the repeated references to it throughout the Bible and the parallels in other ancient Near Eastern sources to many of the details of the Bible's sacrificial system. This system can be understood on several levels, of which we will focus on two.

On one level, sacrifice can be understood as a gift to a god. One of the Hebrew words for sacrifice is *minhah*. In the Bible this word has the general meaning of a gift from an inferior to a superior and can have the nuance of tribute from a vassal to a suzerain (Judg 3.15; 2 Sam 8.2, 6; 2 Kings 17.3; Hos 10.6) or part of an effort to curry favor with someone more powerful (Gen 32.13; 43.11). In religious contexts, a *minhah* is thus a gift to God as superior from the offering individual or community. In sources other than P it can refer to any type of sacrificial offering (for example, in Gen 4.3–4, both Cain's grain offering and Abel's meat offering are called *minhah*); in P, however, it is used exclusively of the grain offering.

As a gift, the sacrifice, whether an animal or other commodity, could have several functions, including appeasing an angry deity, thanking a supportive deity, or motivating a deity to help the offerer. On an even more anthropomorphic level, the slaughtered sacrificial animals and other foodstuffs were a meal for the deity, presented on the altar, which was a kind of table. To the deity were offered the "choice" portions, which were also the fattiest parts and thus easiest to burn. The deity was pleased by the odor of the sacrifice (see, for example, Gen 8.21; Ex 29.18; Lev 1.9). In some types of sacrifice the roasted meat was shared between deity and worshiper, in effect a kind of "communion." Some sacrifices can thus be understood as a shared meal, a ritual of uniting.

In some biblical sources we find a critique of the understanding of sacrifice as a gift or meal for the deity; in Psalm 50, for example, God is quoted as saying:

If I were hungry, I would not tell you,
    for the world and all that is in it is mine.
Do I eat the flesh of bulls,
    or drink the blood of goats?
Offer to God a sacrifice of thanksgiving,
    and pay your vows to the Most High.
Call on me in the day of trouble;
I will deliver you, and you shall glorify me.
    (Ps 50.12–15)

(For further discussion of the relatively rare critiques of the more widely accepted biblical views of sacrifice, especially in prophetic literature, see Box 18.3 on page 319.)

On a second, more functional level, sacrifice can be understood as a collection and distribution system for agricultural products, both animals and crops—in other words, as a form of taxation. It is significant that the three primary pilgrimage festivals (see pages 134–36) are set at the time of the three principal harvests in early spring, early summer, and early fall. At this time, the priests would collect a portion of the harvested crops. It would then be stored in temple treasuries, for distribution to the needy in times of famine or before the next harvest had ripened. During the time of the monarchy, from the tenth to the sixth centuries BCE, when priests were often under direct royal control, the collection system that sacrifices comprised would help centralize the monarchy's power. In addition to agricultural products, on occasion an offering could be real estate (Lev 27.14–25), or even personal labor, as in the dedication of nonpriests to temporary or permanent sanctuary service as Nazirites (see Num 6.2–21; Judg 13.5–7; 1 Sam 1.11, 22).

The practice of tithing had a similar function. According to Leviticus 27.30–33, all agricultural produce and livestock were subject to the **tithe**: That is, ten percent of these commodities were considered as belonging to Yahweh; the Hebrew word usually translated "tithe" literally means "a tenth." In a religious sense, this can be understood as a kind of rent from a tenant to a landlord, for according to Leviticus 25.23 the land itself belonged to Yahweh. Functionally the tithe was a kind of universal taxation, which paid for the maintenance of the clergy and ultimately of the monarchy itself, and also enabled redistribution of goods produced.

Leviticus mentions tithing only in a brief note in the concluding appendix (27.30–33), but it also occurs in P in Numbers 18.21–32, where it is explicitly designated for the Levites, and in a number of other sources dating from almost all periods in the formation of the biblical traditions (see, for example, Gen 14.20; 28.22; Deut 12.6;

Am 4.4; Neh 10.37; Mal 3.10; 1 Macc 3.49). One passage is especially informative. In Samuel's speech describing the negative consequences of the monarchy, a Deuteronomistic composition, he asserts that the king "will take one-tenth of your grain and of your vineyards and give it to his officers and his courtiers. . . . [And he] will take one-tenth of your flocks, and you shall be his slaves" (1 Sam 8.15–17). This, along with evidence from elsewhere in the ancient Near East, suggests that the tithe was a civic as well as a religious obligation, like the *minhah* (see page 139). In a monarchic system, where the king controlled the priesthood, as was the case in Jerusalem, the crown and the Temple were inextricably linked. This is confirmed by an account of the centralization of worship under the Judean king Hezekiah in the late eighth century BCE, part of which involved the collection and storage of tithes in the Temple treasuries (2 Chr 31.5–12), which were adjacent to the palace.

Types of Sacrifices

Leviticus 1–7 is devoted to an elaboration of the principal kinds of sacrifice according to P. The

FIGURE 9.1.   Altar from Beersheba, dated to the eighth or seventh century BCE. The four projections on the top are called "horns" in the Bible; these symbolized strength and also could have been used to hold a grate on which offerings were placed to be burned. The altar is about 5.25 ft (1.6 m) high.

presentation in Leviticus appears to be neither comprehensive nor entirely consistent, and many details remain obscure. In the broadest terms, four principal types of sacrifice are found, which to some extent overlap:

- *The "burnt offering" or "holocaust"* (Lev 1.1–17; 6.8–13): This was an animal sacrifice, in which the whole animal (a bull, ram, male goat, or bird) was slaughtered, its blood splashed on the altar (compare Ex 24.6), and the entire animal burned. The Hebrew word for this type of sacrifice (*ola*) literally means "that which goes up," as pleasant-smelling smoke. The precise function of the burnt offering is not clearly stated.

- *The "grain offering"* (Lev 2.1–16; 6.14–23): This was an offering (a *minhah*, or "gift"; see page 139) of flour mixed with oil and incense. A "token portion" of the offering was consumed by the fire on the altar, and the rest was given to the priests. As is the case with the burnt offering, the precise religious function of the grain offering is not stated.

- *The "sacrifice of well-being"* (Lev 3; 7.11–38) is similar to the burnt offering, in that the blood of the animal was sprinkled on the altar, but in this case only the fatty portions of the animal were burnt, and the rest was shared by the worshiper (7.15–17) and the priests (7.31–36). The meaning of the name of this kind of sacrifice is not entirely clear; the traditional translation of its Hebrew name, *shelamim*, is "peace offering." In Leviticus 7, this type of sacrifice is subdivided into three types of offering: thanksgiving, presumably in response to some prayer answered; fulfillment of a vow; and a voluntary ("free-will") offering, that is, one not required by circumstances or calendar.

- *The "sin offering"* (Lev 4.1–5.13; 6.24–30) and *the "guilt offering"* (5.14–6.7; 7.1–10). In these offerings, a sacrificial animal served as a kind of substitute for an offender. Its blood was sprinkled on the altar and the fatty portions were burnt, but the rest of the carcass was either discarded as profane and burned outside

the sanctuary, or, in some cases, given to the priest who performed the ritual. The purpose of the offering was to remove an offerer's guilt, which was due to either advertent or inadvertent sin or impurity.

Both in Leviticus and elsewhere in the Bible, other types of sacrifices are also prescribed; among these are the "elevation" (KJV: "wave") offering (Lev 7.30), the regular daily offerings (Ex 29.38–42), the weekly offering of twelve loaves of bread (the "bread of the presence" or the "shewbread"; Ex 25.30; Lev 24.5–9), drink offerings or libations (Lev 23.13), and incense offerings. Incense is made from spices and local and imported gum resins that when burned emit a pleasant odor. The sanctuary included an altar exclusively designated for incense (Ex 30.1–10), as did the Temple built by Solomon (1 Chr 28.18). Incense altars have also been found at many Israelite sites, and were apparently used in domestic rituals in private homes, as well as in public ceremonies (see Figure 9.2). Incense served several functions,

FIGURE 9.2.   Incense altar from Tel Miqne (ancient Ekron), dated to the seventh century BCE. About 8 in (20 cm) high, it is considerably smaller than the altar shown in Figure 9.1, but it has the same design, including the four "horns."

both practical and symbolic. On a mundane level, the burning incense would have masked what must have been a terrible stench from the slaughtering and burning of the animals being sacrificed. It probably also served to repel flies and other insects that would have been attracted to the sacrificial precinct. At the same time, because incense was an expensive import, its use would have demonstrated the wealth and prestige of the offerer. Its smoke also symbolized the ascent of the offerer's prayers into the heavenly realm (see Ps 141.2; Rev 8.4).

THE CONSECRATION CEREMONIES AND THEIR AFTERMATH (LEV 8–10)

In Leviticus 8 the divine instructions are interrupted by a resumption of narrative in two connected episodes. The first (Lev 8–9) is the completion of the fulfillment of the divine commands given in Exodus concerning the dedication of the sanctuary and its furnishings and the ordination of the priests (Ex 28–29; 30.26–30; 40.9–15). In Exodus, all of the ritual objects had been constructed and the most sacred objects and places had been consecrated; what remained to be done in carrying out God's instructions to Moses was the ordination of the priests, which is now described. The repeated phrase "as the LORD commanded Moses" (Lev 8.9, 13, 17, 21, 29; 9.10) emphasizes the nature of the narrative as fulfillment. The entire ritual lasted eight days, and Moses himself officiated at its beginning, but once Aaron and his sons were ordained they assumed the priestly functions. These sacrifices are the first sacrifices narrated by P in the Pentateuch, and at their conclusion the divine approval is apparent: "The glory of the LORD appeared to all the people. Fire came out from the LORD and consumed the burnt offering and the fat on the altar" (Lev 9.23–24). The second episode, in Leviticus 10, is another case of priestly rivalry, similar to that in the episode of the golden calf (Ex 32). Two of Aaron's four sons made an incense offering of "strange fire" (NRSV "unholy fire"), probably meaning that they performed an illegitimate rit-

ual. As punishment in kind, they were destroyed when "fire came out from the LORD and consumed them" (10.2). When their bodies had been disposed of, by those not in the direct priestly line (to avoid contamination, as is prescribed in Lev 21.1–5, 10–11), and they had been mourned, Moses gave further instructions to Aaron concerning priestly conduct, including prohibiting the consumption of alcoholic beverages prior to performing their sacred duties.

PURITY AND IMPURITY (LEV 11–15)

A large part of Leviticus, including sections of the Holiness Code, is devoted to instructions concerning the pure and the impure. The traditional translations "clean" and "unclean" are somewhat misleading, for the categories do not deal with either hygiene or cleanliness. Rather, according to the definitions of Leviticus, the "clean" is what is pure, that is, suitable for human use and in some cases also for use in ritual. The unclean, on the other hand, is impure, and unsuitable for either purpose. For example, Leviticus 11 lists those animals that may be eaten and those that may not (a similar but not identical list is found in Deut 14), and Leviticus 12–15 deals with various conditions that cause impurity in persons and in objects.

Various theories have been offered to explain these categories; probably they stem from a combination of factors, including the following:

- *Health:* Some animals may not have been eaten because they were recognized as carriers of disease; among these we can include those that eat other dead animals, such as vultures. Likewise, it may have been observed that people whose diet included pork or shellfish became ill more frequently. Some types of bodily emissions also made a person impure. These include abnormal genital emissions in both males and females and skin diseases. Early peoples probably recognized that these may have been contagious, and so the impure or unclean person was not only prohibited from participating in rituals, but also sometimes quarantined, presumably to prevent spread of the condition to others.

- *Cultural differentiation:* One of the ways that cultures distinguish themselves from other cultures is diet. Thus, for some, animals such as cow, horse, dog, and cat are part of the diet; for others they are taboo, and are never eaten. The pig is a case in point. In the late second millennium BCE, when Israel was beginning to emerge in the land of Canaan, another group, the Philistines, had emigrated there from their homelands in the Aegean (see further Box 13.3 on page 220). The Philistines, unlike the Israelites and most of their neighbors, did not practice circumcision, and they also included the pig as a part of their diet, as archaeological remains of pig bones at predominantly Philistine sites attest. Pig was not generally eaten by the Israelites or the Canaanites, and so both circumcision and avoidance of pig in the diet became cultural markers that distinguished the Israelites from the Philistines. Thus, even though the prohibition against eating pork is found in texts dating from the first millennium, it probably originates earlier, when the Israelites and Philistines were competing for control of the same region. Its preservation provides an example both of how later writers preserved ancient traditions and of how cultures can be conservative, for the Israelites (and subsequently Judaism and Islam) retained this dietary taboo long after the decline of the Philistines, which began in the tenth century BCE.

- *A sense of order:* In a highly influential book, *Purity and Danger: An Analysis of the Concepts of Pollution and Taboo* (1966), the British anthropologist Mary Douglas argued that the distinction between pure (or "clean") and impure (or "unclean") reflects a kind of theoretical order, in which some animals are suited to their respective environments (air, land, water), and others are not. Thus, fish are suited to water because of their fins and scales, but other aquatic creatures, such as shellfish, are not; animals that chew the cud and have divided hooves (such as cows) are permissible, but those that apparently chew the cud but do not have divided hooves (such as camels and hares) or that have divided hooves but do not chew the cud (such as pigs) are not. This aversion to mixing of categories extends to clothing—the Israelites were not to wear clothes made from two different materials (Lev 19.19, specified as linen and wool in Deut 22.11), nor were men to wear women's clothing or vice versa (Deut 22.5)—and to agriculture—a field was not to be sown with two different crops, nor were two different kinds of animals to be bred together nor used together to pull a plow (Lev 19.19; Deut 22.9–10).

- *Relationship to sex and death:* As in most cultures, in ancient Israel taboos existed concerning death and sex. A person becomes impure by contact with a corpse or a dead animal that may not be eaten; by skin disease, which may be understood as mimicking the decay that occurs after death (see Num 12.12); and by loss of fluids considered essential to life, such as semen and blood, especially menstrual blood. Some animals are prohibited because they are connected with death, especially those that eat other dead animals, and the consumption of blood was strictly prohibited.

None of these explanations is entirely satisfactory, and even taking them all into account does not explain all prohibitions and taboos, and those listed in Leviticus and elsewhere in the Bible do not form a comprehensive system. Moreover, only a few of the animals that humans are permitted to eat are considered suitable for sacrifice. This is due to the greater degree of holiness required for the most immediate contact with the divine (see page 146). For similar reasons, although ordinary Israelites were permitted to bury their dead, the high priest was prohibited from any contact with a corpse, even of a member of his immediate family, and from the traditional signs of mourning (Lev 21.10–11).

Those who have contact with impure persons also contract impurity, as for example when a man has sexual intercourse with a menstruating woman (Lev 15.24). The impurity caused by contact with an impure person or object, such as a dead corpse or a dead animal (Lev 11.24, 31, 39), can also affect objects that have contact with them.

Leviticus 13 discusses various skin conditions that make a person impure. The descriptions do not enable precise identification with modern diagnoses, but it is clear that the traditional translation of the Hebrew word *saraat* as "leprosy" is inaccurate; in fact, some scholars question whether actual leprosy (Hansen's disease) was present in the ancient Near East. Rather, the Hebrew word seems to be a general one, referring to various conditions, including boils and other eruptions, psoriasis, and fungal infections. The identification of these conditions was made by the priest, probably because they concerned ritual fitness, and also because in Israel as in much of the rest of the ancient world priests often functioned as medical practitioners. One reason for this is that disease was often considered divinely caused as a punishment for sin. For various conditions the afflicted person was also quarantined for a period, to prevent others from becoming impure by contact (as well as to prevent contagion) and to allow the condition to heal. Likewise, just as skin disease makes a person impure, so its equivalent, such as mildew, makes clothing (13.47–59) and houses (14.33–53) impure.

Leviticus 15 concerns impurity or uncleanness caused by genital discharges. Males become impure both because of abnormal discharges and by normal seminal ejaculation (15.1–15). For the first, which is a medical condition, a period of impurity lasts for seven days after the emission stops, followed by a purification offering. For the second (15.16–18), the impurity lasts for one day, and only a ritual washing is prescribed.

Women are impure for seven days during normal menstrual discharge (15.19–24), although later rabbinic tradition understood the seven-day period to begin after the bleeding had stopped. That is certainly the case with non-menstrual vaginal bleeding (15.25–30); after the bleeding has stopped, the woman is impure for seven days, after which there a purification ritual, as for males with abnormal discharges.

All of this detail is somewhat alien to modern readers, encompassing as it does both practical and religious dimensions. For P, the details of purity were part of a comprehensive way of life that marked the Israelites as a distinct people, chosen by God who himself was considered the author of the regulations. That distinctiveness was expressed in the concept of holiness: "For I am the LORD who brought you up from the land of Egypt, to be your God; you shall be holy, for I am holy" (Lev 11.45). This notion dominates the Holiness Code, which we will consider presently, but first Leviticus discusses another set of rituals, those of the Day of Atonement.

THE DAY OF ATONEMENT

Following the instructions concerning purity and impurity, Leviticus 16 is devoted to what has become the most solemn observance in the Jewish calendar, that of Yom Kippur, the **Day of Atonement**. The ritual serves to purify the priest, the sanctuary, and the people. It is to take place annually on the tenth day of the seventh month (16.29), that is, in the fall according to a spring new year. It is called a "sabbath of sabbaths" (16.31; NRSV: "sabbath of complete rest"); in addition to refraining from work, the Israelites are also to "deny themselves" (16.29), which is later understood to mean a complete fast and perhaps also abstinence from sexual intercourse.

On the Day of Atonement, in addition to sacrificing a bull as a sin offering for Aaron, two goats are also provided, and lots are cast for them. One is dedicated as a sin offering "for Yahweh"; the other is designated as "for Azazel," an obscure term probably referring to some sort of demon, often translated as the "**scapegoat**." The sins of the community are symbolically transferred to this goat, which is then released in the wilderness. The ritual has magical aspects; it may be a kind of partial legitimization of earlier sacrifices to "goat-demons" or satyrs (see Isa 13.21; 34.14; 2 Chr 11.15), which according to Leviticus 17.7 are now forbidden, as well as a symbolic transfer of the community's sin to an animal that is then banished.

For all of its importance in later Judaism, however, both the Day of Atonement itself and the rituals associated with it are given little attention elsewhere in the Bible (exceptions include Lev 23.27–28; 25.9; Acts 27.9; Heb 9.7); Numbers 29.7–11 prescribes a different ritual for the same day.

THE HOLINESS CODE

Since the late nineteenth century, scholars have identified chapters 17–26 of Leviticus as a separate source, termed the **Holiness Code** because of its repeated use of words having to do with holiness (see page 146). This source (often abbreviated as "H") is comparable to other collections of biblical law, especially the Covenant Code (see pages 122–25) and the Deuteronomic Code (see pages 175–80). In some details it also overlaps with these collections, for example, the ritual calendar (Lev 23) and the obligations to the land concerning its sabbath or fallow period (Lev 25).

Until the late twentieth century, the scholarly consensus was that the Holiness Code, while later than the other two collections, is earlier than P, which included it in its final edition of the Pentateuch; a generally accepted date is sometime in the seventh century BCE. It is, however, from the same larger priestly school as P, and thus presumably originated among priests in the Temple in Jerusalem. More recently, some scholars have argued that the Holiness Code is later than most of the rest of P in the Pentateuch and that the editors of the Holiness Code may have been responsible for a revision of P and thus perhaps even for the final formation of the Pentateuch itself. Agreement remains, however, that the two sources (P and H) are distinct, in part because they are not entirely consistent.

Important evidence for the date of the Holiness Code is the close parallels in vocabulary and theme between it and the book of Ezekiel, named for the prophet Ezekiel who was also a priest in the Jerusalem Temple before his exile to Babylonia in 597 BCE. These parallels have led most scholars to conclude that the Holiness Code in some form preceded Ezekiel, although it is also possible that both were independently drawing on established priestly traditions. (See further page 393.)

Like the other collections of laws, the Holiness Code has its own complicated literary history. It has no obvious principle of arrangement and includes both apodictic and casuistic laws. It also contains some repetitions and inconsistencies. The Holiness Code ends with blessings and curses, already familiar to us from their use in ancient Near Eastern treaties (see pages 110–12). The curses seem at times to reflect the experience of exile in the sixth century BCE. For example, Yahweh declares as punishment for disobedience to his commands:

> I will lay your cities waste, will make your sanctuaries desolate, and I will not smell your pleasing odors. I will devastate the land, so that your enemies who come to settle in it shall be appalled at it. And you I will scatter among the nations, and I will unsheathe the sword against you; your land shall be a desolation, and your cities a waste. Then the land shall enjoy its sabbath years as long as it lies desolate, while you are in the land of your enemies; then the land shall rest, and enjoy its sabbath years. (Lev 26.31–34)

This warning is probably to be understood as a kind of prediction after the fact, based on what actually occurred when the Israelites lost control of their land and were taken captive to Babylon. Nevertheless, Yahweh continues, the ancient covenant with Abraham, Isaac, and Jacob will not be abrogated:

> When they are in the land of their enemies, I will not spurn them, or abhor them so as to destroy them utterly and break my covenant with them; for I am the LORD their God; but I will remember in their favor the covenant with their ancestors whom I brought out of the land of Egypt in the sight of the nations, to be their God. (Lev 26.44–45)

The Concept of Holiness

Central to the Holiness Code is the concept of holiness itself, as in the phrase "You shall be holy, for I Yahweh your god am holy" (Lev 19.2) and its variations (20.7, 8, 26; 21.6, 8, 15, 23; 22.9, 16, 32). In fact, words containing the consonants of the root for "holy" (Hebr. *q-d-sh*) occur more than twice as many times in the ten chapters of the Holiness Code as in the other seventeen chapters of the book of Leviticus. English translations obscure this frequency, since words like "sanctuary," "sanctify," "hallow," "consecrate," "dedicate," and "sacred" are all renderings of Hebrew words containing this root.

The primary meaning of the Hebrew word translated "holiness" (*qodesh*) is separation. The holy is that which is separate from the profane, the impure, the ordinary. Thus, for example, Israel is holy because it has been separated by Yahweh from other nations: "You shall be holy to me; for I the LORD am holy, and I have separated you from the other peoples to be mine" (Lev 20.26). As a consequence, to maintain its holiness Israel must separate itself from the practices of other nations: "You shall not do as they do in the land of Egypt, where you lived, and you shall not do as they do in the land of Canaan, to which I am bringing you. You shall not follow their statutes" (Lev 18.3; see also 18.24).

Varying degrees of separation may be categorized according to persons, spaces, and times and visualized as a series of concentric circles (see Figure 9.3).

With regard to persons, in the center is Yahweh himself, who is holy (Lev 11.44; 19.2; etc.). Nearest to Yahweh are the priests, who have the closest contact with Yahweh. The highest-ranking priest during the time of Moses was Aaron, "the priest who is greater than his brothers, on whose head the anointing oil has been poured and who has been ordained to wear the vestments" (Lev 21.10). The successors of Aaron as preeminent priest were called "the great priest," "the chief priest," and later the "high priest." Only this priest was permitted to enter the holy of holies, the innermost sanctum of the tabernacle, and later of the Temple. As a symbolic and perhaps actual ritual designating the holiness of priests is the ceremony of anointing (see Box 9.1). Priests have special obligations concerning purity because of their proximity to the divine. Next are

the Levites, who, although they do not feature in the book of Leviticus, in other sources are a class of minor clergy. The rest of the Israelites form the next group, and they too are holy (see Lev 19.2; also Ex 19.6; Deut 7.6); in P and in the Holiness Code resident aliens are included among them. Finally are other nations, who are least holy or in fact not holy at all, especially the Canaanites.

The degrees of holiness of space mirror those of persons. The "holy of holies" is in the center of the sanctuary (literally, "holy place") and is where the divine presence dwells (Ex 25.8). Only the high priest has access to the holy of holies, and only priests may enter the sanctuary. Within the larger structure of the tabernacle is the courtyard, which the Israelites are permitted to enter. The tabernacle itself is in the camp, from which it is clearly separated. When the Temple is built, these divisions are applied to the holy of holies, its innermost chamber, then the rest of the Temple, the Temple courtyard, and finally the land of Israel, which corresponds to the camp. The land of Israel itself is a "holy land" (see Zech 2.12; Wis 12.3) in the midst of other nations; ultimately it belonged to Yahweh (see Lev 25.23; Jer 2.7) and if the Israelites profaned it they would be expelled from it.

The same model can also be used to explain sacred time. At the center is the sabbath (Lev 23.3). According to P, the origins of the sabbath lay in the divine rest at creation. The land, which belonged to Yahweh, also needed its sabbaths. Less sacred than the sabbath are the "appointed festivals (23.4–44), and less sacred still is what we might call ordinary time.

Prohibited Sexual Relationships

In the Holiness Code, two chapters (18 and 20) are devoted to prohibited sexual relationships. Chapter 18 is introduced by a general statement about how the Israelites were to act differently from both the Egyptians and the Canaanites, implying that such forbidden practices were acceptable among those peoples, although little evidence supports that assertion. The attribution to others of what was considered sexual aberration is also

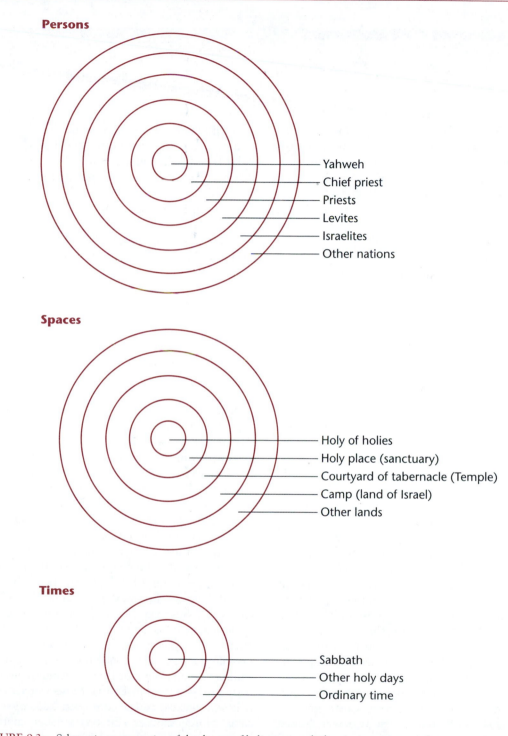

Persons

- Yahweh
- Chief priest
- Priests
- Levites
- Israelites
- Other nations

Spaces

- Holy of holies
- Holy place (sanctuary)
- Courtyard of tabernacle (Temple)
- Camp (land of Israel)
- Other lands

Times

- Sabbath
- Other holy days
- Ordinary time

FIGURE 9.3.   Schematic representation of the degrees of holiness as applied to persons, spaces, and times.

Box 9.1 ANOINTING

In ancient Israel, as in other ancient cultures, anointing with oil was used to consecrate those who had a close relationship with the divine. These included priests and kings, both of whom can be called the "anointed (of the LORD)" (Lev 4.3; 2 Sam 1.14) and had important ritual functions. On occasion, at least, prophets were also anointed (see 1 Kings 19.16; Isa 61.1; Ps 105.15).

The origins of this ritual are uncertain; one suggestion is that it may have served an actual function, to remove bodily parasites that might make a person impure by smearing the entire person with oil. In any case, anointing was more extensive than the symbolic dabbing with oil that is retained in some ecclesiastical and monarchic traditions; note especially Psalm 133, which speaks of

> . . . the precious oil on the head,
>   running down upon the beard,
> on the beard of Aaron,
>   running down over the collar of his robes. (Ps 133.2)

found in the J source (see pages 33 and 164–65), and in fact is a widespread cultural prejudice. The only specific references to non-Israelite rituals are the offering of children to Molech (18.21; 20.1–5; a form of child-sacrifice only partially understood) and necromancy (consulting the dead; 20.6, 27).

The lists of persons with whom sexual intercourse ("uncovering the nakedness of") was prohibited include one's father or mother, father's wife (other than mother), sister, half-sister, stepsister, aunt, or daughter-in-law. Also banned was sex with the sister, daughter, or granddaughter of a sexual partner or with a menstruating woman. Male homosexual intercourse was also forbidden, as was bestiality. For violating these sexual taboos, the penalty was either expulsion from the community (Lev 18.29) or, in some cases in the variant tradition (Lev 20), death.

These lists are not entirely comprehensive, since some obvious omissions exist, such as father-daughter. Moreover, the text is addressed to males and refers only to sexual relationships

implicitly initiated by men with female relatives or relatives-in-law. Thus, for example, Leviticus 18.6 literally says "No man among you shall approach anyone of his own flesh to uncover nakedness" and goes on to specify "the nakedness of your [masc. sing.] father, that is, the nakedness of your mother." Thus, although male homosexual relations are prohibited, female homosexual relations are not mentioned.

Many of the relationships prohibited in Leviticus are attested in biblical narrative. Reuben was condemned because he slept with his father Jacob's wife (not his mother; Gen 35.22; 49.4). Curiously, however, other prohibited relationships are not considered reprehensible: Abraham claimed that Sarah was his half-sister as well as his wife (Gen 20.12); David's daughter Tamar was willing to marry her half-brother Amnon after he had raped her (2 Sam 13.13); Moses' father Amram was married to his aunt Jochebed, who became Moses' mother (Ex 6.20); Jacob married both Leah and Rachel, who were sisters (Gen

Box 9.2 CAPITAL PUNISHMENT

Throughout the legislation in the Torah, the penalty for a wide variety of crimes is capital punishment, which is divinely decreed according to the narrative structure. The modern argument that capital punishment is wrong because the Fifth Commandment states "Thou shalt not kill" is both a misinterpretation of that commandment, which refers to premeditated murder, and a selective disregard of the repeated use of capital punishment throughout biblical law and narrative.

On the other hand, the contrary argument that capital punishment as divinely ordained should continue to be employed is also flawed. It too is selective, since few today would apply it to all cases in which it is prescribed in the Bible, such as for cursing or striking a parent (Ex 21.15, 17; Lev 20.9), violation of the Sabbath (Ex 31.15), or prohibited sexual relationships (Lev 20.10–16).

The usual method of capital punishment was stoning. All members of the community participated, thus instilling a sense of collective responsibility for the carrying out of the death penalty. According to Deuteronomy 17.7, the first stones were to be thrown by the accusing witnesses. Burning is prescribed only for a sexual relationship with both a wife and her mother (Lev 20.14) and, on occasion, for prostitution (Gen 38.24; Lev 21.9).

29.21–30); and Abraham's brother Nahor married his niece (Gen 11.29). All of these unions violate the prohibitions of Leviticus, but they are not questioned. It seems, then, that not all of the prohibitions in Leviticus were always in force in ancient Israel.

A Narrative Interlude: The Case of the Blasphemer (Lev 24.10–23)

Apart from the account of the ordination of the priests and its aftermath in Leviticus 8–10, the only other narrative in Leviticus is the short episode of the blasphemer (24.10–23), which has been inserted into the Holiness Code. A man of mixed Egyptian and Israelite parentage, in a fight with a full Israelite, used "the Name" (Yahweh) in a curse; for this he was incarcerated until Yahweh himself had passed sentence, death by stoning (see Box 9.2).

The divine judgment is followed by more general pronouncements concerning blasphemy and a fuller version of the law of talion (see Box 8.2 on page 126), which is to apply to the resident alien as well as to the Israelite ("the citizen"), and then the sentence is carried out.

EXCURSUS ON WOMEN IN ISRAELITE RITUAL AND LAW

In the sections of Exodus and Leviticus concerning ritual, it is not surprising that women are mentioned only infrequently. The Israelite priesthood was patrilineal, passed from father to son. Women therefore had a much less significant part in Israelite ritual than men; their roles were at best peripheral. We find mention of women "who served at the entrance to the tent of meeting" (Ex 38.8; 1 Sam 2.22) and of women who were singers and dancers in liturgical contexts (Pss 68.25; 148.12; Judg 21.19–21). Limited evidence also shows that women had their own rituals, such as that for Jephthah's daughter (Judg 11.40). On the other hand, women were specifically dispensed from participating in the three pilgrimage festivals, presumably because of their reproductive and domestic functions (see Ex 23.17; 34.23; Deut 16.16). Moreover, a woman's vows could be nullified by her father or husband (Num 30).

This subsidiary status of women in Israelite ritual is paralleled by their subordinate legal status. As we have seen, in Israel's earliest systems, women generally were considered property. The Tenth Commandment (Ex 20.17) lists the neighbor's wife between his house and his slaves and animals as property that is not to be coveted (see further page 116). Other laws describe how daughters were under the control of their fathers, who were paid a bride-price; recall the case of the virgin daughter (Ex 22.16–17; see further page 124). Because a daughter was her father's property, he was permitted to sell her as a slave-wife (Ex 21.7–10), but if she was seduced before her marriage, the seducer was required only to sacrifice a guilt offering; apparently no other penalty applied because of her status as a slave (Lev 19.20–22). These laws starkly illustrate the subordinate position of women in ancient Israel.

As we have seen also, the lists of prohibited sexual relationships in Leviticus 18 and 20 almost exclusively concern males; in fact, the only sexual relationship prohibited to women as if by their own initiative is bestiality (18.23; 20.16). The sexual relationships prohibited to Israelite males included a large number that concerned women that were under the control of and therefore implicitly the property of another man: the man's father's wife, whether his own mother or another wife of his father; his sisters and half-sisters; his uncle's wife; his granddaughters, daughters-in-law, and so forth. This is clear from the formulation "A man who lies with his father's wife has uncovered his father's nakedness" (Lev 20.11; see also 18.7–8)—the father's wife, whether or not she is the mother of the individual who sleeps

with her, is the father's property, and it is his rights that have been infringed upon.

Because Israel was a patriarchal society, property passed from father to sons. Women could only inherit in exceptional cases (see Num 27.1–11; Job 42.15).

The subordinate status of women is illustrated further in the regulations concerning purity. Thus, after the birth of a boy, the woman is impure for seven days, until the boy's circumcision; but after the birth of a girl, she is impure for fourteen days (Lev 12.2–5). Impurity resulting from menstruation is a special case. As we have seen on page 143, many of the regulations concerning purity of individuals have to do with reproductive functions, so the existence of regulations concerning menstruation is not surprising. But modern readers sometimes misinterpret the regulation concerning menstrual impurity because of the frequency of menstruation among contemporary women. Comparative anthropological data suggest that menstruation was relatively infrequent in the life of women in traditional (preindustrialized) societies. Women in such societies tend to marry near the time of menarche, and during their reproductive years are for the most part either pregnant or breast-feeding, which inhibits ovulation. So the number of menstrual periods that a woman might have in her life was relatively small—perhaps as few as ten or twenty—and thus impurity resulting from menstruation was relatively infrequent.

These laws, then, reflect the ethos of the society that produced them. It was a patriarchal society in which women were under the control of males and could be considered their property. Only partially countering this essentially patriarchal view is the repeated mention of both father and mother as those who are to be honored (Ex 20.12; see also Ex 21.15, 17; Lev 19.3; 20.9).

THE ETHICS OF LEVITICUS

Despite all of its seemingly extravagant detail about sacrifices and purity, for the most part exotic if not alien to modern sensibilities, and also despite its reinforcement of women's subordinate status, Leviticus, like other biblical collections of laws, does include a profound humanitarian ethic. Reference to the Exodus experience invites the Israelites to model the divine action in freeing them:

> When an alien resides with you in your land, you shall not oppress the alien. The alien who resides with you shall be to you as the citizen among you; you shall love the alien as yourself, for you were aliens in the land of Egypt: I am the LORD your God. (Lev 19.33–34)

In fact, according to Leviticus, the resident alien, the stranger, was a full member of the community for purposes of ritual. Within the community as well, special attention was to be taken so that the poor and the needy could subsist:

> When you reap the harvest of your land, you shall not reap to the very edges of your field, or gather the gleanings of your harvest. You shall not strip your vineyard bare, or gather the fallen grapes of your vineyard; you shall leave them for the poor and the alien: I am the LORD your God. (Lev 19.9–10)

Finally, Leviticus also includes what later Jewish tradition will identify as one of the primary commandments in the Torah: "You shall not take vengeance or bear a grudge against any of your people, but you shall love your neighbor as yourself: I am the LORD" (Lev 19.18). For the authors of Leviticus, as for later Jewish thinkers, love of neighbor summarized a wide-ranging social justice: When he was in need, one's neighbor, a fellow Israelite, was not to be cheated (Lev 19.13–16), not to be charged interest (25.36), not to be made a debt-slave (25.39). Jesus is reported in quoting this law to have characterized it as one of the two primary commandments in the Torah (Mk 12.31; see also Gal 5.14). Loving one's neighbor as oneself, in effect, was to imitate what has been called the divine preferential option for the poor as manifested in the Exodus itself.

RETROSPECT AND PROSPECT

Leviticus immerses us into an elaborate system of ritual and ritual purity that encompasses all aspects of life. It clearly stems from a very different culture from our own, with its own codes and values, many of which we no longer find compelling or normative, although parts of Leviticus, for better and for worse, continue to be cited in contemporary ethical discussions. It is less clear to what extent the various regulations in Leviticus preserve actual Israelite practices and to what extent they are more a kind of utopian program for the community that P wished to reestablish following the return from exile in Babylon in the sixth century BCE.

In the next chapter we will deal with the book of Numbers, in which the Israelites leave Sinai and resume their journey toward the Promised Land.

IMPORTANT TERMS

Day of Atonement	sacrifice	tithe
Holiness Code	scapegoat	

QUESTIONS FOR REVIEW

1. What are the religious and social dimension of sacrifice?

2. Discuss some theories that help explain the concepts of purity and impurity.

3. What is the primary meaning of "holiness"? How does the concept of holiness apply to person, places, and time?

BIBLIOGRAPHY

Two good commentaries on Leviticus are Baruch A. Levine, *Leviticus* (Philadelphia: Jewish Publication Society, 1989); and Lester L. Grabbe, "Leviticus," pp. 91–110 in *Oxford Bible Commentary* (ed. J. Barton and J. Muddiman; Oxford: Oxford University Press, 2001).

A good survey of the interpretation of the sacrificial system is Gary A. Anderson, "Sacrifice and Sacrificial Offerings (Old Testament)," pp. 870–86 in *Anchor Bible Dictionary*, Vol. 5 (ed. D. N. Freedman; New York: Doubleday, 1992).

For a discussion of the concepts of purity and impurity, see David P. Wright, "Unclean and Clean (OT)," pp. 729–41 in *Anchor Bible Dictionary*, Vol. 6 (ed. D. N. Freedman; New York: Doubleday, 1992); and Drorah O'Donnell Setel, "Purity, Ritual," pp. 633–34 in *Oxford Companion to the Bible* (ed. B. M. Metzger and M. D. Coogan; New York: Oxford University Press, 1993).

For a discussion of the status of women, see Judith Romney Wegner, "Leviticus," pp. 34–44 in *Women's Bible Commentary* (rev. ed; ed. C. A. Newsom and S. H. Ringe; Louisville: Westminster John Knox, 1998), and, for a more general collection of essays, Phyllis A. Bird, *Missing Persons and Mistaken Identities: Women and Gender in Ancient Israel* (Minneapolis: Fortress, 1997), which includes her important essay "The Place of Women in the Israelite Cultus," originally published in 1987.

IN THE WILDERNESS

CHAPTER

10

Numbers

In the book of Numbers we return to the primary narrative theme of the Pentateuch, the journey from Egypt to the Promised Land of Canaan. In the context of the final stage of the journey in Numbers, we also return to some familiar subthemes: a rebellious people, an angry but eventually forgiving deity, and Moses as an intermediary between them. Interspersed in the account of the journey, as elsewhere in the Pentateuch, are divinely given laws and ritual instructions.

THE BOOK OF NUMBERS

Numbers is the most complicated book of the entire Pentateuch, in terms of both its content and its sources. It takes its name from the censuses at its beginning (chaps. 1; 3–4) and near its end (chap. 26); its Hebrew title is taken from one of its opening words, *bemidbar*, meaning "in the wilderness," an accurate designation of the book's narrative setting. After the census and other preparations, in Numbers 10.10 the Israelites leave Mount Sinai and head toward the Promised Land. The central portion of the book, chapters 11–25, describes incidents on their journey, and finally a series of appendixes gives final instruc-

tions by Moses and by Yahweh for the imminent entry into the land.

Within this framework, however, the book is a hodgepodge of disparate, sometimes contradictory material, only loosely held together by narrative and by chronology. In addition to the censuses that give it its name, Numbers includes other lists, itineraries, folklore, etiologies, ritual regulations, battle accounts, laws, geographical descriptions, and genealogies, all in a somewhat haphazard arrangement. In addition to the sources J, E, and P, it also includes material from other sources, notably independent poems that in some cases at least are very ancient. Because Numbers contains such disparate material, we will discuss it thematically.

PREPARATIONS FOR THE JOURNEY

The Census

At the beginning and end of the book of Numbers appears a census list of the Israelites, the first (chap. 1) of the generation that had come out of Egypt and the second (chap. 26) of those who had been born since the Exodus. The numbers given for males twenty years old and over, that is, of an age suitable for military purposes, are 603,550 in the first census and 601,730 in the second. These are of the same order of magnitude as that given for the male participants in the Exodus in Exodus 12.37, 600,000, but like it (see pages 99–100), the numbers are impossibly high. They are also internally unrealistic: If the total of 603,550 males is divided by the number of first-born sons (22,273 according to Num 3.43), then each family would have had some twenty-seven sons! No convincing interpretation has been given for the precision of the numbers, their origins, and why P included them in its narrative. Perhaps the best we can say is that P has incorporated numbers from earlier traditions, which implicitly confirms the divine promise to the ancestors that they would be fruitful and multiply.

Twelve tribes are counted in each census. Because the tribe of Levi had no inheritance, the tribe of Joseph was subdivided into Ephraim and Manasseh to maintain the number twelve (see further page 79). Supplementing the census of the twelve tribes is a separate census of the Levites (Num 3–4; 26.57–62), who number 23,000. Included in the census of the Levites is a precise description of the ritual duties of each Levitical clan.

The Arrangement of the Camp

With the census complete, instructions are given for the organization of the camp (Num 2) (see Figure 10.1). This is a schematic idealization of P's view of ancient Israel, and has little relationship to actual geography. The tent of meeting is in the center, with the priestly houses and then the tribes arranged around it, reflecting their respective degrees of holiness (see pages 146–47). The Temple built by Solomon in the tenth century BCE (see pages 274–77) had its entrance on the east, and so in P's arrangement the east side is the most prestigious. On this side are Moses, Aaron, and the sons of Aaron. Adjacent to them is the tribe of Judah, the dominant tribe in Israel's later history as the kingdom of Judah, flanked by Zebulun and Issachar, Judah's brothers according to the traditional genealogy. The other priestly houses and tribes are assigned positions on the

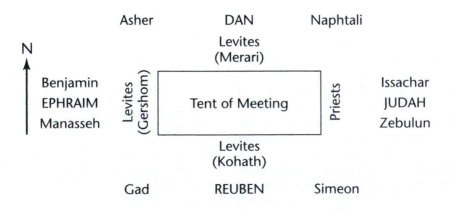

FIGURE 10.1. Plan of the camp of the Israelites as described in Numbers 2.

other three sides. (A somewhat different scheme for the geographical arrangement of the tribes after the return from exile is found in Ezek 48; see further pages 398–99.)

With all of the arrangements made, the Israelites break camp and follow the guidance of the cloud on their journey to the Promised Land (see further Ex 40.36–38 and page 129.)

LAW, RITUAL, AND PURITY

Interspersed throughout Numbers, as is also the case with Exodus, are numerous divinely given regulations. These duplicate or supplement those already found in earlier books and for the most part have been discussed in the preceding chapters in this book. These variant traditions concern the Passover (Num 9.1–14) and the ritual calendar in general (28–29); various types of sacrifices (5.5–10; 15); the rights and responsibilities of the priests and the Levites (18); ritual objects, such as the lampstand (8.1–4) and the silver trumpets (10.1–10); purity (5.1–4; 19.10–22); and an expanded description of the "glory of the LORD," the cloud that covered the tabernacle (9.15–23). Some new material also appears and we will cover this under the categories of law, ritual, and purity. The general principles of source analysis and interpretation discussed in previous chapters are applicable here; most of this new and supplementary material in Numbers is P.

Law

The Wife Accused of Adultery

The longest case law in the Pentateuch concerns the woman suspected by her husband of being unfaithful (Num 5.11–31). Since "she was not caught in the act," the only recourse is to leave the decision up to the deity, and a complicated trial by ordeal (see further page 124) takes place in the tabernacle. The priest mixes "holy water" with dust from the tabernacle floor. The woman then takes an oath, which would have included curses specifying the divinely imposed consequences to her for swearing falsely. These curses are put in writing, and then the priest dissolves the ink with which they were written into the "water of bitterness" and the woman is made to drink it. If she is guilty, then she will apparently suffer a miscarriage and become incapable of having children; if she is innocent, then the "water of bitterness" will have no effect. In either event, her husband will not be charged with any offense.

In this episode we find parallels to the use of an ordeal in cases of suspected adultery in other ancient Near Eastern sources; for example, according to the Code of Hammurapi, "If man's wife should have a finger pointed against her in accusation involving another male, although she has not been seized lying with another male, she shall submit to the divine River Ordeal for her husband."[*]

The biblical case is remarkable for its detail, and the solution of the case has a magical dimension. If the woman is guilty, then she is supposed to become infertile (the precise meaning of the terms used in Num 5.21 is unclear). This divinely caused punishment is less severe than the death penalty, the punishment for adultery that has been witnessed rather than merely suspected (Lev 20.10; Deut 22.22). In fact, some scholars have argued that the entire procedure is a kind of sham, in which nothing really happens to the woman but the husband's suspicions are allayed.

Cities of Asylum

Numbers 35 assigns forty-eight cites to the Levites as their possession, since they have no tribal territory. Among these are six "cities of refuge," three on each side of the Jordan valley. The function of these cities is to provide asylum for someone who has taken another's life, until the matter of guilt can be resolved. If "the congregation" decides that the death was unintentional, then the killer is allowed to live in the city of refuge and is protected from blood vengeance by the vic-

---

[*] Martha T. Roth (trans.), *Law Collections from Mesopotamia and Asia Minor* (2d ed.; Atlanta: Scholars Press, 1997), p. 106.

tim's **"avenger of blood"** (Hebr. *goel*, often translated "redeemer"), that is, his nearest male relative who has legal responsibilities toward the deceased. If the killer leaves the city, he may be killed by the avenger. This situation prevails until the death of the incumbent high priest; after that, the killer is free to return home and vengeance cannot be taken. If the killing was intentional, that is, was a murder, the murderer shall be executed, provided that at least two witnesses testify to his guilt.

This legal convention is P, and a variant tradition appears in Deuteronomy 19.1–11. Its implementation is described in Joshua 20, in which the six cities are named, but we find no examples in the Bible of any of the cities functioning in the way that the legal traditions describe.

Inheritance in the Absence of Male Descendants: The Case of the Daughters of Zelophehad

Inheritance was patrilineal, that is, it went from father to sons, with the oldest son getting twice as much as his brothers (see Deut 21.17). But what if a man died without male offspring? That is the issue in the story of the daughters of Zelophehad in Numbers 27.1–11 and its sequel in 36.1–12. During Moses' division of the land (see pages 170–71), a problem is reported. The head of one of the clans of the tribe of Manasseh, Zelophehad, had no sons but five daughters, who are named Mahlah, Noah, Hoglah, Milcah, and Tirzah. They protest that if they are not given an inheritance, then their family would die out: "Why should the name of our father be taken away from his clan because he had no son?" (27.4). The divinely given decision is that each daughter is to receive an inheritance equal to that of a male descendant of Manasseh. But the women must marry within their tribe, so that inalienable tribal property would not be transferred to another tribe by marriage.

The situation is different from the legendary case of Job, who gave his daughters an inheritance equal to that of their brothers (Job 42.15; see further page 489). Despite the prominence of the women in the narrative, what is at issue here is essentially an adjustment of the patrilineal system of inheritance in a special circumstance: The daughters' inheritance is only temporary, until they too produce sons.

Although this narrative may reflect a legal tradition about how daughters can temporarily receive a paternal inheritance, the narrative context, the division of the land among the tribes, is significant. At least three of the daughters' names are also the names of places known from the Bible and nonbiblical sources, so the primary issue concerns tribal territory more than inheritance by women; here, as elsewhere in the Bible, especially in the books of Genesis and Joshua, geography is personified, with places and regions depicted as individuals.

Ritual

Vows

Two chapters of Numbers are devoted to the details of vows, solemn promises made to the deity. In Numbers 6, regulations are given for the nazirites. These are men or women who dedicate themselves to the deity, usually for a set period, during which they abstain from alcoholic beverages, leave their hair uncut, and, like priests, avoid any contact with a corpse.

The matter of vows also comes up in Numbers 30, which states that vows made by a woman can be nullified by her father or, if she is married, by her husband, provided that he does so in a timely fashion. Since the property that would be offered in sacrifice to fulfill the vow belonged to the father or husband, he would have a material interest in the vow. Divorced or widowed women, who controlled their own property, had no such restriction.

The Priestly Blessing

Added as a kind of appendix to the regulations concerning the nazirites is the blessing to be given to the Israelites by the priests. Literally translated, it reads:

> May Yahweh bless you and may he protect you;
> May Yahweh make his face shine to you,
>   and may he be gracious to you;
> May Yahweh raise his face to you,
> and may he give you peace. (Num 6.24–26)

That Yahweh's shining face could be seen by the worshiper is anthropomorphic, and, although found elsewhere in the Bible (as in Ps 80.3), is somewhat at odds with the view that no one can see God's face and live (for example, Ex 33.20). Similarly anthropomorphic is the raising of the divine face, a metaphor for looking with favor on (see Gen 32.20; Job 42.9). This ancient prayer (see also Mal 1.9; Pss 4.6; 67.1) is still widely used in Jewish and Christian worship. (See also Figure 10.2.)

Priests

Much of the material concerning the priesthood in Numbers, as in Exodus and Leviticus, is P, and it continues to emphasize the privileged status of the priests descended from Aaron and the subordinate status of the Levites. Symptomatic of this privilege is the unusual revelation made directly to Aaron: "The LORD spoke [or said] to Aaron" occurs three times in Numbers (18.1, 8, 20), and only twice elsewhere (Ex 4.27; Lev 10.8). To the earlier material Numbers adds several significant bits of information. One of the most intriguing is the "covenant of salt" that guarantees the priests their share of the offerings (Num 18.19). The phrase seems to be the equivalent of "eternal covenant," probably because of the use of salt as a preservative; it is also applied to the eternal covenant between Yahweh and David, the king of Israel (2 Chr 13.5; compare 2 Sam 23.5; Ps 89.28). Another divine covenant with the priesthood is found in the conclusion to the story of Baal Peor, in which Aaron's grandson Phinehas is rewarded for his actions with "a covenant of peace . . . a covenant of perpetual priesthood" (Num 25.12–13). For P, then, the status of priests was clearly part of a divinely given blueprint for

society, and within the priesthood, the line of Aaron was preeminent. This view was not shared by all: According to Malachi 2.4–5 the covenant of peace is made with the Levites (see also Jer

FIGURE 10.2. This silver amulet was discovered in 1967 in a burial cave on the outskirts of Jerusalem, along with hundreds of pieces of pottery, jewelry, and other artifacts. Unrolled, as shown here, it measures about 0.5 by 1.5 in (1 by 4 cm). It contains a form of the "Priestly Blessing," written in late seventh-century BCE script: "May Yahweh bless and may he keep you, may Yahweh make his face shine upon you and may he give you peace" (see Num 6.24–26). This text is evidence that the blessing was current in ancient Israel; it was incorporated into the book of Numbers in a slightly different form.

33.21), while Nehemiah 13.29 refers to "the covenant of the priests and the Levites," perhaps a harmonization. In any case, tensions existed within the priesthood, as also perhaps between the priests and the laity, tensions that are also apparent in some of the stories of conflict in Numbers discussed on pages 161–66.

Purity

The Red Cow

The ashes to be used in the rituals of purification for those who have had contact with a corpse are produced by the process described in remarkable detail in the first part of Numbers 19. It instructs that a red cow (the traditional translation "red heifer" is inaccurate) be slaughtered "outside the camp," and after some of its blood has been sprinkled toward the camp, its carcass be burned together with cedar, hyssop, and crimson material (as in the case of skin disease—Lev 14.4). The ashes are to be gathered for mixture with "water of purification" to cleanse those who have become impure because of contact with a corpse.

This is an ancient ritual, rich in primal symbolism, which seems to have been secondarily incorporated into the sacrificial system, much like the "goat for Azazel" of the Day of Atonement (see pages 144–45). Like the "goat for Azazel" and also the Passover lamb, the cow becomes a kind of substitute for the human: Its death is the means for preserving life. Much of the symbolism is unclear—it is a female bovine, totally burned (including blood, hide, and dung) but not in a sacrifice, and outside the camp, after some of its blood has been sprinkled seven times in the direction of the tent of meeting. It is to be "red," probably representing blood, the same color as the crimson material and perhaps also the cedar with which it is burned. This obscure ritual is not mentioned elsewhere in the Bible.

THE CHRONOLOGY AND GEOGRAPHY OF THE WANDERINGS

From the return of Moses from Midian to Egypt early in the book of Exodus until the departure of the Israelites from Sinai, a little more than a year elapsed according to the narrative chronology of P, the final editors of the Pentateuch. In the book of Numbers the pace of the chronology increases. Because of the divine decree that none of the generation of the Exodus would be allowed to enter Canaan (see page 162), the Israelites are to wander in the wilderness for some forty years (see Box 8.3 on page 131). During that time Miriam and Aaron both die, as do most of the rest of the generation that had experienced the Exodus. Those forty years are the chronological framework of Numbers, and the wandering itself provides the geographical framework.

But the primary sources, J and P, differ on both chronology and geography. According to the summary of this period in Deuteronomy 2.14, the Israelites were at Kadesh (see below) only briefly, and they wandered in the wilderness some thirty-eight years before they reached the Wadi Zered, the southern boundary of Moab. This chronology, which also is adopted implicitly by J in Numbers, is at odds with that found in P, according to which most of the forty-year period was spent at Kadesh.

As we have seen, one of the organizing devices used by P to advance the narrative of the journey from Egypt to Canaan is the use of an itinerary, in which the places at which they stopped are given; near the end of the book of Numbers, P gives a summary of the entire itinerary (chap. 33). Identification of most of the places named is very difficult, however; to some extent they are locations that were familiar to P in the mid-first millennium BCE. Moreover, P's itinerary is not entirely consistent with that found in J or the book of Deuteronomy.

The location of Kadesh is a good example of the problems. Scholars generally agree that Kadesh, also called Kadesh-barnea, was thought by J to be the impressive site of Tell el-Qudeirat at an oasis in the northern Sinai Peninsula. Excavations at that site have shown that it was a major fortification from the tenth to the sixth centuries BCE, but that there was no settlement prior to that (see Figure 10.3). Obviously this creates problems for any association of Moses and the Exodus generation with the site, no matter

FIGURE 10.3. View of Tell el-Qudeirat in the northeast Sinai Peninsula, traditionally identified as Kadesh-barnea, where the Israelites camped on their journey from Egypt to Canaan. Four springs in the vicinity create an oasis in an otherwise arid environment, and the Arabic name of one of them, Ain Qadis, may preserve part of the site's original Hebrew name. On the right are the remains of a fortress built in the first half of the first millennium BCE.

when the Exodus is dated. We see some hints that the original site of Kadesh was much farther to the east. Numbers 20.16 describes Kadesh as on the border of Edom; this would suit the location of Sinai in that same region of southern Transjordan (see further Box 7.2 on page 108). On the other hand, by the seventh century the Edomites had expanded considerably to the west, and it is possible that Kadesh was on the edge of the territory that they controlled. Finally, the name Kadesh (Hebr. *qadesh*) was a common one, meaning "holy (place)," and is used of a number of sites, both in the Bible in the variant form Kedesh (*Qedesh*) and elsewhere in the ancient Near East. In short, given the data at our disposal, we cannot securely locate Kadesh, and much the

same is true of most of the other places given in the book of Numbers.

REBELLIONS IN THE WILDERNESS

The narrative in the book of Numbers is punctuated by a series of rebellions against both Moses and Yahweh. As we have already seen (pages 105–7), some of these are variants of narratives found before the Sinai sojourn, such as those about the water from the rock and the manna. In Numbers, however, the theme of rebellion is more prominent. (See further Box 10.1.)

Much of the rest of biblical tradition follows the pattern found in the book of Numbers, that the period of the wandering in the wilderness was

Box 10.1 THE REBELLIONS OF THE ISRAELITES IN CHRISTIAN AND MUSLIM SCRIPTURES

The rebellions of the Israelites in the wilderness against God and their divinely designated leader Moses are condemned not only in the Hebrew Bible but also in the New Testament and in the Quran. In both of these later scriptures, however, they are elevated to a kind of inherited character-failing among Jews that led them to reject subsequent divinely sent messengers as well, notably Jesus and Muhammad. Thus, the early Christian Stephen is reported before his martyrdom to have said:

> You stiff-necked people, uncircumcised in heart and ears, you are forever opposing the Holy Spirit, just as your ancestors used to do. Which of the prophets did your ancestors not persecute? They killed those who foretold the coming of the Righteous One, and now you have become his betrayers and murderers. (Acts 7.51–52)

Similar sentiments are found in the Quran; for example:

> And We gave to Moses the Book, and after him sent succeeding Messengers; and We gave Jesus son of Mary the clear signs, and confirmed him with the Holy Spirit; and whensoever there came to you a Messenger with that your souls had not desire for, did you become arrogant, and some cry lies to, and some slay? . . . God has cursed them for their unbelief. (2.81–83)

These later developments are clearly tendentious, and unfortunately have contributed to anti-Semitism among both Christians and Muslims.

---

one of repeated rebellion followed by divine punishment. Psalm 78 is a representative summary:

> How often they rebelled against him in the wilderness
> and grieved him in the desert!
> They tested God again and again,
> and provoked the Holy One of Israel.
> (Ps 78.40–41)

By contrast, some biblical traditions remember the period from the Exodus to the entry into the Promised Land more positively. Using the metaphor of Israel as Yahweh's wife, Jeremiah has him proclaim:

> I remember the devotion of your youth,
> your love as a bride,

> how you followed me in the wilderness,
> in a land not sown. (Jer 2.2)

For Jeremiah, then, the period that Numbers describes as one of rebellion was rather a kind of honeymoon. The same positive spin is found in Hosea, who also speaks nostalgically of Israel's early history with Yahweh, "the days of her youth . . . the time when she came out of the land of Egypt" (Hos 2.15; contrast Hos 11.1–4).

In Numbers, the rebellions begin immediately following the departure from Sinai:

> Now when the people complained in the hearing of the LORD about their misfortunes, the LORD heard it and his anger was kindled. Then the fire of the LORD

burned against them, and consumed some outlying parts of the camp. But the people cried out to Moses; and Moses prayed to the LORD, and the fire abated. (Num 11.1–2)

This brief summary continues a pattern already established in the book of Exodus, one that will be repeated during the journey from Sinai to Canaan.

That rebellion is immediately followed by another, concerning the manna and quail, by the "riffraff" (perhaps the non-Israelites who had joined the Exodus, the "mixed multitude" of Ex 12.38); this is E's version of the same episode found in J and P in Exodus 16. In a nostalgic longing for "the flesh pots" of Egypt (the evocative translation of the KJV in Ex 16.3),

> The riffraff among them had a strong craving; and the Israelites also wept again, and said, "If only we had meat to eat! We remember the fish we used to eat in Egypt for nothing, the cucumbers, the melons, the leeks, the onions, and the garlic; but now our strength is dried up, and there is nothing at all but this manna to look at." (Num 11.4–6)

The divine response is typically angry, and Moses is forced to intercede with Yahweh on the people's behalf, as he had in the episode of the golden calf and elsewhere, and will continue to do.

Rebellion by Miriam and Aaron (Num 12)

Numbers 12, a short chapter largely if not entirely belonging to E, contains an account of a revolt against the leadership of Moses, surprisingly by Miriam and Aaron. They are represented as using as a pretext Moses' marriage to a non-Israelite (called here a Cushite woman; see Box 7.2 on page 108) and claiming that they too had been recipients of divine revelation.

In response, Yahweh declares that Moses had a special status:

> When there are prophets among you,
>   I the LORD make myself known to them in visions;
>   I speak to them in dreams.

> Not so with my servant Moses;
>   he is entrusted with all my house.
> With him I speak face to face—clearly, not in riddles;
>   and he beholds the form of the LORD. (Num 12.6–8)

While other prophets receive authentic revelations in dreams and visions that can be difficult to interpret, the revelation given to Moses is direct—"face to face," or, more literally, "mouth to mouth"; see further pages 188–89. Thus, E develops one of its central themes, the importance of prophecy as a primary mode of revelation, but also recognizes that Moses is no ordinary prophet.

The episode ends with Miriam being punished by affliction with a skin disease. After Moses prays for her, she is healed, but must be quarantined for seven days. As in the episode of the golden calf (Ex 32), Aaron is not punished, even though he is guilty; also, as in Exodus 34, Moses is once again revealed as the preeminent divinely chosen leader. (See Box 10.2.)

The Episode of the Spies (Num 13–14)

The account of Miriam and Aaron's attempted revolt is followed immediately by another story of rebellion, in which J and P are combined. According to P's geography, from Kadesh in the wilderness of Paran (see Num 13.26) Moses sent out twelve spies, one from each tribe, to see if the land of Canaan could be entered directly from the south. The spies penetrated as far north as Hebron, and returned with grapes, pomegranates, and figs: It was a bountiful land! But the spies' report was mixed. A majority advised that the cities were too well fortified and their inhabitants too strong for the Israelites to defeat them:

> The land that we have gone through as spies is a land that devours its inhabitants; and all the people that we saw in it are of great size. There we saw the Nephilim (the Anakites come from the Nephilim); and to ourselves we seemed like grasshoppers, and so we seemed to them." (13.32–33; on the Nephilim, see Box 3.3 on page 34)

Box 10.2 MIRIAM

Numbers 12 is the last episode in which Miriam plays a role; her death is given somewhat perfunctory notice (Num 20.1). Nevertheless, she is a constant if minor presence throughout the Exodus narrative. Like Moses, Miriam is called a prophet (Ex 15.20), and on one occasion, in the story of her revolt with Aaron against Moses' leadership, she is a direct recipient of divine revelation. Exodus 15.20–21 attributes to her the victory song celebrating the defeat of the pharaoh's army, a song taken up by Moses and the other Israelites (Ex 15.1). Traditionally Miriam has also been identified as the unnamed sister who arranged for the infant Moses to be nursed by his mother after the pharaoh's daughter found him in the reeds.

Miriam's relationship to Aaron and Moses is not consistently presented. In Exodus 15.20 (E), she is called "sister of Aaron." According to Exodus 6.20 (P), Moses and Aaron were brothers, which would make Miriam Moses' sister as well, a relationship made explicit in Numbers 26.59 and 1 Chronicles 6.3. In the conflict story of Numbers 12, no sibling relationship between Miriam, Aaron, and Moses is stated, and it is tempting to see behind this narrative three independent leaders, sometimes collaborators, sometimes rivals, who together were the human agents of the Israelites' escape from Egypt, as the prophet Micah recalls:

> For I brought you up from the land of Egypt,
>   and redeemed you from the house of slavery;
> and I sent before you Moses,
>   Aaron, and Miriam. (Mic 6.4)

Only Caleb (in J; in P both Caleb and Joshua) argued that the land should be invaded because the Lord would give them victory. The people, however, followed the view of the spies whose report was unfavorable and again proposed to get a new leader who would bring them back to Egypt. Yahweh again threatened to annihilate all the Israelites and to start afresh with Moses: "I will make of you a nation greater and mightier than they" (14.12). And Moses again intervened, appealing to Yahweh's concern for his reputation and to his character as a merciful deity:

> Now if you kill this people all at one time, then the nations who have heard about you will say, "It is because the LORD was not able to bring this people into

the land he swore to give them that he has slaughtered them in the wilderness." . . . Forgive the iniquity of this people according to the greatness of your steadfast love, just as you have pardoned this people, from Egypt even until now. (14.15–16, 19)

Yahweh relented, but then decreed that none of the generation that had escaped Egypt would be allowed to enter the Promised Land; they would have to wander in the wilderness for forty years—the spies had spent forty days on their mission—until all had died. When the people heard this decree, they acknowledged their sin and decided to invade the land after all. Ominously, however, the ark of the covenant and Moses remained in the camp, and the Israelites suffered a

Box 10.3 THE AMALEKITES

One of Israel's traditional enemies was the Amalekites (see Ps 83.7). According to Genesis 36.12, they were descended from Jacob's brother Esau; the Israelites thus recognized a cultural and perhaps kinship relationship with them. They feature prominently in the narratives of the premonarchic period and of the early monarchy, when both Saul and David had military encounters with them in the late eleventh and early tenth centuries BCE; as Exodus 17.16 puts it, "The LORD will have war with Amalek from generation to generation." In narratives set after the tenth century, they are mentioned only in 1 Chronicles 4.43, which speaks of "the remnant of the Amalekites" in Mount Seir [Edom], who are reported to have been destroyed by members of the tribe of Simeon during the reign of King Hezekiah in the late seventh century.

The Amalekites seem to have been seminomadic herders, especially of camels (1 Sam 27.9; 30.17), whose principal territory was in the Negeb (Num 13.29), the southern region of Judah, although they are also mentioned in connection with southern Transjordan and as far east as Egypt. Their power is suggested by one of the oracles of Balaam (see pages 167–69), which states: "First among the nations was Amalek, but its end is to perish forever" (Num 24.20). According to the book of Judges, the Amalekites were at times allied with other enemies of Israel, including the Kenites (Judg 1.16), the Moabites and Ammonites (Judg 3.13; see Box 13.1 on page 215), and the Midianites (Judg 6.33).

The Amalekites are not mentioned in any nonbiblical source, but in the Bible they are found in a variety of sources from different periods, and it is reasonable to assume that underlying the many references to them is a historical memory of one of the groups with whom the Israelites came into conflict from the twelfth to the tenth centuries BCE. As is true of much of the other material in the Pentateuch, this conflict has been retrojected into the period of the Exodus itself, when the Israelites are reported to have fought the Amalekites on two occasions (Ex 17.8–16; Num 14.45; see also Deut 25.17 and pages 106–7).

---

major defeat at the hands of the Amalekites (see Box 10.3) and the Canaanites. Beginning with this episode, each rebellion that follows results in more deaths, eventually eliminating the generation that had experienced the Exodus.

The episode has several literary functions. It explains, by an extended etiological narrative, why it took the Israelites so long to get from Egypt to Canaan. It also explains the dominance in southern Judah of the descendants of Caleb, who was of Kenizzite, not Israelite, stock (Num 32.12; Josh 14.6). P alters this genealogy and makes Caleb a member of the tribe of Judah (Num 13.6; 34.19). Finally, it prepares the way for Joshua to assume the leadership of the Israelites as Moses' divinely designated successor. Historically, the narrative may preserve a reminiscence of an earlier conquest of Canaan from the south by one or more groups.

The entire episode is reminiscent of the story of the golden calf (Ex 32). Both share the themes of the rejection of Moses' leadership, a divine threat of extermination averted by Moses' intercession, and punishment by death of the guilty parties. The episode of the spies also includes an abridged version of the ancient description of the deity's character as both merciful and punishing (Num 14.18), from the theophany that follows the golden calf episode (Ex 34.6–7).

Rebellions by Priests (Num 16–17)

The parade of rebellions in the wilderness continues in Numbers 16 with a revolt led by priests but including others against the leadership of Moses and Aaron. The core narrative is P, which has somewhat clumsily incorporated an account of another revolt from J.

In J the instigators are Dathan and Abiram, both of the tribe of Reuben. They refused to obey Moses' summons and rejected his leadership:

> Is it too little that you have brought us up out of a land flowing with milk and honey to kill us in the wilderness, that you must also lord it over us? It is clear you have not brought us into a land flowing with milk and honey, or given us an inheritance of fields and vineyards. Would you put out the eyes of these men? We will not come!" (Num 16.13–14)

Moses, they asserted, had failed—he made their lives worse by bringing them to this wilderness from Egypt, which they characterize as like the Promised Land, flowing with milk and honey—but still insisted on his position. The rebels are punished by being swallowed up by a chasm in the earth with their families and descending alive to the underworld, Sheol. Although on one level this is another story of rebellion with disastrous consequences, on another it is an etiology for the decline of the tribe of Reuben, a repeated theme in the Pentateuchal traditions. The original independence of the narrative concerning Dathan and Abiram is clear from the mention of it (but not of the rebellion of Korah) in Deuteronomy 11.6; on the other hand, Psalm 106.17 links the two revolts, following the present text.

The revolt of Korah, combined by P with that of Dathan and Abiram, is another episode of priestly rivalry. A group of Levites led by Korah claimed that since the entire people of Yahweh was a holy people, the special status of Moses and Aaron was unjustified. Moses proposed a test: They should bring incense to the sanctuary, and if Yahweh answered with fire, then they too would be considered chosen. But when the fire from Yahweh came, they and their supporters were burned to death. The fire-holders that they had used, however, were now sacred, and so were incorporated into the sanctuary furnishings as a warning reminder. The next day, when the Israelites complained about this violent retribution, Yahweh sent a plague on the people, which was halted by incense burning only after some 14,700 had died. The entire Exodus generation is gradually being eliminated.

In the sequel in Numbers 17, the status of Aaron was reaffirmed on the very next day: Only his staff produced shoots, blossoms, and almonds (a classic example of a tree of life), and it too was saved as another memorial warning against rebellion. The episode is followed in chapter 18 with an elaboration of the duties of various levels of the hierarchy and their compensation. The priests get the share of the various sacrificial offerings, which are elaborated, while the Levites get the tithes. The tithes of the Levites, however, are also tithed, and this "tithe of the tithe" (Num 18.26) is to be given to the priests. (See further page 140.)

The episode of Korah's revolt is related thematically to other narratives that reflect tension between priestly houses, including those of the golden calf (Ex 32), the strange fire (Lev 10), and the revolt of Aaron and Miriam (Num 12). For P, all of these narratives serve to legitimate the line of priests who claimed Aaron as their ancestral founder.

The Waters of Meribah (Num 20)

Numbers 20.2–13 is a P version of the miracle of water from the rock, a bracketing doublet to the E account of the same event (Ex 17.1–7; see pages

105–6). Like the earlier episode, it is on one level an etiology of a place name. In Exodus that was Massa ("test"); here it is Meribah ("quarrel"; see v. 3: "The people quarreled with Moses"). Although water comes from the rock as it had in the earlier episode, Moses loses his temper, and both Moses and Aaron are condemned by Yahweh: "Because you did not trust in me, to show my holiness before the eyes of the Israelites, therefore you shall not bring this assembly into the land that I have given them" (Num 20.12). This puzzling punishment, hardly proportionate to the offense, is probably an attempt by P to rationalize why Moses, the divinely chosen leader, did not himself complete the journey from Egypt to Canaan; this is only one of several explanations given for that problematic detail (see pages 187–88).

Numbers 20 begins with the death of Miriam at Kadesh and ends with the death and burial of Aaron on Mount Hor (according to P; in Deut 10.6 a different location is given), after his successor, his son Eliezer, has been robed with his father's priestly vestments. Aaron's death, explained by reference to the Meribah episode, continues the account of the elimination of the generation of the Exodus. The death of Moses will not be reported until the end of Deuteronomy, but it is anticipated in the Meribah narrative.

The Bronze Snake (Num 21.4–9)

Another episode of complaint, again about the "miserable bread" (probably a reference to manna, as in 11.6), leads to another divine punishment: "Then Yahweh sent fiery serpents [Hebr. *nehashim seraphim*] among the people, and they bit the people, so that many Israelites died" (Num 21.6). After the people's admission of guilt, Yahweh instructs Moses to make a "seraph" and to place it on a standard or pole, so "Moses made a bronze snake . . . and whenever a snake bit someone, that person would look at the bronze snake and live" (Num 21.9). The bronze snake was thus a kind of sympathetic magic that prevented death by snakebite, similar to the golden mice and tumors that the Philistines made to protect themselves from the plague caused by Yahweh after they had captured the ark of the covenant (1 Sam 5–6) (see Figure 10.4).

The "fiery serpents" have a mythological background; these *seraphim* are winged serpents (see Isa 14.29; 30.6; also 6.2), like the winged cobras represented in Egyptian art. This narrative, probably J, may be an etiology for the ritual use of a bronze snake in the Temple constructed by Solomon in Jerusalem, which legitimates it by connecting it with Moses. According to 2 Kings 18.4, this bronze snake (*nahash nehoshet*) was called Nehushtan, and incense was offered to it. We find no hint of condemnation of the ritual use of the snake in Numbers, nor any suggestion that this sacred object in any way violates the Second Commandment, which prohibited the use of graven images. But its questionable orthodoxy in some circles is indicated by its destruction by the Judean king Hezekiah during his religious reform in the late eighth century BCE (2 Kings 18.4).

FIGURE 10.4.   An image of a snake, found in the ruins of an Egyptian temple near the copper mines of Timna in the Arabah. Made of copper with its head covered with gold foil, it dates to the thirteenth or twelfth century BCE and is about 5 in (12.5 cm) long.

Baal Peor (Num 25)

Following the episode of the prophet Balaam (Num 22–24; see pages 167–69), the Israelites camped at Shittim, on the northern border of Moab, their last stop before the entry into the land. There they had sexual relations with Moabite women and worshiped their deity, Baal of Peor, a regional manifestation at Mount Peor (Num 23.28) of the Canaanite deity Baal.

Both J and P have versions of this incident, and they differ in many details. In J (Num 25.1–5), the "people" prostituted themselves with Moabite women, at whose invitation "Israel yoked itself to Baal-Peor," probably meaning that it engaged in a covenantal relationship with that deity. Yahweh, "a jealous god" (Ex 20.5; 34.14; compare Num 25.11), became angry and commanded Moses to execute the participants.

In the P version (25.6–18), the apostasy is restricted to an Israelite man and a high-ranking Midianite woman, both of whom, while in the "tent" (a rare word probably signifying a religious setting), are killed with a single spear thrust "through the belly" by Aaron's grandson Phinehas. This averts the plague that had afflicted the Israelites, in which 24,000 died. Because of his actions, Phinehas was rewarded with an eternal "covenant of peace" (*berît shalom*) for his descendants in the line of chief priests. Thus, the episode provides yet another example of the divine choice of the line of Aaron as chief priests, in this case through his grandson (see Sir 45.23–25; 1 Chr 6.3–15).

In other biblical traditions, the apostasy at Peor becomes paradigmatic of Israel's rebelliousness after the Exodus. Hosea provides a compelling example:

> Like grapes in the wilderness,
>   I found Israel.
> Like the first fruit on the fig tree,
>   in its first season,
>   I saw your ancestors.
> But they came to Baal-Peor,
>   and consecrated themselves to Shame
>   [a substitution for Baal],
> and became detestable like the object of their
>   love. (Hos 9.10)

The use of the term "love" is probably an allusion to the sexual component of the worship at Baal Peor, also suggested by the detail of the single spear thrust that killed the couple. A later summary in Psalm 106 adds another dimension:

> They attached themselves to the Baal of Peor,
>   and ate sacrifices offered to the dead (Ps 106.28)

In this version, the ritual apparently included a form of ancestor worship (see Deut 26.14).

OPPOSITION ON THE JOURNEY

In addition to the battle with the Canaanites and Amalekites in the episode of the spies, we see a number of other brief encounters with inhabitants of the territories through which the Israelites wish to pass on their journey to Canaan. These narratives follow a pattern: The ruler of the territory through which the Israelites wished to pass refused to allow them to do so; with divine assistance, they defeated him even though he was more powerful than the Israelites. Thus, in fairly rapid succession, the Canaanites living in Arad (21.1–3), the Amorites under the leadership of Sihon (21.21–32), Og the king of Bashan (21.33–35), and the Midianites (31) were defeated; an encounter (but not a battle) also occurs with the Edomites (20.14–21).

These encounters seem to be another set of retroversions into the time of Moses of events later in Israel's history, from its struggles for control of the Promised Land in the late second millennium BCE to events in the first half of the first millennium. At the same time, the groups with whom the Israelites have dealings fit the geography of the narrative; that is, they are largely in southern Transjordan, and no mention is made of other enemies of the Israelites, such as the Philistines and the Arameans.

In constructing these narratives of opposition, the biblical writers made use of a variety of sources, some of which are fragments of ancient poems. In two cases the sources for these poems are given by the biblical writers as a kind of footnote. The defeat of the Moabites, the "people of

Chemosh" (their national deity), is celebrated in a poem that is attributed to the "balladeers" (Num 21.27–30); it is unclear whether either the victors or the balladeers were originally Israelites. The traditional boundary between Israel and Moab also is given in poetic form, from a source called "the book of the wars of Yahweh" (Num 21.14–15); of this source we know nothing more, but its mention testifies to the existence of compositions and probably anthologies that preceded the earliest Pentateuchal sources identified in the Documentary Hypothesis. Other originally independent poems are preserved in a song about a well (Num 21.17–18) and in the oracles of Balaam (see below).

Numbers also describes the defeat of Sihon the king of the Amorites (21.21–32) and Og the king of Bashan in northern Transjordan (21.33–35). In biblical tradition these two legendary kings become the prototypical enemies of the Israelites in their journey to Canaan; thus, in its catalogue of what God had done for Israel, Psalm 135 summarizes the period in the wilderness as follows:

> He struck down many nations
>   and killed mighty kings—
> Sihon, king of the Amorites,
>   and Og, king of Bashan,
>   and all the kingdoms of Canaan—
> and gave their land as a heritage,
>   a heritage to his people Israel. (Ps 135.10–12)

One of the legendary characteristics of Og was his great size: "Now only King Og of Bashan was left of the remnant of the Rephaim. In fact his bed, an iron bed, can still be seen in Rabbah of the Ammonites. By the common cubit it is nine cubits long and four cubits wide" (Deut 3.11). Like other pre-Israelite inhabitants of the land (see Num 13.32–33), Og was a giant; his iron bed, or perhaps his sarcophagus, was enormous—about 13 ft (4 m) long. He is also called one of the Rephaim, another group that dwelt in the land (Gen 15.20; Deut 2.20–21). In other sources, both biblical and nonbiblical, the term is use for the deified dead (see Isa 14.9 [NRSV "the shades"]; on beliefs in life after death, see further pages 493–95).

Balaam the Seer (Num 22–24)

One of the most remarkable passages in the Pentateuch, and also one of the most difficult to analyze, is Numbers 22–24, the narrative of the non-Israelite prophet Balaam who was commissioned by the king of Moab to curse the Israelites, camped at the northern border of his territory, but who ended up blessing them. The chapters feature humor, a talking animal, and ironic reversals, as well as the remarkable introduction of a non-Israelite prophet who was inspired by Yahweh.

Balaam, the son of Beor, a foreign seer, was hired by Balak, the king of Moab, to curse the Israelites. Warned at night by God that the Israelites were blessed, Balaam at first refused the commission, but eventually, with divine permission, went to Moab. At this point God became angry and sent an angel to block the way. Balaam's donkey saw the divine messenger, but Balaam did not, and he beat the donkey to compel it to move forward. The donkey addressed Balaam, reproaching him, and finally Balaam saw the messenger and was allowed to proceed, with instructions to deliver a divinely received message.

Having finally arrived in Moab, Balaam ordered that a sacrifice be prepared, and after it had been offered, he was given his message by God, an oracle of blessing for Israel:

> How can I curse whom God [El] has not cursed?
>   How can I denounce those whom Yahweh has not denounced?
> For from the top of the crags I see them,
>   from the hills I behold them;
> Here is a people living alone,
>   and not reckoning itself among the nations!
> Who can count the dust of Jacob,
>   or number the dust-cloud of Israel?
> Let me die the death of the upright,
>   and let my end be like theirs! (Num 23.8–10)

But a blessing was not what Balak had ordered, and at his request Balaam tried again to curse the Israelites, but repeatedly blessed them in several more divinely revealed oracles, which contain some memorable lines. Among these are:

> God [El], who brought them out of Egypt,
>   is like the horns of a wild ox for them.

Surely there is no enchantment against Jacob,
   no divination against Israel;
now it shall be said of Jacob and Israel,
   "See what God [El] has done!" (Num 23.22–23)

In the King James Version, the last phrase was translated "What hath God wrought!" and was used by Samuel Morse for the first message by telegraph in 1844.

The final set of oracles, against several of Israel's enemies, reiterates its superiority:

The oracle of Balaam son of Beor,
   the oracle of the man whose eye is clear,
the oracle of one who hears the words of God [El],
   and knows the knowledge of the Most High
     [Elyon],
who sees the vision of the Almighty [Shadday],
   who falls down, but with his eyes uncovered:
I see him, but not now;
   I behold him, but not near—
a star shall come out of Jacob,
   and a scepter shall rise out of Israel;
it shall crush the brow of Moab,
   and the skull of all the sons of Seth.
Edom will become a possession,
   Seir a possession of its enemies,
   but Israel will triumph. (Num 24.15–18)

These chapters have been the subject of much scholarly discussion, and no consensus exists on their literary analysis according to the sources of the Documentary Hypothesis. The main narrative, describing the exchanges between Balak, the king of Moab, and Balaam, the seer who blessed Israel, is probably E. Imbedded in this narrative is the satirical episode with the talking donkey who can see what the seer cannot; some have identified this section as J, since it has a much less favorable view of Balaam than the narrative that surrounds it, although several characteristics of it also fit E. The poems themselves were probably originally separate compositions, according to some scholars of an early date, that were put into the mouth of Balaam by the biblical writers. These poems seem to be independent of each other—each has its own introduction—as well as of their surrounding context. They belong to the genre of the "oracles against the nations" used by biblical prophets (see further pages 310–11).

They have been incorporated into the narrative, or perhaps the surrounding narrative has been created to fit them, as is the case elsewhere in Numbers and in other narrative books of the Bible.

Apart from the episode with the talking donkey, the portrayal of Balaam in Numbers 22–24 is positive (as it also is in Mic 6.5)—he received a prophetic revelation from God and delivered it. This is not the case with other references to him in the Bible. Thus, the book of Joshua describes Balaam pejoratively as a "diviner" (what we might call a "psychic"), and reports that the Israelites killed him (Josh 13.22; see also 24.9–10), as also does P (Num 31.8), which furthermore blames Balaam for the apostasy at Baal Peor, the episode that immediate follows in the book of Numbers (see Num 31.16; also Rev 2.14).

Balaam the son of Beor is also known from an important if obscure nonbiblical source, a group of texts discovered in 1967. They are written in a language closely related to Hebrew on plastered walls at the site of Deir Alla in the eastern Jordan Valley and date to the latter part of the eighth century BCE (see Figure 10.5). In these texts, Balaam is described as the "seer of the gods," who receives a revelation of doom (see Box 10.4). Bib-

FIGURE 10.5.   Part of one of the Deir Alla texts, written in an elegant script on plastered walls. These fragmentary texts are written in two colors and tell of revelations given to Balaam the seer.

lical writers seem to have appropriated the character of this Transjordanian seer and made him the proclaimer of a pro-Israelite and anti-Transjordanian message, in effect turning the words of a local visionary against his own people. (For further discussion of the phenomenon of prophecy in the ancient Near East, see pages 297–99.)

The Midianites (Num 31)

At the end of the episode of Baal Peor, Yahweh commanded Moses to "Harass the Midianites, and defeat them" (Num 25.17); that command is carried out in Numbers 31, which describes a major military encounter between the Israelites and the

Box 10.4 EXCERPT FROM THE DEIR ALLA TEXTS

This excerpt from the Deir Alla texts shows both their fragmentary state and their evocative links with many biblical traditions:

> The account of Balaam son of Beor who was a seer of the gods. The gods came to him in the night, and he saw a vision like an oracle of El. Then they said to Balaam son of Beor: Thus he will do . . . hereafter, which. . . . And Balaam arose the next day . . . but he was not able to . . . and he wept grievously. And his people came up to him and said to him: Balaam, son of Beor, why are you crying? And he said to them: Sit down! I will tell you what the Shaddayin have done. Now, come, see the works of the gods! The gods gathered together; the Shaddayin took their places in the assembly. And they said . . . : Sew up, bolt up the heavens in your cloud, ordaining darkness instead of eternal light! And put the dark . . . seal on your bolt, and do not remove it forever! For the swift reproaches the griffin-vulture and the voice of vultures sings out. . . . The whelps of the fox . . . laughs at the wise. And the poor woman prepares myrrh while . . . for the prince a tattered loincloth. The respected one now respects others and the one who gave respect is now respected. The deaf hear from afar . . . and a fool sees visions.[*]

Among themes familiar from the Bible are the divine reversal of ordinary expectations (see, for example, 1 Sam 2.4–8; Lk 1.51–53), the idea of a divine assembly or council of the gods (see page 9), the prophet as witness to the proceedings of that assembly (see page 302), and the title "Shadday," in this case applied to all of the gods (see page 81). Very few texts have been preserved from ancient Israel's contemporaneous immediate neighbors, or for that matter from ancient Israel itself apart from the Bible, because most of them were probably written on perishable materials. The texts that have survived, however, make it clear that these peoples had ideologies, literary genres, and vocabulary similar to those of the Israelites.

---

[*]   Adapted from J. A. Hackett, *The Balaam Text from Deir 'Allā* (Chico, CA: Scholars, 1980), p. 29.

Midianites. As we have seen (in Box 7.2 on page 108), Midian was in the northeast part of Arabia, the probable location of Mount Sinai. Early relations between Midianites and Israelites seem to have been friendly. Moses was married to a Midianite, Zipporah, and in Numbers 10.29 he invited Midianites to join the Israelites in their journey to the Promised Land. These traditions suggest that relations between the two groups were originally peaceful. By the end of the second millennium BCE, however, these camel-riding nomads were attacking the Israelites in raids, and in Judges 6–7 they are defeated by the judge Gideon. That defeat is later called "the day of Midian" (Isa 9.4; see also 10.26; Ps 83.9) and is a quintessential example of Yahweh's military victories on behalf of Israel. The defeat of Midian in Judges is anticipated in Numbers 31, which describes a total rout, the slaughter of all Midianite males, including Balaam, and the capture of their women and children and a great deal of booty.

After the defeat of the Midianites comes a complicated dispute about the spoil from the battle. Moses requires that the women be killed, except for the girls who are virgins; they become slaves. The material goods must be purified and are kept by the warriors, who eventually give some of this plunder to the priests as offerings to Yahweh. Half of the animals and women are given to the warriors, and the other half to the Israelites. Of the warriors' share, one five-hundredth is to be given to the priests to be offered to Yahweh, and of the Israelites' share, one-fiftieth is to be given to the Levites. The numbers are of epic proportions: "six hundred seventy-five thousand sheep, seventy-two thousand oxen, sixty-one thousand donkeys, and thirty-two thousand persons in all, women who had not known a man by sleeping with him" (Num 31.32–35).

PREPARATIONS FOR THE ENTRY INTO THE LAND

The last several chapters of the book of Numbers describe the final preparations for the entry of the Israelites into the Promised Land, the primary theme of the Pentateuch. At the same time, as in the rest of the book, the narrative does not entirely unify the chapters, which include material that is only tangentially relevant, especially more prescriptions concerning law and ritual.

The second census in Numbers 26 sets the stage. After it has been taken and the issue of the daughters of Zelophehad has been resolved (see page 156), Joshua is designated as Moses' successor, although his authority is subject to that of the priests (27.12–23); here P is clearly aware of the importance of Joshua in the book that bears his name (see pages 193–94).

The status and obligations of the tribes of Reuben, Gad, and eastern Manasseh, traditionally viewed as having settled in Transjordan, are the subjects of Numbers 32, which is probably a composite of J and P. According to this chapter, although the eastern boundary of the Promised Land is the Rift Valley (see Num 34.10–12 and pages 53–54), Reuben and Gad decided that Transjordan was suited to raising their numerous cattle and asked Moses to be allowed to settle there. Moses agreed, provided that they commit themselves to assisting the other tribes in their conquest of Canaan proper. The tribe of Machir, one of Manasseh's sons, was given land to their north, in the region known as Gilead. Underlying this and related narratives (Josh 1.12–18; 22, for example) is a historiographical problem. At some point, probably during the late second millennium BCE, Israel included some groups east of the Jordan. When independent kingdoms, such as those of the Moabites, Ammonites, Edomites, and Arameans, emerged east of the Jordan, as did Israel west of the Jordan, the territory of the Transjordanian Israelites came under non-Israelite control. In the genealogical narratives, this is explained by the loss of inheritance, especially in the case of Reuben. But the memory of Israelite control of Transjordanian territory survived, and the loss of some of that territory, notably Gilead, continued to rankle (see 1 Kings 22.3; Am 1.3). Like other narratives in the Pentateuch, then, the distribution of some land east of the Jordan to Reuben, Gad, and part of Manasseh reflects historical realities later than the narrative chronology, but still relatively early in the development of Israel as a distinct political entity.

The account of the wanderings in the wilderness concludes in chapter 33 with a summary of the Israelites' itinerary from Egypt to the plains of Moab (see further page 105). Then in chapter 34 the boundaries of the Promised Land are given, followed by provision of forty-eight cities for the Levites, including the six cities of asylum (see pages 155–56), because they had no inheritance of their own. Finally comes a further discussion of the problem of the daughters of Zelophehad.

RETROSPECT AND PROSPECT

At the end of Numbers, the Israelites under the leadership of Moses have arrived at the border of the Promised Land—"in the plains of Moab by the Jordan at Jericho" (Num 36.13). According to the narrative structure of the Pentateuch presented by P, their religious, legal, and social structures are in place, provided by Yahweh, the same deity who despite their rebellions had guided them from Egypt through the wilderness to this point. For P, these structures are also a blueprint for the community that would return from exile in Babylon in the sixth century BCE.

At the same time, as the book of Numbers reiterates, the Israelites had been a rebellious community, and the divinely imposed punishment for one of its rebellions, the episode of the spies, was that all who had experienced the Exodus would have to die before the nation could enter the Promised Land. Hence they wandered in the wilderness for some forty years, until the entire Exodus generation died, including Aaron and Miriam. Only three individuals who experienced the Exodus were still alive: Caleb and Joshua, the good spies, and Moses himself. Joshua will replace Moses as the leader of the Israelites, for even Moses will die before entering the land, as a punishment for his role in the incident of the waters at Meribah. Before his death, however, he will give a lengthy farewell address, which is in essence the book of Deuteronomy and which we will consider in the next chapter.

IMPORTANT TERMS

avenger of blood   cities of refuge

QUESTIONS FOR REVIEW

1. Compare the narratives of Israel's wilderness sojourn in Numbers with the summary presentations in Psalms 78 and 106.
2. How does the Documentary Hypothesis help explain the complicated geography and accounts of rebellions in Numbers? To what extent does the book of Numbers preserve traditions earlier than J, E, and P?

BIBLIOGRAPHY

A good short commentary on the book of Numbers is Terence A. Fretheim, pp. 110–34 in *The Oxford Bible Commentary* (ed. J. Barton and J. Muddiman; Oxford: Oxford University Press, 2001). For a fuller commentary, see Baruch A. Levine, *Numbers 1–20* (New York: Doubleday, 1993) and *Numbers 21–36* (New York: Doubleday, 2000).

THE END OF THE JOURNEY TO THE PROMISED LAND

CHAPTER

11

Deuteronomy

According to the second book of Kings, during the repairs to the Temple in Jerusalem in 622 BCE, the high priest reported to the royal secretary, "I have found the book of the law in the house of the LORD" (2 Kings 22.8). That book—actually a scroll—was brought to King Josiah, and when he had heard it read (for reading was generally an audible activity in antiquity), he convened

> all the people of Judah, all the inhabitants of Jerusalem, the priests, the prophets, and all the people, both small and great; he read in their hearing all the words of the book of the covenant that had been found in the house of the LORD. The king stood by the pillar and made a covenant before the LORD, to follow the LORD, keeping his commandments, his decrees, and his statutes, with all his heart and all his soul, to perform the words of this covenant that were written in this book. All the people joined in the covenant. (2 Kings 23.2–3)

Inspired by the "book of the law" the king went on to inaugurate a major reform, destroying all shrines to other gods both in Jerusalem and throughout the country and all places of worship of Yahweh except in Jerusalem, and presiding over a national celebration of Passover in the capital city of Jerusalem. Since late antiquity, the "book of the law" that was found in the Temple

has been identified with the biblical book of Deuteronomy, or at least a major portion of it.

THE BOOK OF DEUTERONOMY

Deuteronomy is the fifth and final book of the Torah/Pentateuch; its name, which is Greek in origin, means "second law" and succinctly summarizes its contents. (The book's Hebrew name, "Debarim," means "Words," from 1.1: "These are the words that Moses spoke . . .") Although it is set in the context of the last stage of the journey from Egypt to Canaan, Deuteronomy contains very little narrative. It is rather a lengthy speech given by Moses shortly before his death. In the course of the speech, which resembles a sermon, Moses summarizes the earlier history of Israel, including the promises to the ancestors, the escape from Egypt, the wanderings in the wilderness, the revelation at Horeb (the alternate name for Sinai used by Deuteronomy), and subsequent events. Most of the book, however, is devoted to a representation of biblical law. Not only do we find yet another version of the Ten Commandments (Deut 5.6–21), but chapters 12–26 especially contain Israelite laws concerning criminal, civil, and religious matters, often paralleling and modifying laws found earlier in the Pentateuch.

According to the Documentary Hypothesis, most of Deuteronomy constitutes the Pentateuchal source called D, and D is probably not found outside of Deuteronomy. Precritical tradition identified Moses himself as the author of the book, but for a variety of reasons such an attribution is impossible. The framework narrative itself is set in the third person ("These are the words that Moses spoke to all Israel beyond the Jordan" [1.1]), and the narrator of those words is living on the west side of the Jordan River, in Israel, not east of the Jordan, where Moses died. Moreover, Moses' death and burial are described (chap. 34) and are unlikely to have been written by Moses himself, as even some premodern commentators recognized. Finally, a number of factors indicate that Deuteronomy dates from the eighth century BCE and later in Israel's history, as we shall see.

Genre, Style, and Contents

The book of Deuteronomy on its surface is a distinct genre: It is a farewell address, in which a notable leader speaks to his constituents shortly before his death. Similar speeches are attributed in the Bible to Jacob (Gen 49), Joshua (Josh 23–24), Samuel (1 Sam 12), and David (2 Sam 23.1–7; 1 Kings 2.1–9). The authors of the book of Deuteronomy have taken this genre and have given its fullest exemplar, appropriately, to Moses, the most important human character in the Hebrew Bible.

As is appropriate for a speech, Deuteronomy was intended to be heard:

> Every seventh year, in the scheduled year of remission, during the festival of booths, when all Israel comes to appear before the LORD your God at the place that he will choose, you shall read this law before all Israel in their hearing. Assemble the people—men, women, and children, as well as the aliens residing in your towns—so that they may hear and learn to fear the LORD your God and to observe diligently all the words of this law, and so that their children, who have not known it, may hear and learn to fear the LORD your God, as long as you live in the land that you are crossing over the Jordan to possess. (Deut 31.10–13)

Both because of its genre and because of the setting in which it was intended to be used, Deuteronomy has a style that can best be described as rhetorical. It is intended to persuade, and it does so by repeated use of the same phrases and concepts, which are italicized in the following summary: The *law* that Moses proclaims consists of *commandments*, *statutes*, *ordinances*, *decrees*, and in it the Israelites are urged to *love* God *with all their heart and all their soul*. He *chose* them from *all the nations*, rescued them from Egypt with his *mighty hand and outstretched arm*, because he *loved* them. Therefore the Israelites are to *worship* him *alone*, and not *other gods*, so that he will *bless* them and their *days will be long* in the *land which he is giving them*, which they are *entering to possess*. For it is in this land that he will also *choose a place for his name to dwell*, and it is there that they are to *assemble* regularly for specified *festivals* at which this law will be *read*.

The law that is to be read, however, differs in an important way from that given at Mount Sinai, found earlier in the Pentateuch in the books of Exodus, Leviticus, and Numbers. At Sinai, God spoke; in the book of Deuteronomy, it is Moses who speaks. Deuteronomy thus is an early stage in the continuing process of interpretation. By having Moses promulgate a "second law," the authors of Deuteronomy also implicitly recognized that revelation needs interpretation, as well as adaptation to different historical contexts. That interpretative movement is evident in the complicated literary history of Deuteronomy itself.

Close analysis of Deuteronomy shows that the book consists of not one, but several speeches of Moses, to which are added other materials:

Moses' first speech: 1.1–4.43 (narrator's introduction 1.1–5; narrative appendix concerning the cities of refuge in Transjordan 4.41–43)

Moses' second speech: 4.44–11.32 (narrator's introduction 4.44–5.1)

Moses' reproclamation of the divinely given law: chaps. 12–26

Moses gives instruction concerning the covenant renewal at Shechem: chaps. 27–28

Moses' third speech: chaps. 29–30 (narrator's introduction: 29.1–2)

Supplementary material: narrative (chaps. 31; 32.45–52), poetry (the "Song of Moses," 32.1–44, and the "Blessing of Moses," chap. 33), and the account in chapter 34 of the death of Moses.

In analyzing this composite structure, scholars have dated the sections to different periods. The earliest part, it is generally agreed, is the collection of laws themselves in chapters 12–26, which may be as early as the eighth century BCE, although it shows signs of later editing. These laws have been selected and incorporated into the framework of a speech by Moses; that speech consists essentially of chapters 5–11 and 28 and dates to the eighth or seventh century. To this nucleus was added the material at the beginning and end of the book. The opening chapters (1.1–4.43) are a second introductory speech dating to the sixth century, reflecting the experience of the exile in Babylon after Jerusalem's destruction in 586 BCE; note especially passages such as this:

> I call heaven and earth to witness against you today that you will soon utterly perish from the land that you are crossing the Jordan to occupy; you will not live long on it, but will be utterly destroyed. The LORD will scatter you among the peoples; only a few of you will be left among the nations where the LORD will lead you. There you will serve other gods made by human hands, objects of wood and stone that neither see, nor hear, nor eat, nor smell. From there you will seek the LORD your God, and you will find him if you search after him with all your heart and soul. (4.26–29; see also 28.47–57, 63–68; 29.26–28; 30.1–10)

The final stage in the composition of Deuteronomy was that by the Priestly editors of the entire Torah, also during the sixth century BCE. Just as the book of Genesis begins with the Priestly account of creation (Gen 1.1–2.4a), so the final book of the Torah ends with a Priestly addition to the book of Deuteronomy, describing the death of Moses (chap. 34).

The literary history of the book of Deuteronomy is thus further evidence of the process of interpretation: At several different stages in the nation's history the teaching ("torah"; see Box 11.3 later in this chapter) of Moses was reinterpreted for a new generation living in a different context. (See Box 11.1.)

The Deuteronomic Code

The core of Deuteronomy is the law code found in chapters 12–26. Like the collections of laws found earlier in the Pentateuch (notably the Covenant Code, Ex 20.22–23.33), the **Deuteronomic Code** deals with a variety of topics, including religious ceremonies and ritual purity, civil and criminal law, and the conduct of war. Like those collections, too, it is not comprehensive. Some of what any society would need for its legal system is absent, and the laws found in it do not deal with all possible circumstances, but are probably intended simply as examples.

Arrangement and Structure

The principle of arrangement of these laws is not entirely clear. Laws dealing with the same general topic are often, but not always, grouped together; at times the arrangement appears random. Reflecting the Deuteronomists' own interests, and following the pattern of the Covenant Code, the Deuteronomic Code appropriately begins with a lengthy section on worship (Deut 12; compare Ex 20.22–26). The Israelites are to eliminate all aspects of the worship of other gods and to worship Yahweh only at the place he will choose; there, and only there, may they offer the prescribed sacrifices. This double emphasis on exclusive worship of Yahweh and at one location recurs throughout the Code. The exclusive worship of Yahweh is also a touchstone for deciding whether or not a prophet is false and for punishing even close family members for their apostasy (chap. 13).

Continuing the focus on issues related to ritual, laws concerning the category of holiness follow. These deal at length with permissible food (14.1–21, paralleling material especially in Leviti-

Box 11.1 THE SHEMA

Deuteronomy 6.4–9 is one of the most important texts in Judaism:

> Hear, O Israel: The LORD is our God, the LORD alone. You shall love the LORD
> your God with all your heart, and with all your soul, and with all your might.
> Keep these words that I am commanding you today in your heart. Recite them
> to your children and talk about them when you are at home and when you are
> away, when you lie down and when you rise. Bind them as a sign on your
> hand, fix them as an emblem on your forehead, and write them on the door-
> posts of your house and on your gates.

Known as the "**Shema**," after the opening Hebrew word, which means "hear," this passage, in combination with Deuteronomy 11.13–21 and Numbers 15.37–41, has become
a frequently used Jewish prayer. It expresses the Deuteronomic and subsequent Jewish
commitment to the teaching of Moses, a commitment expressed by repeated daily recita-
tion of the words themselves, by instruction of subsequent generations, and by visual
reminders in the form of phylacteries and mezuzahs, in which the words themselves, written on tiny scrolls, are attached to the arms and head during prayer and to the door of
the home, respectively.

These practices, like the elevation of the Shema itself to the status of something like
a creed in Judaism, are attested in the Second Temple period; note that Jesus is reported
to have called Deuteronomy 6.5 "the greatest and first commandment" (Mt 22.37–38).

Although the opening words are generally interpreted as a ringing affirmation of
monotheism, their original sense was probably "Yahweh is our god, Yahweh alone," an
expression of the exclusive worship of Yahweh also commanded in the Decalogue (Deut
5.7), while implicitly recognizing the existence of other gods (see further page 116).

cus 11.2–23) and with the tithe, which required
that one-tenth of every Israelite's produce be
given for the maintenance of the sanctuary and
the support of religious personnel (14.22–29; see
also Lev 27.30–32; Num 18.21–24). The next section (15.1–18) deals with debts and debt slavery.
Another section on religious rituals (15.19–
16.17) follows, including designation of the three
pilgrimage festivals, which Deuteronomy calls
"Passover/unleavened bread" (16.1, 16), "weeks,"
and "booths"; compare the earlier legislation in
Exodus 23.14–17 and 34.18, 22–23, and the later
in Leviticus 23.

A set of laws concerning the administration of
justice is found in 16.18–17.13, with several apparently unrelated laws concerning purity of religious ritual imbedded in it (16.21–17.7). Then
follow sections pertaining to the king (17.14–20),
the Levites (18.1–8), and prophets (18.9–22), all
of which are discussed further on pages 178–80.
Next are laws concerning cities of refuge (19.1–
13; compare Num 35; Josh 20), war (20.1–20),
and unsolved murders (21.1–9). The final section
of the code is a lengthy assemblage of laws in no
obvious order, dealing mostly with civil and family matters (21.10–25.19). The code ends with in-

structions concerning the harvest rituals of "first fruits" and tithes (26.1–15), and a final rhetorical flourish (26.16–19).

Date and Origin

The date of these laws is unclear, as are their origins. Most likely they stem from earlier collections of laws, like the Covenant Code (Ex 20.22–23.33) and the Ritual Decalogue (Ex 34.10–26). In fact, some of the laws found in Deuteronomy are exact duplicates or nearly so of laws found in Exodus, such as "You shall not boil a kid in its mother's milk" (Ex 23.19; 34.26; Deut 14.21). Others, however, show considerable variation. It is thus not clear whether the laws in Deuteronomy are modifications of these biblical laws or whether they derive from other collections. In any case, the Deuteronomists have selected, modified, and added to their sources in line with their own perspectives. Special attention is given to the central sanctuary as the only permissible place where ordinary sacrifices are to be offered and pilgrimage festivals are to be celebrated. Likewise, a great many of the laws deal with the elimination of worship of other gods and the execution of those who support such worship. Finally, the laws in the Deuteronomic Code are frequently supplemented by references to the narrative setting: Moses' farewell address at the end of Israel's journey to the Promised Land.

FIGURE 11.1.   Biblical law required the use of honest weights and measures (see Lev 19.35–36; Deut 25.13–15). These stone weights, from ancient Jerusalem, are examples of different sizes of weights. Each is marked in ancient Hebrew with its unit.

Social Organization and Values

In our examination of the Covenant Code (pages 122–25), we observed that laws are a window into the values and organization of a society. The Deuteronomic Code, however, appears to represent a utopian society more than an actual one. In its present form the Deuteronomic Code offers something of a populist program for an Israel reconstituted according to an idealized premonarchic period.

At the same time, the Deuteronomists had to take historical realities into account. Although the society they wished to establish was a monarchy, like the society in which they lived, in their program the king's power was limited (see page 179). Thus, justice was to be administered on the local level, rather than by the king (16.18). Likewise, in the discussion of warfare, the king is not mentioned, although priests, civil officials, and military commanders are. Moreover, the true leader in warfare was Yahweh himself, and warfare was thus a kind of holy war.

One feature of this holy war is the "ban," which called for the total extermination both of Canaanites in the land (Deut 20.16–18) and of Israelite towns where idolaters were found (13.12–16). By the Deuteronomists' times, of course, there were no longer any Canaanites as such in the land who posed any sort of a threat either militarily or religiously. Thus, with reference to the Canaanites at least, the "ban" illustrates the Deuteronomists' insistence on exclusive and undefiled worship of Yahweh, but does not necessarily reflect actual practice (see further pages 206–7).

Humanitarian Concerns

The Deuteronomic Code in general has a more humanitarian cast than does the Covenant Code. That earlier collection offered divine action on behalf of the Israelites in Egypt as a model that should inform their relationships with others in similar circumstances, especially "strangers" (NRSV "resident aliens"; see Ex 22.21; 23.9). In Deuteronomy, this appeal to Israel's own experience is emphasized by repetition and by extension. The persons to be shown special attention are the least powerful members of society: slaves, widows, orphans, the needy, and the poor, as well as strangers.

Observance of the law is thus both a response to and an imitation of what Yahweh had done for the Israelites in freeing them from Egypt:

> So now, O Israel, what does the LORD your God require of you? Only to fear the LORD your God, to walk in all his ways, to love him, to serve the LORD your God with all your heart and with all your soul, and to keep the commandments of the LORD your God and his decrees that I am commanding you today, for your own well-being. Although heaven and the heaven of heavens belong to the LORD your God, the earth with all that is in it, yet the LORD set his heart in love on your ancestors alone and chose you, their descendants after them, out of all the peoples, as it is today. Circumcise, then, the foreskin of your heart, and do not be stubborn any longer. For the LORD your God is God of gods and Lord of lords, the great God, mighty and awesome, who is not partial and takes no bribe, who executes justice for the orphan and the widow, and who loves the strangers, providing them food and clothing. You shall also love the stranger, for you were strangers in the land of Egypt. (10.12–19; see also 24.21–22).

Further examples of this humanitarian emphasis are found in modifications made to laws in other collections. Thus, in Exodus 21.2, after six years the Hebrew slave is simply released; in Deuteronomy 15.12–15, he is to be given abundant gifts. Likewise, in Deuteronomy's version of the Ten Commandments, the observance of the sabbath is motivated not by imitation of the divine rest after creation, as in Exodus 20.11, but by humanitarian concern:

> Observe the sabbath day and keep it holy, as the LORD your God commanded you. Six days you shall labor and do all your work. But the seventh day is a sabbath to the LORD your God; you shall not do any work—you, or your son or your daughter, or your male or female slave, or your ox or your donkey, or any of your livestock, or the resident alien in your towns, so that your male and female slave may rest as well as you. Remember that you were a slave in the land of Egypt, and the LORD your God brought you out from there with a mighty hand and an outstretched arm; therefore the LORD your God commanded you to keep the sabbath day. (Deut 5.12–15)

In some cases, however, Deuteronomy seems more restrictive. Thus, the law concerning lost or fallen animals in Exodus 23.4–5 specifies animals belonging to the enemy, whereas the equivalent in Deuteronomy mentions only the "brother" (22.1–4; NRSV "neighbor").

The Levites

One of the significant differences between the Deuteronomic Code and the Priestly traditions is the prominence given to the **Levites**, also called the "levitical priests" and "the priests, the Levites." The evidence in Deuteronomy is difficult to disentangle, at least in part because of the different stages in the book's formation.

The general principle is that the entire tribe of Levi is a priestly tribe, charged with the responsibility for the ark of the covenant, although it has no territory of its own:

> At that time the LORD set apart the tribe of Levi to carry the ark of the covenant of the LORD, to stand before the LORD to minister to him, and to bless in his name, to this day. Therefore Levi has no allotment or inheritance with his kindred; the LORD is his inheritance, as the LORD your God promised him. (Deut 10.8–9; see also 12.12; 14.27; etc.)

In theory, then, the Levites have an exalted status, as the priests who carry the ark (31.9) and teach the law (24.8). This may indicate their participation in the early Deuteronomic school (see page 183). Most of the times they are mentioned in Deuteronomy, however, the Levites are a needy and protected class, often grouped with slaves, strangers, orphans, and widows. This reduced status can be explained in part because of the Deuteronomic reform, in which all worship of Yahweh was to take place at only the central sanctuary. Many Levites who had earned their livelihood by officiating at local shrines would now be unemployed. Added to this is the dominance of a subset of the original tribe of Levi, the priests at the Temple in Jerusalem. Despite the attempts of the Deuteronomists to make all Levites equal as designated teachers and interpreters of the law, the Jerusalem priesthood, which traced its lineage back to Aaron, was able to maintain its hierarchical supremacy. In the book of Leviticus, for example, the Levites are mentioned in only one context, having to do with the "levitical cities" (Lev 25.32–33).

The Law of the King

The Deuteronomic Code contains several noteworthy additions to earlier biblical codes. One, in Deuteronomy 17.14–20, concerns the institution of kingship. The king is to be divinely chosen, an Israelite and not a foreigner. He is forbidden from acquiring large amounts of three different sorts of possessions: horses, presumably for military purposes, especially by trade with the Egyptians in exchange for "the people" (v. 16; perhaps mercenaries); many wives, lest his heart be turned away from the exclusive worship of Yahweh; and silver and gold. Moreover, he is to devote himself to the "words of this law . . . neither exalting himself above other members of the community nor turning aside to the right or to the left, so that he and his descendants may reign long over his kingdom in Israel" (vv. 19–20).

This "law of the king" seems clearly to have been written with specific kings in mind, especially as they are described in the books of Kings. The extravagant acquisition of horses and gold and an enormous harem especially coincides with the description of Solomon's reign (see 1 Kings 3.1; 4.26; 9.28; 10.14–11.8), but trade and alliances with Egypt are mentioned of other kings, and a harem would have been an ordinary part of the royal establishment.

The Deuteronomic "law of the king" thus seems to be a critique of the extravagances of the kings belonging to the dynasty established by David, and also of the ideology attached to that dynasty, in which the king was the adopted son of God and the essential intermediary between God and the people, and in which God had made an unconditional covenant guaranteeing the dynasty in perpetuity (see further pages 277–83).

For the authors of Deuteronomy, writing during the period of the monarchy, although kingship was a divinely sanctioned institution, it was to be severely limited. God's blessing for the people depended not on the king but on the entire nation's observance of the Mosaic covenant. The Deuteronomists, in other words, advocated a reform in which the ideals of the premonarchic period would be combined with the realities of the monarchy. Like many of the prophets, they were reactionaries, but their nostalgia for the past was translated into a detailed program for the present and future.

Prophets

Another innovation in the Deuteronomic version of earlier laws is legislation concerning prophecy. In two unconnected passages Deuteronomy discusses the issue of false prophets. This reflects the Deuteronomists' own close connections with the prophetic movement (see page 183), and also addresses what must have been a chronic problem in ancient Israel: How could one distinguish between true and false prophets?

In the context of the promise of continued revelation to prophets like Moses, Deuteronomy asks the apt question: "How may we recognize a word that the LORD has not spoken?" (18.21), and answers it: "If a prophet speaks in the name of the LORD but the thing does not take place or prove true, it is a word that the LORD has not spoken" (18.22).

That seems clear enough, but earlier in the book a more complicated, and more realistic, criterion is provided:

> If prophets or those who divine by dreams appear among you and promise you omens or portents, and the omens or the portents declared by them take place, and they say, "Let us follow other gods" (whom you have not known) "and let us serve them," you must not heed the words of those prophets or those who divine by dreams, for the LORD your God is testing you, to know whether you indeed love the LORD your God with all your heart and soul. (13.1–3)

This passage introduces a section dealing with those who would promote religious apostasy. It implicitly recognizes that individuals can mislead the community, and it interprets that as a divine test of Israel's obedience (like the wandering in the wilderness; see 8.2). But the passage does not provide a criterion for deciding whether a prophet is true or false: Even a false prophet, the passage suggests, may be sent by Yahweh for his own purposes. Deuteronomy thus does not entirely resolve the issue of false prophecy. (See 1 Kings 22.19–23 for a specific illustration, discussed on pages 302–3.)

Women in the Deuteronomic Code

The treatment of women in Deuteronomy is sometimes less restrictive than in other biblical legislation. Thus, while in the Covenant Code female slaves may be kept in perpetuity (Ex 21.7), in Deuteronomy they are to be freed after six years just like male slaves (Deut 15.17). In the case of adultery, if it takes place outside the city "in the open country," the woman is presumed to be innocent, since her cries for help would not have been heard (Deut 22.25–27); in an analogous case in Leviticus 20.10, however, no exception is made, and both guilty parties are to be executed.

At the same time, it must be recognized that these modifications do not substantially mitigate the essentially patriarchal ethos of ancient Israel, which also characterizes Deuteronomy. To give just one example, the audience of Moses' speeches is addressed in the second-person masculine form, either singular or plural. This variation may simply be stylistic, or it may reflect different stages in the book's composition. But while the masculine plural could be inclusive, referring to both women and men, the masculine singular cannot. Furthermore, women are essentially property, and the Deuteronomic version of the Tenth Commandment (Deut 5.21), while it reverses the order of "house" and "wife" found in Exodus 20.17, still designates the wife as property, along with real estate, slaves, and livestock.

THE ORIGINS OF DEUTERONOMY

Although an early form of the book of Deuteronomy served as the inspiration and the program for the late seventh-century BCE reform of the Judean king Josiah (see page 353), which mandated centralized worship at the Temple in Jerusalem, Jerusalem itself is not mentioned in Deuteron-

omy. The only place explicitly identified as a place of Israel's worship in the book is Shechem, an important tribal center during the premonarchic period and one of the principal cities of the northern kingdom of Israel after the death of Solomon in the late tenth century BCE (see Box 12.2 on pages 204–5). It is at Shechem, in the pass between Mount Ebal on the north and Mount Gerizim on the south, that the tribes are directed to gather for the covenant renewal (Deut 11.29; 27.4, 13). Moreover, the laws concerning kingship in particular, and the book as a whole, make no explicit mention of the Davidic dynasty that ruled in Jerusalem.

A possible reconstruction is that Deuteronomy was the work of a Deuteronomic school that originated in the northern kingdom of Israel prior to its fall to the Assyrians in 722 BCE. This school (see page 183) insisted that Israel had to return to its original ideals, as expressed in the covenant mediated by Moses—united in worship of Yahweh alone at a single national shrine, and faithful to the laws promulgated by Moses. The Deuteronomic school shared the viewpoint of the mid-eighth century northern prophet Hosea:

> Set the trumpet to your lips!
>
> One like a vulture is over the house of the LORD,
>   because they have broken my covenant,
>   and transgressed my law. . . .
> With their silver and gold they made idols
>   for their own destruction. (Hos 8.1, 4)

Among the exiles from the northern kingdom who helped increase Jerusalem's population in the late eighth century BCE would have been the Deuteronomists, who brought with them their traditions in written form. In Jerusalem they established links with scribal and priestly groups, and probably had some influence on the reform and independence movement of King Hezekiah (715–687 BCE). Eventually the Deuteronomists' version of Israel's early legal traditions, the core of the book of Deuteronomy, ended up in the Temple library, where it was discovered during Josiah's reform nearly a century later.

This hypothesis of northern origins is supported by a number of strands of evidence. Like the Pentateuchal source E, also of northern origin, Deuteronomy calls the mountain of revelation Horeb, rather than Sinai, its name in J and P. Also like E, Deuteronomy has an interest in prophecy (see pages 179–80). Especially close connections exist between Deuteronomy and the book of Hosea, a prophet of the northern kingdom. Both speak of the divine love for Israel and insist on the exclusive worship of Yahweh; both also stress the importance of covenant and the need for religious and social reform. These same emphases are found in the Deuteronomistic Historians' accounts of the activity of prophet Elijah, another northern prophet (1 Kings 17–19, 21; see further pages 303–5).

Moreover, as we have seen, in Deuteronomy the Levites have, in theory at least, a high status. This also suggests as point of origin the northern kingdom, where the dominance of the priesthood of the Temple in Jerusalem would not have been accepted. In fact, it is likely that the Levites participated in the early stages of the Deuteronomic school. Consistent also with the hypothesis of northern origins, in the "Blessing of Moses," a poetic catalogue of tribes incorporated into the final form of the book, about four times as many lines are devoted to the dominant northern tribe of Joseph (Deut 33.13–17) as to the dominant southern tribe of Judah (33.7).

Deuteronomy and Assyrian Rule

The book of Deuteronomy appears to originate from a time when Assyrian influence and domination of the Near East was at its height. As we have seen (pages 107–9), one of the legal analogues for the concept of the covenant between Yahweh and Israel is the international suzerainty treaty. Such treaties were used widely in the Near East from the Late Bronze Age onward, and the language used in them pervades biblical tradition. In addition to the Hittite treaties from the late second millennium discussed on pages 109–13, another important group of treaties dates from the time of Assyrian domination of the Near East in the first half of the first millennium. The best preserved and most extensive treaties are those of the

Assyrian king Esarhaddon (681–669 BCE), which were discovered in 1956.

Under Esarhaddon, Assyria was at the zenith of its imperial reach, extending its control even to Egypt. Within the Assyrian empire, smaller entities that were loyal subjects (unlike the northern kingdom of Israel, which had rebelled) were allowed to maintain a quasi-independence, as long as they stayed loyal and paid the requisite tribute. In 672 BCE, arranging for the succession of his son Ashurbanipal after his death, Esarhaddon required his vassals to swear allegiance to the designated heir. Like the earlier Hittite treaties, these vassal treaties, of which several copies have been found, include the identification of the suzerain, a list of divine witnesses, a list of stipulations (couched as conditions), and a lengthy catalogue of curses that will fall on those who break the terms of the treaty. Unlike the Hittite treaties, the vassal treaties of Esarhaddon do not include blessings alongside the curses; Deuteronomy includes both blessings and curses, but the curses are four times longer than the blessings, probably reflecting the exclusive prominence of the curses in the Assyrian texts. The curses in the treaties of Esarhaddon are strikingly similar to those found in Deuteronomy 28 (see Box 11.2).

These parallels, and a number of others, especially of vocabulary, suggest that the authors of Deuteronomy deliberately made use of the Assyrian treaty genre. They would certainly have been familiar with it because of the repeated submissions of kings of both Israel and Judah to Assyrian kings from the mid-ninth century BCE well into the seventh. The Deuteronomists' use of this genre may be viewed as subversive: They were asserting that Israel's authentic status was as vassal not of the king of Assyria but of Yahweh, a relationship solemnized by covenant (for which the Hebrew word is *berît*, which can also mean treaty). To Yahweh was owed exclusive allegiance, and failure to provide it would result in divinely imposed punishments just as severe as those found in the Assyrian vassal treaties.

Several historical contexts from the eighth century BCE on would have been likely times for this message to be proclaimed and reproclaimed. In the

May Shamash, the light of heaven and earth, not give you a fair and equitable judgment, may he take away your eyesight; walk about in darkness! . . . May Venus, the brightest of the stars, let your wives lie in the embrace of your enemy before your very eyes, may your sons not have authority over your house, may a foreign enemy divide your possessions. . . . May Adad, the canal inspector of heaven and earth, put an end to vegetation in your land, may he avoid your meadows and hit your land with a severe destructive downpour, may locusts, which diminish the produce of the land, devour your crops, let there be no sound of the grinding stone or the oven in your houses, let barley rations to be ground disappear for you, so that they grind your bones, the bones of your sons and daughters instead of barley rations. . . . Mother shall bar the door to her daughter, may you eat in your hunger the flesh of your children, may, through want and famine, one man eat the other's flesh, clothe himself in another's skin. . . . May the earth not receive your body for burial, may the bellies of dogs and pigs be your burial place, your days should be somber, your years dark. . . . May all that is good be abhorrent to you, all that is evil be bestowed upon you. . . . May all the gods who are named in this treaty turn your soil in size to be as narrow as a brick, turn your soil into iron, so that no one may cut a furrow in it. Just as rain does not fall from a copper sky, so may there come neither rain nor dew upon your fields and meadows. (E. Reiner [trans.], "The Vassal Treaties of Esarhaddon," pp. 537–39 in *Ancient Near Eastern Texts Relating to the Old Testament* [3d ed.; ed. J. B. Pritchard; Princeton University Press, 1969]).

The LORD will afflict you with consumption, fever, inflammation, with fiery heat and drought, and with blight and mildew; they shall pursue you until you perish. The sky over your head shall be bronze, and the earth under you iron. The LORD will change the rain of your land into powder, and only dust shall come down upon you from the sky until you are destroyed. The LORD will cause you to be defeated before your enemies; you shall go out against them one way and flee before them seven ways. You shall become an object of horror to all the kingdoms of the earth. Your corpses shall be food for every bird of the air and animal of the earth, and there shall be no one to frighten them away. . . . The LORD will afflict you with madness, blindness, and confusion of mind; you shall grope about at noon as blind people grope in darkness, but you shall be unable to find your way; and you shall be continually abused and robbed, without anyone to help. You shall become engaged to a woman, but another man shall lie with her. You shall build a house, but not live in it. You shall plant a vineyard, but not enjoy its fruit. . . . In the desperate straits to which the enemy siege reduces you, you will eat the fruit of your womb, the flesh of your own sons and daughters whom the LORD your God has given you. Even the most refined and gentle of men among you will begrudge food to his own brother, to the wife whom he embraces, and to the last of his remaining children, giving to none of them any of the flesh of his children whom he is eating, because nothing else remains to him, in the desperate straits to which the enemy siege will reduce you in all your towns. She who is the most refined and gentle among you, so gentle and refined that she does not venture to set the sole of her foot on the ground, will begrudge food to the husband whom she embraces, to her own son, and to her own daughter, begrudging even the afterbirth that comes out from between her feet, and the children that she bears, because she is eating them in secret for lack of anything else, in the desperate straits to which the enemy siege will reduce you in your towns. (Deut 28.22–30, 53–57) mid-eighth century the prophet Hosea, whose message was similar to that of Deuteronomy, proclaimed a lawsuit against Israel for its breach of covenant, in part because their foreign alliances implied a rejection of Yahweh's protection:

> Ephraim has surrounded me with lies,
>   and the house of Israel with deceit. . . .
> Ephraim herds the wind,
>   and pursues the east wind all day long;
>   they multiply falsehood and violence;
> they make a treaty with Assyria
>   and oil is carried to Egypt. (Hos 11.12–12.1)

Most significant perhaps are the two assertions of independence from Assyria by kings of Judah, Hezekiah in the late eighth century BCE and Josiah in the late seventh. In both cases severing ties to Assyrian imperial control was accompanied by religious reform, which reestablished the exclusive worship of Yahweh by means of a covenant renewal. It is precisely in these contexts that we have proposed that principal preexilic stages of the formation of Deuteronomy occurred: the beginnings of the Deuteronomic school in northern Israel in the mid-eighth century, probably in association with the prophetic movement; its first full formulation in the southern kingdom of Judah during Hezekiah's reform; and its reformulation after the discovery of the earlier edition during Josiah's reform.

THE DEUTERONOMIC SCHOOL

The authors of Deuteronomy were also the founders of an intellectual movement that had an extraordinary and lengthy influence in the history of ancient Israel and in the development of its literature. This "school" is similar to that which produced the book of Isaiah over several centuries (see pages 331–32) and is analogous to philosophical schools such as Platonism.

The Deuteronomic school, as we have seen, had connections with both the Levitical priesthood and the prophets. It continued to revise its core text, the book of Deuteronomy, as Israel's circumstances changed from autonomous nation to people in exile. It also produced the Deuteronomistic History, the interpretive narrative of Israel's history in the Promised Land based on the ideals of the book of Deuteronomy, a remarkable work covering the books of Joshua, Judges, Samuel, and Kings. This Deuteronomistic History was itself revised several times, much like the book of Deuteronomy (see further page 192).

The Deuteronomic school is also responsible for editing, if not originally collecting, the oracles and autobiographical and biographical reports of several prophets, including Isaiah of Jerusalem ("First Isaiah"), Hosea, Amos, Micah, and Zephaniah. The prophetic book with the closest connection to the Deuteronomists is that of Jeremiah, who himself may have belonged to the Deuteronomic school or been heavily influenced by it. Jeremiah's prophetic career began toward the end of the seventh century, during the reign of Josiah, whose reforms were both inspired by and modeled on the core of the book of Deuteronomy. The book of Jeremiah contains much familiar Deuteronomic language and was edited by Deuteronomic circles (see further pages 367–68).

This Deuteronomic school maintained its core message of fidelity to the teaching ("torah") of Moses, and adapted it to changing circumstances, from the period of Assyrian domination in the late eighth and early seventh centuries BCE to that of the exile, when the Deuteronomists interpreted the catastrophe of the destruction of Jerusalem in 586 BCE and the concomitant loss of Israel's autonomy as a deserved punishment for the nation's failure to observe the requirements of the teaching of Moses (see Box 11.3).

EXCURSUS ON THE CHARACTER AND PERSONALITY OF MOSES

The person of Moses dominates the narrative of the final four books of the Pentateuch. Moreover, Moses and the events associated with him—the escape from Egypt, the making of the covenant, the revelation of the divine name, the wandering through the wilderness—are so central to ancient

Box 11.3 THE MEANINGS OF "TORAH"

One of the characteristic terms used by the latest Deuteronomic editors to refer to the content of the book is as the **"torah"** given by Moses. Apart from three uses in chapter 17 (verses 11, 18, 19), the word "torah" is found mainly in chapters 1, 4, and 31–33, all sections that are generally thought to have come from the latest stage of Deuteronomic editing.

The word "torah" itself occurs more than two hundred times in the Hebrew Bible, and it has a variety of meanings. In its ordinary sense "torah" means teaching or instruction, as in Proverbs 1.8:

> Hear, my child, your father's instruction,
>   and do not reject your mother's teaching [torah].

It is particularly used of divine teaching or instruction throughout the Pentateuch and Deuteronomic literature, and occasionally in the prophets as well. It can have a more specific nuance of precise instructions, or rubrics, as in the legislation concerning sacrifices in Leviticus (6.9, 14, 25; etc.; in all of these cases, NRSV translates "ritual"). By the end of the monarchic period, however, it came to signify something more: a divinely revealed corpus of teaching mediated through Moses—hence, the "torah" of Moses, the teaching or law of Moses.

By the postexilic period, that "torah" was in "book" (that is, scroll) form (Ezra 6.18; Neh 8.19) and was essentially the same as the first five books of the Bible, the Pentateuch, known in Jewish tradition as the Torah. This is what is called "the Law" in the earliest descriptions of the Jewish scriptures (see further the Appendix). By extension the term Torah is then used to refer to the entire body of revelation, including not just the whole Bible but also the "oral teaching" that in Jewish tradition was also revealed to Moses on Sinai, the authoritative interpretation of the written law by the rabbinical sages.

Israel's self-definition that they continue to be appealed to in the historical and prophetic books as preeminent authority and paradigm. It is thus not surprising that until the modern period Moses himself was considered the author of the entire Pentateuch.

Modern critical analysis, however, has analyzed the Pentateuch as composed of different sources. The analysis of these sources in the books of Exodus through Deuteronomy not surprisingly

reveals a number of inconsistencies and contradictions concerning Moses. The sources are combined in P's edition of the Pentateuch, probably in the sixth century BCE, in part because preservation of different traditions was considered more important than superficial consistency of plot and character.

One such inconsistency concerns the relationship between Moses and Aaron. In general, the earlier the source, the greater is Moses' preeminence over Aaron. Conversely, in the latest source, P, the role of Aaron, the ancestor of the Jerusalem priesthood, is more significant and Moses appears diminished. Although Moses occasionally functions as a priest (see, for example, Ex 24.3–8), in the final form of the Pentateuch Aaron is the priest par excellence. Still, even in P, Moses is primary. It is he who receives instructions from Yahweh concerning the priesthood and its rituals and who ordains Aaron as the first high priest.

Another inconsistency concerns Moses' communication with God. A widespread biblical tradition is that no one can see the "face of God" and live; this axiom is generally appealed to on occasions when it is broken (see Gen 32.30; Judg 6.22; 13.22; Isa 6.5). In the case of Moses, it is not surprising that given his unique position, according to some biblical writers he had a special form of communication with God:

> When there are prophets among you,
> I the LORD make myself known to them in
>   visions; I speak to them in dreams.
> Not so with my servant Moses;
>   he is entrusted with all my house.
> With him I speak face to face—clearly, not in
>   riddles; and he beholds the form of the LORD.
>   (Num 12.6–8)

Yet when it comes to describing Moses' actual encounter with God we find some reticence. In Exodus 33, Moses asks Yahweh, "Show me your glory" (v. 18). Yahweh replies, "I will make all my goodness pass before you, and will proclaim before you the name 'Yahweh' . . . but you cannot see my face; for no one can see me and live." Then follows a vivid yet restrained anthropomorphism:

> "See, there is a place by me where you shall stand on the rock; and while my glory passes by I will put you in a cleft of the rock, and I will cover you with my hand until I have passed by; then I will take away my hand, and you shall see my back; but my face shall not be seen." (33.21–23)

Moses will be prevented from seeing Yahweh's face by the divine hand, but he will be allowed to see Yahweh's back. The account of the theophany that follows in Exodus 34.5–9 omits this poignant detail. Still, as the conclusion to the theophany shows, Moses' experience was unique: "The skin of his face shone because he had been talking with God," so that he had to cover his face with a veil (34.29–35). Earlier translators misunderstood the Hebrew of this passage to mean that Moses had "horns," and he is often represented with them in art (see Figure 11.2).

As we have seen (page 96), no mention of Moses or of the events associated with him is found in any contemporaneous sources outside the Bible. Moreover, the presentation of Moses is complicated by the existence of the different Pentateuchal sources. It is therefore risky to speculate about the "historical Moses," and some scholars have argued that Moses is in fact a fictional character. Yet common to all the traditions is the recognition that the period from the Exodus to the crossing of the Jordan (Josh 3–4) was normative. Beliefs and practices developed later were given a greater authority by setting them in that period. The central figure of that period was Moses, and under the layers of tradition plausibly lies a historical individual, although one whose status was clearly enhanced as the traditions developed and were combined.

Thus, although in a superficial reading of the books of Exodus through Deuteronomy Moses transmits and interprets the divinely given instructions (the "torah"; see Box 11.3), in fact, as we have seen, the laws themselves stem from different times and sources. Although Moses has been interpreted as the founder of Israel as a confederation of twelve tribes, we will see that that confederation seems to have come into being only after the entry into the Promised Land following the death of Moses. And although in some sources Moses is apparently presented as a military leader, the dominant view is that it is Yahweh who is responsible for the defeat of Israel's enemies both in Egypt and in the wilderness.

In biblical narrative, Moses emerges as a complex character. Although a stutterer (Ex 4.10), he was also a prophet (Deut 34.10) and even more than a prophet (Num 12.6–8). He stands alone

FIGURE 11.2. Michelangelo's Moses. As often in art, Moses is depicted with horns, a misinterpretation of Exodus 34.29.

as mediator between the people and Yahweh, yet one with considerable diffidence, a characteristic that is introduced at the time of his call (Ex 3–4) and repeatedly shown thereafter. For example, when the people complained of the unappetizing manna, longing instead for the meat, fish, cucumbers, melons, leeks, onions, and garlic that they had enjoyed in Egypt (Num 11.5–6), Moses complained to Yahweh:

> Why have you treated your servant so badly? Why have I not found favor in your sight, that you lay the burden of all this people on me? Did I conceive all this people? Did I give birth to them, that you should say to me, "Carry them in your bosom, as a nurse car-

ries a sucking child," to the land that you promised on oath to their ancestors? Where am I to get meat to give to all this people? For they come weeping to me and say, "Give us meat to eat!" I am not able to carry all this people alone, for they are too heavy for me. If this is the way you are going to treat me, put me to death at once—if I have found favor in your sight—and do not let me see my misery. (Num 11.11–15)

The cumulative portrait we get of Moses in biblical tradition is of a reluctant but gifted leader. And while we have no independent corroboration of Moses' existence, he dominates biblical tradition to such an extent that we can reasonably assume that he existed. Moreover, the presentation of Moses is not that of a model character. He has an Egyptian name and is married to a non-Israelite woman; he may even not have been circumcised at birth (see page 90). His leadership was often challenged, and his anger is often noted, as is Yahweh's anger with him. Biblical writers were certainly capable of presenting an ideal type of leader: as we will see, in the book of the Bible that follows Deuteronomy, Joshua is such a character, as is David in the books of Chronicles (in contrast to his presentation in 2 Samuel). But Moses has complexity and depth, weaknesses as well as strengths.

Underlying the traditions about Moses, then, is probably a historical person. More than any other single individual, this Moses was the human founder of the religion of ancient Israel, whose basis is the idea that Israel was the people of Yahweh. Their relationship is expressed in terms of covenant, with Yahweh metaphorically understood as lord, suzerain, husband, and parent. Israel's covenant obligations are codified in various forms of the Decalogue, in which the divine action in delivering Israel out of Egypt becomes the motive for the exclusive worship of Yahweh and the model for treatment of one's "neighbor."

Moses' Failure to Reach the Promised Land

According to Deuteronomy 34, Moses died before the Israelites entered the Promised Land. For the biblical writers this posed something of a problem: Why would God not allow his faithful servant to fulfill his mission? That the people who had escaped from Egypt were denied entry into the land seems deserved because of their repeated rebellions and disobedience, but we do find exceptions—Caleb and Joshua (Num 32.12)—so why not Moses also?

Various explanations are given to explain this paradox. One is that Moses himself must have done something wrong. Yahweh was a just judge, and if Moses had died, that must have been a punishment, as in the case of the other Israelites. But a punishment for what? According to P, it had something to do with the incident at Meribah. In Numbers 20.1–13, Moses and Aaron are both condemned for having failed to trust in God and to show his holiness to the Israelites. According to this P version of the incident of the water from the rock (summarized in Deut 32.51, also P), when the Israelites complain of thirst, Yahweh instructs Moses and Aaron to take the staff and to tell the rock to provide water. Moses, angered by yet another example of the Israelites' regret at having left Egypt, strikes the rock twice. The water flows, as it does in the earlier version of the same incident (Ex 17.1–7), but immediately thereafter Yahweh decrees Moses' and Aaron's punishment. Rabbinic interpreters explain that Moses had sinned both by striking the rock twice and by not following the divine command to the letter, striking the rock instead of speaking to it. Both of these interpretations seem desperate to preserve the divine reputation for justice.

Deuteronomy offers a different explanation, one followed by Psalm 106.32–33. According to it, Moses is being punished vicariously for the people's sin in the spies episode (see Num 13–14), when the people were reluctant to attack the land: "Even with me the LORD was angry on your account, saying, 'You also shall not enter there'" (Deut 1.37). As a result, despite his repeated requests, Yahweh refuses to allow Moses to enter the land:

At that time, too, I entreated the LORD, saying: "O Lord GOD, you have only begun to show your servant your greatness and your might; what god in heaven or on earth can perform deeds and mighty acts like yours! Let me cross over to see the good land beyond the Jordan, that good hill country and the Lebanon." But the LORD was angry with me on your account and would not heed me. The LORD said to me, "Enough from you! Never speak to me of this matter again! Go up to the top of Pisgah and look around you to the west, to the north, to the south, and to the east. Look well, for you shall not cross over this Jordan. (Deut 3.23–27)

So Moses gets to see the Promised Land, but not to enter it.

The Death and Burial of Moses

Deuteronomy 34, the concluding chapter to the Pentateuch, describes the death and burial of Moses. As Yahweh had decreed, Moses would not be allowed to enter the Promised Land, but he

would be able to see it (see Figure 11.3). So he climbs Mount Nebo, just a few miles east of the outlet of the Jordan River into the Dead Sea, and from there

> The LORD showed him the whole land: Gilead as far as Dan, all Naphtali, the land of Ephraim and Manasseh, all the land of Judah as far as the Western Sea, the Negeb, and the Plain—that is, the valley of Jericho, the city of palm trees—as far as Zoar. The LORD said to him, "This is the land of which I swore to Abraham, to Isaac, and to Jacob, saying, 'I will give it to your descendants'; I have let you see it with your eyes, but you shall not cross over there." (Deut 34.1–4).

And then Moses dies, "at the LORD's command"; the Hebrew literally means "at the mouth of Yahweh," recalling the special intimate knowledge that Moses had of the deity: He knew him "mouth to mouth" (Num 12.8; see Deut 34.10; NRSV:

FIGURE 11.3. Aerial photo view of Mount Nebo, with a view to the east.

"face to face"). In rabbinic tradition this was interpreted literally: Moses died when God kissed him.

The twentieth-century philosopher Martin Buber elaborates on the death of Moses:

> And now Moses ascends Mount Nebo, solitary as he has always been; more solitary than he has ever been before. As he is making his way over the ridge and is mounting to the level summit, he is reminiscent of one of those noble animals which leave their herd in order to perish alone.
>
> According to the Bible he was one hundred and twenty years old; according to our understanding of the sequence of time the years were far less in number. In any case he was an aged man. But as he stands here upon the peak everything within him demonstrates the soul that has not aged. "His eyes were not dimmed, and his freshness had not fled"; that is the speech of a people's memory.
>
> From Nebo you can see the whole of the Jordan depression and beyond. When the air is clear you see the snows of Hermon in the north, and in the West the hills that lie above the Mediterranean; it is Canaan. That is what he sees close before him. . . .
>
> "So Moses the servant of YHVH died there in the Land of Moab at the bidding of YHVH." The Hebrew wording admits of the meaning "by the mouth of YHVH." This, in turn, was elaborated by post-Biblical legend, for which the death of Moses was a favourite theme. But here as ever the Biblical text is far greater than all expansions; greater than the picture of death by the kiss of God is that of the man who has lived by the bidding of this God, and who now also perishes at his bidding.
>
> "And he buried him in the gorge, in the Land of Moab, facing Beth Peor". . . . Although the translation "and one buried him" is permissible, there can be no doubt that YHVH himself is regarded as the digger of the grave for His servant; and therefore "no man knoweth his grave unto this day."[*]

RETROSPECT AND PROSPECT

At the end of Deuteronomy, Israel is poised to return to the Promised Land. Its stirring rhetorical style has an inspiring message: God's love of Israel, expressed in covenant and proven through history, will continue as long as the people are faithful to the teaching of Moses. That will be the dominant theme that the Deuteronomists use to organize the historical narrative that follows in the books of Joshua, Judges, Samuel, and Kings. At the same time, Deuteronomy concludes the Pentateuch, in which later Jewish tradition will enumerate a total of 613 commandments given by God through Moses, the traditional author of the Pentateuch. Obedience to these commandments will form the essence of Jewish tradition—the way of Torah.

In biblical narrative, the end of Deuteronomy is obviously not the end of the plot: The promises to the ancestors have not yet been fulfilled, and the Israelites are not yet in the "land flowing with milk and honey." That fulfillment will take place in the book of Joshua. Yet in another sense, with Deuteronomy we reach what later tradition identified as the end of the primary divine instructions. When the Priestly editors of Israel's earlier traditions concluded the Torah with Deuteronomy, they deliberately established a paradigm for the community in exile: The necessary condition for survival as a people was fidelity to the teaching of Moses. And, since its compilation took place during the period of exile in the sixth century BCE, it is understandable that the Pentateuch ends with Israel still in exile.

One of the principal themes of the Pentateuch, in fact, is the theme of exile and return. This theme pervades the book of Genesis, from the expulsion from the garden of Eden in Genesis 3 through the various wanderings of Israel's ancestors in and out of the Promised Land. The remaining four books of the Pentateuch, Exodus through Deuteronomy, are essentially one long journey home, a journey that for the Priestly writers of the exilic period and others provided a typological anticipation of the hoped-for restoration of Israel during the Babylonian captivity after the destruction of Jerusalem in 586 BCE.

---

[*]   Martin Buber, *Moses: The Revelation and the Covenant* (New York: Harper Torchbooks, 1958), p. 201.

IMPORTANT TERMS

Deuteronomic Code   Shema   torah
Levites

QUESTIONS FOR REVIEW

1. What is the relationship of the book of Deuteronomy to the preceding four books of the Pentateuch? What is its relationship to the books that follow?

2. How do the laws in Deuteronomy differ from those found earlier in the Pentateuch? How can these differences be explained?

3. What are the core messages of the book of Deuteronomy?

BIBLIOGRAPHY

Three good commentaries on Deuteronomy are Richard Clifford, *Deuteronomy* (Wilmington, DE: Michael Glazier, 1982); Richard D. Nelson, *Deuteronomy: A Commentary* (Louisville, KY: Westminster John Knox, 2002); and Jeffrey A. Tigay, *Deuteronomy: The JPS Torah Commentary* (Philadelphia: Jewish Publication Society, 1996).

JOSHUA AND THE CONQUEST OF THE LAND OF CANAAN

CHAPTER

12

Joshua

THE FORMER PROPHETS

In Jewish tradition, the major division of the Bible that follows the Torah (the Pentateuch) is the Prophets, and the Prophets is further divided into two parts: the **Former Prophets**, comprising the books of Joshua, Judges, Samuel, and Kings, and the **Latter Prophets**, consisting of the books that have a prophet's name (Isaiah, Jeremiah, Ezekiel, and the twelve "minor" prophets Hosea through Malachi). Christian tradition has a somewhat different arrangement: The books of Joshua, Judges, Samuel, and Kings likewise follow the Pentateuch, but to them are added the books of Ruth (after Judges), and Chronicles, Ezra, Nehemiah, and Esther (after 2 Kings). (In the Jewish canon, these books are included among the Writings, the last of the three divisions of the Bible; see further the Appendix.)

These different arrangements of books suggest somewhat differing understandings of their contents. The Christian arrangement groups together all the books that contain narrative history, thus providing a relatively continuous chronological sequence, although one with some repetitiveness, since most of the events narrated in Chronicles are also found in Samuel and Kings. It also reflects a tendency to view the narrative history as factual: The historical books contain a record of the past, and what they narrate occurred as described.

The Jewish arrangement links the historical narratives with prophecy, thus understanding them as more than a straightforward account. Rather, they include interpretation, specifically from a divine perspective, implicitly revealed to divinely informed interpreters or "prophets." It is at least a happy coincidence that one of the features of the **Deuteronomistic History**, the books of Joshua, Judges, Samuel, and Kings (see below), is the use of speeches by prophets at key points in the narrative; the ancient nomenclature "Former Prophets" thus turns out to be apt.

THE DEUTERONOMISTIC HISTORY

The Pentateuch ends with Moses dead and Israel camped on the eastern border of the land of Canaan. A central theme of the J tradition, as we have seen, is the promise that Israel will possess that land. It is likely that J originally included an account of how the promise of the land was fulfilled, but J ends abruptly, as do E and P, at the end of the book of Deuteronomy. The original ending of J seems to have been suppressed in the final shaping of the Bible in favor of the narrative of the book of Joshua.

That narrative tells how the promise is fulfilled, but its style, themes, language, and theological perspective are distinctively different from those of J, E, and P. It does share both themes and language with the book of Deuteronomy, however, and so since the mid-twentieth century most scholars have followed the proposal of the twentieth-century German biblical scholar Martin Noth that the books of Joshua, Judges, Samuel, and Kings are part of a larger work, called the "Deuteronomistic History" because of its close connections with the book of Deuteronomy. Deuteronomy itself, in the canonical arrangement, can thus be understood not just as a conclusion to the Pentateuch, but also as a kind of theological and thematic preface to the historical narrative that follows it.

That narrative is the second of three chronologically sequential histories in the Hebrew Bible. It picks up the story where the first, the Pentateuch, ends and continues until the Babylonian captivity in the sixth century BCE. The third is the books of Chronicles, which begin with the genealogy of Adam and, as the latest of the three, concludes with the return of the exiles from Babylon in the late sixth century BCE (see further pages 446–54).

This Deuteronomistic History seems to have undergone several editions. The latest is clearly a product of the exile, which sees almost the entire history of Israel in the land as a pattern of apostasy. This exilic edition of the Deuteronomistic History interprets the destruction of the capitals of the northern kingdom of Israel (Samaria) and the southern kingdom of Judah (Jerusalem) by the Assyrians in the eighth century BCE and Babylonians in the sixth, respectively, the loss of autonomy, and exile as deserved punishments from God for this apostasy. Traces of this exilic perspective can be found throughout the work.

But there were earlier editions as well. One is probably associated with the reign of Josiah in the late seventh century BCE. His rule is prophesied in 1 Kings 13.2: "A son shall be born to the house of David, Josiah by name," and he, it is predicted, would defile the altar on which Jeroboam, the first ruler of the northern kingdom of Israel in the late tenth century, was offering incense, in clear violation of the Deuteronomic doctrine of worship at only one sanctuary. When Josiah does become king, the Deuteronomistic Historians introduce his reign with unalloyed praise: "He did what was right in the eyes of the LORD, and walked in all the way of his father David; he did not turn aside to the right or to the left" (2 Kings 22.2). Moreover, the Deuteronomistic Historians present Josiah as the king during whose reign the "book of the law" was discovered during the repairs to the Temple, and who, inspired by it, inaugurated a sweeping reform to bring the nation into compliance with that book, which was an early form of the book of Deuteronomy. There thus seems to have been an edition of the Deuteronomistic History associated with the reign of Josiah.

But Josiah is not the only king of the Davidic dynasty to be given such praise. His predecessor, King Hezekiah, who ruled in the late eighth and early seventh centuries BCE, is given even more unqualified approval:

He did what was right in the sight of the LORD just as his ancestor David had done. . . . He trusted in the LORD the God of Israel; so that there was no one like him among all the kings of Judah after him, or among those who were before him. For he held fast to the LORD; he did not depart from following him but kept the commandments that the LORD commanded Moses. The LORD was with him; wherever he went, he prospered. (2 Kings 18.3–7)

As we have seen on pages 180–81, the circles responsible for Deuteronomy had northern origins, and it is likely that after the destruction of the northern kingdom in 722 BCE some members of this group—which we have called a "school" analogous to schools of philosophy in ancient Greece—had moved south to Jerusalem. There they seem to have become engaged in King Hezekiah's religious reform (see 2 Kings 18.4; 2 Chr 29–31), and probably during his reign produced an earlier edition of the Deuteronomistic History. Scholars label these three versions of the

Deuteronomistic History DTR^G ("G" stands for the German *Grundschrift*, meaning "basic text"; dated to the late eighth century BCE), DTR[1] (the late seventh century), and DTR[2] (the mid-sixth century).

Two themes of Deuteronomy are prominent in the Deuteronomistic History. One is the exclusive worship of Yahweh as a prerequisite for Israel's continued possession of and prosperity in the Promised Land. Worship of other gods will inevitably result in divine punishment, as the curses in Deuteronomy 28 detail. A second theme is that that worship is to take place only at "the place that the LORD your God will choose" (Deut 12.5; etc.), and for the Deuteronomistic Historians, writing from a Judean perspective, once the ark of the covenant has been moved to Jerusalem by David (2 Sam 6) and installed in the Temple by Solomon (1 Kings 8.1–10), that "place" is the Jerusalem Temple exclusively. A third theme, introduced in the Deuteronomistic History, is that of a covenant made by Yahweh with the dynasty founded by David. We find some tension in the presentation of this theme, for the very institution of kingship is one about which ambivalence is repeatedly expressed.

The subject of the Deuteronomistic History is the experiences of the Israelites in the Promised Land of Canaan, from their entry into it under Joshua to their loss of it in the early sixth century BCE. In composing that history, the Deuteronomistic Historians made use of earlier sources, some of which they mention but which no longer exist. These include "the Book of Jashar" (Josh 10.13; 2 Sam 1.18), "the Book of the Acts of Solomon" (1 Kings 11.41), "the book of the Annals of the Kings of Israel" (1 Kings 14.19; etc.), and "the book of the Annals of the Kings of Judah" (1 Kings 14.29; etc.). In using these named and many other unnamed sources, which not infrequently present very different views, the Deuteronomistic Historians were often more interested in setting down the traditions found in their sources than in a superficial consistency. Thus, they were in a very real sense responsible historians, preserving contradictory traditions despite their own ideological perspective.

That perspective is expressed in a number of speeches by God and by key human characters. These speeches are characteristically free compositions of the Deuteronomistic Historians, a technique employed by other ancient historians, such as the Greek writer Thucydides. In the earlier parts of the Deuteronomistic History, God often speaks directly to individuals, such as Joshua and Samuel. In the later books, for the most part, the divine locutions are put into the mouths of prophets. These prophetic oracles function as an ongoing commentary on the narrative and are an elaboration of the divine promise of continued prophetic guidance found in Deuteronomy 18.15–19.

Covering Israel's history for over six centuries, the Deuteronomistic History is perhaps the earliest extended historical narrative known from antiquity, and it is a complex and subtle document.

THE BOOK OF JOSHUA

The Deuteronomistic History begins with the book of Joshua. In precritical tradition, Joshua himself was thought to be the author of the book that bears his name. Only the verses at the end of the book, which describe his death (24.29–32), were thought to have been written not by Joshua, but by Eleazar the priest, just as Joshua himself was sometimes credited with the last few verses of Deuteronomy, which describe Moses' death. And the last verse of the book of Joshua, which in turn describes Eleazar's death, was attributed to his son Phinehas. In the late nineteenth and early twentieth centuries, some early critical scholars found in the book of Joshua the Pentateuchal sources J, E, D, and P, identified in the Documentary Hypothesis (see pages 23–27), and spoke of a "Hexateuch" ("six books") rather than a Pentateuch ("five books"). The recognition of the existence of the Deuteronomistic History, however, has made it clear that the book of Joshua is part of that larger work, sharing its characteristic language, themes, and perspectives.

The broad outlines of the narrative of the book of Joshua are straightforward. Yahweh appoints Joshua to be Moses' successor, and under Joshua's leadership the Israelites cross the Jordan and capture the entire Promised Land in a series of battles in which Yahweh fights for them. Several chapters are devoted to events in a relatively restricted region—at Gilgal (4.19–5.12), Jericho (5.13–6.27), Ai (7.2–8.29), and Gibeon (9.3–27). Then come more abbreviated accounts of victories over coalitions of southern and northern kings (10.1–11.15), followed by several summaries (11.16–23; 12.1–6, 7–24). With the land captured, Joshua proceeds to divide it among the tribes, first the land east of the Jordan River to the tribes of Reuben, Gad, and half of Manasseh, and then the territory in Canaan proper to the remaining nine and a half tribes. Cities of refuge and Levitical cities are established, and a dispute concerning an altar constructed by the Transjordanian tribes is resolved. Finally, Joshua gathers the tribes together for a farewell address and renews the covenant at Shechem.

As the beginning of the Deuteronomistic History, the book of Joshua appropriately presents a paradigm of how Israel was to live in the land: twelve tribes, with a divinely designated leader, united by covenant in warfare and in worship of Yahweh alone at a single sanctuary—all in obedience to the commands of Moses as found in Deuteronomy. The fulfillment of these commands is the principal theme of the book, as its opening makes clear. As part of his commission to Joshua, Yahweh instructs him:

> Be strong and very courageous, being careful to act in accordance with all the law that my servant Moses commanded you; do not turn from it to the right or to the left, so that you may be successful wherever you go. This book of the law shall not depart out of your mouth; you shall meditate on it day and night, so that you may be careful to act in accordance with all that is written in it. For then you shall make your way prosperous, and then you shall be successful. (Josh 1.7–8)

The book of Joshua ends with a final reference to "the book of the law of God" (24.26), at the conclusion of the covenant ceremony at Shechem; thus the entire book is framed by the theme of the law of Moses.

The character of Joshua himself is a template for the Deuteronomistic Historians' presentation of later kings, notably David, Hezekiah, and especially Josiah, who, like Joshua, "did what was right in the eyes of the LORD, and . . . did not turn aside to the right or to the left" (2 Kings 22.2; see Josh 1.7; 23.6) and who read aloud to "all the people . . . the words of the book of the covenant (2 Kings 23.2; see Josh 8.34–35). Joshua is also a foil to Israel's first king, Saul, who failed to observe the rules of holy war (1 Sam 13–15; see Josh 7) and violated the covenant with the inhabitants of Gibeon (2 Sam 21.1–14; see Josh 9).

Sources

The book of Joshua is not just an ideological program, however. It is also a carefully constructed historical narrative, which incorporates into its final form a variety of ancient sources.

Etiological Narratives

Throughout the book of Joshua, as in other biblical narratives about the more distant past, are etiologies: short narratives that explain by means of the narrative itself the origins of religious rituals, topographical features, genealogical relationships, and other aspects of ancient Israelite life. The book of Joshua includes more of these etiological narratives than any other book of the Bible—twelve of them containing the phrase "to this day." This phrase clearly shows the chronological perspective of the narrator, who is writing at some remove from the events being related.

As in the ancestral narratives in the book of Genesis, these etiological narratives were probably originally independent legends, and the explanations and etymologies that they contain are usually fictive. In Joshua, they most frequently concern features of the landscape and the origins of the ethnic diversity of Israel. Thus, after the defeat of the Canaanite city of Ai, "Joshua burned Ai, and made it forever a heap of ruins, as it is to this day" (8.28), and then, over the body of the king of Ai who had been executed, they "raised . . . a heap of stones, which stands there to this day" (8.29). This conclusion to Ai's conquest shows that the narrative originates as an explanation of the impressive ruins of Ai, which archaeological investigation has shown to be the result of the city's destruction in the mid-third millennium BCE (see Figure 12.1), long before the time of Joshua. The etiological narrative also explains the large mass of stones at the former gateway to the city and implicitly, the name of Ai itself, which means "the ruin." The story of Ai's destruction thus answers the questions: "How did these ruins get here?" and "How did Ai get its name?" It is likely that this etiological legend first existed independently and was connected with Joshua only secondarily, as is also the case with such etiologies as the stones at Gilgal (4.1–9; see pages 207–8).

Another etiological legend is associated with Rahab, the prostitute of Jericho who had sheltered the spies whom Joshua had sent across the Jordan ahead of the Israelites. According to Joshua 6.25, "Rahab the prostitute, with her father's house and all who belonged to her, Joshua spared. She has lived in Israel to this day. For she hid the messengers whom Joshua sent to spy out Jericho." Probably originating as an answer to the question of how a Canaanite group became part of Israel, this note, which concludes the episode of the spies in chapter 2, is remarkable. Like the similar incorporation into Israel of the Gibeonites (chap. 9) and other non-Israelites (see 13.13; 16.10; Ruth), it is inconsistent with the Deuteronomic injunction to kill all Canaanites and not

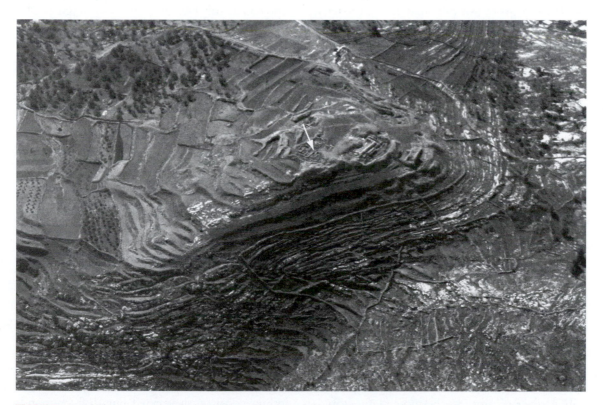

FIGURE 12.1. The ancient mound of Ai. The arrow points to the remains of an unfortified village dating to early in the Iron Age (twelfth century BCE). To its right are the ruins of a large temple from the Early Bronze Age (ca. 2500 BCE), and below that is a large defensive wall of the same period. Between the Early Bronze Age and the Iron Age the site was unoccupied. The description of the city in Joshua 8 thus is historically questionable.

to intermarry with them (Deut 20.16–18; 7.1–4). The Deuteronomistic Historians were not entirely comfortable with this inconsistency, as is shown in the case of Rahab by their locating her and her extended family "outside the camp of Israel" (6.23) and in the case of the Gibeonites by their relegation to the status of temple servants or slaves (9.21, 27).

These two examples, then, illustrate how etiological narratives functioned. They were incorporated into the book of Joshua and contributed to the portrayal of Joshua as the central figure in the story of the conquest of the land. It is more likely, however, as we will see on pages 199–201, that he was originally only a local hero.

Boundary and City Lists

The central section of the book of Joshua (chaps. 13–19) consists of lists of boundaries of the territories of the twelve tribes and of cities contained within those territories (see Figures 12.2 and 13.1). These are followed by two additional lists, of cities of asylum (chap. 20) and Levitical cities (chap. 21). The lists are incorporated into the narrative as Joshua's division of the land, whose conquest was just described in the preceding chapters.

To modern readers, these lists, like the genealogies in Genesis and Chronicles, and similar lists in the Bible and other ancient literature, often seem dry and unimportant. Yet for the ancient audience of Joshua, the lists were clearly of interest. The geographical information they contain is a record of local history and, taken as a whole, forms a kind of map in prose form. More generally, the lists also demonstrate the importance attached to the land of Israel in the Deuteronomistic History in particular, and in the Bible as a whole (see further pages 59–61).

Several things are notable about these lists. The descriptions of the territories assigned to the tribes are not all given in the same detail. In general, that of the tribe of Judah (chap. 15) is the most detailed, and the farther removed from Judah a tribe's territory is, the more perfunctory is its geographical description. This suggests that the lists were compiled in Judah itself. Moreover, archaeological evidence for a number of the places named indicates that they were not settled before the late seventh century BCE, suggesting a date for the lists as a whole during the reign of King Josiah, when they would have been incorporated into a preexilic edition of the Deuteronomistic History.

These lists have their own complicated history, however, and they were not all composed at one time. Rather, different elements were added at various stages, such as the material concerning Caleb (14.6–15; 15.13–19; see also Judg 1.11–15, 20) and the daughters of Zelophehad (17.3–4; see Num 27.1–11).

The boundary descriptions and city lists are followed by two other ancient geographical lists, those of the "cities of asylum" (NRSV: "cities of refuge"; chap. 20) and the Levitical cities, that is, those assigned to the members of the tribe of Levi, who had no tribal territory of their own (chap. 21).

The establishment of the cities of asylum is an example of Joshua carrying out the commands that God had given to Moses (Num 35.9–15) and that Moses had given to Israel (Deut 19.1–13; see also Deut 4.41–43). Six cities are set apart as places to which someone who has killed another unintentionally may flee and be safe from vengeance on the part of the victim's family ("the avenger of blood," 20.3; see further pages 155–56) until the facts of the case have been adjudicated ("until there is a trial before the congregation," 20.6). Six cities of asylum are named, three on each side of the Jordan, roughly equidistant, making them relatively accessible throughout Israel (see Figure 12.2).

The list of the cities of asylum shows signs of later reworking, including the addition of some priestly elements (see page 198), and it is questionable if they ever functioned as places of refuge in ancient Israel. Rather than being an actual ancient record, the list is more likely an example of how the later editors of the book of Joshua used other scriptural traditions as a source. Their primary function is to show how Joshua consistently carried out the commands that God had given to Moses (see 20.2) and to provide an example of how life in the land was to be lived.

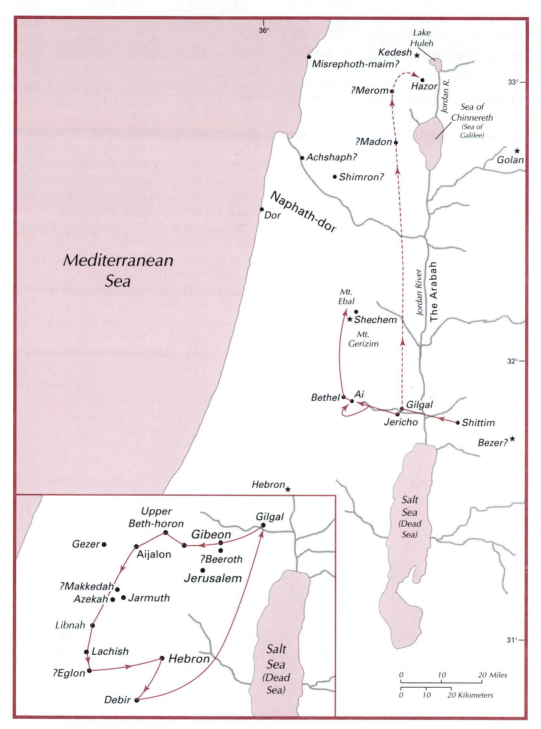

FIGURE 12.2. Map showing the principal sites mentioned in the account of the conquest of the land of Canaan in the book of Joshua. In the main map, the solid line locates the events in chapters 1–8, the dotted line those in chapter 11. The cities of asylum in chapter 20 are starred. The inset shows the events in chapters 9–10.

Chapter 21 is another list of those cities (and their surrounding territory) assigned to the members of the tribe of Levi, who had become dispossessed early in Israel's history in the land (see page 222). Like the cities of asylum, these Levitical cities may also have been an ideal rather than a reality, and the entire chapter also shows signs of priestly reworking. Once again, in establishing them, Joshua is carrying out a command of Moses (Num 35.1–8).

Priestly Material

The final edition of the book of Joshua also includes material that originated in priestly circles. This material was assigned by earlier scholars to the Pentateuchal source P, but most scholars today accept the hypothesis of the Deuteronomistic History discussed on pages 191–93, and so the priestly material must have a different origin, perhaps from the same "priestly" school that eventually produced the P edition of the Pentateuch, but earlier than P in its final form.

An example is an expansion found in chapter 20, which concerns the cities of asylum. In the traditional Hebrew version (the Masoretic Text) of that chapter (although not in other ancient textual traditions), the unintentional killer of another may remain in a city of asylum "until the death of one who is high priest at the time" (v. 6). This expansion brings Joshua 20 into harmony with the legislation concerning the cities of asylum in Numbers 35.25. Moreover, all six of the cities of asylum are also Levitical cities in Joshua 21.

Other examples of priestly reworking of the Deuteronomistic History in Joshua include elaboration of various rituals, frequent references to "the congregation," and the roles assigned to Eleazar in the distribution of the land (Josh 14.1; 17.4; 19.51; 21.1) and to Eleazar's son Phinehas in resolving the issue of the altar in Transjordan (22.13, 30–32).

Narrative Devices

Although the narrative progresses according to a chronological and geographical logic, it often has an artificial literary quality to it, derived in part from the Deuteronomistic Historians' interest in making connections between Moses and Joshua. Take, for example, the sequence of events in chapters 4–5: Joshua and the Israelites cross the Jordan, an event that is explicitly connected with the crossing of the Reed Sea in Exodus 14–15: "The LORD your God dried up the waters of the Jordan for you until you crossed over, as the LORD your God did to the Reed Sea" (Josh 4.23). Like the waters of the Reed Sea, the waters of the Jordan stand up "in a single heap" (Josh 3.13, 16; Ex 15.8; along with Ps 78.13, these are the only biblical occurrences of the rare word translated "heap") (see Figure 12.3). Having arrived in Canaan, the Israelites celebrate the Passover (5.10–12). Then Joshua has a vision of a divine messenger, in which he is instructed: "Remove the sandals from your feet, for the place where you stand is holy" (5.15). The sequence of crossing—Passover—divine appearance reverses the sequence of similar events in the book of Exodus, in which the theophany to Moses in the burning bush (in which he is instructed: "Remove the sandals from your feet, for the place on which you are standing is holy ground" [Ex 3.5]) is followed by the celebration of the first Passover (Ex 12) and the crossing of the Reed Sea (Ex 14).

Likewise, the Moses-Joshua connection lies behind the unexplained changes in the locales of the action. Without explicit account of their travel, the Israelites' base of operation in Canaan shifts from Gilgal (chaps. 4–17; see 4.19; 9.6; 10.7; 14.6), with a brief interlude at Shechem (8.30–35), to Shiloh (chaps. 18–23), and again to Shechem (chap. 24). The move to Shechem in 8.30–35 is motivated not by the logic of the narrative but by the desire to depict Joshua as carrying out the law of Moses in every respect. The many correspondences between Deuteronomy 27 and Joshua 8.30–35 are shown in Box 12.1.

As soon as it is strategically possible, then, Joshua goes to Shechem, where he constructs an altar and writes the law on stones, because for the Deuteronomistic Historians obedience to the commands of Deuteronomy is more important than a logically sequential narrative.

FIGURE 12.3.   A view of the Jordan River near Jericho. The Jordan can be as wide as 100 ft (30 m) and as deep as 11 ft (3.4 m) in the spring, the season when the Israelites are described as having crossed it. Modern diversion of the river and its sources has considerably reduced its flow.

The Characters

Joshua

Joshua is a minor figure in the Pentateuch, figuring in the narrative of the spies (Num 13–14) and in a few passages in which he is Moses' assistant and designated successor; these have been embellished to prepare for his role in the book of Joshua.

In the book of Joshua itself, Joshua is clearly the main character, yet he is one-dimensional. He is consistently presented as the ideal successor to Moses, although he lacks Moses' complexity. Rather, Joshua's career is patterned on that of his predecessor, to make the point that he embodies the essence of the Mosaic tradition: "As the LORD had commanded his servant Moses, so Moses

commanded Joshua, and so Joshua did; he left nothing undone of all that the LORD had commanded Moses" (Josh 11.15). Moses himself is mentioned more that fifty times in the book of Joshua, and his life serves as the model for the Deuteronomistic Historians' presentation of Joshua. Note these parallels, following the order of events in Joshua:

- Joshua sent spies to scout out the land near Jericho (Josh 2), just as Moses had sent spies from the wilderness to scout out the Promised Land (Num 13; Deut 1.19–25).

- Joshua led the Israelites out of the wilderness into the Promised Land through the waters of the Jordan River, which they crossed as if on dry ground because "the waters stood still . . .

Box 12.1 PARALLELS BETWEEN DEUTERONOMY 27 AND JOSHUA 8

On the day that you cross over the Jordan into the land that the LORD your God is giving you, you shall set up large stones and cover them with plaster. . . . You shall write on them all the words of this law when you have crossed over. . . . So when you have crossed over the Jordan, you shall set up these stones, about which I am commanding you today, on Mount Ebal, and you shall cover them with plaster. And you shall build an altar there to the LORD your God, an altar of stones on which you have not used an iron tool. You must build the altar of the LORD your God of unhewn stones. Then offer up burnt offerings on it to the LORD your God, make sacrifices of well-being, and eat them there, rejoicing before the LORD your God. You shall write on the stones all the words of this law very clearly. . . . When you have crossed over the Jordan, these shall stand on Mount Gerizim for the blessing of the people: Simeon, Levi, Judah, Issachar, Joseph, and Benjamin. And these shall stand on Mount Ebal for the curse: Reuben, Gad, Asher, Zebulun, Dan, and Naphtali. (Deut 27.2–8, 12–13; see also 11.29–30)

Then Joshua built on Mount Ebal an altar to the LORD, the God of Israel, just as Moses the servant of the LORD had commanded the Israelites, as it is written in the book of the law of Moses, "an altar of unhewn stones, on which no iron tool has been used"; and they offered on it burnt offerings to the LORD, and sacrificed offerings of well-being. And there, in the presence of the Israelites, Joshua wrote on the stones a copy of the law of Moses, which he had written. All Israel, alien as well as citizen, with their elders and officers and their judges, stood on opposite sides of the ark in front of the levitical priests who carried the ark of the covenant of the LORD, half of them in front of Mount Gerizim and half of them in front of Mount Ebal, as Moses the servant of the LORD had commanded at the first, that they should bless the people of Israel. And afterward he read all the words of the law, blessings and curses, according to all that is written in the book of the law. There was not a word of all that Moses commanded that Joshua did not read before all the assembly of Israel, and the women, and the little ones, and the aliens who resided among them. (Josh 8.30–35)

in a single heap" (Josh 3.16–17), just as Moses led the Israelites out of Egypt through the Reed Sea, which they crossed as if on dry ground because the water "stood up in a heap" (Ex 14.22; 15.8, 19).

- After crossing the Jordan the Israelites celebrated the Passover (Josh 5.10–12), just as they had done immediately before the Exodus (Ex 12).

- Joshua's vision of the "commander of Yahweh's army" (5.13–15) echoes the divine rev-

elation to Moses in the burning bush (Ex 3.1–6).

- When Yahweh was angry with the people for their failure to observe the "ban" fully (see pages 206–7), Joshua successfully interceded (Josh 7.7–10), just as Moses had repeatedly persuaded God not to punish the people (see Ex 32.11–14; Num 11.2; 14.13–19; Deut 9.12–29).

- Obeying divine instructions, Joshua extended his sword, and the Israelites defeated the inhabitants of Ai (Josh 8.18), just as they had defeated the Amalekites as long as Moses stretched out his hand that held the "staff of God" (Ex 17.8–13). In an earlier stage of the narrative in Joshua, the extended sword was a military signal for the troops to emerge from ambush; in the final account by the Deuteronomistic Historians, it becomes another parallel between Moses and Joshua.

- Joshua was the mediator of the renewed covenant between Yahweh and Israel at Shechem (Josh 8.30–35; 24), just as Moses was the mediator of the covenant at Mount Sinai/Horeb.

- Before their deaths, both Moses and Joshua delivered farewell addresses to the Israelites (the book of Deuteronomy and Joshua 23–24, respectively).

These parallels, and others like them, make it difficult to say much about the "historical Joshua." The notice about his grave locates it in the tribal territory of Ephraim (Josh 24.30), and the events described in the most detail, those at Gilgal, Jericho, Ai, and Gibeon, take place in a relatively small region just to the south of Ephraim (see Figure 12.2). It is probable, then, that Joshua was a local hero, like those in the book of Judges, who was magnified and idealized by the Deuteronomistic Historians as the prototype for the ideal ruler of Israel, under whom the nation is united in warfare and in exclusive worship of Yahweh at a central sanctuary and who fully obeys the requirements of the law of Moses.

Rahab

The only other individual who has any significant role in the narrative is Rahab, the prostitute of Jericho (see Figure 12.4). Her importance is immediately suggested by her being named, unlike many other women in the Bible, and also unlike the spies who visit her. For the Deuteronomistic Historians, she is clearly a model believer, even though she is a Canaanite. Echoing the earliest Israelite traditions, she affirms:

> I know that the LORD has given you the land, and that dread of you has fallen on us, and that all the

FIGURE 12.4.   The image of a woman looking out of a window occurs frequently in ancient Near Eastern art and literature. This example is a carved ivory from Nimrud in North Syria dating to the ninth century BCE. Compare the story of Rahab (Josh 2.15–21); see also Judges 5.28, 2 Samuel 6.16, 2 Kings 9.30, and Proverbs 7.6.

inhabitants of the land melt in fear before you. For we have heard how the LORD dried up the water of the Reed Sea before you when you came out of Egypt, and what you did to the two kings of the Amorites that were beyond the Jordan, to Sihon and Og, whom you utterly destroyed. As soon as we heard it, our hearts melted, and there was no courage left in any of us because of you. The LORD your God is indeed God in heaven above and on earth below. (Josh 2.9–11; compare Ex 14–15; Deut 3.6; 4.39)

Her faith in Yahweh leads her to side with the spies against her own people and to deceive the king of Jericho who wants to apprehend them. For the Deuteronomistic Historians, it also serves to legitimate the inclusion of her family into the community of Israel.

Rahab's role in the fall of Jericho may have been more than simply passive. The familiar story of the city's destruction, in which "the wall fell down flat" (Josh 6.20), is difficult to reconcile with the location of Rahab's house, which was built into the city wall (2.15). Moreover, Joshua 24.11 refers to a battle between the Israelites and the rulers of Jericho, unmentioned in Joshua 6. Two independent accounts of Jericho's fall probably exist, then, that in Joshua 6 and another, to which the Rahab story belongs. It is tempting to hypothesize that in the original form of her story Rahab may have acted as a kind of fifth column, opening the city gates to the invading Israelites.

Another aspect to the figure of Rahab is worth reflecting upon. Elsewhere in the Deuteronomistic History, especially in the cases of Samson (Judg 14–16), Solomon (1 Kings 11.1–8), and Ahab (1 Kings 16.31), and in the Bible generally, contact with foreign women is condemned because it could lead to apostasy. Proverbs 23.27–28 is typical:

> For a prostitute is a deep pit;
>   a foreign woman is a narrow well.
> She lies in wait like a robber
>   and increases the number of the faithless.

Yet in Rahab we have a foreign woman, and a prostitute, who is singled out in the story of Israel's conquest of the land as a true heroine. The Deuteronomistic Historians are capable of subtlety and even subversion.

Later writers remember this independent and resourceful woman positively as well. In some postbiblical Jewish traditions she becomes Joshua's wife. The gospel of Matthew lists her as one of the ancestors of Jesus (Mt 1.5), and other early Christian writings recall her extraordinary faith and actions (Heb 11.31; Jas 2.25; 1 Clement 12).

The Gibeonites

One other group of foreigners features in the narrative: the Gibeonites, who successfully deceive the Israelites, making them think that the Gibeonites are from "a very far country" (Josh 9.9). The Israelites make a covenant with them, which Joshua insists be kept, even when it is learned that they lived nearby. They are spared from death but are relegated to religious servitude, working as woodcutters and water carriers for the sanctuary.

The entire narrative (Josh 9) is an etiology, constructed to explain both the inclusion of another Canaanite group into Israel and also their inferior status. Like Rahab, the Gibeonite emissaries express their belief in the power of Yahweh. Moreover, they show a familiarity with Deuteronomic law, which commands the Israelites:

> When you draw near to a town to fight against it, offer it terms of peace. If it accepts your terms of peace and surrenders to you, then all the people in it shall serve you at forced labor. . . . Thus you shall treat all the towns that are very far from you, which are not towns of the nations here. But as for the towns of these peoples that the LORD your God is giving you as an inheritance, you must not let anything that breathes remain alive. You shall annihilate them. (Deut 20.10–11, 15–17)

The Gibeonites are portrayed as clever deceivers, but that is insufficient basis for annihilating them (that is, subjecting them to the "ban"; see pages 206–7). Because of the obligations of covenant, when the Gibeonites are attacked by a coalition of southern Canaanite kings (Josh 10.5), Joshua defeats the kings with divine assistance and proceeds to capture other cities farther south.

The Gibeonites' religious servitude should probably be connected with the listing of Gibeon as one of the Levitical cities (Josh 21.17), and especially with the location of a sanctuary at Gibeon, where Solomon offered sacrifices and received a dream revelation (1 Kings 3.4–5; see also 1 Chr 16.39; 21.29).

History and the Book of Joshua

For much of the history of its interpretation, the narrative of the conquest of the land of Canaan by Joshua and the Israelites was accepted as an accurate account of what had actually taken place. That view, however, was irrevocably altered by modern study of the book and its biblical context and by archaeological evidence.

The total conquest of the land and the exter-mination of the indigenous population are con-tradicted by the Bible itself. In the summary of the conquest, we are told that "Joshua took the whole land . . . and gave it for an inheritance to Israel" (Josh 11.23; compare 11.16–20). Yet shortly thereafter, Yahweh informs Joshua that "very much of the land still remains to be pos-sessed" (Josh 13.1), and the first chapter of the book of Judges describes in detail how several of the tribes failed to drive out the inhabitants of the land, who thus lived alongside the Israelites. Careful analysis of the biblical traditions them-selves, then, suggests that the account of the con-quest in Joshua 1–12 is not to be taken at face value. As we have seen, it is likely that Joshua was originally a local hero of the tribe of Ephraim, and as such was perhaps involved in local victo-ries over Canaanite opponents. But just as Joshua's role has been magnified by the Deuteron-omistic Historians, so too their account of the conquest of the land of Canaan as described in the book of Joshua is unlikely to be historically accurate. That conclusion is confirmed by ar-chaeological data.

Many earlier scholars were inclined to inter-pret the accounts of Joshua more literally and thought that they could relate them to the ar-chaeological record. Thus, ignoring the statement that Israel had burned none of the cities in Canaan except for Hazor (Josh 11.13), it was pro-posed that the extensive destruction layers at sites through Palestine were caused by the Israelite conquest, especially Jericho (Josh 6; see Figure 12.5), Lachish (10.31–32), and Hazor (11.10–13). But subsequent investigation of those sites and others mentioned in the narrative has made it clear that no easy correlation between the ar-chaeological record and the biblical text can be found. This is especially true of the principal lo-cales of the extended narratives of the book of Joshua in chapters 2–9. Gilgal has not been iden-tified, but the cities of Jericho, Ai, and Gibeon were uninhabited at the end of the thirteenth century BCE, which is when a majority of schol-ars would place the time of Joshua (see pages 98–99). Hazor and Lachish were destroyed at

FIGURE 12.5. An aerial view of Tell es-Sultan ("Old Tes-tament Jericho"), showing the disruption of the ancient ruins by erosion and by several archaeological expeditions since 1868. Excavators have found no evidence of occupation at the ten-acre site during the latter part of the Late Bronze Age, the prob-able context for the events narrated in the book of Joshua.

about that time, but probably almost a century apart.

Shechem is a special case (see Box 12.2). It was continuously occupied during the thirteenth and twelfth centuries BCE and suffered extensive de-struction only at the end of the twelfth century, which is probably to be associated with the events described in Judges 9 and in any case is too late for Joshua. Moreover, Shechem is not listed among the cities defeated by the Israelites in Joshua 12.9–24, nor do they ever attack it in the book. Yet Shechem is the locale of the covenant renewal in Joshua 24 (and 8.30–35). If the association of

Box 12.2 SHECHEM IN BIBLICAL TRADITION

The ongoing importance of Shechem (see Figure 12.6) in ancient Israel is evident in its recurrence in a variety of sources set in different periods. It is associated with Abraham (Gen 12.6–8 [J]) and Jacob (Gen 33.20 [E]), both of whom are said to have built altars there. Jacob is also reported to have bought land at Shechem (Gen 33.19 [E]), and this plot was the site of the burial of Joseph according to Joshua 24.32. In Genesis 34 [J], Shechem is the locale of the rape of Jacob's daughter Dinah and its aftermath.

Both its archaeological history and nonbiblical sources make it clear that Shechem was an important religious and political center during most of the second and first millennia BCE. Excavations at Shechem have uncovered a sanctuary that was in almost continuous use from the mid-seventeenth to the late twelfth centuries BCE, and it is tempting to identify some phase of it with the temple of El-berith, or Baal-berith ("El of the covenant," or "Baal of the covenant"; see Judg 8.33; 9.4, 46; the names are probably variant traditions).

Several biblical passages mention a large evergreen oak or terebinth as one of the dominant features of the city's sanctuary. This is "the diviners' oak" in Judges 9.37, a

FIGURE 12.6.   The ancient site of Shechem is strategically located in the pass between Mount Ebal (on the right) and Mount Gerizim (on the left). It was here, according to Joshua 8.30–35 and 24, that the covenant renewal ceremony took place.

term that probably is connected with the "oak of Moreh" (literally, "oak of the teacher") in Genesis 12.6, where it is said to be near the altar that Abraham built, and Deuteronomy 11.30. In Genesis 35.1–4, Jacob, still residing at Shechem, is about to return to Bethel to fulfill the vow he had made when fleeing from Esau. In preparation for that religious act, he instructs his family: "Put away the foreign gods that are among you," and "so they gave to Jacob all the foreign gods that they had, and the rings that were in their ears; and Jacob hid them under the oak that was near Shechem."

Also associated with the sanctuary at Shechem is a large standing stone. It is mentioned in Judges 9.6, in the phrase "the oak of the pillar." Its presence is implied in Genesis 33.20, in which the verb "erected" used there of an altar is elsewhere used typically of standing stones and never of altars.

As we have seen, Shechem suffered no destruction at the end of the Late Bronze Age. Various components of the complex entity that called itself Israel (see pages 223–24) may have had a long-standing association with the site, as a place where the Israelites worshiped alongside their Canaanite neighbors and where one of their ancestors was buried.

Because of Shechem's importance as a northern Israelite city, it is not surprising that it is so central in the book of Deuteronomy, which originated in northern Israel. But because its religious traditions were of questionable orthodoxy for the authors of that book, in it Shechem appears in somewhat disguised form, without being named. But its location is clear: near Mount Ebal and Mount Gerizim, the mountains of the curse and the blessing (Deut 11.29; 27.12–13).

A direct connection with earlier Shechem traditions is made in Joshua 24 by the almost verbatim repetition of the phrase "Put away the foreign gods that are in your midst" (v. 23), by the mention of "the oak in the sanctuary of the LORD" (v. 26), by the large stone which Joshua erects under the oak as a witness to the people's commitment to Yahweh (see also the stones in Josh 8.32), and by the mention of the burial of Joseph's mummified remains (v. 32); note also the construction of an altar in Joshua 8.30. The Deuteronomistic Historians, then, incorporated older elements of tradition—the altar, the oak, the deposition of "foreign gods," the standing stone(s)—and connected them with Joshua. But because of their desire to present Joshua as a model of obedience to the law of Moses, many earlier religious associations are in effect desacralized.

Shechem's continuing importance is evident in 1 Kings 12.1, in which Rehoboam, Solomon's successor as king of Judah, goes to Shechem to be accepted by the northern tribes as their king also. That mission ends in disaster with the secession of the northern tribes, and the first king of the northern kingdom of Israel, Jeroboam I, makes Shechem his first capital (1 Kings 12.25). In the Hellenistic period the Samaritans identified Mount Gerizim as the only legitimate place of worship (see Jn 4.20) and constructed a temple there (see Box 26.1 on page 450).

Joshua with Shechem has any historical basis, and is not merely an example of the Deuteronomistic Historians' showing Joshua carrying out the commands of Moses in Deuteronomy (see pages 198–200), then the Israelites were present at Shechem without having to capture it.

How then are we to understand the account of the conquest in the book of Joshua, if not historically? One way is to see the book itself as a kind of extended etiology, written several centuries after the events it describes in order to answer the question: How did Israel get control of the Promised Land? The answer is a simple one: Yahweh did it, with Joshua as the principal human leader. Their victories, moreover, explain a large number of prominent mounds of ruined cities, like Jericho, Ai, and Hazor. The account of the conquest, then, like other etiologies, is a kind of fiction, and its message is theological rather than historical: Yahweh gave Israel the land, and its continued possession requires obedience to the law of Moses, like that shown by Joshua and the Israelites in the book of Joshua.

Military activity was almost certainly part of the process by which Israel gained control of the land, and it is possible that some of the victories described in Joshua may have occurred—the destruction of Hazor is the one that is most frequently claimed. As we will see in the next chapter, however, the emergence of Israel in Canaan was slow and complicated, also involving the peaceful incorporation of some Canaanites into Israel, and complete control of the Promised Land was not achieved until the end of the eleventh century BCE.

Institutions

The Ban and Holy War

One of the most troubling elements of the book of Joshua is the extermination of indigenous populations—"men and women, young and old" (Josh 6.21)—by the invading Israelites at Yahweh's command. This wholesale slaughter is disturbing not only intrinsically but also because it has been used as a model in subsequent Jewish and Christian history. One example is provided by the English settlers of North America in the seventeenth and eighteenth centuries, who saw themselves as having escaped oppression, crossed a body of water, and arrived in a land that God had given them. In this "providence plantation," their treatment of Native Americans was justified by the practice of extermination found in the book of Joshua.

The Hebrew word translated "devoted to destruction" (Josh 6.17 [NRSV]) or "**ban**" is *herem*, which literally means something prohibited. (The word "harem," the place where women were segregated in traditional Muslim society, is from the same root.) Referring to the spoils of war, it means that which is set apart for Yahweh as exclusively his, and therefore prohibited for any other use. It applies to all spoils, including animals and human beings, as well as inanimate objects. As an institution, the "ban" was also practiced by Israel's neighbors, the Moabites.

According to the book of Deuteronomy, the ban is to be applied to all cities of the land of Canaan. Moses instructs the Israelites that when they defeat the inhabitants of the Promised Land, they "must utterly destroy them" (Deut 7.2; the verb used here is from the same root as *herem*), not letting "anything that breathes remain alive" (20.16). The motivation was to avoid the risk of apostasy, because for the Deuteronomists, Israel was always in danger of corrupting its worship of Yahweh with Canaanite practices. Preservation of Israel's religious and cultural identity was essential, which also explains the general biblical opposition to marriage with non-Israelites. In the frequent oversimplification of the biblical writers, we find the Israelites, whom Yahweh had chosen, and everyone else. As in the account of the killing of the Egyptian firstborn (Ex 12.29–30), no ethical nuances are seen: Non-Israelites were the enemy, and they fully deserved the punishments that were divinely imposed upon them. Thus, as in the accounts of the plagues in Exodus, Yahweh also "hardened the hearts" of the Canaanites "in order that they might be utterly destroyed" (Josh 11.20; see further Box 6.4 on page 91).

Modern scholars have proposed another explanation for the ban, which may also have been operative. The extermination of indigenous populations and their animals may have been a way to avoid contracting diseases carried by them, diseases for which the Israelites as outsiders may have had no acquired immunity. In any case, the ban seems to have been an ideal rarely if ever carried out. In the Deuteronomistic History outside the book of Joshua it figures only in the accounts of the Benjaminite war (Judg 21.11) and of the defeat of the Amalekites (1 Sam 15), where it was not observed.

The ban is one element within what has been called "holy war," a phrase not used in the Hebrew Bible (but see 4 Macc 17.11), although it does refer to the "wars [or "battles"] of Yahweh" (Num 21.14; 1 Sam 18.17; 25.28). Participation in holy war required sexual abstinence (see 1 Sam 21.5; 2 Sam 11.11) and other forms of ritual purity (see Deut 23.9–14). The war was "holy" because Yahweh himself was present, invisibly enthroned on the ark, whose original function may have been some sort of battle palladium (see below), and he fought for Israel.

The Ark and Ritual Procession

Because the book of Joshua was composed late in the monarchy, many of its details concerning institutions and rituals are likely to reflect practices of the time of its composition rather than of earlier Israel. Several aspects of worship, however, seem to reflect traditions from the premonarchic or early monarchic periods.

The ark of the covenant (see pages 126–28) is prominent in the narratives of the crossing of the Jordan in chapters 3–4 and of the capture of Jericho in chapter 6. In both episodes it is the central element in a ritual procession, which is all the more remarkable because this does not reflect practices found in the book of Deuteronomy. Moreover, once the ark was brought to Jerusalem by David in the tenth century, it is seldom mentioned in the descriptions of worship in the Temple in Jerusalem (see page 278). The detailed accounts of the rituals in which the ark is central, then, although like the rest of the book of Joshua heavily edited by the Deuteronomistic Historians, probably preserve aspects of early Israelite ritual procession in which the ark was involved.

The primary setting for these rituals would have been military. This is most clear in the account of the capture of Jericho, in which seven priests blowing on seven horns precede the ark and the army in a procession around the enemy city. They march around it once a day for six days, and then seven times on the seventh day (sab-

bath observance seems not to have been an issue). That this was one of the principal contexts in which the ark was used is confirmed by its appearance in other battle narratives (see 1 Sam 4; 2 Sam 11.11; also Num 14.44–45).

The association of the ark with battle informs the interpretation of the account of the crossing of the Jordan in Joshua 3–4. Again there is a procession, led by the priests carrying the ark, but there are also military overtones. Although in the highly stylized narrative of the Deuteronomistic Historians we find none of the personification of the Divine Warrior found in the related Exodus account or in Psalm 114, the ark is the visible symbol of the presence of Yahweh, who leads the way across the Jordan into the Promised Land and who guarantees victory:

> By this you shall know that among you is the living God who without fail will drive out from before you the Canaanites, Hittites, Hivites, Perizzites, Girgashites, Amorites, and Jebusites: the ark of the covenant of the LORD of all the earth is going to pass before you into the Jordan. (Josh 3.10–11; compare Deut 9.3)

The Sanctuary at Gilgal

Another example of the presence of earlier religious traditions in the book of Joshua concerns the sanctuary at Gilgal. The Deuteronomistic Historians preserve the memory of an installation of sacred stones there (Josh 4), the celebration of the Passover (5.10–12) and probably the ritual of circumcision (5.2–9; see Box 12.3). These references in Joshua, like those in Judges (3.19) and 1 Samuel (7.16; 10.8; etc.), are entirely positive; only in the eighth-century BCE prophets is the worship at Gilgal described negatively (Hos 4.15; 9.15; 12.11; Am 4.4; 5.5; contrast Mic 6.5). Gilgal was therefore an important place of worship and assembly during the premonarchic period, and clearly some of the most important festivals of the tribal confederation took place there, but it is impossible to reconstruct those rituals with any certainty.

An important feature of the sanctuary at Gilgal was the twelve stones that had been erected

Box 12.3 CIRCUMCISION A SECOND TIME?

In Joshua 5.2, the LORD instructs Joshua to "make flint knives and circumcise the Israelites a second time." The use of flint (a kind of quartz) for the procedure, as in Exodus 4.25, instead of bronze or iron, shows the antiquity of the ritual of circumcision (see further Box 5.3 on page 70). But we also see several oddities in this passage.

The first is the phrase "a second time," an anatomical impossibility. That phrase is a gloss, a secondary interpretive addition, found in the traditional Masoretic Hebrew text but not in other ancient textual sources. It was probably introduced to rationalize the failure of the generation that had been born in the wilderness to practice circumcision. According to Genesis 17.9–14, all males descended from Abraham were to be circumcised eight days after their birth, but that reflected a relatively late change in the time of circumcision from puberty to infancy. The original text of Joshua then, like Exodus 4.24–26 (see page 90), preserves earlier custom, in which circumcision was neither universal for all Israelites nor necessarily performed on babies.

A second curious aspect of the passage is the etiology given for the name of a nearby hill, "the hill of foreskins" (5.3). For the Deuteronomistic Historians, so many Israelite males were circumcised that their heaped up foreskins resulted in a permanent, if bizarre, addition to the landscape. The final redactor also connects the ceremony with the name of Gilgal itself, by a somewhat convoluted word association (5.9).

Finally, the ancient Greek translation of the Hebrew Bible includes yet another note concerning the circumcision. In a late addition after Joshua 24.30, the Greek text records that into Joshua's tomb were put the flint knives that had been used in the circumcision ritual at Gilgal. Clearly the entire episode continued to puzzle and fascinate ancient scribes.

there (see Figure 12.7). Its very name is probably derived from the "circle" (Hebr. *gilgal*) formed by the stones. Like so many other features of early Israelite tradition in the book of Joshua, the installation of the stones is attributed to Joshua himself. But they were only a memory by the time of the final edition of the book of Joshua, when they, and the sanctuary in which they were a prominent feature, had fallen into oblivion. To reconcile the earlier tradition with the fact that the stones were no longer visible, the final editor placed the stones not at Gilgal itself, but in the bed of the Jordan (Josh 4.9), where, of course, they cannot be seen.

RETROSPECT AND PROSPECT

Coming in the Deuteronomistic History as it does immediately after the programmatic book of Deuteronomy, the book of Joshua presents a model of how ancient Israel was to live and be governed. Its constitution, as it were, was the teaching of Moses as found in Deuteronomy. Israel was to be a nation governed by one divinely chosen leader, under whose direction the nation would worship Yahweh, and Yahweh alone, and would live its life in strict accordance with the requirements of the laws taught by Moses.

FIGURE 12.7.   An example of a monument of standing stones at Gezer, from the Middle Bronze Age (ca. 1650 BCE); compare Joshua 4.

This message is presented in an artificial narrative, in which disparate ancient sources have been shaped into a kind of theological fiction. The paradigm presented by Joshua is one that will serve the Deuteronomistic Historians in their presentation of the history that follows, a history that details how, for the most part, Israel fell short of that paradigm. A principal exception is King Josiah, whose adherence to the law of Moses has contributed to the portrait of Joshua in the book that bears his name.

In the next book, the book of Judges, the Deuteronomistic Historians present a remarkable contrast, showing how Israel in the premonarchic period repeatedly failed to live up to the model set by the book of Joshua.

IMPORTANT TERMS

ban

Deuteronomistic History

Former Prophets

Latter Prophets

QUESTIONS FOR REVIEW

1. How is the book of Deuteronomy related to the books that precede and follow it?

2. Define the Deuteronomistic History, and describe its principal themes.

3. What are the functions of the etiologies and the geographical lists in the book of Joshua?

4. In the book of Joshua, how is Joshua presented as the successor of Moses?

5. How is the account of the fall of Jericho in Joshua 6 inconsistent with other details in the book and with the archaeological evidence?

6. What is the significance of Shechem in biblical traditions?

7. How is the book of Joshua's account of the conquest of the land of Canaan to be interpreted?

BIBLIOGRAPHY

On the Deuteronomistic History, see the essays collected in Gary N. Knoppers and J. Gordon McConville, eds., *Reconsidering Israel and Judah: Recent Studies on the Deuteronomistic History* (Winona Lake, IN: Eisenbrauns, 2000).

An excellent commentary on the book of Joshua is Richard D. Nelson, *Joshua: A Commentary* (Louisville, KY: Westminster John Knox, 1997); see also Michael David Coogan, "Joshua," pp. 110–31 in *The New Jerome Biblical Commentary* (ed. R. E. Brown et al.; Englewood Cliffs, NJ: Prentice Hall, 1990).

For a discussion of the problem of the historicity of the book of Joshua, see B. S. J. Isserlin, *The Israelites* (Minneapolis: Fortress, 2001), pp. 53–64; and Michael D. Coogan, "Archaeology and Biblical Studies: The Book of Joshua," pp. 19–32 in *The Hebrew Bible and Its Interpreters* (ed. W. H. Propp et al.; Winona Lake, IN: Eisenbrauns, 1990).

THE EMERGENCE OF ISRAEL IN THE LAND OF CANAAN

CHAPTER 13

Judges and Ruth

The book of Judges continues the Deuteronomistic Historians' complex narrative of Israel's history in the Promised Land of Canaan. In the book of Joshua, they presented the ideal: Israel united in worship of Yahweh alone, and united under the leadership of a divinely designated successor to Moses in fighting against their enemies. Immediately following this programmatic presentation, however, the book of Judges gives a sobering and even appalling presentation of the reality, relating how the Israelites repeatedly failed to live up to the ideal by worshiping other gods, by refusing to come to each others' assistance, and even by intertribal warfare. At the same time it provides valuable data for reconstructing the processes by which Israel gradually established its own identity and extended its territorial control. In this chapter we will also examine the book of Ruth, a short fictional narrative set in the time of the Judges.

THE BOOK OF JUDGES

The book of Judges begins with a summary of the successes and, mostly, failures of individual tribes to extend their control over Canaan (chap. 1)

and reports the death of Joshua (Judg 2.8–9 is repeated from Josh 24.29–30). Then follow narratives of the judges themselves (chaps. 3–16). The book concludes with two narratives of the Israelites' failures to observe the religious and social obligations of their covenant with Yahweh (chaps. 17–18 and 19–21).

Jewish tradition identifies Samuel as the author of the book of Judges, but that attribution reflects the ancient tendency to attribute anonymous works to well-known figures. Modern scholars consider the book to be the work of the Deuteronomistic Historians (see pages 191–93). As such, it continues the narrative of Israel's history in the Promised Land of Canaan. The framework provided by the Deuteronomistic Historians for the premonarchic period of the judges is one of repeated apostasy—"the Israelites did what was evil in the eyes of the LORD and worshiped the Baals" (Judg 2.11), followed by inevitable divine punishment, which leads to repentance and finally deliverance. The deliverance is provided by divinely inspired "judges," originally local heroes whose stories have been set into this framework.

In addition to their focus on the consequences of worshiping other gods, another interest of the

Deuteronomistic Historians in the book of Judges is kingship. In the earlier part of the book, kingship is experimented with and divinely rejected (chap. 9), and four times in the book, including its final verse, we are told: "In those days there was no king in Israel; every man did what was right in his own eyes" (17.6; 18.1; 19.1; 21.25). That refrain is ambiguous. "There was no king in Israel" on one level reflects the strong antimonarchic tendency that is repeatedly found in the Deuteronomistic History. Yahweh was Israel's king, as the legal metaphor of covenant implied. In the book of Judges the first attempt to establish human kingship is rejected—"I will not rule over you, and my son will not rule over you; the LORD will rule over you" (8.23)—and the second, the short reign of Abimelech (chap. 9), ends in disaster.

Yet on another level the refrain implies the absence of the centralized control that a monarchy could provide, resulting in constant threats from neighboring entities and internal disunity. Moreover, what "every man" did was often not right "in the eyes of Yahweh" (2.11; 3.7, 12; 4.1; 6.1; 10.6; 13.1). Especially at the end of the book of Judges, in the narrative of the rape of the Levite's concubine and its aftermath (chaps. 19–21), the Deuteronomistic Historians present an alarming picture of Israel in the premonarchic period, a picture of anarchy, civil war, and chaos. Combined with the threat of the Philistines that is evident in the cycle of stories concerning Samson (chaps. 13–16), this conclusion sets the stage for the transformation of Israel's system of government that will be the topic of the books of Samuel that follow.

Sources

The Deuteronomistic Historians incorporated a variety of previously existing sources into their narrative of life in early Israel:

- Folk legends of originally local heroes (the "judges"; see pages 214–15)
- Etiologies of place names, including Hormah (Judg 1.17), Bochim (2.5), Ramath-lehi (15.17), En-hakkore (15.19), and Mahaneh-dan (18.12), and of religious institutions and practices, such as Gideon's altar (6.24), the annual lament for

Jephthah's daughter (11.39–40), and the priesthood at Dan (18.30–31)

- Early poetry, including both short riddles in verse in the Samson cycle (14.14, 18; 15.16) and a lengthy victory hymn, the "Song of Deborah" (chap. 5), generally acknowledged to be one of the oldest parts of the Bible, dating not long after the victory it celebrates.

The Narrative

The book of Judges opens with a double introduction or prologue. The first (1.1–2.5) is a summary of the vicissitudes of several tribes, beginning with Judah. Most of them, we are told, were unable to defeat the Canaanites who lived in the land, and so they coexisted with them. That summary focuses on individual tribes, moving from south to north. This is followed by a second introductory section (2.6–3.6), which reports the death of Joshua and provides a kind of overture to the stories of the judges that follow:

> Then the Israelites did what was evil in the eyes of the LORD and worshiped the Baals. . . . So the anger of the LORD was kindled against Israel, and he gave them over to plunderers who plundered them, and he sold them into the power of their enemies all around. . . . Then the LORD raised up judges, who delivered them out of the power of those who plundered them. . . . But whenever the judge died, they would relapse and behave worse than their ancestors, following other gods, worshiping them and bowing down to them. . . . So the anger of the LORD was kindled against Israel. (Judg 2.11–20)

Chapters 3.7–16.31 are the stories of the judges themselves, and they are presented sequentially, as if one judge followed another. If this were the case, the period of the judges would span more than four centuries, rather than the roughly two centuries between the Exodus in the mid-thirteenth century BCE and the rule of Saul, Israel's first king, which began about 1025. The accuracy of the apparently sequential chronology is also undercut by the formulaic character of many of the judges' terms of office: We are told that after Othniel's defeat of Aram, the land had rest for forty years; likewise, after Ehud eighty years, after Deborah forty years, and after Gideon forty years. Samson is said to have judged Israel for twenty years and Eli for forty (1 Sam 4.18). These numbers are conventional rather than precise. (See further Box 8.3 on page 131.)

Moreover, although in the framework of the Deuteronomistic Historians the hostility of neighboring entities is directed against all Israel, the judges seem to have been primarily local leaders, and their victories are regional rather than national. Except for Jair (Judg 10.3) and Jephthah (11.1), both of whom are from Gilead, no two judges are from the same tribe or region. Overlapping periods of "judging" and of the peace that followed the defeat of an enemy are consistent with this interpretation. Like the summary in chapter 1, the narratives have been organized in part according to a geographical pattern from south to north (see Figure 13.1). The first judge,

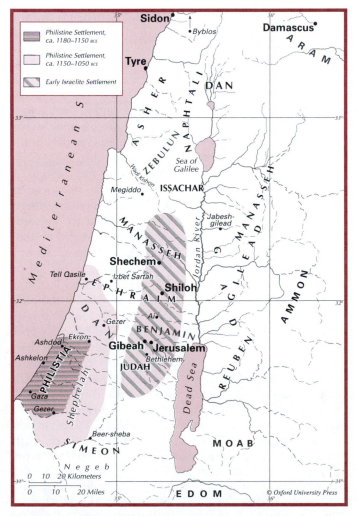

FIGURE 13.1.   Map of tribal divisions during the period of the judges, showing principal areas of Philistine and Israelite control.

Othniel, is from Judah, and then, with some omissions, we have Ehud from Benjamin, Deborah from Ephraim, Gideon from Manasseh, Tola from Issachar, and Jair and Jephthah from Gilead in Transjordan. It is also probably significant that twelve judges in all are named in the book, another indication that the narrative is artificially constructed.

Scholars have traditionally divided the judges into two groups, the "major" judges, those about whom there are more or less extended narratives (Othniel, Ehud, Shamgar, Deborah, Gideon, Jephthah, and Samson), and the "minor" judges, who are given merely perfunctory notice. The careers of the five "minor" judges, Tola and Jair (10.1–5), and Ibzan, Elon, and Abdon (12.8–15), are sketched only briefly, but in contrast to the terms of the six "major" judges, they each "judged Israel" for a precise number of years—twenty-three, twenty-two, seven, ten, and eight, respectively. The only "major" judge who has a similarly precise term of office is Jephthah, who "judged Israel for six years" (12.7). In all of these cases the numbers can reasonably be assumed to be accurate, unlike the formulaic numbers discussed on pages 212–13.

Balancing the double introduction is a two-part concluding narrative following the stories of the judges, the first concerning the shrine of Micah and the migration of the tribe of Dan (chaps. 17–18) and the second relating the rape of the Levite's concubine and its tragic sequel (chaps. 19–21).

The Characters

The Office of Judge

In premonarchic Israel, when "there was no king in Israel," the highest authority at the tribal level was the **judge**. The term "judge" in the Bible has a different meaning from our society, where it refers to those who preside in courts of law. While some of the biblical judges did exercise judicial functions, presumably as interpreters of covenantal law, such as Deborah (Judg 4.5; compare also Samuel in 1 Sam 7.15–17, and Samuel's sons in 1 Sam 8.1–3), most of them acted principally as

military leaders. Although for the Deuteronomistic Historians they are leaders of Israel in its entirety, it is more likely that they were local or tribal leaders who emerged in specific crises. As we have seen, Joshua himself may originally have been such a local leader (see 1 Macc 2.55), whose role was subsequently magnified by the Deuteronomistic Historians into that of Moses' successor and a national hero.

The title "judge" is well attested throughout the ancient Semitic world, from the second millennium BCE onward. It is used of human rulers at Mari in northern Mesopotamia and in Phoenicia, as well as in the Phoenician colony in North Africa at Carthage and of the Moabites (Am 2.3); all of these officials, in widely separated geographical and historical contexts, were administrators whose functions included judicial activity, but which were considerably broader, and some of them were kings. The title "judge" is also applied to deities, including the Canaanite gods Baal and Sea (Yamm), as well as to Yahweh (see, for example, Gen 18.25; Judg 11.27; Isa 33.22). The early twentieth-century sociologist Max Weber dubbed the judges "charismatic leaders," meaning those who arose in times of emergency and were selected because of their ability rather than their lineage or status. This selection is sometimes expressed by the phrase the "spirit of Yahweh came upon" them (Judg 3.10 [Othniel]; 6.34 [Gideon]; 11.29 [Jephthah]; and 13.25, 14.6, 19, and 15.4 [Samson]); the same phrase is used to describe Israel's first kings (1 Sam 10.6; 11.6 [Saul]; and 16.13 [David]). In some cases, the same individuals and deities who are called "judges" are also called "saviors" or "deliverers," that is, those who engaged in successful military activity.

Several individuals in the book of Judges belong to the category of the "trickster," a stock character known in myths and folktales around the world. Tricksters are heroes who by their wits reverse a bad situation to their advantage. They are often outsiders, too, who work for the good of the larger society to whose fringes they have been relegated. Examples from other cultures include Odysseus in the Homeric epics, Loki in Norse mythology, and Coyote in Navajo tradition.

The depiction of the judges is not always one of unqualified approval. Some, like Ehud, and Jael, are presented simply as one-dimensional heroic characters (like Joshua in the book of Joshua, although he is not a trickster). But others, like Gideon and Samson, are more complex, having both good and bad qualities. All succeed, however, by using their wits to defeat an apparently stronger adversary.

Ehud

The first of the "major" judges whose story is told in any detail is Ehud. He was from the tribe of Benjamin, whose name literally means "son of the right hand," but he was left-handed. This trait enables him to trick the Moabite king Eglon into thinking that he is unarmed and to assassinate him as he is presenting the imposed tribute.

The brief narrative includes a fair bit of crude humor, involving Eglon's obesity and his bathroom habits and the stupidity of his courtiers—all contrasted with the clever hero Ehud, who manages to trick his adversaries and then to rally the Israelites so that they defeat the Moabites (see Box 13.1).

Box 13.1 THE MOABITES AND THE AMMONITES

Just east of the Jordan River and the Dead Sea lay the kingdoms of Ammon and Moab, parts of whose territory were assigned to the tribes of Gad and Reuben. Both the **Moabites** and the **Ammonites** are sporadically mentioned in the Bible and in nonbiblical texts from the first half of the first millennium BCE. According to the genealogy at the end of the book of Ruth (4.17; see pages 226–27), King David had a Moabite ancestor.

The Moabite and Ammonite languages are known from a few inscriptions, most notably the stele erected by the Moabite king Mesha (see 2 Kings 3.4 and Figure 17.4) in the mid-ninth century BCE. Both languages are very closely related to each other and to Hebrew. We also know from the Mesha stele that the Moabites shared with the Israelites such institutions as the "ban" (see pages 206–7), and the view that the vicissitudes of their history were a result of the favor or displeasure of their national god (who for the Moabites was Chemosh). Biblical tradition recognizes these cultural connections by making both the Ammonites and the Moabites descendants of Abraham's nephew Lot (Gen 19.36–38).

The relationships between Moab and Israel and Ammon and Israel were often hostile, but given the limited evidence available, these relationships are difficult to reconstruct in detail. According to the books of Samuel, both Saul (1 Sam 11.1–11) and David (2 Sam 12.26–31) defeated the Ammonites, and David captured their capital, Rabbah, located within the modern city of Amman, the capital of Jordan, which preserves the ancient name of Ammon.

It is unclear whether the stories of Ehud's defeat of the Moabites (Judg 3.12–30) and Jephthah's defeat of the Ammonites (11.1–33) have any historical basis. It is likely, however, that the emerging nation-states on both sides of the Jordan were frequently in conflict, and the narratives in Judges may reflect that situation.

Deborah and Jael

Only three women in the extended narratives in the book of Judges are named, Deborah, Jael, and Delilah, and two of them occur in the account of Deborah's judgeship. The first is Deborah herself. We find two accounts of her activities: a prose account from the Deuteronomistic Historians in chapter 4 and an ancient poem in chapter 5, the "Song of Deborah" (see Box 13.2).

Deborah is described as exercising both judicial (Judg 4.4–5) and military (4.10; 5.12, 15) functions, and she is also called a prophet (4.4).

Box 13.2 THE SONG OF DEBORAH

The Song of Deborah (Judg 5.2–31) is a stirring account of a victory of some of the northern tribes over the Canaanites, and it has long been recognized as one of the oldest parts of the Bible. Because of its grammar and content, it probably dates to the twelfth century BCE, roughly contemporary with the events that it describes. This early date accounts for the Song's many obscurities, but despite them it is an important witness to early Israel's beliefs and organization.

The song is a victory hymn, incorporating some elements found in other early biblical poetry, but combining them with specific details of an actual event. Traditional elements include the invocation of Yahweh, the One of Sinai, whose march from southern Transjordan caused convulsions in nature (vv. 4–5; compare Deut 33.2; Ps 68.7–8; Hab 3.3–7), and the catalogue of the tribes (vv. 14–18; compare Gen 49; Deut 33.6–25). To these is added information about the period in which the events occurred, a time when travel was dangerous and life for the agricultural villages that constituted Israel was precarious. It was also a time when apostasy occurred: "When new gods were chosen, then war was in the gates" (v. 8). This line in the ancient poem is a precursor of the later view of the Deuteronomistic Historians that worship of gods other than Yahweh resulted in disaster.

With a somewhat disjointed structure, the song celebrates a victory of some of the tribes of Israel over Canaanite adversaries. That victory is attributed first of all to Yahweh himself and his heavenly army—the "stars" of verse 20—and to human agents—Barak and two women: Deborah herself, and Jael, who killed the fleeing Canaanite general Sisera.

The center of the poem, verses 14–18, is an account of how six of the northern tribes (the southern tribes Judah and Simeon are not mentioned) responded positively to the call to arms, but four did not. Both the names of the tribes and the order in which they are given differ somewhat from other tribal catalogues (notably Gen 49 and Deut 33); note especially the substitution of Machir for Manasseh.

The poem ends with a poignant image of another woman, Sisera's mother, looking out from the city for her son's return in victory, like Hecuba on the walls of Troy waiting for Hector (see also Figure 12.4).

Although some of the other judges are social outsiders, such as Gideon, who is the youngest of his family, and Jephthah, who is the illegitimate son of a prostitute, Deborah's status as a woman does not seem to have been remarkable for the biblical writers. Rather, her roles as judge and prophet are presented matter-of-factly, without attention being given to her gender. Still, Deborah's position as judge stands in contrast to the other women in the book of Judges, who are frequently unnamed and generally dependent upon fathers and husbands, sometimes, as with Jephthah's daughter (11.34–40) and the Levite's concubine (19.24–26), tragically so.

The second named woman in this account is Jael. She too is an outsider, a member of the Kenite clan. The Kenites were a group of metalsmiths, apparently itinerant—Jael lives in a tent. According to some traditions, they had close connections with the Israelites; see 1 Samuel 15.6, and note that Moses' wife is identified as a Kenite in Judges 1.16; 4.11, although elsewhere she is a Midianite or Cushite (see page 108). As is the case with Deborah, in the earliest form of the tradition (Judg 5) Jael's role in the Israelite victory is stated simply, without her status as a woman being noted as unusual; she is simply a hero, paired in verse 6 with one of the judges, Shamgar (Judg 3.31). She entices the fleeing Canaanite general Sisera into her tent, offers him a refreshing drink, and when he collapses "between her feet," kills him by hammering a tent peg through his temple. There is a suggestion of seduction here, for the term "feet" is often a euphemism in the Bible for genitalia.

For the Deuteronomistic Historians, who recast the ancient poem in prose, that Jael is a woman is a further sign that Yahweh ultimately is responsible for the victory: The mighty Canaanite general Sisera will be "sold" by the Lord "into the hand of a woman" (Judg 4.9)—the ultimate degradation.

Gideon and Abimelech

One of the longer narratives in the accounts of the major judges is of Gideon and his family in chapters 6–9. It begins with a notice of raids deep into Israelite territory by the camel-riding Midianites and their allies, both from the east and the south; Israel's earlier link with the Midianites (see pages 169–70) has turned into overt hostility. For the Deuteronomistic Historians, this is a central episode in the premonarchic period, as is indicated by the appearance of a prophet in Judges 6.7–10, who condemns the Israelites for their worship of the "gods of the Amorites" in violation of the covenant made at Shechem (Josh 24.14–15). Gideon's given name was apparently Jerubbaal, which literally means "Let Baal contend" and reflects his father's devotion to that Canaanite deity (6.25); the name is reinterpreted to mean "one who contends with Baal" (6.32). The name "Gideon," meaning "hacker," is apparently a nickname, based on his military prowess, also reinterpreted as "the one who cuts down forbidden ritual objects."

The prophet's oracle is followed immediately by the appearance of a divine messenger (compare Josh 5.13–15), who announces to a reluctant Gideon that through him the Lord will deliver Israel. The divine role will be evident because Gideon is a nobody, an insignificant member of an insignificant clan in Manasseh. As a further sign of divine assurance, fire miraculously consumes the meal, or sacrifice, that Gideon offers the messenger (compare 1 Kings 18.38). As the narrative proceeds, the divine presence continues to be demonstrated by signs, like those given to a similarly reluctant Moses in his initial theophany (Ex 4.1–17). Gideon thus is placed implicitly in the line of Moses and Joshua, as a divinely chosen leader who achieves victories with divine assistance, and he acknowledges the divine rule over Israel by refusing to become a king and the founder of a dynasty (8.22–23).

With cunning strategy Gideon defeats the Midianites, and then ruthlessly punishes those Israelites in Transjordan who had refused him aid. After this, however, Gideon and his family cease being model leaders. Gideon himself manufactures an idol from the Midianite earrings taken as booty, recalling both the episode of the golden calf (Ex 32.2–4) and Achan's appropriation of booty in holy war (Josh 7). Then, when Gideon dies, his son Abimelech kills his many brothers and has himself crowned king at the old sanctuary at Shechem (see Box 12.2 on pages 204–5). This brief experiment with kingship ends in disaster, with Abimelech killed and the tower of Shechem destroyed by fire; all this is caused by an "evil spirit" from Yahweh (9.23)—a dramatic contrast to the "spirit of Yahweh" that had "clothed" Gideon himself (6.34) and inspired other judges, and an anticipation of the divine rejection of Saul (1 Sam 16.14; 18.10; 19.9).

From the perspective of the Deuteronomistic Historians, this episode has a multiple moral: Yahweh alone must be worshiped, he alone is Israel's king who fights on its behalf, and if a human ruler is to be chosen, it is by divine rather than human initiative. Thus, although like the heroes with whom he implicitly is compared Gideon is a shrewd and successful military leader, in the end he is no model.

Jephthah and His Daughter

One of the most poignant tales in the book of Judges is that of Jephthah and his vow (11.1–12.7). Jephthah is another outsider, the illegitimate son of a Gileadite with a prostitute. Expelled from his family, he becomes a successful bandit, so successful, in fact, that when the Ammonites (see Box 13.1) threaten Gilead, as they will repeatedly (see 1 Sam 11.1–4; Am 1.13; Jer 49.1), the Gileadites turn to Jephthah for help, and make him their head. In an initial negotiation, Jephthah details the history of the relationship between Israel and Ammon, summarizing the narrative of the wanderings before Israel entered Canaan, but that fails to allay the Ammonite king's hostility.

A perfunctory account follows Jephthah's defeat of the Ammonites. The narrator is much more interested in Jephthah's rash vow and its consequences. Before the battle, he had promised that if he were successful, he would sacrifice to Yahweh "whoever [or "whatever"—the Hebrew is not specific] comes out of the doors of my house to meet me" (Judg 11.31). When he did return victorious, his daughter came to meet him in the traditional women's victory dance (see Ex

15.20–21; 1 Sam 18.6–7; compare Judg 5.1, 12, and see also page 96).

Although like many other female characters in the Bible Jephthah's daughter is unnamed, the story now becomes hers. She agrees with her regretful father that he must keep his vow, but asks for a respite to lament her unfulfilled life as wife and mother—her "virginity"—with her "companions" (11.37). It is difficult not to impose modern sensibilities on an ancient narrative, not to be horrified by the piety that requires the death of a young woman. Jephthah himself is dismayed at what he must do, as in Greek tradition are, in close parallels, Idomeneus, when after a similar vow he must sacrifice his son, who is the first creature to greet him when he returns from the Trojan War, and Agamemnon, when he sacrifices his and Clytemnestra's daughter Iphigenia. In later retellings of the Greek tales, both Idomeneus and Iphigenia miraculously escape death at their father's hand, but there is no escape for Jephthah's daughter. Were biblical writers and audiences similarly horrified? Perhaps—according to the etiological conclusion of the narrative, her fate was remembered in an otherwise unknown ritual: "For four days every year the daughters of Israel would go out to lament the daughter of Jephthah the Gileadite" (Judg 11.40).

Samson and His Women

The last of the judges is Samson, but he is not a typical judge. He is divinely chosen before his birth, rather than as a divine response to Israelite pleas for help in an immediate crisis. In the pattern of Sarah (Gen 11.30; 16.1), Rebekah (Gen 25.21), Rachel (Gen 29.31), and Hannah (1 Sam 1.2), Samson's mother, who is not named, is unable to have children, but a divine messenger announces to her (and not to her husband, Manoah) that she will conceive (compare Gen 18.1–15; 1 Sam 1.17) and that her son "will begin to deliver Israel from the hand of the Philistines." Moreover, he is to be a "nazirite," bound by vow not to cut his hair (Judg 13.3–5; see Num 6.5). These traditional elements form a kind of editorial prologue to the folktales that follow, in which Samson repeatedly will wreak havoc on the

Philistines, but will be undone by his hair being cut. The note that Samson will begin to deliver Israel from the Philistines anticipates that the conflict between the Israelites and the Philistines will be a long one and prepares for the encounters between them described in 1 and 2 Samuel (see Figure 13.2 and Box 13.3).

Unlike the other judges, who fight Israel's enemies for the sake of the Israelites, Samson's various encounters with the Philistines are personal. He fights alone and never leads the Israelites in battle. For most of the Samson cycle (chaps. 13–16), those solitary encounters have a comic quality. Samson is a preternaturally strong man, like Heracles or Paul Bunyan, and, like them, his strength is more impressive than his common sense, especially in his dealings with women. Yet at the same time he has a kind of naïve shrewdness, which enables him to take advantage of the Philistines repeatedly both by acts of violence and by outwitting them with riddles.

FIGURE 13.2. Captive Philistine warriors, on a relief of Pharaoh Rameses III (1184–1153 BCE).

He is so strong that he can kill a lion with his bare hands and can take three hundred foxes, tie them together in pairs by their tails, put torches between the tails, and release the foxes so that the Philistines' grain fields are set ablaze. He can kill thirty men in an outburst of violence—or even a thousand. Having spent several hours with a prostitute in Gaza, he is able to wrench the city's gate from its foundations and carry it some forty miles and from sea level to over three thousand feet (one thousand meters) above sea level to Hebron. And, at the end of his life, he is able to cause the roof the temple of Dagon to collapse by pushing down its supporting pillars.

In editing these folktales, the Deuteronomistic Historians are careful to explain that Samson is endowed with "the spirit of the LORD" (Judg 13.25; 14.6, 19; 15.14)—he is not just a lusty, amoral giant, but a divinely chosen hero, like the other judges, more or less. Yet at the same time the Deuteronomistic Historians are careful to detail Samson's major flaw, his involvement with foreign (that is, non-Israelite) women. A subtheme of the edited cycle of legends is that such involvement inevitably leads to disaster. The first woman with whom Samson is connected is his unnamed Philistine wife, whom he marries over his parents' objections. The second is the prostitute of Gaza, presumably also a Philistine. The third is Delilah, and although she is not identified as a Philistine, her close connection with the Philistine rulers suggests that she is one as well. In the first case, Samson violates the Deuteronomic prohibition against marriage with non-Israelites (Deut 7.3), and the case of Delilah especially illustrates the warning of Proverbs:

> The lips of a foreign woman drip honey,
>   and her speech is smoother than oil;
> but in the end she is bitter as wormwood,
>   sharp as a two-edged sword. (Prov 5.3–4)

Within the larger context of Judges, Samson's betrayal by Delilah is reminiscent of Jael's murder of Sisera in Judges 4–5.

Samson's victories over the Philistines, although personal, foreshadow those of the Israelites in 1 and 2 Samuel. Samson dies by bringing down

Box 13.3 THE PHILISTINES

One of the groups of **Sea Peoples** who had menaced the coast of Egypt during the twelfth century BCE (see page 221), the **Philistines** settled on the southeast coast of the Mediterranean, where five cities, Gaza, Ashkelon, Ashdod, Gath, and Ekron (see Figure 13.1), became the centers of their power. By the eleventh century they had expanded eastward into Israelite territory. The first tribe affected by this expansion was Dan, which was eventually forced to move far to the north (see Judg 18, and contrast Judg 5.17). Eventually, as described in 1 Samuel, the Philistines came into direct conflict with the Israelites, as both groups vied for control of the territory west of the Jordan River.

Our knowledge of the Philistines comes from three different sources. As one of the Sea Peoples, they are mentioned in Egyptian texts and depicted in Egyptian reliefs of the late second millennium BCE. Archaeologists have uncovered their material culture, one that is distinct from that of the Canaanites and Israelites, with very different ceramic styles, architectural traditions, and dietary habits. Our principal source, however, that helps interpret the Egyptian and the archaeological data, is the Bible, especially the Samson narratives and those in 1 Samuel.

The Philistines had a centralized political organization, a kind of pentapolis. The rulers of their five principal cities formed a collaborative alliance and are described as acting in accord. These "five lords" (Judg 3.3; 1 Sam 6.16) are called in Hebrew *seranim*, a word probably related to the Greek word *tyrannos* (from which the English word "tyrant" is derived), reflecting the Aegean origin of the Philistines. They also seem to have had a standing army, probably augmented by mercenary groups such as that led by David (1 Sam 27.2), as well as a superior metallurgical technology (see 1 Sam 13.19–22), which gave them a further strategic advantage. Unlike most of their contemporaries in the region, their diet included pig as a principal source of protein, and they did not practice circumcision. (See Box 5.3 on page 70.)

According to the book of Judges, the Philistines had consolidated their position along the coast, and had moved to the north and east. Samson's Philistine wife is from Timnah, in the Shephelah on the border with Israelite territory; excavations at the site of Timnah (Tel Batash) have uncovered Philistine occupation there during the late twelfth and eleventh centuries BCE. The Philistines also are reported to have been able to compel Judahites on the border with Philistia to surrender Samson (Judg 15.9–13). The relationships between Philistines and the Israelites seem to have been generally peaceful, however, during the early period of their interaction as described in Judges, and Samson moved freely between his own territory and Philistia. Only during the second half of the eleventh century did the two groups come into repeated armed conflict, as described in 1 Samuel. It was probably during this period that the Samson cycle originated, the Philistines having become such a threat that tales featuring an Israelite hero repeatedly outwitting them became popular.

the temple of the Philistine deity Dagon on thousands of worshipers and on himself. As in the final form of the Exodus narrative (see Ex 12.12), the god of Israel—and his representative—is more powerful than the gods of other nations. This will be demonstrated dramatically when Yahweh himself, invisibly enthroned over the ark, will shatter the statue of Dagon (1 Sam 5.1–5).

As the seventeenth-century English poet John Milton recognized in his verse-drama *Samson Agonistes*, Samson is by the end also a tragic figure. In it, Samson poignantly says:

> Promise was that I
> Should Israel from Philistian yoke deliver;
> Ask for this great deliverer now, and find him
> Eyeless in Gaza, at the mill with slaves,
> Himself in bonds under Philistian yoke. (ll. 38–42)

HISTORY AND THE ISRAELITE CONFEDERATION

The latter part of the thirteenth century BCE and the beginning of the twelfth was a time of major upheaval throughout the regions bordering the eastern Mediterranean. In what was to become Greece, the Mycenaean empire collapsed and its major cities were destroyed; the account of the Trojan War in the Homeric poems probably preserves a memory of part of this process. In Asia Minor, the Hittite empire came to an end, and its major cities, including the capital Hattusha, were also destroyed. Similarly, in northern Mesopotamia the Hurrian kingdom of Mitanni collapsed, and in Cyprus many urban centers were devastated.

We have graphic documentation for this period of chaos from the city of Ugarit, on the northern coast of Syria (see further page 74), where letters were found dating from the last days of the city's existence and describing a desperate situation. One, perhaps not sent before the city was destroyed, is from the king of Ugarit to the king of Cyprus, who is addressed by the honorific title "father":

> Ships of the enemy have come. By fire he has burned my towns and done much evil in my country. My fa-

ther does not know that my troops [and chariots] are all in the Hittite country, and all my ships are stationed in Lycian country. They have not rejoined me yet, and the country is left to itself. Let my father know it: yes, seven enemy ships have come and plundered my land. If there are any enemy ships now in sight, let me somehow know.

The king of Ugarit was a vassal of the Hittite king and, according to the stipulations of their treaty, had to supply troops to his suzerain when called upon; hence his army and navy had been sent to defend the Hittites from the invaders. The source of the threat is also clear: It is attack by sea.

From Egyptian sources of the late thirteenth and early twelfth centuries BCE we learn more of these invaders. Called the "Sea Peoples," they were of Aegean origin and consisted of several different groups, including the biblical Philistines. The Egyptian pharaoh Rameses III (1184–1153 BCE) effectively blocked the Sea Peoples from gaining control of Egypt, but the effort exhausted the Egyptians. They lost control of their empire in Palestine and entered a prolonged period of weakness and internal strife.

The chaos of the period is also evident in the destruction of many major Palestinian cities, including Megiddo, Bethel, Hazor, Gezer, Aphek, Ashdod, Beth-shan, Beth-shemesh, and Lachish, many no doubt at the hands of the Sea Peoples. Egyptian weakness allowed the Philistines to settle on the southeastern coast of the Mediterranean, in the area known today as the Gaza Strip, and the collapse of local urban centers of authority was in part responsible for the emergence of hundreds of new agricultural villages, largely in previous unsettled areas such as the highlands on both sides of the Jordan River. In archaeological terminology, these events correspond to the end of the Late Bronze Age and the beginning of the Iron Age, around 1200 BCE. This periodization, however, implying a change in technology, is misleading, since the use of iron is attested before that date and remained relatively rare for some time after it. Moreover, the events just described spanned many decades, and no single event marks a change.

The mostly unfortified highland villages show some cultural innovations, but also considerable continuity with the preceding Canaanite culture. Some of them were clearly part of Israel, although attempts to identify all of them as Israelite push the evidence too far, since many of the same cultural markers in villages located in territory that the Bible assigns to the Israelites are also found in villages in territories that they never controlled. But clearly the Israelites were part of the picture.

As we have seen, the book of Joshua's account of a rapid and complete conquest of the land of Canaan is contradicted both by other biblical sources and by archaeological data. The process by which Israel gained control of the land was gradual and complex, and scholars dispute its details. What follows is an eclectic synthesis, combining several different scholarly hypotheses and attempting to take into account all the data. My assumption is, in general, that Israel as the biblical writers knew it came into existence in the land of Canaan.

In the premonarchic period, the two centuries that preceded the establishment of dynastic kingship in the late eleventh century BCE Israel was a loosely knit confederation of tribes. Scholars have used various terms to designate early Israel, including "amphictyony," "league," and "confederation." All are essentially Western analogues, and the last is perhaps the most apt, for its etymology suggests both "compact, covenant," from the Latin *foedus*, and the cognate word *fides*, "faith."

The twentieth-century scholar Martin Noth proposed that Israel's organization resembled that of amphictyonies known from ancient Greece. These were leagues connected with a sanctuary, such as Delphi, with each of six or twelve members having responsibility for their collective shrine for a set time each year. The Greek amphictyonies, however, date from the sixth century BCE and later, and the key element, the central sanctuary, is problematic for early Israel, since its primary shrine, the ark of the covenant, was sited at different locations during the premonarchic period. Still, perhaps because of some association with the twelve months of the lunar calendar, the number of twelve tribes seems to have been more or less constant in Israel, although the names and order of the tribes change as their historical circumstances altered. These changes are evident when one compares the tribal catalogues in several poems dating to the premonarchic period: the "Blessing of Jacob" (Gen 49), the "Blessing of Moses" (Deut 33), and the Song of Deborah (Judg 5).

The tribal structure seems to have been organizational and geographical more than ethnic. Most tribes had their own fairly stable territory, although this could change, as in the case of Dan, which was forced to move from the southern coast to northern Galilee, probably because of Philistine expansion (see Judg 18; compare Judg 5.17; 1.34). Levi is a special case. Its territory was lost at a very early stage; when this occurred the Joseph tribe was subdivided into Ephraim and Manasseh to preserve the number twelve. The separate geographical tribal entities, which no doubt also corresponded with extended kinship ties within each tribe, were linked by the developing myth of a common ancestor, Jacob, renamed Israel, whose twelve sons were identified as the ancestors of the individual tribes. Other genealogies linked Jacob with Isaac and Abraham, and, more distantly, with the "descendants" of Terah, through Abraham's brother Nahor (the Arameans; see Gen 22.20–24) and Abraham's nephew Lot (the Moabites and the Ammonites; see Gen 18), and with other descendants of Abraham, through his son Ishmael and his third wife Keturah (various Arabian tribes; see Gen 25.1–18), and of Isaac, through Jacob's brother Esau (the Edomites). The intersecting genealogies show an awareness that all of these groups were part of a cultural continuum, but only the descendants of Jacob had become part of Israel.

In many respects the premonarchic Israelites were indistinguishable from others living in Canaan. The Israelites' material culture—especially their pottery, house plans, agricultural practices, and settlement patterns—was the same as that of their contemporaries on both sides of the Jordan, with the exception of the Philistines. What distinguished them from their contemporaries was the shared commitment, under the mechanism of the "covenant" or contract, to worship only Yahweh, the god of the confederation, and to provide mutual support and defense to each other. In other words, the principle of unity that made these tribes "Israel" was primarily religious and political—in biblical terminology, to love God and to love their neighbors.

Passages in Deuteronomy (especially 27.1–29.1) and Joshua (8.30–35; 24; see page 200) give a stylized version of what must have been the ceremony in which the covenant was renewed. The tribes gathered at a central location such as Shechem. There, before the ark of the covenant, they committed themselves to mutual support and to worship of Yahweh alone; Joshua 24.14–15 presents this as a freely made choice. Part of the covenant ritual, as we have seen, involved the pronouncement of blessings on those who kept its terms and curses on those who did not. Covenant making also included dismemberment of one or more animals, symbolizing the fate of those who broke the covenant.

The composition of the Israelite confederation was complex. One major component of the group that called itself Israel, and that could be identified as a distinct geopolitical entity in Canaan by the end of the thirteenth century BCE (in the Merneptah stela; see pages 98–99), was the group (or groups) that had come out of Egypt. As we have seen, a number of probabilities converge to make it reasonable to conclude that the Exodus was historical: A group of Hebrew slaves escaped from Egypt under the leadership of Moses and attributed their escape to intervention on their behalf by the deity Yahweh. Given the frequent contacts between Canaan and Egypt, it is possible that more than one such escape occurred but that does not affect the basic contour of the biblical tradition.

This group of Hebrew slaves eventually made their way into Transjordan and from there into Canaan. As they settled there, they joined with other groups, some of whom were related by kinship and some not, to form a confederation. Evidence of this composite nature is found in a variety of sources. In the Exodus narratives, the number of the Israelites is augmented by a large group of foreigners (Ex 12.38; NRSV: "mixed crowd"), also called "those gathered in" (Num

11.4; NRSV: "the rabble"). This recognizes, probably retrospectively, that "Israel" was always a complex entity, defined by more than kinship. Complicated kinship links exist between various components of Israel, as expressed by the four different mothers for the twelve sons of Jacob, a kind of fictional genealogy recognizing the complexity of the confederation formed by the "descendants" of those sons.

We should also note the marriage of Moses to a Midianite (or Cushite, for the two terms are synonymous; see Hab 3.7) and the important role of his father-in-law Jethro (or Reuel), the priest of Midian, in shaping Israel's institutions (see further page 224). Despite the hostility of some biblical traditions toward the Midianites (such as the Gideon narrative, Judg 6–7), their connections with Moses, and with Israel, were deeply imbedded. (See further pages 169–70.)

Moving back even earlier in the chronology of biblical narrative, we should also note the association of Israel's ancestors with key political and religious centers in the land, such as Jerusalem, Shechem, Hebron, Beersheba, and Bethel. Although, as we have seen, we have reasons to doubt that the ancestral narratives are historical in a straightforward way, at the very least the incorporation of these ancient Canaanite centers into Israel's story suggests a complex process of assimilation and syncretism.

In the book of Joshua, two etiological narratives explain the inclusion of Canaanite groups within Israel: the family of Rahab, the prostitute of Jericho (Josh 2; 6.22–25), and the Gibeonites (Josh 9; compare Deut 29.11). We should also note in passing such individuals as Shamgar son of Anath (Judg 3.31; 5.6), Ruth the Moabite (see pages 226–27), and Uriah the Hittite (2 Sam 11.3; 23.39), whose names or epithets reveal their "foreign" (that is, non-Israelite) background. In fact, the authors of Deuteronomy, and of the Deuteronomistic History, repeatedly recognize the composite nature of Israel; for example, the membership of "all Israel" at the covenant ceremony in Joshua 8.33 includes "alien as well as native-born" (see also Josh 8.35), and the words of Deuteronomy 27.9—"this day you have become the people of the LORD your God"—imply the addition of new members.

Other evidence for the composite nature of Israel includes the Passover festival, which combines originally distinct agricultural (the unleavened bread) and pastoral (the lamb) elements (see pages 92–93), and some elements in the law codes. Although embedded in the narrative of the Exodus, the earliest Israelite law codes, such as the Decalogue in its various forms (Ex 20.2–17; 34.10–26; Deut 5.6–21) and the Covenant Code (Ex 20.22–23.33), with their references to houses, town gates, fields, and vineyards, come from an essentially permanent agricultural society. As such, they are not entirely new creations, and they share both a general ethos and many details with other ancient Near Eastern law codes.

No Canaanite law codes have yet been discovered, but given the parallels between the biblical laws and those found in such sources as the Code of Hammurapi (see pages 120–22), we should assume that Canaanite legal traditions were similar and that they are the most likely origin for the earliest biblical laws. To put it another way, when the Exodus group joined with Canaanites to form the Israelite confederation, the Canaanites supplied its civil and criminal legal framework (see further pages 123–24). Narrative confirmation of this occurs in the account of how Moses' father-in-law, the Midianite priest Jethro, instructed Moses about the establishment of a judicial system (Ex 18.13–27 [E]). In other versions, the institution of the judiciary is attributed either to God himself (Num 11.16–17 [J?]) or to Moses (Deut 1.9–18); these differences may reflect some embarrassment over the "foreign" origin of the judiciary.

To the legal system brought by Canaanite members to the confederation was added the ethos derived from the Exodus experience: "You shall not oppress a resident alien; you know the heart of an alien, for you were aliens in the land of Egypt" (Ex 23.9; see also Ex 20.2; 22.21; Lev 19.34; Deut 5.15; 10.19; 15.15; etc.). Another important innovation was the concept of egalitarianism, in which all Israelite males were equal before the law.

The cumulative evidence, then, suggests that the Israelite confederation was composed of groups of disparate origin, including Canaanites. What would have motivated such groups to join Israel? One factor must have been the persuasive power of the story of the victories of Yahweh, the god who had rescued Hebrew slaves from Egypt and led them in a triumphant march through southern Transjordan into Canaan. Another would have been the political, military, social, and economic benefits of belonging to the confederation. The principle of mutual support ("love of neighbor") would have provided a powerful incentive for highland villagers at risk from more powerful groups. The egalitarianism of early Israel may have proved attractive to individuals or groups who had found the feudalism of the Late Bronze Age Canaanite city-states oppressive. And the inclusiveness of the confederation would have provided a haven for survivors of the collapse of many of those same city-states.

The Canaanite components of the Israelite confederation explain the material cultural continuities not only between early Israel and its neighbors but also between the Early Iron Age and the preceding Late Bronze Age. Had we only the archaeological record, we would be hard pressed to posit the existence of Israel as a culturally distinct group in the region—a remarkable contrast with the case of the Philistines, with their very different material culture.

The unifying symbol of the confederation was the ark of the covenant, which served as the divine footstool and over which the deity was invisibly enthroned on the cherubim (see Figure 13.3). The ark was housed in a tent, which suggests that it was a moveable shrine, not attached to one sanctuary. In the traditions associated with the ark, it is variously located at Gilgal (Josh 7.6; compare Judg 2.1), Shechem (Josh 8.33), Bethel (Judg 20.26–27, the only explicit mention of the ark in the book of Judges), and Shiloh (1 Sam 3.3). It may have moved from one tribal center to another on a regular basis, accompanied by its officiating clergy, the Levites, although all of the places with which it is explicitly connected are in the territory of Ephraim, and so it may origi-

FIGURE 13.3. A carved ivory knife handle or plaque from Megiddo, dating to the end of the Late Bronze Age (thirteenth–twelfth centuries BCE); it measures 2.2 in (5.7 cm) high. In the first scene, on the right, a Canaanite king returns from battle, with his chariot led by nude captives. In the second, on the left, the king is sitting on his throne whose sides are winged sphinxes, with his feet on a footstool. The throne and footstool are reminiscent of descriptions of the ark of the covenant and the associated cherubim throne of Yahweh. (See also Figure 8.3 on page 127.)

nally have been the sacred symbol of a smaller grouping of tribes. Thus, it is perhaps significant that Joshua is from the territory of Ephraim.

We also see evidence that the ark functioned as a religious symbol in war, representing the invisible presence of Yahweh as divine warrior fighting on behalf of Israel (see further page 128). As the book of Judges suggests, many of these wars were local rather than supraregional, as various groups competed with individual tribes of Israel for control over their territory, and the confederation would often have been victorious, extending its reach by military means. This long and complex process is collapsed into the swift conquest of the land in the book of Joshua.

In the end, however, the confederation proved inadequate as a form of government. It was essentially decentralized, without continuity of leadership though dynastic succession, and the theory of mutual support was seldom operative, as the tribal catalogue in the Song of Deborah demonstrates. Moreover, the professional army of the Philistines proved superior to the volunteer militia of the Israelites, in which the farmers of the settlements, like those of Lexington and Concord in the American Revolution, took up arms only when necessary.

We get a picture both of the relationship of the Israelite confederation to its context and of how it apparently functioned in the tragic story of the Levite's concubine and its aftermath in Judges 19–21. The "concubine" (that is, probably a secondary wife) of an unnamed Levite left him and returned to her father's house in Bethlehem. After an interval, he followed her there, and after a few days set out for his home to the north in Ephraim with his concubine and his servant. Because they left late in the day, they did not get far, reaching only Jerusalem, some six miles (ten kilometers) north of Bethlehem, as evening was approaching. But when the servant suggested to the Levite that they spent the night there, the Levite refused: "We will not turn aside into a city of foreigners, who do not belong to the people of Israel; but we will continue on to Gibeah" (19.12). Gibeah was not far to the north.

The terminology is important, as is the geography. Here, within a distance of about ten miles (sixteen kilometers) on the main north-south road through the Judean hill country, are three cities. Two of them, Bethlehem and Gibeah, "belong to the people of Israel," but Jerusalem, between them, is "a city of foreigners." The material culture of these three settlements would have been the same. What distinguished them was not material but spiritual, not physical but metaphysical. "Belonging to Israel" meant worship of Yahweh alone and special obligations to one's neighbors, that is, fellow Israelites.

As the story continues, the inhabitants of Gibeah failed to live up to their obligations, violating the principles of hospitality and brutally raping the concubine. When the Levite discovered his wife's body at the door of the house where he was staying, he brought her home, and dismembered her, sending one part to each of the twelve tribes. This reminder of the actual ceremony of covenant making (compare 1 Sam 11.7, and see further pages 113–14) stirred the tribes to action, and they united to enforce the punishment—the curse of the covenant ceremony—on the guilty tribe of Benjamin. It is one of the many ironies of the book of Judges that the only time that all the tribes of Israel are reported to have united in warfare (in contrast to the idealized picture in Joshua) is not to attack an enemy that threatens them but to punish one of their own.

For the Deuteronomistic Historians, this concluding episode in the book of Judges portrays the disastrous consequence of anarchy—the narrative begins and ends with the phrase "there was no king in Israel" (19.1; 21.25). Modern readers find another aspect, the tragic fate of the unnamed woman who is the victim of men's actions, including her own husband. Although it is risky to project modern sensibilities back into an ancient text, some details in it prompt the question whether the original narrator and audience would not also have concluded that this kind of ruthless exploitation and gratuitous violence were unacceptable. The scene of the men of Gibeah surrounding the house and demanding that the man visiting its owner be given to them for sexual pleasure is clearly a reprise of the episode of Sodom (Gen 19.1–8), but this time the guilty parties are Israelites rather than other inhabitants of the land. And the poignant description of the brutally raped woman collapsed "at the door of the house, with her hands on the threshold" (Judg 19.27) would have prompted outrage in any culture.

THE BOOK OF RUTH

In the Jewish canon (see Appendix), the book of Ruth is one of the Writings; in many manuscripts it is placed after the book of Proverbs, so that Ruth provides a narrative illustration of the "woman of valor" [NRSV: "capable wife"] with which the book of Proverbs ends (Prov 31.10; the same phrase is used in Ruth 3.11). In the Christian canon, Ruth comes between Judges and 1 Samuel because of its setting "in the days when the judges ruled" (1.1). In this position it interrupts the Deuteronomistic History, to which it does not belong; like the books of Esther and Judith, its genre is historical fiction, with a woman as protagonist (see further Chapter 30). Although Jewish tradition attributed its authorship to Samuel himself, modern scholars are divided over the date of the book, for which almost every period from the tenth to the fourth centuries BCE has been proposed; in any case, it was written some time after the events that it narrates.

The purpose of the book is also unclear. If its genealogical conclusion, which makes Ruth the great-grandmother of King David, is original, the tale may have originated as an explanation of David's mixed ancestry. According to Deuteronomic law, "no . . . Moabite shall be admitted to the assembly of the LORD . . . to the tenth generation" (Deut 23.3); the Moabites (see Box 13.1) were frequent enemies of Israel and Judah in the first half of the first millennium BCE, and David's connection with Moab must have been something of an embarrassment. By presenting Ruth as a model proselyte and by making Naomi the surrogate mother of David's ancestor, the embarrassment is mitigated. If the book dates to the postexilic period, it may be intended to counter a limitation of membership in the community to those of pure lineage (see, for example, Neh 13.1–3).

Whatever its origins and purpose, the tale of Ruth "amid the alien corn" (Keats, "Ode to a Nightingale") is a masterpiece of Israelite narrative. The German Romantic writer Goethe called it "the most charming little whole" of antiquity. As one Israelite writer's view of the premonarchic period, it is remarkable on several counts. Most of the action of the book is furthered by dialogue, which accounts for nearly two-thirds of the text, a higher proportion than in any other book in the Hebrew Bible. Moreover, it is principally a narrative about two women, Naomi the Israelite widow, returning to Bethlehem from Moab with her Moabite daughter-in-law Ruth, also widowed. Together they plot to have Ruth marry Boaz, a wealthy relative of Naomi, so that both women acquire a male protector and, more important, a continuation of their dead husbands' lineage.

These two women dominate the narrative, which gives us a glimpse not only of how ancient Israelite village society functioned but also of the roles available to women in it. That society was clearly patriarchal, with women dependent on their male relatives, in this case husbands and sons. When both Naomi and Ruth are left childless widows, they take the initiative to get a distant relative, Boaz, to marry Ruth, and from the male offspring of this union both women are effectively restored. The legal transaction is conducted at the town's gate, the ordinary place of commerce, judicial proceedings, and informal gatherings (see, for example, Deut 25.7; Job 29.7; Prov 31.23), and the women are not present. But their maneuverings have secured the eventual resolution: Boaz's assumption of a nearer kinsman's obligation to Ruth as the widow of a member of the clan.

Often called "levirate marriage," this legal tradition is also attested in Genesis 38 and Deuteronomy 25.5–10; it provides a specific example of the role of the "redeemer" (Hebr. *goel*), the kinsman whose responsibility it was to assume the position of male protector when the primary head of household had died, especially with regard to property and blood vengeance. Another example of how legal traditions functioned is the practice of gleaning, in which fields and vineyards would not be completely harvested, leaving the residue for the benefit of the marginalized in Israelite society—the poor, widows, orphans, and resident aliens (see Lev 19.9–10; 23.22; Deut 24.19–22). Less clear is the procedure involving the sandal in 4.7; even for the narrator it was a custom no longer in use.

Taken as a whole, the book of Ruth is a remarkable portrait of rural life in ancient Israel, with its scenes of famine and harvest, and of women's lives in that context. The bonds between Naomi and Ruth are deeper than those of ethnicity or religion, and together they manipulate the patriarchal system to their mutual advantage. From such stock, the narrator concludes, Israel's greatest king was born.

RETROSPECT AND PROSPECT

The book of Judges ends with the last occurrence of the phrase "In those days there was no king in Israel; every man did what was right in his own eyes" (21.25). As the immediately preceding episode of the rape of the Levite's concubine and the Benjaminite war shows, what was right in their own eyes was often wrong in the eyes of Yahweh. The experiment with a kind of primitive democracy had failed and had resulted in anarchy.

Although in the book of Judges the Philistines are a problem more for Samson than for all Israel, that will rapidly change. The Philistine threat will directly lead to the establishment of kingship in Israel in the next book, 1 Samuel. The Deuteronomistic Historians are decidedly ambivalent about monarchy, and they present the initial attempt to establish it by Abimelech as an outright rejection of Yahweh's direct rule over Israel. Gideon's refusal to accept dynastic leadership ("I will not rule over you, and my sons will not rule over you; the LORD will rule over you" [Judg 8.23]) anticipates the debate about kingship when monarchy is finally introduced ("they have rejected me from being king over them" [1 Sam 8.7]). Likewise, the fact that Benjamin is depicted so pejoratively in the narrative of the Levite's concubine may prepare readers for 1 Samuel's essentially negative depiction of Saul, Israel's first king, who was a member of the tribe of Benjamin.

The edition of the Deuteronomistic History that was produced in the late seventh century BCE (see page 192) was in part propaganda supporting the religious and political reforms of King Josiah. The religious reforms included a centralization of all worship in Jerusalem, which deprived the Levites at local shrines of their livelihood. The negative presentation of Levites in Judges 17–19, and of the origins of the shrine at Dan (chap. 18), may be inspired by that reform.

On a larger scale, the view of the Deuteronomistic Historians that worship of other gods invariably leads to divine punishment antici-pates their interpretation of the eventual fall of the northern kingdom of Israel to the Assyrians in 722 BCE and ultimately the fall of Jerusalem and Judah to the Babylonians in 586 BCE.

IMPORTANT TERMS

Ammonites

judge

Moabites

Philistines

Sea Peoples

QUESTIONS FOR REVIEW

1. How does the picture of Israelite relationships with the inhabitants of the land of Canaan in the book of Judges differ from that in the book of Joshua?

2. How would you define "Israel" in the period of the Judges? What elements were included in it? What was its structure? What was its principle of unity? How was it related to other groups?

3. What was the role of Yahweh in the period of the Judges according to the Deuteronomistic Historians?

BIBLIOGRAPHY

A good short commentary on Judges is S. Niditch, "Judges," pp. 176–91 in *The Oxford Bible Commentary* (ed. J. Barton and J. Muddiman; Oxford: Oxford University Press, 2001).

For a discussion of the history of the period, see L. E. Stager, "Forging an Identity: The Emergence of Israel," Chap. 3, and J. A. Hackett, " 'There Was No King in Israel': The Era of the Judges," Chap. 4 in *The Oxford History of the Biblical World* (ed. M. D. Coogan; New York: Oxford University Press, 1998).

A good summary of contemporary views about the amphictyony is A. D. H. Mayes, "Amphictyony," pp. 212–16 in *Anchor Bible Dictionary*, Vol. 1 (ed. D. N. Freedman; New York: Doubleday, 1992).

A notable interpreter of narratives concerning women is Phyllis Trible; for the material in Judges, see her essays, "An Unnamed Woman: The Extravagance of Violence [Judges 19:1–30]," pp. 65–91, and "The Daughter of Jephthah: An Inhuman Sacrifice," pp. 93–116 in *Texts of Terror: Literary-Feminist Readings of Biblical Narratives* (Philadelphia: Fortress, 1984).

One of the best commentaries on Ruth is E. F. Campbell, *Ruth* (Garden City, NY: Doubleday, 1975); see also his essay "Ruth, The Book of," pp. 662–64 in *The Oxford Companion to the Bible* (ed. B. M. Metzger and M. D. Coogan; New York: Oxford University Press, 1993).

PART THREE

KINGS AND PROPHETS

THE ESTABLISHMENT OF THE MONARCHY

CHAPTER

14

1 Samuel

Few parts of the Bible are as dramatic or as complex as the books of Samuel and the first few chapters of 1 Kings. On a political level, the books narrate how Israel, with its very existence threatened by growing Philistine power, transformed itself from a loose confederation of tribes into a nation with a dynastic monarchy and a permanent Temple in Jerusalem. As in the period of the judges that precedes, the stories of individuals convey the larger story. The narrative is advanced by accounts of a series of personal conflicts: between Samuel the prophet and Saul, the first king of Israel; between Saul and David, who succeeded him as king; and between David and several of his sons. All of them are vividly portrayed. For ancient audiences, both the characters and the times when they lived were familiar, and so the historians could present a kind of fictionalized historical drama, with frequent use of dialogue. Interspersed with the dialogues are a variety of ancient traditions whose selection and arrangement exhibit a subtle, sophisticated understanding of the historical process.

THE BOOK(S) OF SAMUEL

In Jewish tradition what now appears as 1 and 2 Samuel was originally one book. In the ancient Greek translation of the Jewish scriptures, the Septuagint, this book was divided into two parts, the second beginning immediately after the death of the first king Saul. Together with the books of Kings, 1 and 2 Samuel was understood in the Septuagint as the first part of an extended history of "the kingdoms" of Israel and Judah from the beginning of the monarchy until the fall of Jerusalem in 586 BCE. The books are named for the prophet Samuel, who is the principal character of the early chapters of 1 Samuel. Later tradition attributes the authorship of the books to Samuel as well, based on an interpretation of 1 Chronicles 29.29.

In their final form, the books of Samuel are part of the larger work of the Deuteronomistic Historians (see pages 191–93). In compiling the narrative, they used a number of originally independent traditions, many of which duplicate or contradict each other. One example of such inconsistent traditions concerns the killing of Goliath, the Philistine champion from Gath. In the detailed narrative of 1 Samuel 17, it is David, son of Jesse, who slays the giant, "the shaft of whose spear was like a weaver's beam" (v. 7). But in 2 Samuel 21.19, in a summary of David's battles with the Philistines, the death of the same

Goliath is attributed to Elhanan, son of Jaare-oregim. These traditions are shaped and edited with the distinct theological perspective of the Deuteronomistic Historians, according to which the vicissitudes of the nation result not from the interplay of human personalities and politics but from the actions of the divine covenant partner, who either rewards or punishes Israel in accordance with its observance of the law given to Moses.

1 SAMUEL

Sources

The presence of independent traditions is especially clear in 1 Samuel because of passages that either duplicate or contradict each other. Thus we find three different and not entirely consistent accounts of how Saul was chosen as the first king of Israel: in a private meeting between himself and Samuel (1 Sam 9.1–10.16), in a selection by lot in a public ceremony over which Samuel presided (1 Sam 10.17–27), and as a popular choice following Saul's victory over the Ammonites (1 Sam 11). We also see two narratives of David's introduction to Saul: In 1 Sam 16.14–23 he is a skilled musician whose playing relieves Saul when "the evil spirit from God" comes over him; in the very next chapter, he comes from Bethlehem to the court as an apparent stranger (see 1 Sam 17.55–56) and defeats Goliath. Likewise, after Saul has turned against David, he twice tries to kill him with a spear (1 Sam 18.10–12; 19.10). And toward the end of the book, which is dominated by the narrative of David and Saul's rivalry, David twice spares Saul's life (1 Sam 24; 26).

First Samuel opens with two such independent traditions, whose incorporation shows us the Deuteronomistic Historians at work. In its present form, 1 Samuel 1 is the birth narrative of Samuel, the transitional figure between the confederation and the monarchy. Following a familiar pattern, his mother Hannah, like Sarah (Gen 16.1), Rebekah (Gen 25.21), Rachel (Gen 29.31), and Samson's mother (Judg 13.2), is un-able to have children. In response to her prayer, she does become pregnant, and when her child is born she names him Samuel. As in the earlier cases, this motif highlights the son as divinely designated for an important role. But the details of the birth narrative fit Samuel poorly. His name is explained as derived from Hannah's recognition of his origin: "I have asked him of the LORD" (1 Sam 1.20). The Hebrew root used here is *sha'al*, and it occurs some seven times in the chapter, once in the form *sha'ul* (v. 28), which is the same as Saul's name in Hebrew. It is likely, then, that this was originally Saul's birth-narrative and that it has been transferred to Samuel because, as we will see, the figure of Samuel is central to the purposes of the Deuteronomistic Historians, and also because the final form of 1 Samuel narrative depicts Saul pejoratively in order to enhance David's status.

Another originally independent tradition is the "Song of Hannah" in 1 Samuel 2.1–10. After Samuel has been weaned, his mother Hannah takes him to the sanctuary at Shiloh, where she had made her prayer and an accompanying vow, and dedicates him to the service of Yahweh, giving him to the priest Eli. Then she sings a hymn of thanksgiving. But the hymn includes the anachronistic prayer that Yahweh "give strength to his king, and exalt the power of his anointed" (v. 10). As the book of Judges repeatedly puts it, however, "in those days there was no king in Israel," and so the hymn must date not from Samuel's childhood, before the monarchy had been established, but later, from the time of the monarchy itself. It has been inserted here not only because of an appropriate reference to the reversal of the status of the "barren woman" (v. 5) but also because of its emphasis on divine power. For the original author of the hymn, God exercises control over the lives of individuals and the nation as well, including "his king . . . his anointed." By incorporating the hymn at the beginning of their account of the monarchy, the Deuteronomistic Historians are telling us, in effect, that the outcome of the story about to be told will be positive, especially for those most in need.

Scholars have also identified a number of longer independent sources in 1 Samuel. Like the Pentateuchal sources (see pages 23–27), these are not explicitly delineated in the text, and their existence is thus hypothetical. They include:

- *The Ark Narrative* (1 Sam 4.1b–7.1 and 2 Sam 6): a history of the vicissitudes of the ark of the covenant (see pages 126–28)—its capture by the Philistines, its return to Israelite territory, and its eventual transfer to Jerusalem by David. Samuel himself is not mentioned in this narrative, in contrast with the surrounding material (see 1 Sam 4.1a; 7.2); this is one of the reasons for isolating it as a separate source. The Ark Narrative resembles other ancient accounts of the capture of divine images in war.

- *The History of Saul's Rise* (mainly in 1 Sam 9–14): The Deuteronomistic Historians also probably used an originally independent account of Saul's career, evident especially in passages that treat Saul favorably in contrast to the final negative presentation of him.

- *The History of David's Rise* (embedded in 1 Sam 16–2 Sam 5): a pro-David account of how David became the divinely designated ruler of Israel, replacing Saul, dating no earlier than David's reign and possibly later. In this source Saul is almost always depicted negatively.

In addition, a number of smaller units appear to have existed independently before being incorporated into the Deuteronomistic Historians' account of the establishment of the monarchy. These include proverbs and folk traditions associated with them (for example, 1 Sam 10.11–12; 19.24; 18.7); some poetic compositions, notably the Song of Hannah (see page 232) and the women's victory chant (1 Sam 18.7); some early material taken from royal annals (such as 1 Sam 13.1 [not fully preserved in the traditional Hebrew text]; 14.49–51; 25.43–44); and battle accounts. Although these materials have been shaped by the Deuteronomistic Historians in their final presentation, many appear to preserve authentic historical memory.

Underlying this collage of sources is a clear narrative development, one that effectively presents how Saul became Israel's first king but proved to be unworthy and how David emerged as the divine choice to succeed Saul. The narrative uses set speeches by its principal characters, as well as dialogue, and has an overarching theological perspective.

The Narrative

The birth narrative that opens the book, now connected with Samuel rather than Saul, moves to an account of Samuel's youth in which he is shown to be the only leader in Israel acceptable to God. The nation itself suffers from internal problems and external threats. Eli's sons, the priests at Shiloh, are corrupt, and the capture of the ark by the Philistines is implicitly a divinely sent punishment (see 1 Sam 7.6). According to the Deuteronomistic Historians' rhetoric, as in the period of the judges Israel has been worshiping gods other than Yahweh, and the Philistines are the agents of his anger.

At first the situation seems stable: After their repentance, the Israelites defeat the Philistines, recover the territory that had been captured, and control them during Samuel's life. But Samuel's sons are as corrupt as Eli's had been, and the Israelites request a king from Samuel. Although Samuel is opposed to this request, Yahweh begrudgingly agrees, and Saul is anointed by Samuel. Saul shows his prowess as a leader by defeating the Ammonites, who have been menacing the Israelite city of Jabesh-gilead across the Jordan. The kingship is "renewed" (1 Sam 11.14) at Gilgal. A long and important speech by Samuel follows, in which he again warns the people of the inevitable bad effects of kingship; and Saul's reign officially begins with a now broken archival notice in 1 Samuel 13.1.

The Philistines continue to expand, and much of Saul's early career is devoted to keeping them in check. It is at this point that David appears on the scene. From the moment David is introduced, Saul's stature diminishes. God regrets having chosen Saul, and Samuel secretly anoints David as king. David rapidly rises to eminence in Saul's court and marries one of his daughters. As David's reputation grows, so does Saul's suspicion of him. Much of the latter part of the book recounts Saul's repeated attempts to eliminate David, whom he now perceives as a rival. David, forced to flee from Saul, establishes himself as a kind of bandit leader in southern Judah, working for the Philistines but against other enemies of Israel.

The book of 1 Samuel ends near the same place where the battle between Israelites and Philistines had taken place in chapter 4. Once again the outcome is defeat for Israel. Saul has failed in the primary task for which he was appointed as king in the first place: the containment, if not the defeat, of the Philistines. And once again, Israel's survival is threatened. How that crisis will be resolved is the subject of 2 Samuel.

The Characters

Samuel

Like Joshua, Samuel is an idealized figure. He embodies three principal offices in ancient Israel—priest, judge, and prophet—and is clearly presented as the individual who presided over the transition between Israel as a tribal confederation and Israel as a monarchy. But his exercise of these offices is so stereotypical that it is difficult to penetrate beneath them to his actual historical role or to his character. We find occasional glimpses of Samuel's personality in the narrative—frightened when a boy by a divine revelation at night (1 Sam 3.15), angry when the people's demand for a king appears to be a personal rejection of him (1 Sam 8.4–6), and grieving over Saul's rejection by Yahweh (1 Sam 15.35). For the most part, however, the Deuteronomistic Historians' portrait of Samuel is of an ideal figure who is larger than life.

Samuel is first of all a priest, although not a member of the traditional priestly tribe of Levi; his father, Elkanah, is an Ephraimite. But as a child he is consecrated to the divine service in the shrine at Shiloh, under the tutelage of Eli, who appears almost as a surrogate father (note 1 Sam 3.16). As a priest, Samuel is repeatedly described as offering sacrifices, and when Saul usurps that prerogative, Samuel strenuously objects (1 Sam 13.8–14).

Samuel is also a judge, both in the sense of a local military leader like the heroes of the book of Judges, and also as one who exercised typical judicial functions. 1 Samuel 12.6–17 is a set speech composed by the Deuteronomistic Historians, comparable to the addresses of other leaders at critical occasions in Israel's history (compare the book of Deuteronomy; Josh 23; 24; 1 Kings 8.12–61). In this speech Samuel lists himself alongside Jerubbaal, Barak, and Jephthah (1 Sam 12.11; some ancient traditions read "Samson" for "Samuel" here) as one divinely sent to deliver Israel from its enemies. And this is in fact one of his functions: Under Samuel's leadership, "the hand of the LORD was against the Philistines all the days of Samuel" (1 Sam 7.13). Later events in the narrative, however, make that implausible. Even if occasional Israelite victories in battle occurred under Samuel's leadership, the war was far from over: The conflict between Israel and the Philistines continues in the latter part of 1 Samuel, and the Philistine threat to Israel's existence is not ended effectively until well into David's reign (2 Sam 5.25; 8.1).

Like Deborah, who was both a military leader and a judge in the sense of a magistrate who resolved legal disputes (Judg 4.4–5), Samuel is also depicted as one who "judged Israel all the days of his life" (1 Sam 7.15). His activities as a magistrate, however, as the next verses makes clear, were restricted to a limited region in Ephraim and Benjamin: "He went on a circuit year by year to Bethel, Gilgal, and Mizpeh; and he judged Israel in all these places. Then he would come back to Ramah, for his home was there; he judged Israel there" (1 Sam 7.16–17). These towns are within an eight-mile (sixteen-kilometer) radius, suggesting a local rather than national jurisdiction for Samuel, as with the earlier judges.

The conclusion that Samuel was originally a local leader is reinforced by accounts of his activity as a prophet. The Deuteronomistic Historians have preserved traditions that Samuel was a local "seer" (1 Sam 9.6–20), one who was at least connected with, if not the head of, the wandering group of ecstatics encountered by Saul. Yet in the Deuteronomistic Historians' own perspective, Samuel was the first of many prophets in the period of the monarchy who articulate the Deuteronomistic Historians' view of the failure of Israel to live up to its covenant with God. As such, for the Deuteronomistic Historians, Samuel's activity extended to all Israel; they assert that he was recognized as the recipient of the word of the Lord "from Dan to Beersheba" (1 Sam 3.20), the traditional northern and southern limits of Israelite territory. As a prophet, he relayed the divine judgment on the corrupt priesthood at Shiloh (3.11–14), on the king (1 Sam 12.12–13; 15.22–29; 28.16–19), and on the nation as a whole (1 Sam 8.11–18; 12.7–19). Moreover, as a prophet, like the later prophets Nathan, Elisha, and Isaiah, Samuel is presented as crucial for kingship, functioning both as king-maker, anointing first Saul and then David (although the latter only in private), and as king-breaker, in the case of Saul.

For the Deuteronomistic Historians, Samuel recalls Moses—also priest, judge, and prophet—the idealized leader of early Israel when Yahweh was its king. In the pattern of Moses, he intercedes with God for the people and relays the divine word to them. Samuel thus represents both continuity with the past and innovation, even if that innovation was one over which he only reluctantly presided. An antimonarchical slant is present in the narrative and in the depiction of Samuel: The old system of divinely chosen leaders had been sufficient, and the establishment of the monarchy was another example of Israel's repeated rebellion against divine rule.

We may conclude cautiously that Samuel, like Joshua, was an important local leader who was pivotal in the change in Israel's system of government. His authority was such that his sanction provided the monarch with apparently necessary legitimation, both in fact, in Saul's case, and in theory, in David's. But for the Deuteronomistic Historians, he was one in a continuous line of prophets beginning with Moses who functioned as intermediaries between Yahweh and the peo-

ple, and this idealized role has largely obscured the historical Samuel (see Box 14.1).

Saul

Saul is a complex and ultimately tragic figure. Although he begins his career as a successful military leader, he dies during a rout of his army by the Philistines. Initially selected by God as king in response to the people's request, God soon rejects Saul in favor of David. Saul's daughter Michal and his son and designated successor Jonathan also side with David against their father.

Saul's choice as military leader and king results from his victory over the Ammonites besieging Jabesh-gilead. As with the judges of old, "the spirit of God came upon Saul" (1 Sam 11.6). Using the symbolism of a cut animal to remind the people of their mutual obligations under the covenant (see pages 113–14), he musters the Israelites and leads them in a rout of the Ammonites and is immediately crowned king at the ancient sanctuary at Gilgal. This initial success is followed by a number of important victories against all of Israel's enemies: "against Moab, against the Ammonites, against Edom, against the kings of Zobah, and against the Philistines" (1 Sam 14.47). Even if this summary contains hyperbole, it attests to Saul's frequent successes in battle and must stem from the pro-Saul source called "The History of Saul's Rise."

Because of his personal qualities and his military successes, Saul was a popular leader. When he had been chosen by lot, the people shouted "Long live the king" (1 Sam 10.24), and when he returned victorious from battle with the Philistines, the women of Israel danced and sang, for he brought them security as well as spoil (see 1 Sam 18.6; 2 Sam 1.24).

Saul was also a shrewd leader. For Israel to survive its numerous external threats, especially that posed by the Philistines, it needed a regular fighting force. So Saul created an army. Among his troops were several sons of a Bethlehemite, Jesse, including David. As David's popularity increased, Saul, correctly as it turns out, began to view David as a potential danger to his ambition to establish a dynasty.

Box 14.1 SAMUEL IN OTHER TRADITIONS

Samuel himself is seldom mentioned outside of 1 Samuel. In 1 Chronicles, a number of references establish continuity between Samuel and the worship of Yahweh in the time of David and Solomon. Samuel's sons are listed among the descendants of Levi (6.28, 33; not Ephraim, as in 1 Sam 1.1), thereby eliminating the anomaly, for the Chronicler at least, that a non-Levite could exercise priestly functions. Samuel is said to have appointed the gatekeepers along with David (1 Chr 9.22). Included among the treasures dedicated to the Temple was booty captured by Samuel (26.28), and "the records of the seer Samuel" are given as one of the sources for the reign of David (29.29). All of these references illustrate the continuing tendency to harmonize monarchical institutions with less uniform premonarchic practice, and especially to establish links between David and earlier times, a process that began in David's own time as a way of legitimizing his assumption of power. But coming in the fifth- or fourth-century BCE book of Chronicles (see page 448), they also testify to Samuel's later importance.

This importance is especially clear in Jeremiah 15.1 and Psalm 99.6, which link Samuel with Moses as one of the primary intercessors with Yahweh in Israel's early history; the same theme is implied in 1 Samuel 7.8 and 12.19–25. The summary of Samuel's career in Sirach 46.13–20 is a late example of the heightening of Samuel's role as a pivotal figure.

Once David enters the narrative, the Deuteronomistic Historians' presentation of Saul is overwhelmingly negative. From their perspective, Saul's failure is ultimately because of divine rejection, expressed in Samuel's condemnation and in the replacement of the "spirit of the LORD" by "an evil spirit from the LORD" (1 Sam 16.14). Saul's behavior becomes erratic and homicidal, and the object of his antagonism is David. Modern readers have attempted to diagnose Saul's malady: Was it epilepsy or paranoid schizophrenia? For the Deuteronomistic Historians, no natural explanation is needed: God rejected Saul.

Saul's enmity toward David becomes, as the narrators imply, obsessive. Saul, it appears, will go to any lengths to track David down, and even kills David's supporters, notably the priests of Nob, of whom we are told some eighty-five were slaugh-

tered and their city razed, in a grotesque parody of "holy war" against Israel's enemies. Saul, like the later King Ahab, became one who troubled the land (1 Sam 14.29; 1 Kings 18.18).

Historically, we may conclude that Saul failed because he was unable to deal with the Philistine threat decisively. He died on the battlefield, and although it was by his own hand, heroically. But for the Deuteronomistic Historians, Saul's failure to deal with the Philistines was only symptomatic of a deeper reason: Saul failed because God had rejected him, and nothing he could do would reverse the divine judgment (see Box 14.2).

David

In 1 Samuel, David is almost without exception a heroic figure. In part this is because the Deuteronomistic Historians' principal source for

Box 14.2 POSITIVE ASSESSMENTS OF SAUL

The portrait of Saul in the final form of 1 Samuel is decidedly negative. That judgment is echoed in the summary of Saul's death by the Chronicler:

> So Saul died for his unfaithfulness; he was unfaithful to the LORD in that he did not keep the command of the LORD; moreover, he had consulted a medium, seeing guidance, and did not see guidance from the LORD. Therefore he put him to death and turned the kingdom over to David son of Jesse. (1 Chr 10.13–14)

That this assessment is not entirely valid historically is indicated by the earlier traditions that depict Saul positively, of which two stand out at the end of his life.

Saul had begun his career with a victory over the Ammonites on behalf of the beleaguered inhabitants of Jabesh-gilead east of the Jordan River (1 Sam 11.1–11). According to 1 Samuel 31.11–13, when news of Saul's death and the ignominious display of his body and those of his sons on the walls of Beth-shan reached Jabesh-gilead, men from that city, in a daring night expedition, retrieved the bodies and gave them an unusual although apparently proper burial. That such loyalty to Saul endured some twenty years after the event that motivated it is eloquent testimony to his reputation in his own time.

Another is found in David's lament over Saul and Jonathan, in 2 Samuel 1.19–27. In this remarkable eulogy, Saul's heroism is remembered, and along with Jonathan he is given unqualified praise:

> Saul and Jonathan, beloved and lovely!
>   In life and in death they were not separated.
> They were swifter than eagles,
>   they were stronger than lions. . . .
> How the warriors have fallen,
>   and the weapons of war have perished. (2 Sam 1.23, 27)

While this attitude supports the view of David as devoted completely to Saul rather than as his rival, it also reflects David's own view. In the end, David loved Saul, and this poignant poem, which can reasonably be attributed to David himself, shows it. Certainly it is a much more positive view of Saul than that of the Deuteronomistic Historians' presentation in the final form of 1 Samuel.

David was the "History of David's Rise," a propagandistic presentation of David as the legitimate successor to the divinely rejected Saul. Following a familiar pattern, David is introduced as Jesse's youngest son whom Yahweh chooses with-

out respect to the traditionally dominant status of the firstborn son (1 Sam 16.6–12), as he had earlier chosen Isaac over Ishmael (Gen 17.19–21) and Jacob over Esau (Gen 25.23). Like Saul, David is revealed to Samuel as the one to be anointed. But whereas Deuteronomistic Historians relate Samuel's reluctance to anoint Saul as king, there is no such reluctance in the case of David. Once anointed, the spirit of the Lord comes upon David, as it had come earlier on the judges and on Saul himself.

The dual narratives of David's introduction to the court of Saul continue the theme of divine favor and promote David as a hero of legendary status. In 1 Samuel 16.14–23, David is brought to Saul to provide him relief from "an evil spirit from the LORD." The narrative draws on the tradition of David as a talented poet and musician, "the sweet psalmist of Israel" (2 Sam 23.1 [KJV]; see Box 15.1 on page 250). In 1 Samuel 17, it is David, not Saul or any member of Saul's army, who is able to dispatch the Philistine champion Goliath. David does so relying on both his wit and his piety (see Figure 14.1).

Within Saul's entourage, David quickly rises to prominence. His military successes against the Philistines match those of Saul, provoking Saul's anger and arousing his suspicions of David's ambition. To Saul's dismay, David forms a close relationship with Jonathan, Saul's oldest son and presumed successor. When Saul finally keeps his promise to allow David to marry his daughter Michal for having killed Goliath, she too sides with her husband rather than her father. His popularity with the people grows as well; in a statement anticipating David's eventual rule over both the northern and the southern tribes, we are told in 1 Samuel 18.16 that "all Israel and Judah loved David" (see 2 Sam 5.1–5).

In part because of what is presented as the divine plan, Saul turns against David. For the narrators, David has done nothing to provoke Saul's hostility. Modest and pious, he is the king's loyal servant, who can scarcely believe that the king wishes him dead. He flees for his life, and twice when given the chance to kill Saul, he nobly refuses. He establishes a power base for himself in southern Judah, attacking enemies of Israel while nominally serving as a Philistine vassal.

The only hints of complexity in the presentation of David in 1 Samuel are his apparent willingness to kill his fellow Israelites, in the case of

FIGURE 14.1. Ancient slingers. The story of David killing Goliath with a sling (1 Sam 17) is a legend that illustrates David's military ability. Ancient Near Eastern armies often included slingers, as in this detail from reliefs showing the Assyrian siege of the Judean city of Lachish in 701 BCE. The sling worked by centrifugal force. A leather or cloth pad had thongs attached to it on two sides. The slinger placed the sling stone in the pad, and, holding the two thongs in his hand, whirled the sling around his head, releasing one of the thongs when the sling had achieved sufficient momentum. Skilled slingers were accurate at long distances, as was David when he killed Goliath. (For other scenes from these reliefs, see Figs. 19.3 and 19.4.)

Nabal (1 Sam 25.13, 34), and his service of the Philistines, although even this is presented as a form of loyalty to Israelites by attacking their enemies. As subsequent events in 2 Samuel will show, David is in fact an opportunist, who can be ruthless in using his power to advance his objectives.

David's marriages are politically advantageous, and in some cases even politically motivated. His marriage to Saul's daughter Michal makes him a member of the royal family and provides some legitimacy to his later ascension to the throne. His marriage to Abigail links him to the powerful

Calebite clan in southern Judah around Hebron, the city that will become his first capital (2 Sam 5.1–5), and his marriage to Ahinoam of Jezreel strengthens his connections with the same region.

The portrait of David in 1 Samuel, then, contains hints of what is to come. But his moment has not yet arrived.

Jonathan

David expresses his attachment to Jonathan in the eulogy he gives for Saul and Jonathan after their death:

> I grieve for you, my brother Jonathan;
>   you were very dear to me;
> your love was more wonderful for me
>   than the love of women. (2 Sam 1.26)

These words probably do not suggest a homosexual relationship between David and Jonathan, but they do testify to their closeness. Although Jonathan is essentially a minor character in the drama of David and Saul's rivalry, his loyalty to David is in stark contrast to his father's antagonism. Like everyone, it seems, except Saul, Jonathan recognizes in David the next king. Like his sister Michal, he is on David's side, and his gift to David of his own royal robe is a symbolic transfer of the succession, echoing Samuel's words in 1 Samuel 15.28.

Jonathan is depicted as a heroic warrior, popular with his troops and with the people as a whole. Beyond this we can say little, for the Deuteronomistic Historians' portrayal of Jonathan is shaped by their pro-David, anti-Saul bias.

Women

Although the primary narrative of 1 Samuel consists of the interlocking personal and political dramas of Samuel, Saul, and David, women also figure in the narrative, and the ways in which they are depicted shed light on women's social status. Like the males on whom they are dependent, many of these women are developed literary characters rather than idealized types.

Hannah, who in the final form of the narrative is Samuel's mother (but see page 232), is the first of these vividly portrayed women, and her

story opens the book. She is one of two wives of Elkanah, his favorite (1.5) and probably his first wife, but she is childless, in contrast to Elkanah's other wife, Peninnah, who has several children and taunts Hannah. Hannah deals with this circumstance with initiative, reminiscent of similarly situated women in the ancestral narratives in Genesis. Like Rebekah (Gen. 25.22–23) and Jacob's favorite wife Rachel (Gen. 29.30; 30.22), she prays to God directly for fertility, and her prayer is heard. She dedicates her firstborn, Samuel, to the service of the Lord at the shrine at Shiloh, and subsequently she has five more children (2.21). Although it is clear that Hannah shares the larger society's values of a woman's validation through childbearing, especially of a male, within the roles that Israelite society assigned to women she is very much an independent actor.

Another woman who demonstrates independence is Michal, Saul's daughter and David's first wife. While her marriage is an arranged one—she was given by her father to David—Michal's loyalty to and love for her husband motivate her to side with him rather than with her father. In a scene reminiscent of Rahab's assistance to the Israelite spies (Josh 2), Michal helps David escape her father's murderous plans and, like Rachel (Gen 31.34–35), deceives her father using "teraphim" (NRSV: "household gods").

A third woman who acts independently and who subverts the traditionally subservient role of the wife is Abigail. Her husband, who has the pejorative nickname Nabal, meaning "fool," refuses to provide the outlaw David with food for his men. David is prepared to retaliate, but Abigail averts the disaster by bringing the requested supplies herself, in a caravan reminiscent of Jacob's gifts to Esau (Gen 32.13–21). In a flowery speech, Abigail pleads with David to be merciful and expresses her conviction that David will be king because God is on his side. David relents, and in swift succession Nabal dies and David marries Abigail.

HISTORY

As has been true for all of the material in the Bible we have considered so far, no nonbiblical sources can be linked directly with the events and individuals mentioned in 1 Samuel. Constructing history from narratives such as these, which are characterized by invented dialogue, focused on individual and family relationships, and cast in the ideological perspective of the Deuteronomistic Historians, continues to be a speculative enterprise. Yet some evidence does exist, not least of which is the end result: the ancient Israelite monarchy from the tenth to the sixth centuries BCE. A transition from the loose confederation of tribes to that monarchy must have taken place, and the narrative in 1 Samuel presents an imaginative reconstruction of the early stages of that transition, in the persons of Samuel, the last leader of the old order; Saul, the first king; and David, waiting in the wings to be Saul's successor.

Toward the end of the second millennium BCE, at the beginning of the Iron Age, a period of weakness existed both in Egypt and in northern Mesopotamia, the two areas that for centuries had wrestled for control of the lands between them. This power vacuum enabled the city-states of the previous Late Bronze Age to consolidate their power into nations that were small by comparison with Egypt or Assyria, but larger than their predecessors. Fragmentary evidence from both biblical and nonbiblical sources suggests that in this period such states as Tyre, Damascus, Ammon, Moab, and others became nation-states, ruled by kings. Rivalry among these states and the continuing absence of a more powerful imperial presence enabled Israel also to become a monarchy "like all nations" (1 Sam 8.5). The immediate background for this change is the Philistine threat.

First Samuel presents a Philistine territorial expansion beyond their original borders eastward into the Negeb, northward along the coast, and northeastward into the hill country that was Israel's home. Philistine garrisons are reported at Geba, at Michmash, near Socoh, in the Jezreel Valley, and at Bethlehem. The archaeological record confirms this expansion. While not all of the sites where evidence of Philistine occupation is present are mentioned in the Bible, and not all of the places associated with the Philistines in the Bible have been excavated or show evidence of Philistine presence, the general pattern is consistent. Recognizable Philistine pottery in large quantities (that is, more than could be explained by occasional trading contacts) is found beyond the Philistine homeland at sites in the vicinity of Beersheba and at the important Philistine site of Tell Qasile near modern Tel Aviv, and significant levels of Philistine occupation can be found at such sites as Gezer, Timnah (Tel Batash), and Beth-shemesh.

Shiloh is another case in point. Although 1 Samuel mentions only the Philistine capture of the ark of the covenant, other biblical sources indicate that the city of Shiloh was also destroyed by the Philistines (see Ps 78.60–64; Jer 7.12, 14), an event correlated with a destruction dating to the mid-eleventh century BCE uncovered by excavations at Shiloh. While the numbers of troops involved were probably not very large in this and other engagements, Israel and the Philistines were in a state of virtually continuous war as they competed for control of the same territory.

This was the context for the emergence of the monarchy: The old institutions of the Israelite confederation, with its lack of standing army and its decentralized authority, were insufficient to deal with the Philistine threat. Yet those institutions were not replaced wholesale. The transition from confederation to monarchy was gradual, in part because of opposition such as that personified in Samuel.

Doubtless other factors contributed to a more centralized system of government, including population increase in the hill country and concomitant socioeconomic pressures. Trade with neighboring kingdoms would have led to the formation of a merchant class, who would have wanted security for their commerce. Moreover, increased specialization of occupations rather than familial self-subsistence would have required regional stability.

At most Israelite sites we find no significant difference in material culture and organization between the late eleventh and the late tenth centuries BCE. The only exception may be the remains of a structure dated to the late eleventh century BCE at Tell el-Ful, just north of Jerusalem, which some scholars have identified as a fortress built by Saul. If so, it is the only archaeological feature directly associated with Israel's first king. In any case, Saul's rule was only the beginning of the gradual transformation of Israel, and not surprisingly we find almost no evidence of its early stages in the archaeological record.

Nor is the chronology secure. The biblical numbers themselves are confused and apparently incomplete. The earliest direct connection between biblical and nonbiblical sources is the raid of the Egyptian pharaoh Shishak in 924 BCE, which according to 1 Kings 14.25 took place in the fifth year of the reign of Solomon's son Rehoboam (see further page 289). Working backward from this date and accepting as more or less accurate the round number of forty years given for the reigns of both David and Solomon, we can arrive at an approximate chronology for the first three kings of Israel as follows:

Saul	ca. 1025–1005 BCE (the original number of years in 1 Sam 13.1 is not recoverable; a twenty-year reign is found in later nonbiblical sources)
David	ca. 1005–965 BCE
Solomon	ca. 968–928 BCE (according to 1 Kings 1, Solomon was crowned before David's death)

On the basis of this chronology, the events described in 1 Samuel date to the second half of the eleventh century BCE.

The extent of the territory over which Saul ruled is debated. Minimally, it included his home base in Benjamin, Ephraim, and regions to their north and east; this at least was the extent of the area briefly ruled by his son Ishbaal (see 2 Sam 2.9). He probably had at least sporadic control of a wider area; the narrative depicts him as active from Amalek in the southwest to Gilead in the northeast (see Figure 14.2).

The only independent written source that we have for Saul's reign is 1 Samuel, and it is informed by the Deuteronomistic Historians' concern with divine intent. Once Saul has become king, less attention is paid to the larger context of the political and military events in the nation as a whole and more is given to personalities. As a result, we cannot be sure of the details of Saul's kingship. Some of the evidence that may be gleaned concerning Saul's reign and the early reign of David fits a model known from other cultures as a chiefdom rather than a true monarchy. Whether or not the actual title of "king" is appropriate to Saul, that is how later writers understood his role, and although Saul's reign marks only the beginning of the Israelite monarchy, the narrative preserves details of some of the changes that this new form of government brought.

Institutions

The Family and the Roles of Women

On the level of family ("the house of the father"), clan, and tribe, social organization continued much as it had in the preceding period of the judges. The head of the household was the de facto ruler of his domestic domain, exercising control over the means of sustenance and over sons, wives, daughters, and servants and slaves.

Life for women was much as it had been during the days of the confederation and as prescribed in the ancient legal codes. Women's primary functions lay within the family, and their status was as the property of their fathers and husbands. As property, women were also spoils of war (1 Sam 27.9; 30.3–5, 22).

In 1 Samuel, women are typically daughters, wives, and mothers, who implicitly find their fulfillment in these roles and who seldom act independently of the males upon whom they depend. Following traditional patterns, Saul decides whom his daughters will marry. Although his older daughter Merab has been promised to David, he gives her to someone else (18.17–19). He also gives his younger daughter Michal to David (18.20–29), and after the rupture between David and Saul, Saul then gives her to another man (25.44).

Although her husband loves her, Hannah's life is incomplete until she has children. As in the depiction of the ancestral period in Genesis, men often had more than one wife, and this polygyny

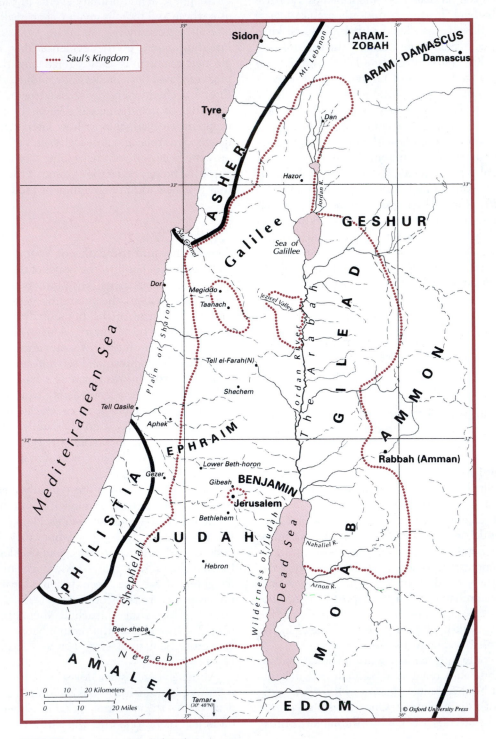

FIGURE 14.2.   Map of Saul's kingdom.

could lead to rivalry between the wives. The taunts of Peninnah to Elkanah's other wife Hannah echo the tension between Sarah and Hagar (Gen 16.4–6; 21.9–11) and between Leah and Rachel (Gen 30.1–24).

Yet within these social constraints, women occasionally exercise initiative. Michal defies her father and rescues David. Abigail defies her husband and assists David, and, as a widow, is free to act on her own in accepting David's offer of marriage.

Women did occasionally have public roles. They functioned as secondary officiants in the worship of Yahweh at Shiloh (1 Sam 2.22) and sang victory songs to greet returning warriors (18.6–7). The woman of Endor is an apparently independent medium (28.7–25). The episode in which she figures serves two purposes for the Deuteronomistic Historians: to provide a further rationale for the divine rejection of Saul, as one who violated Yahwistic observance by consulting the dead (see Deut 18.10–11), and also to restate through the dead Samuel himself the divine choice of David. Saul's death, which will occur almost immediately, is predicted and is deserved.

Succession

Within the family, according to ancient traditions, the oldest son was the primary heir. The same principle of patrilineal succession also prevailed in the larger society, no doubt modeled on the family. The priesthood was hereditary; so too was the office of magistrate ("judge"), at least in the case of Samuel's sons (1 Sam 8.1). The resistance to such succession expressed in the book of Judges by Gideon (Judg 8.22–23) seems to have been exceptional, if not an ideological bias on the part of the Deuteronomistic Historians with their continuing insistence that it was God who ultimately chose leaders and that the divine choice was not dependent upon patrilineal descent or other human conventions.

This principle of succession was naturally extended by Saul to his oldest son Jonathan, whom Saul intended to become king after him; when Jonathan was killed in the battle at Mount Gilboa that closes 1 Samuel, another of Saul's sons was recognized as his successor by the northern tribes

(2 Sam 2.8–10). Widespread social change was thus not a feature of Saul's rule.

The Army

The major innovation of the early monarchy was the army. One of the weaknesses of the tribal confederation was its lack of a permanent, professional military. Reliable ancient traditions in the book of Judges make it clear that individual tribes and groups of tribes relied on a volunteer militia. But this militia proved unable to deal with the Philistine threat, as Saul perspicaciously recognized. Soon after having assumed power as king, he established a standing army. In fact, the first observation that the Deuteronomistic Historians make after the notice of Saul's accession is that he "chose three thousand out of Israel" (1 Sam 13.2; see also 14.52).

Some of these troops were under Saul's personal command, and others were under his son Jonathan and his cousin Abner; the leadership of the army was thus controlled by Saul through his family. Although poorly equipped (1 Sam 13.22), they formed the nucleus of a fighting force that would probably have been supplemented as occasion required by volunteers. Conscription does not yet seem to have been institutionalized.

This army's primary loyalty was to the king rather than to Israel more generally, and it was called the "servants of Saul" (18.5, 30; 22.17). The troops were paid for their services by exemption from taxes (1 Sam 17.25) and apparently by land grants (1 Sam 8.14–15). They also shared in the booty taken from defeated enemies. The army was comprised of different groups, one of which is called the "runners" (22.17; NRSV: "guard"), also a term used for a contingent of David's army. Some of these soldiers functioned as the king's personal bodyguards.

David followed Saul's example, forming a cadre of soldiers, including mercenaries, whose loyalty was to him personally rather than to some larger entity. They seem to have subsisted by a kind of banditry, like Jephthah (Judg 11.3). Later he hired himself and his private army to the Philistines, which reflects their military worth. In employing David, the Philistines were perhaps also motivated by a desire to keep this unpredictable outlaw under their oversight. In any case, the notice that the Philistines hired David and his "men" is a detail that has the ring of fact, since it is one of the few negative notes about David in 1 Samuel and is unlikely to have been invented by the Deuteronomistic Historians. The Deuteronomistic Historians go to some lengths to insist that David's raids were directed only against Israel's enemies rather than at parts of Israel itself and that David did not join the Philistines against Israel in the battle in which Saul died. Apparently David's activity as a mercenary for the Philistines was something of an embarrassment for the Deuteronomistic Historians, but it was a well-known tradition that they could not ignore.

Religion

The picture of Israelite worship in 1 Samuel continues that of the period of the judges. The principal places of worship were local shrines, each presided over by its own priesthood. Only Shiloh seems to have functioned as a supraregional religious center. According to the Ark Narrative the ark was located there, perhaps in a permanent structure (called a "temple" in 1 Sam 1.9; 3.3; compare 3.15), although for ceremonial occasions at least the ark may have been located in a tent associated with the temple. The presence of the ark could have made Shiloh the site of the great pilgrimage feasts for many Israelites during this period. Although the apparently special status of Shiloh in 1 Samuel may derive from the Deuteronomistic Historians' preoccupation with a central sanctuary, as decreed in Deuteronomy (12.5; etc.), it also seems to reflect the actual situation, as references to Shiloh in later writings presume (Ps 78.60; Jer 7.12; see also Judg 21.19). Yahweh was clearly worshiped at Shiloh and at a number of other sites, one of which, probably at Ramah, has a "high place" (NRSV: "shrine"). And, according to the Ark Narrative, in the premonarchic era the ark of the covenant was the confederation's most important sacred object. Once captured by the Philistines, however, it disappears from the narrative. (The only exception is a mention in the traditional Hebrew text of 1 Sam 14.18, where

following other ancient traditions we should almost certainly read "ephod.")

The priests' primary responsibility was to officiate at worship, with each local shrine having its own priesthood. The priesthood at Shiloh was hereditary: Eli and his sons were both priests there, and his grandson Ahitub continued the family line of priests, based at Nob after Shiloh's destruction, as did Ahitub's grandson Abiathar. Samuel is also depicted as a priest, offering sacrifice at a number of locations and jealous of his priestly prerogatives according to the Deuteronomistic Historians' tendentious account of the rejection of Saul (1 Sam 13.8–15). Ordinary people made offerings, which were supervised by the priests, who earned their livelihood from their share of the sacrifice. Saul himself officiated at a sacrifice; this is interpreted by the Deuteronomistic Historians as a usurpation of priestly functions, when Samuel announces that God has rejected Saul (1 Sam 13.9). He also officiates at another sacrifice, but is not condemned (1 Sam 14.31–35). Both of the next two kings, David and his son Solomon, are similarly described as offering sacrifices, and Saul's assumption of priestly functions may anticipate later monarchic efforts to control the entire religious establishment.

Priests, like diviners, also interpreted the divine will by their use of the Urim and Thummim (14.36–42) and the ephod (30.7; compare 14.18). Little is known about what these devices looked like or how they worked, but they apparently gave positive or negative responses to a question asked, and presumably because the result was unpredictable, they were thought to reveal divine intent. (See further page 298.)

Deities other than Yahweh must have been worshiped as well, as they had been in the era of the Judges and would continue to be during the later monarchy. The passage in 1 Samuel 7.3–4, in which the Israelites are described as worshiping the Canaanite deities Baal and Astarte, is so formulaic that its historicity is questionable. But some other evidence does exist, notably from personal names. Saul, Jonathan, and David each gave one of their sons names containing the element "baal," which can mean simply "master," as a title of Yahweh, but more probably refers to the Canaanite god.

The only named religious festival in 1 Samuel is that of the new moon (20.5; see Num 28.11–15). Neither the sabbath nor any of the great pilgrimage festivals of Passover, Weeks, and Booths is referred to explicitly by name, although some scholars have identified the annual festival at Shiloh in which Elkanah and Hannah participate (1 Sam 1.21) as the festival of Booths. Again, however, we must recall that the Deuteronomistic Historians are not writing social history, and the absence of observances and institutions attested in other periods does not mean that they were not present in the early monarchy as well.

We see little evidence for the practice of necromancy, consulting the spirits of the dead, in ancient Israel, but like other aspects of popular religion that were deemed unacceptable by the biblical writers it was probably not uncommon. The prohibition in Deuteronomy 18.11 testifies to its existence, and in the eighth century BCE the prophet Isaiah will condemn those who "consult the ghosts and the familiar spirits . . . for teaching and for instruction" (Isa 8.19; see also 65.4). Although forbidden, necromancy was considered efficacious. The best example of the practice in the Bible is Saul's consultation of the medium at Endor. In the narrative, Samuel does rise from the grave to speak to Saul, and Sirach 46.20 interprets this postmortem revelation as authentic prophecy.

First Samuel also contains valuable data about the phenomenon of prophecy in early Israel. Prophecy is attested elsewhere in the ancient Near East: in Mesopotamia in texts from the second millennium BCE, in Phoenicia in the eleventh century BCE, and in a number of sources from the first millennium. The details vary considerably, but the ancients maintained a consistent view that certain individuals had a special channel of communication with the gods. These individuals were understood as messengers of divine knowledge or intention, mediated through them to individuals and groups in the larger society.

Not surprisingly, the Bible also uses a variety of terms for prophets and in describing their ac-

tivities and functions. The Deuteronomistic Historians view certain prophets as special revealers of Yahweh's will, and as we have seen its presentation of Samuel belongs to this category, which could be called "high" prophecy. Especially noteworthy in this regard is the account of Saul's rejection in 1 Samuel 15. Samuel's speech, with its insistence that obedience to divine commands is more important than ritual offerings (vv. 22–23), is strongly reminiscent of later prophetic utterances (see Box 18.3 on page 319), and his symbolic interpretation of Saul's tearing of his robe (vv. 27–28) recalls the symbolic meaning given to ordinary gestures and phenomena by prophets to follow.

But the Deuteronomistic Historians have preserved other traditions of how prophets functioned in society, and we have two pieces of evidence in 1 Samuel. The first is Samuel himself, who is not just a prophet in the more exalted sense, but also, or perhaps originally, a seer, the sort of person one consulted when, for example, looking for lost animals, as Saul did in 1 Samuel 9.5–10. Later the term seer may even have a pejorative connotation (like "psychic"), as in Amos 7.12. Many such local visionaries, consulted by ordinary people whose needs were more immediate than the issues that later prophets often addressed, must have been functioning. To some extent, these seers overlapped in function with the priests in their use of divination to discern the divine will.

In 1 Samuel we also learn that prophets were not always solitary. Some formed their own associations or guilds, known as "the sons of the prophet" (NRSV: "company of the prophets"). Similar prophetic guilds are attested later in the monarchy (see 1 Kings 20.35; 2 Kings 2.3; etc.). Their leader, known as their "father," was apparently a teacher in the techniques of prophesying, from the mundane to the sublime. These include, for some at least, the use of music to reach a kind of ecstatic state (see 1 Sam 10.5; 2 Kings 3.15–19), in which the prophets, and apparently others under their influence, would exhibit abnormal behavior (see 1 Kings 18.28–29). Such ecstatic prophetic activity is elsewhere in the ancient Near East and appears to be the case with Saul's dealings with the "sons of the prophets." In his first encounter, in 1 Samuel 10.10, Saul, although not a prophet himself, exhibits ecstatic behavior, and this is further demonstration that Yahweh is with him. In the second encounter, in 19.20–24, which takes place after Saul's rejection, the Deuteronomistic Historians' view of his behavior may be more negative.

The Deuteronomistic Historians thus have taken folk traditions about Samuel the local seer and leader of a band of prophets and expanded them into a presentation of Samuel as one of the preeminent prophets in Israel's history, the messenger of the deity to both king and people. On God's behalf he presides over the choice and ceremonial anointing of both Saul and David, as his prophetic successors Nathan and Elisha are reported to do for other kings later in the Deuteronomistic History, and, in a pattern that will become familiar, he announces the divine judgment of doom on the nation for its rejection of Yahweh as their true king. (See further page 301.)

RETROSPECT AND PROSPECT

Preoccupied as they are with the personal dramas of Samuel, Saul, and David, the Deuteronomistic Historians pay little attention to the development of social institutions in 1 Samuel. But the details that they provide in passing, as it were, are valuable nuggets. In part this may be because the Deuteronomistic Historians are not writing a social history but are presenting a theological perspective on the establishment of the monarchy through the vehicle of narrative of the principal characters. In part, as well, little change probably occurred. The early monarchy under Saul, restricted to a relatively small territory, did not yet entail the more pervasive social change that 1 Samuel 12 anticipates. Nor did Saul, as king, manage to consolidate as much power in his hands as did his successors.

Why did Saul fail? According to the Deuteronomistic Historians it was because the divine favor left him and was transferred to David. But as we

have seen, the Deuteronomistic Historians' view is colored by their pro-David sources. The specific occasion of the rejection is presented as Saul's offering of sacrifice, implicitly a priestly task, but one that other kings also did without censure. Such episodes as the slaughter of the priests of Nob, if they have any basis in fact, would have created disenchantment but not necessarily opposition. Ultimately, perhaps, Saul's failure was military: He was unable to contain the Philistines, in part because he squandered his military resources pursuing David. When Saul died in the battle with the Philistines at Mount Gilboa, he had failed in the primary task that had motivated the people to choose him as king. And David, a proven warrior with his own army, was poised to assume the kingship and to succeed where Saul had failed.

An unresolved tension can be seen in the Deuteronomistic Historians' presentation of the beginning of the monarchy in 1 Samuel. Kingship has not yet solved the problem of the Philistines: First Samuel ends almost as it began—with a terrible defeat of the Israelite army by the Philistines. The tension is also evident in the ambivalent attitude toward the monarchy itself. Structurally this ambivalence is expressed in the alternation of passages that are negative toward the establishment of the monarchy (8.1–22; 10.17–27; 12.1–25) and passages that are positive (9.1–10.16; 11.1–15).

Yet God has a plan—that is the perspective of the Deuteronomistic Historians, thematically announced in the Song of Hannah. Monarchy in general, and especially David's kingship, are part of that plan. In the opening chapters of 1 Samuel, God is, so to speak, on stage himself, speaking to Samuel repeatedly—but only to Samuel, revealing his intentions. Once David has been anointed, the divine plan has been set in motion, and God moves offstage.

Unlike the book of Judges that precedes and the books of Kings that follow, the Deuteronomistic Historians in 1 (and 2) Samuel are not preoccupied with the nation's failure to worship Yahweh exclusively. Israel's defeats are not explained as divine punishment for worshiping other gods, but the divine hand is still present. This may ultimately be the key to understanding the Deuteronomistic History: How were the historical facts—Saul's failure, David's assumption of the throne—to be explained in terms of the divine purpose? Had the seeds of the ultimate failure of the monarchy already been sown?

Since 1 Samuel is part of a larger work, we will have to wait for the complete fulfillment of the prophecies of judgment on the priesthood of Eli (1 Sam 2.27–36; 3.11–14; see 1 Kings 2.27) and of the dire consequences of kingship (1 Sam 8.11–18; 12.14–15). Kingship will be at best a mixed blessing, as Israel's subsequent history will demonstrate, and the Deuteronomistic Historians are writing from that perspective of hindsight. Yet the monarchy will have its glorious moments as well, and that too, for the Deuteronomistic Historians, must be divinely ordained.

For the Deuteronomistic Historians, neither Saul's fall nor David's rise were ultimately caused by their own weaknesses and strengths: It was the Lord's doing; the Lord was first with Saul, and then with David. With a king, as without a king, God was guiding the nation.

QUESTIONS FOR REVIEW

1. How do the Deuteronomistic Historians incorporate different and even inconsistent traditions into their work, and how does this contribute to their presentation of the period of the early monarchy?

2. What factors led to the establishment of the monarchy in ancient Israel? What were the reasons for opposition to it?

3. How do the delineations of the characters of Samuel, Saul, and David reveal the perspectives of the Deuteronomistic Historians?

4. What is the theological problem that arose with the establishment of kingship in Israel?

5. How did ancient Israelite society change during the early monarchy as described in 1 Samuel?

BIBLIOGRAPHY

Good commentaries on 1 Samuel include Robert L. Cohn, "1 Samuel," pp. 245–61 in *HarperCollins Bible Commentary* (ed. J. L. Mays; San Francisco: Harper & Row, 2000); Jo Ann Hackett, "1 and 2 Samuel," pp. 85–95 in *The Women's Bible Commentary* (ed. C. A. Newsom and S. H. Ringe; Louisville, KY: Westminster John Knox, 1992); and P. Kyle McCarter, Jr., *I Samuel* (Garden City, NY: Doubleday, 1980).

For a careful survey of the historical context, see Carol Meyers, "From Kinship to Kingship: The Early Monarchy," Chap. 5 in *The Oxford History of the Biblical World* (ed. M. D. Coogan; New York: Oxford University Press, 1998).

For summaries of the career of Saul, see Diana V. Edelman, "Saul," pp. 989–99 in *The Anchor Bible Dictionary*, Vol. 5 (ed. D. N. Freedman; New York: Doubleday, 1992); and David M. Gunn, "Saul," pp. 673–81 in *The Oxford Companion to the Bible* (ed. B. M. Metzger and M. D. Coogan; New York: Oxford University Press, 1993).

An excellent reconstruction of the life of David is Steven L. McKenzie, *King David: A Biography* (New York: Oxford University Press, 2000).

THE REIGN OF DAVID

2 Samuel, 1 Kings 1–2, and Psalm 132

The book of 1 Samuel ends with the death of Saul. Now the focus shifts to David, who will soon become Saul's successor. The reign of David had far-reaching consequences for ancient Israel and beyond, especially for Judaism and Christianity. Because of its importance, the material pertaining to the **United Monarchy** (the reigns of David and Solomon, which lasted for most of the tenth century BCE) is covered in both this chapter and the next.

2 SAMUEL

Second Samuel continues the narrative of 1 Samuel without interruption because the two books were originally one (see page 231). Still, the death of Saul at the end of 1 Samuel is a logical place for the division that was eventually made, and David's reign is the exclusive focus of 2 Samuel. David's death, however, does not occur until 1 Kings 2. This shows that the books of Samuel and Kings were also divided only later, as does the presence of a source, "The Succession Narrative of David" (see page 249), which extends from 2 Samuel 9 to 1 Kings 2.

The focus of 2 Samuel and the first two chapters of 1 Kings, then, is on David. As the narrative develops, the complexity of David's character that had only been hinted at in 1 Samuel is laid out clearly. He is the divinely chosen king, yet he comes to power as the result of carefully calculated political and military moves. The Lord is with him, yet he repeatedly incurs divine wrath. And most strikingly, having been presented in 1 Samuel as a heroic figure, in this material David is almost an antihero—often absent from the battlefield, duped by his son, forced into exile, and, at the end of his life, impotent and senile.

Sources

As in 1 Samuel, the Deuteronomistic Historians made use of a variety of sources in composing the narrative of David's reign in 2 Samuel. Chapters 1–5 continue "The History of David's Rise," culminating in his becoming king over both Judah and Israel; embedded in this source are smaller units of tradition of several kinds, including David's lament over Saul and Jonathan (see further page 237). The Ark Narrative is concluded in 2 Samuel 6 with the account of David bringing the ark of the covenant to Jerusalem.

The major source that scholars have identified is in 2 Samuel 9–20 and 1 Kings 1–2. Like other "sources" in the Bible, especially in the Pentateuch and the Deuteronomistic History, it is hypothetical—that is, it does not exist independently from its biblical context. This source is called the "**Succession Narrative**" because its main theme may be viewed as providing an explanation of why Solomon became his father David's successor; some scholars also call it the "Court History of David." This narrative describes in detail the events that led to the birth of Solomon by Bathsheba, the death of Solomon's older brothers Amnon and Absalom, and, in 1 Kings 1–2, how Solomon rather than Adonijah assumed the throne. Like earlier narratives in 1 Samuel, it is a kind of historical fiction, containing invented dialogue that moves the action along. It also uses foreshadowing: Characters introduced early on recur later. It is an extraordinarily well-written composition, in which even minor characters are distinctly portrayed. It also has a high level of verisimilitude and can plausibly be dated not long after the events it narrates.

Inserted into the Succession Narrative at the end of 2 Samuel are a number of originally independent units, arranged in a symmetrical pattern:

- A narrative, in 21.1–14, of how seven of Saul's surviving sons and grandsons (and David's possible rivals) were killed. Some scholars think that this was originally connected with 2 Samuel 9. The account attributes the death of Saul's sons only indirectly to David; it is the inhabitants of Gibeon who actually carry out the execution, with royal sanction. Only Mephibosheth, Saul's grandson and Jonathan's son, is spared.

- A list, in 21.15–22, of David's heroes in his wars against the Philistines. These too seem to have taken place earlier in his reign.

- A royal hymn of thanksgiving, in chapter 22 (also found in the book of Psalms as Psalm 18; see further Box 16.2 on page 276). Its prose introduction relates it to events throughout David's career. Parts of the hymn recall the Song of Hannah at the be-

ginning of 1 Samuel and Nathan's dynastic oracle in 2 Samuel 7.

- A second hymn, in 23.1–7, called "the last words of David." Similar poetic compositions at the ends of their lives are also attributed to Jacob (Gen 49) and Moses (Deut 32–33). Like them, this poem contains archaic features, but its attribution to David is debated (see Box 15.1).

- A second list, in 23.8–39, of David's heroes with summaries of their exploits, which includes his elite warriors, "the Thirty."

- A narrative, in chapter 24, of the census undertaken by David and its disastrous consequences.

Interspersed with these sources are compositions of the Deuteronomistic Historians themselves and shorter poetic pieces and archival notices. The whole, as shaped by the Deuteronomistic Historians, forms a coherent narrative of David's reign.

The Narrative

As the book opens, David gets news of Saul's death. He is chosen as king by the tribe of Judah and makes his capital at Hebron, the traditional site of the tombs of Israel's ancestors (see Gen 23; 25.9–10; 49.29–32). Saul's son, Ishbaal, rules in the north. With the assassinations of Ishbaal's general Abner and Ishbaal himself, David is accepted as king by the northern tribes as well, and he moves his capital farther north to Jerusalem, to which he brings the ark of the covenant. (See Figure 15.1.)

Because "the LORD gave victory to David" (2 Sam 8.6, 14), the king is able to defeat his enemies and succeeds in subjugating not only the Philistines but also the other nations that could threaten Israel. Among these are the Ammonites, to the east of Israel across the Jordan River. The Ammonite campaign is the context for David's adulterous affair with Bathsheba, the wife of Uriah the Hittite.

The affair with Bathsheba marks a shift in the book's perspective. From this point on David is

Box 15.1 DAVID'S COMPOSITIONS

David's reputation as poet and musician in the books of Samuel increases in later biblical and postbiblical tradition. In 1 Chronicles, David is credited with organizing the elaborate rituals of the Temple, and especially its music. One tradition even holds that David invented musical instruments (see Am 6.5; 1 Chr 23.5; 2 Chr 7.6; 29.26; Ps 151.2), and in later art he is typically shown holding a lyre.

The book of Psalms is a collection of hymns, most of which were used in worship in the Temple. Seventy-three of the 150 psalms in the Hebrew Bible are attributed to David, six times more than to anyone else. This reflects David's reputation more than historical reality, since some of the psalms attributed to David mention the Temple, which was not constructed during his lifetime, and allude to events that happened long after his life. The tendency to attribute psalms to David is analogous to associating legal traditions with Moses, and it continues in postbiblical literature. In the ancient Greek translation of the Hebrew scriptures, the Septuagint, all 150 psalms are attributed to David, and a manuscript of the Psalms from the Dead Sea Scrolls credits David with composing 4,050 songs.

Underlying this development must be a historical memory: David was a great poet. Scholars disagree about whether any of David's poems have actually survived, but two that have a good chance of stemming from David himself are the lament over Saul and Jonathan in 2 Samuel 1.19–27 (see Box 14.2 on page 237) and "the last words of David" in 2 Samuel 23.1–7; the latter includes this striking image:

> One who rules over people justly,
>   ruling in the fear of God,
> is like the morning light at sunrise,
>   a morning without clouds,
>   making the grass sparkle after rain. (vv. 3–4)

largely at the mercy of events rather than directing them. Unable to control his sons, and incapable of rendering justice to the nation as a whole, David is ousted from his throne by Absalom and forced to flee in disgrace across the Jordan. This is a narrative of sexual betrayals, murders, and tragedy, in sharp contrast to the triumphant beginnings of David's story in 1 Samuel and the early chapters of 2 Samuel.

The revolt of Absalom is the centerpiece of this narrative. It begins with the rape of Absalom's sister Tamar by her half-brother Amnon, for which Absalom kills Amnon. Forced to flee from the court, Absalom bides his time until, at the instigation of David's general Joab, he is allowed to return. He forms his own cadre of soldiers, and with popular support has himself anointed king at Hebron, David's first capital. David is forced to flee in disgrace. Absalom's rule is sabotaged, however, by David's supporters, and David's superior strategy results in the defeat of Absalom's troops and his death at Joab's hand.

FIGURE 15.1. According to 2 Samuel 2.12–17, supporters of David met supporters of Saul's son Ishbaal (Ishbosheth) "at the pool of Gibeon," where twelve champions from each side met in combat. All were killed, and in the larger battle that followed David's army was victorious. Excavations at ancient Gibeon uncovered this large reservoir cut into the limestone bedrock in the early Iron Age. Its diameter is 37 ft (11.25 m), and seventy-nine steps around the perimeter lead down 82 ft (25 m) to the bottom. This is the pool referred to in 2 Samuel 2.3 and also in Jeremiah 41.12.

David returns to Jerusalem, only to face another revolt, by a northerner, Sheba, which is quickly suppressed. The Deuteronomistic Historians interpret these events as divine retribution for David's having taken Uriah's wife Bathsheba and having arranged his murder. We see an ironic symmetry here: Sexual offense leads to murder and exile for both Absalom and David.

Throughout 2 Samuel, David himself is removed from the violence that surrounds him, but the Deuteronomistic Historians lay the blame squarely at his feet. David was apparently unwilling to employ violence to further his cause against Saul in 1 Samuel, but now he allows his subordinates to eliminate Saul's survivors ruthlessly, and his proxies are responsible for the deaths of Uriah,

Absalom, and Sheba. The implication is that David himself is ultimately guilty.

The narrative ends with David a pathetic figure, politically and sexually impotent, at the mercy of his court and an unwitting participant in the events that lead to Solomon's succession.

The Characters

David

David is the most important individual in the Hebrew Bible after Moses (see Figure 15.2). More space is devoted to him and to compositions attributed to him than to anyone except Moses, and the actions David took and the policies he instituted had a profound effect on the literature, his-

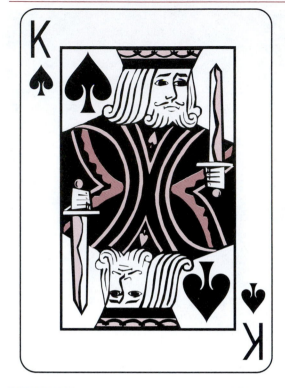

FIGURE 15.2. No contemporaneous portraits of David exist. In Western art he is frequently depicted with a sword, as in this image from a deck of cards, and sometimes with a lyre as well. The face cards were originally designed to teach ancient history; in addition to David, the king of spades, other characters from the Bible are Rachel and Judith, two of the queens.

tory, and religion of ancient Israel and on Judaism, Christianity, and Islam. David is also the most fully developed character in the Hebrew Bible, thanks in large part to the Succession Narrative, whose depiction of him is unusually detailed and candid. The biblical writers—and the ancient Israelites, we can presume—were clearly fascinated and troubled by this man, and the result is a vivid portrait of a complex individual, with all his strengths and weaknesses, one who was cunning, opportunistic, loyal, and passionate—and the greatest king in Israel's history.

Among David's many talents were those as a poet and a musician. This is an early and enduring tradition (see Box 15.1). In the ancient world, poetry and music were part of the same creative

art: Poems were generally sung, with lyrics and music composed by the same person. The first narrative about David, in 1 Samuel 16, highlights his musical abilities: He is so skilled that when he plays the lyre, the evil spirit leaves Saul. Second Samuel contains poems attributed to David at the beginning and end of the book (1.19–27; 22; 23.1–7), bracketing his reign as it were with highlights of this aspect of his talents.

David also was a gifted warrior and military tactician. His legendary strategic sense has been seen in 1 Samuel, in the accounts of his killing of Goliath and of his repeated escapes from Saul. He headed a small mercenary army, whose services the Philistines employed. Once he became king, he swiftly employed this military ability to defeat or at least contain both the rival house of Saul and the enemies of Israel, beginning with the Philistines (2 Sam 5.17–25) and continuing with the Moabites, the Arameans, the Edomites, and the Ammonites. And when his son Absalom revolted against him, once again David emerged victorious. While some of the episodes in which David's strategic skill is featured have sagalike embellishments, especially the account of the killing of Goliath, without a doubt David was an exceptional warrior.

Perhaps the most striking of David's many talents is his brilliance as a politician. In 1 Samuel, he is presented as able to keep both Israelites and Philistines convinced that he is on their side. His only failure, perhaps, was his rupture with Saul, but for the Deuteronomistic Historians that is part of a larger divine plan and David has no culpability for the rupture.

In 2 Samuel, immediately after Saul's death, David's political adroitness led to his being crowned king of Judah, although initially perhaps as a Philistine vassal. He then arranged for his first wife, Saul's daughter, to be returned to him, probably to bolster his claim to the throne, and within a few years won the allegiance of the rival northern kingdom of Israel, which was ruled by Saul's son Ishbaal (Ishbosheth). In the Deuteronomistic Historians' narrative, it is David's subordinates, and particularly Joab, the commander of his army, who are responsible for eliminating Ishbosheth and his supporters, but it is unlikely that this would have happened without David's direction and consent.

With the rival rule of Saul's son disposed of, David was crowned king of the northern tribes as well. Then he undertook a step that both shows his political shrewdness and would have enduring consequences for Israel and beyond: He captured Jerusalem and made it his capital. To further unify the kingdom and to enhance his legitimacy as its ruler, he brought the old religious symbol of tribal unity, the ark of the covenant, to the city. In a literal sense, Yahweh was with David (2 Sam 7.3) because David brought Yahweh to Jerusalem. With a dual focus on monarch and deity, Jerusalem became both city of David and city of God (see further Box 15.2).

It is at this point that the Succession Narrative begins, and we see the dark side of David. This is hinted at in the opening line of the Bathsheba episode: "It was the springtime, the time when kings go forth to war . . . but David remained in Jerusalem" (2 Sam 11.1). If David had been acting as a king should, the implication is, he would have been in the battlefield with the ark and the army, not in his capital.

This implicit condemnation is made clear by what follows: the adulterous affair with Bathsheba and the murder by proxy of her husband Uriah. When Bathsheba informed David that she was pregnant, David cunningly arranged for her husband to return from the battlefield and repeatedly tried to get him to go home, and, in the biblical euphemism, to wash his feet—that is, to have sexual intercourse with Bathsheba, so that Uriah would appear to have fathered the child. But Uriah, one of David's elite warriors ("the Thirty"), was pious—sexual abstinence was a requirement of holy war, and he would not enjoy luxury while the troops were camped in the open. So David sent him back to the front with a sealed message to Joab that was Uriah's death warrant: "Set Uriah in the forefront of the hardest fighting, and then draw back from him, so that he may be struck down and die" (2 Sam 11.15).

David was a sinner—but one capable of repentance. The prophet Nathan used a parable of immoral expropriation to elicit David's judgment, and then turned that judgment on David himself: "You are the man!" (2 Sam 12.7). David in his reply did not equivocate: "I have sinned against the LORD" (12.13). In the classic biblical mode of divine retribution, David was punished through the fatal illness of his child with Bathsheba. Later, in the episode of the census in 2 Samuel 24, David again displayed his capacity for repentance—one of the reasons that led so many of the psalms that express penitence being attributed to him (see further Box 15.1).

The antiheroic portrait of David is developed further in the events that follow. He is presented as an overindulgent father, unwilling to punish either Amnon for the rape of Tamar or Absalom for his revolt. During the revolt itself, while continuing to demonstrate his shrewdness by having Hushai serve as a fifth column in the court of Absalom in Jerusalem, he is at the same time a somewhat pathetic figure, "weeping . . . and walking barefoot" as he left the city (2 Sam 15.30), with Shimei, a relative of Saul, throwing dirt and stones at David and cursing him (16.5–13).

Despite his failings, however, David was a successful king. Unlike Saul he was able to deal with the Philistine threat effectively, and also unlike Saul he was able to establish a dynasty, one that would endure, if not eternally, at least for some four centuries. And so David, the major—and complex—character in the fictionalized account of the Succession Narrative, was also a major—and complex—figure historically: extraordinary poet, successful warrior, brilliant politician, and greatest king of Israel.

David's Sons

Seventeen sons by various wives are attributed to David in the lists of 2 Samuel 3.2–5 and 5.13–16 (the variant lists in 1 Chr 3.1–9 and 14.3–7 give nineteen). Infant mortality was high in antiquity, and many children, like David and Bathsheba's first son, would not have lived very long, so it is not surprising that we know little about many of David's sons except their names. Because of its central theme—the question of succession—several of them figure prominently in the Succession

Narrative: One after another, sons of David are killed or displaced, leading in 1 Kings 1 to the coronation, during David's lifetime, of Solomon, one of his younger sons, as David's successor.

The first son is Amnon, who as the oldest son would have succeeded his father. His calculating deception of his father and his rape of his half-sister Tamar in 2 Samuel 13 comes immediately after David's affair with Bathsheba and his arranging the death of her husband Uriah: Like father, like son, the narrator implies. David's response was to do nothing to Amnon, "because he loved him, for he was his firstborn" (2 Sam 13.21). But in an equally calculating act, Absalom, Tamar's brother and Amnon's half-brother, killed Amnon.

Absalom was exiled for his fratricide. He was eventually allowed to return, and, perhaps having harbored resentment against David during his exile, immediately set on the course of action that culminated in his coup d'état. Absalom seems to have had many of his father's qualities, such as political savvy and personal charm, but in the end he was no match for David, and he came to a disgraceful and grotesque end.

Solomon, the second child of David and Bathsheba, has two names. At birth he is given the name Solomon, but the narrator tells us that Nathan, instructed by Yahweh, named him Jedediah, "beloved of Yahweh," because "Yahweh loved him" (2 Sam 12.24). Almost at the outset of the drama its outcome is implied, which is Solomon's succession to the throne after his father, although this does not in fact occur until 1 Kings 1 (see further page 267).

Women

As in 1 Samuel, several of the women connected with the royal family are portrayed vividly. Michal, Saul's daughter and David's wife, is eventually returned to David, but her affection for and loyalty to him seem to have waned since they were separated. In 2 Samuel 6, she bluntly disparages David for his indecent dancing before the ark and is effectively dismissed by him with a curt if not cruel retort denigrating her father.

Bathsheba is a complex character. Although in the events that lead to David marrying her she is portrayed almost passively, in the conclusion to the Succession Narrative she is an active participant in the machinations that lead to Solomon's coronation. Some interpreters have suggested that her role in the affair with David was less than innocent, but the skillful author of the Succession Narrative leaves this to the reader to decide.

Tamar, too, is a passive, if attractive, figure, one whose rape by her half-brother is narrated with considerable pathos. Our glimpse of her is brief, ending with the poignant image of "a desolate woman, in her brother Absalom's house" (2 Sam 13.20).

Another woman worthy of note is Saul's concubine Rizpah. Like Antigone, the daughter of Oedipus, in Greek myth, she risks royal displeasure to prevent the unburied bodies of her own two sons and the five sons of Saul's daughter Merab from being defiled. Her courageous action inspires David to give proper burial to the remains of Saul and Jonathan as well to those of the seven just executed (2 Sam 21.10–14).

History

The period covered by 2 Samuel and 1 Kings 1–2 coincides with the reign of David, which can reasonably be dated to about 1005–965 BCE (see page 241). As is the case for narratives set in earlier times, we have no contemporaneous nonbiblical sources that refer to any of the persons or events in 2 Samuel, but one significant nonbiblical datum does exist. David, and his successor Solomon, had an alliance with the king of Tyre in Phoenicia, Hiram. According to 2 Samuel 5.11, "King Hiram of Tyre sent messengers to David, along with cedar trees, and carpenters and masons who built David a house." But David and Hiram's relationship involved more than supplying the famous Lebanese cedar for the construction of David's palace. According to 1 Kings 5.1, after Solomon's accession to the throne, Hiram sent his servants to Solomon, for "Hiram had always loved [NRSV: "been a friend to"] David." This is not merely an expression of affection, but the technical language of a formal treaty relationship. Hiram and David, as two of the most powerful rulers of the Levant at the time, had formed a political alliance, a relationship that continued during the reign of Solomon (see 1 Kings 5.1–12) and was the beginning of an ongoing connection between the royal houses of Tyre and Israel.

No contemporaneous sources mention Hiram, but he is treated at length in the writings of Flavius Josephus, the first-century CE Jewish historian. Citing earlier Phoenician sources, Josephus gives a detailed account of the relationship between Hiram and David and Solomon, including the chronological note that Solomon built the Temple 143 years before the Phoenicians founded Carthage in north Africa in the late ninth century BCE. So the biblical tradition that Hiram and David, and subsequently Hiram and Solomon, were treaty partners is supported, and for the first time we have a direct correlation of biblical data and chronology with nonbiblical sources. These correlations will become more frequent as the history of Israel continues.

As was also the case for Saul's brief reign, we have no archaeological remains that can be dated with certainty to the time of David. In Jerusalem, a large stepped-stone structure at the northeast corner of the city of David that had been attributed to the reigns of David or Solomon is now thought to be several centuries earlier, although it may have been repaired in the tenth century BCE (see 2 Sam 5.9; 1 Chr 11.8) (see Figure 15.3). The 52-foot (16-meter) vertical shaft on the east side of the city of David, discovered by the British engineer and explorer Charles Warren in 1867, is often identified as the shaft up which Joab is reported to have climbed in 2 Samuel 5.8, but it is now thought to be a natural fissure that was never used to draw water.

Some indirect archaeological evidence does exist, however. Beginning in the tenth century BCE, large quantities of imported ceramics make their appearance at Israelite sites, especially a finely made pottery that is called "Cypro-Phoenician ware." Scientific analysis has shown that these ceramics were usually imported from the Phoenician cities along the coast of the Mediterranean.

FIGURE 15.3. Stepped stone structure on the east side of the city of David in Jerusalem. Constructed toward the end of the Late Bronze Age as part of a terrace system to provide more space for building, it probably was repaired in the tenth century BCE. It probably formed part of the Millo (literally, "fill") mentioned in 2 Samuel 5.9 and 1 Kings 9.15, and if so it is the only structure in Jerusalem that can be dated to the time of David and Solomon.

This correlates nicely with the biblical accounts of trade between Tyre and Israel. Because such imported pottery would have been a luxury item, it confirms the picture of Israelite prosperity during the reigns of David and Solomon, as does the increased frequency of iron artifacts, also luxury items made from imported ore. Still further archaeological evidence is the increase in fortified settlements. Especially important are several dozen fortresses in the central Negeb just south of Judah proper, probably constructed during the tenth century as part of an effort to control the lucrative southern trade route from the Red Sea and Arabia.

Both Tyre and Israel took advantage of a kind of power vacuum in the region. Since the end of the second millennium BCE, Egypt, weakened by its struggles both with the Sea Peoples and with Libya and suffering from internal divisions, was unable to exercise its traditional control over the southern Levant. And in Mesopotamia, the home of other powers that frequently sought to control the region, the dominant state, Assyria, was pre-occupied with maintaining order in its own territory and in Babylonia to its south and would not move to expand its influence in the Levant until the ninth century BCE. These circumstances enabled the rise of independent states, and under David Israel was able to dominate its near neighbors, except for Tyre, with which it shared common interests. (See Figure 15.4.)

As had Israel, these neighboring states had moved or were moving toward monarchic rule. Kings, or their equivalent, are reported in the biblical record, not only for Tyre, but also for Ammon (see 1 Sam 10.27; 2 Sam 12.26), the Aramean states of Zobah (2 Sam 8.3) and Hamath (2 Sam 8.9), and the northern Transjordanian states of Geshur (2 Sam 3.3) and Maacah (2 Sam 10.6). Although no independent witness to any of this can be found, the archaeological record shows some evidence of the same movement toward centralization in those regions in the tenth century BCE, as it also does for Damascus and Moab and, at the same time or perhaps somewhat later, for Edom.

For biblical writers, the United Monarchy, the reigns of David and Solomon, was a golden age, like Augustan Rome or Elizabethan England. Its success is presented as the result of divine favor and the fulfillment of the promise to Abraham: "To your descendants I give this land, from the river of Egypt to the great river, the river Euphrates" (Gen 15.18). Those maximalist boundaries for the "Promised Land" are echoed in a list of David's conquests: "Edom, Moab, the Ammonites, the Philistines, Amalek, and . . . Zobah" (2 Sam 8.12). Taking these statements literally,

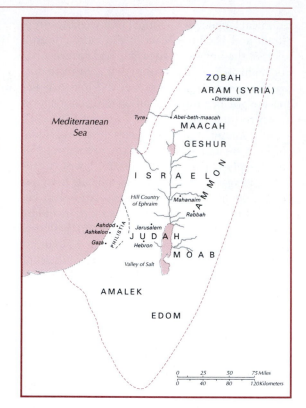

FIGURE 15.4. Map of the territory controlled by David and Solomon.

scholars have often spoken of a "Davidic empire," which controlled most of the Levant. According to 2 Samuel, the Philistines were permanently subjugated (see 2 Sam 5.17–21, 22–25; 8.1; 21.15–22) and became vassals of Israel, as did Edom, Moab, Ammon, and several Aramean kingdoms, as least for a time. Vassal status required both loyalty and regular payment of tribute, one source of the wealth that Israel enjoyed during this period. Only Tyre was not subject to Israel's control: Hiram and David were equals ("brothers"; see 1 Kings 9.13; Am 1.9), and the treaty between them was a parity treaty.

It now seems unlikely that Israel's power over the territories that surrounded it was as wide-reaching or as continuous as this. Nevertheless, underlying the apparently exaggerated claims is a historical kernel: David, and later Solomon, were the most important rulers of their day in the southern Levant, and during their reigns Israel enjoyed a security and prosperity that would never be equaled.

A major factor in Israel's ascendancy was its political unity. When Saul died, David was immediately recognized as his successor by the southern tribe of Judah, where even while Saul was alive he had carefully built a power base. In the north, Saul's son Ishbaal (Ishbosheth) succeeded his father. The inevitable conflict between the two sides ended when David's partisans murdered both Ishbaal and the commander of his army, Abner, and David was recognized as king by the northern tribes

as well. A deep fault line existed between north and south in ancient Israel, and for most of the tenth century BCE, David and his successor Solomon were able to paper over the division. Although the United Monarchy would last for less than a century—after Solomon, the north and the south were again divided into separate kingdoms—during that period Israel enjoyed a unity that would be remembered as ideal. That unity was enhanced by the move of the capital to Jerusalem and by the transfer of the ark to the capital, making it the religious center of the kingdom (see Box 15.2).

Box 15.2 JERUSALEM

Jerusalem's enduring status as holy city up to the present originates in David's actions. Although within the traditional boundaries of the tribe of Judah, Jerusalem did not come under Israelite control until its capture by David. Prior to this it had been a Jebusite enclave (see Josh 15.63; Judg 19.10–12), with a history of occupation dating back several centuries. David made this city, centrally located near the border between the northern tribes and Judah, the capital of his kingdom. Because it had not been part of Israel, it had no prior tribal loyalty, and it became the "**city of David**." The subsequent transfer of the ark of the covenant to Jerusalem also made it "the city of God."

David's successor Solomon built the Temple in Jerusalem, and in it he placed the ark. So Jerusalem became the place of worship for all Israelites. Destroyed in 586 BCE, the Temple was rebuilt in the late sixth century BCE and rebuilt again in the late first century BCE by Herod the Great. This last was the Temple destroyed by the Romans in their capture of Jerusalem in 70 CE. All that remained was the massive platform constructed by Herod on which the Temple stood, and part of this platform's retaining wall, known as the Western Wall or the Wailing Wall, became the most sacred shrine of Judaism.

Because Jesus was a Jew, he went to Jerusalem to celebrate the Passover, and it was there, during Passover, that he was arrested, executed, and buried. The city thus became holy for Christians because it was the locale for the events at the end of Jesus' life.

For Muslims, too, Jerusalem is holy, not just because of its association with Abraham (see page 76), David, and Jesus, all of whom are repeatedly mentioned in the Quran, but especially because according to Muslim tradition, Muhammad was miraculously taken from Mecca to Jerusalem and from Jerusalem to heaven to converse with God. So, for Islam, Jerusalem is the third holiest city, after Mecca and Medina, and it is called in Arabic simply *al-Quds*, "the Holy (City)."

Institutions

The Family

Given the importance of the extended-family unit ("the house of the father") in ancient Israel, it is not surprising that families are central to the account of David's reign. The "house of Saul" continued to be a factor for some time after Saul's death. His oldest surviving son, Ishbaal, inherited his father's throne, and for a brief time ruled Israel, in the north, while David ruled in Judah, in the south. In the account of Absalom's revolt, Saul's grandson through Jonathan, Mephibosheth, was accused of wishing to regain his grandfather's throne, and even if untrue, the accusation shows how the house of Saul continued to be a preoccupation for David. The threat posed by the house of Saul was finally ended with the killing of Saul's surviving male offspring, except for Mephibosheth, who was spared because of David's covenant with his father Jonathan (2 Sam 21.7), and whose lameness would probably have prevented him from ruling in any case (compare Lev 21.18).

The rivalry between the families of Saul and David extended to collateral members. Sons, nephews, and cousins shared in the power of the head of the family. Some of David's sons were appointed priests (see pages 259–61). Both Saul and David appointed close relatives as heads of their military: Abner, Saul's first cousin, and Joab, David's nephew. We frequently find bloody conflict between these leaders. In the struggle between David and Ishbaal, Abner killed Joab's brother Asahel (2 Sam 2.18–23), and when given the opportunity not long after, Joab killed Abner (3.26–27). This not only eliminated a potential rival of Joab and a threat to David (3.23), but also fulfilled Joab's obligation to avenge the death of his brother.

Blood vengeance for wrongs committed against a member of the family (see page 156) recurs in the Succession Narrative. Absalom killed Amnon for the rape of his sister Tamar (2 Sam 13.28–29), and in the staged petition of the wise woman of Tekoa that leads to David forgiving Absalom, blood vengeance is precisely the issue.

The importance of the extended-family unit is also clear in the issue of succession to the throne. In the north, Saul was succeeded by his son Ishbaal, yet David's concern to reclaim Michal, his first wife and Saul's daughter, was part of an effort to win the allegiance of the supporters of the house of Saul. The issue of who will succeed David dominates the Succession Narrative. In the ideology of the Davidic dynasty, it is the dynasty itself that is divinely chosen, but the messy process of succession itself is left to the family members to sort out.

The Roles of Women

Although they are frequently independent actors in the narrative, in the social context that forms the background for the narrative women are generally depicted in terms of their relationships to men, especially their husbands, fathers, and brothers. As Michal had been subject to her father Saul's authority, upon his death she was under the control of her brother Ishbaal, Saul's successor as head of the family and as king. Ishbaal took Michal from Paltiel, her second husband, and returned her to David, her first husband, and no hint is given of her reaction, although Paltiel is described as distraught (2 Sam 3.12–16). David's interest in Michal seems at this point to be more political than affectionate: Regaining the dead king Saul's daughter as his wife enhanced his claim to the throne. The final mention of Michal occurs in the account of the bringing of the ark to Jerusalem, and it is highly pejorative. She reproaches David for his dancing before the ark, and David reproaches her. The scene concludes tersely: "Michal the daughter of Saul had no children until the day of her death" (2 Sam 6.23). Why? Because David no longer had sexual relations with her, or because God had made her infertile? The narrator does not tell us.

Royal wives and concubines constitute a special category. Control of the royal harem was apparently a crucial sign of political power. The clearest example is Absalom's taking possession "in the sight of all Israel" of the ten concubines whom David had left in Jerusalem (2 Sam 16.22), a public demonstration that David was no longer in charge. The same view presumably motivated Abner's intercourse with Saul's concubine Rizpah (2 Sam 3.7), and, after David's death, Adonijah's request that he be given David's concubine Abishag (1 Kings 2.17), which Solomon immediately interpreted as a virtual coup and ordered Adonijah killed. David himself, we are told, had taken control of Saul's harem (2 Sam 12.8), part of his careful maneuvering to legitimate his rule. These women are considered only pawns in the power politics that surround them; their own feelings are unreported, reflecting their inferior status.

Some women, however, do have considerable influence, although not as part of the patriarchal power structure. For example, in the Succession Narrative (which features women so prominently that some scholars have even suggested that it was written by a woman), two of these are "wise" women, who have considerable standing within their communities. Both the woman from Tekoa (2 Sam 14.2–20) and the woman from Abel of Beth-maacah (2 Sam 20.16–22) are able to affect the course of events by their wisdom and to influence the men to whom they are formally inferior. Bathsheba too emerges as a woman of influence, notably at the end of the Succession Narrative. (On the roles of queens and queen mothers, see pages 295–97.)

Royal Administration

Second Samuel contains two lists of David's appointees, in 8.16–18 and 20.23–26. Although these may simply be variants stemming from different sources, their placement toward the beginning and the end of David's reign may be significant, reflecting changes that occurred as his rule continued. In either case, they appear to contain authentic archival material probably dating back to the time of David himself. The first list gives the following officials:

- Joab, son of Zeruiah (David's sister): over the army
- Jehoshaphat: "recorder" (perhaps the equivalent of a "prime minister," although the precise function of this office is unclear)

- Zadok and Abiathar (correcting the text's Ahimelech; see 2 Sam 20.25): priests. On Zadok, see pages 260–61; Abiathar was Eli's great-grandson who had survived Saul's massacre of the priests at Nob and had joined David's side (1 Sam 22.20).
- Seraiah: "secretary" (or "scribe") (the name of this person has variants; see 1 Kings 4.3)
- Benaiah: over the Cherethites and Pelethites (the foreign mercenary component of the army that served as the palace guard). Benaiah was one of David's most prominent warriors (see 2 Sam 23.20), and under Solomon would become commander of the entire army (1 Kings 4.4).
- David's sons: priests

In managing his kingdom, David built on the foundations that had been laid by Saul, beginning with a professional army. The first official mentioned is Joab, David's nephew, who was in charge of the army; the position of this office in the list reflects the importance of military actions at the beginning of David's reign. We see another military official, too: Benaiah, the head of the mercenaries. Shared military responsibilities would have served as a check on Joab's power.

This first list contains two sets of priests: Zadok and Abiathar, and David's sons (see pages 260–61). As with the military, the presence of more than one priestly official would have enhanced royal control and diminished the status of the officeholder.

The second list is found in 2 Samuel 20.23–26:

- Joab: over the army
- Benaiah: over the Cherethites and Pelethites
- Adoram: over the forced labor
- Jehoshaphat: "recorder"
- Sheva: "secretary" (perhaps the same person as in the first list; his name is attested in various forms)
- Zadok and Abiathar: priests
- Ira the Jairite: David's priest

In this list is one new official, responsible for the "forced labor," apparently conscripts consisting of war captives, subjugated populations, and perhaps Israelites. He would have been responsible for public building projects such as the repairs of Jerusalem's fortifications and the construction of David's palace (see 2 Sam 5.9, 11).

Another telling monarchic innovation is the census (2 Sam 24). According to the narrative, its purpose seems to have been to ascertain the number of males able to be drafted into the army, although the figures given (v. 9) are impossibly high. The census also demonstrates a royal attempt to impose further centralization on the kingdom, such as that anticipated in 1 Samuel 8.11–18, by assessing the population's resources for taxation and labor. As such, the census was opposed by some elements in the administration, including Joab, and for the Deuteronomistic Historians it was sinful, probably because it implied a lack of confidence in God, who should have been trusted to provide for Israel.

To what extent the increased complexity of administration of the kingdom affected ordinary life is difficult to say. The case of the woman of Tekoa (2 Sam 14.4–11), although a ruse, and the scene of Absalom intercepting petitioners to the king (2 Sam 15.2–4) suggest that centralized royal administration of justice had begun to replace local procedures, although not entirely satisfactorily.

It is important to keep in mind the scale. Israel proper was a relatively small entity, roughly some 9,000 mi^2 (23,000 km^2) in area (see further page 47), and Jerusalem under David covered only some 15 acres (6 hectares), with a population of only a few thousand. This small size makes the accounts of close personal relationships, such as those between Absalom and subjects seeking redress of grievances, plausible if historically improvable.

Religion

David continued the pattern that had been set by Saul, increasing his control over religious institutions. At his initiative the ark of the covenant, which appears to have been languishing in obscurity, was brought to the new capital, and once again was reportedly used as a protective divine symbol, a palladium, in battle (2 Sam 11.11). In the account of the ceremony in which the ark was brought to Jerusalem, David is clearly the principal celebrant, wearing the ephod (elsewhere a priestly vestment), offering sacrifices, and leading the ritual procession with dance and probably song as well (2 Sam 6.12–19).

Such royal leadership in religious ritual is also recorded for David in 2 Samuel 24.25, as it is for Saul (1 Sam 13.9; 14.35) and for Solomon (1 Kings 3.3; 8.5, 14, 55, 62). Only Saul's usurpation of priestly functions is viewed negatively (1 Sam 13.10–14) because of the Deuteronomistic Historians' bias against him. In fact, throughout the monarchy, kings continued to be identified and to act as priests (see 2 Kings 16.13; Ps 110.4), like their counterparts elsewhere in the ancient Near East.

Direct royal control of the priesthood is indicated by the presence of priests in the lists of David's officials (see page 259). The first priests listed in 2 Samuel 8.16–18 are Zadok and Abiathar. Abiathar was a descendant of the priestly line of Eli and one of David's early supporters. Zadok's background is less clear. One suggestion is to connect Zadok with the line of Aaron; Abiathar and the entire Eli priesthood would have been in the line of Moses. Under this hypothesis, David's appointment of priests from different families was another strategic move, giving priests from the two main and arguably rival priestly houses positions in the hierarchy of the new capital. An alternative is to connect Zadok with the indigenous priesthood of the Canaanite deity El in Jerusalem. The occurrence of the element "zedek" in the names of kings of pre-Israelite Jerusalem (Melchizedek, Gen 14.18; Adonizedek, Josh 10.1) is certainly striking, especially since Melchizedek is also called a priest (see also Ps 110.4). Under this second hypothesis, the appointment of Zadok would also have been strategic: incorporating the religious traditions of Jebusite Jerusalem and thus enhancing the allegiance of its inhabitants to David.

Further down in the list is also the note that "David's sons were priests" (2 Sam 8.18). That the king's sons served as priests is elsewhere unattested, and this notice, along with the mention of the otherwise unknown Ira the Jairite as "David's priest" in the second list (2 Sam 20.26), indicates that the priesthood was not yet either hereditary or confined to one lineage. It also makes the identification of Zadok as a non-Aaronid more plausible.

Prophets continue to be depicted as functioning during the reign of David. Given the Deuteronomistic Historians' use of prophets as periodic commentators on the events from the perspective of the Deuteronomic law, it is difficult to be sure to what extent prophecy had emerged as a routinized office during the early monarchy. Two prophets appear in 2 Samuel, Nathan and Gad. Neither is given a formal introduction, presuming the audience's familiarity with the institution of prophecy. Nathan appears in several roles. Like Samuel, he functions as king-maker. He announces the divine decree guaranteeing the dynasty of David (2 Sam 7.1–17), and he is central in the events that lead to Solomon's coronation (1 Kings 1), although perhaps significantly this takes place without explicit mention of the divine choice. Both Nathan and Gad, again like Samuel, transmit the divine judgment to the king on his transgressions, Nathan in the matter of Bathsheba and Uriah (2 Sam 12.1–15) and Gad in the matter of the census (2 Sam 24.10–14). For the Deuteronomistic Historians, the presence of prophets in the royal court is unremarkable, and it is likely that in broad outline this corresponds to historical reality. At the very least, it is consistent with accounts of prophets later in the monarchic period, when they were actively engaged with kings, both in the northern kingdom of Israel (Elijah, Elisha, Amos, Hosea) and in the southern kingdom of Judah (Isaiah, Jeremiah).

Because of the narrative's focus on the royal court, and also because of the Deuteronomistic Historians' preoccupation with centralized worship, little information is given concerning worship outside of Jerusalem after the ark has been brought to the capital. The only exceptions are Absalom's sacrifice at Hebron (2 Sam 15.7–12) and the sanctuary at Gibeon where Saul's descendants were killed (2 Sam 21.6, 9). The latter is particularly interesting, for Gibeon apparently continued to be a place of worship in Solomon's time (see 1 Kings 3.4), and independent evidence exists for worship there during David's time as well (1 Chr 16.39; 21.29), although its authenticity has been questioned. These sparse references suggest that centralized worship was a theoretical ideal of the Deuteronomistic Historians rather than an actual practice; the Deuteronomistic Historians did not rewrite their sources to make them conform to that ideal.

Royal Ideology

Reflecting their programmatic interest in the Davidic dynasty and in the Temple, the Deuteronomistic Historians insert into the narrative of David's reign an important passage that sets forth for the first time the ideology of kingship as they understood it. We will explore this ideology more fully in the next chapter, but here we will examine its elaboration in 2 Samuel 7.

This chapter is placed immediately after the establishment of the capital in Jerusalem and the ark's transfer there. It opens with a notice of David's military successes (to be elaborated in 2 Sam 8), followed by David expressing a desire to build a temple ("house") for Yahweh, since he himself already lives in a lavish palace ("a house of cedar"; see 2 Sam 5.11). The prophet Nathan expresses his approval, but Yahweh has other views, and Nathan receives an oracle to communicate to David: Yahweh does not want a temple, but he will guarantee the security of Israel and the dynasty ("house") of David unconditionally and in perpetuity, even if David's successor(s) act wrongly. Moreover, it is David's successor who will build the temple, and who will be the deity's son—to be punished like a child if he "commits iniquity," but never to lose the deity's "steadfast love," a phrase that suggests a covenant relationship (see 1 Kings 8.23; Ps 89.28; Isa 55.3). David's response to the prophet's message is a lengthy prayer praising Yahweh for all he has done for Israel and asking for continued blessing on David's dynasty (his "house").

The chapter is complex, and it shows evidence of layering of traditions. At least two stages can be detected. The first is a strong statement of divine opposition to building the Temple at all (vv. 5–7), reminiscent of the opposition to the establishment of the monarchy in the first place in 1 Samuel. To this is joined a divine promise of "rest" for Israel and for David and a promise of a dynasty to succeed David. To use the language of the text, David's desire to build a "house" for Yahweh is rebuffed. Yahweh will build a "house" for David instead. Then, somewhat awkwardly, in verse 13 we are told that David's successor "shall build a house" for Yahweh—despite Yahweh's just expressed negative view of such construction—and the dynastic promise is elaborated. This last part (vv. 13–16) appears to be a second stage in the development of the oracle, which in part contradicts the first.

In its final form, 2 Samuel 7 provides a further example of the Deuteronomistic Historians at work. They preserve inconsistent traditions, in part presumably because these traditions exist and are known and in part because they implicitly recognize that history is not a neat progression of causes and effects. The composite result highlights the Deuteronomistic Historians' view of the centrality of the Temple, while preserving a more qualified and nuanced view that questions the Temple's very existence. (See further Box 15.3.)

RETROSPECT AND PROSPECT

The Deuteronomistic Historians present a remarkably candid account of David's rule, drawing mostly on originally independent sources and only occasionally interrupting it with their own commentary. That account is informed by their conviction that, for all his flaws, David was the divinely designated ruler. In fact, in the rest of the books of Kings, all of his successors on the throne of Judah will be measured against the standard of David's unwavering fidelity to Yahweh, and few will meet it. Yet the Deuteronomistic Historians' portrait of David is far from uncritical, unlike that of the Chronicler. In the account of David's reign in Chronicles, which uses 2 Samuel as its principal source, the events in the

Succession Narrative that cast David in a negative light are simply omitted, as they are in most of the rest of the Bible; the relatively late titles that are found at the beginning of Psalms 3 and 51 are exceptions to this tendency. On the other hand, as in 1 Samuel, where ambivalence toward the establishment of the monarchy was expressed by the juxtaposition of different sources, so too in the account of David's reign by the Deuteronomistic Historians, their attitude toward David is decidedly mixed. This is true both in the composite 2 Samuel 7, with its conflicting views of the construction of the Temple, and especially in the Succession Narrative.

Thematic and linguistic connections between the Yahwist tradition (J) in Genesis and the Succession Narrative have led some scholars to suggest that they were written by the same author, or were even parts of a single work. For example, both J and the Succession Narrative have a tragic tale of fratricide—Cain and Abel, and Absalom and Amnon, respectively. Both also include narratives about women named Tamar (Gen 38; 2 Sam 13)—two of the only three women with this name in the Bible (the third is Absalom's daughter, doubtless named for his sister; 2 Sam 14.27).

As we have seen, the boundaries of the land promised to Abraham in J (Gen 15.18–21) correspond to the boundaries of the territory under the control of David and Solomon—and only during their reigns was this promise fulfilled. Moreover, in his choice as his first capital of Hebron, Abraham's burial place (see Gen 23; 25.9–10), David seems to have deliberately linked himself with Israel's ancestor to enhance his legitimacy as king.

The theme of exile from the Promised Land that is so prominent in Genesis—Abraham, Isaac, Jacob, Joseph, and finally Jacob's entire family all leave the land, at least for a time—is also found in the account of David's flight from Jerusalem during the revolt of Absalom. Yet like the ancestors of Israel, and, in the end, Israel itself, David returns to the land, and to Jerusalem.

Yet those connections, while tantalizing, are only suggestive. The most that can be inferred from them is that David's accession to the throne

Box 15.3 **PSALM 132**

Psalm 132 includes an ancient account of the bringing of the ark to Jerusalem independent of 2 Samuel 6 and a treatment of the covenant with David different in an important detail from that found in 2 Samuel 7. The psalm has two thematically linked parts. In the first (vv. 1–10), David's oath to bring the ark to Jerusalem is recalled, and the search for the ark and its transfer to Jerusalem is summarized, with a reference to the ark hymn from Numbers 10.35–36 (see further page 128). In the second (vv. 11–18), Yahweh's reciprocal oath to David states the essentials of the covenant with David: an enduring dynasty and the choice of **Zion** (a frequent poetic term for Jerusalem).

One of the many remarkable aspects of this psalm is that it contains the only reference to the ark of the covenant in the entire book of Psalms. Although the psalm was doubtless used in rituals in the Temple in Jerusalem, it is essentially a commemorative hymn, recalling David's action and the divine promise. The absence of the ark in other psalms suggests that once installed in the Temple by Solomon, the ark was no longer central in the religious language of Jerusalem.

Moreover, the psalm contains no mention of the Temple itself, and the language of the covenant with David in verse 12 is conditional:

> If your sons keep my covenant
> and my decrees that I shall teach them,
> their sons also, forevermore,
> shall sit on your throne.

In 2 Samuel 7.16 implicitly, and in Psalm 89.28–37 explicitly, however, the covenant with David is unconditional: No matter how his successors behave, Yahweh says, the dynasty will last forever.

All of these observations suggest that the psalm is very old, probably going back to the time of David himself. It preserves an early stage of the royal ideology of the David's dynasty, when the Temple had not yet been built and the covenant between Yahweh and David was understood to be conditional.

---

and the subsequent development of a dynastic monarchy that made extravagant claims for itself intrigued and even disturbed biblical writers. To put it somewhat differently, both the Succession Narrative and the apparent allusions to it in J raise questions: To what extent could David's successes—and ultimately Israel's—be attributed to divine guidance rather than to David's own ma-

neuvering, and, if David—and Israel—were in some sense chosen, then how could their failures be reconciled with their providential destiny?

The Deuteronomistic Historians offer no easy answers to these questions. The divine perspective is only rarely provided, and always through editorial note or prophetic mediation—Yahweh is not really a character in the narrative, as he was in earlier parts of the Deuteronomistic History and in the Pentateuch. Prophetic pronouncements directly attributed to God are Nathan's oracles in 2 Samuel 7 and 12 and Gad's in 2 Samuel 24. All three function to give divine pronouncements at crucial stages of the ongoing narrative, and, like the speeches of Samuel in 1 Samuel, share an ambivalent view of the monarchy. In 2 Samuel 7, as we have seen, the Deuteronomistic Historians preserve in Nathan's oracle evidence of opposition to building the Temple. Nathan's second oracle, in 2 Samuel 12, interprets the chaos in David's family that will ensue as divine punishment for David's adultery with Bathsheba and the murder of her husband. Gad's oracle in 2 Samuel 24 interprets the census as instigated by God as a punishment against Israel for some unspecified sin. Notably, each of these prophetic oracles contains implicit or explicit critique of the actions of the king. But we see no dramatic theophanies here, except in David's hymn in 2 Samuel 22. That poem uses the familiar language of the convulsions of nature that accompany Yahweh's appearance in earthquake and fire, darkness and thunder—language that is totally absent in the rest of the book. Yet in the history of David's rule—however that rule was achieved, however troubling were its details, however immoral were David's own actions—the Deuteronomistic Historians see, even if ambiguously, the hand of God.

The final edition of the Deuteronomistic History was a product of the exilic period in the sixth century BCE, after Jerusalem had been captured and destroyed and the Davidic dynasty had come to an end. In the final Babylonian siege of Jerusalem in 586 BCE, the last descendant of David to rule, King Zedekiah, fled the city in disgrace, only to be captured and taken in chains to Babylon, never to return. David's flight from Jerusalem anticipates that of Zedekiah. But David did return from exile, and for the exilic audience of the Deuteronomistic History, that was a basis for hope in the darkest time in Israel's history.

IMPORTANT TERMS

city of David

Succession Narrative

United Monarchy

Zion

QUESTIONS FOR REVIEW

1. What is the cumulative portrait we get of David in 2 Samuel?

2. What are the themes of the Succession Narrative? What are its attitudes toward kingship? Are they similar to or different from the attitudes of other parts of 2 Samuel?

3. During the reigns of David and Solomon, Israel was the most important state in the Levant, a political prominence unequalled until the time of Herod the Great (40–4 BCE). What circumstances permitted the formation of the "Davidic empire"? What was the extent and nature of its control?

4. Give reasons why David benefited from the transfer of the ark of the covenant to Jerusalem.

BIBLIOGRAPHY

In addition to works by Hackett, McKenzie, and Meyers (see the bibliography to Chapter 14), see also P. Kyle McCarter, Jr., *II Samuel* (Garden City, NY: Doubleday, 1984); David M. Gunn, "David," pp. 153–56 in *The Oxford Companion to the Bible* (ed. B. M. Metzger and M. D. Coogan; New York: Oxford University Press, 1993); Jerome Murphy-O'Connor, "Jerusalem: History," pp. 349–52 in *The Oxford Companion to the Bible* (ed. B. M. Metzger and M. D. Coogan; New York: Oxford University Press, 1993); and Barbara Geller Nathanson, "Jerusalem: Symbolism," pp. 352–56 in *The Oxford Companion to the Bible* (ed. B. M. Metzger and M. D. Coogan; New York: Oxford University Press, 1993).

THE REIGN OF SOLOMON

1 Kings 1–11 and Psalm 89

In this chapter we will consider the reign of Solomon, David's son and successor. Many of the themes of the Deuteronomistic History discussed in earlier chapters are elaborated further here, including the status of Jerusalem as the central place of worship, especially in the Temple that Solomon built. But like their presentation of David, the Deuteronomistic Historians give us a very mixed picture of Solomon's rule, including the notice that toward its end the king strayed from one of the primary principles of the teaching of Moses, the exclusive worship of Yahweh.

THE BOOKS OF KINGS

The books of Kings continue the narrative by the Deuteronomistic Historians of Israel's history in the Promised Land. The separation of the books of Kings from the books of Samuel and the later division of Kings into two books is artificial, as the continuities between the various parts make clear. For example, 1 Kings 1–2 continues the Succession Narrative that begins in 2 Samuel (see page 249), and 2 Kings 1 continues the narrative about the prophet Elijah that begins in 1 Kings 17.

As in the books of Samuel, the Deuteronomistic Historians have shaped various sources into a coherent chronological narrative informed by their perspective. That perspective is that Israel's prosperity and even survival in the land is dependent upon their observance of the law of Moses as found in the book of Deuteronomy, and especially in their obedience to the command to worship Yahweh alone, and only at the place that he has designated. Failure to do so, as prophets repeatedly warn throughout the books of Kings, will inevitably result in punishment, which for the Deuteronomistic Historians is ultimately exile.

1 KINGS 1–11

Sources

In compiling a narrative of Solomon's reign, the Deuteronomistic Historians incorporated a variety of originally independent sources:

- The conclusion of the Succession Narrative in 1 Kings 1–2, which narrates how Solomon became king and eliminated his rivals and their supporters.

- Detailed descriptions of the Temple, its furnishings, and various metal objects used in its rituals, in 1 Kings 6 and 7.

- Annalistic notices, presumably originating in royal archives such as "the Book of the Acts of Solomon" mentioned in 1 Kings 11.41. These include a list of royal officials (4.1–6) and descriptions of the administrative districts into which the kingdom was divided (4.7–19) and the labor force for the building of the Temple, palace, and other royal projects (5.13–18; 9.15–24).

- Wisdom traditions, originating in the royal court, summarized in 1 Kings 4.32–33.

- Royal legends, such as the accounts of the Solomonic judgment concerning the two children of the prostitutes (3.16–28) and the visit of the queen of Sheba (10.1–13).

These sources are combined with a number of Deuteronomistic compositions, including:

- Solomon's dream at Gibeon (1 Kings 3.3–15), where he prays for wisdom and is promised it as well as riches. This prayer echoes that of David in 2 Samuel 7.18–29, another composition of the Deuteronomistic Historians.

- The account of the dedication of the Temple (1 Kings 8), with Solomon's lengthy prayer acknowledging that the people's sins may cause divine punishment in the form of military defeat, drought, famine, and exile, and requesting compassion when they pray for forgiveness at the sanctuary God has chosen.

- A concluding summary of Solomon's reign (1 Kings 11.1–40), in which it is predicted that Solomon's worship of other gods, blamed on his foreign wives, will result in the division of the kingdom.

The Narrative

These elements are combined into a coherent yet complex narrative that both recognizes Solomon's accomplishments and points out the theological and political problems that his rule entailed. It is clearly a selective narrative, as the reference to the "rest of the acts of Solomon . . . written in the Book of the Acts of Solomon" (1 Kings 11.41) indicates. Moreover, it is a narrative with a decidedly mixed view of Solomon. He succeeds David as king not as the result of explicit divine choice, but through palace intrigue. And his reign ends with a negative account of his worship of other gods. Yet between these brackets Solomon is portrayed as a wise and pious ruler. The overall effect is to present Solomon as a complex character, like his father, and the combination of different sources reveals this complexity.

The narrative opens with the conclusion of the Succession Narrative. David's sexual impotence (see page 251) leads his oldest surviving son Adonijah to attempt to have himself crowned as king with the support of the army commander Joab and the priest Abiathar. But another faction in the court, led by the prophet Nathan and Solomon's mother Bathsheba and supported by the palace bodyguard, the Cherethites and the Pelethites, persuades the ailing David to name Solomon as his successor, and in a hasty coronation Nathan and Zadok the priest anoint Solomon as king.

David gives final instructions to Solomon in a composite speech (1 Kings 2.2–9), which urges, in Deuteronomistic style, fidelity to the law of Moses and commands Solomon to kill Joab for the murder of Abner (see 2 Sam 3.22–30) and Amasa (2 Sam 20.8–10), and also to kill Shimei, a relative of Saul who had cursed David during Absalom's revolt (2 Sam 16.5–8; 19.16–23). After a brief notice of David's death and the chronology of his reign, the Succession Narrative concludes with an account of Solomon's systematic and ruthless elimination of his rival Adonijah and his supporters, including Joab, and of Shimei. Although the narrative attempts to justify Solomon's actions by attributing them to David, to modern sensibilities at least this is self-serving, and may be deliberate Solomonic propaganda.

A series of essentially unrelated episodes follows, illustrating Solomon's piety, wisdom, and accomplishments. In the course of a sacrifice at Gibeon, Yahweh appears to Solomon in a dream and, in response to Solomon's request for wisdom in governing, grants him both wisdom and wealth (1 Kings 3.3–15). His wisdom is shown by the folk tale of his resolution of the case of the two prostitutes and their infants (3.16–28) and by his international reputation (4.29–34), and his wealth is illustrated with archival details about the administration of the kingdom and its prosperity (4.1–28).

These apparently incidental materials in fact set the stage for the account of the building and dedication of the Temple, which is the centerpiece of the Deuteronomistic Historians' narrative of Solomon's reign. The account has three parts, the first dealing with the details of the construction of the Temple (1 Kings 5–6), and the second with the metalwork associated with the Temple (7.13–51). Between these first two sections is a more perfunctory account (7.1–12) of the construction of the various buildings that comprised the palace complex, even though its construction took nearly twice as long as that of the Temple.

The third part of the section devoted to the Temple is a lengthy account of the Temple's dedication (8.1–9.9). This includes a description of the bringing of the ark of the covenant into the Temple, various prayers by Solomon in typical Deuteronomistic style, and a twofold divine speech, reiterating the promise of an eternal dynasty yet warning that the Temple will be destroyed and the people sent into exile if they worship gods other than Yahweh.

The narrative of Solomon's reign continues with further accounts of his building projects and of his international relations (9.10–28; 10.13–29), into which is set an account of the visit of the queen of Sheba (10.1–13), an episode that exemplifies both his wisdom and his international reputation.

A summary conclusion to the narrative concerning Solomon begins with a critique of his marriages with "foreign women," who, we are told, led him to worship other gods. For this apostasy, in the Deuteronomistic pattern of sin and punishment, God decrees that after Solomon's death the kingdom will be divided (11.1–13). Then follows an account of opposition to Solomon both from such

vassal states as Edom and Damascus and from Jeroboam, a northerner who is proclaimed by an anonymous prophet to be the instrument of divine punishment and the future ruler of what will become the northern kingdom of Israel after Solomon's death. The narrative ends with a brief notice of the chronology of Solomon's reign, of his death, and of his successor.

The Characters

Solomon

The main character is of course Solomon. But the sources used by the Deuteronomistic Historians, and their own compositions, rarely contain the vivid dialogue found in the narratives in 1 and 2 Samuel. We do find two exceptions. First, in the conclusion of the Succession Narrative (1 Kings 2.13–46), Solomon is an active participant in the elimination of his rival Adonijah and his supporters, David's nephew and general Joab, and Shimei. Second, in resolving the dispute over the dead child (3.16–28), Solomon exhibits a shrewd practical wisdom. The rest of Solomon's reported speeches—in his dream at Gibeon (1 Kings 3.6–9), in his correspondence with Hiram (5.2–6), in his dedication of the Temple (8.12–21, 23–61)—are set pieces that are formulaic articulations of the Deuteronomistic Historians' views but reveal little of Solomon's personality.

Another facet of Solomon's character intimated by the Deuteronomistic Historians is his penchant for luxurious living. Solomon had been raised in the court, and the peace accomplished by David had brought prosperity that increased during Solomon's reign. Using presumably archival material, the Deuteronomistic Historians include in their portrait of Solomon's court two striking catalogues of his lifestyle. The first is a record of the daily consumption at the court: "Solomon's provision for one day was thirty cors of choice flour, and sixty cors of meal, ten fat oxen, and twenty pasture-fed cattle, one hundred sheep, besides deer, gazelles, roebucks, and fatted fowl" (1 Kings 4.22–23). The second includes a description of the court furnishings:

King Solomon made two hundred large shields of beaten gold; six hundred shekels of gold went into each large shield. He made three hundred shields of beaten gold; three minas of gold went into each shield; and the king put them in the House of the Forest of Lebanon. The king also made a great ivory throne, and overlaid it with the finest gold. The throne had six steps. The top of the throne was rounded in the back, and on each side of the seat were arm rests and two lions standing beside the arm rests, while twelve lions were standing, one on each end of a step on the six steps. Nothing like it was ever made in any kingdom. All King Solomon's drinking vessels were of gold, and all the vessels of the House of the Forest of Lebanon were of pure gold; none were of silver—it was not considered as anything in the days of Solomon. For the king had a fleet of ships of Tarshish at sea with the fleet of Hiram. Once every three years the fleet of ships of Tarshish used to come bringing gold, silver, ivory, apes, and peacocks. (1 Kings 10.16–22)

That wealth was a sign of divine favor is a biblical cliché, found also in the account of Solomon's dream at Gibeon (1 Kings 3.13), and this is one level of meaning here: The extraordinary riches of Solomon's palace confirmed that he was the divinely chosen ruler. But we may also detect both a hint of disapproval of the excess and an authentic memory of a king who enjoyed a life of conspicuous consumption—well-fed, sitting on a lavish ivory throne, with exotic animals roaming freely in the palace gardens. (See further Box 16.1.)

Women

Although the primary focus of 1 Kings 1–11 is on Solomon, women are significant minor characters. Bathsheba has emerged as an important power because of her alliance with the prophet Nathan and the priest Zadok, and, after Solomon's coronation, because of her position as queen mother (see further pages 295–97). She is the essential intermediary between King David and Nathan (acting as proxy for Solomon) and between King Solomon and Adonijah. Her role as intermediary is reminiscent of that of the "wise women" earlier in the Succession Narrative (2 Sam 14.2–20; 2 Sam 20.16–22).

Abishag, David's last concubine and the object of Adonijah's request, is a passive agent in the interplay of sex and politics that permeates the Succession Narrative (see pages 295–97). But by telling us of her presence when Bathsheba and Nathan go to David to advance Solomon's succession, the Deuteronomistic Historians invite readers to consider the feelings of both women.

Women also serve to reveal Solomon's character, as in his arbitration of the dispute between the prostitutes and in the visit of the queen of Sheba. The same is true of his wives. The size of Solomon's harem is extraordinary—seven hundred wives and three hundred concubines. It is not the size itself that is explicitly condemned, but the fact that many of these women were foreigners, who, with Solomon's support and even participation, continued to worship their native deities. Although no doubt many of Solomon's marriages furthered his international diplomacy, such as his marriage to the daughter of the king of Egypt (1 Kings 9.16), that is of only passing interest to the Deuteronomistic Historians. For them, as in Deuteronomy 7.3–4, foreign women are a danger because they instigate apostasy.

Other Characters

Only in the conclusion to the Succession Narrative (1 Kings 1–2) are other characters developed, and as elsewhere in that source by means of dialogue. Nathan's adept exploitation of David's frailty succeeds in having David designate Solomon as his successor. Adonijah's efforts to gain the throne end in his murder. Joab challenges Solomon to violate the sanctity of the altar where he has sought sanctuary and remains defiant until his death.

History

As is the case with David, we find no independent corroboration for Solomon's reign, and, apart from Hiram, the king of Tyre (see pages 254–55), no individual or event mentioned in the biblical sources is attested in contemporaneous nonbiblical sources. A convergence of probabilities suggests that at least the broad outlines

Box 16.1 SOLOMON IN LATER TRADITION

In Chronicles, Solomon's role as builder of the Temple is subordinated to David's, who according to the Chronicler originated and carefully planned both the Temple and its worship. Yet like his source in 1 Kings, the Chronicler devotes several chapters to the details of the Temple's construction.

Solomon's legendary wisdom is already evident in Kings, in the narratives of the two prostitutes (1 Kings 3.16–28) and of the visit of the queen of Sheba (10.1–10), and in the summary of Solomon's compositions: "He composed three thousand proverbs, and his songs numbered a thousand and five. He would speak of trees, from the cedar that is in Lebanon to the hyssop that grows in the wall; he would speak of animals, and birds, and reptiles, and fish" (1 Kings 4.32–33). This passage explains the later attribution to Solomon of part of the book of Proverbs (see 1.1; 10.1; 25.1); of the book of Ecclesiastes, whose author pseudonymously identifies himself as "the son of David, king in Jerusalem" (Eccl 1.1); and of the book known as the Wisdom of Solomon. (For discussion of these books, see pages 472–75, 488–93, and 518–22.) Attributing later writings to past worthies was a widespread practice in antiquity, as we have already seen with Moses and David.

Solomon is also credited with the authorship of the Song of Solomon (1.1), a loosely linked series of love poems that is difficult to date but which most scholars assign to the postexilic period (see pages 495–97). The tradition of Solomonic authorship is based in part on the repeated occurrence of Solomon's name in the text (1.5; 3.7, 9, 11; 8.11–12), but Solomon is not the male lover who speaks in the poems; rather, he is referred to by the speaker (see 8.12). An additional reason for attributing these love poems to Solomon may be the legendary size of Solomon's harem in 1 Kings 11.3. Much later postbiblical tradition also conjectures a sexual relationship between the queen of Sheba and Solomon.

Despite his reputation as a prolific writer (see Sir 47.15–17), however, only two biblical psalms (72; 127) are attributed to Solomon, but in postbiblical literature, such works as the Odes of Solomon and the Psalms of Solomon have Solomon as their pseudonymous author.

of Solomon's accomplishments are historically rooted and that his reign can be dated in the mid-tenth century BCE, approximately 968–928 (see further page 289). These dates allow for some coregency with David, as indicated in the narrative that has Solomon anointed king before David's death.

Solomon is depicted as the ruler whose reign continued the era of peace and prosperity that David had inaugurated and who constructed the Temple in Jerusalem, where worship was carried out until its destruction by the Babylonians in 586 BCE. Because David's conquests had brought peace to the region (see Figure 15.4 on page 256), no military activities are reported during Solomon's reign until its end, when there were signs that Israel's control over its subject states was weakening (1 Kings 11.14–25) and the northern part of the kingdom was becoming restive (1 Kings 11.26–40). That peace also enabled the extension of trade. Much of this trade was with Tyre, Israel's close ally to the north, which provided both raw materials and technical expertise for Solomon's building projects. Solomon is also reported to have joined Hiram, the king of Tyre, in exploiting the lucrative Red Sea trade route, with Hiram providing nautical expertise and Solomon the financing as well as the port of Ezion-geber in his own territory; this maritime venture was unusual for the ancient Israelites. The visit of the queen of Sheba, a region in southwestern Arabia, should be understood as related to this trade. Commerce in horses and chariots is also reported with Asia Minor (1 Kings 10.26–29).

This trade, along with the tribute from the vassal states that bordered Israel and taxes in kind collected internally, brought great wealth to the capital city and enabled Solomon to finance extensive building projects in Jerusalem and elsewhere. Principal among these public works was the construction of a royal quarter in Jerusalem. Solomon expanded the city of David to the north, doubling its size, and in this expansion he constructed a royal quarter, an elaborate complex that included residences for the king and his wives, administrative buildings, and the Temple (see Figure 16.1).

Archaeological evidence from the early first millennium BCE provides parallels not only for the tripartite longitudinal plan of the **Temple of Solomon**, with its innermost chamber reserved for the deity and the priests, but also for its incorporation into a royal complex, which was considerably larger than the Temple. The same evidence also illustrates many details of its construction (see Figure 16.2). The scale is important to keep in mind. The Temple's footprint was only about 30 by 100 ft (9 by 30 m). Even with its expansion under Solomon, Jerusalem was a city of only about 25 acres (10 hectares) with some 5,000 inhabitants, and the population of the kingdom as

a whole was probably less than 100,000. The grandiose descriptions, then, can give a misleading impression. Israel under Solomon was the most important power in the region, controlling trade routes and neighboring kingdoms. This brought relatively great wealth into the city, but it was still a relatively provincial backwater in comparison to the larger capitals of Egypt and Mesopotamia. And when these powers moved to reassert their control over the Levant, Israel was no match. This would happen soon after Solomon's death, when the Egyptian Pharaoh Shishak invaded Palestine (see page 289).

According to 1 Kings 9.15, Solomon built not only the Temple and his palace but also the wall of Jerusalem and the strategically situated cities of Hazor, Gezer, and Megiddo. Although the dates for the archaeological strata in question are disputed, a majority of scholars agree that gates and attached city walls with the same plan at the latter three sites were constructed in the tenth century BCE and can plausibly be interpreted as evidence of centralized planning by Solomon's administration. Significantly, in Ezekiel's restored Temple, modeled on the Solomonic Temple where Ezekiel had served as a priest, the description of the gates has the same features (Ezek 40.6–16). A number of other key cities were also fortified during the tenth century, further evidence for the centralization that occurred during the reigns of David and Solomon. The broad outline of the narrative, then, is historically correct, and many details in it are supported by archaeological data (see Figures 16.3 and 16.4).

Institutions

Royal Administration

Comparing the list of Solomon's officials (1 Kings 4.1–6) with those of David (see pages 259–60) is instructive. The first position is that of the priest, reflecting the increased importance of the religious establishment with the building of the Temple. It is held by Azariah, the son of Zadok, whose father had been appointed by David and who had supported Solomon against Adonijah. The second position is held by "secretaries," probably

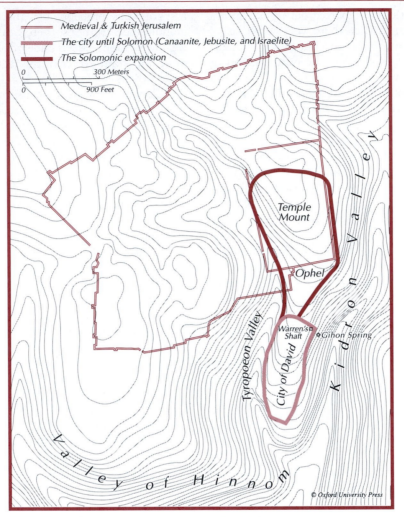

FIGURE 16.1. Jerusalem in the time of David and Solomon.

because of the increased record-keeping required for the administration of the kingdom. Next comes the "recorder," Jehoshaphat, who had served in the same capacity under David. The position of army commander has moved from first to fourth position, probably because David's subjugation of Israel's neighbors had brought security. This is held by Benaiah, who had supported Solomon's accession and who been the head of David's bodyguards; he replaced Joab, who had sided with Adonijah and whom Solomon had killed. Further down the list are two sons of

Nathan, one "over the officials" and another serving both as "priest and king's friend," the latter title probably meaning a close royal advisor; if their father is Nathan the prophet, this shows his continuing influence in the court, although he himself is not mentioned after the account of Solomon's accession. Finally is an official in charge of the palace and another in charge of the forced labor; the latter, Adoniram, is probably the same person as Adoram, who held this post under David and continued to do so under Solomon's successor Rehoboam (1 Kings 12.18).

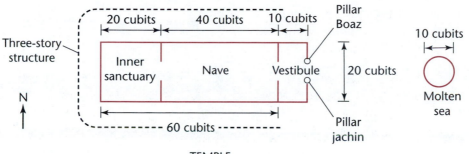

TEMPLE

FIGURE 16.2. Plan of the Temple of Solomon as described in 1 Kings 6 (1 cubit = 1.5 ft [.45 m]).

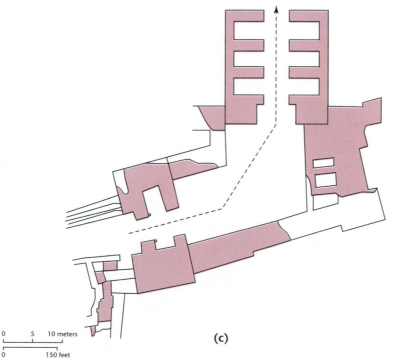

FIGURE 16.3. Plans of six-chambered gates at Gezer (a), Hazor (b), and Megiddo (c), three cities that Solomon is reported to have constructed. According to Ezekiel, the gates of the Temple had the same plan. The arrows show the route into the city.

273

FIGURE 16.4. The foundations of the Solomonic gate at Gezer (see Figure 16.3), looking out from the city to the south.

In this administrative structure, the king was the apex of authority, with political, military, and religious officials under his direct control.

According to 1 Kings 4.7–19, the kingdom was divided into twelve districts, excluding Judah, with an official appointed for each district to collect provisions for the royal court (see Figure 16.5). Two of these district officials were married to daughters of Solomon, indicating the close ties between the officials and the king. The districts in the list only partially correspond to the old tribal boundaries, reflecting changes in the administration of the kingdom that replaced the old tribal divisions, the economic resources of those districts, and the territory actually under direct royal control rather than an idealized geography. The census undertaken by David may have been the first step in the creation of these districts. The omission of Judah from the list of districts may be significant; in the breakup of the kingdom that followed Solomon's death, the northern tribes claimed that their burden was excessive (1 Kings 12.4). Judah may have been administered separately, with an advantageous status.

Religion

Like his predecessors Saul and David, Solomon is described as personally offering sacrifices (1 Kings 3.3–4, 15; 8.63; 9.25). This occurs first at "the principal high place" at Gibeon, not far to the northwest of Jerusalem. The worship at "high places" was generally unacceptable to the Deuteronomistic Historians, since it violated the principle of centralized worship in Jerusalem and often involved worship of other deities (see 1 Kings 11.7). It is probably allowed in this case because the Temple had not yet been built. (See further Box 16.2.)

The Temple

The centrality given to the Temple in 1 Kings 5–8 reflects the Deuteronomistic program, in which

Mediterranean
Sea

ASHER

NAPHTALI

Hazor
• VIII

BASHAN

33°

IX

NAPATH-DOR

IV   ISSACHAR
X

Dor •

Megiddo •   • Jezreel

Taanach •   • Beth-shean
V

• Hepher   • Arubboth

• Socoh   Abel-meholah •

GILEAD   VI

• Ramoth-gilead

III

EPHRAIM

I

32°

VII

• Mahanaim

XI

Shaalbim •
Gezer •   BENJAMIN
Makaz •   II   • Elon
• Gibeon

Beth-shemesh •   JERUSALEM

XII

Hebron •

JUDAH   Dead
Sea

31°

0   10   20 Miles

0   10   20 Kilometers

35°   36°

FIGURE 16.5.   The administrative districts of Solomon's kingdom.

Box 16.2 THE "ROYAL PSALMS"

One of the principal categories identified by form-critical analysis of the Psalms (see further pages 460–66) is that of the "royal psalms." These hymns, especially Psalms 2, 18, 20, 21, 45, 72, 89, 101, 110, 132, and 144, have the king as their central figure, often the speaker. They were composed for and used at various occasions, including coronations (Pss 2; 110) and royal weddings (Ps 45). Most of the other royal psalms belong to form-critical categories widely used in the book of Psalms, including petition (for example, Pss 20; 144), lament (Pss 89; 101), and thanksgiving (Pss 18; 21). In these psalms, the king himself or the community on behalf of the king asks God for help or expresses gratitude for help given.

Like most of the Psalms, these royal psalms are difficult to date, but their existence is important evidence of the continuing role of the kings in worship.

there was only one legitimate place for the worship of Yahweh: the city that he had chosen, Jerusalem, and the Temple that he had commanded, or at least allowed, to be built. This centrality is indicated by the formal introduction to the account of the Temple's construction, which connects it with the Exodus: "In the four hundred eightieth year after the Israelites came out of the land of Egypt, in the fourth year of Solomon's reign over Israel . . . he began to build the house of the LORD" (1 Kings 6.1; the actual chronology is questionable). The importance of the Temple for the Deuteronomistic Historians is indicated further by the detailed descriptions of the Temple (1 Kings 6) and of its furnishings (1 Kings 7.13–51). Moreover, the descriptions are consistent with those found both in 2 Chronicles 3–4 (which, to be sure, uses 1 Kings as a source, but did not copy it slavishly and has some independent details) and in Ezekiel 40–42, Ezekiel's plan for a restored Temple. We have, in other words, three separate witnesses to the particulars of the Temple, which served as the center of worship in Jerusalem for nearly four centuries.

We can thus be fairly sure what the Temple looked like. Many details of the building itself and

of its furnishings are paralleled in the archaeological record from the same period. Much of the symbolism is derived from the Canaanite mythology that informed the ideology of the Davidic monarchy (see pages 277–84), and this symbolism had few roots in older premonarchic tradition. Note especially the Great Bronze Sea, symbolizing perhaps the primeval cosmic waters of chaos, and the twelve bulls that supported the sea, like the "lions, oxen, and cherubim" on the ten bronze stands (1 Kings 7.29)—this is scarcely consistent with the Decalogue's prohibition of the making of "graven images" (Ex 20.4). The live trees planted in the Temple's courtyard (see Pss 52.8; 92.12–13) and the architectural ornamentation representing palms and flowers (1 Kings 6.29) recalled the myth of the garden of Eden, the garden of God that was a widespread Canaanite tradition. The same is probably true of the cherubim, both those carved on the walls, doors, and stands (1 Kings 6.29, 32, 35; 7.29, 36), and perhaps the gigantic cherubim over the ark as well. Even if there were cherubim in some form associated with the ark in the premonarchic period, which some scholars question, those in the Temple were constructed specially for that purpose by Solomon (1 Kings 6.23–28). Made of solid wood and overlaid with gold, they were 15 ft (4.5 m) high and had a wingspan of the same distance and were certainly not portable. (For illustrations of the details of the Temple, see the color section following page 300.)

The priests and temple personnel were royal appointees, and maintenance of the Temple was a royal function. The king himself offered sacrifice at least occasionally. The Temple and its furnishings, then, were the expression of a state religion.

EXCURSUS: THE IDEOLOGY OF THE DAVIDIC MONARCHY

The influence of the Davidic monarchy on the formation of biblical traditions was considerable, an influence that is not surprising given the dynasty's more than four-hundred-year duration. A major part of this influence is what can be called the "**royal ideology**," that cluster of concepts that both derived from and supported and shaped the institution of the monarchy. Because of the complex nature of biblical traditions, we see no single explicit formulation of the royal ideology as such, but elements are found throughout the Bible, especially in the historical books, the prophets, and the Psalms. Each of these sources, of course, has its own literary history, and so a process of abstraction runs the risk of collapsing what were originally separate and even inconsistent perspectives. But because the royal ideology is so pervasive, it is appropriate to summarize its main features here.

The king was chosen by God, with whom he had a special relationship described by the metaphor of sonship. The divine oracle in 2 Samuel 7 speaks of David's successor in this way: "I will be his father, and he will be my son" (v. 14). This language is a projection of the dominant social construct of Israelite, and indeed ancient Near Eastern, society in general, that of a family presided over by a patriarch. Sonship was not understood literally, so that the king was considered divine. Rather, using the familial

metaphor, it expressed a special and mutual relationship of obligation between deity and monarch; as we have seen (page 113), the father-son metaphor is used as well to describe the relationship of suzerain to vassal.

The father-son metaphor also occurs in Psalm 2, whose genre is a coronation hymn. After a quotation of a divine proclamation—"I have set my king on Zion, my holy hill"—the king speaks:

> I will tell of the decree of Yahweh:
> He said to me, "You are my son;
>   today I have begotten you." (v. 7)

The "decree" is proclaimed on the day the king is crowned, the day that, by adoption as it were, the king becomes a son of God by virtue of his becoming king. The same idea probably also lies behind Isaiah 9.1–7, in which, again on the day of coronation, the members of the council of the gods celebrate the addition of a new member to their assembly:

> For unto us a child is born,
>   unto us a son is given. (Isa 9.6 [KJV])

Another model used for the relationship between God and the king was that of covenant: In this contractual metaphor, God committed himself to the Davidic dynasty. This **Davidic covenant** was at first perhaps conditional:

> If your sons keep my covenant
>   and my decrees that I shall teach them,
> their sons also, forevermore,
>   shall sit on your throne. (Ps 132.12; see Box 15.3 on page 263)

But soon the agreement came to be expressed in unconditional terms:

> When he commits iniquity, I will punish him with a rod such as mortals use, with blows inflicted by human beings. But I will not take my steadfast love from him, as I took it from Saul, whom I put away from before you. Your house and your kingdom shall be made sure forever before me; your throne shall be established forever. (2 Sam 7.14–16)

The covenant that guaranteed the dynasty became an "everlasting covenant" (2 Sam 23.5)—and hence the dynasty would never end, and its capital city and the Temple in that city would never be destroyed. God had chosen Jerusalem as his home, as he had chosen the dynasty, and both would endure forever.

The language of sonship and of eternal covenant was nothing less than a revolution in ancient Israel's self-understanding, a presumably deliberate effort to replace the premonarchic understanding of the relationship between Israel as a whole and its God. In the older system, Israel itself was God's son (Ex 4.22), and its relationship with God was direct; in the newer royal ideology, the king was the essential mediator between God and people. In Psalm 72, significantly one of only two biblical psalms attributed to Solomon, the prosperity of the nation and of its crops was linked with the king's rule, rather than with the conduct of the people as in the Ten Commandments (Ex 20.12) and in the blessings and curses associated with the Sinai covenant (Lev 26.3–45; Deut 28). This interposition of the king between God and people was reflected in the plan of Jerusalem in Solomon's expansion of the city: The palace complex was sited between the Temple and the city proper, where the populace lived.

Moreover, the covenant between Israel and God was conditional: Israel's prosperity depended on continued obedience to the stipulations of the covenant (see Ex 19.5). But the Davidic covenant was eternal and unconditional: God guaranteed the continuation of the dynasty in perpetuity, without regard for the kings' conduct.

Symptomatic of the substitution by the Davidic covenant of the Sinai covenant is how in the royal ideology Mount **Zion**—the poetic term for Jerusalem—replaces Mount Sinai as the locus of revelation:

> Out of Zion, the perfection of beauty,
>   God shines forth. . . .
> before him is a devouring fire,
>   and a mighty tempest all around him.
>   (Ps 50.2–3; see also Isa 4.5 and compare Ex 19.16–18)

And, in a remarkable shift, it is from Zion, not Sinai, that "instruction" (*torah*) comes (Isa 2.3).

Given its importance in Pentateuchal traditions, it is also remarkable that Sinai (or Horeb, the alternate name of the mountain of the revelation to Moses in the Pentateuchal traditions E and D) is mentioned only nine times outside the Pentateuch. Its disappearance from the literature concerning the period of the monarchy parallels that of the ark of the covenant. Bringing the ark to Jerusalem had served to legitimate David's kingship: The Lord was with David (2 Sam 7.3) in a very real sense because David had brought the ark to the capital; the ark was, so to speak, co-opted. And the ark, the visible sign of the divine presence, made the Temple Yahweh's home. But once installed in the innermost chamber of the Temple, the ark was virtually forgotten. In the Psalms, many of which were hymns used in worship at the Temple, the ark is referred to only once, in the account of its recovery by David (Ps 132.8). Nor is the ark mentioned in any of the prophets except in Jeremiah 3.16, which tellingly says: "It shall not come to mind, it shall not be remembered." Apart from the ark itself, the rituals of the Jerusalem Temple, as well as its architecture and ornamentation, had few links with earlier Israelite tradition.

A major purpose of the royal ideology was religious and political centralization. Premonarchic Israel had been decentralized, a loose confederation of tribes united by commitment to worship Yahweh alone and to mutual support. The unifying symbol of the confederation had been the ark of the covenant, a moveable object understood both as the footstool for the invisible god and as the container for the tablets of the covenant that expressed the tribes' commitments. The permanent installation of the ark in the Temple was part of the shift from a decentralized to a centralized system of religious observance. Royal control of the rituals of the kingdom was part of the larger program of political centralization. The palace complex was the seat of government, and associated with it was an emerging aristocracy, which often thrived by exploitation of those it ruled.

In the royal Judean ideology, then, deity, king, and city were linked; Yahweh proclaims: "I will defend this city to save it, for my own sake and for the sake of my servant David" (Isa 37.35). The

Box 16.3 **THE PSALMS OF ZION**

Another category of Psalms that scholars have identified is those that share the theme of God's choice and protection of Jerusalem, and its status as the "holy city." This category includes Psalms 46, 48, 76, 84, 87, and 122. The speaker is either the community as a whole (Ps 48) or an individual (Pss 84; 122). These psalms illustrate the city's role in worship in ancient Israel and express belief in its exalted status and impregnability. They are examples of the "songs of Zion" (Ps 137.3) that were remembered in grief after the city's destruction in 586 BCE.

In addition to these psalms, the importance of Jerusalem may be discerned in its mention in more than thirty other psalms, as Zion, Salem, or Jerusalem.

---

plan of Jerusalem as expanded by Solomon reflected this ideology, as did many details of the Temple's design. The two pillars flanking the entrance to the Temple had the symbolic names of Jachin and Boaz: God had chosen to make his home in the dynastic Temple in Jerusalem, and he would establish it (Jachin) with his strength (Boaz) forever. (See further Box 16.3.)

Many elements of the ideology of the Davidic monarchy are found throughout the ancient Near East. In the prologue to his famous code, the eighteenth-century BCE Babylonian king Hammurapi speaks of himself as "the one who makes affluence and plenty abound," and a letter addressed to the seventh-century BCE Assyrian king Ashurbanipal reads:

> [The sun god] Shamash and [the storm god] Adad have established for the king my lord, for his kingship over the lands, a happy reign: days of justice, years of equity, heavy rains, waters in full flood, a thriving commerce.[*]

The same ruler also says of himself:

> After [the gods] had caused me to take my throne . . . Adad sent his rains, Ea opened his fountains, Ea opened his springs, the grain grew five cubits high. . . . In my reign there was fullness to overflowing, in my years there was plenteous abundance.[†]

These examples find echoes in Psalm 72:

> Give the king your justice, O God,
>   and your righteousness to a king's son.
> May he judge your people with righteousness,
>   and your poor with justice.
> May the mountains yield prosperity for the people,
>   and the hills, in righteousness. . . .
> May there be abundance of grain in the land;
>   may it wave on the tops of the mountains;
>   may its fruit be like Lebanon;
> and may people blossom in the cities
>   like the grass of the field. (Ps 72.1–3, 16)

In the late second millennium BCE texts from Ugarit, this and other elements of the Davidic royal ideology are also found. In the epic named

---

[*]   W. L. Moran (trans.), in J. B. Pritchard, *Ancient Near Eastern Texts Relating to the Old Testament* (Princeton, NJ: Princeton University Press, 1969), p. 627.
[†]   Adapted from D. D. Luckenbill, *Ancient Records of Assyria*, Vol. II (Chicago: University of Chicago Press, 1927), par. 769.

for him, Kirta, the king, is the "son of El," the high god, who is the guarantor of the dynasty. As "son of El," Kirta was a member of, or at least present at meetings of, the divine council, the assembly of the gods. The prosperity of Kirta's subjects depended on his own well-being: When he became ill, the crops failed. He also exercised priestly functions in offering sacrifices.

The ideology of the Davidic monarchy, then, was a particular Israelite expression of this broader Near Eastern understanding of kingship. The immediate source of the ideology can only be conjectured. One obvious possibility is that it came from Tyre. The Phoenicians of Tyre were direct descendants of the second-millennium BCE Canaanites; their chief deities were originally Canaanite, and they inherited other aspects of religion and social and political concepts as well. The king of Tyre, Hiram, was an ally of both David and Solomon, and he supplied raw materials and specialists for the construction of the Temple. The plan of the Temple, in fact, followed a typical Canaanite design and has close parallels from Syria (see Figures 16.6 and 16.7). Many of the details of the Temple furnishings are also paralleled in Phoenician art. It is likely, then, that Phoenician—originally Canaanite—concepts and formulations lie behind the royal ideology of the Davidic monarchy.

Of interest in this connection is the identification of Mount Zion as Zaphon, the home of the Canaanite storm-god Baal, which was located on the northern coast of Syria. Psalm 48, a hymn of Zion that celebrates "the city of our God, which God establishes forever" (v. 8), describes Jerusalem in these phrases:

> His holy mountain, beautiful in elevation,
>   is the joy of all the earth,
> Mount Zion, the heights of Zaphon,
>   is the city of the great king. (vv. 1–2)

The alternate translation of "the heights of Zaphon" as "in the far north" obscures the connection, but also implies a Canaanite background, for Jerusalem is not a northern city in any ordinary geography.

Some influence may have come from the Canaanite sacred traditions of Jerusalem itself, which until its capture by David had not been part of Israel. One clue is the name of David's priest Zadok. His genealogy is inconsistently presented in different sources; it seems that he was not from one of the main priestly families, although later writers did connect him with Aaron (see 1 Chr 6.1–8), which may be a legitimation after the fact. It is possible that Zadok was a priest of the Jebusite city (see page 216) whom David appointed as one of his priests and whose family eventually became the most prominent of the groups of priests attached to the Temple. Under this hypothesis Zadok would have been one source for the royal ideology, which took hold so rapidly in the United Monarchy.

The most sustained treatment of the royal ideology is found in Psalm 89. In its final form, this hymn dates either to the end of the monarchy or to the exilic period, but it incorporates much older traditions. It begins with an introduction (vv. 1–4) giving its main theme: praise of Yahweh, especially for his covenant with David. Then follows a section (vv. 5–18) praising Yahweh as the head of the council of the gods, the one who, like Baal in Canaanite tradition and Marduk in *Enuma elish* (see pages 5–7 and 101–2), destroyed the primeval sea, and then, like Marduk, created the world.

The hymn continues the praise with a section describing the divine choice of David to rule (vv. 19–37). David is guaranteed defeat of all his enemies, he is the firstborn son of Yahweh, and he shares the divine task of keeping the watery forces of chaos in check:

> I will crush his foes before him
>   and strike down those who hate him . . .
> I will set his hand on the sea;
>   and his right hand on the rivers.
> He shall cry to me: "You are my Father,
>   my God, and the rock of my salvation!"
> I will make him the firstborn,
>   the highest of the kings of the earth.
>   (vv. 23–27)

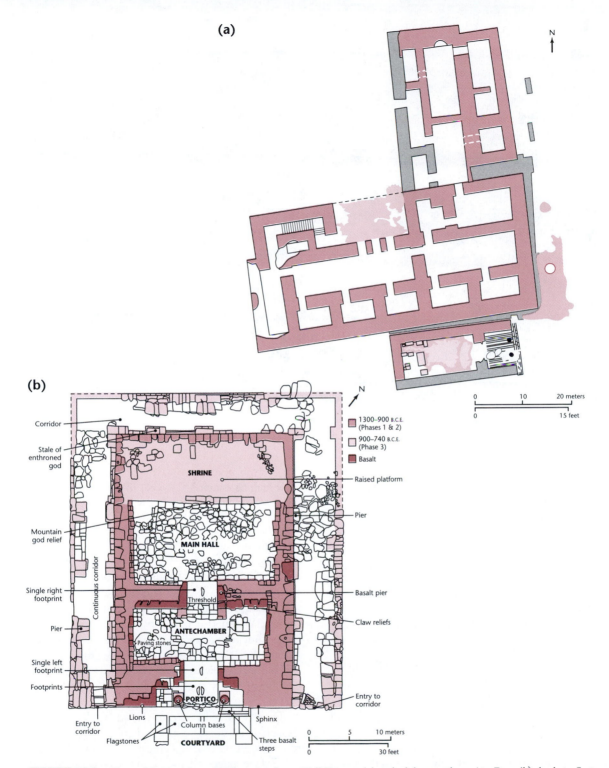

FIGURE 16.6. Plans of the temple and palace complex at Tell Tayinat (a) and of the temple at Ain Dara (b), both in Syria and dating to the early first millennium BCE. In (a), the temple is at the bottom, attached to a much larger royal complex, as in Solomonic Jerusalem. The plans of both temples are similar to that of the Jerusalem Temple (see Figure 16.2). Carved into the threshold stones of the Ain Dara temple are giant footprints, probably symbolizing the deity taking possession of the holy place.

281

FIGURE 16.7.   The Ain Dara temple (see Figure 16.6b).

Moreover, the king's rule is confirmed by an unconditional covenant:

> Forever I will keep my steadfast love for him,
>   and my covenant with him will stand firm.
> I will establish his line forever,
>   and his throne as long as the heavens endure.
> If his children forsake my law
>   and do not walk according to my ordinances,
> if they violate my statutes
>   and do not keep my commandments,
> then I will punish their transgression with the rod
>   and their iniquity with scourges;
> but I will not remove from him my steadfast love,
>   or be false to my faithfulness.
> I will not violate my covenant,
>   or alter the word that went forth from my lips.
> Once and for all I have sworn by my holiness;
>   I will not lie to David.
> His line shall continue forever,
>   and his throne endure before me like the sun.

> It shall be established forever like the moon,
>   an enduring witness in the skies. (vv. 28–37)

This hymn is remarkable for what may be called its high mythology. Also remarkable is what is missing: No reference is made to any of the individuals or events of Israel's history—the ancestors, Moses, the Exodus, the Sinai covenant, the ark—that are so central in the Pentateuchal narratives. When the Israelites asked Samuel for a king, they requested a king "like all nations" (1 Sam 8.5), and that is what they got: a dynastic monarchy whose ideology was essentially Canaanite, only slightly connected with Israel's earlier traditions.

There was resistance to the royal ideology, although it is usually expressed subtly. Opposition to the building of the Temple found in 2 Samuel 7.5–7 (see pages 261–62) may have prevented

David from building the Temple himself. Noteworthy in that passage is Yahweh's expressed preference for a tent rather than a house of cedar: In Ugaritic myth, a house of cedar is built for Baal after his defeat of Sea and his installation as king of the gods. This implicit hostility to the overly close identification of Yahweh and Baal will become explicit in the ninth- and eighth-century BCE prophets Elijah and Hosea (see pages 304 and 321).

Themes of the J tradition in the primeval history can be also read as criticism of the royal ideology. In the tale of the garden of Eden (Gen 2–3), in the mythic fragment concerning the marriages of the sons of God and human women (6.1–4), and in the story of the tower of Babel (11.1–9), J stresses that there is an uncrossable boundary between the divine and the human exists and that any attempt to breach that boundary will be met with punishment. The tower of Babel narrative itself may be read on one level as a condemnation of the building of the Temple.

Some prophets would appeal to Israel's pre-monarchic traditions as primary. For Hosea, it was not the king who was the deity's firstborn son, but Israel:

> When Israel was a child, I loved him,
>   and out of Egypt I called my son.
>   (Hos 11.1; compare Jer 3.19)

And some prophets could be ruthless in their denunciation of the extravagant claims of the monarchies of Israel and Judah, like Amos in the eighth century BCE:

> Woe to those who are at ease in Zion,
>   and for those who feel secure on Mount
>   Samaria,
> the notables of the first of the nations,
>   to whom the house of Israel resorts! . . .
> Therefore they shall now be the first to go into exile,
>   and the revelry of the loungers shall pass away.
>   (Am 6.1, 7)

Likewise, in the late seventh century BCE, Jeremiah, in his "Temple Sermon" (7.1–14), attacked the idea that the divine presence in the Temple was a guarantee of security. That, said Jeremiah, was a lie, as could be learned from the ruins of Shiloh to the north of Jerusalem, where the ark had been located before its capture by the Philistines (1 Sam 4.11) and their destruction of Shiloh itself.

The attitude of the Deuteronomistic Historians toward the royal ideology of the David monarchy is decidedly ambivalent. While the repeated theme of the book of Judges—"In those days there was no king in Israel: everyone did what was right in their own eyes"—has a kind of wistful nostalgia for an earlier time, the space devoted by the Deuteronomistic Historians to the rise of the monarchy in 1 Samuel and to its four-hundred-year history in 2 Samuel and 1 and 2 Kings reveals a much more complex understanding. On the one hand, under the monarchy the nation as a whole and particularly its rulers failed to live up to the primary requirement of the law given by God to Moses as the Deuteronomistic Historians understood it: exclusive worship of Yahweh. Yet the religious centralization introduced by David and Solomon and later renewed by King Hezekiah in the late eighth century BCE and King Josiah in the late seventh was fully in concert with the insistence of the book of Deuteronomy on worship only at a central sanctuary. And the repeated praise of David, Hezekiah, and Josiah by the Deuteronomistic Historians indicates that for them not all kings were bad. Still, one of the unifying threads throughout Deuteronomy and the entire Deuteronomistic History from Joshua to the end of 2 Kings is a pattern of sin and punishment, a pattern that, especially from the perspective of the destruction of Jerusalem in 586 BCE, clearly calls into question the claim of the Davidic monarchy to have an unconditional and eternal covenant. For the Deuteronomistic Historians, the Davidic monarchy was responsible for its own destruction, even if its claims to be divinely chosen had some merit. Thus, while recognizing the divine choice of the house of David, the Deuteronomistic Historians still maintained the priority of the Sinai covenant. (See further Box 16.4.)

Box 16.4 THE ROYAL IDEOLOGY IN LATER TRADITIONS

Even after the end of the Davidic dynasty in 586 BCE, elements of the royal ideology continued to have a formative role in later Jewish and Christian traditions. Both the Essenes, in the Dead Sea Scrolls, and the earliest Christians, in the New Testament, applied the language of divine sonship to a future leader or messiah.

The term "**messiah**" itself is derived from royal nomenclature. In Israel, as elsewhere in the ancient Near East, objects and persons whose function or office brought them especially close to the divine were smeared with oil (see Box 9.1 on page 148). Kings, priests, and at least occasionally prophets (see 1 Kings 19.16; Isa 61.1) were anointed, and in the Hebrew Bible the term "anointed one" (Hebr. *mashiah*) is used only of past or present leaders. Both Saul (1 Sam 24.6; 2 Sam 1.14) and David (2 Sam 19.21; 23.1) are called "the anointed of Yahweh," and the title is also used to refer to kings in general in several of the royal psalms (2.2; 18.50; 20.6; 28.8; 89.38, 51) and elsewhere (for example, 1 Sam 2.10; Lam 4.20).

In Hellenistic Judaism the term "messiah" was applied to a future leader sent by God to restore autonomy to Israel, whose rule would inaugurate an era of peace and prosperity like that enjoyed under David. Earlier prophetic sayings were reinterpreted to describe him. So the anointed one, or "messiah" (the English transliteration of the Hebrew term), was to be a descendant of David (see Isa 11.1, 10; Jer 23.5–6; Ezek 34.23–24), fulfilling the promise of an eternal dynasty to David in 2 Samuel 7.16. Like David, he would be born in Bethlehem (see Mic 5.2).

The early Christians believed that Jesus was this messiah. One of the titles used for him was "Christ," from the Greek word *christos*, which is originally simply a translation of Hebrew *mashiah*, "anointed one." They also made use of biblical traditions in their formulations of that belief. So Jesus was born in Bethlehem (see Mt 2.5–6), was called "son of David," and, like the Davidic kings, was "son of God." Not surprisingly, several of the royal psalms are applied to him in the New Testament.

The royal ideology also survives in the hope for a restored, or new, Jerusalem, in which the promises attached to the city would be fulfilled. In Western political theory, the concept of "the divine right of kings" is based in part on the biblical precedent of the Davidic monarchy.

RETROSPECT AND PROSPECT

Like the entire Deuteronomistic History, the account of Solomon's reign is informed by the perspective of hindsight. This is especially the case with Solomon's final prayer at the dedication of the Temple, which refers to the Temple's destruction and to exile. Those events are interpreted by the latest stage of the Deuteronomistic History as fully deserved punishment for failure to observe the requirements of the law of Moses, a failure of which Solomon was especially guilty.

Although he was the builder of the Temple, he "did not observe what the LORD had commanded" (1 Kings 11.10).

The book of Deuteronomy has only one passage dealing with kingship, the "law of the king" in Deuteronomy 17.14–20:

> When you have come into the land that the LORD your God is giving you, and have taken possession of it and settled in it, and you say, "I will set a king over me, like all the nations that are around me," you may indeed set over you a king whom the LORD your God will choose. . . . Even so, he must not acquire many horses for himself, or return the people

to Egypt in order to acquire more horses, since the LORD has said to you, "You must never return that way again." And he must not acquire many wives for himself, or else his heart will turn away; also silver and gold he must not acquire in great quantity for himself.

The reign of Solomon as presented by the Deuteronomistic Historians is the principal example of failure to live up to this ideal; indeed, the prohibitions expressed in Deuteronomy seem to be based on Solomon's rule, which for the Deuteronomistic Historians was in the end a moral disaster despite its accomplishments.

IMPORTANT TERMS

Davidic covenant   **royal ideology**   **Zion**

messiah   **Temple of Solomon**

QUESTIONS FOR REVIEW

1. Discuss the ways in which religion and politics were intertwined in the physical and ideological description of Solomonic Jerusalem.

2. What were the strengths and weaknesses of Solomon's reign?

3. Describe the "royal ideology" and how it differed from the older, premonarchic views of the Israelite confederation.

BIBLIOGRAPHY

A good short commentary on 1 Kings is P. Kyle McCarter, Jr., "1 Kings," pp. 305–22 in *Harper's Bible Commentary* (ed. J. L. Mays; San Francisco: Harper & Row, 1988). For a longer commentary, see Mordechai Cogan, *1 Kings* (New York: Doubleday, 2000).

In addition to the essay by Meyers (see the bibliography to Chapter 15), for a summary of Solomon's career, see Tomoo Ishida, "Solomon," pp. 105–13 in *The Anchor Bible Dictionary*, Vol. 6 (ed. D. N. Freedman; New York: Doubleday, 1992).

For a summary of ancient Israel's views of kingship

and monarchy in its ancient Near Eastern context, see
Baruch Halpern, "Kingship and Monarchy," pp. 413–16
in *The Oxford Companion to the Bible* (ed. B. M. Metzger
and M. D. Coogan; New York: Oxford University Press,
1993).

For a discussion of the Solomonic Temple and ar-

chaeological parallels to its features, see Elizabeth Bloch-
Smith, " 'Who is the King of Glory?' Solomon's Temple
and Its Symbolism," pp. 18–31 in *Scripture and Other Ar-
tifacts: Essays on the Bible and Archaeology in Honor of
Philip J. King* (ed. M. D. Coogan et al.; Louisville, KY.:
Westminster John Knox).

THE DIVIDED KINGDOMS OF ISRAEL AND JUDAH FROM THE LATE TENTH TO THE EARLY EIGHTH CENTURIES BCE

CHAPTER
17

1 Kings 12–2 Kings 14

The Deuteronomistic Historians narrate in varying degrees of detail the parallel histories of the two kingdoms that followed the United Monarchy that had flourished under David and Solomon. These were the **northern kingdom of Israel**, ruled by a succession of dynasties until its conquest by the Assyrians in 722 BCE, and the **southern kingdom of Judah**, ruled by the Davidic dynasty until its conquest by the Babylonians in 586 BCE. The Deuteronomistic Historians, it must be recalled, were writing in Judah after the fall of the northern kingdom, and their presentation of that northern kingdom is almost entirely negative. Moreover, their history of the divided monarchies is highly selective. The reigns of some kings are treated only perfunctorily, while considerable space is devoted to material that coincided with the ideological perspective of the Deuteronomistic Historians. They also devoted considerable space to the activities of various prophets, especially Elijah and Elisha, and this chapter will discuss the phenomenon of prophecy in some detail.

HISTORY

Biblical Sources

The primary body of data for the history of Israel during the period of the Divided Monarchy is the Deuteronomistic Historians' account in the books of Kings. These historians in turn relied on earlier sources, including:

- *Royal annals*: In the concluding formulas for the reigns of almost all of the rulers of Israel and Judah, references are made to the "book of the days of the king of Israel [or: Judah]." These serve as footnotes, in which the Deuteronomistic Historians give one of their sources. The royal annals no longer survive, but they presumably resembled such chronicles known from other cultures, especially Assyria and Babylonia.

- *Prophetic legends*: Throughout the books of Kings, the Deuteronomistic Historians incorporate into their narrative folkloric legends concerning prophets. These legends seem originally to have been oral, although it is impossible to know in what form the Deuteronomistic Historians knew them.

In organizing their narrative, the Deuteronomistic Historians used a dominant theme: the obligation of Israel to observe the requirements of the teaching of Moses, especially the worship of Yahweh alone. Failure to do so inevitably resulted in divinely imposed punishments, and that is the repeated interpretation by the Deuteronomistic Historians of internal and external events in the histories of the kings of Israel and Judah.

That interpretation of historical events as divinely controlled is often expressed in the books of Kings by prophets, and prophetic predictions and their fulfillment punctuate the narrative, providing a running commentary on it. Thus, the division of the kingdom after Solomon is prophesied in 1 Kings 11.29–40 by Ahijah as a punishment for Solomon's worship of other gods, and the fulfillment of this prophecy is recorded in 1 Kings 12.15. An anonymous "man of God" prophesies in 1 Kings 13.2 the contamination of the altar at Bethel by King Josiah, and that prophecy is fulfilled in 2 Kings 23.15–20. Ahijah predicts the ignominious end of the house of Jeroboam I in 1 Kings 14.7–14, and the fulfillment is duly noted in 15.29–30. The prophet Jehu, the son of Hanani, predicts the end of the Baasha's dynasty in 1 Kings 16.1–4, and that is fulfilled in 16.7 and 16.12. Elijah prophesies the deaths of Ahab and Jezebel in 1 Kings 21.17–29, and the fulfillment of that prediction is repeatedly noted (2 Kings 9.36; 10.10, 17). Elijah also predicts the death of Ahab's successor Ahaziah in 2 Kings 1.4 and 1.16, and that prophecy is fulfilled immediately (2 Kings 1.17). Elijah's successor Elisha prophesies the repeated defeats of Israel by the Aramean king Hazael in 2 Kings 8.12, and that prophecy is fulfilled in 2 Kings 13.3. Elisha's representative prophesies both that Jehu will terminate the house of Ahab and the death of Jezebel in 2 Kings 9.7–10, and he does so in 2 Kings 9.36.

In all of these cases, the explicit reason for the judgments of doom is failure to observe the teaching of Moses, especially by worshiping other gods. Most of the prophetic judgments summarized here have to do with the northern kingdom of Israel. From the perspective of the Deuteronomistic Historians, writing originally in Jerusalem, the capital of the southern kingdom of Judah, the northern kingdom was an unrelieved moral disaster, beginning with Jeroboam I. In fact, the entire history of the northern kingdom was irrevocably contaminated by the "sins of Jeroboam," a phrase that is used more than a dozen times between 1 Kings 14.16 and 2 Kings 15.28.

Closely related to this negative assessment of the northern kingdom are repeated positive statements about the Davidic dynasty in Jerusalem. The divine promise of an enduring dynasty (see 2 Sam 7.11–16) will be kept, "for the sake of my servant David and for the sake of Jerusalem, which I have chosen" (1 Kings 11.13; see also 1 Kings 11.36; 15.4; 2 Kings 8.19; 19.34).

The Deuteronomistic Historians, then, are writing an ideologically biased history, in which they have revised older prophetic legends to express their negative view of the northern kingdom of Israel and their essentially positive view of the southern kingdom of Judah.

The books of Kings were used as a source for the other narrative history of Israel in the Bible, the books of Chronicles, which give additional information not found in the books of Kings, some of which may be historically accurate. In the period treated in this chapter, such additional information includes the lists of fortified cites built by Rehoboam and lists of his wives and sons (2 Chr 11.5–23; for the latter, compare the list of the sons of Jehoshaphat, 2 Chr 21.2–4); the composition of the Egyptian pharaoh Shishak's army (2 Chr 12.3); and details concerning the reigns of Asa (2 Chr 14), Jehoshaphat (2 Chr 17; 19; 20), and Amaziah (2 Chr 25).

Nonbiblical Sources

Another important source is nonbiblical records. By the late tenth century BCE, direct correlations begin to occur between the Bible and other ancient Near Eastern texts. To some extent this is ominous: The more frequent the mention of Israel and Judah and their rulers in nonbiblical records, the more they were threatened by the great powers to their north and south, as well as by their more immediate neighbors. By the late tenth century BCE, the Assyrians in northern Mesopotamia had resumed their drive toward imperial conquest of the entire Near East, and Egypt also had regained some of its power. Israel and Judah were caught between the two.

The earliest direct correlation between biblical and nonbiblical sources concerns the invasion of Palestine and Transjordan by the Egyptian pharaoh Shishak (Shoshenq I) in the late tenth century BCE. According to 1 Kings 14.25, in the fifth year of Rehoboam, Solomon's successor as king of Judah, Shishak "came up against Jerusalem . . . and took away the treasures of the house of the LORD and the treasures of the king's house." Second Chronicles 12.4 adds other details, including that Shishak captured the fortified cities of Judah. Shishak's own records list over 150 cities captured in an Asiatic campaign, including such familiar places as Gibeon, Mahanaim, Penuel, Taanach, and Megiddo. At Megiddo was found a fragment of a stela with Shishak's name on it, presumably part of a victory monument erected after his capture of the city. There is also archaeological evidence of the destruction of a number of cities in the late tenth century BCE. Why did Shishak invade the regions to the north of Egypt? Probably in an effort to reassert Egyptian sovereignty over them, taking advantage of the weakness of both Israel and Judah immediately after their split when Solomon died.

Shishak is the first Egyptian pharaoh named in the Bible. In narratives of earlier times, none of the pharaohs with whom Abraham, Joseph, the Israelites in Egypt, and Moses dealt is named. If the Deuteronomistic Historians had wanted to be vague here, they had ample precedent. But they are not, and so we have a direct correlation between the Bible and contemporaneous nonbiblical sources. Moreover, because our knowledge of Egyptian chronology is fairly secure, we also have an absolute date. Shishak died in 924 BCE. His Asiatic campaign is dated by the biblical historians to the fifth year of Rehoboam, who must therefore have assumed the throne no later than 928 BCE, a date that enables us to give an approximate chronology for his predecessors (see further page 241).

Three kings of Israel from the ninth and early eighth centuries BCE are named in the annals of Assyrian kings, generally as defeated or as paying tribute: Ahab, Jehu, and Jehoash. Moreover, two rulers of states neighboring Israel are mentioned both in the Bible and in nonbiblical records: Hazael, king of Aram-Damascus (2 Kings 8.15), and Mesha, king of Moab (2 Kings 3.4; see further pages 293–94).

These contemporaneous correlations and the chronological data they include confirm the historicity of the broad outlines of the biblical narrative and provide a relatively secure chronology for the kings of Israel and Judah (see Box 17.1). In reconstructing the history of the Divided Monarchy, therefore, we have occasional corroborative evidence from outside the Bible, but our principal source is the Deuteronomistic Historians' narrative found in the books of Kings.

Synthesis of Biblical and Nonbiblical Sources

Much of the treatment in the books of Kings of the century and a half between the death of Solomon and the accession of Jeroboam II as king of Israel (788 BCE) is perfunctory, drawing mostly on royal annals and consisting mainly of notices of accession and succession. Each king's reign is assessed according to the ideological standards of the Deuteronomistic Historians. Because of the incomplete and selective nature of the documentation, it is impossible to construct a detailed history of the events in this period. A number of battles and encounters mentioned in Assyrian and other nonbiblical sources go unmentioned in the Bible, and likewise most events mentioned in the Bible are not documented elsewhere.

Following the death of Solomon, what had been a united monarchy immediately divided into two separate kingdoms, Judah in the south, ruled by Solomon's son Rehoboam (928–911 BCE), and Israel in the north, ruled by Jeroboam (928–907), one of Solomon's officials who had rebelled against him. According to the biblical writers, the union between north and south had been fragile at best, and the fault line that divided the two opened again at Solomon's death. The reasons given by the Deuteronomistic Historians for the split are probably essentially correct. Solomon's construction of an oriental court in the grand

Box 17.1 CHRONOLOGY OF KINGS OF ISRAEL AND JUDAH LATE TENTH TO MID-EIGHTH CENTURIES BCE

Kings of Israel	Kings of Judah	Events
Jeroboam I (928–907)	Rehoboam (928–911)	
Nadab (907–906)	Abijam (Abijah) (911–908)	Invasion of Shishak (924)
Baasha (906–883)	Asa (908–867)	
Elah (883–882)		
Zimri (882)		
Omri (882–871)		
Ahab (871–852)	Jehoshaphat (870–846)	Battle of Qarqar (853)
Ahaziah (852–851)	Jehoram (Joram) (851–843)	
Jehoram (Joram) (851–842)	Ahaziah (Jehoahaz) (843–842)	
Jehu (842–814)	Queen Athaliah (842–836)	
Jehoahaz (817–800)	Jehoash (Joash) (836–798)	
Jehoash (Joash) (800–784)	Amaziah (798–769)	
Jeroboam II (788–747)	Azariah (Uzziah) (785–733)	

Date ranges are for reigns, not life spans. Overlapping dates indicate coregencies. Vertical lines show genealogical connections.

style had been paid for by high taxes and forced labor, and the northern tribes seem to have paid more dearly than had Judah. Resistance to Solomon's extravagance developed during his reign, and Rehoboam's refusal at least to promise reform made the break final.

From this point onward, Judah and Israel went their separate ways. Their relationship was generally one of rivals, although they were allies periodically. Israel was the larger, more populous, and more powerful of the two. Neither was able to maintain the allegiance of the neighboring kingdoms that had been under the control of David and Solomon, and these kingdoms, especially Aram-Damascus, grew in strength and made frequent incursions into Israel's territory (see Figure 17.1).

The first ruler of the northern kingdom of Israel, Jeroboam I, moved quickly to solidify his control. Installed as king at the ancient tribal center of Shechem (see Box 12.2 on pages 204–5), he soon moved his capital to Penuel, another site associated with Israel's ancestral traditions (see Gen 32.30–31), and, perhaps after Shishak's with-

drawal, to Tirzah, which remained the capital of the northern kingdom until Omri moved it to the city of Samaria.

Much of the space devoted by the Deuteronomistic Historians to Jeroboam's reign concerns his establishing two royal shrines, one at Bethel near the southern boundary of his kingdom and one at Dan near the northern boundary. The reason for this action is clearly given: to discourage worship by his subjects in Jerusalem, the capital of the rival kingdom. But it was Yahweh ("who brought you up out of the land of Egypt"—1 Kings

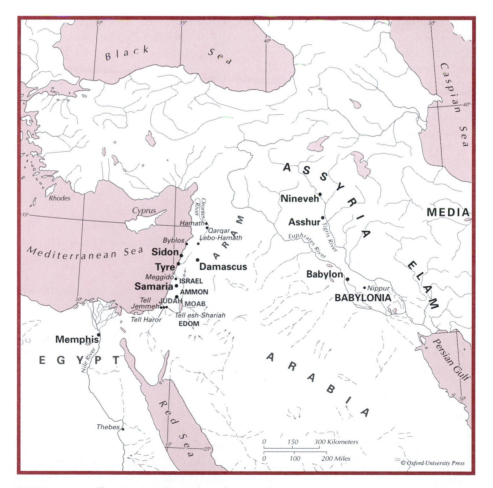

FIGURE 17.1. The Near East during the early first millennium BCE.

12.28) who was worshiped at the two shrines, enthroned on a calf following an ancient tradition. For the Deuteronomistic Historians, this action of Jeroboam became his "sin" (1 Kings 12.30; see page 288) because it violated the principle of a central sanctuary for all Israel and because in their tendentious interpretation it was a form of idolatry. This interpretation is also found in Hosea (8.4–6; 10.5–6), who had connections with the Deuteronomic movement. (See further pages 181–83; for further discussion of the golden calf, see pages 130–33.)

Jeroboam's counterpart in Judah, Solomon's son Rehoboam, engaged in a systematic defensive buildup, fortifying major cities on his borders. This may have been in anticipation of the campaign of Shishak, and also because of repeated conflict with Jeroboam (see 1 Kings 14.30; 15.6). Rehoboam was succeeded by his son Abijam (also called Abijah), and then by his grandson Asa. Asa's long reign is described in only a few verses. During it, apparently, conflict with Israel continued, and the king of Israel, Baasha, fortified the town of Ramah, just a few miles north of Jerusalem. To counter this threat, Asa formed an alliance with Ben-hadad, the king of Aram-Damascus on Israel's northeastern border. Baasha was forced to withdraw from Ramah when the Arameans attacked several cities in Israel.

The stability provided to Judah by the dynastic principle that son succeeded father on the throne was never as accepted in the northern kingdom of Israel. In Israel, in the period of eighty-seven years from the accession of Jeroboam I (928 BCE) to that of Jehu (842 BCE), ten kings belonging to five different families ruled, and four of those ten were killed during coups (see Box 17.1). Jeroboam I was succeeded by his son Nadab, who ruled for only two years and was killed in a coup by Baasha, while the Israelite army was laying siege to the Philistine city of Gibbethon. History then repeated itself, as Baasha's successor Elah was assassinated by Zimri after a short reign. Zimri ruled for only seven days; when the army commander Omri was proclaimed king by his troops, again at Gibbethon, Zimri committed suicide.

The dynasty of Omri, consisting of four kings during the mid-ninth century BCE, was one of the most powerful in the history of the northern kingdom. Omri moved the capital to **Samaria** (1 Kings 16.24), where he and his successor Ahab constructed a lavish royal city whose details have been illuminated by archaeology. Israel's political and economic power was enhanced by an alliance with the Phoenician kingdom of Tyre to the north, an alliance cemented by the marriage of Ahab to Jezebel, the daughter of the Tyrian king Ethbaal. A similar marriage resulted in some Israelite control of Judah, when Athaliah, Ahab's daughter, married Jehoram, the crown prince of Judah.

During the mid-ninth century BCE, Israel and Judah were allies, often against Aram-Damascus, the northern kingdom's chief rival among the states of the region. The Deuteronomistic Historians introduce their account of the first attempt to regain control of the city of Ramoth-gilead in Transjordan with the statement: "For three years Aram and Israel continued without war" (1 Kings 22.1), apparently an unusually long period of peace. According to the narrative in the books of Kings, at least ten major military encounters occurred between Israel and Aram from the reign of Ahab (871–852 BCE) to that of Jehoash (800–784 BCE), and in most of them the Arameans were victorious. During the long reign of the Aramean king Hazael (ca. 845–810 BCE) especially, the Arameans extended their control as far south as Philistia, and under the threat of a siege of Jerusalem, Jehoash the king of Judah was forced to pay tribute (2 Kings 12.17–18).

In 1993 and 1994, fragments of a stone monument with an Aramaic inscription were discovered at Dan, on Israel's northern border (see Figure 17.2). The inscription is dated to the mid- to late ninth century BCE and describes a defeat of Israel and Judah by an Aramean king whose name is missing, but who may be Hazael. The stela was erected at Dan as a monument to his victory. The king attributes both his assumption of the throne and the victory to his national deity, the storm-god (Baal) Hadad, and mentions the "house of David"—the earliest nonbiblical reference to

FIGURE 17.2. Fragments of an Aramaic inscription found at Tel Dan in northern Israel. In it an unnamed ninth-century BCE king of Aram reports that he defeated a king of Israel and mentions the "house of David" (the highlighted words on the lower right). Carved in stone, it is 12.5 in (32 cm) high on the right.

David and to the dynasty that he founded—and perhaps (the name is broken) King Ahaziah of Judah. The details of the conflict referred to in the stela do not match any biblical data.

When threatened from outside, however, the rival states of Israel and Aram could cooperate. This was the case in 853 BCE. Assyrian records describe a major battle in that year at Qarqar on the Orontes River in northern Syria between the Assyrian king Shalmaneser III and a coalition of southern forces, including contingents from Damascus and Hamath in Syria, from Byblos and Arvad in Phoenicia, and from Ahab, king of Israel. That encounter was inconclusive, and the same coalition fought against Shalmaneser several more times. Not until 842 BCE could Shalmaneser claim victory, celebrated in the famous "Black Obelisk," which depicts Jehu, the king of Israel who had succeeded in ousting Omri's dynasty, bowing in submission as he paid tribute (see Figure 17.3). None of this is reported in the Bible; even Shalmaneser himself is unmentioned. Subsequently, payment of tribute is reported to the Assyrian king Adad-nirari III (811–783 BCE) by Jehoash (Joash) of Israel; again, neither the tribute itself nor the Assyrian ruler is mentioned in the Bible.

The situation is somewhat different with an important Moabite text, the **Mesha Stela**, discovered in 1868 (see Figure 17.4). In it, King Mesha of Moab recounts, "Omri, king of Israel . . . oppressed Moab for many days, for Chemosh [the Moabite national deity] was angry at his land. And his son succeeded him, and also said, 'I will oppress Moab.' . . . But I triumphed over him and his house." The rest of this relatively lengthy text describes Mesha's capture of seven thousand Israelites and of ritual objects. All of these he "devoted to destruction." The word used is the same as Hebrew *herem*, "ban" (see pages 206–7); here we see just one of the close correspondences between Israelite and Moabite religious language and practice.

An account of the relationship between Moab and Israel in the late ninth century BCE from an Israelite perspective is found in 2 Kings 3. According to this narrative, which is part of the larger cycle of stories concerning the prophet Elisha (see pages 303–5), Ahab's son Jehoram joined forces with the king of Judah, Jehoshaphat, and the king of Edom in order to regain control over Moab from Mesha, who had stopped paying the annual tribute of 100,000 lambs and the wool of an equal number of sheep (see 2 Kings 1.1; 3.5). The battle was joined, and the Moabites were on the verge of defeat when Mesha sacrificed his own son. "Great wrath came upon Israel" and the coalition was forced to retreat.

Both texts agree on the essentials: The northern kingdom of Israel controlled Moab for a time, but Moab successfully revolted and recovered its independence in the second half of the ninth century BCE. But it is difficult to correlate the details, and the texts may be referring to different events in what must have been a lengthy struggle between Moab and Israel. Moreover, omissions remind us of the need to interpret both texts cautiously. Second Kings 3 mentions neither the capture of thousands of Israelites and much booty nor the loss of Israelite territory in Transjordan,

FIGURE 17.3. A panel from the "Black Obelisk" of King Shalmaneser III of Assyria, showing King Jehu of Israel bowing before Shalmaneser. Carved ca. 825 BCE, it is the only contemporaneous picture of an Israelite ruler.

all mentioned in the Mesha Stela. But the Mesha Stela mentions neither a near defeat of the Moabites nor the human sacrifice that provoked the Israelites' rout.

The general picture that emerges from this spotty documentation is a time of intense rivalry and occasional cooperation between the smaller kingdoms of the southern Levant, all in the shadow of the Assyrian advance.

INSTITUTIONS AND SOCIETY

Because of the highly selective nature of the Deuteronomistic Historians' account of the history of Israel and Judah after the death of Solomon, we cannot get a detailed picture of how primary institutions and society in general functioned during this period. Two categories, however, are worth noting.

The Army

From the very beginning of the monarchy, military leadership was often a path to political power. Both Saul and David became king in part at least because of their military successes, and in the northern kingdom of Israel several kings assumed power in military coups, no doubt because of their positions in the army. Thus, Baasha plotted against Jeroboam I's successor Nadab on the battlefield. His successor Elah was assassinated by Zimri, "commander of half his chariots" (1 Kings 16.9), and Zimri's seven-day rule ended when Omri, the commander of the army, was acclaimed as king on the battlefield and Zimri committed suicide (1 Kings 16.15–18). Likewise, both Jehu (2 Kings 9.5) and Pekah (2 Kings 15.25) were military officers who successfully conspired to oust the reigning king. The professional army, then, which had been responsible for Israel's survival at

FIGURE 17.4.   Stela erected by King Mesha of Moab to commemorate a victory over Israel in the mid-ninth century BCE. It is about 3.5 ft (1.1 m) high.

the beginning of the monarchic period, also was the source of much upheaval throughout it.

According to Shalmaneser III's account of the battle of Qarqar (see page 293), King Ahab of Israel contributed two thousand chariots and ten thousand infantry to the coalition that opposed him. Although these appear to be round numbers, and may be exaggerated, archaeological evidence exists that confirms the importance of chariots in Israel in the ninth century BCE. At Megiddo, in a level dating to the ninth century, excavators uncovered two complexes of pillared buildings with large open courtyards that have

plausibly been identified as stables with attached chariot parks or exercise yards, with a capacity of about two hundred horses (see Figure 17.5). Similar structures are found elsewhere, and with two or three horses per chariot, Ahab could have had a chariot force numbering at least in the hundreds.

Queens and Queen Mothers

The ideologically structured and highly selective narrative of the Deuteronomistic Historians in the books of Kings gives only a few glimpses of the roles of women in ancient Israel. They appear occasionally throughout the narrative, as mothers, widows, and wives, and most of them are unnamed. Because of the focus on kings and their deeds, the most prominent women are members of the royal families.

In the Davidic dynasty that ruled over Judah, the mother of almost every king from Rehoboam onward is named in the formulaic summary of the king's reign (see, for example, 1 Kings 14.31); by contrast, the mother's name of only one of the kings of Israel, Jeroboam I, is given. One of these women is explicitly called *gebira*, a title that literally means "powerful woman," and that is often translated as "queen mother." Concerning Maacah, the mother of King Asa, we are told that the king "removed his mother Maacah from being *gebira*, because she had made an abominable image for Asherah," the Canaanite goddess (1 Kings 15.13; 2 Chr 15.16). This brief comment suggests that the position held some status, and that the woman who held it could be removed from office. Four other times in the Bible the title is bestowed upon women who are not named in the immediate context, once of an Egyptian princess (1 Kings 11.19), twice of a member of the royal family in the last days of the Judean monarchy (Jer 13.18; 29.2; in both cases probably Nehushta: see 2 Kings 24.8), and once of a member of the royal family of the house of Omri, in the northern kingdom (2 Kings 10.13; almost certainly Jezebel).

Jezebel, the Tyrian princess who married Ahab, king of Israel, was one of the most power-

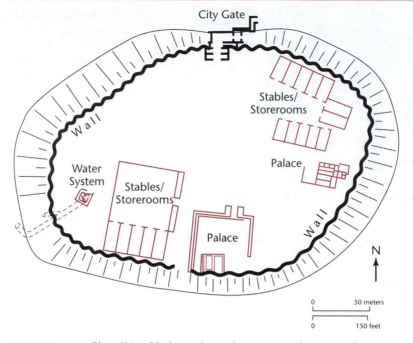

FIGURE 17.5.   Plan of Megiddo during the ninth century BCE, showing two large complexes that were used as stables and probably also as storerooms.

ful and notorious women of monarchic times. As the king's consort she presided over her own religious establishment—"the four hundred fifty prophets of Baal and the four hundred prophets of Asherah, who eat at Jezebel's table" (1 Kings 18.19)—and was responsible for eliminating rival prophets of Yahweh (1 Kings 18.4; 19.2). She also exercised her own power over local judicial processes in the episode of Naboth's vineyard, when she arranged for Naboth's execution on false charges (1 Kings 21.1–14). After Ahab's death she remained a formidable power, as is clear in the account of Jehu's revolt. When Jehu approached the royal residence in Jezreel, Jezebel prepared to meet him: "She painted her eyes, and adorned her head, and looked out of the window. As Jehu entered the gate, she said, 'Is it peace, Zimri, murderer of your master?'" (2 Kings 9.30–31). For the revolt to succeed, Jezebel had to be eliminated. For the Deuteronomistic Historians, of course, Jezebel is the quintessence of evil, and that is how she is re-

membered in later tradition: Revelation 2.20 speaks of her namesake as "that woman Jezebel, who calls herself a prophet and is teaching and beguiling my servants to practice fornication and to eat food sacrificed to idols." But we cannot fail to admire the courage and bravado of the queen who meets her death defiantly and in full regalia.

Another powerful woman of the monarchic period was Athaliah, a princess of the royal house of Israel (and perhaps Jezebel's daughter) who became the wife of the Judean king Jehoram and mother of his successor Ahaziah. When her son was killed during the revolt of Jehu, she assumed the throne, the only woman in Israelite history to have ruled on her own. She ruled Judah for six years, but was killed during an uprising in which Jehosheba, Ahaziah's sister, the wife of the high priest (2 Chr 22.11), and perhaps Athaliah's own daughter, played a crucial role.

Thus the king's wife and the king's mother could exercise considerable power in ancient

Israel, as we have already seen in the case of Solomon's mother Bathsheba (see page 269).

EXCURSUS ON PROPHECY

In most cultures from antiquity to the present persons have been recognized as having the ability to interpret phenomena considered to be beyond ordinary human comprehension. These phenomena include such natural occurrences as the movement of the heavenly bodies, the flight of birds, and the appearance of an animal's liver and other organs, as well as apparently random events, such as the casting of lots, dice, or arrows (see Figure 17.6). Such persons also can function as interpreters of dreams and as mediums who have the ability to communicate with the dead. Some have apparently magical powers and the ability to heal and even to restore the dead to life. In most of these capacities they function as intermediaries and channels of communication between the natural and the supernatural orders. Thus, apparently random phenomena can be interpreted as controlled by the gods and as containing a divinely

revealed message. We see a spectrum of functions here, from the mundane to the most profound forms of communication with the divine. Such individuals are attested widely in the ancient Near East, and in ancient Israel as well. While their techniques and behaviors are often culture-specific, they no doubt believed, and their contemporaries believed, that they had special abilities derived from their association with the divine.

Consistent with the extensive nonbiblical ancient Near Eastern evidence are repeated biblical references to such persons outside of Israel. Note, for example, Ezekiel's description of how the king of Babylon would decide whether to attack Jerusalem or the Ammonite capital Rabbah first: "For the king of Babylon stands at the parting of the way, at the fork in the two roads, to use divination; he shakes the arrows, he consults the teraphim, he inspects the liver" (Ezek 21.21). Likewise, the Moabites (Num 22.7), the Philistines (1 Sam 6.2), the Egyptians (Isa 19.3), and others made use of various forms of **divination**, including necromancy, the consultation of the dead.

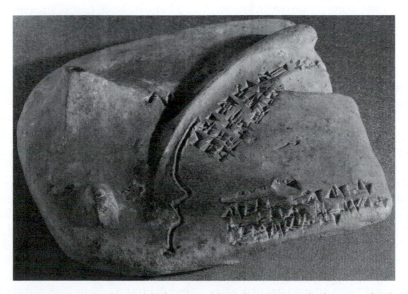

FIGURE 17.6. A clay model of an animal liver, from Syria in the late second millennium BCE, measuring about 4.3 in (11 cm) wide. Such models were used for teaching divination throughout the ancient Near East.

In one of the most widely attested forms of divination in ancient Israel, lots were cast, or sacred objects such as the Urim and Thummim and the ephod were employed, to give answers to questions that could be answered by either "Yes" or "No." This type of divination was used to decide on a course of action (1 Sam 30.7), to choose a leader (1 Sam 10.20–21; see also Acts 1.26), and to determine a guilty party when the material evidence was inclusive (1 Sam 14.41–42; Jon 1.7). In all of these cases, the result was considered to be from Yahweh:

> The lot is cast into the lap,
>   but the decision is the LORD's alone.
> (Prov 16.33; see also Josh 7.14.)

The Urim and Thummim, and the ephod with which they were connected, formed part of the vestments of the priests. These objects are not fully understood. The Urim and Thummim were apparently thrown like dice (see 1 Sam 14.42). Their connection with the priesthood is significant, although also not entirely clear. Deuteronomy 33.8 identifies the entire tribe of Levi as those who used this form of divination; P, however, restricts it to the high priest (Ex 28.30; Lev 8.8). In any case, the connection with priestly functionaries clearly indicates the divine role in rendering judgment.

Other forms of divination were also practiced in ancient Israel. The prophet Elisha, for example, instructs King Jehoash in the use of arrows as a kind of magical act to assure victory (2 Kings 13.15–19). Necromancy, the consultation of the dead, is also attested. When Saul consulted the woman of Endor, a medium, she was able to conjure up the spirit of the dead Samuel (1 Sam 28.14). The practice of necromancy was apparently popular, as its repeated condemnation suggests (see, for example, Lev 19.31; Deut 18.11; Isa 8.19).

At what we may call the "high" end of the spectrum of interpreters are the individuals known from the Bible as the **prophets**. It is important to recognize at the outset that distinctions between prophets and other interpreters of divine will were often not sharply drawn. Deuteronomy provides a helpful starting point:

> No one shall be found among you who makes a son or daughter pass through fire, or who practices divination, or is a soothsayer, or an augur, or a sorcerer, or one who casts spells, or who consults ghosts or spirits, or who seeks oracles from the dead. (Deut 18.10–11)

The association of these practices, which might be included under the category of magic, with prophecy is suggested by their position immediately before a discussion of prophecy in Deuteronomy 18.15–22. That is to say, the ancients had many ways of ascertaining the will of the god(s), and prophecy was one of them.

Like other forms of interpretation of the supernatural, prophecy is found throughout the ancient Near East. The evidence is incomplete because of the accidents of preservation and discovery, but phenomena like prophecy are known from Byblos in Phoenicia, Hamath and Mari in Syria, and Assyria, and span the period from the early second millennium to the mid-first millennium BCE. Biblical evidence also supports this picture of prophecy among Israel's neighbors. Thus, the Bible refers to "the four hundred fifty prophets of Baal and the four hundred prophets of Asherah" (1 Kings 18.19; see also 2 Kings 10.19) who were part of the entourage of Jezebel, the Phoenician wife of King Ahab of Israel, and describes their activity simply as "prophesying." (The NRSV translation at 1 Kings 18.29, "they raved," is a pejorative misinterpretation.)

One of the closest correlations between biblical and nonbiblical evidence concerns the prophet Balaam. According to Numbers 22, Balaam, the son of Beor, is a Syrian diviner hired by the king of Moab to curse Israel. But he is a true prophet who speaks the word that has been revealed to him, blessing for Israel and destruction of its enemies. He is one "who hears the words of El [NRSV: God], who sees the vision of Shadday [NRSV: the Almighty]" (Num 24.4) and who apparently receives his revelations in some sort of a trance (Num 24.4, 16), often at night (Num 22.8, 13, 19–20), like the prophets Samuel (1 Sam 3.3) and Nathan (2 Sam 7.4). While the entire portrait of Balaam is colored by the biblical writers' experience of prophecy in Israel, the essential elements of the depiction of Balaam in the Bible are also found in the eighth-century BCE Deir Alla texts. In them, the "seer" Balaam, the son of Beor as in the Bible, receives a vision from El at night that reveals a disaster decreed by the "Shaddayin," who are members of the divine council. (See further pages 167–69.)

Like similar specialists in other ancient and modern cultures, prophets could employ unusual techniques. One involves the use of music. In 2 Kings 3, King Jehoram leads a coalition against Moab, and on their march they are without water. Elisha is summoned, and says, "Get me a musician." The text continues: "And then, while the musician was playing, the power of the LORD came on him" (2 Kings 3.15). The band of prophets with whom Saul has two encounters also uses music. When they "prophesy" (the NRSV translation "fell into a prophetic frenzy" is misleading) these prophets use "harp, tambourine, flute, and lyre playing" (1 Sam 10.5; see also 1 Chr 25.1) to reach an ecstatic state,

a state that is contagious: Both Saul, and later his messengers, also begin prophesying, and on the second occasion Saul strips off his clothes (1 Sam 19.23–24). Another example of unusual behavior is attributed to the prophets of Baal, who, when they prophesied, "cried aloud and . . . cut themselves with swords and lances until the blood gushed out over them" (1 Kings 18.28); compare the similar practice of self-laceration by prophets of Yahweh in Zechariah 13.4–6. These accounts of ecstatic activity should probably be connected with the symbolic actions known as "prophetic gestures" attributed to some of the classical prophets, such as Ezekiel lying on his side for a total of 430 days (Ezek 4.4–8). (See Box 17.2.)

Prophets in Ancient Israel

Terminology

Not surprisingly, given the diversity of their lives and activities, various terms are used to describe

Box 17.2 PROPHETS IN LATER TRADITIONS

Prophecy continued to be an important phenomenon in the later developments of the monotheistic traditions, especially in Christianity and Islam. Throughout the Gospels both John the Baptist and Jesus are identified as prophets, and in earliest Christianity prophecy was a recognized, and sometimes criticized, phenomenon. The book of Revelation, as its name implies, is the account of a vision by John while he "was in the spirit on the Lord's day" (Rev. 1.10). In subsequent Christian history, various individuals have identified themselves as recipients of divinely revealed messages. Notable examples are Nostradamus, Joseph Smith (the founder of The Church of Jesus Christ of Latter Day Saints [the Mormons]), and, since 1870, Roman Catholic popes.

In the Quran, the line of those with whom God communicated begins with Adam and continues through Noah, Abraham, Isaac and Ishmael, Jacob, David, Solomon, John the Baptist, and Jesus. This parade of messengers ends with Muhammad, the last and greatest of the prophets, who received his first revelation in a cave outside of Mecca during the "night of power." As in Judaism and Christianity, some branches of Islam believe in continuing revelation to specially designated individuals.

Israelite prophets. The English word "prophet" comes from Greek and literally means "spokesperson." It expresses the understanding that the prophets were delivering divinely sent messages. The primary content of these messages, as we have suggested, was interpretation of phenomena and events from a divine perspective. This notion of interpretation is implicit in the use of prophetic pronouncements by the Deuteronomistic Historians in the books of Samuel and Kings as a kind of running commentary on the historical narrative and also in the canonical division of the Bible in Jewish tradition, which groups together as the "Prophets" both the historical books (Joshua, Judges, 1 and 2 Samuel, and 1 and 2 Kings) and the books named after individual prophets (the books of Isaiah through Malachi); see further the Appendix.

The most frequently used term in the Bible itself is the Hebrew word *nabi'*, usually translated as "prophet." Its etymology is not entirely clear, but the most likely origin is from a word meaning "to call"; a *nabi'* is thus someone called by the deity. Another frequently used title of prophets, "man of God," expresses the same essential idea. That designation is used of Moses, Samuel, Shemaiah, Elijah, and Elisha, as well as of several anonymous prophets (see 1 Sam 2.27; 1 Kings 13.1; 20.28) and, significantly, of Yahweh's messenger who announces the conception and birth of Samson to Manoah and his wife (Judg 13.6–8). The prophets, in other words, had the same status as the divine messengers (later to be designated "angels"; see Box 30.3 on page 534) who appear in biblical tales: They were spokespersons for Yahweh himself.

Modes of Revelation

How did the prophets receive their messages? The exact mode of revelation is a recurring question in many religious traditions. For a god or gods to communicate with humans, such communication must be possible, but at the same time the deity's essential otherness must also be preserved. One way of dealing with this paradox, ultimately the problem of immanence and transcendence, is the mythological device of messengers from the di-

vine to the human. Another is to express the mode of revelation metaphorically. The two most common metaphors in the prophetic literature are those of speech and vision. The metaphor of speech draws on the understanding of the prophets as messengers, who transmit a divine word they have received to an individual, to a group (such as the royal family, the priests, or other prophets), to Israel as a whole, and sometimes to other nations as well. The metaphor of vision is reflected in another title used of the prophet, that of "seer" or visionary. A "seer" transmitted to the audience a vision, a dream, or the proceedings of the divine council. That the prophet as seer was endowed with preternatural vision is shown by the story of the nearly blind Ahijah who can recognize his disguised royal visitor (1 Kings 14.4–6); the paradoxical figure of the blind seer is widely attested in world cultures. Sometimes the two metaphors are explicitly combined, as in Amos 1:1: "The words of Amos . . . which he saw concerning Israel."

Types of Prophets

The phenomenon of prophecy in ancient Israel is extraordinarily diverse. Some prophets, probably most, were trained professionals who earned their livelihood as prophets. The Bible mentions groups of prophets gathered around a leader, who can be called their "father," as were both Elijah (2 Kings 2.12) and Elisha (2 Kings 13.14), and perhaps others as well. These "sons of the prophet(s)" were presumably members of a kind of guild, presided over by a master prophet who instructed his apprentices, as the translation "company of (the) prophets" in the New Revised Standard Version suggests. Samuel, who is a complex figure in his own right, also is presented as the leader of such a group (1 Sam 19.20; note also 1 Sam 10.12), and Isaiah may have been one as well (Isa 8.16 mentions his "disciples").

How did prophets earn their living? Some were consulted to resolve specific problems by individuals who presumably paid a fee (see Num 22.7), like Saul visiting the "seer" Samuel when he was looking for his father's missing animals (1 Sam 9.6–10). Others functioned in a ritual ca-

JERUSALEM IN BIBLICAL TIMES

The single most important place in the Bible is Jerusalem, the capital of ancient Israel and then Judah and Judea throughout the first millennium BCE. Because of its importance in the Bible, it has remained a holy city for Jews, as well as for Christians and Muslims. This section is intended to help readers visualize ancient Jerusalem and to illustrate its continuing importance. (See further Box 15.2 on page 257.)

PLATE 1: AERIAL VIEW OF JERUSALEM FROM THE SOUTH. (Compare Figure 16.1 on page 272.) In the foreground is the city of David, which formed the nucleus of ancient Jerusalem. The large rectangular enclosure above it is the Muslim sanctuary built on the Temple mount, approximately the site of Solomon's Temple. In the center of that enclosure is the Dome of the Rock, an octagonal shrine with a gold dome.

PLATE 2: A RECONSTRUCTION OF THE EXTERIOR OF SOLOMON'S TEMPLE. The horned altar of sacrifice (2 Chr 4.1) is on the right, and the great bronze sea (1 Kings 7.23–26) is on the left. (For plan, see Figure 16.2 on page 273.) This reconstruction, like that in Figure 3, is based on descriptions in the Bible and similar structures elsewhere in the Levant. (See further pages 274–77 and Figure 16.6 on page 286.) (Reconstruction: © L. E. Stager; illustration: C. Evans)

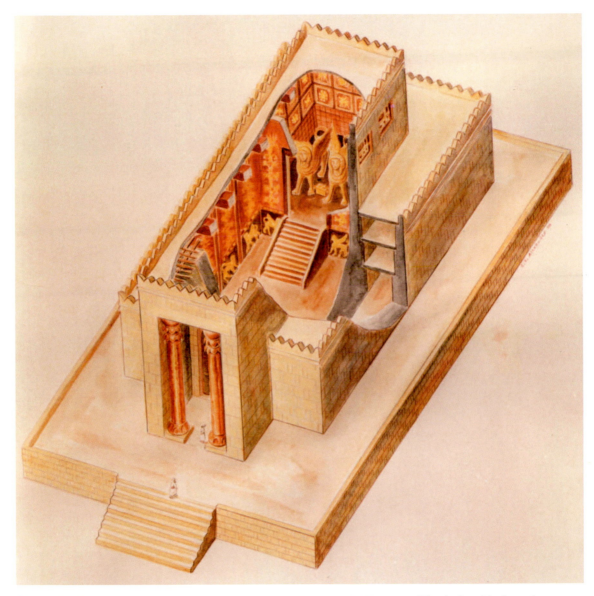

PLATE 3: CUTAWAY SHOWING THE INTERIOR OF SOLOMON'S TEMPLE. The holy of holies, the inner-most room that contained the cherubim and the ark, is at top. (Reconstruction: © L. E. Stager; illustration: C. S. Alexander)

PLATE 4: A RITUAL STAND FROM TAANACH IN NORTHERN ISRAEL. The stand is about 21 in (54 cm) high and dates to the tenth century BCE. Like the Temple of Solomon from the same period, it is decorated with a variety of motifs from ancient Near Eastern art, including, from the top, a bull calf between two stylized columns with a sun disk above it; two gazelles flanking a tree of life (compare Figure 1.4 on page 14), with a lion on either side; two sphinxes or cherubim; and a nude goddess, again with a lion on either side (compare Figure 1.5 on page 17).

PLATE 5: A BRONZE OFFERING STAND FROM CYPRUS. Dating to the eleventh century BCE, this stand was probably used for burning incense and was wheeled, like the ten bronze stands in Solomon's Temple. This stand is about 12 in (30 cm) high, considerably smaller than those described in 1 Kings 7.27–37. The side shown depicts a seated woman playing a lyre (compare Figure 18.5 on page 321), with two musicians standing in front of her (see further pages 466–68).

PLATE 6: AN ORNATE IVORY PANEL DE-PICTING A CHERUB OR SPHINX. Dating to the eighth century BCE, it comes from Cyrus, is about 6.25 in (16 cm) high, and was originally attached to the side of a chair (compare Figure 18.3 on page 317). This miniature piece is a good illustration of the biblical cherubim that formed the throne on which Yahweh was invisibly seated. (See also Figures 8.3 on page 127 and 13.3 on page 225).

PLATE 7: SPHINX FROM THE TEMPLE AT AIN DARA IN SYRIA. Carved in basalt, a dark volcanic stone, the sphinx is immediately to the right of the main entrance of this structure, as if to guard it. It is about 20 in (50 cm) high and dates to the early first millennium BCE. The temple's plan (see Figure 16.6b on page 281) is similar to that of Solomon's Temple.

PLATE 8: FOOTPRINTS AT AIN DARA. Carved into the threshold stones of the Ain Dara temple are giant footsteps, over 3 ft (1 m) long, probably symboliz-ing the deity taking possession of the holy place.

PLATE 9: DEPICTION OF JERUSALEM IN THE LATE EIGHTH CENTURY BCE. This reconstruction, looking west, is based on details in the Bible and archaeological data and shows the expansion of the city under King Hezekiah (see pages 329–30). The Temple is in the upper right-hand corner. (Reconstruction: © L. E. Stager; illustration: C. S. Alexander)

PLATE 10: FORTIFICATION WALL OF JERUSALEM. The foundations of this wall are all that survive, but they are still about 10 ft (3 m) high and more than 23 ft (7 m) wide. The wall was constructed in the late eighth century BCE by King Hezekiah to incorporate the "Second Quarter" of the city within its defenses, in preparation for the invasion of the Assyrian king Sennacherib, which occurred in 701 BCE (see 2 Chr 32.5 and pages 342–43). The Dome of the Rock, on the Temple mount, is at the top.

PLATE 11: VIEW OF JERUSALEM FROM THE WEST, LOOKING TOWARD THE MOUNT OF OLIVES IN THE BACKGROUND. Three of the most sacred shrines of the three monotheistic religions are visible in this photograph. On the left is the large dome that forms part of the Church of the Holy Sepulcher, the traditional site of the burial of Jesus. In the center is the Dome of the Rock, the Muslim shrine covering the rock from which the prophet Muhammad is reported to have ascended to heaven. The Dome of the Rock is built on the platform on which stood the Jewish Temple destroyed by the Romans in 70 CE. A retaining wall of this platform, to the right and just below the Dome of the Rock, is known as the "Western Wall" or the "Wailing Wall," and for centuries it has been a place of prayer and pilgrimage for Jews.

pacity; to these "cultic" prophets we should probably attribute oracular pronouncements and divine responses to prayer, such as those found in psalms. It is significant that at least two prophets, Jeremiah and Ezekiel, were also priests.

Alongside the professional prophets were also amateurs. The clearest example is Amos. When the priest at Bethel ordered Amos to return to his home in Judah, Amos replied: "I am no prophet, nor a son of a prophet; but I am a herdsman, and a dresser of sycamore trees, and the LORD took me from following the flock, and the LORD said to me, 'Go, prophesy to my people Israel'" (Am 7.14–15). Amos is saying, in effect, that he is not a professional: He is not a member of a prophetic school ("a son of a prophet"), and he has his own livelihood. But he is still a prophet because of the divine call that he received. (See further page 313.)

The Relationship of Prophets and Kings

As elsewhere in the ancient Near East, in the biblical record prophets are closely connected with kings. Some prophets, it is clear, were supported by various monarchs: In addition to the prophets of Baal and Asherah in the court of Jezebel and Ahab (see page 298), we have a large number of individuals who are depicted as belonging to the royal establishment, including Nathan, Gad, Isaiah, and Jeremiah.

The phenomenon of prophecy in ancient Israel is more or less coterminous with that of kingship. References to the phenomenon of prophecy are relatively rare in narratives of the premonarchic period. In the Pentateuch, apart from the discussion in the Deuteronomic Code (Deut 13.1–5; 18.15–22; see pages 179–80), we find only five mentions of prophets. Four of these—having to do with Abraham (Gen 20.7); Miriam (Ex 15.20); the seventy elders and Eldad and Medad, who prophesied briefly (Num 11.24–30); and in the discussion of Moses' special relationship with God when Aaron and Miriam challenged his authority (Num 12.6)—are in the Elohist source (E), which we have dated to the ninth or perhaps the eighth century BCE (see page 26), and are one of its hallmarks. The last is in the conclusion to

Deuteronomy (34.10)—the only explicit designation of Moses as a prophet in the Pentateuch. Prophets are also rarely found in the books of Joshua and Judges—once of Deborah (Judg 4.4) and once of an anonymous prophet (Judg 6.8). Only beginning with the narrative of the establishment of the monarchy does prophecy become more frequent. The scarcity of such references in narratives set in earlier times reflects the links between prophecy and kingship, as does the decline of prophecy after the end of the monarchy, in the exilic and postexilic periods.

One of the functions exercised by prophets was to designate the divinely chosen ruler, and as such they are frequently described as participating in coronation rituals. Thus, Samuel anointed both Saul and David (1 Sam 10.1; 16.13), and Nathan was a key participant in Solomon's coronation (1 Kings 1.38–39). Likewise, Ahijah appointed Jeroboam I as the first king of the northern kingdom of Israel (1 Kings 11.31), and Elisha appointed Hazael as king of Aram (2 Kings 8.13) and sent one of his associates to anoint Jehu as king of Israel (2 Kings 9.6), in both cases carrying out a command given to his predecessor Elijah (1 Kings 19.15–16). It is also likely that it was a prophet who announced the divine choice of the king, as in Psalm 2.7–9 and Isaiah 9.2–7. (See further page 277.) At the same time, however, at least according to the Deuteronomistic Historians, the prophets functioned not just as king-makers, but also as king-breakers, being actively involved in the process of succession by communicating divine rejection of a ruler. Moreover, many prophets, even some court prophets, are depicted as independent of the kings, and they could be harshly critical of individual kings and occasionally of the entire institution of monarchy as well.

Women Prophets

Although most of the named prophets are men, it is clear that women were also prophets. During the period of the monarchy, the best example is the prophet Huldah (2 Kings 22.14). Other named women prophets are Miriam (Ex 15.20), Deborah (Judg 4.4), and Noadiah (Neh 6.14). In all of these cases, that the prophets were women is not pointed out as unusual (see also Lk 2.36). Other evidence for women as prophets included the unnamed wife of Isaiah, herself identified as a prophet (Isa 8.3; it is gratuitous to interpret her title as simply honorific—the equivalent of "Mrs. Prophet"). In his vision of the "day of Yahweh" (see Box 18.2 on page 316), the prophet Joel speaks of Yahweh pouring out his spirit on the entire population:

> Your sons and your daughters shall prophesy,
>   your old men shall dream dreams,
>   and your young men shall see visions.
> Even on the male and female slaves,
>   in those days, I will pour out my spirit.
>   (Joel 2.28–29)

In this vision of restoration, the gift of prophecy—including dreams (see Jer 23.25) and visions—will be universal, rather than restricted to a narrow group or a specific socioeconomic class; again, the inclusion of women is apparently not remarkable.

Micaiah

The episode of Micaiah in 1 Kings 22 illustrates several aspects of the previous discussion. In planning an attack on Aram for its taking of the Israelite city of Ramoth-gilead, the king of Israel, who is unnamed but is probably Ahab, asks Jehoshaphat the king of Judah to join him. Jehoshaphat agrees but suggests that they consult the prophets to inquire for the word of Yahweh. The king of Israel summons four hundred prophets, probably court prophets, and asks them: "Shall I go up against Ramoth-gilead, or shall I refrain?" (1 Kings 22.6). Prophets were often asked this sort of question: What was the divine perspective on a course of action? The four hundred prophets, led by Zedekiah, replied: "Go up; for the LORD will give it into the hand of the king" (1 Kings 22.6). Suspicious, perhaps, at this unanimity, Jehoshaphat asks if there is any other prophet who might be consulted, and in due course Micaiah arrives on the scene. He is probably an independent prophet, not a court prophet, but one frequently consulted by the king.

At first he agrees with the four hundred, but when pressed delivers an ominous oracle: "I saw all Israel scattered on the mountains, like sheep that have no shepherd; and the LORD said, 'These have no master; let each one go home in peace'" (1 Kings 22.17).

Micaiah goes on to explain how it is that the other prophets gave a false prophecy:

> Therefore hear the word of the LORD: I saw the LORD sitting on his throne, with all the host of heaven standing beside him to the right and to the left of him. And the LORD said, "Who will entice Ahab, so that he may go up and fall at Ramoth-gilead?" Then one said one thing, and another said another, until a spirit came forward and stood before the LORD, saying, "I will entice him." "How?" the LORD asked him. He replied, "I will go out and be a lying spirit in the mouth of all his prophets." Then the LORD said, "You are to entice him, and you shall succeed; go out and do it." So you see, the LORD has put a lying spirit in the mouth of all these your prophets; the LORD has decreed disaster for you. (1 Kings 22.19–23)

Micaiah claims to have been a witness to the deliberations of the divine council, in which Yahweh decided to send his prophets a false communication. Other prophets make a similar claim. Isaiah also has a vision of the divine council as it deliberates:

> In the year that King Uzziah died, I saw the Lord sitting on a throne. . . . Seraphs were in attendance above him. . . . Then I heard the voice of the Lord saying, "Whom shall I send, and who will go for us?" And I said, "Here am I; send me!" (Isa 6.1–2, 8)

Likewise, Jeremiah attacks the false prophets, challenging the source of their message:

> Thus says the LORD of hosts: Do not listen to the words of the prophets who prophesy to you; they are deluding you. They speak visions of their own minds, not from the mouth of the LORD. . . . For who has stood in the council of the LORD so as to see and to hear his word? . . . I did not send the prophets, yet they ran; I did not speak to them, yet they prophesied. But if they had stood in my council, then they would have proclaimed my words to my people. (Jer 23.16, 18, 21–22)

But this is not the situation in 2 Kings 22, where Yahweh is deliberately deceiving his own prophets.

As Deuteronomy 13.1–3 indicates (see pages 179–80), it was not always easy to decide whether a prophet's words were to be followed. But, as in Deuteronomy 18.22, the authenticity of Micaiah's revelation is shown by the outcome: The king of Israel is killed in the battle.

Finally, the Micaiah episode illustrates the chronological focuses of biblical prophecy. The prophets interpreted past, present, and immediate future events, but less frequently the distant future. To understand the prophets' messages, therefore, it is essential to understand the historical contexts in which they spoke.

THE LEGENDS OF ELIJAH AND ELISHA

Beginning in 1 Kings 17, the Deuteronomistic Historians have incorporated a large amount of folkloristic material concerning the two northern prophets Elijah and Elisha. This material is interspersed in the ongoing chronological narrative and lasts until the death of Elisha in 2 Kings 13.20. The independent origin of this material is evident in a number of ways. Elijah enters the narrative in 1 Kings 17.1 with minimal introduction, as though he were a character already well known to the Deuteronomistic Historians' audience. Also, many of the events are described as miraculous, an aspect generally not characteristic of the Deuteronomistic Historians.

The careers of the two prophets are intertwined: Elisha is Elijah's divinely designated successor, and he completes the assignments given to Elijah at Mount Horeb (1 Kings 19.15–16; see 2 Kings 8.7–15; 9.1–13). Nevertheless, the cycles of stories about them seem to have been originally separate, as is suggested by the presence of a number of doublets in which each prophet performs a similar action. Both raise a widow's son to life (1 Kings 17.17–24; 2 Kings 4.18–37), both multiply food (1 Kings 17.14–16; 2 Kings 4.1–7; 4.42–44), both prophesy the death of Jezebel (1 Kings 21.23–24; 2 Kings 9.10), both part the waters of the Jordan with their prophet's mantle (2 Kings 2.8, 14), and both are addressed as "My father, my father" at their deaths (2 Kings 2.12; 13.14).

Many folkloristic elements are found here: the extraordinary transportation of the prophet from one place to the next (1 Kings 18.12) and from this life to the next (2 Kings 2.11); the almost comic use of animals (2 Kings 2.23–25); and all sorts of miracles: some mundane, such as the recovery of an axe head from the Jordan River (2 Kings 6.1–7) and the neutralizing of poison in a stew (4.38–41), others less so, including healing the sick, restoring the dead to life, and calling fire from heaven. These folkloristic elements are more frequent in the narratives about Elisha.

These folkloristic traditions have been reworked by the Deuteronomistic Historians, especially in the case of the Elijah narratives. In doing so, the Historians develop several themes. One is the presentation of Elijah as a new Moses, fulfilling the promise made by Moses in Deuteronomy: "The LORD your God will raise up for you a prophet like me from among your own people; you shall heed such a prophet" (Deut 18.15). Like Moses, Elijah parted the water (2 Kings 2.8; compare Ex 14.21), built an altar to Yahweh (1 Kings 18.32; compare Ex 24.4), was instructed by God to appoint his successor (1 Kings 19.16; compare Num 27.12–23; Deut 31.23), and ended his life east of the Jordan River (2 Kings 2.9; compare Deut 34.5).

Like Moses, too, Elijah experienced a theophany on Mount Horeb (the alternate name of Mount Sinai). Fleeing from Jezebel, Elijah spent forty days and forty nights journeying to the same mountain where Moses also spent forty days and forty nights. Elijah returned to the same cave where Moses had seen God's back: The Hebrew says literally that Elijah came to "the cave" (1 Kings 19.9)—probably referring to the "cleft in the rock" where Moses had been covered by the divine hand as God passed by (Ex 33.22). But Elijah's experience of the divine presence was qualitatively different from that of Moses. When God appeared to Moses on the mountain, so too did the mythological elements of the appearance of the storm-god: thunder and lightning, thick cloud, fire, smoke, and earthquake (Ex 19.18; Deut 4.11–12; 5.22). The same natural phenomena are present when Yahweh appears to Elijah, but they are not manifestations of the divine presence:

> Now there was a great wind, so strong that it was splitting mountains and breaking rocks in pieces before the LORD, but the LORD was not in the wind; and after the wind an earthquake, but the LORD was not in the earthquake; and after the earthquake a fire, but the LORD was not in the fire. (1 Kings 19.11–12)

After the fire, however, was "a sound of sheer silence" (1 Kings 19.12 [NRSV; the KJV is more allusive: "a still small voice"]). In this remarkable passage, several important points are being made. First, no matter how Yahweh was said to have revealed himself in the remote past, in the experience of the prophet Elijah, and of the Israelites to whom he preached, the divine was not so dramatically accessible. Although it was Yahweh who brought the rain that ended the drought (1 Kings 18.1, 41–45), he was now not just a storm-god, like Baal, whose powerlessness Elijah had just demonstrated in the contest on Mount Carmel (1 Kings 18.17–40). Rather, Yahweh revealed himself as an almost hidden God; as the author of the book of Job puts it, "How small a whisper do we hear of him" (Job 26.14).

A second theme in the Elijah stories is the insistence on the exclusive worship of Yahweh. In the northern kingdom especially, from the Deuteronomistic Historians' perspective, worship of other deities was rife and would have disastrous consequences. Like Joshua at Shechem (Josh 24.15), in the contest on Mount Carmel Elijah offered the assembled people a choice: "If Yahweh is God, follow him; but if Baal, follow him" (1 Kings 18.21). Although Elijah was a prophet in the northern kingdom of Israel, the Israel symbolized by the altar he constructed on Mount Carmel with twelve stones was the older Israel, the twelve-tribe confederation, which preceded the monarchy and whose constitution was the Sinai covenant, which required that Yahweh alone be worshiped. Elijah's name itself appropriately means "My God is Yahweh."

We find an important development here. In Israel's earlier traditions, Yahweh was the preeminent deity (see Ex 15.11; Deut 32.8), more powerful than the other gods whom he ruled. Now those gods, and Baal in particular, are shown to be powerless. The dramatic contest between Elijah and the prophets of Baal has a satiric dimension. He urges them: "Call with a loud voice! Surely he is a god; maybe he is in a meeting, or he is relieving himself, or he is on a journey, or perhaps he is asleep and must be awakened" (1 Kings 18.27). The prophets of Baal do call on their deity, but "there was no voice, no answer, no response" (1 Kings 18.29). The only god who answers is Yahweh, "the god of Elijah" (2 Kings 2.14), and the fire from heaven that he sends shows him to be the true god.

Although presented in a folkloristic context, this is clearly a movement toward monotheism: The only god with power is Yahweh, and he is implicitly the only god. Ramifications of this developing monotheism are also found in the divine instructions to Elijah at the end of the theophany:

> Go, return on your way to the wilderness of Damascus; when you arrive, you shall anoint Hazael as king over Aram. Also you shall anoint Jehu son of Nimshi as king over Israel; and you shall anoint Elisha son of Shaphat of Abel-meholah as prophet in your place. (1 Kings 19.15–16)

Elijah is instructed to anoint three persons: Hazael, Jehu, and Elisha. The naming of Elisha as Elijah's successor is saying in effect that the old prophet's career is nearing an end, a conclusion that he seems not to be pleased with, to judge from the abrupt way that he passes his authority on to Elisha (1 Kings 19.19–20). In fact it is not Elijah but his successor Elisha who will carry out the first two commands, designating Hazael as king of Aram (2 Kings 8.13) and sending one of his servants to anoint Jehu as king of Israel (2 Kings 9.1–10). As we have seen, a prophet's designation of a new ruler, even during the lifetime of a sitting king, has precedents (see 1 Sam 16.1–13; 1 Kings 1.38–39). But with the command to anoint a new king over Aram we enter upon a new understanding of Yahweh's role in history. For the first time, a prophet is instructed to become involved in the internal politics of a nation outside Israel. If Yahweh is the only deity, then it follows that he has an interest in what goes on throughout the world. And, as the episode of Naaman, the Aramean court official whom Elisha healed, shows, that can lead to conversion to the worship of Yahweh by non-Israelites (2 Kings 5). This understanding of Yahweh as the "lord of history" will become more explicit in pronouncements of prophets that follow.

To the interwoven themes of incipient monotheism and of Yahweh's rule of the world is added another that will become characteristic of the preaching of many prophets, that of social justice. The episode of Naboth's vineyard (1 Kings 20) makes this point. The abuse of royal power by Jezebel to gain control of privately owned property desired by her husband, King Ahab, was, for the Deuteronomistic Historians, a telling example of the problems with the monarchy. Among the "ways of the king" against which the prophet Samuel had warned the people when they requested a king is that "he will take the best of your fields and vineyards and olive orchards" (1 Sam 8.14). Now, some two centuries later, through proxies, a king takes an Israelite's vineyard, and in doing so is guilty of violating not just the social order, in which property rights were essential, but also three of the Ten Commandments, by committing false witness, murder, and expropriation of property. For these sins, the prophet Elijah proclaims the divine judgment— the destruction of the dynasty and an ignominious death for Jezebel, which are in effect the curses attached to the violation of the covenant. (See Box 17.3.)

Box 17.3 ELIJAH IN LATER TRADITION

Because he was taken up to heaven without dying (like Enoch in Gen 5.24), Elijah becomes a major figure in later Jewish and Christian literature. The book of Malachi ends with an apocalyptic prediction of Elijah's return: "Lo, I will send you the prophet Elijah before the great and terrible day of the LORD comes. He will turn the hearts of parents to their children and the hearts of children to their parents, so that I will not come and strike the land with a curse" (Mal 4.5–6; see also Sir 48.10). In subsequent Jewish and Christian tradition, the return of Elijah is anticipated before the coming of the Messiah in the apocalyptic end of history, "the day of the Lord." At every Passover table, a cup of wine is poured for Elijah, and the door outside is opened to see if he is there, because according to Jewish tradition it is at Passover that Elijah will announce the coming of the Messiah. Likewise, traditionally a chair is set out for Elijah at a boy's circumcision, so that he may witness the family's observance of the ritual.

Early Christian writers identified John the Baptist as Elijah, because he heralded the coming of the Messiah, fulfilling Malachi's prophecy (see Mt 11.10). Many of the miracle stories of Jesus' ministry also seem to be based on the Elijah narratives, including healing of the sick, raising the dead, multiplying food, calling fire from heaven, and ascending to heaven.

RETROSPECT AND PROSPECT

Having devoted considerable space to a detailed history of the early monarchy in 1–2 Samuel and 1 Kings 1–11, the Deuteronomistic Historians move briskly through the first century and a half of the Divided Monarchy, focusing on repeated prophetic interpretations of the failures of the northern kingdom especially to observe the requirements of the teaching of Moses. In so doing, they reinforce their view that the vicissitudes of the histories of Israel and Judah, and events beyond their borders as well, are ultimately controlled by Yahweh for his own purposes.

Those events include the repeated defeats of both kingdoms by neighboring states, and although the Assyrians will not be mentioned until 2 Kings 15.19, we know from nonbiblical sources that their imperialistic ambitions are beginning to have profound effects. This will become more apparent in the eighth century BCE, as we will see in the next chapter.

IMPORTANT TERMS

divination	northern kingdom of Israel	Samaria
Mesha Stela	prophet	southern kingdom of Judah

QUESTIONS FOR REVIEW

1. Discuss the importance of nonbiblical records for understanding the history of Israel and Judah.

2. Describe some of the ways in which prophets in the ancient Near East and in Israel functioned.

3. What was the relationship between prophecy and kingship?

BIBLIOGRAPHY

Excellent commentaries on the books of Kings are Mordechai Cogan, *1 Kings* (New York: Doubleday, 2001); and Mordechai Cogan and Hayim Tadmor, *II Kings* (New York: Doubleday, 1988). A good summary of the history of this period is Edward F. Campbell, "A Land Divided: Judah and Israel from the Death of Solomon to the Fall of Samaria," Chap. 6 in *The Oxford History of the Biblical World* (ed. M. D. Coogan; New York: Oxford University Press, 1998).

For an introduction to prophecy in ancient Israel, see Patrick D. Miller, *The Religion of Ancient Israel* (Louisville: Westminster John Knox, 2000), pp. 174–89; and David L. Petersen, *The Prophetic Literature: An Introduction* (Louisville: Westminster John Knox, 2002).

For a summary of interpretations of the prophet Elijah, see Jerome T. Walsh, "Elijah," pp. 463–66 in *Anchor Bible Dictionary*, Vol. 2 (ed. D. N. Freedman; New York: Doubleday, 1992).

THE NORTHERN KINGDOM OF ISRAEL IN THE EIGHTH CENTURY BCE

CHAPTER

18

2 Kings 14–17, Amos, and Hosea

The eighth century BCE was a period of turmoil and change. As the Assyrians moved toward Egypt in their ambition to control the entire Near East, the northern kingdom of Israel, like many other states in the region, was absorbed into the Assyrian empire, and the independence of the southern kingdom of Judah was curtailed severely. This is the context for the prophets Amos and Hosea, and also Isaiah and Micah, who will be treated in the next chapter. Here we will focus on the northern kingdom.

HISTORY

As is the case for the ninth century BCE, the highly selective biblical account of the history of the northern kingdom of Israel in the eighth century is supplemented by nonbiblical sources, principally Assyrian inscriptions. Payment of tribute to the Assyrian king Tiglath-pileser III (747–727 BCE; he is sometimes called Pul in the Bible [2 Kings 15.19; 1 Chr 5.26]) is reported by Menahem, Pekah, and Hoshea, three of the last four kings of Israel, and by Jehoahaz (Ahaz) of Judah, and Tiglath-pileser claims to have deposed and exiled King Pekah and to have installed Hoshea

in his place. Assyrian sources also provide a secure chronology for the events of the period (see Box 18.1).

The Assyrian advance into the Levant paused toward the end of the ninth century BCE, as the Assyrians dealt with problems in other regions of their empire. Especially in Urartu (biblical Ararat, roughly the same as modern Armenia), the Assyrians were preoccupied with local attempts to gain independence; six campaigns are reported during the ten-year reign of Shalmaneser IV (783–773 BCE). Assyria also suffered from plagues and internal revolts.

These events diminished for a time Assyria's immediate interest in the Levant. As a result, during the first half of the eighth century BCE both Israel and Judah enjoyed considerable independence and prosperity. The threat against Israel from its Aramean neighbors to the northeast diminished because of conflict between the Aramean states of Damascus and Hamath. Judah apparently was able to regain some control over the Edomites, Ammonites, and Philistines (see 2 Chr 25–27).

The most important rulers of the period were Jeroboam II of Israel (788–747 BCE) and Uzziah of Judah (785–733, although during the last

Box 18.1 CHRONOLOGY OF THE EIGHTH CENTURY BCE

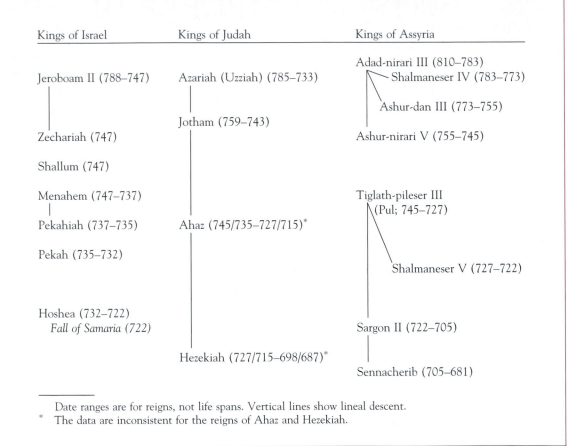

Kings of Israel	Kings of Judah	Kings of Assyria
		Adad-nirari III (810–783)
		Shalmaneser IV (783–773)
Jeroboam II (788–747)	Azariah (Uzziah) (785–733)	
		Ashur-dan III (773–755)
	Jotham (759–743)	
Zechariah (747)		Ashur-nirari V (755–745)
Shallum (747)		
Menahem (747–737)		Tiglath-pileser III
Pekahiah (737–735)	Ahaz (745/735–727/715)*	(Pul; 745–727)
Pekah (735–732)		
		Shalmaneser V (727–722)
Hoshea (732–722)		
Fall of Samaria (722)		Sargon II (722–705)
	Hezekiah (727/715–698/687)*	
		Sennacherib (705–681)

Date ranges are for reigns, not life spans. Vertical lines show lineal descent.
* The data are inconsistent for the reigns of Ahaz and Hezekiah.

decades of his long reign he was quarantined because of serious illness, and his son Jotham and then his grandson Ahaz were corulers with him). The Deuteronomistic Historians give the long reign of Jeroboam only perfunctory attention, covering it in a mere seven verses (2 Kings 14.23–29), and, probably because of Assyrian preoccupation elsewhere, we find no mention of Jeroboam in Assyrian sources. According to 2 Kings 14.25, he restored Israelite territory in the north and east, in Aram and Transjordan (see Am

6.13–14). Moreover, it was during his reign that the prophets Amos and Hosea were active, and archaeological evidence confirms the picture they provide of prosperity (see Figure 18.1).

Illustrative are some remains from Samaria, the capital of the northern kingdom of Israel founded by Omri in the ninth century BCE, especially a collection of more than two hundred fragments of carved ivories that were used as a decorative veneer on walls and furniture (see Figures 18.3 and 18.4 on page 317). At Samaria we have only

FIGURE 18.1. Impression of a seal inscribed in Hebrew "Belonging to Shema, the servant of Jeroboam." The original seal, which was about 1 in (2.7 cm) high, was elegantly engraved and dates to the reign of Jeroboam II, king of the northern kingdom of Israel in the mid-eighth century BCE.

the ivories, not the walls or furniture, and although their precise stratigraphic context is no longer recoverable, evidence from elsewhere in the ancient Near East enables us to understand their function and to date them on art-historical grounds to the ninth and eighth centuries. A number of architectural fragments also testify to the luxury that characterized Samaria.

All this changed in 745 BCE when a usurper, Tiglath-pileser III, assumed the throne of Assyria. He swiftly imposed his control over Urartu and immediately resumed the Assyrian drive toward Egypt. As he moved south, he exacted tribute from many of the kings of the region, including Menahem of Israel, making them his vassals, and also continued the practice of his predecessors, going back to the thirteenth century BCE, of deporting conquered populations. It was Assyrian practice to exile significant numbers of the populace of the territories they had conquered to other parts of their empire and to resettle the conquered territories with outsiders. This separated the conquered from their homelands, diminishing the likelihood of nationalistic uprisings, and provided a source of labor for royal building projects and for cultivating previously undeveloped regions.

In a futile attempt to block Tiglath-pileser, several of the small states in the region formed a coalition in 734 BCE. These included the king of Aram-Damascus, Rezin, and the king of Israel, Pekah, who tried to persuade Ahaz, king of Judah, to join them. He refused and became an Assyrian vassal, requesting assistance from Tiglath-pileser. (For further discussion of these events, called the Syro-Ephraimite War, see pages 336–39). Assyrian reprisal against the coalition was swift, and Damascus fell in 732. The Assyrians also occupied parts of the northern kingdom of Israel and helped Hoshea oust Pekah as its king. In a pattern that would soon repeat itself in Judah, Hoshea, although initially a loyal Assyrian vassal, eventually rebelled against Assyria during the uncertainty that followed Tiglath-pileser's death in 727. But once his son and successor, Shalmaneser V, had secured power, he besieged Samaria, the capital of the northern kingdom of Israel, and captured it in 722. He and his successor, his brother Sargon II, reduced Samaria to ruins and made the northern kingdom an Assyrian province.

For the Deuteronomistic Historians, writing from the perspective of the southern kingdom of Judah as well as of their own theological bias, the fall of the northern kingdom of Israel was the inevitable result of its continual apostasy, and so it is not surprising that they devote much space to its fall. The account in 2 Kings 17 consists largely of sermonizing on the reasons for the fall—principally the worship of deities other than Yahweh. According to the Deuteronomistic Historians, the inhabitants of the northern kingdom had persisted in this practice from the time of Jeroboam I in the late tenth century BCE, despite repeated prophetic warnings. At the same time, the account includes a number of historical details, including the location of the cities to which the Israelites were exiled—"in Halah, on the Habur, the river of Gozan," in northern Mesopotamia, and "in the cities of the Medes" to the east of the Tigris River (2 Kings 17.5). We are also told that to the former northern kingdom, now an Assyrian province, the Assyrians transferred various foreign peoples from elsewhere in their empire (2

Kings 17.24). These newcomers continued to worship their own native deities, but apparently worshiped Yahweh as well.

PROPHETIC BOOKS AND "CLASSICAL" PROPHECY

Beginning in the eighth century BCE, the nature of the prophetic material that we have changes significantly. In addition to prophetic legends like those about Elijah and Elisha preserved in the Deuteronomistic History, we also begin to have collections of material about and by individual prophets, which have been collected and edited in separate prophetic "books," known as the **Latter Prophets** in Jewish tradition.

In the Bible, these books are arranged somewhat arbitrarily in rough order of length, from the longest to the shortest. This arrangement by length of text is also found in other collections of religious texts, for example, the letters of Paul in the New Testament and the suras of the Quran. Thus, the Latter Prophets begins with the "**Major Prophets**," the long books of Isaiah (sixty-six chapters), Jeremiah (fifty-two chapters), and Ezekiel (forty-eight chapters). (In most Christian canons, the book of Daniel is placed next, but it should not be identified as a prophetic book, as Jewish tradition recognizes in placing it in the third section of its canon, the Writings; see further page 456 and the Appendix.) Then comes a separate collection, the "Book of the Twelve" (see Sir 49.10) or the "**Minor Prophets**," shorter books ranging in length (but not in order) from Hosea with its fourteen chapters to Obadiah, only one chapter. Based in part on the amount of text that could conveniently fit on a single scroll, there were thus four scrolls of the prophets: Isaiah, Jeremiah, Ezekiel, and the Twelve.

Within the "Book of the Twelve," the order was more fluid, as comparison of different ancient manuscripts indicates. The arrangement found in current Bibles follows one ancient tradition and is roughly chronological. First come those prophets dated to the early Assyrian period: Hosea, Amos, Obadiah, Jonah, and Micah; Joel

is undated, but it is placed before Amos because of links with it (see further page 441). These are followed by prophets that are set in the later Assyrian period: Nahum, Habakkuk, and Zephaniah. Last come those set in the Persian period: Haggai, Zechariah, and Malachi.

Each of the fifteen books of the Latter Prophets has its own literary and editorial history, which is often complicated, especially for the longer books. In general, the books include three types of materials:

- *Biographical materials about the prophet, in the third person.* These make it clear that the collection and editing of the prophetic books was completed by persons other than the prophets themselves.
- *Autobiographical materials, in the first person.* Some of these may go back to the prophet in question.
- *Oracles, or speeches, by the prophets.* These are usually in poetic form, and draw on a wide variety of genres, including covenant lawsuit, oracle against the nations, judgment oracle, messenger speech, song, hymn, call narrative, lament, law, proverb, symbolic gesture, prayer, wisdom saying, and vision.

The prophetic books, then, are anthologies. Within each we often find no clear principle of arrangement. For example, an account of the prophet's call is often put at the beginning of the book, as in Jeremiah, Ezekiel, and Hosea. Sometimes, however, it occurs elsewhere, as in Amos (7.15) and, according to some scholars, in Isaiah (chap. 6; see further pages 333–34). As this suggests, the material within each prophetic book is not necessarily arranged in chronological order.

Sometimes material is arranged by theme or by genre. A good example is the "**oracle against the nations.**" Many of the prophetic books include these prophetic pronouncements, essentially divine judgments against nations other than Israel. Generally clustered together, they are found in Isaiah 13–23, Jeremiah 46–51, Ezekiel 25–32, Amos 1–2, Zephaniah 2.4–15, Zechariah 9.1–8, and Obadiah and Nahum in their entirety. The origins of this genre are obscure but may be related to the sorts of oracles that would be pronounced in time of war (as in 2 Kings 13.17). The first prophetic use of the oracles against the nations occurs in Amos, who may in fact have originated the genre. As they now stand, these oracles vividly express the prophetic belief that Yahweh controlled all of history. Other principles of arrangement will be apparent as we consider individual books, including the use of refrains and of catchwords, in which two originally unrelated passages are juxtaposed because both include an identical or similar word.

The emergence of collections of written prophecies attributed to individual prophets in the eighth century BCE is a significant development. The book of Chronicles refers to "the records" of "the seer Samuel," "the prophet Nathan," and "the seer Gad" (1 Chr 29.29), but in part because that book is a postexilic creation it is difficult to know if such earlier prophetic collections actually existed. Beginning in the eighth century, however, we have references to the writing down of prophetic oracles, notably in Isaiah (8.1–2, 16; 30.8), in Jeremiah (especially chap. 36), and in Ezekiel (for example, 43.11). This begins at the very time when evidence from ancient Hebrew inscriptions suggests that literacy was becoming widespread in ancient Israel. It is likely, then, that the emergence in the mid-eighth century of this new type of literature, the collection of a prophet's oracles, was a result of this increasing literacy. Once written down, the collections were then edited and augmented, by the prophets' disciples, in some cases by the Deuteronomic school, and perhaps even by the prophets themselves.

AMOS

The Book of Amos

Like most other prophetic books, the book of Amos is an anthology containing a variety of materials of different genres, some of which can be attributed to Amos himself. A number of larger units are identifiable; these are interspersed with shorter judgment oracles. The larger units include:

- *Oracles against the nations* surrounding Israel and against Israel itself (1.3–2.16). This is the largest single unit in the book, occupying a prominent position and setting out themes that will be developed and alluded to in the following chapters.
- *Oracle concerning prophecy* (3.3–8).
- *Addresses to groups in Israel*, including the women of Samaria (4.1–3) and the wealthy in Samaria and Jerusalem (6.1–7; 8.4–8), and to Israel as a whole (3.1–2, 13–15; 4.4–12; 5.1–7; 5.10–17).
- *Visions*: Five visions express divine judgment on Israel. Four of them begin with the formula "This is what the LORD God showed me"—locusts (7.1–3), fire (7.4–6), a plumb line (7.7–9), and a basket of summer fruit (8.1–3)—and the fifth begins "I saw Yahweh standing beside the altar" (presumably at Bethel; 9.1–4). The vision of summer fruit requires explanation: The words for "fruit" and for "end" (8.2) were similarly pronounced in ancient Israel; the meaning of the vision is explained by the pun, a type of wordplay considered high art. These five visions have a climactic arrangement, in which Yahweh is first moved to mercy by the prophet's entreaties, but then pronounces irrevocable doom. But the five visions are not found in an uninterrupted sequence. After the first three visions, which are first-person narratives, comes a third-person account of the confrontation at Bethel in 7.10–17. The visions resume in 8.1–3 with the basket of summer fruit, but then a collection of shorter judgment oracles intervenes (8.4–14) before the final vision in 9.1–4.
- *Confrontation at Bethel* (7.10–17), a third-person narrative describing how Amos's preaching at the royal sanctuary of Bethel was met by opposition from its priest.
- *Hymnic fragments*: Scattered throughout the book of Amos are several hymnic fragments (4.13; 5.8–9; 9.5–6), resembling in language

and theme some of the psalms and other hymns preserved in the Bible. These fragments share the refrain "Yahweh is his name" and emphasize the deity's actions as creator.

The arrangement of these parts is sometimes thematic, sometimes more superficial. One important organizing principle seems to have been the catchword. Thus, the placement of the hymnic fragment in 5.8–9 is probably due to the occurrence of the word "turn" in both 5.7 and 5.8. Other verbal connections between originally distinct units occur in 3.9–11 and 3.12 ("Samaria") and 5.1 and 5.4 ("house of Israel"). Another organizing principle is repetition, such as the phrase "Hear this word" (3.1; 4.1; 5.1) and the proclamation of "Woe" (NRSV "Alas"; 5.18; 6.1).

A majority of scholars think that not all of the material in Amos goes back to the prophet himself, but was added later by ancient editors of the book. Two probable examples of such later additions are:

- *The oracle against Judah* (2.4–5): Although it begins with the same formula and includes the same punishments as the preceding oracles against other nations, this oracle seems to be rhetorical prose rather than the poetry used in the others; it also contains Deuteronomistic clichés: "They have rejected the law of the LORD, and have not kept his statutes, but they have been led astray by the same lies after which their ancestors walked" (2.4). Moreover, since the following oracle is directed against Israel in the sense of all Israel (see 2.9–10 and page 314), rather than the just the northern kingdom, an oracle specifically directed against Judah seems inappropriate. This oracle may have been added after the destruction of the northern kingdom, to emphasize that the words of Amos applied to Judah as well.
- *The oracle of promise to David* (9.11–15): The references to the "booth of David" that has "fallen" and is in "ruins" (9.11), to "ruined cities" and a restored Israel (9.14), and to "the remnant of Edom" (9.12) suggest that this epi-

logue to the book of Amos dates from a period later in the history of Judah, perhaps after the destruction of Jerusalem and of the Davidic dynasty in 586 BCE. Elsewhere Amos is not concerned with the house of David (now a more fragile "booth") as such, yet these verses predict its restoration along with abundant fertility in the Promised Land.

These likely later additions to the book show its continuing relevance for subsequent audiences and also provide glimpses of early interpretations of Amos's original words.

The Life of Amos

The superscription (the opening historical note) to the book of Amos dates the prophet's career to the reigns of Jeroboam II of Israel, who died in 747 BCE, and of Uzziah of Judah, who relinquished the throne in 759 because of illness (see 2 Kings 15.5) and died in 733. The superscription further dates Amos's preaching to "two years before the earthquake" (Am 1.1). This earthquake, also referred to in Amos 8.8, 9.1, and 9.5 and Zechariah 14.5, was a major catastrophe, as archaeological evidence at both Hazor and Samaria shows. None of this meager information enables us to date Amos's prophetic career precisely, but it took place around 750 and probably lasted no more than a decade.

The book of Amos gives us some information about the prophet. He was from Tekoa, in Judah, some 10 miles (16 km) south of Jerusalem. Most of his preaching was directed against the northern kingdom and was delivered there. We know from ancient inscriptions that dialectal differences existed between the Hebrew of Judah and that of the northern kingdom of Israel. Amos's southern background, therefore, would have been obvious to his audience.

Amos was a sheep and cattle herder (1.1; 7.14–15). The word used to describe him in 1.1 means not just a shepherd, but a wealthy owner of a large number of sheep. The same word is used in this sense in Ugaritic, and in the Bible of Mesha, the king of Moab reported to have paid as an annual tribute to the king of Israel 100,000 lambs and the wool of an equal number of rams (2 Kings 3.4). Amos was also a farmer, raising sycamore figs (7.14). Although the sycamore fig is inferior to the true fig, it could be cultivated on a large scale (see 1 Chr 27.28). Thus, the older view that Amos sympathized with the needy because of his own impoverished background no longer seems likely.

Amos claims to be a true prophet, one "taken" from his livelihood in response to a divine summons (7.15). But he was not a professional prophet; hence his denial: "I am not a prophet nor a son of a prophet" (7.14), meaning that he was not a member of a prophetic school nor one who had undergone extensive training (see further pages 300–301).

The Message of Amos

The first major unit in the book of Amos is the series of oracles in which the nations surrounding Israel and then Israel itself are condemned for their violation of covenant (Am 1.3–2.16). The passage begins with six (or seven, if Judah is included; see page 312) patterned condemnations of Damascus (Aram), Philistia, Tyre, Edom, Ammon, and Moab. For the first four there we see an alternating geographical pattern: from northeast to southwest to northwest to southeast. Each of these nations is condemned for particular crimes: Aram and Ammon for their harsh occupation of Gilead, originally Israelite territory (see Josh 17.6; Judg 5.17; 1 Kings 22.3; Ps 60.7); Philistia and Tyre for what appears to be slave traffic with Edom; Edom for some vague aggression; and Moab for an offense against its southern neighbor Edom.

These six nations all border Israel and Judah, and also were either controlled by or allied with Israel during the reigns of David and Solomon in the tenth century BCE. Such control or alliance would have been expressed formally in terms of treaty or covenant, like that between Hiram, king of Tyre, and David and Solomon. In the oracle against Tyre, that Phoenician state is indicted "because they did not remember the covenant of brothers" (Am 1.7), language that recalls the formal parity treaty between Tyre and Israel (1 Kings 5.12) and the language used by Hiram to address Solomon, "my brother" (1 Kings 9.13). Likewise, Edom is condemned for mistreatment of "his brother" (Am 1.11), probably referring to Israel as occasional covenant partner of Edom, and also reflecting the traditional genealogical relationship between their ancestors, Jacob (Israel) and Esau (Edom; see Gen 25.19–34).

In this context, even though the specific historical allusions are often no longer recoverable, a good interpretation of these oracles against the nations, the earliest examples of the genre in prophetic literature, is that Yahweh as the deity who presided over the various treaties or covenants that bound these nations to Israel is now, like the divine witnesses in Hittite and Assyrian treaties, enforcing the curses for violation of covenant. The punishment proclaimed in the divine speeches in Amos 1–2 is destruction of the capital and other cities of the nation being condemned, and often both exile of its inhabitants and annihilation of its ruling family.

These detailed predictions of impending military disasters are in themselves not remarkable. Assyrian policy for some time had been the systematic deportation of conquered populations and the destruction of their cities. Although the Assyrians are not explicitly named in Amos as the agents of the disasters, in the mid-eighth century BCE it would not have taken divine revelation to anticipate the continuation of the Assyrian conquest of the Levant. What is more significant is what is being claimed here: The disasters will be Yahweh's doing, for he controls all history for his own purposes, in these cases to punish nations that have violated the terms of covenants in which he was a principal deity. (See Figure 18.2.)

One can only imagine the nationalistic enthusiasm that these divine judgments proclaimed by the prophet would have aroused in an Israelite audience, whose history since the late tenth century BCE had been largely one of losses to regional entities that they had once controlled. But these oracles against foreign nations are only the prelude to the main focus of the divine wrath:

FIGURE 18.2.   Part of a relief of the Assyrian king Tiglath-pileser III, shown in his chariot in the lower panel. The upper panel shows a fortified city on the left, from which, on the right, captives and cattle are being taken. The cuneiform text between the two panels names the city, Astartu, probably biblical Ashtaroth in northern Transjordan, which the Assyrians captured in 732 BCE.

For three sins of Israel,
    and for four, I will not revoke the punishment.
    (2.6)

Initially the precise meaning of Israel is uncertain—it could mean just the northern kingdom. But the continuation of the oracle makes it clear that it refers to all Israel, the twelve-tribe entity, not divided into the northern kingdom of Israel and the southern kingdom of Judah:

I brought you up out of the land of Egypt,
    and led you forty years in the wilderness,
    to possess the land of the Amorite. (2.10)

This interpretation is confirmed by the judgment speech that immediately follows the oracle against Israel:

> Hear this word that the LORD has spoken against you, O people of Israel, against the whole family that I brought up out of the land of Egypt:
>
> You only have I known
>   of all the families of the earth;
> therefore I will punish you
>   for all your iniquities. (3.1–2)

Israel is even more guilty of covenant violation than the other nations, for Israel had a unique relationship with Yahweh. The use of the verb "to know" ("You only have I known . . .") alludes to the Sinai covenant, both because of its connotation of sexual intimacy, recalling the marriage analogue for the covenant (see page 113), and also because the verb was a technical term in ancient treaties for mutual recognition by both parties of their obligations to each other.

The offenses of which Israel is accused are primarily social:

> They sell the righteous for silver,
>   and the needy for a pair of sandals—
> they trample the head of the poor into the dust of
>   the earth,
>   and push the afflicted out of the way;
> father and son go in to the same girl,
>   so that my holy name is profaned;
> they lay themselves down beside every altar
>   on garments taken in pledge;
> and in the house of their God they drink
>   wine bought with fines they imposed. (2.6–8)

The precise details of these offenses are not always clear, but what is clear is that Israel is guilty of pervasive injustice toward the innocent, the poor, and young women. The oracle goes on to condemn Israel for corrupting some of its most sacred personnel: the nazirites, who took vows to abstain from wine (see Num 6.1–4; Judg 13.4; 1 Sam 1.11), and the prophets, who, like Amos (7.13, 16), were ordered to stop prophesying. The consequence is inevitable: Like the other nations, Israel will be punished, its army ineffective and scattered. What had been anticipated by the

prophet's audience as a "day of Yahweh" in which Yahweh acting on Israel's behalf attacked its enemies would now be a day when Yahweh turned against Israel (see Box 18.2).

As the initial oracle against Israel indicates, Amos is concerned principally with the Israel that Yahweh brought out of Egypt. The references to the Exodus (Am 2.10; 3.1; 5.25; 9.7) provide an essential context for understanding a principal component of the prophet's message. Israel is guilty of breaking its primary contract with God, the Sinai covenant, and so the curses that were attached to that covenant will be executed. That covenant had two aspects: correct worship of Yahweh and of Yahweh alone (love of God) and just treatment of fellow Israelites (love of neighbor). Amos does refer to improper forms of worship, especially at the sanctuary at Bethel (3.14; 4.4; 5.5–6), and to profanation of the sabbath and other aspects of Israel's sacred life (2.8, 12; 8.5), but more attention is given to the second aspect of the covenant. In considerable detail, Amos emphasizes that Israel has failed in its primary obligation to provide for the powerless: The poor are trampled into the ground (2.7; 4.1; 5.11; 8.4) and deprived of justice (2.6; 5.12; 8.6). This exploitation of the poor is perpetrated by the wealthy elite, and Amos is ruthless in his denunciation of the ruling class:

> Woe to those who are at ease in Zion.
>   and to those who feel secure on Mount
>   Samaria. . . .
> Woe to those who lie on beds of ivory,
>   and lounge on their couches,
> and eat lambs from the flock,
>   and calves from the stall;
> who sing idle songs to the sound of the harp,
>   and like David improvise on instruments of music;
> who drink wine from bowls,
>   and anoint themselves with the finest oils . . .
> Therefore they shall now be the first to go into exile,
>   and the revelry of the loungers shall pass away.
>   (6.1, 4–7)

In this passage, Amos attacks the conspicuous consumption of the elite in the capital cities of Samaria and Jerusalem, whose wealth was acquired at the expense of the poor and the needy; even David is indirectly condemned (see Figures

Box 18.2 THE DAY OF THE LORD

Amos is the first prophet to use the term "the day of Yahweh" (NRSV: "the day of the LORD"), and it becomes an important concept in subsequent prophetic and apocalyptic literature. Its primary imagery seems to be military: the **day of the Lord** is that day when Yahweh as the divine warrior will come to fight against his enemies (see Jer 46.10; Joel 2.11). Often those enemies are also Israel's enemies, and the day of Yahweh will be a day of victory for Israel; the day of the Lord thus can be included in oracles against the nations (see pages 310–11), as in Isaiah 13, Ezekiel 30, and Jeremiah 46.

In Amos and in other prophets, Israel can be included among the enemies of Yahweh. Because the vengeance of Yahweh would be directed against Israel itself, the prophet warns his audience:

> Is not the day of the LORD darkness, not light,
>   and gloom with no brightness in it? (Am 5.20)

The "day of the LORD" develops in later Jewish and Christian apocalyptic literature into the idea of a day of judgment at the end of the world, as, for example, in Malachi 4.1–3; see further pages 441–42.

18.3 and 18.4). Amos also attacks the royal ideology, according to which the divine choice of the capital was a guarantee of security. That supposed guarantee is illusory: Like the elite of the capitals of Israel's neighbors, the members of the royal establishment will also be exiled. Israel's special relationship with Yahweh is no guarantee of special treatment:

> Are you not like the Ethiopians to me,
>   O people of Israel? says the LORD.
> Did I not bring Israel up from the land of Egypt,
>   and the Philistines from Caphtor and the
>   Arameans from Kir?
> The eyes of the Lord GOD are upon the sinful
>   kingdom,
>   and I will destroy it from the face of the earth.
>   (9.7–8)

Israel must learn that Yahweh is the one who controls all of history, and that it is therefore not unique. If it fails to live up to its covenant obligations, he will treat it like any other "sinful kingdom."

One of Amos's most brutal attacks is directed against the women of Samaria. Playing on the use of animal titles for nobility, Amos refers to the women of Samaria as fat cows, like those raised in Bashan, a region east of the Sea of Galilee famous for its cattle (see Ps 22.12). Because of their participation in the oppression of the underprivileged, they will be punished by being slaughtered, becoming like sides of beef on a butcher's hook, with the scraps used for bait (Am 4.1–2).

The vehemence of Amos's attack on the establishment is the background for the confrontation between Amos and the royally appointed priest Amaziah at Bethel, one of the principal sanctuaries of the northern kingdom (Am 7.10–17). Accusing Amos of treason, Amaziah tells him to return to Judah. Amos replies with a judgment against the priest himself: Amaziah's family will be destroyed, with his wife reduced to prostitution, and Amaziah himself will die in ex-

FIGURE 18.3. One of the ivories from Samaria, dating to the reign of Jeroboam II in the mid-eighth century BCE. About 4 in (10 cm) high, it shows a sphinx in a lotus thicket. Ivories such as this were used as decorative inlays on furniture (see Figure 18.4).

ile in an unclean land, where he will be unable to carry out his priestly functions.

So great is the divine anger against the Israelites that Yahweh will no longer accept prayers and sacrifices from them. In a scathing denunciation of Israelite ritual, the prophet expresses the divine disgust at Israelite religious practices:

> I hate, I despise your festivals,
>   and I take no delight in your solemn assemblies.
> Even though you offer me your burnt offerings and
>   grain offerings,
>   I will not accept them;
> and the offerings of well-being of your fatted
>   animals
>   I will not look upon.

FIGURE 18.4. Part of an Assyrian relief of the mid-seventh century BCE, showing a queen sitting on a throne. The throne is decorated with carvings, probably ivory inlays like that shown in Figure 18.3.

Take away from me the noise of your songs;
   I will not listen to the melody of your harps.
But let justice roll down like waters,
   and righteousness like an ever-flowing stream.
   (5.21–24)

The word used for "festivals" is used in the liturgical calendars for the great pilgrimage feasts of Passover, Weeks, and Booths (see Ex 23.14–17; Deut 16.1–17; and pages 134–36), and the word for "songs" is used in the titles of many of the psalms. All of the Israelites' rituals—their sacrifices, their festivals, their hymns—are unacceptable to Yahweh (see Box 18.3).

What Yahweh demands from the Israelites is not religious observance, but social justice: "Let justice roll down like waters, and righteousness like an ever-flowing stream" (Am 5.24). The political and religious establishments have caused the breakdown of the premonarchic egalitarian ideal. As Gandhi remarked, "Those who say that religion has nothing to do with politics do not know what religion means," and it is no coincidence that Rev. Martin Luther King, Jr., quoted Amos 5.24 in his famous "I have a dream" speech on the steps of the Lincoln Memorial in Washington, DC, in 1963.

HOSEA

The Book of Hosea

The book named after the prophet Hosea is the longest of the twelve Minor Prophets, and, like the book of Amos, it is an anthology comprised of a variety of materials. Larger units in the book include the following:

- A biographical account of Hosea's marriage, and its use as an analogue for the relationship between Yahweh and Israel (chaps. 1–2).

- An autobiographical account of Hosea's marriage (chap. 3), which is probably related to the preceding biographical account. Some scholars have interpreted chapters 1 and 3 as referring to the prophet's relationship with two different women.

- Oracles of judgment against Israel, and especially against the northern kingdom, often called Ephraim (the dominant northern tribe,

named after one of Jacob's two grandsons through Joseph), for its failure to live up to the requirements of its covenant with Yahweh by worshiping other gods and not carrying out the social requirements of the Ten Commandments. These oracles have been gathered into what appear to be two separate collections, 4.1–12.1 and 12.2–14.9, each of which has a positive if vague assurance of restoration toward its conclusion.

The principles of arrangement of the two collections that form the latter part of the book (chaps. 4–14) are largely unclear. Sometimes catchwords seem to be used, and sometimes the arrangement appears to be thematic. Because the oracles either lack specifics or allude to events not known from other sources, we cannot be sure if they are arranged in some sort of chronological sequence.

As with Amos, we find evidence of later additions to the book of Hosea. Some of these are editorial, such as the superscription (Hos 1.1) and the conclusion (14.9), which is a generalization typical of wisdom literature (see further pages 468–72). Others concern Judah, although since Judah as well as Israel is the object of Hosea's attacks, particular cases are disputed. Most likely to be later additions are 1.7, 3.5, and 11.12, all of which speak positively about Judah or the Davidic dynasty, and 11.11, which describes a return from exile like homing pigeons or doves. As in Amos, these additions show that the prophet's message was considered relevant in later times.

The Life of Hosea

The career of Hosea is dated by the superscription (Hos 1.1) to the reign of Jeroboam II of Israel (788–747 BCE) and to the reigns of kings of Judah from Uzziah to Hezekiah, spanning most of the eighth century BCE. The latter seems historically unlikely, and no specifics in the book show familiarity with the details of the fall of the northern kingdom to the Assyrians in 722. Most scholars, therefore, date Hosea's career to the third quarter of the eighth century, a little after that of Amos.

Box 18.3 **PROPHETIC ATTACKS ON RITUALS**

A recurring theme in prophetic literature is an attack on Israelite rituals. It is found first in Amos (5.21–25), and also in Isaiah (1.10–17; 66.1–4; see also 58), Jeremiah (6.20–21; 7.21–26), Hosea (6.4–6), and Micah (6.6–8), as well as in Psalms 50 and 51. As in Amos 5.21–25, the rejection of sacrificial offerings and prayers can be categorical:

> What to me is the multitude of your sacrifices?
>   says the LORD;
> I have had enough of burnt offerings of rams
>   and the fat of fed beasts;
> I do not delight in the blood of bulls,
>   or of lambs, or of goats. (Isa 1.11)

In other passages, the message seems to be that religious observance is less important than interior submission to the divine will, as in 1 Samuel 15.22–23:

> Has the LORD as great delight in burnt offerings and sacrifices,
>   as in obedience to the voice of the LORD?
> Surely, obedience is better than sacrifice,
>   and attentiveness than the fat of rams.
> For rebellion is the sin of divination,
>   and insubordination is the iniquity of idolatry.

In interpreting these attacks on ritual, scholars have generally taken two approaches, typically reflecting their own religious backgrounds. For many Protestant scholars, these passages are an attack on ritual itself, or at least on the elaborate rituals of ancient Israel. For others from more liturgical traditions, such as Jews, Roman Catholics, Orthodox Christians, and Episcopalians, these verses do not reject elaborate forms of worship entirely, but simply worship that is not accompanied by an inner disposition of full obedience to divine commands, including especially love of neighbor.

Particularly puzzling is the prophetic assertion that sacrifices and rituals were not part of Israel's earliest experience. Amos's rhetorical question, "Did you bring to me sacrifices and offerings the forty years in the wilderness, O house of Israel?" (5.25), is echoed by Jeremiah's statement: "For in the day that I brought your ancestors out of the land of Egypt, I did not speak to them or command them concerning burnt offerings and sacrifices" (Jer 7.22). These passages clearly contradict the overwhelming evidence of the Pentateuch and other sources that sacrifice was part of Israel's religious observance in the earliest periods. These statements are the more remarkable because in the ancient world grain and animal sacrifices were ubiquitous. Perhaps this is simply prophetic exaggeration. Jeremiah goes on to proclaim: "But this command I gave them, 'Obey my voice, and I will be your God, and you shall be my people; and walk only in the way that I command you, so that it may be well with you'" (7.23). One interpretation, then, is that sacrifice as such was not being attacked, but the merely formal observance of ritual obligations. As satisfying as this may be, however, it does not resolve the problem of what seems to be the plain sense of Amos's and Jeremiah's insistence that the period immediately after the Exodus was devoid of sacrifice.

Although the book tells us nothing of Hosea's background, the frequent references to places and events in the northern kingdom, as well as some peculiarities of language, indicate that Hosea himself was a northerner. According to the biographical narrative in chapter 1, Hosea's wife was named Gomer. Earlier interpretations that Gomer was a prostitute, or even a sacred prostitute, are now generally rejected: The word "prostitute" (Hebr. *zonah*) is never used directly of her, and the related word *zenunim* (Hos 1.2; 2.2) is better translated "promiscuity" rather than "harlotry" or "whoring" (NRSV), although when applied to Israel the sense of prostitution is not inappropriate: Israel has sold herself to her lovers for a prostitute's wages (9.1), and even hires them (8.9). Gomer and Hosea's three children are given symbolic names: Jezreel, which can be an ordinary

name (as in 1 Chr 4.3), but here recalls Jehu's extermination of the dynasty of Omri at Jezreel (see 2 Kings 9–10); Not-loved; and Not-my-people. The autobiographical narrative in chapter 3 is probably an alternate version of the prophet's marriage, or a sequel to the preceding narrative.

That marriage was apparently a stormy one, if chapters 1–3 describe what actually occurred. But because throughout these chapters the prophet's marriage serves as an analogy for the relationship between Yahweh and Israel, biographical details are difficult if not impossible to disentangle from their metaphorical use. If Hosea became aware of his wife's infidelity only after they had become married, that would parallel the relationship between Yahweh and Israel, which also started off well (see 2.15), but the symbolic names of at least the last two children would not necessarily make

Box 18.4 MARRIAGE IN ANCIENT ISRAEL

The book of Hosea provides important evidence concerning marriage in ancient Israel. It includes what may be an ancient Israelite marital vow: "I will take you for my wife forever; I will take you for my wife in righteousness and in justice, in steadfast love, and in mercy. I will take you for my wife in faithfulness" (Hos 2.19–20). It also includes what may be a divorce formula: "She is not my wife, and I am not her husband" (2.2).

The relationship between husband and wife was clearly one of unequal power, in which the husband initiated both marriage and divorce (see further Deut 24.1–4). The woman's father was also a central figure, setting the terms of the marriage and fixing the bride-price. Under this arrangement, the future husband paid the woman's father for his daughter, whose control then passed from her father to her husband (see page 150). The woman called her husband "lord," using the Hebrew terms *adon* or *baal* (see Hos 2.16; Prov 12.4; 2 Sam 11.26). Marriage is repeatedly celebrated by the biblical writers, but usually from the male perspective; the Song of Solomon is a notable exception that includes the female voice (see further pages 495–97).

The use of marriage as a metaphor for the exclusive relationship between Yahweh and Israel implies that a wife could have only one husband, and we find no examples of one wife with multiple husbands (polyandry) in the Bible. But the Bible contains many examples of men having more than one wife (polygyny), and until a relatively late period monogamy does not seem to have been the ideal.

sense. If the prophet was aware that his wife was promiscuous before they married, then the analogy with Yahweh and Israel is less apt. We must keep in mind that the purpose of the two narratives is not to help us in a quest for the historical Hosea. Rather, they are a parable of sorts, an object lesson whose primary content is about Yahweh and Israel rather than Hosea and Gomer. (See Box 18.4.)

The Message of Hosea

Hosea is best known for his extended use of the marriage metaphor to describe the relationship between Yahweh and Israel. This metaphor is probably implicit in the concept of covenant; the Hebrew word *berît*, traditionally translated "covenant," is used both of the relationship between Yahweh and Israel and of the marriage contract (as in Prov 2.17; Mal 2.14; see further page 113). Both Jeremiah (2.2; 3.1–5) and Ezekiel (chap. 16) will use this metaphor as well, and it is implied in other passages (such as Isa 5.1–7; 62.5).

The use of the marriage metaphor has several dimensions. One is that Yahweh loves Israel. That attachment will endure, despite Israel's repeated infidelities by worshiping other gods. In Hosea's own case, his wife Gomer was unfaithful, yet he did not ultimately reject her. It must also be recognized how daring Hosea's use of this metaphor was. The Canaanite deity Baal, widely worshiped in the northern kingdom of Israel, was the storm-god who brought the winter rains that made agricultural produce and herds abundant. Baal was also closely associated with the goddess Asherah, another fertility-deity (see Figure 18.5). By identifying Yahweh as Israel's husband, Hosea implicitly makes Yahweh a sexual deity, and also a god who provides fertility:

> She did not know
>   that it was I who gave her
>   the grain, the wine, and the oil. . . .
> Therefore I will take back
>   my grain in its time,
>   and my wine in its season;
> and I will take away my wool and my flax,
>   which were to cover her nakedness. (Hos 2.8–9)

FIGURE 18.5. Drawing of one of the graffiti found on fragments of a large storage jar at Kuntillet Ajrud in the northern Sinai and dating to the eighth century BCE. The Hebrew inscription mentions "Yahweh of Samaria and his Asherah," who may be the two figures beneath the inscription, with Yahweh on the left and the goddess Asherah on the right. If so, then this is a rare if crude depiction of Yahweh and an expression of popular belief that he had a divine wife.

Another metaphor used by Hosea for the relationship between Yahweh and Israel is that of parent and child:

> When Israel was a child, I loved him,
>   and out of Egypt I called my son.
> The more I called them,
>   the more they went from me;
> they kept sacrificing to the Baals,
>   and offering incense to idols.
> Yet it was I who taught Ephraim to walk,
>   I took them up in my arms;
>   but they did not know that I healed them.
> I led them with cords of human kindness,
>   with bands of love.
> I was to them like those who lift infants to their
>   cheeks.
>   I bent down to them and fed them. (11.1–4)

Although some details of the translation of the Hebrew of these verses are uncertain, the imagery of God as parent is clear (see Box 18.5).

This metaphor is relatively rare in the Hebrew Bible. It is used in Exodus 4.23, where Moses is instructed to say to the pharaoh: "Thus says the LORD: Israel is my firstborn son. I say to you, 'Let

Box 18.5 GOD AS PARENT: FATHER OR MOTHER?

Some feminist interpreters have suggested that the image of God as parent in Hosea 11.1–4 probably refers to the mother rather than the father. Certainly maternal imagery is used of God occasionally in the Bible; note especially Isaiah 66.13:

> As a mother comforts her child,
>   so I will comfort you. (See also Isa 42.14; 46.3–4; 49.15.)

In fact, one of the words for love (Hebr. *rahamim*; note also the adjective *rahum*, "merciful, loving"), including God's love, is etymologically connected to the word for "uterus" (Hebr. *rehem*), and God can be described as the one who gave birth to Israel (see Num 11.12; Deut 32.18; Isa 49.15), as well as to aspects of the entire world (Job 38.29). (See further Box 23.3 on page 414.)

The image of God as parent in Hosea 11.1–4 is gender-neutral, and so could refer to either father or mother or both. It is probably an overstatement to suggest that childcare as described in the passage was principally the task of women; fathers also are depicted as being responsible for the raising of children. Several passages refer to God just as father (for example, Isa 63.16; 64.8; Mal 1.6), including in his role of creator (see Mal 2.10). Thus, although it is a mistake to presume that every nonspecific reference to a parent is to a father, many certainly are, and others (for example, Isa 1.2; 30.9) probably are. In the case of Hosea 11.1–4, we have what may be an allusion to and hence an early interpretation of the passage in Jeremiah 31.9:

> I have become a father to Israel,
>   and Ephraim is my firstborn. (See also Jer 31.20.)

In this case, God is father, and if this is an allusion to Hosea 11.1–4, then that passage too probably had the same meaning.

---

my son go that he may serve me. If you refuse to let him go, I will kill your firstborn son.'" Like the metaphor of marriage, that of parent-child suggests not just familial intimacy but also a covenant relationship; note especially 2 Kings 16.7. As also in the marriage metaphor, Hosea sees God's relationship to Israel as characterized by love (11.1, 4). Like a loving parent, God loves Israel, and this is reason for hope for the future of the relationship, as 14.4 indicates: "I will love them freely, for my anger has turned from them."

Like a forgiving spouse or parent, God forgives Israel, because he loves it.

Jeremiah also combines the two metaphors of parent and spouse:

> I thought
>   how I would set you among my children,
> and give you a pleasant land,
>   the most beautiful heritage of all the nations.
> And I thought you would call me, My Father,
>   and would not turn from following me.
> Instead, as a faithless wife leaves her husband,

so you have been faithless to me, O house of
Israel,
  says the LORD. (Jer 3.19–20)

Like other prophets, Hosea condemns Israel for
a number of interrelated offenses. Both sections
of the oracles on judgment begin with a "lawsuit"
(NRSV: "indictment"). The Hebrew word used
here is *rîb*, often used in the Bible in ordinary legal contexts not having to do with God. In several prophets, beginning with Hosea, the
"**covenant lawsuit**" forms a distinct genre, in
which Yahweh sues Israel for breach of contract,
that is, for violation of the Sinai covenant. The
first occurrence in Hosea sets the tone for what
follows:

Hear the word of the LORD, O people of Israel;
  for the LORD has a lawsuit against the inhabi-
    tants of the land.
There is no faithfulness or loyalty,
  and no knowledge of God in the land.
Swearing, lying, and murder,
  and stealing and adultery break out;
  bloodshed follows bloodshed.
Therefore the land mourns,
  and all who live in it languish;
together with the wild animals
  and the birds of the air,
  even the fish of the sea are perishing. (4.1–3)

The words for swearing, lying, murder, stealing,
and adultery refer to the Ten Commandments,
the text of Israel's primary contract or covenant
with Yahweh. Israel has broken its contract, and
so the curses that formed part of the covenant for-
mulary are being implemented in the form of natural disasters. The same word *rîb* is also used at
the beginning of the final section of the book:

The LORD has a lawsuit against Israel [correction
  for "Judah"],
  and will punish Jacob according to his ways,
  and repay him according to his deeds. (Hos
12.2)

The theme of covenant is central in the book
of Hosea and is a key to its interpretation. The
Israelites have repeatedly "broken my covenant
and transgressed my law" (8.1), worshiping other
gods, showing lack of confidence in Yahweh by

making foreign alliances and building fortifications, and denying social justice. Hosea focuses
especially on forbidden worship: the worship of
gods other than Yahweh and the making of
graven images, such as the calves of Samaria and
Bethel.

Another breach of covenant was making foreign alliances. These implied a lack of confidence
in Yahweh's ability to act on Israel's behalf, and
probably also involved swearing allegiance to or
at least acknowledging the power of other gods in
treaty-making ceremonies. Hosea condemns Israel for its alliances with both Egypt and Assyria:

Ephraim has become like a dove,
  silly and without sense;
they call upon Egypt, they go to Assyria. . . .
Woe to them, for they have strayed from me!
  Destruction to them, for they have rebelled
  against me! (Hos 7.11, 13)

For the last decade of its existence, the northern
kingdom of Israel vacillated between loyalty to
Assyria as its vassal and rebellion against it, sometimes in league with Egypt. The sketchy account
of the book of Kings gives several specific examples of such policy shifts, and there may have been
others. For Hosea, these foreign entanglements
were another form of infidelity: "Ephraim has bar-
gained for lovers" (8.9). The result would be the
same as for apostasy—divine punishment in the
form of exile from the Promised Land, with a terrible ironic twist: "Ephraim shall return to Egypt,
and in Assyria they shall eat unclean food" (9.3;
see also 8.13; 11.5). The covenant curse of exile
in a foreign land will be either a reversal of the
Exodus, a return to Egypt, or a deportation to Assyria, where, like the priest Amaziah (Am 7.17),
the exiles will be unable to maintain their ritual
purity.

For Hosea, another example of lack of trust in
Yahweh is the monarchy. Hosea takes a decidedly
antimonarchical stance, at least toward the rulers
of the northern kingdom of Israel. "They made
kings, but not through me" (Hos 8.4): The kings'
claim that they were divinely chosen is rejected;
"They devour their rulers" (7.7): From the death
of Jeroboam II in 747 BCE to the fall of Samaria

in 722, six kings belonging to five different families ruled, and four of those six kings were assassinated by their successors. Part of the divine punishment will be a return to kingless rule (3.4), for "Samaria's king shall perish" (10.7). (See Figure 18.6.)

Hosea refers repeatedly to traditions concerning Israel's ancestors; for example:

> The LORD has an indictment against Judah,
>   and will punish Jacob according to his ways,
>   and repay him according to his deeds.
> In the womb he tried to supplant his brother,
>   and in his manhood he strove with God.
> He strove with the angel and prevailed,
>   he wept and sought his favor;
> he met him at Bethel,
>   and there he spoke with him. . . .

FIGURE 18.6. One of the Samaria ostraca—records written on pieces of broken pottery dating to the mid-eighth century BCE. This one, which measures 2.75 by 4 in (7 by 10 cm) and is written in a flamboyant Hebrew script, is an instruction to pay a quantity of barley.

> Jacob fled to the land of Aram,
>   there Israel served for a wife,
>   and for a wife he guarded sheep. (Hos 12.2–4, 12)

These verses are clearly connected with traditions found in Genesis, which, in a somewhat different order, recount Jacob's birth (Gen 25.19–26), his wrestling with God (Gen 32.22–32), his revelation at Bethel (28.10–21), and his service to Laban (Gen 29–31). We may also note in passing that the presence of these traditions in Hosea is evidence that they are not entirely fictional creations of the postexilic or Hellenistic periods (see pages 79–81). The point of this historical retrospective seems to be that Jacob (Israel) exhibited questionable character from the beginning, cheating his brother and challenging God, and that this pattern continued in the history of Ephraim, Jacob's grandson and the poetic name for the northern kingdom, and of Judah (if this is the original reading), Jacob's son whose name was also that of the southern kingdom.

Hosea also refers to the Exodus:

> By a prophet the LORD brought Israel up from Egypt,
>   and by a prophet he was guarded. (12.13)

The prophet who brought Israel out of Egypt is Moses; in calling him a prophet, Hosea shows familiarity with other northern traditions, especially E and D. The prophet who "guarded" Israel is perhaps a reference to Samuel or Elijah, but more likely Moses as well, because of the poetic stylistic device known as synonymous parallelism (see further page 461). Both E and Deuteronomy emphasize the role of prophets as mediators of divine revelation, and the preeminent prophet in both is Moses, as in Hosea. Other references to the Exodus are scattered through the book of Hosea.

As we have already seen (on pages 181–83), a close connection is found between Hosea and the Deuteronomic movement, which originated in the northern kingdom of Israel in the second half of the eighth century BCE. Like Deuteronomy, Hosea emphasizes the divinely given "torah" ("teaching"; see Hos 4.6; 8.1, 12; and Box 11.2

on page 184) and the covenant between Yahweh and Israel. Both Hosea and Deuteronomy stress the divine love for Israel, a love that is like that of a parent (see page 322 and compare Deut 14.1; 32.5–6, 20), and share an insistence on the exclusive worship of Yahweh. For Hosea, as in Deuteronomy, the penalty for violation of covenant is the fulfillment of the treaty curses. Hosea describes Yahweh metaphorically in the most gruesome terms: He is like maggots or a disease, eating away at Israel (5.12–13), he is Israel's predator (5.14; 13.7–8) and hunter (7.12).

Although Hosea is best known for his extended use of the marriage metaphor to describe the relationship between Yahweh and Israel, only a part of the book that bears his name is concerned with that analogy. Like his contemporary Amos, Hosea anticipated the conquest of the northern kingdom of Israel by the Assyrians, and he interpreted that imminent catastrophe as a deserved punishment carried out by Yahweh. Still, although Yahweh was justifiably angry, like a husband whose wife was unfaithful or a parent whose child had rebelled, Yahweh was also a loving god, and Hosea anticipated a restoration of the relationship between Yahweh and Israel.

RETROSPECT AND PROSPECT

For Amos and Hosea, as for the Deuteronomistic Historians, the northern kingdom of Israel was doomed. Historically, of course, it was doomed because it stood in the way of Assyria's imperial ambitions; the Assyrians would not allow that, and their conquest of Israel was predictable. But from the religious perspective of Amos and Hosea, as from that of the Deuteronomistic Historians, Israel was doomed because it had failed to live up to its covenant obligations with Yahweh, and it was he who was ultimately responsible for the Assyrian onslaught. Although neither Amos nor Hosea mentions the events of 722 BCE, when the Assyrians captured and burned Samaria, the capital of the northern kingdom of Israel, and exiled many of its inhabitants, that end was consistent with their view.

Although Judah escaped, it would not be for long, for it too stood in the way of the Assyrian advance. From 722 BCE onward, the focus of the biblical writers is exclusively on the southern kingdom of Judah, and the question that pervades the literature of the next century and a half is: Would Judah learn from the mistakes of the northern kingdom?

IMPORTANT TERMS

covenant lawsuit	Latter Prophets	Minor Prophets
day of the LORD	Major Prophets	oracle against the nations

QUESTIONS FOR REVIEW

1. What is the nature of the books of the prophets, and how are they arranged?

2. How did Amos and Hosea interpret the impending Assyrian campaigns and conquests?

3. Discuss the uses that Amos and Hosea make of earlier biblical traditions.

4. Why do Amos and Hosea condemn the Israelites for lack of social justice?

BIBLIOGRAPHY

For the history of the period, see the work by Campbell cited in the bibliography to Chapter 17; for a commentary on 2 Kings see the work by Cogan and Tadmor listed in same place.

A good introduction to the prophetic books is David L. Petersen, *The Prophetic Literature: An Introduction* (Louisville: Westminster John Knox, 2002).

A good short commentary on Amos is Julia Myers O'Brien, "Amos," pp. 648–52 in *The HarperCollins Bible Commentary* (ed. J. L. Mays; San Francisco: HarperSanFrancisco, 2000).

A good short commentary on Hosea is John Day, "Hosea," pp. 571–78 in *The Oxford Bible Commentary* (ed. J. Barton and J. Muddiman; Oxford: Oxford University Press, 2001). A thoughtful discussion of Hosea's use of the marriage metaphor is Tikva Frymer-Kensky, "The Wanton Wife of God," pp. 144–52 in *In the Wake of the Goddesses: Women, Culture, and the Biblical Transformation of Pagan Myth* (ed. New York: Fawcett Columbine, 1993).

THE KINGDOM OF JUDAH IN THE EIGHTH AND EARLY SEVENTH CENTURIES BCE

CHAPTER

19

2 Kings 15–20, 2 Chronicles 29–32, Isaiah 1–39, and Micah

The focus of this chapter is Judah in the decades before and after the fall of Samaria in 722 BCE. Although threatened by hostile armies on two occasions, Judah's capital, Jerusalem, did not suffer the fate of its sister capital to the north, Samaria, but it too became subject to Assyrian imperial control. This paradox challenged biblical writers, who interpreted both Jerusalem's deliverance and its submission as the work of Yahweh.

HISTORY

The Assyrian campaigns that culminated in the conquest of the northern kingdom of Israel in 722 BCE also affected Judah. During the reign of the Assyrian king Tiglath-pileser III (745–727), Judah's king Ahaz (735–715) chose to be an Assyrian vassal rather than to join the various coalitions that opposed the Assyrian advance. This status as vassal continued for several decades, during the reigns of Tiglath-pileser's successors Shalmaneser V (727–722) and Sargon II (722–705). But when Sargon died, Ahaz's son, the Judean king Hezekiah (715–687), asserted his independence. Sargon's successor Sennacherib (705–681) responded by attacking in force, and Judah had no choice but to resubmit to Assyrian rule.

Judah was only one of Assyria's concerns, however. A major preoccupation was with Babylon, Assyria's powerful neighbor to the south. Babylon had been taken over by Tiglath-pileser III earlier in the seventh century BCE, but Assyria's hold on Babylon remained tenuous. For a decade during the reign of Sargon, in fact, Assyria lost control to the Babylonian ruler Marduk-apla-iddina, known in the Bible as Merodach-baladan. But a series of campaigns by Sargon and Sennacherib culminated in the destruction or at least the capture of Babylon itself in 689 BCE. (See Box 19.1.)

For these events in the last third of the eighth century BCE we have a number of different sources, almost an embarrassment of riches. The Bible contains a variety of contradictory perspectives on the events, especially those affecting Judah. Assyrian sources are also abundant for the period recording the payment of tribute in 734 BCE to Tiglath-pileser by Ahaz, king of Judah, and, as we have seen, describing the capture and destruction of Samaria in 722. For the next two decades Assyrian records make no mention of Judah, but Sennacherib's lengthy account of his third campaign to the west in 701 includes a long section on the devastation of Judah and the siege of Jerusalem in that year. Supplementing this

Box 19.1 CHRONOLOGY OF THE EIGHTH AND SEVENTH CENTURIES BCE

Kings of Judah	Kings of Assyria	Events
Azariah (Uzziah) (785–733)*		
Jotham (759–743)		
Ahaz (745/735–727/715)†	Tiglath-pileser III (745–727)	
	Shalmaneser V (727–722)	
		Fall of Samaria (722)
	Sargon II (722–705)	
Hezekiah (727/715–698/687)†	Sennacherib (705–681)	
		Invasion of Sennacherib (701)
Manasseh (698/687–642)		

Date ranges are for reigns, not life spans. Overlapping dates indicate coregencies. Vertical lines show lineal descent.

*   Azariah (Uzziah) was apparently quarantined for much of his reign with a skin disease, and Jotham and Ahaz ruled while he was still alive.

†   The data are inconsistent for the reigns of Ahaz and Hezekiah.

narrative is a series of extraordinary reliefs from Sennacherib's palace at Nineveh depicting in vivid detail the capture and destruction of Lachish, one of the principal Judean cities. Archaeological evidence supplements these sources. Excavations at Lachish have confirmed the essential accuracy of the Assyrian reliefs, and, as we will see, discoveries in Jerusalem can also be connected with Sennacherib's campaign. The king of Judah during most of this period was Hezekiah, who ruled for nearly thirty years.

THE REIGN OF HEZEKIAH

Hezekiah came to the throne either in 727 BCE, just before the Assyrian conquest of the northern kingdom of Israel, or, more likely, in 715, soon after that event, and he ruled until either 698 or, more likely, 687. The dates given in the Bible for his reign are inconsistent.

For the Deuteronomistic Historians, Hezekiah was one of the most important kings of Judah; in fact, "there was no one like him among all the kings of Judah after him, or among those who were before him" (2 Kings 18.5). From their ideological perspective, this was true because of Hezekiah's fidelity to the Deuteronomic Code concerning exclusive and pure worship of Yahweh:

> He did what was right in the sight of the LORD just as his ancestor David had done. He removed the high places, broke down the pillars, and cut down the sacred pole. He broke in pieces the bronze serpent that Moses had made, for until those days the people of Israel had made offerings to it; it was called Nehushtan. . . . He held fast to the LORD; he did not

depart from following him but kept the commandments that the LORD commanded Moses. (2 Kings 18.3–4, 6)

Other reasons for this affirmative judgment are also evident. Judah had been an Assyrian vassal at least since the time of Hezekiah's father Ahaz in 734 BCE, and at first, it seems, Hezekiah followed his predecessor's lead. In 705, however, the Assyrian king Sargon II died in battle, and the most pressing problem for his successor Sennacherib was to maintain control over Babylon. Presumably to take advantage of this Assyrian preoccupation with Babylon, Hezekiah decided to withhold tribute and allied himself with Egypt and Ethiopia, and probably with Babylon as well. This distancing from Assyria amounted to a declaration of independence from Assyrian sovereignty.

Hezekiah's rebellion had disastrous consequences. Sennacherib attacked Judah with devastating force, creating economic and social catastrophe. Hezekiah avoided the destruction of the capital, Jerusalem, only by abject submission and payment of enormous tribute. For the rest of his reign, and during the reign of his son and successor Manasseh (687 [698]–642 BCE), Judah was a loyal Assyrian vassal. Not until Assyria itself came under attack in the late seventh century BCE would Judah regain any real independence.

Both in Kings (2 Kings 18–20) and in Chronicles (2 Chr 29–32) a disproportionate amount of space is given to Hezekiah, and so we are better informed about his reign than about those of most other kings. What emerges from these sources is a picture of a daring nationalist. The destruction of the northern kingdom had apparently resulted in an influx of refugees into Judah (see 2 Chr 30.25) and especially into its capital, Jerusalem. It is estimated that by the end of the eighth century BCE both the size and the population of Jerusalem were four times larger than they had been during Solomon's reign in the mid-tenth century, from some 25 acres (10 hectares) to more than 100 acres (40 hectares) and from five thousand inhabitants to as many as twenty thousand (see Figure 19.1 and Plate 9 in the color section following p. 300). Hezekiah exploited this situation to reestablish the centralized Judean monarchy, extending his control to parts of what had been the northern kingdom (now an Assyrian province). Accompanying and supporting this policy was a religious revival. The originally northern traditions of the Deuteronomic movement, which had been associated with such prophets as Hosea (see pages 183 and 324–25), were reinterpreted and revised in Judah and given a Judean slant. Aspects of worship in Jerusalem and throughout the kingdom were reformed in accordance with the Deuteronomic regulations. These changes, of course, were made under royal auspices, further strengthening the power of the monarchy. Thus, the destruction of locales where illegitimate worship was practiced, the "high places" (2 Kings 18.4; 2 Chr 31.1), for which there is archaeological evidence, and the concomitant centralization of worship in Jerusalem, meant that the complicated sacrificial system, which in part served to redistribute meat and grain, was now entirely under royal control.

The Deuteronomists and the monarchy seem to have been kindred spirits, each using the other to their own advantage. That at least is the implication of the scholarly hypothesis that the first edition of the Deuteronomistic History was produced under Hezekiah (see further page 192). Inspired by the king's commitment to the principles of their movement, the Deuteronomists compiled an ideologically informed history of Israel, according to which the separation of north and south was a disaster and the divine choice of the Davidic monarchy, and its current ruler, were emphasized.

In the Chronicler's idealized account of these events, which reshaped the narrative in 2 Kings but also drew upon other sources, the reform includes a celebration of Passover in Jerusalem, to which the northern tribes were also invited (2 Chr 30). The festival thus expressed the unity of the nation, as well as the extension of royal control to the former northern kingdom.

Because of the abundance of the evidence, it is possible that our understanding of Hezekiah's importance is skewed. More likely, however, is that the attention given to Hezekiah in biblical and in Assyrian sources is recognition that his

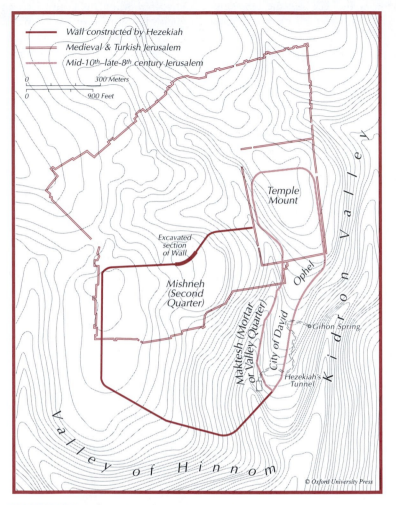

FIGURE 19.1.   Plan of Jerusalem in the late eighth century BCE.

reign was pivotal. An important contemporary of Hezekiah was the prophet Isaiah.

ISAIAH

The Book of Isaiah

With its sixty-six chapters, the book of Isaiah is the longest of the prophetic books, and one of the longest books in the entire Bible. Until the late nineteenth century the entire book was generally considered the work of the prophet whose name is found at its beginning, Isaiah son of Amoz, who lived in Jerusalem in the late eighth and early seventh centuries BCE. Some premodern scholars, including Ibn Ezra in the thirteenth century and Baruch Spinoza in the seventeenth, recognized some problems with this assumption, and further work in the eighteenth and nineteenth centuries culminated in the commentary on Isaiah by the German scholar Bernhard Duhm in 1892. Duhm found three principal parts to the book: **First Isaiah**, chapters 1–39, the bulk of which could be dated to the time of Isaiah of Jerusalem, **Second** (or Deutero-) **Isaiah**, chapters 40–55, dating to the sixth century BCE, and **Third** (or Trito-) **Isaiah**, chapters 56–66, up to a century later. Most modern scholars agree with this analysis.

This analysis of the book of Isaiah shares several presuppositions and conclusions with the critical analysis of the Pentateuch (see pages 22–29). It assumes that an eighth-century BCE prophet in Jerusalem could not have known about the particulars of sixth-century history, such as the fall of Jerusalem to the Babylonians in 586 BCE, repeatedly mentioned in Isaiah 40–55; the rise to power of the Persian king Cyrus the Great in 559, explicitly mentioned in Isaiah 44.28 and 45.1; and his defeat of Babylon in 539, mentioned in Isaiah 47 and 48.14. These specific historical references show that parts of the book were written after these events. This critical judgment does not allow for the possibility that the prophets could, under divine inspiration, know of events in the distant future. That is more in the realm of theology, but at least it should be said that the rise of a king in Persia who would conquer Babylon would have made little sense to an eighth-century Judean audience, for whom Persia was unknown and Babylon no threat at all.

In any case, the consensus of scholars is that the book of Isaiah is the result of a lengthy process of formation, which began with the collection of oracles of Isaiah of Jerusalem. To this nucleus later writings were attached, and many additions were made to its early parts. The entire body of literature shares a common vocabulary, frequently referring to Yahweh as "the holy One of Israel" and making repeated mention of "justice" and "righteousness," and is pervaded by the view that Jerusalem/Zion is central to Yahweh's plans.

Beginning in the latter part of the twentieth century, some scholars have focused more on the final form of the book of Isaiah than on its hypothetical literary history. This type of criticism, often called "canonical criticism," emphasizes the traditional shape of the book and stresses its unifying themes rather than its compositional history. It recognizes that communities of faith from the late biblical period onward viewed the book of Isaiah as a single work containing a coherent and divinely inspired message. This approach also stresses that the processes that led to the final form of the book were not just mechanical editing, using scissors and paste as it were, but the result of a living intellectual tradition.

The School of Isaiah

Within First Isaiah are several references to the writing down of the prophet's words. Typical is Isaiah 30.8:

> Go now, write it before them on a tablet,
>   and inscribe it on a scroll,
> so that it may be for the time to come
>   as a witness forever.

The prophet's words are recorded and preserved, so that their truth may be confirmed by events subsequent to the prophetic proclamation. The same process is found in 8.1–3, the prediction of the birth of Maher-shalal-hash-baz, and in 8.16: "Bind up the testimony, seal the teaching among my disciples"—the prophetic message, having been written on papyrus, is rolled up, tied with string, and sealed, presumably to be opened at a later time to prove its truth, as is also the case in Habakkuk 2.2–3. Moreover, the message is entrusted to the prophet's "disciples," presumably those responsible for collecting and preserving the prophet's oracles, like Jeremiah's scribe Baruch a century later (see Jer 36 and page 376); the tradition that Isaiah himself was a writer is also found in 2 Chronicles 26.22.

We can therefore conclude that Isaiah had disciples, something like the "sons of the prophet" of earlier tradition (see pages 300–301), and that around him or after his death a kind of school of thought formed, like the Deuteronomic School that we have identified earlier (see page 183). In fact, we should note the close connections between Isaiah and the Deuteronomists: Isaiah is the only one of the "Latter Prophets" with any prominence in the Deuteronomistic History, in 2 Kings 19–20, and those chapters were also incorporated into the developing book of Isaiah. (The only other of the latter prophets even mentioned is Jonah, in 2 Kings 14.25; see further pages 525–26.)

It was this Isaianic school that scholars think was responsible for the composition and addition of new material to the original collection of narratives and oracles of the eighth-century BCE prophet Isaiah of Jerusalem. Like the schools of Greek philosophy, these disciples continued the style and viewpoint of their founder, in a remarkably consistent yet developing stream that lasted for several centuries. This Isaianic school not only added material to the earlier prophet's work but also constantly revised it, an indication that later generations would consider the prophet's original words as relevant for them as well. (We will discuss on pages 408–14 and 427–28 the parts of the book of Isaiah called Second Isaiah and Third Isaiah.)

First Isaiah (Isaiah 1–39): Contents

The nature of the book of Isaiah as an anthology is clear from its length, from the arrangement of the materials in it, and from overlaps within the book and with other biblical books. Note especially the following overlaps:

- Isaiah 2.2–4 = Micah 4.1–4, with only slight variations (Zion's centrality in a new age)
- Isaiah 15–16 = Jeremiah 48 (the oracle against Moab)
- Isaiah 36–39 = 2 Kings 18.13–20.19; the editors of the book of Isaiah have incorporated into it the account of the invasion of Sennacherib from the Deuteronomistic History

Moreover, what seems originally to have been a poem with several stanzas and a common refrain ("For all this his anger has not turned away, and his hand is stretched out still") has been divided. The refrain occurs first in 5.25, and then again in 9.12, 9.17, 9.21, and 10.4. The first stanza has been separated from the body of the oracle by the material in 6.1–9.7.

The principles of arrangement of First Isaiah are neither chronological nor self-evident, as an outline of its contents shows; within each of these larger divisions is evidence of later additions.

- *Chapters 1–12*: A series of oracles, primarily against Israel, interspersed with autobio-

graphical and biographical narratives. The material found in these chapters refers to events throughout the late eighth and early seventh centuries BCE, in no apparent chronological order. These include a vision of the prophet in the year of the death of King Uzziah (most likely 733 BCE), found in 6.1–13; the account of the attack on Jerusalem by the combined forces of Israel and Aram, in 734 (chaps. 7–8); references to the Assyrian destruction of the northern kingdom of Israel in 722 (9.8–21; 10.11); a coronation hymn, probably for Hezekiah's accession in 715 (9.2–7); and references to the invasion of Sennacherib in 701 (1.7–9; 10.5–11). At the same time, this material has been reworked as part of the lengthy process of the book's formation. Chapter 1 can plausibly be viewed as a kind of overture to the book of Isaiah as a whole, setting forth themes and introducing vocabulary that will recur throughout the book. The opening chapters of Isaiah also contain material that is later than the eighth century. These additions include the eschatological visions of a glorious future in chapters 2 and 11 (significantly, chap. 2 has its own introductory note) and the concluding hymnic interludes in chapter 12.

- *Chapters 13–23*: Oracles against foreign nations. These oracles are an extended elaboration of the genre first found in Amos 1–2 (see page 314). This section includes oracles against Babylon (chap. 13) and its king (14.3–21). A late eighth-century BCE oracle against Babylon by Isaiah of Jerusalem is not inconceivable, given the diplomatic contact between Hezekiah and the Babylonian king Merodach-baladan, as both rebelled against Assyrian control (see page 329 and 2 Kings 20.12 [= Isa 39.1]). In Isaiah 13.17–22, however, mention is made of the Medes, who were located in the region east of Mesopotamia (modern Iran) and were involved in the overthrow of the Babylonians in the mid sixth-century BCE; reference is also made to Babylon's fall. At least in part, then, if not in its entirety, the oracle against Babylon is to be dated to the sixth century, no earlier than the Babylonian conquest of Judah.

- *Chapters 24–27:* The "Isaiah apocalypse," a highly mythological account of the divine judgment of the end-time, probably written no earlier than the sixth century BCE (see further pages 438–39).

- *Chapters 28–33:* Miscellaneous oracles, generally concerned with Judah and Ephraim and their relationships with Egypt.

- *Chapters 34–35:* More postexilic additions, consisting of an attack on Edom, which was apparently an ally of Babylon during the attack on Jerusalem in 586 BCE (see Ps 137.7; Lam 4.21; Obadiah; Ezek 35.5–6), and a description of the return of the exiles from Babylon through a transformed wilderness, anticipating the fuller treatment of this theme in Second Isaiah (see pages 410–11).

- *Chapters 36–39:* The narrative of the Deuteronomistic Historians, borrowed from 2 Kings. Its position at the end of the book of "First" Isaiah, rounding it off, as it were, provides some ancient confirmation of the scholarly consensus that what follows is later in origin.

The Life of Isaiah

The book of Isaiah gives us some information about the prophet himself. According to the superscription, the opening historical note, his prophetic career occurred during the reigns of the kings of Judah from Uzziah to Hezekiah, that is, in the second half of the eighth and the beginning of the seventh centuries BCE. He was married, and his wife was probably also a prophet; the interpretation of "prophetess" in Isaiah 8.3 as simply an honorary title, "Mrs. Prophet" as it were, is less likely. They had several children, who, like those of the prophet Hosea and his wife Gomer (see page 320), had symbolic names: "I and the children whom the LORD has given me are signs and portents from the LORD of Hosts, who dwells on Mount Zion" (8.18). These children are Shear-jashub ("A remnant will return"; 7.3; see 10.21–22), Maher-shalal-hash-baz

("Quickly the booty, hastily the spoil"; 8.1–3), and probably Immanuel ("God is with us"; 7.14; see further Box 19.3 later in this chapter); all three names have both positive and negative significance in the book. The prophet also seems to have had "disciples" (8.16), who probably constitute the beginning of the "school of Isaiah" discussed on pages 331–32.

Judging from the frequent encounters between Isaiah and the kings Ahaz and Hezekiah, it is plausible that Isaiah was a kind of court prophet, like Nathan in David's time (see page 261). As such, Isaiah seems to have been involved in the coronation of Hezekiah as Ahaz's successor, as Nathan was in the case of Solomon (1 Kings 1.45); see further page 334. Like Nathan, too, Isaiah was an independent voice, criticizing as well as supporting the political and religious establishment in Jerusalem. Judging from the prominence of the prophet both in the book that bears his name and in 2 Kings, Isaiah was apparently a major figure in the history of Judah during the late eighth century BCE (see Box 19.2).

The Message of Isaiah

The superscription to the book of Isaiah describes its contents as "the vision . . . which he saw" (1.1). Unlike the books of Jeremiah and Ezekiel, however, the book of Isaiah does not open with an account of the call of the prophet. What has sometimes been identified as an inaugural vision or call comes well into the book, in chapter 6. The account of the vision includes the first precisely dated historical reference in the book (6.1: "the year that King Uzziah died," probably 733 BCE) and is in the first person, so that although it draws heavily on traditional themes and genres, it at least presents itself as the prophet's autobiography, even if it is not actually so. According to the chronology we have adopted here, that vision would have occurred after the events described in the subsequent chapters, and thus it is not an inaugural vision or call. To this vision have been added references to later events, including Sennacherib's devastation of Judah in 701 (6.11) and probably

Box 19.2 ISAIAH IN LATER TRADITION

A postbiblical writing, "The Martyrdom and Ascension of Isaiah," describes the death of Isaiah in some detail. During the reign of Hezekiah's successor, the wicked King Manasseh, under satanic influence, forces Isaiah, Micah, Joel, Habakkuk, and other prophets to flee to the Judean wilderness. But they are betrayed to the king by a Samarian, a descendant of the prophet Zedekiah (1 Kings 22.11, 24), and Manasseh orders that Isaiah be sawed in two (see Heb 11.37). A related tradition is found in the Talmud.

Not surprisingly given its length, the book of Isaiah is one of the most frequently quoted in the New Testament, as it also is among the Essene works among the Dead Sea Scrolls (see Box 29.2, page 508). Both the early Christians and the Essenes saw themselves as communities fulfilling the book's eschatological vision.

to the Babylonian deportations of the early sixth century BCE (6.12–13).

In the vision Isaiah describes himself as present for a meeting of the divine council, like Micaiah (1 Kings 22.19–23) and later Jeremiah (Jer 23.18, 22). That meeting occurs in the Temple, which was the earthly manifestation of the divine home, and whose location in Jerusalem was part of the royal ideology. The prophet sees Yahweh sitting on his throne, with the members of his assembly present. Addressing the council, Yahweh asks: "Whom shall I send, and who will go for us?" (Isa 6.8). Unlike Moses (Ex 3–4) and Jeremiah (1.6), Isaiah is not a reluctant prophet; he volunteers to be the council's emissary: "Here I am; send me!" (6.8). The task he is given, however, dampens his enthusiasm. He is instructed to deliver a message to "this people" (not "my people") that they will reject, and, in words often found in laments (see further pages 461–64), plaintively asks "How long, Lord?" The answer is no more comforting:

> Until cities lie waste
>   without inhabitant,
> and houses without people,
>   and the land is utterly desolate. (Isa 6.11)

The message of Isaiah, then, like that of other prophets, includes dire pronouncements of divine judgment.

Juxtaposed with the proclamations of doom, however, are lyrical passages, such as Isaiah 9.2–7. In that oracle, which later Christian interpretation understood as a messianic prophecy, the prophet proclaims the decree of the divine council on the occasion of a coronation, probably that of Hezekiah:

> For a child has been born for us,
>   a son given to us;
> authority rests upon his shoulders;
>   and he is named
> Wonderful Counselor, Mighty God,
>   Everlasting Father, Prince of Peace.
> His authority shall grow continually,
>   and there shall be endless peace
>   for the throne of David and his kingdom.
> He will establish and uphold it
>   with justice and with righteousness
>   from this time onward and forevermore.
> (Isa 9.6–7)

Adopted as a divine son (see pages 277–78), the newly crowned king is given throne names that describe the deity's enduring support of the dynasty founded by David. In fact, the royal ideology that proclaimed an eternal divine guarantee both for the dynasty and for its capital city is a significant theme in Isaiah.

That divine guarantee, however, did not mean that the royal establishment was free to ignore the obligations of social justice. The prophet did not hesitate to condemn the monarchy and the Jerusalem establishment for their social inequities:

The LORD rises to argue his lawsuit;
  he stands to judge the peoples.
The LORD enters into judgment
  with the elders and princes of his people:
It is you who have devoured the vineyard;
  the spoil of the poor is in your houses.
What do you mean by crushing my people,
  by grinding the face of the poor?
    says the Lord GOD of hosts. (3.13–15)

Here Isaiah employs the metaphor of the lawsuit (Hebr. *rîb*) for breach of contract, which first appears in Hosea (see page 323). But the party sued by Yahweh is now the leadership of the community—"the elders and princes," who are guilty of the same kinds of social injustice for which Amos had condemned the nation as a whole (Am 2.6–7).

Thus, although Jerusalem (Zion) is a central component of the divine plan, she has become a whore because its leaders accept bribes and no longer give the least powerful, orphans and widows, their legal rights (1.21–23; see also 5.23). Nevertheless, after the divine judgment, Zion will once again be called "the city of righteousness, the faithful city" (1.26; compare 1.21).

Even the most lyrical passages can also express divine judgment, as is the case with the "Song of the Vineyard" in Isaiah 5.1–7. Drawing on what seems to have been a popular love song, the passage makes it a parable of Yahweh's unrequited love for Israel. Using one of the most frequent biblical metaphors, the song identifies Israel as Yahweh's beloved, his vineyard (see Song 4.12; 8.12), which he had carefully tended. Yet after all that Yahweh had done for Israel, it failed to fulfill his requirements. Using wordplay, the prophet proclaims:

he expected justice [Hebr. *mishpat*],
  but there was only bloodshed [*mishpah*];
righteousness [*sedaqa*],
  but there was only a cry [*se'aqa*]! (5.7)

Isaiah's insistence on social justice continues that of his prophetic predecessors. Echoing the views of Amos and Hosea (see Box 18.3 on page 319), he insists that religious ritual is not the primary obligation:

When you stretch out your hands,
  I will hide my eyes from you;
even though you make many prayers,
  I will not listen;
  your hands are full of blood.
Wash yourselves; make yourselves clean;
  remove the evil of your doings
  from before my eyes;
cease to do evil,
  learn to do good;
seek justice,
  rescue the oppressed,
defend the orphan,
  plead for the widow. (Isa 1.15–17)

Failure to "seek justice" inevitably will bring upon Israel the divinely caused curses resulting from covenant disobedience. For Isaiah those curses will take the form of Assyrian invasion. In texts that can be connected with the events of 734 and 701 BCE, the prophet has a distinct attitude toward Assyria, expressed most clearly in 10.5–7:

Ah, Assyria, the rod of my anger—
  the club in their hands is my fury!
Against a godless nation I send him,
  and against the people of my wrath I command him,
to take spoil and seize plunder,
  and to tread them down like the mire of the streets.
But this is not what he intends,
  nor does he have this in mind;
but it is in his heart to destroy,
  and to cut off nations not a few.

In the prophetic view, it is Yahweh who is ultimately responsible for historical events. Whatever the Assyrians' intentions, ultimately they are simply an instrument in the divine hands, a weapon used in the punishment of Judah.

This same perspective is found in the speech by the Rabshakeh, the Assyrian official during the siege of Jerusalem in 701 BCE. Although the speech itself is probably a literary creation, it makes the same point: "Is it without the LORD that I have come up against this land to destroy it? The LORD said to me, 'Go up against this land, and destroy it.'" (Isa 36.10).

The vicissitudes of the kingdoms of Israel and Judah can be viewed both historically, as part of the Assyrian imperial drive toward dominance of the entire ancient Near East, and in the view of the prophets as part of a divine plan. This theological perspective, shared by the Deuteronomic school (see page 183), sees historical events as essentially part of a divine justice, a theodicy, in which Yahweh is rewarding or punishing the nation for its failure to trust in him and to observe his commandments.

The prophet Isaiah's intimate involvement in the events of his own times is evident in the sieges of Jerusalem in 734 and 701 BCE.

THE SIEGE OF JERUSALEM IN 734 BCE

Reconstructing the events of the late 730s BCE requires synthesis of several different sources, including the fragmentary records of the Assyrian king Tiglath-pileser III and, in the Bible, the telescoped and occasionally inconsistent accounts found in 2 Kings 16, 2 Chronicles 28, and the book of Isaiah, especially chapters 7–8. Here is a likely scenario, one accepted by most scholars.

In 734 BCE, as Tiglath-pileser moved to reestablish Assyrian control over the smaller kingdoms of the Levant, several of them, including Aram of Damascus (Syria) and the northern kingdom of Israel (often called Ephraim in prophetic texts), and probably Tyre, Ashkelon, and Edom, formed a coalition in an attempt to block the Assyrian king's advance. Judah apparently refused to join this coalition. To force it to do so, the kings of Aram and Israel, Rezin and Pekah, laid siege to Jerusalem, in what is called the **Syro-Ephraimite War**. The siege may have been accompanied by devastation of the kingdom of Judah outside the capital, as suggested in 2 Chronicles 28.5–7. The intention of the kings of Aram and Israel was to depose the newly crowned king, Ahaz, and to replace him with "the son of

Tabeel," who would presumably join their anti-Assyria coalition. "The son of Tabeel" cannot be further identified with certainty, but he probably was a member of the Judean ruling family and thus a descendant of David.

Ahaz was a young ruler, only twenty years old, and he had just become king. With Jerusalem under siege, he made a strategic decision. To remove the threat to his throne and to his capital, he requested assistance from Tiglath-pileser. According to the Deuteronomistic Historians, that request was couched in the formal language of submission as a vassal: "I am your servant and your son. Come up, and rescue me from the hand of the king of Aram and from the hand of the king of Israel, who are attacking me" (2 Kings 16.7).

Ahaz's submission to Tiglath-pileser is confirmed by a notice in Assyrian sources that he paid tribute in 734 BCE. All three biblical sources (2 Kings 16; 2 Chr 28; Isa 7–8) present Ahaz's submission to Assyria in a bad light—at the very least as a lack of trust in Yahweh, if not outright apostasy—and this perspective has colored their presentation of what happened. This is especially the case with Isaiah.

In a complicated group of interrelated passages in chapters 7–8, the book of Isaiah deals with the crisis of 734 BCE. The first, 7.1–17, is a third-person narrative of two encounters between Ahaz and Isaiah, including the prophet's proclamation of a "sign": the birth of a boy named Immanuel and the return of peace and prosperity to Judah in that child's early years. Then follow in 7.18–25 what appear to be several oracles that expand the themes of the preceding passage while referring to later events, such as the fall of Samaria in 722 and the invasion of Sennacherib in 701. Chapter 8, which is entirely in the first person, like chapter 6, opens with a prediction of the birth of another boy (8.1–4). This is followed by condemnation of Judah for its alliance with Assyria (8.5–10) and by three shorter units, having to do with confidence in Yahweh (8.11–15), preservation of the prophet's word (8.16–18), and condemnation of those who prefer to consult the dead (8.19–22; see page 297).

In the first of the two encounters (Isa 7.3–9), the prophet advises the king not to panic because of the attack by the kings of Aram and Israel. His message is "Be quiet, do not fear" (7.4)—that is, do not do anything, but trust in Yahweh. To reinforce this advice, in a second encounter (7.10–17) the prophet gives the king a sign: The child of a pregnant woman apparently present at the scene would be a son, who would be given the symbolic name **Immanuel** ("God is with us") (see Box 19.3). The guarantee that that name implied would be evident soon: Within a few years after the birth of the child ("by the time he knows how to refuse the evil and choose the good"), "he shall eat curds and honey"—that is, the land

would enjoy almost mythical abundance and return to the peace and prosperity that had characterized the United Monarchy in the tenth century BCE, before "Ephraim departed from Judah." A variation on that message is found in the account of the conception, birth, and symbolic naming of the prophet's son Maher-shalal-hash-baz in 8.1–4.

King Ahaz apparently rejected the prophet's advice, and it is here that we can plausibly insert the account in 2 Kings 16.5–9 of Ahaz's request to Tiglath-pileser for help and his submission to him as a vassal. Soon thereafter, it seems, Isaiah

Box 19.3 THE IDENTITY OF IMMANUEL

Because of its use in the New Testament, Isaiah 7.14 is one of the most discussed verses in the Hebrew Bible. The identities of the pregnant woman and of her future son, whom the prophet names Immanuel, are not given in the text, nor are they essential for understanding the "sign" that the child's birth, naming, and early life communicate.

Modern scholars generally identify the child either as a son of King Ahaz, probably his successor Hezekiah (see 2 Kings 18.1), or as a son of the prophet Isaiah and his wife, also a prophet. Hezekiah is prominent in the book of Isaiah, as is the divine guarantee of the Davidic dynasty, and he may indeed be the child who is the sign. But the chronology of Hezekiah's reign is confused (see Box 19.1). According to 2 Kings 18.1 he was twenty-five years old when he assumed the throne; whether that was in 727 BCE (following 2 Kings 18.1) or 715 (following 2 Kings 18.13, the chronology preferred here), he would have been born at least several years before the events of 734.

It is more likely, then, that Immanuel was the son of Isaiah and his wife, the "prophetess" (see page 333), like Maher-shalal-hash-baz in 8.1–3. The parallels between 7.14 and 8.3 are instructive: In both a pregnant woman is to give birth to a son with a symbolic name. The medieval Jewish commentators Ibn Ezra and Rashi also give this interpretation.

In the gospel of Matthew (1.22–23), in part because of the translation into Greek of the Hebrew word for young woman, *almah*, as *parthenos* ("virgin"), Immanuel is identified as Jesus, and the young woman as his mother Mary. The Hebrew of Isaiah 7.14 does not use the technical term for "virgin," but rather a more general word, and also uses the past tense: "The young woman has (already) conceived." Matthew thus uses a mistranslation of the text of Isaiah as a vehicle to express early Christian belief in the divine origin of Jesus and thus in his mother's virginity.

Box 19.4 SENNACHERIB'S THIRD CAMPAIGN (701 BCE) ACCORDING TO THE ASSYRIAN ANNALS

In my third campaign, I marched against Hatti [northern Syria]. The awesome splendor of my lordship overwhelmed Lulli, king of Sidon, and he fled overseas and disappeared forever. The terrifying nature of the weapon of [the god] Ashur overwhelmed his strong cities, Greater Sidon, Lesser Sidon, Bit-zitti, Zarephath . . . Achzib, Acco . . . and they bowed in submission at my feet. I installed Taba'lu on the throne as king over them and imposed upon him tribute and dues for my lordship payable annually without interruption.

The kings of Amurru [the West], all of them—Minihimmu of Samsimuruna, Tuba'lu of Sidon, Abdiliti of Arvad, Urumilki of Byblos, Mitinti of Ashdod, Puduili of Beth-Ammon, Chemosh-nadbi of Moab, Ayarammu of Edom—brought me sumptuous gifts, rich presents, fourfold, and kissed my feet.

As for Sidqa, king of Ashkelon, who had not submitted to my yoke, I deported and sent him to Assyria, together with his family gods, he, himself, his sons, his daughters, his brothers, and all his descendants. I set Sharruludari, son of Rukibti, their former king, over the people of Ashkelon and imposed upon him the payment of tribute and presents to my lordship; he now bears my yoke.

In the course of my campaign, I surrounded and conquered . . . cities belonging to Sidqa, who did not submit quickly, and I carried off their spoil. The officials, the nobles, and the people of Ekron who had thrown Padi, their king, who was under oath and obligations to Assyria, into iron fetters and handed him over in a hostile manner to Hezekiah, the Judean; because of the offense they had committed they were afraid. The kings of Egypt, and the bowmen and chariot corps and cavalry of the kings of Ethiopia assembled a countless force and came to their [the Ekronites'] aid. . . . Trusting in [the god] Ashur, my lord, I fought with them and inflicted a defeat upon them. I besieged and conquered Eltekeh and Timnah and carried off their spoil. I assaulted Ekron and slew its nobles and official who had stirred up rebellion and hung their bodies on watchtowers all about the city. The citizens who had committed sinful acts, I counted as spoil and the rest of them, who had not sinned, I ordered their release. I freed Padi, their king, from Jerusalem, and set him on the throne as king over them and imposed tribute for my lordship upon him.

As for Hezekiah, the Judean, who had not submitted to my yoke, I besieged forty-six of his fortified walled cities and surrounding small towns, which were without number. Using packed-down ramps and by applying battering rams, infantry attacks by mines, breeches, and siege machines, I conquered them. I took out 200,150 people, young and old, male and female, horses, mules, donkeys, camels, cattle, and sheep, without number, and counted them as spoil. Himself I locked him up within Jerusalem, his royal city, like a bird in a cage. I surrounded him with earthworks, and made it unthinkable for him to exit by the city gate. His cities which I had despoiled, I cut off from his land, and gave them to Mitinti, king of Ashdod, Padi, king of Ekron, and Silli-bel, king of

Gaza, and thus diminished his land. I imposed upon him in addition to the former tribute, yearly payment of dues and gifts for my lordship.

He, Hezekiah, was overwhelmed by the awesome splendor of my lordship, and he sent me after my departure to Nineveh, my royal city, his elite troops and his best soldiers, which he had brought into Jerusalem as reinforcements, with 30 talents of gold, 800 talents of silver, choice antimony, large blocks of carnelian, beds (inlaid) with ivory, armchairs inlaid with ivory, elephant hides, ivory, ebony-wood, boxwood, garments with multicolored trim, garments of linen, wool dyed red-purple and blue-purple, vessels of copper, iron, bronze, and tin, chariots, siege shields, lances, armor, daggers for the belt, bows and arrows, countless trappings and instruments of war, together with his daughters, his palace women, his male and female singers. He also dispatched his personal messenger to deliver the tribute and to do obeisance.[*]

---

[*]   Translation adapted from M. Cogan and H. Tadmor, *II Kings* (New York: Doubleday, 1988), pp. 337–39.

---

went back to the king with a different interpretation of the original sign, the name Immanuel. Because Ahaz had rejected the divine assurance and had sought help from Assyria, Yahweh would give them Assyria. Using a dire metaphor, because they had rejected the divinely given water supply of Jerusalem—"the waters of Shiloah that flow gently" (8.6)—Yahweh would send them the waters of the Euphrates River, in the Assyrian heartland:

> Therefore, the Lord is bringing up against it the mighty flood waters of the River, the king of Assyria and all his glory; it will rise above all its channels and overflow all its banks; it will sweep on into Judah as a flood, and, pouring over, it will reach up to the neck; and its outspread wings will fill the breadth of your land, O Immanuel. (Isa 8.7–8)

The name of the child had originally been a positive sign: God is with us, to save and protect us. Now it becomes ominous: God is with us, but now to punish, in the person of the "king of Assyria and all his glory." That attack would occur in 701 BCE.

THE ASSYRIAN INVASION OF JUDAH IN 701 BCE

In 701 BCE Sennacherib invaded Judah. For this campaign we have several sources. Each must be interpreted, for none is an objective account of the events, and synthesizing them is a classic exercise in interpretation. Let us begin with the sources themselves.

Assyrian Sources

In the Taylor Prism, now in the Oriental Institute of the University of Chicago, Sennacherib gives his own account (see Box 19.4). In it he describes a whirlwind campaign south through the Levant, in which he accepted submission and accompanying tribute from a majority of the kings of the states of the region and punished those who did not submit (see Figure 19.2). Among the latter was Hezekiah, king of Judah, whose territory was brutally taken over and whose capital, Jerusalem, was besieged. According to Sennacherib, these measures compelled Hezekiah to surrender, and also to pay an enormous tribute.

In addition to this text, we also have a vivid depiction of the siege and capture of one of the main fortified cities of Judah, Lachish, in reliefs that decorated a large room in Sennacherib's palace at Nineveh. Curiously, the Prism text does not mention Lachish, although the city on the reliefs is identified in a kind of caption (see Figure 19.3).

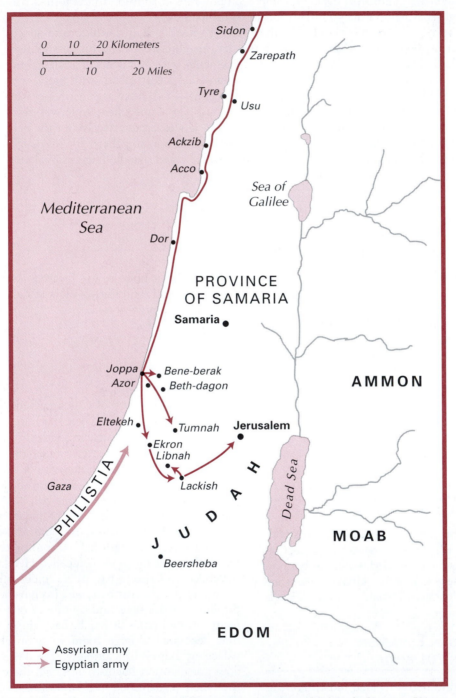

FIGURE 19.2.   Map of the campaign of the Assyrian king Sennacherib in the Levant in 701 BCE.

FIGURE 19.3. The Assyrian king Sennacherib at the Judean city of Lachish, from reliefs in his palace at Nineveh. The cuneiform inscription at the upper left reads "Sennacherib, king of the world, king of Assyria, sitting on his throne and reviewing the booty from Lachish." The king's face has been mutilated, perhaps during the capture of Nineveh by the Babylonians in 612 BCE.

2 Kings 18–20

Scholars have identified two different sources in the Deuteronomistic Historians' account of Hezekiah's reign in 2 Kings. The first is a matter-of-fact, annalistic account of Sennacherib's invasion:

> In the fourteenth year of King Hezekiah, King Sennacherib of Assyria came up against all the fortified cities of Judah and captured them. King Hezekiah of Judah sent to the king of Assyria at Lachish, saying, "I have done wrong; withdraw from me; whatever you impose on me I will bear." The king of Assyria demanded of King Hezekiah of Judah three hundred tal-

ents of silver and thirty talents of gold. Hezekiah gave him all the silver that was found in the house of the LORD and in the treasuries of the king's house. At that time Hezekiah stripped the gold from the doors of the temple of the LORD, and from the doorposts that King Hezekiah of Judah had overlaid and gave it to the king of Assyria. (2 Kings 18.13–16)

This brief account, often called the A-source, corresponds closely to that of Sennacherib himself, although the Assyrian version gives many more details.

The A-source is followed by a very different set of narratives. Called the B-source, it actually consists of two parallel accounts of communications between Sennacherib and Hezekiah and the latter's reactions. The first (B^1) is 2 Kings 18.17–19.9a, and probably concludes with 19.36–37; the second (B^2) is 2 Kings 19.9b–35. In the first, a delegation of Assyrian officials appears before the walls of Jerusalem and, addressing first Hezekiah's representatives and then the city's inhabitants directly, challenges Hezekiah's trust in Yahweh. Although the speech is part of an invented dialogue, it is remarkable for its detailed attack on Hezekiah's policy of centralization of worship. How can Hezekiah rely on Yahweh, if it is his shrines that the king destroyed? Reflecting the prophetic view that Yahweh controlled historical events, the speech goes on to observe that if the Assyrians are present, it must be because Yahweh has sent them; resistance is therefore futile. Although the king is disheartened, the prophet Isaiah gives him assurance: "Do not be afraid. . . . I will cause him [the king of Assyria] to fall by the sword in his own land" (2 Kings 19.6–7).

In the second encounter, Sennacherib sends Hezekiah a letter after the conquest of Lachish. Again, Sennacherib challenges the people's trust in Yahweh: "Do not let your God on whom you rely deceive you by promising that Jerusalem will not be given into the hand of the king of Assyria" (2 Kings 19.10). And, as he had earlier, he refers to the Assyrian victories over all other lands and the apparent weakness of their gods. Because the letter repeats much of the speech of the Assyrian envoy (the Rabshakeh) in the previous episode, most scholars interpret the two as variations (hence, B^1 and B^2). Hezekiah's response to this communication is a pious prayer for Yahweh's help, and in response the prophet Isaiah delivers an oracle of deliverance. The B-source concludes with a direct divine intervention: "That very night the angel of the LORD set out and struck down one hundred eighty-five thousand in the camp of the Assyrians; when morning dawned, they were all dead bodies" (2 Kings 19.35).

This composite B-source has the character of prophetic legends, like those found earlier in the Deuteronomistic History. In it the prophet Isaiah is a central figure, advising Hezekiah to trust in Yahweh. And, according to this source, Hezekiah does so; his piety contrasts with that of his predecessor Ahaz, who had trusted in Assyria rather than in Yahweh.

So different in tone and in detail are the A- and B-sources that some conservative scholars have argued, because the biblical account should be taken at face value, that there must have been two campaigns of Sennacherib: one in 701 BCE, described in the A-source and in Sennacherib's annals, ending in an Assyrian victory; and another, recounted in the B-source but not in any surviving Assyrian record, ending in an Assyrian defeat. Most contemporary scholars, however, have rejected this "two-campaign hypothesis," recognizing that the biblical tradition here, as elsewhere, simply juxtaposes two different accounts of the same event.

2 Chronicles 32

Although largely reproducing its source in 2 Kings, the Chronicler's narrative of the events of 701 BCE provides details not found elsewhere, especially concerning Hezekiah's preparations for the attack. We are told that Hezekiah repaired and added to Jerusalem's fortifications (2 Chr 32.5), and also that he redirected the waters of the Gihon Spring to the west of the city of David (2 Chr 32.30). This expands on the notice in 2 Kings, which reports less clearly that "he made the pool and the conduit and brought water into the city" (2 Kings 20.20).

Isaiah

References to Sennacherib's invasion are found throughout First Isaiah. Perhaps the most poignant, and most telling, is that found in Isaiah 1:

> Your country lies desolate,
>   your cities are burned with fire;
> in your very presence
>   aliens devour your land;
>   it is desolate, as overthrown by foreigners.
> And daughter Zion is left
>   like a booth in a vineyard,

like a shelter in a cucumber field,
   like a besieged city.
If the LORD of hosts
   had not left us a few survivors,
we would have been like Sodom,
   and become like Gomorrah. (Isa 1.7–9)

This passage depicts in poetic form the devastation that accompanied the Assyrian onslaught. All the cities outside Jerusalem were burned, and Jerusalem itself was left standing like a ramshackle guard's hut in a vineyard or field.

The book of Isaiah also reproduces 2 Kings 18–20 in Isaiah 36–39, with one notable omission: The Isaiah version omits the account in 2 Kings 18.14–16 (the A-source described earlier) of Hezekiah's surrender and payment of tribute, making it appear that Sennacherib's arrogant assault on Yahweh's home was punished by the deity himself. It also adds another prayer of Hezekiah during his illness, in the sequel to the B-source (Isa 38.9–20). The result is a consistent narrative that emphasizes Hezekiah's piety and that implicitly contrasts him with Ahaz, who had not followed the prophet Isaiah's advice during the earlier siege of Jerusalem.

FIGURE 19.4. Another detail from the reliefs in Sennacherib's palace at Nineveh, showing the city of Lachish under siege. At the left, an Assyrian battering ram attacks the city's gate as the defenders send down arrows, torches, and stones. At the lower right, captives leave the gate, headed for exile.

Archaeological Evidence

At many Judean sites a massive destruction layer has been connected convincingly with Sennacherib's campaign in 701 BCE, which, according to both Assyrian and biblical sources, devastated Judah. These sites include Ramat Rahel, Timnah, Arad, possibly Beersheba and Ziklag, and especially Lachish. Excavations at Lachish have confirmed to a remarkable level of detail the depiction of the destruction of Lachish in the reliefs from Nineveh. The fortifications and the Assyrian siege ramp as depicted on the reliefs especially coincide with the excavated remains (see Figure 19.4).

Discoveries in Jerusalem contribute further to our understanding of the events of the late eighth century BCE. Considerable evidence exists for an eighth-century expansion of the city beyond the fortified limits of the city of David, especially to its west. Some of this expansion can be attributed to an influx of refugees from the northern kingdom of Israel, especially after its destruction by the Assyrians in 722 BCE. This expanded area, called the "Second Quarter" (2 Kings 22.14; Zeph 1.10), was fortified by Hezekiah (see 2 Chr 32.5; Isa 22.10), and parts of these fortifications have been discovered (see Plate 10 in the color section following page 300). Also connected with Hezekiah's defensive preparations for the anticipated Assyrian attack on his capital was the construction of a water tunnel (see Box 19.5).

Synthesis

Recognizing that each source constitutes data that need to be interpreted, it is possible to synthesize them. Having neutralized the unrest in

Box 19.5 HEZEKIAH'S TUNNEL

One of the earliest modern discoveries in Jerusalem was the underground water conduit known as **"Hezekiah's Tunnel"** or the "Siloam Tunnel" (see Figure 19.5). This construction, which is over 1,700 ft (500 m) long, is a major feat of ancient engineering. Its purpose was to divert the city's main source of water, from the Gihon Spring in the Kidron Valley on the lower northeastern slopes of the city of David to the Siloam Pool on the southwest, which was enclosed by the newly constructed fortifications. The city's water supply would therefore have been protected from enemy attack or poisoning. (See Figure 19.1.)

On the wall of the tunnel itself, near its southern end, an inscription was found in 1880 carved in elegant Hebrew script, one of the very few monumental texts from the monarchic period (see Figure 19.6). Now incomplete, it describes how the teams of workers, starting from opposite sides, finally met:

FIGURE 19.5. The interior of Hezekiah's Tunnel, constructed in preparation for the Assyrian attack of 701 BCE. Marks left by the picks of the ancient workers are visible on the sides and roof of the tunnel.

> And this was the manner of the breakthrough: While [the stonecutters] were still wielding the ax, each man toward his fellow, and while there were still three cubits to be [cut through, they heard] the sound of each man calling to his fellow, for there was a seam in the rock to the right [and the left]. And on the day of the breakthrough the stonecutters struck, each man toward his fellow, ax against ax, and the waters flowed from the source to the pool, for twelve hundred cubits. And one hundred cubits was the height of the rock above the head of the stonecutters.[*]

The tunnel thus seems to have been constructed in some haste, a conclusion confirmed by details of the construction.

---

[*]   Adapted from translation by P. K. McCarter, Jr., page 114 in *Ancient Inscriptions: Voices from the Biblical World* (Washington, DC: Biblical Archaeology Society, 1996).

FIGURE 19.6.   The ancient Hebrew inscription from Hezekiah's tunnel, describing how it was dug. It measures about 20 × 26 in (50 × 66 cm).

Babylon, Sennacherib briefly turned his attention to his western frontier, and in a swift campaign subdued the coastal cities, and then the rebellious kingdom of Judah, whose king, Hezekiah, had withheld the required tribute and fomented unrest among other states in the region.

The campaign against Judah had several stages. First, the fortified cities of the kingdom were captured—forty-six in all, according to Sennacherib's count. Then Sennacherib laid siege to and captured the major southern Judean city of Lachish, where he established his headquarters. Finally, having devastated the Judean countryside, he turned his attention to Jerusalem, some 20 miles (32 km) northeast of Lachish. With his kingdom decimated and his capital under siege and cut off from food supplies, Hezekiah soon surrendered, and later sent a heavy tribute to the Assyrian capital at Nineveh.

As this event was retold, however, the survival of Jerusalem came to be interpreted as divinely accomplished. After all, if Yahweh was responsible for the Assyrian onslaught, as the Deuteronomistic and prophetic interpreters had argued, then he was also responsible for the failure of the Assyrians to capture and destroy Jerusalem. Most other cities in the Levant that had not submitted to Assyrian rule, including Samaria, had been destroyed, but not Jerusalem. So the deliverance of Jerusalem came to be understood as a miracle that demonstrated the divine guarantee of the city itself and of the Davidic dynasty whose capital it was.

MICAH

The Book of Micah

The seven chapters of the book named for Isaiah's contemporary, the prophet Micah, consist of oracles of judgment against Judah interspersed with oracles of restoration, as the following outline of the book's contents shows:

1.1	Superscription
1.2–2.11	Oracles of judgment
2.12–13	Oracle of restoration
3.1–12	Oracles of judgment
4.1–5.15	Oracles of restoration
6.1–7.6	Oracles of judgment
7.7–20	Oracles of restoration

Like other prophetic books, the book of Micah was expanded in later times as its message was continued to be thought relevant. For example, many scholars understand 7.8–10 to refer to the destruction of Jerusalem in 586 BCE, and the mention of rebuilding of Jerusalem's walls in 7.11 to refer to the activity of Nehemiah in the fifth century BCE. In this editorial process, also, material from other sources was added to the collection, including 4.1–4, which as noted earlier is almost identical to Isaiah 2.2–4.

The Life of Micah

Micah's career is dated by the book's editorial introduction to the reigns of Jotham, Ahaz, and Hezekiah, approximately the second half of the eighth century BCE, dating that is confirmed in the book itself by references to the fall of Samaria in 722 BCE (1.6) and to the Assyrian attack on Jerusalem in 701 (1.8–16). He was therefore a contemporary of his fellow Judean Isaiah. But while Isaiah was from Jerusalem, Micah was from the smaller town of Moresheth-gath in southern Judah and is considerably more hostile toward the capital than was Isaiah. The book gives no other details about the prophet's life.

The Message of Micah

Even though it is a relatively short book, Micah uses a variety of genres, including lament (1.8–16; 7.8–10), theophany (1.3–4), and hymnic prayer of petition and confidence (7.14–20). Like Hosea and Isaiah, Micah also includes an example of the covenant lawsuit (see page 323), in which Yahweh sues Israel for breach of contract (6.1–8). The lawsuit begins with an address to the mountains and hills, reminiscent of the "olden gods" in the lists of divine witnesses of the suzerainty treaties (see further pages 110–12):

> Hear what the LORD says:
> Rise, plead your case before the mountains,
>   and let the hills hear your voice.
> Hear, you mountains, the lawsuit of the LORD,
>   and you enduring foundations of the earth;

> for the LORD has a lawsuit with his people,
>   and he will contend with Israel. (Mic 6.1–2)

The lawsuit continues with a summary of what Yahweh had done for Israel from the Exodus to the entry into the Promised Land, echoing the historical prologue of the treaties:

> O my people, what have I done to you?
>   In what have I wearied you? Answer me!
> For I brought you up from the land of Egypt,
>   and redeemed you from the house of slavery;
> and I sent before you Moses,
>   Aaron, and Miriam.
> O my people, remember now what King Balak of
>   Moab devised,
>   what Balaam son of Beor answered him,
> and what happened from Shittim to Gilgal,
>   that you may know the saving acts of the LORD.
>   (Mic 6.3–5)

It concludes with the requirement of justice and "kindness," that is, covenant fidelity, rather than sacrifice (see further Box 18.3 on page 319):

> With what shall I come before the LORD,
>   and bow myself before God on high?
> Shall I come before him with burnt offerings,
>   with calves a year old?
> Will the LORD be pleased with thousands of rams,
>   with ten thousands of rivers of oil?
> Shall I give my firstborn for my transgression,
>   the fruit of my body for the sin of my soul?"
> He has told you, O mortal, what is good;
>   and what does the LORD require of you
> but to do justice, and to love kindness,
>   and to walk humbly with your God?
>   (Mic 6.6–8)

One indication of the importance of Micah's message is its being referred to in Jeremiah 26.18. Written over a century later, Micah's judgment on Jerusalem (Mic 3.12) is quoted in Jeremiah's defense by some of his contemporaries:

> Micah of Moresheth, who prophesied during the days of King Hezekiah of Judah, said to all the people of Judah: "Thus says the LORD of hosts,
>   Zion shall be plowed as a field;
>   Jerusalem shall become a heap of ruins,
>   and the mountain of the house a wooded height."
> Did King Hezekiah of Judah and all Judah actually put him to death? (Jer 26.18–19)

Box 19.6 THE KING FROM BETHLEHEM

In 5.2–5, the book of Micah predicts the rise of a ruler from Bethlehem. Clearly this is to be a new David, for David also was born in Bethlehem (1 Sam 17.12). At the same time, the passage is an implicit attack on the Jerusalem aristocracy. Jerusalem will be replaced as the seat of dynasty by the smaller, relatively insignificant town of Bethlehem.

In Matthew 2.5–6, this passage is quoted in connection with the birth of Jesus in Bethlehem, identifying him as the Messiah. John 7.42, on the other hand, while familiar with the passage's messianic interpretation, does not apply it to Jesus.

Just as Hezekiah did not sentence Micah to death for his prophecy of doom, the argument goes, neither should King Jehoiakim sentence Jeremiah to death for his prediction of Jerusalem's destruction. This is a rare instance of one biblical book explicitly quoting another. (See also Box 19.6.)

RETROSPECT AND PROSPECT

In the last four decades of the eighth century BCE, Jerusalem had been under siege twice and had not fallen. The royal ideology was apparently true: Yahweh had chosen Jerusalem as his home, and the Davidic dynasty as his designated rulers. Quoting the prophet Isaiah speaking in the name of Yahweh, the Deuteronomistic Historians put it this way: "I will defend this city to save it, for my own sake and for the sake of my servant David"

(2 Kings 19.34 = Isa 37.35). Moreover, unlike Ahaz, Hezekiah had apparently trusted in Yahweh rather than in Assyria and had also been faithful to the Deuteronomic program of reform, and Yahweh had rewarded him with deliverance.

At the same time, Hezekiah's revolt against Assyria and the subsequent invasion of Sennacherib inaugurated what in many respects was a dark age in the history of Judah. The kingdom would not recover for many decades, although the message of the prophets, especially of Isaiah, was preserved. That message linked continuing divine protection to observance of the covenant, and especially to social justice. Would Judah continue to heed the prophetic warnings and learn from the experience of the northern kingdom of Israel? That question would not be answered for another century.

IMPORTANT TERMS

Immanuel	Hezekiah's Tunnel	Syro-Ephraimite War
First Isaiah	Second Isaiah	Third Isaiah

QUESTIONS FOR REVIEW

1. Why is Hezekiah given such high praise in the book of Kings?
2. Describe the interactions between the prophet Isaiah and the kings of Judah.
3. How do the various biblical and nonbiblical accounts of the siege of Jerusalem by Sennacherib differ from each other, and what is the significance of those differences?

BIBLIOGRAPHY

For good summaries of the history of the period, see the concluding pages of the essay by Edward F. Campbell cited in the bibliography to Chapter 17 and the opening sections of Mordechai Cogan, "Into Exile: From the Assyrian Conquest of Israel to the Fall of Babylon," Chap. 7 in *The Oxford History of the Biblical World* (ed. M. D. Coogan; New York: Oxford University Press, 1998). An excellent summary and synthesis of the various sources for Sennacherib's campaign is found in Cogan and Tadmor, pp. 246–51 (see the bibliography to Chapter 17). For a minority view, which takes the biblical narrative more literally as describing two separate events, see A. Kirk Grayson, "Sennacherib," pp. 1088–89 in *Anchor Bible Dictionary*, Vol. 5 (ed. D. N. Freedman; New York: Doubleday, 1992).

For an introduction to the interpretation of the book of Isaiah, see Christopher R. Seitz, "Isaiah, Book of (First Isaiah)," pp. 472–88 in *Anchor Bible Dictionary*, Vol. 3 (ed. D. N. Freedman; New York: Doubleday, 1992). See also his *Isaiah 1–39* (Louisville: Westminster John Knox, 1993).

A good introduction to the book of Micah is Delbert R. Hillers, "Micah, Book of" pp. 807–10 in *Anchor Bible Dictionary*, Vol. 4 (ed. D. N. Freedman; New York: Doubleday, 1992).

JUDAH IN THE SEVENTH CENTURY BCE: THE END OF ASSYRIAN DOMINATION

2 Kings 21–23, 2 Chronicles 33–35, Zephaniah, Nahum, and the Prayer of Manasseh

At the beginning of the seventh century BCE, the Assyrian empire was approaching the pinnacle of its power, but by the end of the century the Assyrians had disappeared from the scene. In the jockeying that attended the collapse of the Assyrian empire, several states vied for dominance, and, as usual, Judah was caught in the balance. This was the era of two important Judean kings, Manasseh, Hezekiah's son and successor, a loyal Assyrian vassal, and Josiah, Manasseh's grandson, who took advantage of Assyrian weakness to once again assert Judah's independence and to carry out a religious reform.

HISTORY

Having disposed of the irritation posed by the rebellious Judean king Hezekiah and having regained control of Babylon, the Assyrians continued their drive toward imperial control of the entire Near East. They achieved this goal in 663 BCE when the Assyrian army captured the Egyptian capital of Thebes in Upper (southern) Egypt. Under the kings Esar-haddon (681–669) and Ashurbanipal (669–627), the Assyrian empire was at its peak. But, overextended, by the last

quarter of the seventh century BCE its decline was rapid. (See Figure 20.1.)

Egypt declared its independence from Assyria under Psammetichus I in 655 BCE, although relations between the two powers continued to be friendly. From the mid-seventh century BCE on outbreaks of unrest occurred in Babylon, Assyria's powerful southern subject. The principal catalyst for Assyria's demise was probably the death of Assurbanipal in 627. Because of internal struggles in the succession to Ashurbanipal, Assyrian central power was weak. Taking advantage of this, Nabopolassar, a general, assumed the throne of Babylon in 626, and by 620 had taken charge of all of Babylonia. Meanwhile, the Medes, from the region east of the Tigris, invaded central Assyria and soon allied themselves with Babylon. In 612 their combined forces attacked and looted Nineveh, the Assyrian capital.

Probably fearing a decrease in their own independence if the Babylonians succeeded in eliminating the now weakened Assyrians, the Egyptians intervened several times on the Assyrian side, but to no avail. All that remained was to complete the takeover of Assyrian territory, which the Babylonians accomplished in 609 BCE; we find no mention of Assyria as an imperial

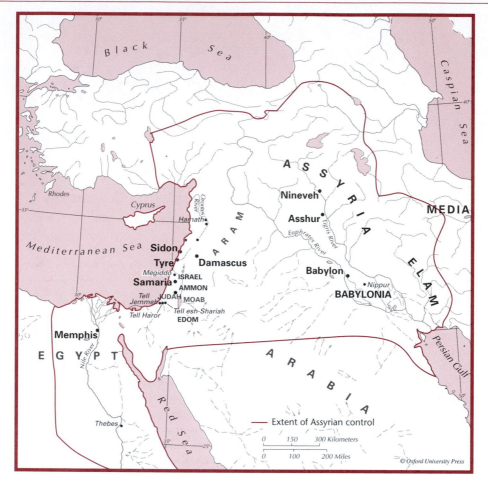

FIGURE 20.1.   Map of the Assyrian empire at its greatest extent in the first half of the seventh century BCE.

power after 608. In 605, the Egyptians, now fighting alone and probably seeking to extend their own sphere of control northward, challenged the Babylonians in Syria, but they were defeated soundly. The Assyrian empire had become the Neo-Babylonian empire, ruled first by Nabopolassar and then by his son and successor Nebuchadrezzar II (in the Bible also called Nebuchadnezzar; 605–562).

In Judah, Hezekiah's son Manasseh ruled for nearly five decades and seems to have been a loyal vassal of the Assyrian kings. Assyria's preoccupa-

tions elsewhere meant that after the mid-seventh century BCE Judah was essentially on its own. Following the brief reign of Amon, Josiah came to the throne and eventually, following the example of his great-grandfather Hezekiah in the previous century, decided to take advantage of Assyrian weakness and effectively declared his independence.

When the Egyptian army under Neco II was heading north, probably to assist the tottering Assyrians as well as to extend Egyptian control over the Levant, Josiah decided to try to block the ad-

Box 20.1 CHRONOLOGY OF THE SEVENTH CENTURY BCE

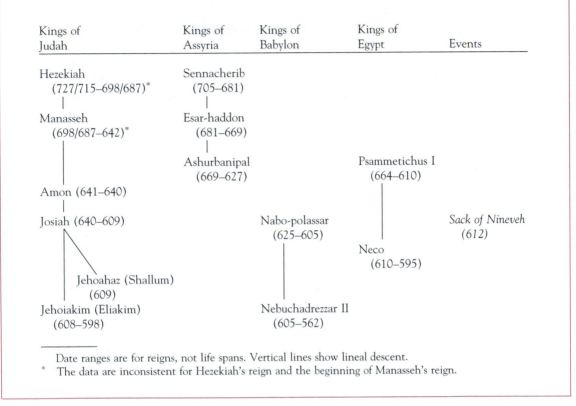

Kings of Judah	Kings of Assyria	Kings of Babylon	Kings of Egypt	Events
Hezekiah (727/715–698/687)*	Sennacherib (705–681)			
Manasseh (698/687–642)*	Esar-haddon (681–669)			
	Ashurbanipal (669–627)		Psammetichus I (664–610)	
Amon (641–640)				
Josiah (640–609)		Nabo-polassar (625–605)		*Sack of Nineveh (612)*
			Neco (610–595)	
Jehoahaz (Shallum) (609)				
Jehoiakim (Eliakim) (608–598)		Nebuchadrezzar II (605–562)		

Date ranges are for reigns, not life spans. Vertical lines show lineal descent.
* The data are inconsistent for Hezekiah's reign and the beginning of Manasseh's reign.

vancing Egyptian army and was killed, presumably in battle, at Megiddo in 609 BCE. Josiah's son Jehoahaz succeeded him, but after only three months Neco replaced him as king of Judah with another of Josiah's sons, Jehoiakim (Eliakim), who in effect became an Egyptian vassal.

It is symptomatic of the selective nature of our sources that the two great biblical histories of the Israelite monarchy, the books of Kings and Chronicles, make no mention of the great Assyrian king Ashurbanipal and that Assyrian and Egyptian records make no mention of Josiah. In fact, Assyrian sources become spotty as the empire disintegrates, and there is no mention of Ju-

dah in Assyrian sources after 643 BCE. (See Boxes 20.1 and 20.2.)

THE REIGN OF MANASSEH

Manasseh was king of Judah for nearly half a century, longer than any other ruler in the Davidic dynasty, yet for that long reign we have little documentation. The Deuteronomistic Historians dispose of it in a mere eighteen verses consisting largely of Deuteronomistic clichés (2 Kings 21.1–18), and their interest is almost entirely in condemning Manasseh's religious apostasy. From

Box 20.2 ASHURBANIPAL'S LIBRARY

The great Assyrian king Ashurbanipal had a fascination with the past, and during his forty-two-year reign he sponsored the collection and copying of older texts for his library at Nineveh. His aggressive acquisitions policy resulted in a carefully catalogued library of as many as twenty thousand tablets consisting of at least fifteen hundred different works. The collection included myths, such as *Enuma Elish* and *Gilgamesh*; hymns; prayers; and medical, mathematical, ritual, divinatory, and astrological texts, alongside all sorts of administrative documents, letters, and contracts. The discovery of these tablets in the mid-nineteenth century by Hormuzd Rassam, and their decipherment soon after, provided the modern world its first detailed glimpse of the languages and literature of ancient Mesopotamia, and their connections with biblical traditions soon became apparent (see pages 5–10, 15–17, and 40–41). It is tempting to see in Josiah's reform (see pages 353–55) the same sort of nostalgia that motivated Ashurbanipal to assemble his library.

the Deuteronomistic perspective, Manasseh was the worst of the kings of Judah, contrasting sharply with both his predecessor Hezekiah and his successor Josiah.

To this stereotypical and negative portrait of Manasseh the book of Chronicles provides some variation. According to it, Manasseh was arrested by the king of Assyria (2 Chr 33.11). While in prison he repented of his apostasy and was returned to his throne by divine intervention; from this point onward, the Chronicler asserts, Manasseh was a pious and model ruler (2 Chr 33.12–19). This story may have a historical basis; evidence can be found of other kings having been summoned to Assyria. For the Chronicler, however, this episode serves as an implicit explanation of Manasseh's long reign, which must have been the result of divine favor. The place of Manasseh's imprisonment was Babylon, and although that city was then under Assyrian control, its mention seems historically questionable. At any rate, Manasseh's detention in Babylon, his repentance, and his restoration to Judah are a kind of prototype for the experience of the nation as a

whole in the sixth century BCE. The additions in Chronicles to the account of Manasseh's reign serve as the basis for "The Prayer of Manasseh," an individual lament (see pages 461–63) composed late in the biblical period and included among the canonical books by most Eastern Orthodox churches (see Appendix).

It was during Manasseh's reign that Assyria's power was at its height, and he is twice mentioned in Assyrian sources as providing materials for the construction of a palace in the Assyrian capital at Nineveh and troops for the capture of the Egyptian capital at Thebes. Assyrian dominance over Judah is illustrated by the presence of Assyrian forts on the kingdom's southern boundary, at Tell Jemmeh (probably Arza), Tell esh-Shariah (Tel Sera; probably Ziklag), and Tel Haror (possibly Gerar).

Given the tendentious, and limited, character of the sources, it is difficult to know exactly what Manasseh's policies were. For the most part, he seems to have been a loyal Assyrian vassal. He also seems to have reversed many aspects of his father Hezekiah's religious reform, a reversal that may have been popular with his subjects. Most significant perhaps, is his survival: During his long reign we know of no attacks on Judah, and the dynasty remained secure. The era of Manasseh, then, was a period of relative calm, even if Judah's power was limited.

Manasseh was succeeded on the throne by his son Amon, whose brief two-year reign was cut short by a palace coup. According to the Deuteronomistic Historians, the conspirators themselves were killed by "the people of the land," who installed Amon's son Josiah on the throne (2 Kings 21.23–24).

THE REIGN OF JOSIAH

Josiah became king at the age of eight, in 640 BCE, and he ruled for some three decades. The account of Josiah's reign in the Deuteronomistic History (2 Kings 22.1–23.30) is almost entirely devoted to his religious reform, which it dates to the eighteenth year of his reign. According to 2 Chronicles 34.3, however, that reform began some years earlier, which may be a more accurate view.

According to 2 Kings 22, during repairs to the Temple, a "book"—more precisely, a scroll—was found in the Temple archives. This "book of the law" (2 Kings 22.8) inspired the king to begin a comprehensive reform. He restricted the worship of Yahweh to Jerusalem and purged the kingdom and especially the capital of the worship of gods other than Yahweh. This royal zeal extended into the territory of the former northern kingdom, the Assyrian province of Samaria (2 Kings 23.15–20). The reform was capped with a national celebration of the Passover.

Since the early nineteenth century, following the suggestion of the German scholar Wilhelm de Wette, the scroll found in the Temple has been identified as some form of the biblical book of Deuteronomy, a suggestion that had been made earlier by some medieval scholars as well. As we have seen (on pages 174–75), Deuteronomy has its own complicated history, but its origins lie in northern Israel, and an early form of the book probably was brought to Jerusalem with the

refugees from the Assyrian destruction of the northern kingdom in 722 BCE. There it served as the inspiration for the reform of Josiah's predecessor Hezekiah (see pages 328–29), and it is at least plausible that having been deposited in the Temple library it was forgotten or neglected during the period of Assyrian domination, the first three-quarters of the seventh century BCE. Having been discovered, whether by accident or by design, it reportedly inspired Josiah to undertake a reform; when hearing it read to him, he tore his clothes in the traditional sign of mourning, an appropriate reaction to the dire curses and punishments found in Deuteronomy (for example, chaps. 27–28).

Our primary source for Josiah's reform is 2 Kings 22–23, hardly an objective account. The books of Kings are part of the Deuteronomistic History, a product of the Deuteronomic school that interpreted Israel's history in the land in light of the principles laid down in Deuteronomy. Thus, in Deuteronomy, Moses commanded the Israelites to "do what is right in the eyes of the LORD" (Deut 13.18; see also 6.18; 12.25, 28; 21.9), and neither they nor their kings should "turn to the right or to the left" (Deut 5.32; see also 17.20; 28.14). Throughout the books of Kings, when they are measured against this standard, most rulers of both Israel and Judah fall short. A few kings of Judah are given qualified approval: These did "what was right in the eyes of Yahweh," but failed to remove the "high places" where illicit worship was carried out (1 Kings 15.11; 2 Kings 12.2; 14.3; 15.3–4, 34). Only two kings, Hezekiah and Josiah, are given unqualified approval by the Deuteronomistic Historians. As we have seen on pages 192–93 and 329, it is likely that the first edition of the Deuteronomistic History was produced during Hezekiah's reign. A second edition was produced during the reign of Josiah. For the Deuteronomistic Historians, like some of his predecessors, Josiah "did what was right in the eyes of the LORD" (2 Kings 22.2). But only of Josiah is it said that "he walked in all the way of his father David; he did not turn aside to the right or to the left" (2 Kings 22.2). Moreover, unlike most of his predecessors, Josiah destroyed the high places, in accord with Deuteronomic law. In fact, many of the details of Josiah's reform in 2 Kings 22–23 are phrased in language that recalls the laws of Deuteronomy.

For the Deuteronomists of Josiah's time, his reign was a climax. During it, Israel returned to the ideals of the teaching of Moses as promulgated in Deuteronomy. The Deuteronomistic History, in its major edition produced during Josiah's reign, begins with the book of Deuteronomy as a program: Israel's prosperity, even its survival, in the land of Canaan, is contingent upon its obedience to the teaching of Moses—his torah (see Box 11.2 on page 184). In that land, they are to observe the Passover and other festivals and to worship Yahweh, and Yahweh alone, at one central sanctuary. When they choose a king,

> he shall have a copy of this law written for him in the presence of the levitical priests. It shall remain with him and he shall read in it all the days of his life, so that he may learn to fear the LORD his God, diligently observing all the words of this law and these statutes, neither exalting himself above other members of the community nor turning aside from the commandment, either to the right or to the left, so that he and his descendants may reign long over his kingdom in Israel. (Deut 17.18–20)

Immediately after the book of Deuteronomy comes the book of Joshua, which shows how the program of Deuteronomy was to work: all Israel, united under one divinely designated leader, united in worship at a single divinely designated sanctuary, united in exclusive worship of Yahweh alone, united in observing the Passover, and united in warfare against its enemies. The character of Joshua himself is an ideal type that can be understood on one level as a prototype of Josiah.

The books of the Deuteronomistic History following Joshua—Judges, 1 and 2 Samuel, and 1 and 2 Kings—relate the successes and, mostly, failures of the Israelites to live up to this program. But the Deuteronomistic Historians of the late seventh century BCE present a paragon of fidelity to the teaching of Moses in King Josiah, "who turned to the LORD with all his heart, with all his soul, and with all his might" (2 Kings 23.25; compare 23.3; Deut 6.5; 11.13). According to the Deuteronomistic Historians, Josiah's coming had been foreseen by a prophet centuries before in an attack against the newly established sanctuary at Bethel: "O altar, altar, thus says the LORD: 'A son shall be born to the house of David, Josiah by name; and he shall sacrifice on you the priests of the high places who offer incense on you, and human bones shall be burned on you'" (1 Kings 13.2). This prophetic pronouncement is a major clue to the purpose and date of the Josianic edition of the Deuteronomistic History: It was written in support of Josiah's reform. It is thus a kind of propaganda, with a distinct theological bias. At the same time, as we have continually seen, the authors of the Deuteronomistic History are no mere ideologues: They are also historians, who often include information from sources that is inconsistent with their own perspective.

In this reform, we are told, the king had the support of the Temple priesthood, who may even have initiated the reform in an effort to centralize their own power. Support also came from the prophet Huldah, who predicted that because of his repentance the king would, in due course, die in peace (2 Kings 22.20). Her prediction proved wrong, but somewhat surprisingly was not revised in the light of Josiah's untimely end in battle against the Egyptian pharaoh Neco at Megiddo.

It is difficult to assess the actual historical importance of Josiah, since the primary textual source we have is the Deuteronomistic History. Archaeological data provide some further clues. We see considerable evidence of extensive building or refortifying key sites throughout Judah from the mid-seventh century BCE onward, suggesting that as Assyrian control diminished, the Judean monarchy began to extend its reach. This activity is especially evident on the kingdom's eastern and southern borders, as it was threatened by other states, which were also taking advantage of Assyrian weakness to expand their territories. A reasonable conclusion, then, is that although the Deuteronomistic Historians' account of Josiah's reign is exaggerated by their ideological program and perhaps shaped by memories of Hezekiah's earlier reform, it has some historical basis: Josiah took advantage of the brief interlude between Assyrian and Babylonian domination to extend Judah's control beyond the restricted borders that had been established early in the seventh century after the invasion of the Assyrian king Sennacherib.

Reflecting the perspective of the Deuteronomistic History, the second-century BCE writer Ben Sira remembered Josiah in this way:

> The name of Josiah is like blended incense
>   prepared by the skill of the perfumer;
> his memory is as sweet as honey to every mouth,
>   and like music at a banquet of wine.
> He did what was right by reforming the people,
>   and removing the wicked abominations.
> He kept his heart fixed on the Lord;
>   in lawless times he made godliness prevail.
> Except for David and Hezekiah and Josiah,
>   all of them were great sinners,
> for they abandoned the law of the Most High.
>   (Sir 49.1–4)

Josiah's reign ended in disaster, if not tragedy. When the Egyptian pharaoh Neco headed north, Josiah attempted to block his advance at the famous site of Megiddo (see Box 20.3), and in the battle he was killed, notwithstanding Huldah's prophecy. At his funeral, the Chronicler tells us:

> All Judah and Jerusalem mourned for Josiah. Jeremiah also uttered a lament for Josiah, and all the singing men and singing women have spoken of Josiah in their laments to this day. They made these a custom in Israel; they are recorded in the Laments. (2 Chr 35.24–25)

The prophet Jeremiah was a major figure during Josiah's reign and in the events that followed, and we will consider his role in the next chapter.

THE BOOK OF ZEPHANIAH

According to its editorial heading (1.1), the superscription, the prophet Zephaniah was active during the reign of Josiah. In his genealogy one of his ancestors was named Hezekiah, but whether this was the king of Judah with that name is not stated. Otherwise we know nothing about the prophet.

The book of Zephaniah, one of the "minor prophets," consists of a series of divine pronouncements of judgment on Judah and Jerusalem (1.4–2.3; 3.1–8) and on the nations (2.4–15), including Assyria (2.13–15). Like many of the prophetic books, Zephaniah concludes with a message of hope, when Zion's fortunes will be restored (3.9–20).

The book of Zephaniah makes use of a number of earlier prophetic themes and genres, including oracles against the nations (see pages 310–11) and a call to repentance. Zephaniah also contains a fully developed form of the motif of the "day of the LORD" (1.7, 14–18; see further Box 18.2 on page 316). As in Amos, that day will be a day of doom, primarily for Judah, but also for nations surrounding it, such as the Philistines (Zeph 2.3), and, in fact, for the whole world (1.18; compare 1.2–3). This is because Yahweh is the only god with power, and he will be universally recognized as such:

> The LORD . . . will shrivel all the gods of the earth,
>   and to him shall bow down, each from its place,
>   all the islands of the nations. (Zeph 2.11)

While this is not yet a fully developed strict monotheism, it continues the viewpoint of earlier prophets that Yahweh's domain extends far beyond Israel, in fact to the entire world.

The judgment on Judah is based on the now familiar prophetic critiques of false worship and social injustice. But this judgment is linked by its placement with that on the rest of the world; the oracles against the nations (2.4–15) are sandwiched between two condemnations of Judah and Jerusalem (1.4–2.3; 3.1–8). Especially shocking is the juxtaposition of Nineveh, Assyria's capital, with Jerusalem, Judah's capital. Both will be made desolate, for both rebelled against Yahweh's authority. Assyria boasted, "I am, and there is no one else" (2.15), and Jerusalem's leaders—its officials, prophets, and priests—were corrupt (3.3–4).

Zephaniah refers to various prohibited practices—worship of Baal and other deities (1.4–6)—and to more obscure rituals—"leaping over the threshold" (1.9). Although such apostasy and syncretism were supposedly abolished during Josiah's reform—and hence the activity of Zephaniah would be dated to early in Josiah's

Box 20.3 MEGIDDO AND ARMAGEDDON

Josiah's attempt to block the Egyptian advance in 609 BCE took place at **Megiddo**, a strategic site that defended a major pass from the coastal road to the interior (see Figure 20.2). Because of its location, many battles took place at Megiddo from ancient to modern times. In the mid-fifteenth century BCE, the Egyptian pharaoh Thutmoses III defeated a coalition of Canaanite kings there, and, according the Judges 5.19, it was at "the waters of Megiddo" that Israelites led by Deborah defeated "the kings of Canaan." More recently, Megiddo was the site of a decisive battle between British and Turkish forces for control of Palestine in 1918.

Because of the number of battles fought there, in the book of Revelation Megiddo, rendered as Armageddon (from the Hebr. *har Megiddo*, "mountain of Megiddo"), is made the site of the final eschatological battle between the forces of good and evil (Rev 16.16).

FIGURE 20.2.   Aerial view, looking west, of the impressive site of Megiddo, showing its strategic location.

reign—practices like these clearly continued, as their condemnation in Jeremiah and Ezekiel makes clear. At best, therefore, we can conclude that the substance of Zephaniah's oracles date to

the last few decades of the seventh century BCE. The absence of mention of Babylon, which by the end of the century was a major power, suggests a date earlier rather than later in that period.

The experience of the Babylonian exile gave occasion for a reapplication of the original message of the prophet to a new context, and the conclusion to the book of Zephaniah, a later addition, has close affinities with the literature of the late sixth century BCE, celebrating Jerusalem's restoration and the return of its exiles (see further Chapter 23).

THE BOOK OF NAHUM

The book of Nahum, some forty-eight verses in length, is one of the shortest of the minor prophets, and nothing is known about the prophet himself. As its title, "an oracle concerning Nineveh," suggests, it is devoted entirely to an attack on Assyria and especially its capital city, Nineveh, and is an expanded example of the oracle against the nations. It dates originally to the late seventh century BCE: It mentions the Assyrian conquest of Thebes, the capital of Egypt, which occurred in 663 BCE, and refers to the destruction of Nineveh, which occurred at the hands of the Medes and Babylonians in 612. The nucleus of the book reasonably can be dated shortly after, or perhaps shortly before, that event. Like other prophetic books, however, Nahum was revised in subsequent generations. It especially shows some connections with Second Isaiah; note, for example, Nahum 1.15 and Isaiah 40.9 and 52.7.

Adopting the general prophetic view that Yahweh is responsible for all events in history, the book opens with hymnic praise of Yahweh as the divine warrior whose dramatic theophany affects the entire cosmos (1.2–8). Then follow a confusing group of pronouncements, some of which apparently are directed against Assyria (1.9–2.2). The dominant section of the book is the detailed description of the sack of Nineveh (2.3–3.19). It captures in vivid detail the horror of ancient warfare, as in this somewhat free translation in the NRSV:

The crack of whip and rumble of wheel,
    galloping horse and bounding chariot!
Horsemen charging,
    flashing sword and glittering spear,
piles of dead,
    heaps of corpses,
dead bodies without end—
    they stumble over the bodies! (Nah 3.2–3)

The book of Nahum is a celebration of the fall of Assyria, a message of comfort for Israel, Judah, and others who had experienced the "endless cruelty" (3.19) of the Assyrians. It is thus a sustained and unrelieved expression of intense nationalism, without any ethical nuances. In Nahum, as C. S. Lewis observed of the psalms, "the spirit of hatred which strikes us in the face is like the heat from a furnace mouth." Indeed, in Nahum, as in many of the psalms, we find an intensity of hatred of the enemy, by which the audience is to be "comforted," for that is the meaning of Nahum's name.

RETROSPECT AND PROSPECT

Since the mid-eighth century BCE Judah had survived Assyria's imperial control over the Near East. Unlike most other kingdoms in the region, it had managed to maintain a quasi-independence, and the dynasty founded by David continued to rule in Jerusalem, which also escaped conquest and destruction. And now Assyria itself had been destroyed. For many, the defeat of their enemy and their own survival seemed to confirm the royal ideology, according to which Yahweh had chosen the dynasty, and that both it and its capital, which he had made his own home, would be secure forever.

In the next few decades, however, swiftly moving events would prove that optimism wrong. For the prophets as for the Deuteronomistic Historians, all that happened was ultimately Yahweh's doing; the problem was that the divine intentions were not always easy to decipher.

IMPORTANT TERM

Megiddo

QUESTIONS FOR REVIEW

1. What effects did the collapse of the Assyrian empire have on Judah?

2. What were the political and religious components of Josiah's reform? How were they related?

BIBLIOGRAPHY

For commentaries on 2 Kings, see the bibliography to Chapter 17. For a summary of the history of the period, see Mordechai Cogan, chap. 7 in *The Oxford History of the Biblical World* (ed. M. D. Coogan; New York; Oxford University Press, 1998).

The classic statement of the arguments for a Josianic edition of the Deuteronomistic History is by Frank Moore Cross, "The Themes of the Book of Kings and the Structure of the Deuteronomistic History," pp. 274–89 in *Canaanite Myth and Hebrew Epic: Essays in the History of the Religion of Israel* (Cambridge, MA: Harvard University Press, 1973).

A good recent commentary on Zephaniah is that by Adele Berlin, *Zephaniah* (New York: Doubleday, 1994).

An excellent brief commentary on Nahum is Peter Machinist, "Nahum," pp. 665–67 in *The HarperCollins Bible Commentary* (ed. J. L. Mays; San Francisco: Harper-SanFrancisco, 1998).

THE FALL OF JERUSALEM

*2 Kings 23.31–25.30, 2 Chronicles 36, Habakkuk,
Jeremiah, and the Letter of Jeremiah*

The momentum of the forces leading to Judah's destruction increased. The circumscribed kingdom where the Davidic monarchy still ruled was caught up in larger struggles, between a dying Assyria, a resurgent Egypt, and a rising Babylon, and Judah would inevitably be the loser. Just over two decades after the untimely death in 609 BCE of King Josiah, in whom so much hope had been placed, the dynasty founded by David over four hundred years earlier came to an end and Jerusalem and its Temple had been destroyed, all at the hands of the Babylonians (see Box 21.1). Because these events were so significant, it is not surprising that the Bible preserves a number of perspectives on them, not just in 2 Kings and 2 Chronicles, but also in the books of Jeremiah and Ezekiel, both of whom were participants in the events, and elsewhere throughout biblical tradition, for example, in the book of Lamentations and some of the psalms. In the next several chapters we will examine the events themselves and the varied reactions and responses to them.

HISTORY

With the final defeat of the Assyrians and their Egyptian allies in the battle of Carchemish in 605

BCE, the Babylonians under Nabo-polassar's successor Nebuchadrezzar II (604–562) moved quickly to contain Egypt, which was attempting to regain control over the Levant. In 604 they captured the strategic city of Ashkelon, near Egypt's northern border, and in 601 moved farther south. From this point onward, Egypt was neutralized and largely restricted to its own borders, although unlike the Assyrians, the Babylonians never succeeded in conquering Egypt (see Figure 21.1).

In Judah, the three-month reign of Josiah's successor Jehoahaz ended when the Egyptian pharaoh Neco replaced him with his brother, Eliakim (608–598 BCE), whose throne name was Jehoiakim, probably given him by the Egyptians as a symbol of their control (see Box 21.2). Jehoiakim was at first a loyal Egyptian vassal, but when the Babylonians attacked the Egyptian frontier, he became a Babylonian vassal. When the Babylonians withdrew, however, Jehoiakim rebelled against the king of Babylon, refusing to pay the requisite tribute. As Nebuchadrezzar was preparing to reassert his control over Judah, Jehoiakim died and was succeeded by his son Jehoiachin, a confusingly similar name.

Jehoiachin was king in 597 BCE, during the first Babylonian siege of Jerusalem, which ended with

Box 21.1 CHRONOLOGY OF THE LATE SEVENTH AND EARLY SIXTH CENTURIES BCE

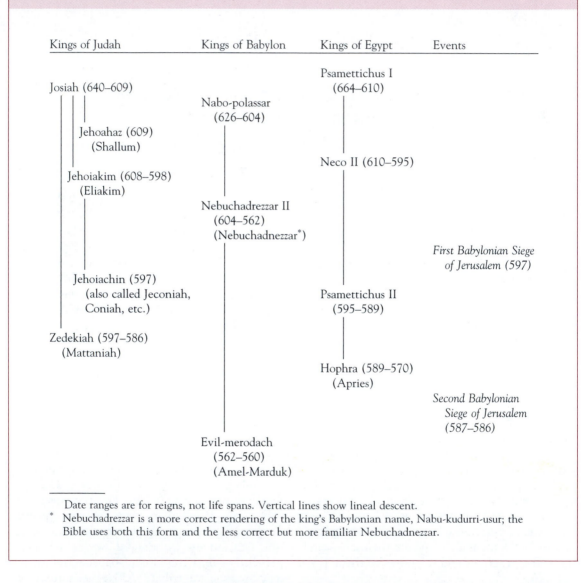

Kings of Judah	Kings of Babylon	Kings of Egypt	Events
		Psammetichus I (664–610)	
Josiah (640–609)	Nabo-polassar (626–604)		
Jehoahaz (609) (Shallum)			
Jehoiakim (608–598) (Eliakim)		Neco II (610–595)	
	Nebuchadrezzar II (604–562) (Nebuchadnezzar*)		
			First Babylonian Siege of Jerusalem (597)
Jehoiachin (597) (also called Jeconiah, Coniah, etc.)		Psammetichus II (595–589)	
Zedekiah (597–586) (Mattaniah)			
		Hophra (589–570) (Apries)	
			Second Babylonian Siege of Jerusalem (587–586)
	Evil-merodach (562–560) (Amel-Marduk)		

Date ranges are for reigns, not life spans. Vertical lines show lineal descent.
* Nebuchadrezzar is a more correct rendering of the king's Babylonian name, Nabu-kudurri-usur; the Bible uses both this form and the less correct but more familiar Nebuchadnezzar.

his surrender and subsequent exile to Babylon along with, we are told, several thousand of the elite. The Babylonians apparently ransacked the Temple and royal treasuries but did not destroy the city, and Nebuchadrezzar appointed another

son of Josiah, Mattaniah, as king, renaming him Zedekiah.

Like Hezekiah and Josiah with Assyria, and his more immediate predecessor Jehoiakim, Zedekiah asserted his independence from Babylon, proba-

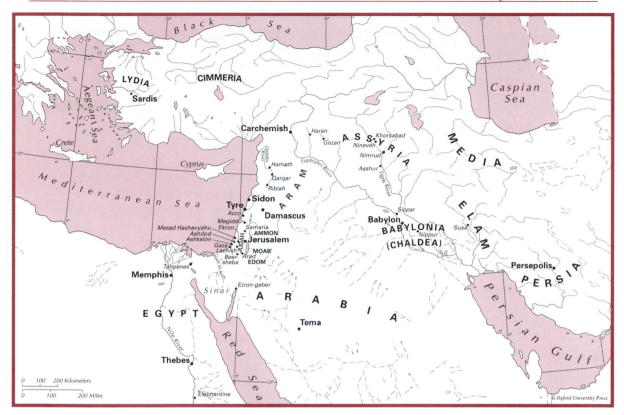

FIGURE 21.1.   Map of the Neo-Babylonian empire.

bly around 590 BCE, perhaps encouraged by other small states in the region (see Jer 27.3). Babylonian reprisal was swift. In 587 Nebuchadrezzar's army laid siege to Jerusalem again. The Babylonian attack on the city was joined by a number of now loyal vassal states of Babylon in the Levant, including Aram, Moab, Ammon, and Edom. In the summer of 586, weakened by famine, the city fell. The king was captured as he fled and was taken as a prisoner to Babylon. The royal quarter was razed, and more of the elite were deported.

For most of this history our primary sources are biblical, especially the Deuteronomistic History in the book of Kings and the book of Jeremiah, both of which we will examine in detail later in this chapter; further information is provided by references in Ezekiel and Chronicles. Nonbiblical textual sources are scant and fragmentary. The

most important is the "Babylonian Chronicles," cuneiform tablets that give annalistic accounts of the reigns of Babylonian rulers in the late seventh and sixth centuries BCE. The relevant tablet dealing with the reign of Nebuchadrezzar describes his conquest of Ashkelon in 604 BCE, and also his attack on Jerusalem in 597: "Year 7: The king . . . encamped against the city of Judah, and on the second of Adar, he captured the city and he seized its king. A king of his choice he appointed there; he took heavy tribute and carried it off to Babylon."* The corresponding section dealing with the second attack on Jerusalem in 587–586 is missing. Finally, broken tablets found in the ruins of Nebuchadrezzar's palace in Babylon list rations delivered to various captives under a kind of house arrest, including Jehoiachin, who is called "king of Judah," and his five sons.

---

* Trans. M. Cogan and H. Tadmor p. 340 in II Kings (New York: Doubleday, 1988).

Box 21.2 THRONE NAMES OF KINGS OF JUDAH

Several kings of Judah are identified as having throne names in addition to the names given them at birth, much as in the Roman Catholic Church, a pope assumes a different name after he has been elected. When Eliakim is appointed king by the pharaoh Neco, "Neco changed his name to Jehoiakim" (2 Kings 23.34), and when Nebuchadrezzar appointed Mattaniah as king in place of Jehoiachin, "he changed his name to Zedekiah" (2 Kings 24.17). It is possible to interpret these name changes as expressions of a suzerain's control over the vassal whom he had just appointed, but evidence exists that at least some of the earlier kings of Judah also had throne names. Both Jehoiakim and Zedekiah were sons of Josiah, like their predecessor Jehoahaz, whose name is also given as Shallum (Jer 22.11; 1 Chr 3.15). In the eighth century BCE, Uzziah's birth name is apparently Azariah. Finally, it is possible that Solomon was also a throne name; at birth the prophet Nathan named him Jedidiah (2 Sam 12.25). (Other variations in royal names, such as Ahaziah/Jehoahaz, Joram/Jehoram, Joash/Jehoash, and Jehoiachin/Jeconiah/Coniah, are simply alternate spellings.)

Excavated sites also provide considerable evidence for the events of this period. Nebuchadrezzar's campaign to the south in 604 BCE caused massive destruction levels at important coastal cities, notably Ashkelon. Excavations at Lachish show a refortification of the city ruined by the Assyrian king Sennacherib in 701; this city (called Level II) was destroyed in the Babylonian campaign of 587–586. Among the ruins of the gate of this level were a number of inscribed potsherds, or ostraca, known as the Lachish letters. One of them contains this poignant message sent to the Judean garrison at Lachish from an unnamed location: "May (my lord) know that we are watching for the fire-signals of Lachish, according to all the signs which my lord has given, for we can no longer see (the signals of) Azekah." This correlates nicely with Jeremiah 34.6–7, which describes the situation shortly before the letter was sent:

> Then the prophet Jeremiah spoke all these words to Zedekiah king of Judah, in Jerusalem, when the army

of the king of Babylon was fighting against Jerusalem and against all the cities of Judah that were left, Lachish and Azekah; for these were the only fortified cities of Judah that remained.

The letter implies that Azekah has already been captured. Jerusalem, too, shows evidence of destruction in 586, including a widespread layer of ashes among which were found arrowheads both of the Judean defenders of the city and of its attackers (see Figure 21.2).

The Last Kings of Judah

Three of the last four kings of Judah were sons of Josiah; the other, Jehoiachin, was his grandson. The first, Jehoahaz (also called Shallum), was deposed after a rule of only three months by Pharaoh Neco, who replaced him with his brother Jehoiakim (originally Eliakim; see Box 21.2). Jehoiakim was first a vassal of Egypt, but after 604 BCE he switched his allegiance to Babylon. When he tried to assert his independence, Nebucha-

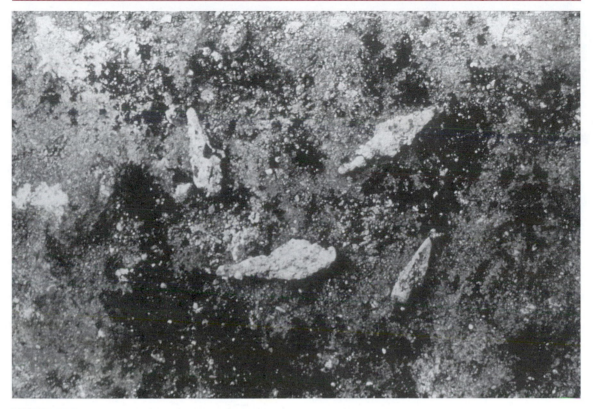

FIGURE 21.2. A layer of ashes from the Babylonian destruction of Jerusalem in 586 BCE (see 2 Kings 25.9). These remains, found adjacent to the city's fortifications, include arrowheads of two types: one used by the attackers of the city on the upper left and three of local origin, used in vain by the city's defenders.

drezzar prepared to retaliate, but before he actually attacked, Jehoiakim died. Although the book of Kings devotes only a few verses to Jehoiakim's reign, it receives more attention in the book of Jeremiah. There he is depicted as a king

> who builds his house by unrighteousness,
>   and his upper rooms by injustice;
> who makes his neighbors work for nothing,
>   and does not give them their wages,
> who says, "I will build myself a spacious house
>   with large upper rooms,"
> and who cuts out windows for it,
>   paneling it with cedar,
>   and painting it with vermilion. (Jer 22.13–14)

Jehoiakim's character is revealed further in the famous passage in Jeremiah in which the king systematically burns the papyrus scroll on which

Baruch, Jeremiah's scribe, had written down the prophet's words (Jer 36.22–25). The contrast between Jehoiakim's reaction to hearing a scroll read and that of his father Josiah is striking. When Josiah "heard the words of the book of the law, he tore his clothes" (2 Kings 22.11); in the case of Jehoiakim however, "neither the king, nor any of his servants who heard all these words, was alarmed, nor did they tear their clothes" (Jer 36.24).

Jehoiakim died in 598 BCE and was succeeded by his son and Josiah's grandson Jehoiachin. During Jehoiachin's brief reign of three months in 597 Nebuchadrezzar launched his first attack on Judah proper, laying siege to Jerusalem and taking into captivity in Babylon the king, the queen mother, and a large number of the royal establishment, some ten thousand persons in all (2 Kings 24.12, 14; somewhat different numbers are given in 2 Kings 24.15–16 and in Jer 52.28). Among those deported among the priests was the prophet Ezekiel (see pages 386–87). The resources of the Temple treasury were also used to pay tribute. In place of Jehoiachin, Nebuchadrezzar installed his uncle, Josiah's son Mattaniah, as king, and gave him the throne name Zedekiah.

Zedekiah was the last of the Davidic dynasty to rule, and his reign lasted for eleven years. His status as king may have been compromised by the presence of his nephew and predecessor in Babylon, since for some biblical writers, at least, Jehoiachin was still considered the legitimate king. The Deuteronomistic Historians end their account of Israel's history in the Promised Land not with a description of Zedekiah's situation in Babylon but with this surprising notice:

> In the thirty-seventh year of the exile of King Jehoiachin of Judah, in the twelfth month, on the twenty-seventh day of the month, King Evilmerodach of Babylon, in the year that he began to reign, released King Jehoiachin of Judah from prison; he spoke kindly to him, and gave him a seat above the other seats of the kings who were with him in Babylon. So Jehoiachin put aside his prison clothes. Every day of his life he dined regularly in the king's presence. For his allowance, a regular allowance was given him by the king, a portion every day, as long as he lived. (2 Kings 25.27–30)

Ezekiel, too, dates his inaugural vision as with reference to "the fifth year of the exile of King Jehoiachin" (Ezek 1.2). As we will see (on page 387), Ezekiel's prophetic ministry took place entirely in Babylon, and so it is possible that at least among the exiles in Babylon Jehoiachin continued to be thought of as the legitimate ruler. Zedekiah, then, may not have had full support from his subjects.

At first Zedekiah was a loyal vassal of the Babylonians, but at some point, probably around 590 BCE, with the support of the neighboring states of Edom, Moab, Ammon, Tyre, and Sidon (see Jer 27.3), he stopped paying tribute to Nebuchadrezzar. Neither he nor his advisors had learned from the failed rebellion of his predecessor Jehoiakim or from the earlier rebellion of Hezekiah against the Assyrians. The Babylonians retaliated with a full-scale attack on Jerusalem. After a lengthy siege, the city was captured and burned, and Zedekiah was taken prisoner and sent to Babylon. This was the end of the Davidic dynasty.

The Fall of Jerusalem

The fullest version of the Deuteronomistic Historians' account of the fall of Jerusalem is in Jeremiah 52, a more detailed version than that in 2 Kings 24.18–25.30 and Jeremiah 39. The account opens with a formulaic summary of the reign of Zedekiah and the judgment of the Deuteronomistic Historians on him: "He did what was evil in the eyes of the LORD, just as Jehoiakim had done. Indeed, Jerusalem and Judah so angered the LORD that he expelled them from his presence" (Jer 52.2–3 = 2 Kings 24.19–20). From the perspective of the Deuteronomistic Historians, the fall of Jerusalem was a deserved punishment for the sins of the king and of the nation as a whole. But how precisely did Yahweh punish them? The account continues with a straightforward narrative of the city's siege, capture, and destruction, which begins with a succinct statement of the proximate cause: "Zedekiah rebelled against the king of Babylon" (Jer 52.3 = 2 Kings 24.20). This juxtaposition of theological and historical perspectives is reminiscent of that found for the invasion of Sennacherib during the reign of Hezekiah (2 Kings 18.13–16; 18.17–19.37; see further pages 339–44).

The actual account of Jerusalem's siege and destruction is selective in its details. The siege lasted a year and a half. Finally, with the city suffering from famine, the army and the king fled, heading east toward Jericho and the fords of the Jordan River, probably intending to take refuge in Transjordan. The Deuteronomistic History begins with the Israelites under Joshua's leadership crossing the Jordan from the east and with divine help conquering Jericho. Now the Deuteronomistic Historians, in a literary irony, depict Zedekiah, the last ruler of the Davidic dynasty, moving in the opposite direction and being captured by the Babylonians in the vicinity of Jericho.

Zedekiah's sons were executed at Nebuchadrezzar's headquarters in Syria. Like their imperial predecessors the Assyrians (see Isa 36), the Babylonians must have been aware of the propaganda of the Davidic dynasty; elimination of the heirs to the throne would end the notion of divinely granted eternal rule. Then Zedekiah was blinded, so that the last sight of the last descendant of David to sit on the throne was the execution of his own sons. Finally he was taken in chains to Babylon.

The plundering of the Temple and its furnishings by the Babylonians is described in considerable detail, poignantly recalling the lengthy account of their construction and manufacture during Solomon's reign (1 Kings 6–7). Much of Jerusalem's population was also taken to Babylon, joining those who had been deported in 597 BCE. Some were allowed to remain in Judah, however, and tension between them and the Babylonian exiles would become a significant problem in subsequent decades.

The Deuteronomistic History ends on an ambiguous note. On the one hand, Jerusalem and its Temple have been destroyed. Yet, we are told, one of the descendants of David, Jehoiachin, was released from captivity and, although still in Babylon, was called "king" (2 Kings 25.27). It is unclear if we are to interpret this as a faint expression of hope for the survival of the Davidic monarchy from the final editors of the Deuteronomistic History or if it is simply an endnote.

THE BOOK OF HABAKKUK

The short book of Habakkuk is one of the books of the Minor Prophets, placed between Nahum and Zephaniah, a location that along with later traditions suggests a date during the early Babylonian period. This is a hypothesis because, unlike most other prophetic books, Habakkuk has no superscription providing information about the prophet and when he lived. But Habakkuk 1.6 does refer to the rise of Chaldeans, another

term for the Babylonians. Since the book makes no explicit mention of the attacks on Jerusalem or the exile of its inhabitants to Babylon in 597 and 586 BCE, it probably dates to the Babylonian campaign at the end of the seventh century BCE.

The book is formally divided into two parts, "the oracle that the prophet Habakkuk saw" in chapters 1–2, and "a prayer of the prophet Habakkuk" in chapter 3. The first part is a dialogue between the prophet and Yahweh, in which prophetic laments about the violence being done to the righteous (1.2–4; 1.12–2.1) alternate with divine responses (1.5–11; 2.2–19). These conclude with five curses on the Babylonians, who are apparently responsible for the suffering that has occurred, although they are not explicitly named.

The third chapter of the book is a hymn describing in archaic mythological language the triumph of Yahweh as the divine warrior. It is reminiscent of such earlier Israelite poems as Exodus 15, Judges 5, and Psalm 18, but whether it is a truly ancient poem added to the "oracle of Habakkuk" or a late monarchical imitation of archaic poetry is disputed. The hymn celebrates the awe-inspiring divine appearance, which causes upheaval in nature; from it the author takes heart, for even in the midst of disaster God provides ultimate victory.

Nothing is known about the prophet Habakkuk himself, but later legends developed about him. In the apocryphal addition to the book of Daniel called "Bel and the Dragon" (see page 540), the prophet Habakkuk is miraculously transported from Judea to bring a bowl of stew to Daniel, who is in the lions' den in Babylon (Bel 33–39), and in a first-century CE writing called "The Lives of the Prophets," Habakkuk's journey to and return from Babylon is interpreted as a sign of the return of the exiles. One of the best preserved of the Dead Sea Scrolls (see Box 29.2 on page 508), is a "pesher," or verse-by-verse commentary, on Habakkuk from the first century BCE, which interprets the first two chapters of the book as a detailed prediction of the early history of the Essene community in the second century BCE and the conflict between its leader, the "teacher of righteousness," and the Jerusalem establishment, led by the "wicked priest," as well as of the conquest of Palestine by the Romans, called the "Kittim," in 63 BCE.

JEREMIAH

The Book of Jeremiah

Placed after the book of Isaiah, probably because the three longest prophetic books are arranged in chronological order, the book of Jeremiah also shows evidence of a complicated literary history. We find repetitions (see, for example, Jer 7.1–15 and 26.1–9, and Jer 39 and 52) as well as a bewildering variation among ancient texts, almost as if Jeremiah were a work in progress to which later generations felt free to add their own touches, adding new and rearranging existing material. A significant difference in length and in arrangement is seen between the traditional Hebrew text (the Masoretic Text) and the ancient Greek translation (the Septuagint). The Greek is one-eighth shorter than the Masoretic Text, and the second half of the book has a very different arrangement in the two textual traditions. These differences are also found in fragments of different Hebrew manuscripts of Jeremiah among the Dead Sea Scrolls. The complicated literary history of the book may be an indirect reflection of the chaos of the time, but it also reveals a kind of open-ended understanding of a "book." Rather than being a finished composition, it was rather something like a hypertext, which subsequent authors and editors felt free to revise and to expand. The same process can be detected in other biblical books, notably the book of Job (see pages 480–83).

Contents

In the version of the book of Jeremiah found in the traditional Hebrew text (followed by the NRSV and most other translations), the contents of the book can be summarized as follows:

- *Chapters 1–25*: The nucleus of the collection, consisting largely of poetic oracles directed against Judah, Jerusalem, its inhabitants, and its rulers. Many scholars have identified this collection, which is substantially the same in the Septuagint, as the "first scroll" that Jeremiah dictated to Baruch (see Jer 36.4 and Box 21.5 on page 376). The reference to "everything written in this book" (25.13) near the end of this section may imply that it originally stood alone. The section begins with the usual editorial introduction, the superscription (1.1–3), and a lengthy account of the call of the prophet and his inaugural visions (1.4–19), which serves as a kind of overture to the book as a whole, introducing themes and vocabulary that will recur often (see further page 370). The material that follows appears to have no clear order, but is an almost random assortment of oracles of judgment and laments, interspersed with prose narratives and speeches.

- *Chapters 26–29*: Several dated prose narratives of encounters between Jeremiah and various members of the establishment, especially other prophets.

- *Chapters 30–33*: "The book of consolation." Like many of the earlier prophets, the book of Jeremiah contains passages of hope and comfort for the future. Much of this section has affinities with the later sixth-century BCE oracles of Second Isaiah (see pages 408–14).

- *Chapters 34–45*: More prose narratives, mostly dated to the reign of Zedekiah and after the fall of Jerusalem in 586 BCE.

- *Chapters 46–51*: Oracles against the nations. As in Amos, Isaiah, and Ezekiel, these oracles against foreign nations (see pages 310–11) are clustered together. The nations that are the subjects of the oracles are Egypt (chap. 46), Philistia (47), Moab (48), Ammon (49.1–6), Edom (49.7–22), Aram-Damascus (49.23–27), the Transjordanian Arabian tribes of Kedar and Hazor (49.28–33), Elam (49.34–39), and Babylon (50–51). Some of the material in these oracles is formulaic: The oracle against Edom also contains verses similar to verses in Obadiah (compare Jer 49.9 and Obad 5; Jer

49.14–16 and Obad 1–4; see further page 386), and parts of the oracle against Moab are similar to that in Isaiah 15–16. Moreover, some material in Jeremiah is repeated elsewhere in the book; for example, parts of the prose section of the oracle against Edom (49.19–21) are also found in that against Babylon (50.44–46). At the same time, however, Jeremiah modifies the traditional genre to take into account the events of the late seventh and early sixth centuries BCE. The longest oracles of this genre in the book are against those nations that most affected Judah during the tumultuous events of that period, namely Egypt, Edom, and Babylon.

- *Chapter 52*: An appendix to the book, taken from the Deuteronomistic History (see 2 Kings 24.18–25.30), that narrates the fall of Jerusalem and its aftermath.

Since the early twentieth century, commentators on the book of Jeremiah have identified three major types of material in it: poetic oracles, often thought to have been composed by Jeremiah himself (designated Source A), biographical narratives about the prophet, perhaps by his scribe Baruch (Source B), and later Deuteronomistic editing and expansion, often in the form of prose discourses attributed to the prophet (Source C). Recently, however, scholars have been less confident that any of this disparate material can be directly linked to the prophet himself.

Jeremiah and the Deuteronomists

It is clear that the Deuteronomic school edited the book of Jeremiah, as it did other prophetic books. The account of Zedekiah's reign and of the Babylonian capture of Jerusalem in Jeremiah 52 essentially duplicates that of the Deuteronomistic Historians in 2 Kings 25, much as the account of Hezekiah's reign in 2 Kings 18–20 is reproduced in Isaiah 36–39. Because Jeremiah was a contemporary of Josiah and of his reform, which was inspired by the Deuteronomic school (see page 183), it is not surprising that we find pronounced

connections between the book of Jeremiah and the Deuteronomic school.

Throughout the book of Jeremiah we find phrasing characteristic of the book of Deuteronomy, especially in the prose oracles (Source C). Thus, for example, Egypt was an "iron furnace" (Deut 4.20; Jer 11.4); the mighty hand and outstretched arm of Yahweh that had brought Israel out of Egypt (see Deut 4.34; 5.15; Jer 32.21) are now directed against Jerusalem (Jer 21.5) because in the land that Yahweh gave them to inherit (Deut 12.10; Jer 3.18; 12.14), they have "gone after other gods" (Deut 6.14; 8.19; Jer 7.6; 11.10; 13.10) "under every green tree" (Deut 12.2; Jer 2.20) and have listened to prophets who spoke what Yahweh had not revealed (Deut 18.20; Jer 29.23). The same overarching theological perspective on divine justice, or theodicy, is also found in both books: Israel's continued control of the Promised Land depends upon its observance of the torah, the teaching of Moses, and failure to do so will inevitably result in divinely inflicted punishment, including exile.

At the same time, however, while using Deuteronomic language, Jeremiah seems to articulate a kind of disillusionment with the failure of Josiah's reform that had been inspired by the Deuteronomic movement: "Judah did not return to me with her whole heart, but only in pretense" (Jer 3.10). As a consequence, the language of Deuteronomy is ironically reversed. Deuteronomy had offered a choice:

> See, I have set before you today life and prosperity, death and adversity. If you obey the commandments of the LORD your God that I am commanding you today, by loving the LORD your God, walking in his ways, and observing his commandments, decrees, and ordinances, then you shall live and become numerous, and the LORD your God will bless you in the land that you are entering to possess. But if your heart turns away and you do not hear, but are led astray to bow down to other gods and serve them, I declare to you today that you shall perish; you shall not live long in the land that you are crossing the Jordan to enter and possess. I call heaven and earth to witness against you today that I have set before you life and death, blessings and curses. Choose life so that you and your descendants may live, loving the LORD your

> God, obeying him, and holding fast to him; for that means life to you and length of days, so that you may live in the land that the LORD swore to give to your ancestors, to Abraham, to Isaac, and to Jacob. (Deut 30.15–20)

But because of Israel's failure to keep the divinely given commandments, the choice between blessing and curse, between life and death, is now reduced to a matter of survival:

> Thus says the LORD: See, I am setting before you the way of life and the way of death. Those who stay in this city shall die by the sword, by famine, and by pestilence; but those who go out and surrender to the Chaldeans who are besieging you shall live and shall have their lives as a prize of war. For I have set my face against this city for evil and not for good, says the LORD: it shall be given into the hands of the king of Babylon, and he shall burn it with fire. (Jer 21.8–10)

The Life of Jeremiah

According to the book's superscription (1.1–3), Jeremiah's long career lasted from the thirteenth year of Josiah (627 BCE) to the fall of Jerusalem in 586; the second half of the book also contains explicit references to the last four kings of Judah (see, for example, 21.1 [Zedekiah]; 22.11 [Shallum (Jehoahaz)]; 22.18 [Jehoiakim]; 22.24 [Coniah (Jehoiachin)]), as well as to events in the life of the prophet during their reigns (for example, 24.1; 25.1; 26.1; 27.1). The superscription also tells us that he was from a small village a few miles north of Jerusalem, Anathoth, and that he was a priest.

Until the late twentieth century, a majority of scholars used the many narrative and historical details in the book to construct a biography of the "historical Jeremiah." More recently it has seemed to many that while biography is surely one intention of the book, the prophet is more a literary character in the book than an actual historical person. A middle ground is perhaps the best course. While it is probably futile to try to reconstruct from the book's detailed notices an exact chronology of the prophet's life and of the oracles themselves, it is unnecessarily skeptical to

conclude that nothing about the prophet is historically accurate.

Jeremiah's existence is beyond question, as is the fact that he lived in the tumultuous times of the late seventh and early sixth centuries BCE. Like Isaiah, he was involved deeply in the politics of his day and apparently paid a high price: ridicule, rejection, persecution, imprisonment, and exile. At the same time, the literary character of Jeremiah personifies the sufferings of the inhabitants of Judah and Jerusalem during the final years of the Davidic monarchy, and, perhaps, especially of the minority who disagreed with the last kings of Judah in their rebellion against the Babylonians and their failure to continue the Deuteronomic reform. He may be compared to the character of Socrates in the Dialogues of Plato, in which the historical person of Socrates becomes a literary character who serves as a vehicle for expressing Plato's ideas. (See also Box 21.3.)

An example of the complex relationship between (auto)biography and history is the account of the prophet's call in Jeremiah 1. This first-person account, placed appropriately at the beginning of the book, narrates a dialogue between Yahweh and Jeremiah. Yahweh announces to the prophet that he had been chosen as a "prophet to the nations" from before birth. The prophet objects, claiming inability to speak because of his youth. Yahweh replies with a mild rebuke:

> Do not say, "I am only a boy";
>   for you shall go to all to whom I send you,
>   and you shall speak whatever I command you.
> Do not be afraid of them, for I am with you to deliver you. (Jer 1.7–8).

Then Yahweh touches Jeremiah on the mouth, and says:

> Now I have put my words in your mouth.
> See, today I appoint you over nations and over kingdoms,
>   to pluck up and to pull down,
>   to destroy and to overthrow,
>   to build and to plant. (Jer 1.9–20)

This "call" is followed by two visions, which Yahweh interprets for the prophet. The first

Box 21.3 JEREMIAH IN POSTBIBLICAL TRADITION

The figure of Jeremiah features prominently in later tradition. Details concerning the end of his life are found not only in the book of Jeremiah but also in various apocryphal books. One of these additions to Jeremiah's biography concerns the ark of the covenant, the primary religious object of ancient Israel that had been enshrined in the innermost room of the Temple built by Solomon (see pages 126–28 and 274–77). The ark is mentioned in the prophetic books only in Jeremiah 3.16; there, in an oracle of restoration, Yahweh speaks of the return to Zion, but without the ark:

> And when you have multiplied and increased in the land, in those days, says the LORD, they shall no longer say, "The ark of the covenant of the LORD." It shall not come to mind, or be remembered, or missed; nor shall another one be made.

But what happened to the ark in 586 BCE? According to one tradition, Jeremiah removed it from the Temple before the destruction of Jerusalem. Drawing perhaps on the absence of the ark in the account of the looting of the Temple by the Babylonian army (2 Kings 25.13–17; Jer 52.17–23), the authors of 2 Maccabees, a work written about 100 BCE (see further pages 510–11), report that ancient records tell of the prophet taking the tent and the ark to Mount Nebo, "where Moses had gone up and seen the inheritance of God" (2 Macc 2.4; compare Deut 34.1–6). In a cave there Jeremiah deposited the sacred objects and sealed its entrance, declaring "The place shall remain unknown until God gathers his people together again and shows his mercy" (2 Macc 2.7). From time to time various explorers have gone in search of the "lost ark," but none have ever recovered it, except in the movies.

In a variant legend, found in a late first-century CE apocalyptic writing called 2 Baruch, an angel removes the ark (called "the mercy seat"; see page 127) and other sacred objects from the Temple before other angels set Jerusalem ablaze. The sacred paraphernalia are deposited in the earth, to remain there until Jerusalem is restored (2 Bar 6). Yet another version of the fate of the ark is in the early second-century CE work called 4 Baruch, which in some manuscripts has the title "The Things Omitted from Jeremiah the Prophet."

One of the Apocrypha, "The Letter of Jeremiah," draws on the tradition that Jeremiah wrote letters, such as that to the exiles in Babylon (Jer 29). This brief work, probably written in the third or second century BCE, is a highly stylized polemic against the worship of idols: "[T]hey are not gods, so do not fear them" is a refrain that with variations occurs eight times in the book. The Letter of Jeremiah draws on passages such as Jeremiah 10.2–15 and Isaiah 44.9–20 and incidentally contains the only biblical reference to cats (v. 22). It is included in the Roman Catholic canon as chapter 6 of the book of Baruch (see further the Appendix), but many modern Bibles print it separately.

Later tradition also identifies Jeremiah as the author of the book of Lamentations, a group of dirges on the destroyed Jerusalem (see further pages 382–84). Likewise, to Jeremiah's scribe Baruch were also attributed subsequent writings, especially the apocryphal book of Baruch (see pages 511–12).

(1.11–12) is of an almond branch (Hebr. *shaqed*), and the interpretation is based on wordplay: Yahweh is watching (*shoqed*) over his word to make it happen. The second vision (1.13–14) is of a pot on a fire, tilted so that its hot contents are spilling toward the south; this is interpreted as disaster coming from the north against Judah. Then follows a lengthy expansion of the second vision (1.15–19), in which Yahweh proclaims his judgment on Jerusalem and Judah in the form of invasions from the north and reassures the prophet that he will be with him, making him "a fortified city, an iron pillar, and a bronze wall, against the whole land" (Jer 1.18).

What appears at first reading to be a revealing glimpse of a prophet's awareness of his vocation becomes on closer examination a carefully constructed composite of themes and genres found repeatedly in biblical literature. The notion that an individual has been designated since before birth is implicit in the narratives of miraculous conception of Isaac (Gen 18.9–15; 21.1–2), Esau and Jacob (Gen 25.21), Joseph (Gen 30.1, 22), Samson (Judg 13), and Samuel (1 Sam 1), and is specifically applied to one with a divine mission in Isaiah 49.1 and 49.5. Jeremiah's reluctance to accept the divine commission is reminiscent of similar objections given by Moses (Ex 4.10) and Gideon (Judg 6.15), and his excuse that he is only a boy recalls Samuel's age when he received his call (1 Sam 3). The promise of divine presence is found in the cases of Moses (Ex 3.12), Joshua (Josh 1.5), and Gideon (Judg 6.16). The touching of the mouth also takes place in the cases of Isaiah (Isa 6.7) and, implicitly, Ezekiel (Ezek 3.1–3). The revelation of successive visions to a prophet occurs in Amos, and also in Zechariah; in both, as in Jeremiah, the phrase "What do you see?" occurs (Am 7.8; 8.2; Zech 4.2; 5.2). The connections with the call of Moses in Exodus 3–4 are especially striking. Jeremiah is identified as another Moses, as Deuteronomy had proclaimed: "I will raise up . . . a prophet like you. . . . I will put my words in his mouth, and he will speak to them everything that I have commanded" (Deut 18.18). Moreover, like Moses, Jeremiah will experience rejection and will plead with and complain to Yahweh. Finally, both Moses and Samuel are in the consciousness of the authors of the book of Jeremiah, as the reference to them in 15.1 indicates. Thus, although it is presented as an autobiographical account, the opening chapter of Jeremiah is in fact a literary composition that alludes to earlier traditions and genres.

At the same time, the first chapter of Jeremiah serves as a kind of overture, in which themes that will be more fully developed later in the book are first presented. These include vocabulary used repeatedly in the rest of the book, as this example (in which italicized words also occur in Jer 1) illustrates:

> At one moment I may *declare* concerning a *nation* or a *kingdom*, that I will *pluck up* and *break down* and *destroy* it, but if that nation, concerning which I have spoken, turns from *its evil*, I will change my mind about the *disaster* that I intended to bring on it. And at another moment I may *declare* concerning a *nation* or a *kingdom* that I will *build and plant* it, but if it does evil in my sight, not listening to my voice, then I will change my mind about the good that I had intended to do to it. (18.7–10)

The prophet's awareness of his vocation, and his complaints about it and divine reassurance, will receive fuller attention in the "confessions" of Jeremiah (see pages 371–72). Reference will also be made to other visions, of the figs in chapter 24, and of the true prophet's presence as an eyewitness to the proceedings of the divine council (23.18–22). The ominous second vision, of a pot spilling its hot contents southward, is echoed in the repeated references to foes from the north, the source of "evil and destruction" (4.6; 6.1; see also 6.22; 10.22; 25.9). Finally, Jeremiah's role as a "prophet to the nations" is elaborated both in the oracles against the nations (chaps. 46–51) and in the divine condemnation of Judah's neighbors, as in chapter 25.

The opening chapter of Jeremiah, then, is no simple excerpt from "Jeremiah's diary," as earlier scholars sometimes thought; it is, rather, a carefully constructed literary piece that presents Jeremiah as one in the line of previous divinely sent messengers and also serves to set forth some of the book's main themes. The same analysis applies to two other distinctive features of the book, the "confessions" of Jeremiah and his prophetic gestures.

The "Confessions" of Jeremiah

Since the early twentieth century, scholars have characterized several passages in Jeremiah as "**confessions**"; these are clustered in the first major section of the book, in 11.18–12.6, 15.10–21, 17.14–18, 18.18–23, and 20.7–18. Many scholars have viewed these passages as soliloquies that provide insight into the prophet's psyche—his deep unhappiness with the message he was commissioned to deliver, his prayers for divine retribution on those who opposed and persecuted him, and his enduring commitment to the divine call although it was not something he had sought. More recently, these passages have been interpreted as

biography rather than autobiography, or, more accurately, like the account of Jeremiah's call in chapter 1, as a kind of fictional autobiography.

The "confessions" are in fact variations on a genre found principally in the psalms and in the book of Job, that of the individual lament (see further pages 461–63). Many of the elements that characterize the individual lament are also found in Jeremiah's confessions, including an address to God, a detailed exposition of the petitioner's complaint, a plea for divine help, cursing of the petitioner's enemies, an expression of confidence that God will come to the petitioner's assistance, and a hymnlike thanksgiving. Much of the wording in the "confessions" is also found in other laments (see Box 21.4). Sometimes, moreover, the parallels are exact, as in "For I hear the whis-

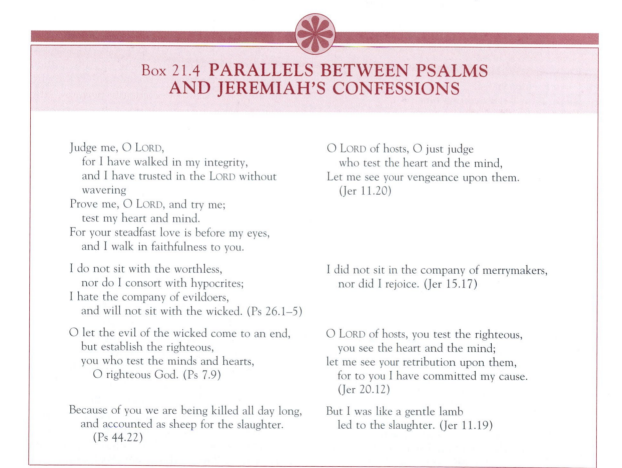

Box 21.4 PARALLELS BETWEEN PSALMS AND JEREMIAH'S CONFESSIONS

Judge me, O LORD,
    for I have walked in my integrity,
    and I have trusted in the LORD without
    wavering
Prove me, O LORD, and try me;
    test my heart and mind.
For your steadfast love is before my eyes,
    and I walk in faithfulness to you.

O LORD of hosts, O just judge
    who test the heart and the mind,
Let me see your vengeance upon them.
    (Jer 11.20)

I do not sit with the worthless,
    nor do I consort with hypocrites;
I hate the company of evildoers,
    and will not sit with the wicked. (Ps 26.1–5)

I did not sit in the company of merrymakers,
    nor did I rejoice. (Jer 15.17)

O let the evil of the wicked come to an end,
    but establish the righteous,
    you who test the minds and hearts,
      O righteous God. (Ps 7.9)

O LORD of hosts, you test the righteous,
    you see the heart and the mind;
let me see your retribution upon them,
    for to you I have committed my cause.
    (Jer 20.12)

Because of you we are being killed all day long,
    and accounted as sheep for the slaughter.
    (Ps 44.22)

But I was like a gentle lamb
    led to the slaughter. (Jer 11.19)

pering of many: Terror is all around!" (Ps 31.13; Jer 20.10).

At the same time, while using traditional language, the "confessions" of Jeremiah do have a particularity reflecting the prophet's own experiences as the book reveals them to us. One theme that recurs in the "confessions" is that of Jeremiah's prophetic vocation. In the "confessions" he maintains his insistence that he had been called by Yahweh: "It was the LORD who made it known to me, and I knew" (11.18; compare 1.5); also:

> Your words were found, and I ate them,
>   and your words became to me a joy
>   and the delight of my heart. (15.16; see also 17.16)

Perhaps the most striking language used to describe the prophet's sense of his vocation is that of seduction and rape:

> O LORD, you seduced me,
>   and I was seduced;
> you overpowered me,
>   and you prevailed. . . .
> If I say, "I will not mention him,
>   or speak any more in his name,"
> then within me there is something like a burning fire
>   shut up in my bones;
> I am weary with holding it in,
>   and I cannot. (Jer 20.7, 9)

Overwhelmed by his mission, Jeremiah curses the day of his birth, in words similar to those used by Job after the loss of his children and his property (Job 3):

> Cursed be the day
>   on which I was born!
> The day when my mother bore me,
>   let it not be blessed!
> Cursed be the man
>   who brought the news to my father, saying,
> "A child is born to you, a son,"
>   making him very glad.
> Let that man be like the cities
>   that the LORD overthrew without pity;
> let him hear a cry in the morning
>   and an alarm at noon,
> because he did not kill me in the womb;
>   so my mother would have been my grave,
>   and her womb forever great.

> Why did I come forth from the womb
>   to see toil and sorrow,
>   and spend my days in shame? (Jer 20.14–18)

It is relevant that Job is a fictional character (see further pages 479–80); thus the laments uttered by Jeremiah may be more a literary composition forming part of the biography of the character of Jeremiah than necessarily his own words.

Prophetic Gestures in Jeremiah

One of the ways that prophets communicated their message was by performing symbolic actions (see further page 299); a large number of these "**prophetic gestures**" are attributed to Jeremiah. These include:

- Remaining unmarried because the disaster about to occur will be terrible for both children and their parents (Jer 16.1–9). This is similar to Ezekiel's not mourning the death of his wife because it will occur in the context of the overwhelming loss of life when Jerusalem is destroyed (Ezek 24.15–27). It also recalls, by way of contrast perhaps, the metaphorical interpretation of the marriage of the prophet Hosea (Hos 1–3; see pages 320–21). For all three prophets, marriage had symbolic significance.

- The purchase of a jug (Jer 19). Jeremiah is instructed to take the jug and to smash it in a public place; so too, he proclaims, Yahweh will "break this people and this city, as one breaks a potter's vessel, so that it can never be mended" (19.11).

- The wearing of an animal's yoke on his neck (Jer 27–28). This gesture is directed toward the kings of Moab, Edom, Ammon, Tyre, and Sidon, who had come to Jerusalem to form a coalition with the king of Judah, Zedekiah, against the Babylonian king Nebuchadrezzar. The message is transparent: They will all become subjects of the Babylonian king—"Bring your necks under the yoke of the king of Babylon, and serve him and his people, and live" (27.12). This gesture leads to an encounter in which a prophet who opposes Jeremiah, Hananiah, breaks the yoke, proclaiming that

Yahweh will "break the yoke of King Nebuchadnezzar of Babylon from the neck of all the nations within two years" (28.11). This episode recalls the encounter between the prophets Micaiah and Zedekiah in 1 Kings 22 and contributes to the portrait of Jeremiah as the true prophet through whom Yahweh speaks (see 23.18, 22).

- The purchase of a plot of land in Anathoth, Jeremiah's hometown. Set within the "book of consolation," this action is a symbolic guarantee that after Jerusalem has been punished for its evil ways, "houses and fields and vineyards shall again be bought in this land" (32.15; see also 32.42–44).

Other prophetic gestures are more difficult to interpret, like the purchase and hiding of a linen loincloth (13.1–11) and burying stones in Egypt (43.8–13). We also see prophetic interpretations of ordinary events, akin to Samuel's interpretation of Saul's tearing his robe (1 Sam 15.27–28). Into this category fall such episodes as the potter starting over again when the pot on which he has been working was spoiled (Jer 18.1–12) and the destruction of the scroll on which the prophet's words had been written (chap. 36; see also Box 21.5).

As with the "confessions," it is difficult to know to what extent these accounts of symbolic actions are authentic historical events or whether they form part of Jeremiah's literary biography. The same is true of the notice that Jeremiah was forcibly taken to Egypt with some of the survivors of the destruction of Jerusalem (Jer 43.6), which becomes the occasion for a series of attacks (43.7–44.30) on those who had hoped to escape further Babylonian attack; Egypt, the prophet is instructed to say, will be no refuge from Nebuchadrezzar and from the divine punishment for persistent idolatry.

The Message of Jeremiah

The book of Jeremiah is complex, and it contains perspectives that at first glance seem inconsistent. It is plausible to understand the message of the prophet as developing in tandem with the changing political situation in Judah during the late seventh and early sixth centuries BCE. In this understanding, at first the prophet would have encouraged, perhaps even actually been linked to, the reform of Josiah, and he offered a message of repentance to be followed by divine reward. When the reform failed and Josiah died at Megiddo, Jeremiah's message shifted to one of inexorable doom. At the same time, however, the prophet continued to maintain that Yahweh would not entirely abandon his people.

Typical in many respects of Jeremiah's message is the famous "Temple Sermon," found in Jeremiah 7.1–15, with expansions in 7.16–8.3. The prophet is instructed to stand at the entrance of the Temple, and there to announce Yahweh's conditions for continued possession of the Promised Land: "Amend your ways and your doings, and then I will dwell with you in this place. Do not trust in these deceptive words: 'This is the temple of the LORD, the temple of the LORD, the temple of the LORD'" (Jer 7.3–4). Unfortunately, Judah had relied on the divine protection apparently guaranteed by the royal ideology, which asserted that because Yahweh had chosen the Davidic dynasty, neither it nor its capital, Jerusalem, could ever be destroyed: "I will defend this city to save it, for my own sake and for the sake of my servant David" (Isa 37.35). The visible sign of this guarantee was the Temple, Yahweh's own home. This promise of protection had been, it seemed, proven true by earlier events, especially the sieges of Jerusalem in 734 and 701 BCE (see pages 336–44). And during the long period of Assyrian domination of the Near East from the ninth to the seventh centuries BCE, Jerusalem was one of the few capital cities not to be captured and destroyed by the Assyrians. But this ideology, said Jeremiah, is a lie. Judah's survival is not guaranteed by the supposedly unconditional Davidic covenant; rather, it is dependent on observance of the nation's primary contract, the Sinai covenant, as stipulated in the Ten Commandments. But the Judeans, trusting in the royal ideology, "steal, murder, commit adultery, swear falsely, make offerings to Baal, and go after other

FIGURE 21.3. Several ceramic female fertility figures with an average height of about 5.5 in (14 cm). Figurines like these have been found at many sites in Judah, including Jerusalem, dating to the first half of the first millennium BCE. They illustrate the worship of other gods, and in particular of the "queen of heaven," condemned by Jeremiah (Jer 7.9, 18).

gods that you have not known, and then come and stand before me in this house, which is called by my name, and say, 'We are safe!'" (Jer 7.9–10) (see Figure 21.3).

The conditional nature of this warning suggests that it was given before the inevitable end was apparent: From the prophet's perspective, Judah still had a chance to learn from the punishment inflicted on the northern kingdom of Israel. To survive, however, Judah had to change its conduct:

> If you truly act justly one with another, if you do not oppress the alien, the orphan, and the widow, or shed innocent blood in this place, and if you do not go after other gods to your own hurt, then I will dwell with you in this place, in the land that I gave of old to your ancestors forever and ever. (Jer 7.5–7)

As the narrative chronology of the book continues, the moment for repentance, for moral change, passes, and what remains is to interpret the full fury of the implacable divine rage.

Therefore thus says the LORD of hosts: Because you have not obeyed my words, I am going to send for all the tribes of the north, says the LORD, even for King Nebuchadrezzar of Babylon, my servant, and I will bring them against this land and its inhabitants. . . . And I will banish from them the sound of mirth and the sound of gladness, the voice of the bridegroom and the voice of the bride, the sound of the millstones and the light of the lamp. This whole land shall become a ruin and a waste. (Jer 25.8–11)

In biblical tradition, Moses was repeatedly able to intercede for Israel when Yahweh threatened it with destruction. Now, however, Jeremiah is prohibited from trying to dissuade Yahweh from his purpose: "As for you, do not pray for this people, do not raise a cry or prayer on their behalf, and do not intercede with me, for I will not hear you" (Jer 7.16).

In the rapid sequence of events in the beginning of the sixth century BCE, Jeremiah is presented as a minority voice. When the Babylonians exiled King Jehoiachin and several thousand of the nobility to Babylon in 597 BCE, some prophets encouraged the exiles to think that their stay in Babylon would be brief, but Jeremiah dissented:

> Thus says the LORD: Do not listen to the words of your prophets who are prophesying to you, saying, "The vessels of the LORD's house will soon be brought back from Babylon," for they are prophesying a lie to you. Do not listen to them; serve the king of Babylon and live. (Jer 27.16–17)

Expanding on this command to serve the king of Babylon, who himself is Yahweh's servant (Jer 25.9; 27.6), Jeremiah writes a letter to those in Babylon:

> Thus says the LORD of hosts, the God of Israel, to all the exiles whom I have sent into exile from Jerusalem to Babylon: Build houses and live in them; plant gardens and eat what they produce. Take wives and have sons and daughters; take wives for your sons, and give your daughters in marriage, that they may bear sons and daughters; multiply there, and do not decrease. But seek the peace of the city to which I have exiled you, and pray to the LORD on its behalf, for in its welfare you will find your welfare. For thus says the LORD of hosts, the God of Israel: Do not let the prophets and the diviners who are among you deceive you, and do not listen to the dreams that they dream, for it is a lie that they are prophesying to you in my name; I did not send them, says the LORD. (Jer 29.4–9)

The phrase "seek the peace of the city where I have sent you into exile" is telling. In one of the "Songs of Ascents" (see further page 457), hymns sung by pilgrims as they approached the city of Jerusalem, the pilgrims were exhorted to "pray for the peace of Jerusalem" (in the alliterative Hebr., *shaalu shalom yerushalayim*) because it was there that "the thrones for judgment were set up, the thrones of the house of David" (Ps 122.5–6). But now Jerusalem's doom is sealed, and the exiles are instructed to pray for Babylon: "Seek the peace [*dirshu et-shalom*] of the city to which I have exiled you."

Despite Jeremiah's insistence on an inescapable divine judgment, we also see a positive counterpoint throughout the book. This is signaled at the beginning of the book, in the description of Jeremiah's mission, which was not just "to pluck up and to pull down, to destroy and to overthrow," but also "to build and

to plant" (Jer. 1.10). The paradoxical juxtaposition of verbs of destruction and construction anticipates the many passages in Jeremiah in which there is reason for hope. The designation of Jeremiah 30–33 as a "book of consolation" underemphasizes the other positive passages in the book. Jeremiah's message was not one of unrelieved doom:

> I will set my eyes upon them for good, and I will bring them back to this land. I will build them up, and not tear them down; I will plant them, and not pluck them up. I will give them a heart to know that I am the LORD; and they shall be my people and I will be their God. (24.6–7)

In part we may trace this message of hope back to the original covenant metaphor, in which Yahweh was Israel's parent and husband, a metaphor developed in detail in the book of Hosea. As Israel's parent and spouse, Yahweh loved Israel, and that love would endure despite Israel's disobedience and adultery. Jeremiah refers to these metaphors in several passages:

> I remember the devotion of your youth,
> your love as a bride,
> how you followed me in the wilderness,
> in a land not sown. (Jer 2.2)
> Have you not just now called to me,
> "My father, you are the friend of my youth—
> will he be angry forever,
> will he be indignant to the end?" (Jer 3.4)
> I have loved you with an everlasting love;
> therefore I have continued my faithfulness
> to you.
> Again I will build you, and you shall be built,
> O virgin Israel! (31.3–4; see also 31.20)

In fact, echoing the antiphonal hymns of Israel's worship, the book of Jeremiah asserts:

> The LORD is good,
> for his steadfast love endures forever!" (33.11;
> see Pss 118; 136)

In this optimistic tone, the book of Jeremiah anticipates destruction of the Babylonians and their allies who are responsible for Jerusalem's fall, as well as the city's restoration, the return of the exiles, and the renewal of the Sinai covenant, written, as Deuteronomy urges, on the hearts of the restored Israel (Jer 31.31–34; compare Deut 6.6).

Box 21.5 JEREMIAH AND THE HISTORY OF BOOKMAKING

According to Jeremiah 36.2, the prophet was instructed to "take a scroll and write on it all the words" that Yahweh had spoken. "Then Jeremiah called Baruch son of Neriah, and Baruch wrote on a scroll at Jeremiah's dictation all the words of the LORD that he had spoken to him" (Jer 36.4). When the scroll was complete, it made its way to the king, who showed his contempt for the prophet's words by systematically burning the scroll column by column as each column was read. So Jeremiah dictated another scroll to Baruch.

This episode contains remarkable details about ancient writing, reading, and bookmaking. The scrolls were apparently of papyrus, since burning a leather scroll in a small brazier would have been difficult and would have caused a horrible stench. The texts on them were written in columns, as is attested in the Dead Sea Scrolls and in other ancient manuscripts. Also, as was generally true throughout the ancient world, reading was done aloud; in fact, the Hebrew word usually translated "read" literally means "call" or "speak aloud." Finally, as was also the practice elsewhere, formal documents, at least, were written by specially trained scribes, in this case Baruch, the son of Neriah. As Jeremiah's scribe, he wrote down the prophet's dictated words on both the first and the second scrolls (Jer 36.4, 32) and also served as the custodian of Jeremiah's deed to the property at Anathoth (Jer 32.12).

The presence of this positive tone in Jeremiah is another indication of the nature of the book as a literary work, to which each generation added its own perspective. Its formation continued into the exilic period, when, as we will see in the following chapters, hopes for the future developed, even in the midst of catastrophe. (See Box 21.5.)

RETROSPECT AND PROSPECT

The events of 586 BCE were a turning point in the history of ancient Israel. The fall of Jerusalem marked the end of autonomous con-trol of the Promised Land for centuries to come. The Temple was destroyed, and along with it the sense of unconditional divine protection. The dynasty founded by David ceased to rule. As the scholar Yehezkel Kaufmann observed, "The fall of Jerusalem is the great watershed of the history of Israelite religion. The life of the people of Israel came to an end; the history of Judaism began"[*]

How would the survivors of the catastrophe react to it? Already in Jeremiah we see tension between the exiles in Babylon and those who remained in Judea. This tension would increase during subsequent decades, with each group claiming to be the "true Israel."

---

[*] Yehezkel Kaufman, *The Religion of Israel* (trans. and abridged by M. Greenberg; New York: Schocken, 1972), p. 447.

IMPORTANT TERMS

confessions of Jeremiah   prophetic gestures

QUESTIONS FOR REVIEW

1. What are the connections between Jeremiah and the Deuteronomic school, and how can they be explained?

2. How does Jeremiah interpret the events of the late seventh and early sixth centuries BCE?

3. To what extent is it possible to construct a biography of the prophet Jeremiah?

BIBLIOGRAPHY

For a summary of the events of the period, see Mordechai Cogan, "The Final Decades of the Judean Monarchy," in Chapter 7 of *The Oxford History of the Biblical World* (ed. M. D. Coogan; New York: Oxford University Press, 1998).

Two good short commentaries on Jeremiah are Thomas W. Overholt, "Jeremiah," pp. 538–76 in *The HarperCollins Bible Commentary* (ed. J. L. Mays; San Francisco: HarperSanFrancisco, 2000), which takes a more traditional approach; and Kathleen M. O'Connor, "Jeremiah," pp. 487–528 in *The Oxford Bible Commentary* (ed. J. Barton and J. Muddiman; Oxford: Oxford University Press, 2001), which is representative of more recent interpretations of the book. A convenient collection of articles sampling the history of modern interpretation of Jeremiah is Leo G. Perdue and Brian W. Kovacs, eds., *A Prophet to the Nations: Essays in Jeremiah Studies* (Winona Lake, IN: Eisenbrauns, 1984).

For Habakkuk, see Marvin A. Sweeney, "Habakkuk," pp. 668–70, and for the Letter of Jeremiah, see Daniel J. Harrington, "Letter of Jeremiah," pp. 787–88, both in *The HarperCollins Bible Commentary* (ed. J. L. Mays; San Francisco: HarperSanFrancisco, 2000).

PART FOUR

EXILE AND RETURN

AFTER THE FALL: JEWS IN JUDAH AND BABYLON

CHAPTER

22

Lamentations, Psalm 137, Obadiah, and Ezekiel

From the first exile of Judeans to Babylon in 597 BCE and ever since, Judaism has been a religion with two distinct geographies. One continued to be the Promised Land, and especially Judah's capital Jerusalem. But a significant number and eventually a majority of what we may now call Jews (a word derived from the name "Judah") were no longer living in Judah, but had been forcibly exiled to Babylon or had fled elsewhere. Those who had been dispersed, the **Diaspora**, frequently found themselves in tension with those who remained in Judah. The beginnings of that tension are evident as we look further at responses to the destruction of Jerusalem by the Babylonians in 586.

HISTORY

Our knowledge of Jews in both Judah and Babylon in the decades after the fall of Jerusalem is fragmentary at best, and our only written source is the account of the Deuteronomistic Historians in Jeremiah 40–41, summarized in 2 Kings 25.22–26. In Judah, the Babylonian ruler Nebuchadrezzar put one of the nobility, Gedaliah, in charge. His headquarters were at Mizpah, an im-

portant premonarchic center 8 miles (13 km) north of Jerusalem, presumably because Jerusalem had been destroyed. Among his supporters, apparently, was the prophet Jeremiah. After only a few months, however, a group led by Ishmael, a member of the royal family, assassinated Gedaliah and his entourage. This was followed by a countercoup in which Ishmael was killed and its leaders fled to Egypt. The subsequent deportation of more Judeans by the Babylonians in 582 BCE, mentioned in Jeremiah 52.30, may have been a reprisal for this short-lived revolt.

Many Judeans stayed in the land, however, and were able to harvest their crops. While some major cities, especially those that served as fortresses, notably Jerusalem and Lachish, had been at least partially destroyed, others continued to be occupied, and some of the destroyed cities were resettled, although mostly by squatters—"the poorest of the land" (Jer 40.7; 52.16).

This largely rural population would form the nucleus of a restored Judean community, whose claims to the land would come into conflict with the eventual returnees from Babylonian exile. Some exiles, among them the prophet Ezekiel, considered themselves to be the true Israel, with whom Yahweh himself had gone into exile, while those left in the land were among the guilty. The exiles seem to have created the notion of an "empty land," a land devoid of inhabitants, which some modern scholars have adopted. Archaeological evidence, however, suggests a more nuanced view. Although much of the population of Judah, and especially the elite from Jerusalem, had been taken into captivity in Babylon, others remained in Judah. To these Judean survivors we should attribute some of the literature of this period, including the book of Lamentations and probably the final edition of the Deuteronomistic History, as well as, perhaps, the editing of various prophetic works, including Jeremiah.

THE BOOK OF LAMENTATIONS

The book of Lamentations is a collection of detailed and sustained reactions to the fall of Jerusalem in 586 BCE, in which a poet or poets lament the destruction of the city. According to ancient postbiblical tradition, the book was written by Jeremiah, perhaps on the basis of such passages as 2 Chronicles 35.25, in which laments for the dead King Josiah are said to have been composed by the prophet, and Jeremiah 9.1, in which the prophet expresses his grief for Israel's fate. This traditional view accounts for the placement of Lamentations after Jeremiah in the Christian canon; in the Jewish canon it is one of the "Five Scrolls," grouped with the Song of Songs, Ruth, Ecclesiastes, and Esther (see further the Appendix). Modern critical scholars, however, generally have concluded that the prophet was not its author.

Using the funeral dirge as a genre, the book expresses grief for the ruined city of Jerusalem in a series of five separate and perhaps originally independent poems, the first four of which are acrostics (see Box 22.1).

We have examples of dirges for deceased individuals in David's laments for Saul and Jonathan (2 Sam 1.17–27) and for Abner (2 Sam 3.33–34). In Lamentations, the poet (or poets, for it is difficult to determine if the five separate poems in the book had more than one anonymous author) grieves for Jerusalem, personified as a dead person, or sometimes as one who has been bereaved. As in the funeral dirge, the former beauty and strength of the personified city are contrasted with her present appearance and state.

The destruction of cities was a frequent phenomenon in the ancient world, and we have a number of examples of the lament for a destroyed city from the ancient Near East, mainly from early Sumerian literature dating to the late third and early second millennia BCE. Presumably the lack of later examples of the genre is because of the vagaries of discovery. As in the Sumerian laments, the dirges in Lamentations have a theological dimension: The destruction of the city is attributed to the action of the city's deity, who was angry at it:

> The Lord has become like an enemy,
>   he has destroyed Israel. (Lam 2.5)
> The LORD gave full vent to his wrath;
>   he poured out his hot anger,
> and kindled a fire in Zion
>   that consumed its foundations. . . .
> It was for the sins of her prophets
>   and the iniquities of her priests,
> who shed the blood of the righteous
>   in the midst of her. (Lam 4.11, 13)

The punishment that Yahweh inflicted on Jerusalem is vividly described; in language that may be offensive to modern sensibilities, Jerusalem is variously depicted as a dead woman and as a widow and mother who has been stripped naked. (See further Box 22.3.)

In general, Lamentations reflects the dominant biblical view that what had happened to Jerusalem was a deserved punishment. But it is expressed with considerable poignancy, contrasting the royal ideology's claim that the city was invincible with its present state in ruins:

> [The LORD] has broken down his booth like a
>   garden,
>   he has destroyed his tabernacle;
> the LORD has abolished in Zion
>   festival and sabbath,
> and in his fierce indignation has spurned
>   king and priest.
> The Lord has scorned his altar,
>   disowned his sanctuary;
> he has delivered into the hand of the enemy
>   the walls of her palaces. (Lam 2.6–7)

Box 22.1 ACROSTIC POEMS

An **acrostic** is a poem in which the first letters of successive lines form a word or pattern. Such acrostics were favorites in antiquity as well as in more recent times, and those found in the Bible are alphabetic acrostics. Each is divided into verses or stanzas, and each verse or stanza begins with a successive letter of the twenty-two letters of the Hebrew alphabet. The alphabetic structure of such a poem served to aid the reciter's memory, and also perhaps to indicate that in the poem the author attempted to cover the entire range of what could be said on any given topic—from A to Z, as it were.

The book of Lamentations contains four alphabetic acrostics in its first four chapters; it is perhaps not a coincidence that chapter 5, although not an acrostic, also has twenty-two verses. The most elaborate acrostic in Lamentations is chapter 3, in which each stanza has three lines and each line begins with the same letter. Other alphabetic acrostic poems in the Bible are Psalms 9–10, 25, 34, 37, 111, 112, 119, and 145; Proverbs 31.10–31 (the praise of the "woman of power"); Nahum 1.2–8 (an incomplete acrostic); and Sirach 51.13–30 (praise for Wisdom). The most elaborate is Psalm 119, which is also the longest chapter in the Bible. Each stanza of this tour de force contains eight verses, and the first letter of each verse is the same letter in the Hebrew alphabet, with *aleph*, the first letter, beginning each of the eight lines in the first stanza, *beth*, the second letter, beginning each of the eight lines of the second stanza, and so on. Moreover, we see a complicated variation of a number of key terms, such as law, commandments, statutes, ordinances, and precepts. Taken as a whole, then, Psalm 119 is a comprehensive hymn praising the Torah.

Most translations do not attempt to replicate the form of the acrostic poems in the Bible. One that does, using the English alphabet, is by Ronald Knox, itself something of a tour de force.

The book concludes on an ambiguous note:

But you, O LORD, reign forever;
    your throne endures to all generations.
Why have you forgotten us completely?
    Why have you forsaken us these many days?
Restore us to yourself, O LORD, that we may be
    restored;
    renew our days as of old—
unless you have utterly rejected us,
    and are angry with us beyond measure.
    (Lam 5.19–22)

In other ancient cultures, the defeat of a nation meant that its deities were less powerful than those of the conqueror, and so the logical reaction was to worship the conqueror's gods. The end of the book of Lamentations wrestles with this dilemma. Even in the midst of the trauma of Jerusalem's fall, the poet expresses faith in Yahweh's supremacy but is at a loss to explain how that can be reconciled with what has occurred.

Although no specific details enable precise dating of the poems that comprise the book of Lamentations, most scholars reasonably assume that they were written in Judah not long after the fall of Jerusalem in 586 BCE. A different perspective on the fall of the city, that of the exiles in

Babylon, is found in Psalm 137 and also in Ezekiel.

THE JEWS IN BABYLONIA

Other than passing reference in fragmentary Babylonian records to the exiled King Jehoiachin and his sons (see page 361), our only source for the status of the Judeans in Babylonia in the sixth century BCE is the Bible. That the community eventually flourished there, probably in unwitting compliance with the prophet Jeremiah's command to "build houses . . . plant gardens . . . multiply there" (Jer 29.5–6), we know from the fifth-century BCE records of the banking house of Murashu in Nippur, a city near Babylon. Among the many principals and witnesses in documents recording loans, leases, and other transactions were Jews, who were full participants in the commercial life of the city, illustrating how Babylonia became one of the major centers of Jewish life and learning for centuries to come.

About ancient Babylonia we know much more. Babylon and other cities under the patronage of the Babylonian kings were carefully planned and lavish urban centers, unlike anything the Judeans had ever seen (see Box 22.2 and Figure 22.1). But their amazement would have been tempered by grief at what they had left behind.

Box 22.2 NEBUCHADREZZAR'S WONDERS

During his reign of more than four decades, Nebuchadrezzar rebuilt a number of cities in his kingdom. Special attention was devoted to Babylon, located on the Euphrates River some 60 miles (95 km) south of modern Baghdad. First established as the capital of Babylonia in the reign of Hammurapi in the eighteenth century BCE, Babylon continued to be a major urban and cultural center for the next three thousand years. Nebuchadrezzar sponsored a major restoration of the city to enhance its status as the capital of his empire, and at the time of the arrival of the Judean exiles, the city's area is estimated at more than 3 square miles (8 km²) and its population at a quarter of a million. By contrast, the population of Jerusalem in the early sixth century BCE before its destruction was probably no more than ten thousand. The fifth-century BCE Greek historian Herodotus, who claims to have visited Babylon in the course of his travels throughout the Near East, described it as a city more carefully planned than any other he had seen—considerable praise from a Greek!

One of the seven wonders of the ancient world was the "hanging gardens" of Babylon, a terraced plantation constructed by Nebuchadrezzar as part of his palace, according to legend for his wife Amytis, a princess from Media who was homesick for her mountainous home. Nebuchadrezzar's grandeur is also remembered in the name of the largest-size bottle of wine: A "nebuchadnezzar" has a volume of some 15 liters. Smaller sizes are named after Jeroboam I of Israel (3 liters), Rehoboam of Judah (4.5 liters), the long-lived Methuselah of Genesis 5.25–27 (6 liters), the Assyrian king Salmanazar (Shalmanezer; 9 liters), and one of the last rulers of Babylon, Balthazar (Belshazzar; 12 liters).

FIGURE 22.1. One of the gates of the city of Babylon excavated by archaeologists in the late nineteenth century is the "Ishtar Gate." Made of multicolored glazed bricks showing dragons, bulls, and other mythological creatures, it is a sample of Babylon's magnificence in the sixth century BCE and of artistic sources that probably informed the prophet Ezekiel's visions. This reconstruction in the Berlin Museum contains the original bricks, but the structure itself is only an approximation.

PSALM 137

Most of the psalms are difficult to date, for they usually articulate individual or communal piety in general terms without reference to specific historical events or contexts (see further page 460). One of the few exceptions is Psalm 137, which tells us in its opening words that its author had been one of the exiles "by the rivers of Babylon." These rivers are probably the irrigation canals that had been maintained in Mesopotamia from prehistoric times to provide water from the Euphrates and Tigris rivers for agriculture. The poet recalls the situation of the exiles in Babylonia, overpowered by grief when remembering

Jerusalem. To add to the grief, their Babylonian captors taunted the Judeans, urging them to sing "one of the songs of Zion" (Ps 137.3). "O you Jews, from Judah," we can imagine the Babylonians saying, "sing us one of your psalms, which tells how Jerusalem is an impregnable city, never to be captured or destroyed, protected by Yahweh as his own home, the city of God" (see, for example, Pss 46; 48).

The response to this taunting is the plaintive question: "How can we sing the LORD's song in a foreign land?" (Ps 137.4). That was the problem for the exiles: how to continue to worship Yahweh, when so many of his promises made apparently had been broken. The ultimate answer to the question is the transformation of the religion of Israel into Judaism, which is the focus of this and subsequent chapters. The poet's answer, however, is simply a curse against himself: May his hand that strums the strings of the lyre and his tongue that sings the words become crippled and useless if he does not continue to make Jerusalem, Yahweh's home, the center of his life. So, in exile, the Jews in Babylon longed for Zion. Within a few decades, as we will see, some did return, but many did not, and eventually these members of the Diaspora established houses of prayer and community centers that came to be called **synagogue**s. Since ancient times synagogues have been designed so that when the worshipers pray they are facing in the direction of Jerusalem. One way to continue to sing the songs of Zion was to make it a focus of worship.

The psalm ends with a violent plea for divine vengeance on the Babylonians and their vassals the Edomites for the destruction of Jerusalem in 586 BCE. The participation of the Edomites is alluded to in other sources; the latest and most explicit form of the tradition that Edom participated in the Babylonian attack on Jerusalem is found in 1 Esdras 4.45, which refers to "the temple which the Edomites burned when Judea was laid waste by the Chaldeans." This contradicts the statement in 2 Kings 25.9 that blames the Babylonians for the fire.

OBADIAH

The book of Obadiah shares the unrelieved hostility of the singer of Psalm 137 toward Edom. Obadiah is the shortest book in the Hebrew Bible, and its mere twenty-one verses are entirely devoted a single topic, the divine judgment on Edom, Judah's longtime rival and neighbor to the southeast. It is thus a freestanding example of the oracle against a foreign nation, like Nahum's attack on Assyria. The book concludes with a report of the forthcoming "day of Yahweh" (see Box 18.2 on page 316), when Edom will be punished for its participation in the destruction of Jerusalem. The judgment on Edom, the book an-

ticipates, will be carried out by an Israel returned from exile and restored to its ancient borders. The mood is one of vindictiveness, along with glee in the reversal of fortunes, when the once defeated Israelites will be victorious and the once powerful Edomites brought low.

From the perspective of the otherwise unknown author of Obadiah, the hostility between Israel and Edom had a long history, going back to the sibling rivalry between their respective ancestors Jacob and Esau. That hostility is also evident in the repeated attacks on Edom elsewhere in prophetic literature. Edom is the subject of the oracles against the nations in Amos 1.11–12, Jeremiah 49.7–22, and Ezekiel 25.12–14 (see also Ezek 35) and of attacks in other genres in Isaiah 34 and 63.1–6 and Lamentations 4.21–22. We have already noted the close connection between the book of Obadiah and the oracle against Edom in Jeremiah 49 (see pages 366–67). Clearly a literary relationship existed between the two, but the precise nature of that relationship is uncertain: Did one borrow from the other, or do both share a common source?

Although the book of Obadiah contains few specific details, most scholars date its nucleus to the sixth century BCE, not long after the fall of Jerusalem in 586 BCE, although a date in the next century is also possible.

EZEKIEL

The prophet Ezekiel, it is recorded, was a priest who had been exiled to Babylon along with other Judean elite in 597 BCE. The book attributed to him is the most unusual of the prophetic books, as rabbinic tradition recognized when it debated whether or not the book should even be admitted to the canon of scripture. It contains elaborate and sometimes fantastic visions, yet its arrangement is more orderly than prophetic books of comparable length. Ezekiel has been called a surrealist, and he is that. He is also, in the end, an optimist, who believes that the relationship between Yahweh and Israel will be restored.

The Book of Ezekiel

Unlike the other long prophetic books that precede it, Isaiah and Jeremiah, the book of Ezekiel is mostly prose, not poetry. Also unlike those books, it is arranged in a strict chronological order, as the dates throughout the book indicate. The book opens with the prophet's inaugural vision in 593 BCE ("the fifth year of the exile of King Jehoiachin," 1.2) and concludes with the vision of the restored Jerusalem in 573 ("in the twenty-fifth year of our exile," 40.1). The only disruption of this order is 29.17, dated to 571.

The book is cast almost entirely in the first person and presents itself as an autobiographical narrative; only 1.2–3, a kind of editorial note, is in the third person. That note indicates that the book has been shaped by editorial activity, although probably less so than other prophetic books. Another indication of editorial activity may be the correction to the oracle predicting the Babylonian destruction of Tyre. In chapter 26, in an oracle dated to 587 BCE, the prophet predicts the fall of Tyre to Nebuchadrezzar. That did not occur, despite a thirteen-year siege, and in 29.17–20, the latest dated oracle in the book, the prophet announced that although Nebuchadrezzar did not capture Tyre, Yahweh would give him Egypt as a kind of consolation prize; that did not occur either.

The book of Ezekiel has an orderly arrangement, as the following outline shows:

Chapters 1–3	The call of the prophet
4–24	Oracles of judgment against Judah and Jerusalem
25–32	Oracles against the nations
33–39	Oracles of restoration, including a further oracle against Edom (35) and two against Gog of Magog (38–39)
40–48	Vision of the restored Temple and the return to the land

Previous generations of scholars often attributed much of the book to a series of disciples and editors, rather than to the prophet himself; one influential study in the early twentieth century proposed that less than one-seventh of the book could be traced back to Ezekiel. Many scholars today, however, are less radical and attribute most of the book's contents to the prophet.

The Life of Ezekiel

Most contemporary scholars accept the autobiographical form of the book at face value, that is, as the work of the prophet Ezekiel himself, who in it tells us a great deal about himself and is often idiosyncratic in thought and phrasing. It seems unnecessarily skeptical to attribute the book to some anonymous author who constructed around a little known figure a detailed fictional autobiography. The chronology of the book is consistent with the view that Ezekiel himself was its primary author. We find no references to datable events or persons after the reign of Nebuchadrezzar, which ended in 562 BCE. The correction of the prophecy on Tyre in chapter 29 is also an indication that the substance of the book dates from the period given by the chronological notices.

According to the book, Ezekiel was exiled to Babylonia during the first deportation by Nebuchadrezzar in 597 BCE. This makes him a contemporary of the prophet Jeremiah, although while Jeremiah preached in Judah, Ezekiel's prophetic career took place entirely in Babylonia. As with Jeremiah, however, the historical context of his life shaped his message. That context included not only exile, but also the fall of Jerusalem and the destruction of the Temple in which, presumably, Ezekiel had served as a priest.

In the fifth year of his exile, he experienced his first prophetic revelation, "by the river Chebar" (1.1–2), to the south of Babylon, perhaps in the vicinity of ancient Nippur. He was probably thirty years old (1.1). He was the first prophet to receive a call outside the Promised Land, an important distinction because for Ezekiel, the divine presence was no longer linked to the land, but rather was with the exiles in Babylon. The audience for Ezekiel's words is clearly his fellow exiles; whenever those living in Jerusalem are spoken about, it is in the third person.

Like the prophet Muhammad in Muslim tradition, in his call Ezekiel is presented with a scroll containing the message he is to deliver, "and written on it were words of lamentation and mourning and woe" (2.10). He is instructed to eat the scroll, and, like Jeremiah, he found that although the words he was given to deliver were terrible, the scroll itself was sweet (see Jer 15.16; 1.9). The eating of the scroll is a metaphor: The prophet has internalized the divine message. At the same time it is also a guarantee that, unlike what happened to Jeremiah's scroll (Jer 36.23), this scroll cannot be destroyed.

The eating of the scroll is the first of a number of prophetic gestures by Ezekiel that can only be termed bizarre. These include speechlessness (3.26; 33.22; compare Ps 137.6), lying on his side for lengthy periods (4.4–6; the numbers given resist interpretation), shaving his head (5.1; an especially unusual action for a priest—see Lev 21.5 and compare Ezek 44.20), and eating while trembling (12.18). Others are more reminiscent of the symbolic actions of other prophets, like packing a bag and pretending to go into exile (12.3–7) and not mourning for his deceased wife (24.16–27). Behaviors such as these have led to various modern diagnoses of the prophet's physical or mental condition, such as epilepsy or catatonic schizophrenia. More fringe interpretations include the suggestions that Ezekiel's behaviors and visions were drug induced (perhaps by the eating of the scroll) or that he had contact with extraterrestrial visitors (the inaugural vision would then be of a UFO!). But since socially abnormal and ecstatic behaviors were part of prophetic activity throughout the Near East (see page 299), it probably goes beyond the evidence to label Ezekiel's condition with a specific diagnosis. It is also possible that he was engaged in a kind of performance art, in which he expressed his message by means of dramatic actions and attitudes. In any case, whether the prophet's gestures were physiologically or psychologically caused, or calculated for dramatic effect, or purely literary devices rather than events that actually occurred, the message was what was important.

In constructing that message, the prophet reveals himself to be an immensely learned individual, and also one deeply rooted in the priestly traditions of the Jerusalem Temple. In the course of the book, he uses elaborately developed and sustained metaphors that can even be called allegories, including the vine (15; 19.10–14), the lioness and her offspring (19.2–9), the eagles (17), the sword (21), metallurgy (22.18–22), shepherds (34), and others discussed in detail later in this chapter. So characteristic are these extended metaphors of his preaching that the prophet was called "a maker of allegories" (NRSV; 20.49); the Hebrew word translated "allegories" (*meshalim*) has a range of meanings that includes all kinds of literary genres from proverbs (as in Ezek 18.2; Prov 1.1) to parables, fables, and allegories (Ezek 17.2; 24.3). More than any other prophetic book as well, Ezekiel refers repeatedly to the major characters and events of Israelite tradition, including Noah and Job (14.14, 20), Abraham (33.24), Jacob (37.25), the Exodus and wanderings in the wilderness (20.5–26), and David (34.23; 37.24). Throughout the book, however, while drawing on more ancient themes and traditions, the prophet shows himself to be an extraordinarily creative writer. He was a visionary, even a mystic, and his elaborate description of the restored Jerusalem became a model for subsequent writers.

The book of Ezekiel tells us nothing of the end of the prophet's life, but as is the case with Jeremiah, later legends developed. According to some of them, Ezekiel was murdered in Babylonia by those who opposed his teaching.

The Message of Ezekiel

The Inaugural Vision

The account of Ezekiel's call to be a prophet opens the book and extends from 1.3 to 3.15, making it the longest exemplar of the genre in the prophetic corpus. Also the most unusual of the call narratives, it introduces readers to the character of the material that follows.

In the inaugural vision, Ezekiel observes a great storm cloud coming from the north. The storm cloud is a sign of a theophany, a divine appearance (see Job 38.1; 40.6; Ps 18.7–15; Isa 29.6; Nah 1.3), and the north is the mythological location of the storm-god's home (see Ps 48.2; Isa 14.13;

and page 280). In the midst of the cloud the prophet sees four living creatures, later identified as the cherubim (10.15, 20) who were the guardians of the throne of Yahweh (see Ex 25.18–22; Pss 80.1; 99.1). In Ezekiel's description of these heavenly beings they are fantastic hy-

brids, each with four wings and four faces. The sources of Ezekiel's vision include the cherubim that were found in the Temple (1 Kings 6.23–28); the widespread motif in Mesopotamian art of such winged beings as guardians of entrances, palaces, and temples (see Figure 22.2); and, more re-

FIGURE 22.2.   A colossal statue of a guardian deity, depicted as a composite creature with a bull's body, a human head, and wings. Such statues were frequently located at the entrances to Assyrian and Babylonian buildings and may have been a source for Ezekiel's description of the "four living creatures" (Ezek 1.5–11). This example is from the late eighth century BCE and is about 10 ft (3 m) high.

motely, the winged sphinxes of Egyptian art, which were widely copied throughout the Levant. The wings on all of these creatures suggest mobility, which, as we will see, was a central concept in Ezekiel's understanding of the deity (see also Ps 18.10 = 2 Sam 22.11).

The vision is reminiscent of Isaiah's vision of the deity in Isaiah 6 and of the claim by several prophets to have been eyewitnesses to the proceedings of the divine council over which Yahweh presided (see page 302). Reflecting the emphasis on the transcendence of the deity that is characteristic of the Priestly tradition, Ezekiel couches his vision of the deity in circumlocutions: "This was the appearance of the likeness of the glory of the LORD" (1.28). Ezekiel then hears the divine voice speaking, although he never sees Yahweh directly.

The prophet is addressed in 2.1, and more than ninety times throughout the book, as "son of man" (NRSV: "mortal"). This means simply "a human being," contrasting the prophet with the transcendent deity; only later, as in the book of Daniel, does the term develop an apocalyptic connotation (see Box 30.4 on page 542). The message he is given, like that given to his predecessor Isaiah, is one of divine judgment on the "rebellious house" of Israel—"words of lamentation and mourning and woe" (2.5–10).

The Sins and Punishment of Israel

In Ezekiel's repeated pronouncements of the divine judgment upon Israel, the primary offenses of which the nation is guilty have to do with idolatry and ritual impurity. The Israelites have worshiped idols throughout the land and have defiled the sanctuary of Yahweh with forbidden forms of worship in the Temple in Jerusalem. These are described in explicit detail: the images of "creeping things and loathsome animals" (8.10), the "women . . . weeping for Tammuz" (8.14), the ancient dying and rising god of Mesopotamia, and the worship of the sun (8.16). The priests are especially guilty, for they have failed to maintain the boundaries between sacred and profane, between clean and unclean (22.26).

Ezekiel places less emphasis on issues of social justice than his prophetic predecessors, and when he does so it is usually in general terms, for example:

> The land is full of bloody crimes;
>   the city is full of violence. (7.23; see also 9.9; 12.19)

Even the extended discussion of "honest balances" concerns their use in measuring sacrificial offerings in the restored Temple (45.10–17; compare Am 8.5). Nevertheless, as in the Sinai covenant as interpreted by Priestly tradition, an individual's obligations to God and to his neighbor are linked:

> If a man is righteous and does what is lawful and right—if he does not eat upon the mountains or lift up his eyes to the idols of the house of Israel, does not defile his neighbor's wife or approach a woman during her menstrual period, does not oppress anyone, but restores to the debtor his pledge, commits no robbery, gives his bread to the hungry and covers the naked with a garment, does not take advance or accrued interest, withholds his hand from iniquity, executes true justice between contending parties, follows my statutes, and is careful to observe my ordinances, acting faithfully—such a one is righteous; he shall surely live, says the Lord GOD. (18.5–9; see also 22.6–12)

In fact, Jerusalem is so pervasively sinful that even if three of the legendary righteous individuals of antiquity lived in it—Noah, Danel (a hero of Ugaritic epic, not the hero of the book of Daniel), and Job—the city would not be saved (14.14; contrast Gen 18.22–33). In this connection, Ezekiel addresses the problem of individual responsibility in a new way. Ancient Israelite legal tradition presumed a notion of collective family guilt. The Ten Commandments speak of Yahweh as one who "punishes children for the iniquity of parents to the third and fourth generation" (Ex 20.5; 34.7; Deut 5.9; see also Num 14.18). To this traditional view, Ezekiel responds by saying that only "the person who sins shall die. A child shall not suffer for the iniquity of a parent, nor a parent suffer for the iniquity of a child" (18.20). In other words, divine justice is absolutely equitable; it is not "the way of the LORD that is unfair" but the ways of Israel (18.25, 29). Ezekiel thus interprets the exile to Babylon and the destruction of Jerusalem as deserved punishments for the sins of those who themselves committed them (see Box 22.3).

Ezekiel and Jeremiah

The prophets Jeremiah and Ezekiel were contemporaries; both were deeply affected by the deportations of Judeans to Babylonia and the destruction of Jerusalem by the Babylonians in 586

BCE, but from different vantage points. Until his emigration to Egypt in the late 580s, Jeremiah was in Judah, witnessing the catastrophe personally, while Ezekiel had been taken to Babylonia in the first deportation of 597 and learned of Jerusalem's destruction only secondhand. References to letters sent between Jerusalem and Babylon by Jeremiah and others (Jer 29.1, 25) indicate that communication existed between the Judeans and the exiles in Babylonia. Additionally, Jeremiah's apparent knowledge of events there (Jer 29.15), and

Box 22.3 YAHWEH AS VIOLENT SPOUSE

Ezekiel 16 and 23 are an extended elaboration of the metaphor of Jerusalem (and Samaria, the capital of the northern kingdom of Israel) as Yahweh's unfaithful wife, a metaphor also used by Hosea (chap. 2) and Jeremiah (2.20–25; 3.1–3, 20; 13.20–27). These chapters are troubling if not offensive to many modern readers, especially women. In them, the prophet describes almost pornographically how Yahweh found Jerusalem as an abandoned infant, raised her, and when she had reached sexual maturity, married her. But she proved unfaithful, and, more than a whore, was nymphomaniacal in her pursuit of other lovers, whom she paid for their sexual favors. As a consequence, she will be punished in the presence of her lovers, stripped naked in public and then given a stoning and slashed with swords, her children killed and her houses destroyed. The same punishment had been given to her equally promiscuous sister Samaria to the north, and Jerusalem should have learned from that.

Although the passages are metaphorical, developing in lurid detail the covenant analogy of Yahweh as husband and Israel as wife, they reflect a patriarchal society in which women were property and in which, apparently, violence against adulterous women was acceptable. This reading is confirmed by the moralizing addition in Ezekiel 23.48 that the passage is a warning to all women that infidelity will be severely punished. But what are modern readers to make of a depiction of Yahweh as a jealous and possessive husband and abuser, for whom, in classic batterer mode, the violence is followed by release of tension: "I will satisfy my fury upon you, and my jealousy shall turn away from you; I will be calm, and will be angry no longer" (16.42)?

The same perspective is also found, somewhat less graphically, in Lamentations, and even in Hosea, where the wayward wife is to be punished. Although Ezekiel 16 ends on a positive note, like Hosea 2, it also exemplifies the patriarchal worldview that pervades the Bible, and thus for many readers raises profound questions about the status of the Bible as an authoritative guide.

the report of Jerusalem's fall brought to Ezekiel (Ezek 33.21), clearly indicate communication between the two groups. Thus, although Jeremiah and Ezekiel were in different locations, it is reasonable to assume that they had some knowledge of each other's prophecies.

That assumption is confirmed by the many connections between the two books. These connections include references in both books to the word that the prophet was given by Yahweh to deliver being put in his mouth (Jer 1.9; 15.16; Ezek 3.1–3); the image of the prophet as sentinel (Jer 6.17; Ezek 3.17; 33.7; see also Hos 9.8); and the metaphor of the northern and southern kingdoms as sisters (Jer 3.6–14; Ezek 23). Both prophets agree that because of its sins, Jerusalem's doom was inevitable and deserved. Both quote the proverb about generational guilt—"The parents have eaten sour grapes, and the children's teeth are set on edge" (Jer 31.29; Ezek 18.2)—and both reject its implicit absolution of the present generation: If they are being punished, it is for their own sins. Both attack false prophets who predicted peace (Jer 6.14; 23.14–22; Ezek 13.10–16). Both envision a restoration of divine love for Israel after its punishment, speaking of a renewed covenant (Jer 31.31–34; Ezek 34.25; 37.26) in which Yahweh will again say, "You shall be my people, and I will be your God" (Jer 30.22; Ezek 36.28). For Jeremiah, this covenant will be written on their hearts, instead of on stone tablets as it had been previously (Jer 31.31–33; compare Ex 31.18; 34.1; Deut 9.10–11). Perhaps playing with this conceit, Ezekiel announces that their stony hearts must be removed and replaced by hearts of flesh (Ezek 11.19–20; 36.26–27). Finally, both Jeremiah and Ezekiel announce that Yahweh himself will remove the corrupt shepherds of his flock and will shepherd them himself (Jer 23.3–6; Ezek 34.1–22), although both books also allow for the restoration of the Davidic line (Jer 30.9; Ezek 34.23–24; 37.24–25).

As we have seen in the previous chapter, the book of Jeremiah has a complex literary history, whereas Ezekiel is probably for the most part the work of a single individual. It is therefore hazardous to try to determine in which direction the

influence from one to the other went. At the very least, however, it is clear that there was a compatibility between them that was recognized, if not by the prophets themselves, then by those who edited their books.

Ezekiel and Priestly Traditions

Since he was a priest in the Temple in Jerusalem, it is not surprising that we find a number of connections between Ezekiel and various aspects of priestly tradition, even though Ezekiel unsparingly condemned the corruption of the Jerusalem priesthood of his day (as, for example, in 22.26). Scholars have long observed an overlap of language and themes between Ezekiel and both the P(riestly) source of the Pentateuch (see page 27) and the Holiness Code (Lev 17–26; see pages 145–47), which the final Priestly editors incorporated into their work. Thus, a characteristic phrase of P is "be fruitful and multiply" (see, for example, Gen 1.28; 9.1; 47.27; Ex 1.7); in Ezekiel this occurs in reverse order, "multiply and be fruitful" (Ezek 36.11). Similarly, in P's Exodus narrative, a reason given for the various signs and wonders is so that both the Israelites and the Egyptians may "know that I am Yahweh" (Ex 6.7; 7.5; 14.4, 18; 16.12; 29.46; 31.13), and the same phrase is used more than sixty times in Ezekiel. A final example is the phrase "eternal [NRSV: "everlasting"] covenant," which occurs eight times in P, of the various covenants made by God with Noah, Abraham, Isaac, the Israelites, and Aaron and Phinehas and their descendants, and in Ezekiel 16.60 and 37.26, both times of the restored relationship between Yahweh and Israel. The same phrase is used twice in Jeremiah (32.40; 50.5), also of the renewed covenant, and occasionally elsewhere in the Bible (for example, Isa 55.3; 61.8; Ps 105.10); its clustering in P, and in Ezekiel and Jeremiah, suggests at the very least some cross-fertilization between those traditions.

Some broader themes of the P tradition are also found in Ezekiel. One is the special status given to the descendants of Aaron through Zadok, a chief priest under David and the sole holder of that office under Solomon, as opposed to the Levites. Thus, in the restored Temple, "the priests who have charge of the altar . . . are the descendants of Zadok, who alone among the descendants of Levi may come near to the LORD to minister to him" (40.46). The Levites, on the other hand, as elsewhere in P, are demoted to the status of lesser clergy (44.10–14). This hierarchy is reflected in the distribution of the land, where the Temple and its immediate environs shall be restricted to the Zadokite priests, and an adjacent area is given to the Levites, farther removed from the Temple itself (45.1–5; 48.9–14).

We also find important connections of theme and vocabulary between Ezekiel and the Holiness Code (Lev 17–26). So close, in fact, are the Holiness Code and some passages in Ezekiel that some scholars have suggested that Ezekiel himself was the author of the Holiness Code. This is less likely than that both Ezekiel and the Holiness Code drew on the same body of laws, collected and preserved by the Jerusalem priesthood and eventually codified into the Holiness Code. Both Ezekiel and the Holiness Code describe various offenses as profaning the holy name of Yahweh (Lev 20.3; 22.2, 32; Ezek 20.39; 36.20–22; 39.7; 43.7–8). Also, the sins catalogued in Ezekiel 18.5–17 and 22.6–12, for example, seem very close to offenses prohibited in the Holiness Code, and the description of the restored Israel in Ezekiel 34.25–31 has a number of verbal connections with the rewards for obedience in Leviticus 26.3–13. Finally, like the Holiness Code, Ezekiel stresses the requirements of ritual holiness, which the Israelites have repeatedly violated, but which will be observed in the restored Temple.

Given the lack of consensus among scholars concerning the dates of both P and the Holiness Code, it is impossible to determine whether the prophet Ezekiel was familiar with them in more or less their present form. But even if in their final form both are to be dated later than Ezekiel, the position taken in this book (see pages 27 and 145), there can be no doubt that they had a considerable prehistory and that at the very least Ezekiel, who was also a priest, was familiar with the traditions that eventually became P and the Holiness Code.

The "Glory of Yahweh"

One of the recurring themes in the book of Ezekiel is the "glory of Yahweh" and its mobility. The phrase "the glory of Yahweh" is also characteristic of the P tradition in the Pentateuch, where it denotes the light-filled cloud that both revealed and concealed the divine presence, called, according to JE, "the pillar of cloud by day and the column of fire by night" (Ex 13.21). This "glory of Yahweh" had accompanied the Israelites during the Exodus and on their journey to the Promised Land (Ex 40.34–38).

This "glory of Yahweh" was associated with the ark of the covenant, the moveable sacred throne and footstool of God. When the ark was captured by the Philistines, the wife of the high priest, as she was dying in premature childbirth, named her newborn son Ichabod, which means "Where is the glory?" She said, "The glory is departed from Israel: for the ark of God is taken" (1 Sam 4.22). According to the Deuteronomistic Historians, when Solomon dedicated the newly constructed Temple in Jerusalem, "the glory of Yahweh filled the temple of Yahweh" (1 Kings 8.11).

In a vision dated to 592 BCE, Ezekiel sees the glory of Yahweh on the move again, as it had been in premonarchic and early monarchic Israel. (See Figure 22.3.) It leaves the innermost room of the Temple, the Holy of Holies, and moves slowly from the Temple doorway (9.3; 10.4) to its gate (10.19) and then leaves the Temple entirely, pausing on the Mount of Olives as it heads east, toward Babylon (11.23). The Temple has not yet been destroyed, so this probably refers to the first deportation, in 597. Jerusalem is no longer the city of God, for Yahweh has gone into exile with his people. Ezekiel was one of those deported, and from his perspective those remaining in the land were among the guilty, and the land would have to be punished for their sins by being made a wasteland (33.29).

Those who had not been exiled, but who remained in the land, claimed that the land had been given to them as it had formerly been given to Abraham (33.23), and that it was the exiles who were guilty. This claim is rejected by Ezekiel (11.15). The vision of the glory leaving the Tem-

FIGURE 22.3. Drawing of a tenth- or ninth-century BCE Assyrian tile, showing the Assyrian deity Ashur surrounded by a radiant disk among rain clouds, proceeding into battle over a man in a chariot, perhaps the Assyrian king. This depiction informs the description of the "glory of Yahweh" in Ezekiel on the move with his people to Babylon.

ple and heading east means that Yahweh is no longer to be found in Jerusalem, but rather is with the exiles, the "remnant of Israel" (11.13) in Babylon.

Finally, in his vision of the restored Jerusalem, when the Temple would be rebuilt, the prophet saw:

> The glory of the God of Israel was coming from the east; the sound was like the sound of mighty waters; and the earth shone with his glory. The vision I saw was like the vision that I had seen when he came to destroy the city, and like the vision that I had seen by the river Chebar; and I fell upon my face. As the glory of the LORD entered the temple by the gate facing east, the spirit lifted me up, and brought me into the inner court; and the glory of the LORD filled the temple. (Ezek 43.2–5)

In the prophet's vision, Yahweh will return from Babylonia with his people and take up residence

in a restored Temple, as he had at the dedication of the Temple built by Solomon.

The Oracles against the Nations (Chaps. 25–32)

Like his prophetic predecessors, Ezekiel makes use of the genre of the "oracle against the nations," and, as in Amos, Isaiah, and Jeremiah, they are clustered in one section, chapters 25–32. A fairly perfunctory treatment, in prose, is given of Ammon, Moab, Edom, and Philistia (chap. 25), with special attention to the role of the Ammonites and the Edomites as participating in and rejoicing at the fall of Jerusalem in 586 BCE.

Prolonged attention is given to the Phoenician city of Tyre, on the Mediterranean just north of Israel's traditional boundary. In several poetic oracles in chapters 26–28, replete with details of Tyrian mythology and commerce, the city's destruction by Nebuchadrezzar is foretold. Built on an island, Tyre was strategically located "in the heart of the seas" (28.2). Like Jerusalem, Tyre was a city "perfect in beauty" (27.3), was linked to the mythological garden of Eden (28.13), and also was thought to be impregnable. Like the Davidic monarchs, the kings of Tyre also seem to have claimed divine status (28.2), and they were ceremonially adorned with precious stones (28.13), like the high priest (Ex 28.17–20). In an extended metaphor in Ezekiel, the island city of Tyre is compared to a ship laden with goods from all over the eastern Mediterranean, reflecting its far-flung commerce (see Figure 22.4). But like a ship, it too will be wrecked, to the dismay of its sailors and the amazement of its trading partners. In fact, although the Babylonians laid siege to Tyre and forced its surrender, they never did succeed in capturing it; not until the fourth century BCE did

the Greeks under Alexander the Great do so. Reflecting the failure of the prophecy to be fulfilled is a kind of footnote in 29.17–21, according to which, as a kind of consolation prize for his failure to capture Tyre, Yahweh gave Nebuchadrezzar Egypt instead.

Egypt too is the subject of a series of oracles, in chapters 29–32. In the tumultuous decades before the fall of Jerusalem in 586 BCE, Egypt had imposed its rule on Judah, and some kings had sought alliances with Egypt to counter the Babylonians. Now Egypt's rulers will be defeated just as Yahweh defeated the primeval dragon of chaos, to which the pharaoh is compared (29.3–4; compare Job 40.15–41.34, and see further Box 28.3 on page 487). The oracles against Egypt, which are in both prose and poetry, show a detailed knowledge of Egyptian geography and conclude with a description of the arrival of the pharaoh

FIGURE 22.4. A picture of a Phoenician ship from a relief in the palace of the Assyrian king Sennacherib, dating to about 700 BCE. The maritime commerce of the Phoenicians is described in Ezekiel 27.

in the underworld, concerning which, of course, the Egyptians had their own elaborate views.

Israel Restored

According to the chronological framework of the book, early in 585 BCE news reached the exiles in Babylon that Jerusalem had fallen (Ezek 33.21–22; compare 24.25–27). Ezekiel's mouth was opened, and his ability to speak returned (see 3.26). The rest of the book is a series of visionary oracles about the future, beginning with alternating negative and positive oracles and concluding in chapters 40–48 with a detailed vision of Jerusalem and the Temple restored and the entire Promised Land occupied by Israel.

Chapter 34 is an extended oracle against the human rulers of Israel, corrupt shepherds whose regime has ended. Now a new age will come, in which Yahweh himself will be the shepherd of his flock. At the same time, in a somewhat confusing way, leadership will be directly in the hands of a "prince" (34.24), a new David (see Box 22.4).

Two vivid and extended metaphors in chapter 37 articulate Ezekiel's vision of restoration. The first is that of the valley filled with human bones (vv. 1–14). Following divine instructions, Ezekiel "prophesies," whereupon the bones are arranged in proper anatomical order, then covered with muscles and skin, and finally given the breath of life. Just so, Yahweh announces, shall Israel be brought back to life. The passage is clearly parabolic and does not mean actual resurrection of the dead, a concept that will not develop for several centuries (see page 495).

The second metaphor is that of the two sticks in 37.15–28. The prophet is to take a stick inscribed

Box 22.4 LEADERSHIP IN THE RESTORED COMMUNITY

In its vision of the restoration, the book of Ezekiel focuses on proper worship in the rebuilt Temple and seems to suggest a kind of theocracy, in which religious and political leadership would be combined. Yet a number of passages refer to a kinglike leader, a new David (34.23–24; 37.22–25). It is possible that these are evidence of later additions to the book; certainly the statements in 34.15 that Yahweh himself will be the shepherd and in 34.23 that David will be the shepherd are, on the surface at least, inconsistent.

Apparently either Ezekiel, or his editors, was willing to accept a restoration of the monarchy, but one with limited powers. Although Ezekiel does occasionally use the word "king" (Hebr. *melek*) for past, present, and future rulers of Israel, as does Jeremiah, the term "prince" (Hebr. *nasi'*) is much more frequent, a term also found in P for the leaders of Israel in the time of Moses. Ezekiel's preference for this term, then, probably means that the ruler's office in the restored community would be more limited than it had been in Judah historically. The prince is clearly subordinate to the priests, whose position at the center of the city indicates their status. In contrast to the plan of Solomonic Jerusalem, in Ezekiel's vision of a restored Jerusalem the Temple would not be part of a royal quarter and the ruler's territory would be somewhat removed from the Temple; moreover, the ruler would have a circumscribed role in ritual. The prince, then, would have a restricted, perhaps exclusively administrative, function, while at the same time preserving the Davidic lineage and the promises attached to it.

with the name of the southern kingdom of Judah and another inscribed with that of Ephraim (the northern kingdom of Israel) and hold them in his closed hand so that they appear to be one stick. The meaning of the parabolic action is clear: The nation that had been divided into two kingdoms in the late tenth century BCE will be reunited, under the rule of a descendant of David, guaranteed by an eternal covenant that combines elements of both the Sinai and the Davidic covenants.

This restoration will be preceded by punishment of Israel's oppressors, Edom and "the Gog of the land of Magog" (chaps. 38–39; see Box 22.5). After divine victory over these enemies, Israel will be fully restored, in a kind of utopia, "like the garden of Eden" (36.35).

Jerusalem Restored

In Ezekiel 40–48 we see the beginning of what is called apocalyptic literature: a detailed description of the end-times, revealed by a divine mes-

senger (see further pages 436–37). Although earlier prophets had spoken vaguely of a positive future following divine punishment, in Ezekiel we have for the first time a detailed description of this future age (see Figure 22.5).

Central to the prophet's vision of the future is Jerusalem, and central to Jerusalem is its Temple. This reflects the ideology of the Davidic line and of the priests who served in the dynastic Temple that Solomon had constructed. Jerusalem was believed to be the "navel" of the earth, its center, as it were (38.12; see also 5.5). Much of the depiction of the "new Jerusalem" is devoted to a detailed set of specifications for the restored Temple, its furnishings, and the rituals to be performed in it. Access to the restored Temple is to be restricted to Israelites, with foreigners barred from admission (44.9). The idea of separation of the sacred from the profane will also apply to the priests, who are to lay aside their linen vestments when they have finished their sacred tasks and to

Box 22.5 GOG OF MAGOG

The account of the restoration of Israel includes a description of the punishment of its oppressors, especially Edom in chapter 35, an expansion of the shorter oracle in 25.12–14, and the defeat of the mysterious Gog of the land of Magog in chapters 38–39. Since antiquity many attempts have been made to identify Gog, from the similar sounding Gyges, king of Lydia in Asia Minor in the seventh century BCE, with Napoleon, Hitler, and the Soviet Union. The latter is based on an improbable identification of Gog's title, *rosh meshek* (literally, "head of Meshek"), as a cipher for Russia and Moscow. Most likely, however, Gog is a veiled reference to Nebuchadrezzar, the king of Babylon.

The announcement of divine judgment is set in the context of the restoration of Israel, and so a final battle between the deity and the forces of evil becomes a commonplace of apocalyptic literature (see further page 436), as in the book of Revelation, in which the defeat of Satan and the nations of Gog and Magog immediately precedes the descent from heaven of the "new Jerusalem" (Rev 20.7–21.2). Thus, although identification with Nebuchadrezzar and Babylon is probable, Gog and Magog come to symbolize all the forces that interfere with the divine plan, and their defeat is described in highly mythological language.

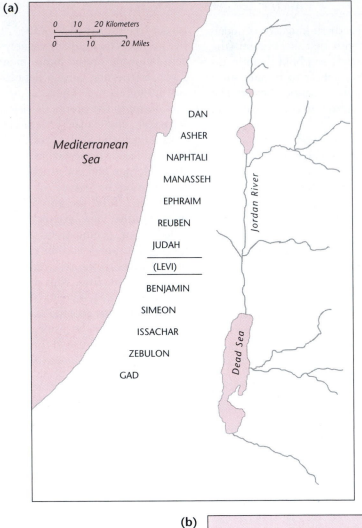

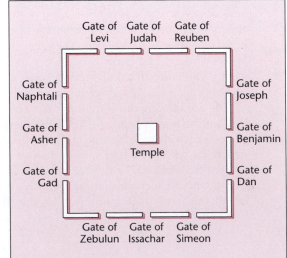

FIGURE 22.5. Schematic representations of Ezekiel's conception of the geography of a restored Israel (a) and a restored Jerusalem (b).

observe all the requirements of Levitical law (44.20–27).

The specifications for the restored Temple are clearly derived from the actual Solomonic Temple, in which Ezekiel had ministered as a priest, as presumably are the mythological components of the description as well. Among the latter we may point out especially the understanding of the Temple as an earthly facsimile of the divine home on the cosmic mountain. These mythological elements are found at the beginning, where we are told that the Temple is set on a very high mountain (40.2), and at the end (47.1–12), where a healing, fertile river flows from the base of the Temple. As this river moves eastward, it becomes progressively deeper, and on its banks are trees that supply fruit and medicinal leaves year-round. When the river reaches the Dead Sea, it will render that barren body of water fresh, so that fish will thrive in it as they do in the Mediterranean. This theme will be reused more in later Jewish and Christian apocalyptic literature (see Zech 14.8; Rev 22.1–2).

The Land Restored

To the priests is assigned the land immediately surrounding the sanctuary. Part of this district, but farther from the Temple, is given to the Levites; unlike the historical situation, in which the Levites were a landless tribe (see pages 198 and 222), in Ezekiel's vision they too have a territorial allotment. Next is land for the prince, on the west and the east, and then the allotments for the twelve tribes, in a roughly symmetrical arrangement. In contrast to the actual historical geography, however, the tribes are distributed on both sides of the Holy City, with Judah and six tribes to the north, and Benjamin and four other tribes to the south. Judah and Benjamin, which had been part of the kingdom of Judah, are set immediately adjacent to the sacred and royal territories, although their actual geography is re-versed, with Judah now north of Jerusalem and Benjamin to its south. Moreover, tribal holdings are restricted to the land west of the Jordan, in contrast both to the division of the land according to the book of Joshua and the actual historical situation, in which tribes such as Reuben, Manasseh, and Gilead claimed territory east of the Jordan.

This geography has a practical dimension: Parts of the holy city are set aside for ordinary uses, for houses, and as agricultural land (48.15–20). For the most part, however, the description is idealized, even utopian. The land is to be divided equally among the twelve tribes, with Jerusalem in its center. The city has twelve gates, one for each of the tribes, symbolizing the unity of the restored community. Finally, the city is given a new name, signifying the return of the divine presence: "Yahweh is there" (48.35)

RETROSPECT AND PROSPECT

In Ezekiel's vision, exile is not a permanent condition, for Yahweh will lead his people from Babylon back to the Promised Land. This theme of a new Exodus will be elaborated in the remarkable poetry of Second Isaiah (see pages 410–11). But alongside the optimism with which the book of Ezekiel ends is, as found in the literature of the sixth century BCE, evidence of developing tensions over the ownership of the Promised Land, and especially over the identity of the true Israel. Ezekiel and Jeremiah were in agreement: Those who had not been exiled were bad figs, so bad that they must be destroyed; the exiles are the good figs, whom Yahweh will restore to the land (Jer 24). Those who remained in the land, however, felt differently. When some of the exiles returned, later in the sixth century, these conflicting views would have to be addressed; from their resolution would emerge various facets of what we can now call early Judaism.

IMPORTANT TERMS

acrostic   Diaspora   synagogue

QUESTIONS FOR REVIEW

1 How do the book of Lamentations and Psalm 137 express some of the emotional reactions to the fall of Jerusalem?

2. What is distinctive about Ezekiel's interpretation of the fall of Jerusalem?

3. What kind of a future does Ezekiel envision for Israel?

BIBLIOGRAPHY

For a brief summary of the history of the period, see M. Cogan, "The Babylonian Exile: Continuity and Change," in Chapter 7 *The Oxford History of the Biblical World* (ed. M. D. Coogan; New York: Oxford University Press, 1998).

A good short commentary on Lamentations is Norman K. Gottwald, "Lamentations," pp. 577–82 in *The HarperCollins Bible Commentary* (ed. J. L. Mays; San Francisco: HarperSanFrancisco, 2000). A lengthier commentary is Delbert R. Hillers, *Lamentations: A Commentary*, 2d ed. (New York: Doubleday, 1992). A feminist perspective on the book is provided by Kathleen O'Connor, "Lamentations," pp. 187–91 in *The Women's Bible Commentary* (ed. C. Newsom and S. Ringe; Louisville: Westminster, 1998).

For Obadiah, see the useful summaries by Robert P. Carroll, pp. 496–97 in *A Dictionary of Biblical Interpretation* (ed. R. J. Coggins and J. L. Houlden; Philadelphia: Trinity Press International, 1990); and by David L. Petersen, pp. 189–91 in *The Prophetic Literature: An Introduction* (Louisville: Westminster John Knox, 2002).

A good short commentary on Ezekiel is Robert R. Wilson, "Ezekiel," pp. 583–602 in *The HarperCollins Bible Commentary* (ed. J. L. Mays; San Francisco: HarperSanFrancisco, 2000).

RETURN FROM EXILE

Ezra 1–2 and Isaiah 34–35 and 40–55

The fall of Jerusalem in 586 BCE stimulated the survivors, especially those who had been deported to Babylonia, to rethink their understanding of Israel and of its relationship to Yahweh. In this chapter we will examine three works that are examples of such rethinking. We will begin with a summary of the history of the period, which saw the defeat of the Babylonian empire by the Persian king Cyrus the Great and his permission for Judean exiles to return to Jerusalem.

HISTORY

The long and successful reign of Nebuchadrezzar II in Babylon (604–562 BCE) ended with his death. Nebuchadrezzar's immediate successor was his son Amel-Marduk (562–560; called Evil-merodach in the Bible). Amel-Marduk is known principally for his release of King Jehoiachin from prison in the first year of his reign (2 Kings 25.27); the Judean monarch, who had been deported in 597, would by then have been in his mid-fifties, having spent some more than three decades under house arrest in Babylon. Amel-Marduk's short reign ended when he was assassinated by his brother-in-law Nergal-sharezer (also known as

Neriglissar). Nergal-sharezer ruled for only five years (560–556); his son Labashi-Marduk succeeded him, but was also assassinated after a few months, and an outsider, Nabonidus, became the last king of Babylon.

Nabonidus (556–539) BCE is one of the most mysterious figures in ancient history. He was apparently not a member of the royal family, and the circumstances under which he came to the throne are unclear. Beginning in 553, he spent a decade away from Babylon, first in Syria and then at Tema in Arabia, perhaps to secure Babylonian control over trade routes to the west and southwest. During his absence, his son Belshazzar was coregent in Babylon. Belshazzar is a major character in the second-century BCE biblical book of Daniel, which erroneously identifies him as the son of Nebuchadrezzar (an error repeated in the later book of Baruch; see further pages 511–12 and 538).

Although Nabonidus is not mentioned in the Bible, he fascinated later writers, and legends developed about his prolonged absence from Babylon, attributing it to illness, madness, or eccentric piety. The description of Nebuchadrezzar in the book of Daniel as one who "was driven away from human society, ate grass like oxen, and his body was bathed with the dew of heaven, until his hair grew as long as eagles' feathers and his nails became like birds' claws" (Dan 4.33) is derived from these probably fanciful explanations of Nabonidus's absence. One of the Dead Sea Scrolls, "The Prayer of Nabonidus," expands on the description in Daniel with an autobiographical account in which the king describes how his illness was cured after his prayer for forgiveness to the true God; this is similar to the prayers of the Judean kings Hezekiah after his illness (Isa 38.9–20) and Manasseh during his captivity (Prayer of Manasseh) (see further page 352).

After the reign of Nebuchadrezzar, the Neo-Babylonian empire faced problems in addition to those of succession. Like their predecessors the Assyrians, the Babylonians were probably overextended, and thus vulnerable. The principal threat came from their east, in the Iranian plateau. There two related groups, the Medes and the Persians, had coalesced in 550 BCE under the leadership of Cyrus, who had become king of Persia in 559. Cyrus posed an immediate and eventually fatal challenge to the Neo-Babylonian empire. He attacked Babylonia in 539, and after a battle at Opis, near modern Baghdad, Nabonidus was captured. Cyrus then entered the capital city of Babylon in triumph the same year. This conventionally marks the beginning of what is called the "Persian period" in ancient Near Eastern history,

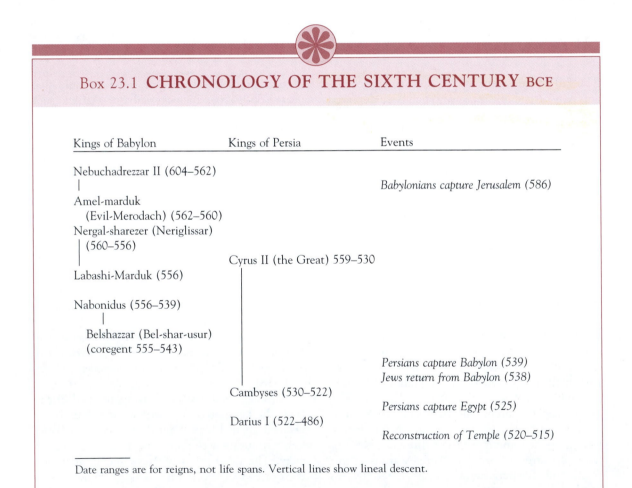

Box 23.1 CHRONOLOGY OF THE SIXTH CENTURY BCE

Kings of Babylon	Kings of Persia	Events
Nebuchadrezzar II (604–562)		Babylonians capture Jerusalem (586)
Amel-marduk (Evil-Merodach) (562–560)		
Nergal-sharezer (Neriglissar) (560–556)		
	Cyrus II (the Great) 559–530	
Labashi-Marduk (556)		
Nabonidus (556–539)		
Belshazzar (Bel-shar-usur) (coregent 555–543)		Persians capture Babylon (539) Jews return from Babylon (538)
	Cambyses (530–522)	Persians capture Egypt (525)
	Darius I (522–486)	Reconstruction of Temple (520–515)

Date ranges are for reigns, not life spans. Vertical lines show lineal descent.

which lasted until the conquests of Alexander the Great in 332 BCE.

With reference to the history of Judah and Judaism, the period from 586 to 539 BCE is often referred to as the exilic period, and the era that follows, the Persian period, is also known as the postexilic period (see Box 23.1).

For all of this history we have a variety of sources, each of which has its own bias. These include, in addition to the Bible, some Babylonian records and extensive Persian texts. Especially important are the Greek historians, beginning with Herodotus, for whom the Persians were a major topic. Persia and Greece vied for control of the eastern Mediterranean throughout the fifth and fourth centuries BCE, a conflict that finally ended with the Greek conquest of the entire Near East by Alexander the Great and his capture of the

Persian capital of Persepolis in 330 BCE. For over two centuries, then, the Persians were the primary power in the Near East, and this had profound effects on the status of the Jews, both in Babylonia and in Judah, which became the Persian province of Yehud. (See Figure 23.1.)

Of the situation of the exiles in Babylon during the sixth century BCE we have little information. The principal biblical narrative for the return itself is in the book of Ezra, which has its own complicated literary history and which we will examine later (see pages 431–32). Ezra 1 sets the stage for the return of the Judeans from exile:

> In the first year of King Cyrus of Persia, in order that the word of the LORD by the mouth of Jeremiah might be accomplished, the LORD stirred up the spirit of King Cyrus of Persia so that he sent a herald through-

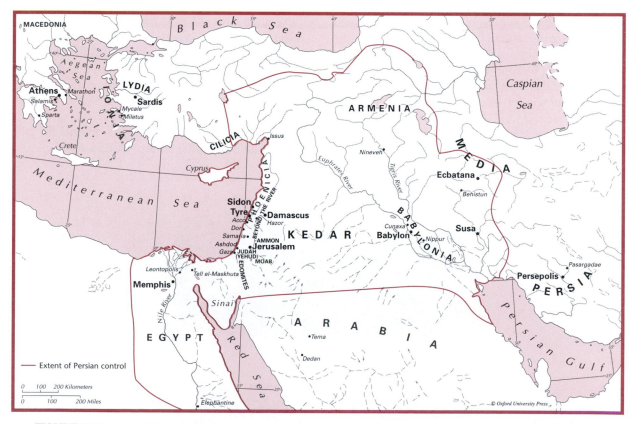

FIGURE 23.1.   Map of the Persian empire.

out all his kingdom, and also in a written edict declared: "Thus says King Cyrus of Persia: The LORD, the God of heaven, has given me all the kingdoms of the earth, and he has charged me to build him a house at Jerusalem in Judah. Any of those among you who are of his people—may their God be with them!—are now permitted to go up to Jerusalem in Judah, and rebuild the house of the LORD, the God of Israel—he is the God who is in Jerusalem; and let all survivors, in whatever place they reside, be assisted by the people of their place with silver and gold, with goods and with animals, besides freewill offerings for the house of God in Jerusalem." (Ezra 1.1–4; see also 2 Chr 36.22–23)

According to this account (a different version of the decree is given in Ezra 6.2–5), in 538 BCE, a year after assuming control of Babylon, Cyrus undertook to rebuild the Temple in Jerusalem. For that purpose he allowed any exile who wished to return and also allowed those who did not return to contribute to the rebuilding. Ezra 1 goes on to relate how Cyrus gave the returnees the original Temple paraphernalia that Nebuchadrezzar had captured. Then, in Ezra 2, a census was taken, with a total of "forty-two thousand three hundred sixty, besides their male and female servants, of whom there were seven thousand three hundred thirty-seven; and . . . two hundred male and female singers" (Ezra 2.64–65); the numbers are apparently inflated.

The returnees were led by Sheshbazzar, "the prince of Judah" (Ezra 1.8), and included Zerubbabel, a grandson of King Jehoiachin and thus a descendant of David, and Jeshua, a priest (2.2); all three become principal figures in the early restoration (see pages 420–21). According to Cyrus's decree in Ezra 1, he attributed his imperial rule to "Yahweh, the god of heaven," who had commanded him to "build a house in Jerusalem." The claim by a foreign ruler to be obeying Yahweh's instructions, although it sounds improbable, may be authentic. We may recall how in the narrative of the siege of Jerusalem by the Assyrians in 701 BCE, the representative of the Assyrian king reportedly claimed that the attack on Judah had been ordered by Yahweh (2 Kings 18.25; Isa 36.10). The presentation of Cyrus as inspired by Yahweh and apparently his devout worshiper is consistent with Persian imperial propaganda. The "Cyrus Cylinder," found in Babylon in 1879, is a first-person narrative in which Cyrus describes himself as one whom Marduk, the principal deity of Babylon, had chosen to be ruler and ordered to march to Babylon, and who restored there the worship of the gods that had been neglected during the time of Nabonidus (see Figure 23.2).

It is likely, however, that Cyrus's original decree was altered by the authors of Ezra for their

FIGURE 23.2.   The Cyrus Cylinder. Inscribed in Babylonian cuneiform writing, this fired clay cylinder is about 9 in (23 cm) long. In it the Persian king Cyrus the Great relates how he captured Babylon at the command of its god Marduk.

own purposes. In their version of the decree, they allude to the Exodus. The mention of the silver and gold vessels along with gifts recalls how as the Israelites were about to leave Egypt, they "asked the Egyptians for jewelry of silver and gold, and for clothing, and the LORD had given the people favor in the sight of the Egyptians, so that they let them have what they asked" (Ex 12.35–36). It is also possible that the census of the returnees is a deliberate parallel to the census taken at the beginning of the book of Numbers, as the Israelites resumed their journey toward the Promised Land. With these parallels in mind, Cyrus is thus presented as the opposite of the pharaoh of the Exodus story. Linking the return from Babylon and the Exodus is a prominent theme in Isaiah 40–55, to which we will soon turn. First, however, we will reexamine two major works that were also products of the exilic period; in both the theme of exile is prominent.

THE PRIESTLY SOURCE OF THE PENTATEUCH

One work that plausibly can be dated to the mid-sixth century BCE is the Pentateuchal source known as P (see page 27). As an important component of ancient Israelite society, the priests, especially those who had served in the Temple in Jerusalem, continued to have a significant role during the exilic period, even though their primary context, the Temple itself, no longer existed. As we have already seen, a prime example is the activity in Babylonia of Ezekiel, who was a priest as well as a prophet (see pages 386–88).

The date of P is a controversial issue in contemporary biblical scholarship, with proposals ranging from the eighth to the fourth centuries BCE. Scholars generally agree that P includes some old material, sometimes, in fact, very old material, such as the memory of the worship of the Canaanite deity El Shadday by Israel's ancestors (see Ex 6.2–3 and pages 81 and 90). There is also a consensus that the divinely given instructions in P concerning religious observances and ritual generally reflect practices in the Temple in Jerusalem, build by Solomon in the mid-tenth century and destroyed by the Babylonians in 586 BCE. Finally, most scholars concur that after the destruction of the Temple the earlier traditions were reshaped, or at least edited, to reflect changing circumstances.

Given the importance in ancient Israel of the priesthood, especially the priesthood in the Temple in Jerusalem, it is reasonable to speak of a kind of priestly school, analogous to those that we have identified in connection with the Deuteronomists and with Isaiah. The products of this priestly school include stages of the P source identified by the Documentary Hypothesis, from its original assemblage to its final edition (see page 27), and some of the independent sources incorporated into it, notably the Holiness Code (pages 145–46). Given the connections between Ezekiel and P, it is also reasonable to associate Ezekiel himself with the priestly school. One stage in the formation of P was the time of the exile in Babylon, and the position taken in this book is that this was the principal stage.

A number of pieces of evidence converge to support an exilic date for this major stage of P. One is the many connections between P and Second Isaiah (Isa 40–55), another work of the exilic period, which we will examine later in this chapter. Nearly half of all of the occurrences in the Bible of the words translated "create" (Hebr. *bara'*) and "redeem" (Hebr. *ga'al*) are in P and in Second Isaiah. Like P, and also like Ezekiel, Second Isaiah repeatedly refers to the "glory" of Yahweh and to his holiness. Other shared vocabulary includes the words *tohu* and *bohu* (NRSV: "formless void"; see Gen 1.2; Isa 45.18–19; 34.11) and frequent references to "darkness" and "beginning." There are also coincidences of theme, especially that of monotheism. In P's creation narrative in Genesis 1, only God is responsible for creation; other mythological entities known from Babylonian myth and elsewhere, while alluded to, are not explicitly mentioned; in the case of the sun and moon, worshiped as divine by the rest of the ancient Near East, P studiously avoids even naming them, calling them "the greater light" and the "lesser light" (Gen 1.16) and reducing them to just another result of God's creative words. This is in effect a kind of monotheism, and it parallels Second Isaiah's fuller elaboration of the same theme.

Furthermore, as we have seen (on pages 7–10), P seems to have a detailed knowledge of Babylonian literature, especially *Enuma elish*, which contains one of the Babylonian mythic accounts of creation to which P can be interpreted as providing an alternative. P's familiarity with *Enuma elish* most plausibly was acquired in Babylonia itself.

In addressing the Judean exiles in Babylonia, P is concerned not only with the past, but also with their present situation and even their future. How could the community preserve its religious identity "in a foreign land" (Ps 137.2)? P answers this question by stressing continued fidelity to Yahweh by observances such as the sabbath, the dietary laws, and circumcision. These observances are not dependent on being in the land of Israel or on institutions such as the Temple or the monarchy. Rather, the Judeans, the Jews, no matter where they might be, could keep the sabbath, circumcise their sons, and maintain purity in diet and in other matters. Moreover, as we have seen, in the books of Exodus, Leviticus, and Numbers P presents a kind of utopian program for the future, consisting of virtual blueprints for the sacred architecture and of rubrics for the rituals of the "assembly." It sets this program in the context of a people outside its home, on a journey back to the land promised to their ancestors. In the chronology of the narrative in which it is set, this is the generation of the Exodus; in terms of P's audience, it is the generation in exile in Babylon.

As we will see later (on page 433), in the mid-fifth century BCE the leader Ezra brings to Judah from Babylonia the "book of the law of Moses" (Neh 8.1; see also Ezra 7.6). Since late antiquity this book has been identified as the Torah, the first five books of the Bible, which according to the Documentary Hypothesis was given its definitive form by P. Even if, as some scholars argue, the book that Ezra brought back to Judah was not identical with the final form of the Torah, it is

reasonable to assume that it was at least a substantial and authoritative stage in the formation of what would become the Torah, a version that had been shaped in Babylon some time before Ezra's mission.

One of the themes of P is that of exile and return, under divine guidance, to the land promised to Abraham, Isaac, and Jacob. That theme is introduced in the narratives of the primeval history and recurs in the ancestral narratives in Genesis 12–50. The plot of the rest of the Pentateuch is essentially the extended narrative of the journey home from Egypt. The eventual return of the exiles from Babylon is thus anticipated in the return of other individuals and groups to their homes in the Promised Land.

The Babylonian exile itself is also referred to in P, which interprets it as a deserved punishment for the people's repeated disobedience. Thus, Leviticus 26 states at length:

> But if, despite this, you disobey me, and continue hostile to me, I will continue hostile to you in fury. . . . And you I will scatter among the nations, and I will unsheathe the sword against you; your land shall be a desolation, and your cities a waste. . . . But if they confess their iniquity and the iniquity of their ancestors, in that they committed treachery against me and, moreover, that they continued hostile to me— so that I, in turn, continued hostile to them and brought them into the land of their enemies; if then their uncircumcised heart is humbled and they make amends for their iniquity, then will I remember my covenant with Jacob; I will remember also my covenant with Isaac and also my covenant with Abraham, and I will remember the land. For the land shall be deserted by them, and enjoy its sabbath years by lying desolate without them, while they shall make amends for their iniquity, because they dared to spurn my ordinances, and they abhorred my statutes. Yet for all that, when they are in the land of their enemies, I will not spurn them, or abhor them so as to destroy them utterly and break my covenant with them; for I am the LORD their God; but I will remember in their favor the covenant with their ancestors whom I brought out of the land of Egypt in the sight of the nations, to be their God: I am the LORD. (Lev 26.27–45)

The cumulative evidence indicates, then, that one moment in the crystallization of traditions that are called P was the time of the exile in Babylon, the sixth century BCE. For the exiles, P's message was one of hope and optimism, coupled with insistence on faithful observance of the traditions associated with Moses.

THE EXILIC EDITION OF THE DEUTERONOMISTIC HISTORY

Another school active in the exilic period was that of the Deuteronomists, who produced another revision of their major work, the Deuteronomistic History, as well as of the book of Deuteronomy (see pages 180–83 and 191–93). In their account of the history of Israel in the land, from the time of the conquest under Joshua to the destruction of Jerusalem, the Deuteronomistic Historians used as principal themes the requirement of strict fidelity to the teaching of Moses, and especially that of worshiping Yahweh alone. The failure of the people to do so inevitably resulted in their punishment by Yahweh.

Thus, the explanation of the Deuteronomistic Historians for the disasters that befell both the northern kingdom of Israel in 722 BCE and the southern kingdom of Judah in 586 was the classic one of divine justice, or theodicy. According to the theological explanation of the events of 586, "Jerusalem and Judah so angered Yahweh that he cast them from his presence" (2 Kings 24.20), and they were exiled and the Temple in Jerusalem was destroyed. The nation had failed to live up to the requirements of the teaching of Moses, and in consequence the covenant curses had come upon them. Those curses included exile: "The LORD will scatter you among all peoples, from one end of the earth to the other; and there you shall serve other gods, of wood and stone, which neither you nor your ancestors have known" (Deut 28.64).

Yet although their primary focus was the past, the Deuteronomists were also concerned with the future. Sprinkled throughout the exilic edition of the book of Deuteronomy and the Deuteronomistic History are passages that urge repentance and express a veiled optimism. Solomon's second prayer at the dedication of the Temple is representative of such passages:

> If they sin against you—for there is no one who does not sin—and you are angry with them and give them to an enemy, so that they are carried away captive to the land of the enemy, far off or near; yet if they come to their senses in the land to which they have been taken captive, and repent, and plead with you in the land of their captors, saying, "We have sinned, and have done wrong; we have acted wickedly"; if they repent with all their heart and soul in the land of their enemies, who took them captive, and pray to you toward their land, which you gave to their ancestors, the city that you have chosen, and the house that I have built for your name; then hear in heaven your dwelling place their prayer and their plea, maintain their cause and forgive your people who have sinned against you, and all their transgressions that they have committed against you; and grant them compassion in the sight of their captors, so that they may have compassion on them, for they are your people and heritage, which you brought out of Egypt, from the midst of the iron furnace. (1 Kings 8.46–51; see also Deut 4.25–31; 30.1–10)

That hope in divine forgiveness and compassion may also be present in the exilic conclusion of the Deuteronomistic History:

> In the thirty-seventh year of the exile of King Jehoiachin of Judah, in the twelfth month, on the twenty-seventh day of the month, King Evil-merodach of Babylon, in the year that he began to reign, released King Jehoiachin of Judah from prison; he spoke kindly to him, and gave him a seat above the other seats of the kings who were with him in Babylon. So Jehoiachin put aside his prison clothes. Every day of his life he dined regularly in the king's presence. For his allowance, a regular allowance was given him by the king, a portion every day, as long as he lived. (2 Kings 25.27–30)

The release of Jehoiachin from prison in 561 BCE may have revived the hope for a restoration of the Davidic dynasty among some of the exiles. Other passages, also to be dated to the sixth century BCE, express a similar hope:

> On that day I will raise up
>   the booth of David that is fallen,
> and repair its breaches,

and raise up its ruins,
and rebuild it as in the days of old. . . .
I will restore the fortunes of my people Israel,
and they shall rebuild the ruined cities and inhabit them;
they shall plant vineyards and drink their wine,
and they shall make gardens and eat their fruit.
I will plant them upon their land,
and they shall never again be plucked up
out of the land that I have given them,
says the LORD your God. (Amos 9.11,
14–15)

The hope of return would soon become a reality, when Cyrus the Great conquered Babylon
in 539 BCE. The most exuberant reaction to that
event is found in Isaiah 40–55.

ISAIAH 40–55

One of the most important conclusions of
eighteenth- and nineteenth-century historical-
critical scholarship was that the biblical book of
Isaiah is not a single work dating from the time
of the prophet Isaiah of Jerusalem in the late
eighth and early seventh centuries BCE, but rather
is composed of writings from several different periods. In addition to the material going back to
Isaiah of Jerusalem, known as First Isaiah and
found in much of Isaiah 1–39 (see pages 330–33),
scholars identified two other major parts of the
book, **Second Isaiah** (also called "Deutero-
Isaiah"; Isa 40–55), and Third Isaiah (Trito-
Isaiah; Isa 56–66). In this chapter we will deal
with Second Isaiah.

A number of factors show that Second Isaiah
is later than First Isaiah. The historical situation
implicit in the book is entirely different. In First
Isaiah the principal enemy was Assyria; in Second Isaiah it is Babylon, which in the late seventh century BCE replaced Assyria as the dominant power in the Near East; Assyria is mentioned
only once in Second Isaiah (Isa 52.4). In First Isaiah, Jerusalem was under siege but never was destroyed; in Second Isaiah the city has been destroyed and will be restored, and the exile to
Babylon (586 BCE) has taken place. Finally, Second Isaiah (but not First Isaiah) twice mentions

Cyrus, the king of Persia, and describes him in
glowing terms usually reserved for Israel's own
leaders: He is the "anointed" of Yahweh, his
"shepherd," chosen by Yahweh to destroy Babylon and to rebuild the Temple (Isa 44.28–45.1)
(see Figure 23.3). Another significant difference
is that in First Isaiah the prophet is named and is
a major character in both autobiographical and
biographical accounts, but in Isaiah 40–66 the
speaker is anonymous and we are given no details
about his life or his family. The historical references suggest that Second Isaiah is to be dated to
the mid-sixth century.

In Third Isaiah the historical context has
changed again. Despite some links in style with
the previous chapters of Second Isaiah, Third
Isaiah does not make use of Second Isaiah's frequent description of an imminent return from exile in Babylon as a second Exodus. By the time of
Third Isaiah the return has already taken place
(see especially Isa 56.8) and the audience is situated in Judah rather than in Babylonia. The Temple seems to have been rebuilt (56.7) or at least
was under reconstruction (66.1), and worship
seems to be taking place there (66.3–4). A ma-

FIGURE 23.3.   The tomb of Cyrus the Great, located in
Pasargadae in Iran. At its base it measures about 48 by 44 ft
(14.6 by 13.4 m). According to an ancient source, the inscription on the tomb said in part: "I am Cyrus, who founded the
Persian empire and ruled over Asia. Please let me keep this dirt
that covers my body."

jority of modern scholars have therefore concluded that Isaiah 56–66 dates somewhat later than Second Isaiah, in the late sixth or early fifth century BCE; we will consider these chapters in more detail on pages 427–28.

Despite the general agreement that chapters 40–66 of the book of Isaiah were not written by the eighth-century BCE prophet, more recent scholarship has also observed that since very ancient times the various parts of Isaiah were viewed as one book and that the parts share many links of vocabulary and theme. One prominent example is the designation of Yahweh as "the holy one of Israel," which occurs over thirty times in Isaiah but only infrequently elsewhere in the Bible. Throughout the entire book of Isaiah as well, Jerusalem (Zion) is a unifying theme, as are the concepts of justice and righteousness. A repeated phrase that connects the various parts of the book is "do not fear," as also does the presence of a "sign" (Isa 55.13). One explanation of these links is that there was something like a "school of Isaiah," a kind of intellectual movement that was active for several centuries, as we have suggested earlier (pages 331–32). This school not only would have preserved and edited the original oracles of the eighth-century prophet, but also would have continued after his death and written new compositions in his style, applying his original message to new situations. This resulted in the addition of various sections to the original collection, including not only Second Isaiah (chaps. 40–55) and Third Isaiah (chaps. 56–66), but also chapters 24–27, 34–35, and 36–39 (taken from the Deuteronomistic History in 2 Kings 18–20). The chapters that form Second Isaiah are thus the product of what we may consider a school of the prophet Isaiah, comparable to the schools or movements that produced the Priestly source and the Deuteronomistic History.

Closely connected with Second Isaiah are two sections in the earlier part of the book of Isaiah: chapters 24–27, often called "the Isaiah Apocalypse" (see further pages 438–39), and chapters 34–35, comprising an oracle against Edom (chap. 34; compare Ps 137.7–9 and Obadiah) and an account of the return from exile (chap. 35). The latter have close verbal parallels with chapters 40–55; note especially:

> The wilderness and the dry land shall be glad,
>   the desert shall rejoice and blossom;
> like the crocus it shall blossom abundantly,
>   and rejoice with joy and singing. (Isa 35.1–2;
>   compare 41.18–19; 51.3)

> And the ransomed of the LORD shall return,
>   and come to Zion with singing;
> everlasting joy shall be upon their heads;
>   they shall obtain joy and gladness,
>   and sorrow and sighing shall flee away.
>   (Isa 35.10 = 51.11)

Because Second Isaiah is anonymous, it is difficult to know exactly when and where it was written. The majority scholars think that the author of Second Isaiah was writing in Babylonia, like his predecessor Ezekiel, probably around 540 BCE, shortly before or after the city's capture by Cyrus. Certainly the author was familiar with Babylonian ritual and religious traditions, but no specific indications make the Babylonian option certain, although it is more likely. The other principal option is that it was composed in Judah, perhaps in Jerusalem itself. But little attention is given to the situation in Judah, and so the primary audience was most likely the exiles themselves.

Structure

As in much of the rest of prophetic literature, it is difficult to discern a principle of arrangement for the various parts of Second Isaiah, or even to delineate those parts with precision. Scholarly attempts to do the latter range from as many as several dozen distinct units to just a few. A closely related issue is the delineation of prose and poetry. In Second Isaiah, as in other prophetic books, most of the oracles are in poetry. Many scholars, but not all, have classified some passages as prose, especially 44.9–20.

The lack of consensus illustrates the complexity of the evidence and the precariousness of any single solution. Perhaps it is sufficient to say that the author of Isaiah 40–55 makes use of a variety of genres. In doing so, the author freely adapts and transforms them, like a composer's variations on another composer's theme. To put it somewhat differently, we perhaps should consider Second Isaiah as an interlocking series of oracles with an overall thematic unity but without a strictly logical and rhetorical development.

Themes

In its sixteen chapters, Second Isaiah reuses language and themes found in earlier biblical traditions. For example, we find a reference to Noah and to the divine promise made to him that the world would never again be destroyed by a flood (Isa 54.9; Gen 9.11); several references to Abraham and Sarah (Isa 41.8; 51.1–3), including the promise that Abraham's descendants would be as numerous as the grains of sand on the seashore (Isa 48.19; Gen 22.17; 32.12); an obscure reference to Jacob (Isa 43.27; see Hos 12.2–4); and a reference to the eternal covenant with David (Isa 55.3; see Ps 89.28–29).

We will examine three principal themes of Second Isaiah: its description of the return from exile as a new Exodus, its presentation of the "servant of Yahweh," and its explicit monotheism.

A New Exodus

The central theme of Second Isaiah, its unifying thread as it were, is that of the imminent return from Babylon as a new Exodus. The author imagines this return as a ritual procession to Zion led by Yahweh himself. The importance of this theme is indicated by its strategic placement at the beginning (Isa 40.3–5) and the end (55.12–13) of the book, as well as its use throughout Second Isaiah.

The return to Zion is linked repeatedly with Israel's earlier journey under divine guidance from Egypt to Canaan. When Yahweh brought the Israelites out of Egypt, he was their shepherd, guiding "his people . . . in the wilderness like a flock" (Ps 78.52). Now, according to Second Isaiah, reprising an image already used by Jeremiah (31.10) and Ezekiel (34.11–16), he will lead his flock once again (Isa 40.11).

Yet, while resembling the earlier journey from Egypt to Canaan, the return from exile will be qualitatively different: It will be something "new" (Isa 42.9; 43.19). Thus, whereas in the original Exodus the participants left "in great haste" (Ex 12.11; Deut 16.3), the participants in this journey will "not go out in haste" (Isa 52.12). The region through which the Israelites had passed on their journey from Egypt to Canaan had been a "great and terrible wilderness, an arid wasteland" (Deut 8.15; see also Num 21.5; Deut 32.10). In this new Exodus, the vast desert between Mesopotamia and the Promised Land will be transformed into an Edenic paradise, forested (Isa 41.19) and in bloom (35.1–2), with the trees clapping their hands for joy as the procession passes (55.12). The returnees will travel on a level road, with every valley filled and every hill made low (40.4). In the first Exodus, water was divinely provided but scarce. This time it will be everywhere: There will be rivers in the desert (43.19), with springs in abundance and the wilderness itself a pool of water (41.18; 49.10).

Making use of mythology, Second Isaiah links this new Exodus with Yahweh's earlier acts, especially his defeat of the waters of chaos before his creation of the world. In Isaiah 51.9–11, the poet addresses Yahweh's powerful arm (see Deut 4.34; Ps 136.12; Jer 32.17), urging it to rouse itself for battle as it had in the days of old, when he defeated the primeval waters, here called Rahab (as in Ps 89.10) and "the dragon" (see Isa 27.1). In a telescoping of chronology characteristic of mythological language, the poet coalesces the primeval battle with two reflexes of the same event, the escape of the Israelites from Egypt through the Sea of Reeds and the return from Babylon:

> Was it not you who cut Rahab in pieces,
>   who pierced the dragon?
> Was it not you who dried up the sea,
>   the waters of the great deep;
> who made the depths of the sea a way
>   for the redeemed to cross over?
> So the ransomed of the LORD shall return,
>   and come to Zion with singing;
> everlasting joy shall be upon their heads;

they shall obtain joy and gladness,
and sorrow and sighing shall flee away.
(Isa 51.9–11)

We thus see a consistency in the divine action, and at the same time something new. While repeatedly alluding to the earlier Exodus, in a lovely paradox the poet exhorts his listeners: "Do not remember the former things, or consider the things of old" (Isa 43.18).

The Servant of Yahweh

In his brilliant commentary on Isaiah, first published in 1893, the German scholar Bernhard Duhm isolated four passages as distinct, the "**servant songs**" or the "songs of the servant of Yahweh." In the first song (Isa 42.1–4), the servant is called the chosen one, to whom Yahweh has given his spirit, as he did to the judges of old, to "establish justice" throughout the world, in a nonviolent way. In the second song (49.1–6) the servant himself speaks to the entire world, and, like Jeremiah (Jer 1.5), identifies himself as one called by God before birth. In the third song (50.4–11), the servant speaks again, and, in words reminiscent of the "confessions" of Jeremiah (see pages 371–72), declares his confidence in divine help even in the face of physical persecution. Finally, the fourth servant song (52.13–53.12) continues this theme of the suffering of the servant, relating how despite his innocence the servant was oppressed "like a lamb that is led to the slaughter," but his suffering is surrogate—he is like the scapegoat (Lev 16; see pages 144–45), bearing the guilt of the people. Duhm hypothesized that these songs had been composed by another author and added to Second Isaiah at a later stage. Modern scholars are less inclined to view them as independent compositions, but Duhm's characterization has framed subsequent interpretation.

The identification of the servant is perhaps the most challenging issue in the interpretation of Second Isaiah. Two principal approaches have been taken. In the first, the servant is an individual, and a number of candidates have been proposed. From Israel's more distant past, these include Moses; from the late eighth and early seventh century BCE, Hezekiah the king of Judah;

from the sixth century, Jehoiachin the king of Judah, Jeremiah the prophet, Cyrus the king of Persia, Zerubbabel, and the anonymous prophet who wrote Second Isaiah himself. In Jewish tradition the servant was sometimes identified as a messianic figure of the future. In the New Testament (for example, Mt 8.17; Lk 22.37; Acts 8.32–35; 1 Pet 2.21–22; see also Mt 12.17–21) Jesus is explicitly identified as the "suffering servant" (a phrase that does not actually occur in the Bible) of the last servant song (Isa 52.13–53.12). For this reason, the view that Jesus is the servant was the dominant precritical Christian view, as in Handel's *Messiah*, where much of Second Isaiah in general and the "servant songs" in particular are incorporated into the libretto.

In other parts of the Bible, the title "servant of the LORD" is used of a number of individuals in Israel's history, including Abraham (Gen 26.24), Moses (Num 12.7; Josh 1.1), Joshua (Josh 24.29), David (2 Sam 3.18; 1 Kings 11.13; Isa 37.35; Ps 89.20), Job (Job 1.8), and, remarkably, even the Babylonian king Nebuchadrezzar (Jer 25.9). The term "servant" as applied to one divinely chosen is thus not unusual, and the description of the servant draws on preexisting biblical tradition, but none of the persons just mentioned seems a suitable identification for the servant in Second Isaiah because there the servant is more a figure of the present and the immediate future than of the past.

A second line of interpretation is to see the servant as a kind of literary figure, a personification of the nation of Israel, regarded as an individual as is often the case elsewhere in the Bible. This identification is supported by the text itself:

And he said to me, "You are my servant,
Israel, in whom I will be glorified." (Isa 49.3)

But the occurrence of "Israel" in this verse is puzzling, since in the following verses the servant is commissioned by the deity

to bring Jacob back to him,
and that Israel might be gathered to him . . .
to raise up the tribes of Jacob
and to restore the survivors of Israel.
(Isa 49.5–6)

Because of this apparent inconsistency, some scholars have argued that the reference to Israel in verse 3 should be deleted. Throughout Second Isaiah, however, Israel is explicitly identified as the servant of the Lord several times (for example, 41.8; 44.1; 48.20). Thus, if we consider the "servant songs" as an integral part of the entire work rather than later additions, the best identification of the "servant" is Israel itself, personified as a kind of prophet; as Jeremiah had been called from before birth to be "a prophet to the nations" (Jer 1.5), so now Israel also has been destined to be a "light to the nations" (Isa 42.6; 49.6; 51.4), that is, a prophet to the rest of the world.

The poet uses the personification of Israel as a prophetic servant of Yahweh fluidly, and at times the servant does seem to be distinct from Israel. Perhaps the prophet was incorporating his own experience, so that some of the passages describing the servant are autobiographical, or perhaps the poet had in mind not all Israel, but a restored Israel, the "remnant" of First Isaiah (10.20–22; 46.3). In this interpretation, the suffering of the innocent during the catastrophe of 586 BCE and its aftermath was the "punishment that made us whole" (53.5).

The variety of possible interpretations makes clear that there is no certain identification of the servant, and we should also allow for the possibility that the ambiguity is deliberate. On one level, the servant can be understood as an individual, or a group within Israel; on another, the servant can refer to Israel itself, understood both collectively and as an individual. As such, having experienced a kind of redemptive suffering, the servant has been commissioned divinely to bring "salvation . . . to the ends of the earth" (49.6), so that, it is implied, all nations may acknowledge the only God.

Monotheism

In Second Isaiah, for the first time in the chronology of biblical literature, we get a clear statement of monotheism, the belief that there is no god other than Yahweh, the god of Israel. In Second Isaiah, monotheism is not expressed in abstract philosophical terms, for Second Isa-

iah is poetry rather than treatise. Moreover, the monotheistic principle is not entirely new; rather, it had been developing for some time (see Box 23.2).

The concept of monotheism is clearly expressed in Isaiah 44.6:

> I am the first and I am the last;
>> besides me there is no god. (see also 43.11; 44.8;
>> 45.5, 21)

Monotheism is developed in Isaiah 44.9–20, a satire on the making and worship of idols and perhaps the only prose passage in Second Isaiah. In it, the foolishness of idolaters is elaborated, such as the carpenter who carves an idol from a tree and worships it, and then with the rest of the wood makes a fire and cooks himself a meal: "A deluded mind has led him astray, and he cannot save himself or say, 'Is not this thing in my right hand a fraud?'" (Isa 44.20). The satirical depiction of idolaters, also found in Jeremiah (2.27–28; 10.1–16; 51.17–18) and Psalm 115, becomes a favorite motif of later biblical writers, as in the Letter of Jeremiah (see Box 21.3 on page 369), and Bel and the Dragon, one of the additions to the book of Daniel (see page 540).

In Genesis 1, P alludes to *Enuma elish*, the Babylonian account of creation by the god Marduk after his defeat of Tiamat, implicitly offering a monotheistic alternative to the Mesopotamian myth: As the sole deity, it was Yahweh who defeated the primeval forces of chaos and created the world (see further pages 7–10). Second Isaiah makes this explicit. In the Babylonian new year festival at which *Enuma elish* was recited, the statue of Marduk along with that of his son Nabu (biblical Nebo) was carried in procession to his temple. Referring to Marduk by his title Bel, Second Isaiah asserts that this need to be carried "on weary animals" (Isa 46.1) demonstrates Marduk's powerlessness:

> [The statue] cannot move from its place.
> If one cries out to it, it does not answer,
>> or save anyone from trouble. (Isa 46.7)

By way of contrast, in the procession of the returnees to Zion, Yahweh is not carried; rather, he

Box 23.2 THE DEVELOPMENT OF MONOTHEISM

In Israel's early legal system, as expressed in the Decalogue, the text of its contract or covenant with Yahweh, the Israelites were commanded not to worship other gods, but no unequivocal statement was made about Yahweh being the only god (Ex 20.3; Deut 5.7; see page 116). Rather, in bringing Israel out of Egypt he had shown his superiority to other gods (Ex 12.12; 15.11), as he also had in defeating the forces of chaos and creating the world (Ps 89.5–14).

In the preexilic prophets, the "oracles against the nations" (see pages 310–11) implied Yahweh's rule over the entire world. For Isaiah of Jerusalem in the late eighth century BCE, even mighty Assyria was a mere instrument in Yahweh's hands (Isa 10.5). One stimulus for this development was the increasingly frequent attacks on and ultimately the conquest of both the northern kingdom of Israel and the southern kingdom of Judah by the Assyrians and the Babylonians. The prophets interpreted these attacks not as the result of Yahweh's inferiority to the more powerful gods of other nations, but as his use of those nations to punish Israel and Judah for having violated their covenant with him.

In Second Isaiah the concept of Yahweh's superiority is taken to its logical conclusion: If Yahweh was responsible for what happened to Israel, if Assyria, and then Babylon, and finally Cyrus, were all instruments in the divine hand, if Yahweh was directing history for his own purposes, then not only was he more powerful than other gods, but other gods in fact did not exist, as Second Isaiah repeatedly proclaims. The development of explicit monotheism thus can be understood as a further response to the catastrophe of the destruction of Jerusalem in 586 BCE.

Monotheism thus became the defining characteristic of Judaism, followed by Christianity and Islam. The ancient words of the Shema were reinterpreted as a monotheistic declaration—"The LORD our God, the LORD is one" (Deut 6.4; see further Box 11.1 on page 176), reiterated in the pronouncement of Paul—"for us there is one God, the Father, from whom are all things and for whom we exist" (1 Cor 8.6), and in the Muslim profession of faith—"There is no god except God."

carries Israel, after having given birth to it (46.3) (see Box 23.3).

It was Yahweh, not Marduk, who defeated primeval chaos, the "great deep" (Isa 51.10; see page 9); it was Yahweh, not Marduk, who created the world (40.12), who formed light and created darkness (45.7). Moreover, unlike Marduk, he did this alone, without the assistance of other deities (44.24); unlike Marduk, Yahweh is neither the offspring of other gods nor did he father any (43.10). Yahweh's supreme power is demonstrated in his care for Israel, which at this historical moment has also involved designating Cyrus as his anointed agent of the return of the exiles to Zion (Isa 45.1), part of a divine plan that reaches back to creation:

Box 23.3 FEMALE IMAGES OF GOD

Yahweh, the god of Israel, is generally described in the Bible as a male deity. The grammatical forms used for him are always masculine, and he is frequently depicted in predominantly male images, for example as a king, a warrior, a husband, and a father. Scattered throughout the Bible, however, are also female images of Yahweh, and such images are clustered in Second and Third Isaiah. In his speeches Yahweh compares himself to a woman in labor whose long wait is over (Isa 42.14), as one who not only fathered but also gave birth to his children (Isa 45.9–12; compare Num 11.12). The metaphor is most explicit in Isaiah 49.14–15:

> Zion said, "Yahweh has forsaken me,
>   my Lord has forgotten me."
> Can a woman forget her nursing infant,
>   or show no compassion for the child of her belly?

Third Isaiah gives an example of another feminine image of God, that of the midwife (66.9; compare Ps 22.9–10).

Although the depiction of Yahweh as mother and midwife is relatively infrequent, it reminds us that all language used of the divine is metaphorical. (See further Box 18.5 on page 322.)

For I am God, and there is no other;
    I am God, and there is no one like me,
declaring the end from the beginning
    and from ancient times things not yet done.
    (Isa 46.9–10)

At the same time Second Isaiah seems to suggest that other deities exist. Yahweh is the creator of the heavenly army (Isa 40.26). In an imaginary courtroom, Yahweh summons to the Babylonian deities to trial (Isa 41.1–2; compare Ps 82), but, when he questions them (41.21–23), like Baal in Elijah's contest on Mount Carmel (1 Kings 18.20–29; see pages 303–5), they are silent (Isa 41.28). Many scholars have also recognized in the plural imperatives of Isaiah 40.1–2 ("Comfort ye . . .") an address by Yahweh to the members of the divine council, the assembly of the gods over which Yahweh presided; at this coun-

cil meeting, as in 1 Kings 22.20–22, various members of the council speak (Isa 40.3, 6). Given Second Isaiah's explicit monotheism, however, all of these references to other gods, like P's allusion to the divine council in its account of creation (Gen 1.26), are literary convention rather than an expression of polytheistic belief.

RETROSPECT AND PROSPECT

From its opening words commanding comfort for Jerusalem to its closing statement guaranteeing that the divine purpose will be fulfilled, Second Isaiah has an exuberant optimism. Babylon will be defeated by Cyrus, the exiles will return, and Jerusalem will be restored to a place of "joy and gladness" (Isa 51.3).

One of the leaders of the returning exiles was Zerubbabel, a grandson of King Jehoiachin and thus a descendant of David, and among some of the returnees there must have been an expectation that this too was part of the divine plan, that the Davidic dynasty would be restored. A permanent Temple had been part of Israel's life since it had been built by Solomon in the mid-tenth century BCE, but the reconstruction of the Temple is mentioned only once in Second Isaiah (44.28). Moreover, although P gives elaborate descriptions of the tabernacle and its rituals, in P's narrative of the journey from Egypt to Canaan that tabernacle is a portable structure suitable for a people on the move. But in Ezra 1 rebuilding the Temple is a primary concern of the returnees, and it becomes an important focus of the literature of the late sixth century.

When the exiles did return, the expectation of a restoration of the monarchy, along with Second Isaiah's optimism and P's careful program for reestablishing worship, all met the cold realities of the actual situation in Judah. Tensions also developed among various groups—the returning exiles, those who had remained in the land, and those who remained in exile, both in Babylon and elsewhere—and, despite the promise, or at least the assertion, of Persian support, rebuilding the Temple proved not to be an easy task. In the next chapter we will examine the literature concerned with the decades immediately following the return from Babylon.

IMPORTANT TERMS

Second Isaiah   servant songs

QUESTIONS FOR REVIEW

1. How did the policies of the Persians toward conquered peoples differ from those of the Babylonians?

2. How does the Pentateuchal source P deal with the problems raised by the destruction of Jerusalem and the exile in Babylon?

3. How did the Deuteronomistic Historians revise their work in light of the exile?

4. How does Second Isaiah reinterpret earlier biblical traditions in response to the events of the sixth century BCE?

BIBLIOGRAPHY

A good summary of the Persian period is Mary Joan Winn Leith, "Israel among the Nations: The Persian Period," Chap. 8 in *The Oxford History of the Biblical World* (ed. M. D. Coogan; New York: Oxford University Press, 1998; pb 2001).

For commentaries on Ezra, see the bibliography to Chapter 25.

For commentaries on Second Isaiah, see Richard J. Clifford, *Fair Spoken and Persuading: An Interpretation of Second Isaiah* (New York: Paulist, 1984; rp. Academic Renewal, 2002); and Christopher R. Seitz, "The Book of Isaiah 40–66," pp. 307–551 in *The New Interpreter's Bible*, Vol. 6 (ed. L. E. Keck; Nashville: Abingdon, 2001).

For a sketch of the development of monotheism, see Baruch Halpern, "Monotheism," pp. 524–27 in *The Oxford Companion to the Bible* (ed. B. M. Metzger and M. D. Coogan; New York: Oxford University Press, 1993); and for its significance in Second Isaiah, see "Monotheism in Isaiah 40–55," pp. 179–94 in Mark S. Smith, *The Origins of Biblical Monotheism: Israel's Polytheistic Background and the Ugaritic Texts* (New York: Oxford University Press, 2001).

On feminine imagery used of God, see Carol Meyers, "Female Images of God in the Hebrew Bible," pp. 525–28 in *Women in Scripture* (ed. Carol Meyers; Boston: Houghton Mifflin, 2000).

PART FIVE

RECONSTRUCTION AND CONSOLIDATION

THE EARLY RESTORATION

CHAPTER 24

Ezra 3–6, 1 Esdras, Haggai, Zechariah 1–8, and Isaiah 56–66

The Jews in exile in Babylonia were allowed to return to their homeland after Cyrus the Great's capture of Babylon in 539 BCE. What the returnees encountered, however, was not nearly as glorious as Second Isaiah had proclaimed. The community in Judea was divided, and Jerusalem was in shambles. The reconstruction of the Temple would take several decades, and that of the city nearly a century. There were struggles over leadership, and tensions existed both between the returnees and those who had not gone into exile but had remained in Judah and between the returnees and other neighboring peoples. In this chapter we will look at the history of the return and the early restoration, including the rebuilding of the Temple in the late sixth century BCE.

HISTORY

Cyrus the Great, the king of Persia who had captured Babylon and allowed those of the Jewish exiles who wished to return to do so, died in battle in 530 BCE and was succeeded by his son Cambyses, who completed the imperial designs of his father by capturing Egypt. Cambyses died under mysterious circumstances in 522 on his way back

from Egypt and was succeeded by a distant cousin and commander in his army, Darius I, who ruled until 486. (For a chronology, see Box 23.1 on page 402; see also Figure 24.1)

For information about the Jewish communities both in the Diaspora and in Judah during the latter part of the sixth century BCE, our only primary source is the Bible, especially the books of Ezra, Haggai, and Zechariah. Unfortunately, these three works do not give a coherent picture and are incomplete and often allusive rather than specific. Moreover, neither the details nor the chronology are entirely consistent in these sources. As a result, in reconstructing the events we can often make only educated guesses.

The return described at the beginning of the book of Ezra seems to have been of a small group. According to Ezra 3, as soon as they arrived in Jerusalem the returnees built an altar in order to reestablish the regular sacrifices to Yahweh. Then, "in the second year after their arrival" (Ezra 3.8), with appropriate ceremonies, they started the reconstruction of the Temple, to replace the Temple that had been built by Solomon in the mid-tenth century BCE and destroyed by the Babylonians in 586 BCE. But when the foundation of the Temple was laid, the attendees had mixed emotions:

FIGURE 24.1.   The Persian king Darius I seated on his throne, with his son Xerxes behind him, on a relief at the royal palace in Persepolis.

Many of the priests and Levites and heads of families, old people who had seen the first house on its foundations, wept with a loud voice when they saw this house, though many shouted aloud for joy, so that the people could not distinguish the sound of the joyful shout from the sound of the people's weeping. (Ezra 3.12–13)

Clearly the new Temple's foundations were not nearly as magnificent as those of the first. For reasons not given, work on the reconstruction was half-hearted at best, if it did not come to a complete halt. Some of the returnees were apparently more preoccupied with their own needs and comfort than with work on the Temple (see Hag 1.4). There was also local opposition. It is difficult to describe the parties and politics of Judah in this period and in the subsequent century because our sources are so fragmentary, but one important group was clearly the returnees, who claimed that the reconstruction had the support of Cyrus and Cambyses. Another group identified as "the adversaries of Judah and Benjamin" (Ezra 4.1) offered their assistance, asserting that they too were worshipers of Yahweh, although they had been settled in the former northern kingdom of Israel by the Assyrians (see 2 Kings 17.24–28); their offer was rebuffed. A third group was the "people of the land," a phrase that in this period proba-

bly means Judeans who had not been taken into exile. They seem to have tried to use their influence with the Persian court to disrupt the reconstruction.

Early in the reign of Darius I, about 520 BCE, work on the rebuilding of the Temple resumed under a dual leadership. Political authority lay with Zerubbabel, who, like Sheshbazzar, the leader of the returnees in 538, had the title of "governor," a designation of the top official in a province in the Persian imperial system. Also like Sheshbazzar, Zerubbabel was a descendant of Jehoiachin (Jeconiah), the king of Judah who had been exiled to Babylon in 597. Religious authority lay with the high priest Jeshua (also called Joshua, a variant of the same name). This shared leadership and their efforts to reconstruct the Temple had the support of two prophets, Haggai and Zechariah (Ezra 5.1).

According to the book of Ezra, Persian imperial support for the restoration was confirmed by Darius, in response to a query from Tattenai, the governor of the province of "Beyond the River," that is, the province west of the Euphrates River, roughly the Levant. Apart from the Persian kings themselves, Tattenai is the only individual in the biblical sources for this period to be mentioned in a contemporaneous nonbiblical text. That support was not just political, but also financial, according to the book of Ezra: Tattenai was to pay for the cost of the reconstruction and also to supply materials for sacrifices. This account is consistent with Persian policy elsewhere: In Babylon, Cyrus restored the proper worship of Marduk, its principal deity, and in Egypt, Cambyses and Darius sponsored the reestablishment of local sanctuaries and priestly schools. As in Judah, the Persian kings thus both gained the support of local authorities and at the same time exercised imperial control over them.

The reconstruction now proceeded relatively swiftly, and in 515 BCE the Temple was dedicated. The rebuilt Temple is often called the "**Second Temple**," and the "Second Temple period" in Jewish history lasts from the late sixth century BCE to 70 CE, when Jerusalem was captured by the Romans and the Temple (which had been rebuilt again in the late first century BCE by Herod the Great) was destroyed. In the restored Temple, rituals resumed, in conformity with "the book of Moses" (Ezra 6.18). Immediately thereafter, the Passover was celebrated by the returnees, along with "all who had joined with them and separated themselves from the pollutions of the nations of the land" (Ezra 6.21). The latter group of participants presumably means those who had remained in the land, but who were willing to accept the religious authority of the leaders, especially as it related to qualifications for membership in the community. We get glimpses of a less restrictive attitude in some of the oracles of Third Isaiah (see page 428 and in the books of Chronicles (see pages 448–49).

At this point a hiatus occurs in the biblical sources until the mid-fifth century BCE. We have no further information about Zerubbabel and Jeshua, nor, as previously, is there any mention in Persian sources of the tiny province of Judah (also called Yehud). From the Persian perspective Judah was a relatively unimportant part of their empire; scholars estimate that the entire population of Judah at this time was perhaps no more than ten thousand persons, and that of Jerusalem perhaps fewer than a thousand.

EZRA 3–6

Ezra and Nehemiah lived in the fifth century BCE, and we will discuss them and the structure of the books that have their names on pages 431–36. Here we will focus on Ezra 3–6, a narrative history of the events of the late sixth century, from the return from Babylon to the dedication of the restored Temple in Jerusalem, and our principal source for those events.

The chronology of this section of the book of Ezra is confused. For example, Ezra 6.22 mentions the king of Assyria, either a deliberate anachronism or simply a mistake, for Assyrian rule had ended in the previous century. Also, the account of the reconstruction of the Temple moves abruptly from the reign of Darius to that of his successor Ahasuerus (Xerxes) in Ezra 4.6, then quotes correspondence of the next Persian king, Artaxerxes I, in 4.7–23, only to return to the time of Darius in 4.24. (For a chronology, see Box 25.1 on page 431.) The correspondence belongs with the debate concerning the activity of Nehemiah in the mid-fifth century BCE, as he undertook to rebuild Jerusalem's fortifications (see further pages 433–34).

It is precisely at this point in the narrative, Ezra 4.8, that the language of the text switches from Hebrew to **Aramaic** (see Box 24.1), only to return to Hebrew in Ezra 6.19. Another Aramaic section, also quoting a royal letter, appears in Ezra 7.12–26.

An important theme of the narrative sections of Ezra 3–6 is the reestablishment of proper worship and the reconstruction of the Temple. The first step was the building of the altar, upon which the prescribed sacrifices were then regularly offered as the principal holy days were observed (Ezra 3.2–6). Then, under priestly supervision, the Temple was built. Like its predecessor the Temple of Solomon, this Temple was constructed using imported cedars from Lebanon (Ezra 3.7; see 1 Kings 5.6–10). At the foundation-laying ceremony, the hymnic refrain celebrating God's covenant fidelity to Israel was sung (Ezra 3.11; see Pss 118; 136). Paralleling the account of the building of the altar and the

Box 24.1 ARAMAIC

A few small parts of the Jewish scriptures are not written in Hebrew (and thus the term "Hebrew Bible" is not strictly accurate), but in a related language called Aramaic. These are Ezra 4.8–6.18 and 7.12–26, Daniel 2.4b–7.28, Jeremiah 10.11, and two words in Genesis 31.47.

Aramaic is one of the Semitic languages, originally spoken in Aram, roughly the same as modern Syria. During the first half of the first millennium BCE Aramaic came to be used as a kind of lingua franca, an international language of diplomacy and commerce. This was the result in part of the Assyrian practice of deporting the elite of conquered regions, so that Aramaic-speaking persons from Syria came to be spread throughout the Assyrian empire. Thus, during the siege of Jerusalem in 701 BCE (see pages 339–44), the representatives of the Judean king Hezekiah asked the representative of the king of Assyria: "Please speak to your servants in the Aramaic language, for we understand it; do not speak to us in the language of Judah within the hearing of the people who are on the wall" (2 Kings 18.26). The implication is that the aristocrats spoke Aramaic, as did the Assyrian envoy, but ordinary people in Jerusalem could not understand it.

Gradually the use of Aramaic spread. During the Persian period it is widely attested in inscriptions from throughout the Persian empire, as far east as India and as far west as Asia Minor, and especially in Egypt, where the climate allowed hundreds of papyri written in Aramaic to be preserved. The use of Aramaic for official Persian documents in the book of Ezra is thus historically accurate, although many scholars question whether all of the documents are themselves authentic.

It was during the Persian period in the fifth and fourth centuries BCE and the subsequent Hellenistic period that Aramaic replaced Hebrew as the ordinary spoken language of Palestine. It remained so well into the Common Era, although, as the result of the conquests of Alexander the Great and the rule of his successors (see pages 499–501), Greek replaced Aramaic as the lingua franca of the region, a status it maintained until the Arab conquest in the seventh century CE.

Thus, Aramaic was the ordinary spoken language of Galilee in the first century CE, and the Gospels, which were written in Greek, quote Jesus speaking Aramaic on several occasions. Many of the Dead Sea Scrolls (see Box 29.2 on page 508) were also written in Aramaic, including the earliest known "targums," or translations of the scriptures from Hebrew into Aramaic. So pervasive was the presence of Aramaic that texts of the Hebrew Bible came to be written with Aramaic characters, and the Aramaic script remains the usual way of printing Hebrew.

Later in the Roman period Aramaic developed into Syriac and other dialects, and small communities in Syria and Iran still speak a form of Aramaic.

Box 24.2 THE BOOKS OF ESDRAS

The Bible has two books of Esdras, the Greek rendering of the Hebrew name Ezra. The book of 1 Esdras (also sometimes called 3 Esdras) is a composite work, consisting of excerpts from the books of 2 Chronicles, Ezra, and Nehemiah in a somewhat different order, with a number of minor variants along with some added material:

1 Esdras 1	=	2 Chronicles 35.1–36.21
2.1–15	=	Ezra 1.1–11
2.16–30	=	Ezra 4.6–24
5.7–46	=	Ezra 2
5.47–73	=	Ezra 3.1–4.5
6–7	=	Ezra 4.24–6.22
8.1–9.36	=	Ezra 7–10
9.37–55	=	Neh 7.73–8.12

This use of earlier texts is an example of how ancient writers could work, freely quoting, abridging, rearranging, and supplementing them; we will see other examples in the books of Chronicles and Job (see pages 447–48 and 482–83). The book probably dates to the second century BCE.

The principal addition is in 1 Esdras 3.1–5.6, a charming tale whose basis is a riddle: What is the strongest force in the world? Three members of the personal bodyguard of the Persian king Darius each argue in turn that wine, the king, and women are the strongest force. The third guard adds to his argument that in fact truth is the strongest force of all because it is a manifestation of God. This third speaker is identified parenthetically (1 Esdr 4.13) as Zerubbabel, and the king rewards him by offering to give him whatever he wants. Zerubbabel replies that he wants the king to fulfill his promise to assist the reconstruction of the Temple in Jerusalem. The king agrees and gives orders to that effect. Thus a popular tale has been revised to make its hero the leader of the reconstruction.

Several other postbiblical writings have Ezra's name attached to them; one of them, 2 Esdras, is discussed in Box 25.3 on page 443.

laying of the foundation (Ezra 3.1–13) is the account of the dedication ceremony when the rebuilding was complete (6.16–22). The priesthood was installed, and the Passover was celebrated with joy. For the author of Ezra, this is truly a restoration.

THE BOOK OF HAGGAI

Among the leaders mentioned by the book of Ezra are the prophets Haggai and Zechariah (Ezra 5.1; 6.14), both of whom actively supported the reconstruction of the Temple under Zerubbabel and

Jeshua. Two of the twelve books of the "Minor Prophets" are named for them, which we will now consider.

The book of Haggai is one of the shortest of the Minor Prophets. It consists of a third-person narrative that contains four oracles delivered by the prophet, all dated to a brief period, during the last few months of 520 BCE, the second year of the reign of Darius I. The book gives no other biographical details about the prophet.

As the book opens, in the late summer of 520, the Temple has not been rebuilt, although the houses of the leaders, the governor Zerubbabel and the high priest and Joshua (as Jeshua is called in this book), are luxurious enough. As a result, the community has not fared well, for Yahweh has caused a drought. Inspired by the prophet's words, the reconstruction starts, and Haggai continues to encourage the leaders, assuring them that "the latter splendor of this house shall be greater than the former" (Hag 2.9). He also addresses the disappointment of those who had known the Solomonic Temple: "Who is left among you that saw this house in its former glory? How does it look to you now? Is it not in your sight as nothing?" (Hag 2.3; see also Ezra 3.12).

When the Temple's foundation is being laid, the prophet pronounces Yahweh's blessing on the community and, in an extravagant conclusion, on its leader:

> Speak to Zerubbabel, governor of Judah, saying, I am about to shake the heavens and the earth, and to overthrow the throne of kingdoms; I am about to destroy the strength of the kingdoms of the nations, and overthrow the chariots and their riders; and the horses and their riders shall fall, every one by the sword of a comrade. On that day, says the LORD of hosts, I will take you, O Zerubbabel my servant, son of Shealtiel, says the LORD, and make you like a signet ring; for I have chosen you, says the LORD of hosts. (Hag 2.21–23)

The language recalls that of the "day of Yahweh" (see Box 18.2 on page 316) and is an example of early apocalyptic imagery that we will explore in the next chapter. With these concluding words, the book of Haggai seems to support the hopes for a reestablishment of the Davidic monarchy.

Jeremiah had spoken of Jehoiachin, the king who had been exiled to Babylon in 597 BCE, as a rejected signet ring (Jer 22.24). The book of Kings ends with the mention of the release of Jehoiachin from prison. Zerubbabel was a grandson of King Jehoiachin, and thus a descendant of David. Now he was the "governor of Judah" (Hag 1.1), who, like David, had been chosen by Yahweh (see 2 Sam 6.21; 1 Kings 8.16; Ps 78.70; Deut 17.15). Zerubbabel is addressed by Yahweh as "my servant," just as David had been (2 Sam 7.5; Ps 89.3, 20; Ezek 37.24), and he is called a signet ring, like Jehoiachin. Thus, Haggai strongly implies but does not explicitly state, Zerubbabel would preside over a restored Davidic kingdom under divine protection.

In the book of Haggai, then, we get a detailed look at one brief period in the early restoration, and also at one particular viewpoint.

ZECHARIAH 1–8

As is the case with the book of Isaiah, modern scholars have detected at least two distinct hands at work in the book of Zechariah. Chapters 1–8 of the book deal with the late sixth century BCE, especially the issues of leadership in the restored community in Judah and the reconstruction of the Temple. Chapters 9–14, on the other hand, are different in style and content and seem to come from a later period. Here we will consider Zechariah 1–8, often called "**First Zechariah**"; for Zechariah 9–14 ("Second Zechariah"), see pages 439–40.

According to the chronology given at the beginning of the book, Zechariah and Haggai were contemporaries; like Haggai, Zechariah's prophetic career began in 520 BCE, and according to subsequent dates given in the book (1.7; 7.1) it continued for at least two more years. Nothing else is known about the prophet; even his genealogy is confused: Zechariah 1.1 identifies him as the son of Berechiah the son of Iddo, while Ezra 5.1 gives his father's name as Iddo. The structure of the book is more straightforward than its contents. It opens with an introductory oracle

(1.2–6) in which the prophet urges his listeners not to follow the rebellious pattern of their ancestors in disobeying divine commands. Then follow eight visions (1.7–6.15), and First Zechariah concludes with oracles about fasting (7.1–14; 8.18–19) and about Jerusalem (8.1–17, 20–23).

The most unusual part of Zechariah 1–8 is the eight visions in the first six chapters. These visions are interlocking, with recurring themes and imagery. Like the visions of Amos (see page 311) they are clearly symbolic, and like those of Ezekiel (see pages 388–90) they are revealed by a divinely sent messenger (NRSV: "angel"). But their elaborate symbolism marks a new stage in the development of prophetic discourse and anticipates apocalyptic literature, in which the divine plan for the future, sometimes even the distant future, is revealed by a messenger using elaborate and even fantastic images (see further pages 436–37).

The first vision (Zech 1.7–17) illustrates the character of the visions. Like that in chapter 4, this vision takes place at night, a frequent time for revelations to prophets (see 1 Sam 3.3; 2 Sam 7.4). The prophet sees a man riding a red horse, among some myrtle shrubs, perhaps a natural corral, among which are three more horses of different colors. The prophet's interpreter, the divinely sent messenger, explains that the task of the horsemen, like that of the *satan* in the book of Job (Job 1.7; 2.2; see further Zech 3.1–2 and Box 28.1 on page 483), is to "patrol the earth." They report that the earth is at peace. The messenger then addresses Yahweh directly, asking when Jerusalem will be restored, and Yahweh replies with a comforting promise that the Temple will be rebuilt and prosperity will return. The same images recur in the eighth vision (6.1–8): Horses of different colors, in this case pulling chariots, represent the four winds, which also patrol the earth.

The second vision (Zech 1.18–21) is of four horns, representing the nations that scattered the Jews, principally the Babylonians. They will be destroyed by four metalsmiths, also agents of Yahweh. Horns are symbols of power, and the use of horns to represent nations will recur in the book of Daniel (7.7–8, 24; 8.6–8, 20–21; see also Ps

75.10). Yahweh then proclaims again that he will punish the nations that destroyed Jerusalem.

In the third vision (2.1–5), the prophet sees another divine messenger, who has a measuring line to determine the dimensions of the restored Jerusalem. This is reminiscent of Ezekiel's vision of a messenger who measures the restored Temple (Ezek 40–42).

The fourth (chap. 3) and fifth (chap. 4) visions use symbolic language to affirm the divine choice of Joshua (as Jeshua is called in this book) and of Zerubbabel. The prophet is assured that Zerubbabel, who began the reconstruction of the Temple, will see it to completion and that Joshua had been vindicated in the divine council, declared ritually pure, and given the appropriate priestly attire.

The sixth vision (Zech 5.1–4) also alludes to Ezekiel. Like Ezekiel (Ezek 2.9–10), the prophet sees a scroll, but this time it is an enormous flying scroll containing curses on thieves and on those who swear falsely. The dimensions of the scroll, 20 cubits by 10 cubits, are identical to those of the vestibule of the Temple of Solomon (1 Kings 6.3), indicating the importance of the Temple for Zechariah.

The seventh vision (5.5–11) is of a woman named "Wickedness," who is taken in a covered container from Judah to Babylon (called Shinar; see Gen 10.10), like an evil genie confined in a jar.

The cumulative message of the visions is of a divine plan being carried out: Babylon destroyed, Jerusalem and the Temple restored, and divinely chosen leaders ruling the community. The shared nature of that leadership from the prophet's perspective is clear. Both Zerubbabel and Joshua are called "sons of oil" (Zech 4.14), an unusual phrase implying that they had been anointed, as were both kings and priests in preexilic Israel (see Box 16.4 on page 284). But the prophet uses a careful circumlocution (the NRSV translation "anointed ones" is misleading), perhaps to avoid explicitly claiming royal status for Zerubbabel, whose official Persian title was "governor." Zerubbabel is also called "the Branch" (3.8; 6.12), a title that could have been understood to mean that in him the Davidic monarchy had been restored (see Isa 4.2; Jer 23.5; 33.15; compare Isa 11.1). His restoration of the Temple would also have been appropriate for a royal figure, since throughout the ancient Near East temple building was a demonstration both of a king's power and of divine favor.

Zerubbabel and Joshua are further described as two olive trees on either side of an intricate lampstand, for they "stand by the lord of the whole earth" (4.14). This is elaborated in 6.9–15, in which an admittedly confused text also mentions a "counsel of peace between the two of them," perhaps implying some tension in the shared leadership.

Zechariah 7–8, dated to the fourth year of Darius (518 BCE) (see Figure 24.2), consists of several loosely connected oracles. They contrast Jerusalem's deserved punishment with its restored state:

> Jerusalem shall be called the faithful city, and the mountain of the LORD of hosts shall be called the holy mountain. Thus says the LORD of hosts: Old men and old women shall again sit in the streets of Jerusalem, each with staff in hand because of their great age. And the streets of the city shall be full of boys and girls playing in its streets. . . . They shall be my people and I will be their God, in faithfulness and in righteousness. (Zech 8.3–5, 8)

The last phrases echo the marriage formula in Hosea (2.19–20).

According to Zechariah, people from all over the world will come to this restored Jerusalem to worship Yahweh (Zech 8.20–23). This reiterates a

FIGURE 24.2. A relief of the Persian king Darius I at Behistun, in Iran, from about 520 BCE. The king is the largest figure, facing defeated enemies. Above, the symbol of the Persian deity Ahura Mazda blesses the king. Surrounding the picture, which is cut into a cliff face several hundred feet above ground level, are inscriptions in three languages: Persian, Elamite, and Babylonian. The discovery of these texts in 1835 enabled the decipherment of Babylonian cuneiform in the 1850s.

theme found in Second Isaiah, and may be a counter to the narrower understanding of the community found in Ezekiel 44.9 and in the book of Ezra. First Zechariah, thus, is essentially an elaboration of themes in the book of Haggai, which includes what seems to be a somewhat broader view of membership in the restored community.

ISAIAH 56–66

As we have already mentioned (see pages 330–31 and 408–9), chapters 56–66 of the book of Isaiah seem to be from a different era than either First Isaiah or Second Isaiah. Since the late nineteenth century, this section has been called "**Third Isaiah**" (or "Trito-Isaiah"). As in Second Isaiah, Jerusalem has been destroyed (for example, Isa 58.12; 64.10–11) and there is a promise that the exiles will return (56.8, 60.4), but there are also passages in which the Temple has been restored and is functioning (56.5, 7; 66.6). Third Isaiah thus seems to be a work of the early postexilic period, rather than of the preceding exilic period, the time of Second Isaiah. A date in the late sixth century BCE, after the completion of the Temple in 515 BCE, is likely, although sometime in the fifth century is also possible. No specific historical references make the date more precise.

Third Isaiah is also difficult to date and to interpret because of its frequent quotations of and allusions to earlier biblical materials; we will observe the same phenomenon in Second Zechariah (see pages 439–40). The author (or authors) of Third Isaiah make use of Hosea, Jeremiah, First Isaiah, and especially Second Isaiah. As examples we may note the following parallels:

[W]hen I called, no one answered,
    when I spoke, they did not listen. (Isa 66.4)

[W]hen I spoke to you persistently, you did not listen, and when I called you, you did not answer. (Jer 7.13)

Nations shall come to your light,
    and kings to the brightness of your dawn.
Lift up your eyes and look around;

they all gather together, they come to you;
your sons shall come from far away,
    and your daughters shall be carried on their nurses' arms. (Isa 60.3–4; see also 66.12)

I will soon lift up my hand to the nations,
    and raise my signal to the peoples;
and they shall bring your sons in their bosom,
    and your daughters shall be carried on their shoulders. (Isa 49.22)

This use of quotations and allusions contributes to an apparent lack of structure in Third Isaiah. Like some other postexilic writings, it seems to be a kind of collage of originally independent units that are connected only loosely. Some of its themes and vocabulary link it with the entire book of Isaiah, such as the centrality of Jerusalem/Zion (named in over a dozen verses in Isa 56–66), the phrase "holy one of Israel" (60.9, 14), and the presence of a sign (66.19). For this reason, the oracles in Third Isaiah, or at least their editing, can be attributed to the school of Isaiah discussed earlier (pages 331–32 and 408–9).

The viewpoints of Third Isaiah are at times different from those of Haggai and Zechariah. One oracle seems to express opposition to the rebuilding of the Temple:

Thus says the LORD:
Heaven is my throne
    and the earth is my footstool;
what is the house that you would build for me,
    and what is my resting place? (Isa 66.1)

This is reminiscent of Yahweh's refusal to allow David to build him a Temple (2 Sam 7.5–7; see pages 261–62). It is also inconsistent with other passages in Third Isaiah that describe the Temple and the offerings there more positively, such as Isaiah 60.7, which describes the Temple as Yahweh's "glorious house," and 56.7, which calls it a "house of prayer" where sacrifices will be accepted. Such inconsistency is doubtless due to the composite nature of Third Isaiah.

Third Isaiah makes no reference to the apparent hope of some Judeans for a restoration of the Davidic monarchy. Zerubbabel is not mentioned either, as is also the case with other narratives set after 515 BCE, but because our sources for the late sixth and early fifth centuries are so fragmentary it is risky to conclude much from this absence.

In some of the oracles in Third Isaiah we find a more inclusive view of the restored community than that attributed to Zerubbabel and Jeshua in the book of Ezra. According to Third Isaiah, the community is to be one in which even eunuchs are included (56.3–5), a rejection of the requirement of physical wholeness found in Deuteronomy 23.1. As in Zechariah 8.20–23, foreigners from all nations are also to be included (56.3–7; 66.18–23), a point of view that will become a major issue of contention in the fifth century BCE (see Ezra 9.1–2; Neh 9.2; 13.23–27).

One group of foreigners, however, is singled out for divine vengeance: the Edomites, whose participation in the Babylonian destruction of Jerusalem in 586 BCE had been condemned earlier in the book of Psalm 137 and Obadiah (see pages 385–86). In Isaiah 63.1–6, Yahweh describes himself returning from battle with his garments stained by Edomite blood, as if he had been treading grapes to extract their juice for wine; in the famous paraphrase of Julia Ward Howe, he has been "trampling out the vintage where the grapes of wrath are stored."

Like some of its prophetic predecessors (see Box 18.3 on page 319), Third Isaiah also emphasizes the importance of social justice over ritual observance:

> Is not this the fast that I choose:
>   to loose the bonds of injustice,
>   to undo the thongs of the yoke,
> to let the oppressed go free,
>   and to break every yoke?
> Is it not to share your bread with the hungry,
>   and bring the homeless poor into your house;
> when you see the naked, to cover them,

> and not to hide yourself from your own kin?
> Then your light shall break forth like the dawn,
>   and your healing shall spring up quickly;
> your vindicator shall go before you,
>   the glory of the LORD shall be your rear guard.
> Then you shall call, and the LORD will answer;
>   you shall cry for help, and he will say, Here I
>   am. (Isa 58.6–9)

The conclusion of this passage also illustrates Third Isaiah's optimism about the restored community in Jerusalem, the center of "the new heavens and the new earth" that Yahweh will bring to pass (Isa 65.17; 66.22).

RETROSPECT AND PROSPECT

More exiles had returned, and the Temple had been rebuilt under the leadership of the Persian appointed governor Zerubbabel and the high priest Jeshua and with the support of the prophets Haggai and Zechariah. In some circles, at least, a hope existed that the Davidic monarchy would be restored, perhaps even in the person of Zerubbabel. But Zerubbabel disappears from the scene, and that hope was disappointed. The idea of a future Davidic ruler, a messiah, would have to be postponed to a more remote future.

Moreover, despite the rebuilding of the Temple, the situation is Judah was unstable. The physical restoration of Jerusalem and the social restoration of the community would need to continue, and questions about the composition of that community would have to be resolved. These issues became pressing in the mid-fifth century BCE, which is when the biblical sources resume their narrative, and to which we will turn in the next chapter.

IMPORTANT TERMS

Aramaic

First Zechariah

Second Temple

Third Isaiah

QUESTIONS FOR REVIEW

1. How did the returned exiles from Babylon relate to others in the land in the late sixth century BCE?

2. Why was it important for the Temple to be rebuilt?

3. What was the nature of leadership in the restored community?

4. What is the significance of Zerubbabel's ancestry?

BIBLIOGRAPHY

For commentaries on the book of Ezra and for a summary of the history of the period, see the bibliography to Chapter 23. A good introduction to 1 Esdras is T. C. Eskenazi, "I Esdras," pages 344–47 in *Dictionary of Biblical Interpretation* (ed. J. H. Hayes; Nashville: Abingdon, 1999); for a fuller commentary, see Sara Japhet, "1 Esdras," pages 751–70 in *The Oxford Bible Commentary* (ed. J. Barton and J. Muddiman; Oxford: Oxford University Press, 2001).

Two good commentaries on Haggai and Zechariah are Carol L. Meyers and Eric M. Meyers, *Haggai, Zechariah 1–8* (New York: Doubleday, 1987); and David L. Petersen, *Haggai and Zechariah 1–8: A Commentary* (Philadelphia: Westminster, 1984).

For Third Isaiah, see the commentary by Christopher R. Seitz in the bibliography to Chapter 23.

JUDAH IN THE FIFTH CENTURY BCE

*Ezra 7–10, Nehemiah, Isaiah 24–27, Zechariah 9–14,
Joel, Malachi, and 2 Esdras*

In this chapter we will consider first events in Judah in the fifth century BCE and then various writings from that period included among the prophets, many of which belong to an early stage of a genre called "apocalyptic." The restored community in Jerusalem continued to experience difficulties and internal disputes, and perhaps in part because of this more and more hope focused on the distant future.

HISTORY

During his long reign, Darius I (522–486 BCE) consolidated Persian control over regions already conquered and sought to extend it, especially to the north and east. Darius's successor, his son Xerxes, moved to expand the empire further, especially to the west. This meant a confrontation with the city-states of Greece, principally Athens and Sparta. Both sides won a number of battles, with the Persians even setting fire to the Acrop-

olis in Athens at one point. The Persians were defeated in a land battle in 490 at Marathon about 25 miles (40 km) northeast of Athens, and a decade later, although they won a famous land battle at Thermopylae about 80 miles (130 km) north of Athens, some of the Persian navy was lost near the island of Salamis about 25 miles (40 km) west of Athens. The presence of the Persians in force on the Greek mainland showed their power, but the fact that the Greeks were able to defeat them some of the time also showed the Persians' vulnerability. Neither side was able to conquer the other decisively, and the conflict continued for another century and a half. (See Box 25.1 and Figure 25.1.)

These events had little recorded effect on the tiny province of Judah and have left scant traces in biblical literature. As was the case for the latter part of the sixth century BCE, there is no continuous biblical narrative. Instead, we are dependent on several incomplete and sometimes inconsistent sources, and any reconstruction of what may have occurred is necessarily tentative. After the rebuilding of the Temple in the late sixth century BCE, discussed in the previous chapter, we know little until the mid-fifth century, which is when most scholars date the missions of Ezra and Nehemiah. In the books named for them we have a brief glimpse into life in Judah.

THE BOOKS OF EZRA AND NEHEMIAH

In the Hebrew Bible the books of Ezra and Nehemiah form one unit; in Christian Bibles since late antiquity they usually have been divided into two books. Most modern scholars consider these books to be a single work. The two parts get their names from their principal characters, Ezra and Nehemiah, both of whom are vividly portrayed. The entire work probably was written in the late fifth or early fourth century BCE. The contents can be outlined as follows:

Ezra 1–2: The return from exile (see pages 403–5)

Ezra 3–6: The early restoration (see pages 421–23)

Ezra 7–10: The mission of Ezra, including a first-person memoir (7.27–9.15)

Nehemiah 1.1–7.5: Nehemiah memoir

Nehemiah 7.6–73: List of returnees (almost identical to that in Ezra 2)

Nehemiah 8.1–12.26: Ceremonies of renewal, to which are added a census of Jerusalem residents and other lists

Nehemiah 12.27–13.31: Resumption of Nehemiah memoir

FIGURE 25.1. Portion of a relief in the audience hall of Darius I in his capital city Persepolis. It depicts subjects from various parts of the Persian empire in their distinctive clothing bringing tribute. Shown here are Scythians in the upper register, bringing a stallion, bracelets, and clothing, and Lydians in the lower register, bringing vases and cloth. The figures are about half life-size.

As this outline indicates, Ezra-Nehemiah is a composite work, compiled from a number of different sources, a conclusion supported by the use of Aramaic rather than Hebrew in Ezra 4.8–6.18 and 7.12–26 (see Box 24.1 on page 422). There are also frequent shifts from third-person narrative to apparently autobiographical accounts. The latter are more likely a kind of fictional autobiography, like the first-person narratives in some of the prophets, although it is possible that they are derived from actual writings of Ezra and Ne-

hemiah themselves. Because the opening verses of the book of Ezra duplicate the concluding verses of 2 Chronicles, many scholars have concluded that there was a literary relationship, perhaps even the same author, for the books of Chronicles, Ezra, and Nehemiah. We will return to this issue in Chapter 26.

The work covers a considerable period, beginning in the second half of the sixth century BCE and continuing well into the fifth. But the two parts of the work overlap, and chronological problems exist. A major issue is the dates of the missions of Ezra and Nehemiah and their relationship. Nehemiah's first mission is dated from the twentieth to the thirty-second year of Artaxerxes (Neh 5.14). Nearly all modern scholars agree that this was Artaxerxes I, which would date Nehemiah's activity in Jerusalem from 445 to 433 BCE; some unspecified time after that he returned from the Persian capital to Jerusalem for a second mission (Neh 13.6). Ezra's mission is dated to the seventh year of Artaxerxes (Ezra 7.7), but there were several Persian kings with that name (see Box 25.1). It cannot be Artaxerxes IV, whose reign lasted only two years. A majority of modern scholars, following the sequence in the books themselves, place the mission of Ezra earlier than that of Nehemiah, in the reign of Artaxerxes I in 458, and that is the position taken here. A minority of scholars have placed the mission of Ezra during the reign of Artaxerxes II, in 398, and consider the references to Ezra and Nehemiah as contemporaries (Neh 8.9; 12.26) to be later additions.

Although Nehemiah, like Zerubbabel in the sixth century BCE, has the official title of "governor," as is the case for both Zerubbabel and Jeshua no mention of either Nehemiah or Ezra is made in any contemporaneous nonbiblical sources.

The Mission of Ezra

According to the introduction to the account of his mission, Ezra was a member of a priestly family and "a scribe skilled in the *torah* of Moses" (Ezra 7.6). With the Persian king's sanction, Ezra traveled to Jerusalem with a sizable entourage of "leaders from Israel" (7.28) in order to impose the requirements of the divinely given commandments, especially those concerning marriage with "foreign" women. Apparently such intermarriage was frequent, for it took several months to identify all the men who had done so. The ending of the book of Ezra is abrupt, and its last few words obscure, but an ancient tradition interprets them to mean that the "foreign" women and their children were sent away or at least ostracized from the community.

Ezra is mentioned again in Nehemiah 10 as the leader of a lengthy ceremony of renewal, at which the "book of the *torah* of Moses" is read, and during which the fall festival of Booths is celebrated. The ceremony concludes with a commitment by all "to walk in God's *torah*, which was given by Moses the servant of God, and to observe and do all the commandments of the LORD" (Neh 10.29). Three particulars are mentioned: no intermarriage, sabbath observance, and support of the Temple personnel with tithes of agricultural produce and an annual tax of one-third of a silver shekel (about 0.13 oz [3.8 gr]).

Although the details of the renewal are not entirely consistent with the prescriptions of the Torah in its present form, it is likely that the text that Ezra brought from Babylonia and that served as the basis for the renewal was some form of P's edition of the Torah, the first five books of the Bible (see page 406).

Ezra's mission, which apparently extended over several years, was thus primarily religious, although it had important social components. Authority seems to have lain not with those who had earlier returned to Jerusalem and Judah, or had never left, but with the leaders of the Diaspora in Babylonia. Especially important is the issue of intermarriage, to which we will return.

The Missions of Nehemiah

According to the sequence of events in the books of Ezra and Nehemiah, Ezra's moves toward religious revival and conformity were encouraged by Nehemiah in two missions, the first as governor of Judah for twelve years, and then during a brief return sometime later. According to the highly embellished first-person memoir, Nehemiah had held the important position of king's cupbearer, and at his own initiative sought royal approval to go to Jerusalem and rebuild it. On his arrival, an inspection tour revealed how dire the situation was: All of the city's defenses were in ruins. The description of Nehemiah's tour by night of the walls and the city gates cannot be correlated with archaeological data from Jerusalem, but the picture we get is of a relatively small city, with a population of no more than a few thousand.

Nehemiah began the reconstruction of the city's walls, but immediately faced opposition. Some was internal and apparently led by prophets, one of whom, Noadiah, was a woman (Neh 6.14). Presumably they and others in Jerusalem resented the imported authority of Nehemiah, and probably that of Ezra as well. More opposition came from the leaders of neighboring provinces, Tobiah the Ammonite, Geshem the Arab, and Sanballat the Horonite. The last of these is also mentioned in a contemporaneous nonbiblical source, the Elephantine papyri (see Box 25.2), in which he is identified as the governor of Samaria. Nehemiah skillfully foiled their plots, and the walls were rebuilt.

Why would the Persians have permitted and perhaps even encouraged the refortification of Jerusalem? From 460 to 454 BCE, a revolt against Persian rule took place in Egypt, a revolt supported by Persia's rival Athens. For the Persians, it would have made strategic sense to strengthen Jerusalem, a city not far to the north of Egypt.

Why was there such opposition from Judah's neighbors? They may have been suspicious that the leaders of a revived Jerusalem would attempt to extend their control over the surrounding region.

That control was not just political but religious and social. Close relationships had existed between the Judeans and their neighbors, many of whom were worshipers of Yahweh. In the time of Zerubbabel, the Samarians had wanted to assist in the reconstruction of the Temple, for they too were worshipers of Yahweh, but they were rebuffed (Ezra 4.1–3). Tobiah, who may also have had the title "governor," was a Yahwist, as his name, which means "Good is Yah(weh)," indicates, and further evidence of his piety as well as of his status is his having a special room in the Temple precinct (Neh 13.7). Two of Sanballat's sons mentioned in a papyrus from Elephantine, Delaiah and Shelemiah, also had Yahwistic names. Moreover, both Tobiah and Sanballat were linked with important Judean families: Tobiah's wife was the daughter of Shecaniah, who belonged to an important priestly family; Tobiah's son was married to the daughter of Meshullam,

Box 25.2 THE ELEPHANTINE PAPYRI

The Murashu texts give us a glimpse of Jews in Babylonia in the fifth century BCE (see page 384). We get a similar picture of life in the Diaspora from another collection of texts, several dozen contracts and letters from Elephantine in southern Egypt, where there had apparently been a colony of Jewish mercenaries and their families for several centuries. The texts were written on papyrus in Aramaic, which had become the lingua franca of the Persian empire (see Box 24.1 on page 422), and date mostly to the second half of the fifth century BCE. From them we get a picture of generally observant Jews, worshipers of Yahweh, who had built a temple in which animals were sacrificed, kept the sabbath and celebrated Passover, and consulted with their fellow Jews in Judah and Samaria for advice and support. Their brand of Judaism was not entirely orthodox, however, since they also seem to have worshiped other deities alongside Yahweh, or at least intermarried with non-Jews who worshiped them.

one of Nehemiah's supporters (Neh 6.18); and Sanballat's daughter was married to a son of the high priest (Neh 13.28).

The Issue of Intermarriage

In this context, the issue of intermarriage has considerable complexity. Although the Jewish community had been traumatized and challenged by the events of 586 BCE, it had managed not only to survive, but also to redefine itself and to restore its Temple. For some, the only way to maintain their identity was to insist on ethnic and religious purity. Exogamy, marriage outside one's group, inevitably weakens a group's identity. The children of Judeans who had married Ammonite, Moabite, and Ashdodite women, we are told, "could not speak the language of Judah, but spoke the languages of various peoples" (Neh 13.24). So the insistence of Ezra and Nehemiah that their version of Yahwism was the only legitimate one was reasonably motivated, a defense against assimilation.

Part of that defense was the strict prohibition of intermarriage outside the group that defined itself as the true Israel. That prohibition had strong precedents in the sacred traditions that had been collected, edited, and shaped in Babylon. Nehemiah 13.26 refers to the apostasy that resulted from Solomon's marriages with foreign women, and intermarriage is a recurring theme throughout Genesis and the Deuteronomistic History. It is also found in Ezra's speech, in which he quotes the divine commandments:

> "The land that you are entering to possess is a land unclean with the pollutions of the peoples of the lands, with their abominations. They have filled it from end to end with their uncleanness. Therefore do not give your daughters to their sons, neither take their daughters for your sons, and never seek their peace or prosperity, so that you may be strong and eat the good of the land and leave it for an inheritance to your children forever." (Ezra 9.11–12)

This is not a verbatim quotation, but it echoes words found in Leviticus (18.24–30) and in Deuteronomy (7.3–4). In this new historical context, the implication is striking: The Promised Land and those who are living there, even if they are also worshipers of Yahweh, are viewed as unclean. So, because "the book of Moses" excluded Ammonites and Moabites from the "assembly of God" (Deut 23.3, quoted in Neh 13.1), all those of foreign background were separated from Israel (Neh 13.3). The need to determine who belonged to Israel and who was "foreign" is one explanation of the censuses and other lists of persons in the books of Ezra and Nehemiah (Ezra 2, paralleled in Neh 7; see also Ezra 7.1–5; 8.1–20; 10.18–43; Neh 10.1–27; 11.3–24; 12.1–43).

The issue of intermarriage reveals a community deeply divided on questions of identity and on where authority lay. To some extent these are a continuation of earlier tensions. After the first deportation in 597 BCE, Jeremiah referred to the exiles as "good figs" and those who remained in the land as "bad figs" (Jer 24). In the same period, those in the land claimed that because they had not been taken to Babylon, they had not been punished by God; it was the exiles who were the guilty ones. Ezekiel, himself an exile, emphatically rejected that view (Ezek 11.14–21). After the decree of Cyrus in 538 BCE, Jews returning from Babylon established a shared religious and political leadership under Jeshua and Zerubbabel (see pages 420–21). Now, in a similar diarchy, Ezra and Nehemiah came from Mesopotamia to impose standards on those in the Promised Land.

In the books of Ezra and Nehemiah we have mainly the perspective of one side, that of leaders from the Diaspora who sought to impose their views on those living in Judah, including some who must have been descended from the first returnees. As we have seen, there was opposition to this insistence on religious and ethnic purity. Some opposition came from those whose motives may have been mixed, like Sanballat and Tobiah, who although worshipers of Yahweh were vying for power with Nehemiah. Other opposition came from some prophets. And more opposition must have come from those directly affected by the prohibition against intermarriage, who were told that they had to separate from their wives and children.

The books of Ezra and Nehemiah represent only one perspective on the issue of intermarriage. The Bible does contain others. For example, Ruth the Moabite became the great-grandmother of King David (see pages 226–27), and the marriage of Esther to the king of Persia seems not to have bothered the original writer of her story (see further pages 529–30).

APOCALYPTIC LITERATURE

Beginning in the postexilic period and continuing into the Common Era developed a genre of literature known as "**apocalyptic**," from a Greek word meaning "to uncover, to reveal." The Hebrew Bible contains a few examples of this genre, most of which have been incorporated into larger books; one is found in the New Testament, the book of Revelation; and many more occur in postbiblical Jewish and Christian literatures.

The apocalyptic genre was popular in the late biblical and postbiblical periods, and the form uses many variations. Grouped together, these works have a number of common elements, although not all of them occur in every work. The elements are:

- A revelation to a designated human by a heavenly messenger or in a vision or dream. The messenger may be either an angelic messenger, or someone who, like Enoch (Gen 5.24) and Elijah (2 Kings 2.11), was taken into heaven before death and is now returning with a communication from God concerning the end-time.

- A detailed explication of the past and present, often in coded language.

- A description of the end-time, along with a chronology indicating when it will occur, often thought to be in the near future.

- A pronounced dualism, contrasting good and evil, light and darkness, life and death, and present and future.

- Pessimism about the present, but optimism for the future based on the expectation of an ultimate divine victory and the subsequent transformation of the cosmos—"new heavens and a new earth" (Isa 65.17; 66.22; Rev 21.1).

- The incorporation of mythic traditions in which the end-time resembles the beginnings of the cosmos, especially the battle between the creator deity and the primeval forces of chaos. In a terrible final battle, the deity will be ultimately victorious, as he was in battle before creation.

- Imagery that is surreal, even fantastic, rather than realistic.

A growing majority among scholars think that apocalyptic literature developed out of prophecy. It is significant that except for the book of Daniel (see pages 536–37) all of the apocalyptic passages in the Hebrew Bible are present in books of the prophets. Moreover, although most of the writings of the preexilic prophets were concerned with interpreting the past, the present, and the immediate future from a divine perspective, most of them include passages that describe a more remote and glorious future, a restoration of divine favor after judgment; examples are Hosea 14.4–8, Amos 9.9–15, Isaiah 2.2–4 (=Mic 4.1–4), and Jeremiah 30–31. Such passages often occur at the end of prophetic books, and it is likely that many are later editorial additions. Nevertheless, their incorporation into the prophetic books is evidence of a commonality between prophecy and apocalyptic literature.

Many of the features of apocalyptic literature listed here are also found in earlier prophetic literature. A clear line of development can be traced from oracles in Amos, Hosea, First Isaiah, and Jeremiah concerning imminent punishment, and occasionally forgiveness, by Yahweh to the more elaborate revelation by a heavenly messenger of a restored Jerusalem in Ezekiel 40–48, and finally to the fully worked-out examples of apocalyptic literature in Daniel 7–12 and the book of Revelation.

Prophecy and apocalyptic literature also share ways of expressing the concept of revelation. Several prophets claim to have received their message because they witnessed or even participated in a meeting of the divine council, such as Micaiah (1 Kings 22.19–23), Isaiah (Isa 6.1–13), and

Jeremiah (Jer 23.18–22). The prophets thus are messengers from the divine council, and especially its presiding deity, to their audiences. This is closely related to the idea of a heavenly messenger, an image widely attested in the ancient Near East and found throughout biblical literature. In sixth-century BCE prophecy, the heavenly messenger becomes a frequent medium of revelation, as in Ezekiel 40–48, in which he discloses to the prophet the details of the new Jerusalem and its restored Temple, and Zechariah 1–6, in which the prophet's visions are accompanied by and interpreted by such a messenger. The same element is found frequently in apocalyptic literature (for example, Dan 9.21–23; 10.11–12; Rev 17.1; 21.9–10; see further Box 30.3 on page 534).

Another link between prophecy and apocalyptic literature is revelation through visions and dreams. Examples of prophetic visions are found in Amos (Am 7.1–9; 8.1–9.4), Isaiah (Isa 6.1), and Jeremiah (Jer 1.11–13) and in more developed form in Ezekiel (Ezek 1.4–28; etc.) and Zechariah (Zech 1.8–6.8). As was the case for the prophets Nathan (2 Sam 7.4) and Zechariah (Zech 1.8), revelations could occur at night, presumably in dreams. Both visions and dreams become frequent modes of revelation in apocalyptic literature, as in Daniel (Dan 7.1), and, like the visions and dreams of ordinary persons, those of apocalyptic writers are often surreal, bizarrely combining elements of reality and fantasy. The meanings of these visions and dreams are provided by a heavenly interpreter.

Among the sources that apocalyptic writers used were a variety of biblical genres and ancient Near Eastern mythology. The concept of the "day of the LORD" (see Box 18.2 on page 316) used in earlier prophets to describe divine judgment on Israel and Judah in the near term because of their failure to observe divine commands is quite naturally developed by apocalyptic writers into a more remote day of universal judgment not just on Israel but on the entire world. As apocalyptic literature developed, its writers drew on other sources, especially the literature of a Persian religious movement known as Zoroastrianism, in which a far-reaching dualism was expressed by contrasting war and peace, light and darkness, and good and evil. During the Hellenistic period beginning in the late fourth century BCE, Greek ideas were incorporated into apocalyptic vocabulary as well.

The origins of apocalyptic literature, then, are to be found in preexilic biblical prophecy. In literature of the sixth century BCE, especially in Ezekiel, Isaiah 40–55, Isaiah 56–66, Haggai 2, and Zechariah 1–8 (see pages 386–99, 408–14, and 423–28), we are in a transition phase between prophecy and apocalyptic literature, and this literature has been called "protoapocalyptic." By the fifth century BCE, some literature that looks more like the later apocalyptic literature found in the books of Daniel and Revelation has developed; this literature is sometimes called "early apocalyptic," and we will look at it in detail later in this chapter.

The fall of Jerusalem in 586 BCE and the Babylonian exile were traumatic for those who experienced them, and many scholars have seen such moments of crisis as the setting for apocalyptic movements. Imaginative conception of a better future would have been natural for those whose present was apparently hopeless. This explanation does fit some early apocalyptic literature, and some later as well, notably the book of Daniel during the persecution of Antiochus IV in the early second century BCE, and perhaps also the book of Revelation during persecutions of Christians during the late first century CE. Not all apocalyptic literature, however, can be so precisely dated, and it is likely that having developed as a genre, it was used by writers of various times and places even if they were not alienated from their immediate circumstances.

Finally, we should note that apocalyptic literature has had a fascination for readers of later eras, who have often attempted to read it literally and to see especially in its detailed chronologies a divinely revealed timetable for the end of the present world in their own lives. None of these precise interpretations, however, has (so far) been accurate.

In Chapter 30, we will examine the only example of fully developed apocalyptic in the

Hebrew Bible, Daniel 7–12. In the rest of this chapter we will examine some early apocalyptic literature included in books of the prophets. Scholars have dated many of these works to the fifth century BCE, largely on indirect evidence, since none of them mentions either Ezra or Nehemiah or any of the activities and events connected with them.

THE "ISAIAH APOCALYPSE" (ISA 24–27)

The book of Isaiah in its final form (see further pages 330–33 and 408–9) includes four chapters (Isa 24–27) that most scholars identify as an early example of the apocalyptic genre. Written at least for the most part in poetry, this **"Isaiah Apocalypse"** vividly describes the end-time, when all creation will be under the divine judgment: the earth withered, the heavens languishing, and human society disordered, with no distinctions between priest and laity, owner and slave, lender and debtor. On that day—the day of the Lord—Yahweh will finally defeat his primeval adversary "Leviathan the fleeing serpent, Leviathan the twisting serpent, and he will kill the dragon that is in the sea" (27.1; see further Box 28.3 on page 487). At the sound of a great war-trumpet, the scattered Israelites will be gathered from their lands of exile and return to Jerusalem to worship Yahweh on his holy mountain (27.13). There they will enjoy a lavish feast (25.6), while the unnamed "city of chaos" (24.10) will be in ruins. In this new age, Death, the god of the underworld, who in Ugaritic myth swallowed the storm-god Baal, will himself be swallowed up (25.8) and Yahweh's people who had died will be restored to life:

> Your dead will live, their bodies will rise up.
>> O dwellers in the dust, awake and sing for joy
>> . . . the earth will give birth to those long
>> dead. (26.19)

The Hebrew of this verse is notoriously difficult, but if this translation is correct, then this is the earliest biblical example of belief in the resurrection of the dead (see further page 495).

Although it contains several elements typical of the genre of apocalyptic literature, Isaiah 24–27 is not a fully developed apocalypse. Unlike later apocalyptic literature, the chapters lack a systematic chronology, and events occur almost at random rather than in a narrative sequence. Rather, Isaiah 24–27 appears to be a collection of originally independent shorter poems, linked by the theme of the end-time, but haphazardly arranged. Confirming this interpretation is the presence of several hymns that are interspersed in the chapters (25.1–5, 9–12; 26.1–6).

These poems have been incorporated into the book of Isaiah, with which they share a number of themes and vocabulary, not only with the preceding chapters but also with Second Isaiah. Two examples will illustrate these links. In both Isaiah 17.6 and 24.13, the fall harvest of olives and grapes is referred to metaphorically. In the first passage, the image is used to describe the almost total destruction of the northern kingdom of Israel, of which there will be only a few survivors: "Gleanings will be left in it, as when an olive tree is beaten" (Isa 17.6). In the second, in which several of the same and relatively rare words are used, the particular has become universal, and the metaphor applies to the whole world:

> For thus it shall be on the earth
>> and among the nations,
> as when an olive tree is beaten,
>> as at the gleaning when the grape harvest is
>> ended. (24.13)

A second example of shared vocabulary occurs in Isaiah 27, which reprises a metaphor from earlier in the book. In Isaiah 5.1–7, Yahweh announced that he would destroy his vineyard, "the house of Israel and the people of Judah," for they had been false, and thorns and briars would overgrow it. That threat is reiterated in 27.4, but then the passage moves on to an echo of Isaiah 11, which promises that "a shoot shall come out of the stump of Jesse, and a branch shall grow out of his roots" (Isa 11.1). This refers to the restoration of the Davidic monarchy under a new ruler. In 27.6, however, the image is much wider: It is Israel itself that will take root, blossom, put forth shoots, and fill the whole world with fruit.

Taken as a whole, the chapters comprise too short a unit to say with certainty that this is another product of the school of Isaiah (see pages 331–32 and 409). Perhaps its author or authors, familiar with Isaiah, composed some variations in apocalyptic mode on the themes of Isaiah; this naturally would have led later editors to incorporate it into the final canonical book of Isaiah. In contrast to both First Isaiah and Second Isaiah, however, Isaiah 24–27 lacks precise historical references. For example, the identifications of the city of chaos (24.10), the lofty city (26.5), and the fortified city (27.10) remain obscure. This makes Isaiah 24–27 difficult to date, although sometime in the early postexilic period, perhaps in the fifth century BCE, is likely.

ZECHARIAH 9–14

The second part of the book of Zechariah (chaps. 9–14, often called **"Second Zechariah"** (or "Deutero-Zechariah") has a somewhat different character than the first (chaps. 1–8; "First Zechariah"). As is the case with the book of Isaiah, materials written in more than one era have been combined into the book of Zechariah. First Zechariah (see pages 424–27) is internally dated to the late sixth century BCE. Second Zechariah has no specific datable references to events or individuals, but a majority of scholars date it to the fifth century BCE.

Second Zechariah has two parts, each with the heading "oracle" (9–11; 12–14). Taking their lead from these headings, some scholars have further divided Zechariah 9–14 into Second and Third Zechariah. The last book in the Minor Prophets, the book of Malachi, also has the heading "oracle," perhaps indicating an ancient editorial linking of the end of the book of Zechariah with Malachi, despite their somewhat different contents.

The two oracles in Second Zechariah are loosely linked by a common theme, the "day of the Lord," itself a concept found in earlier prophetic writings (see further Box 18.2 on page 316). This theme is developed, however, in a variety of genres and smaller units, some in prose and others in poetry. In general, the first oracle (chaps. 9–11) describes how Yahweh will defeat Israel's neighboring nations and bring back the exiled Israelites, but to an as yet uncertain future because of corrupt and ineffective leadership. The second oracle (chaps. 12–14) principally concerns restoration: Jerusalem will be cleansed and "the LORD my God will come, and all the holy ones with him." The land will be transformed into a level plain, with no night, and Jerusalem will be the seat of the divine rule over all the earth. As in the mythology of other ancient Near Eastern deities, living waters will flow from Yahweh's sacred mountain year-round, not just in the rainy season. All nations will come to Jerusalem to observe the festival of Booths. As this summary indicates, much of Second Zechariah is concerned with the future and has many apocalyptic features.

This summary necessarily glosses over the many obscurities in Second Zechariah. One of the reasons that Second Zechariah is so difficult to date and to interpret is its frequent quotation of and allusions to earlier prophetic traditions, as was also the case with Third Isaiah (see page 427). Using the genre of the oracle against the nations (see pages 310–11), the book describes Yahweh's devastation of the nations surrounding Jerusalem; this material is closely related to Amos 1–2. As a result, political entities are mentioned as if existing even though they were no longer important in the fifth century BCE, when the book was probably written, such as the northern kingdom of Israel (called Ephraim; see Zech 9.10) and Assyria (10.11). There is also a reference to Ionia (Zech 9.13; Hebr. *Yawan*, the Greek cities on the western coast of Asia Minor; NRSV: "Greece"), which became important only after the fall of Assyria in the late seventh century BCE. Some scholars have seen in this reference evidence for an even later date, in the Hellenistic period that began in the late fourth century, but the same region is mentioned in Ezekiel 27.19, and the Greek colonies in Ionia unsuccessfully revolted against Persian rule in the early fifth century BCE. The reference to Ionia, then, is not specific enough to require dating the book later.

The links between Zechariah 9–14 and the preceding chapters of the book are not as close as those among the various parts of the book of Isaiah, although there are some. Both parts of Zechariah make frequent allusion to earlier biblical traditions, and there are some repeated phrases and images, such as the special connection between the people and Yahweh (Zech 8.8; 13.9) and the expectation that all nations will worship Yahweh in Jerusalem (8.20–23; 14.16).

Like other early apocalyptic literature of the exilic and postexilic periods, Second Zechariah anticipates a new era. Yahweh will defeat the enemies of his people, restore them to their land, and establish peace and prosperity. In this new era, as also in Ezekiel 34 (see further Box 22.4 on page 396), the worthless shepherds will be removed (Zech 10.3; reiterated in a symbolic action by the prophet himself in 11.4–17). Jerusalem is urged to rejoice (Zech 9.9; compare Zeph 3.14; Zech 2.10), and the writer goes on to speak of a new ruler:

> Lo, your king comes to you;
>   triumphant and victorious is he,
> humble and riding on a donkey,
>   on a colt, the foal of a donkey.
> He will cut off the chariot from Ephraim
>   and the war-horse from Jerusalem;
> and the battle bow shall be cut off,
>   and he shall command peace to the nations;
> his dominion shall be from sea to sea,
>   and from the River to the ends of the earth.
>   (Zech 9.9–10)

This leader, like the ideal Israelite king of old, will have a universal rule; the last two lines in this quotation are from Psalm 72.8, a preexilic prayer for the king. If the translation "humble" is correct, it may indicate a character trait of the king, as one who, like the people he will rule, has been humbled (see Isa 51.21; 54.11). An alternative is to understand the word as an obscure royal epithet without the connotation of humility. The description of the king as riding on a donkey probably should not be understood as further indication of the king's humble character, for evidence exists that in ancient Israel the donkey (or mule) was a royal animal (see, for example, Gen 49.10–11 and also 2 Sam 18.9; 1 Kings 1.33).

Despite obscurities in the text, this clearly refers to a future ruler. Some apparently continued to hope that the Davidic dynasty would be restored, a hope that had not been fulfilled in the person of Zerubbabel in the late sixth century BCE, nor in the fifth century BCE, despite prophets who asserted, "There is a king in Judah!" (Neh 6.7). In part because of these disappointments, the restoration of the monarchy in the person of a future king was included in the apocalyptic account of the end-time and became an important element in the development of the concept of the Messiah in postbiblical Judaism and in Christianity (see Box 16.4 on page 284). In the latter connection we should note the application of these verses to Jesus in the gospels (Mt 21.5; Jn 12.15).

The book of Zechariah ends with the mysterious phrase: "There will be no Canaanite in the house of the LORD of hosts on that day" (Zech 14.21). This may refer to the exclusion of non-Israelites from the recently restored community, also a concern of the book of Ezra. An alternative is to understand the term "Canaanite" as "merchant," a meaning derived from the maritime commerce of the coastal Canaanites and their successors the Phoenicians and used a few times elsewhere in the Bible (for example, Prov 31.24; Zeph 1.11; and according to a common emendation Zech 11.7, 11). In this interpretation, the Temple, and in fact all of Jerusalem, will be sacred to Yahweh. This verse also seems to have been in the Gospel writers' minds, in the account of Jesus overturning the tables of the merchants in the Temple after his entry into Jerusalem (Mt 21.12; Mk 11.15; Lk 19.45; Jn 2.13–16).

Second Zechariah thus describes a definitive divine defeat of Israel's traditional enemies, a glorious restoration of the monarchy, and Jerusalem restored to its status as center of the world in an Edenic landscape. The projection of these events into a distant future, however, is another indication that the writer's present was troublesome.

THE BOOK OF JOEL

The short book of Joel is one of the Minor Prophets and is placed between the books of Hosea and Amos, perhaps because parts of a verse near the end of Joel (3.16) and one near the beginning of Amos (1.2) are identical. Another apparent quotation from Amos is Joel 3.18 (see Am 9.13), and both Amos (7.1–3; see also 4.9) and Joel describe a plague of locusts.

The book of Joel falls naturally into two parts:

- *1.2–2.27*: A vivid account of an infestation of locusts, interpreted as a form of divine punishment that can be stopped by a communal ritual of repentance. This section resembles laments found in the book of Psalms and elsewhere, and like them it concludes with an assurance of divine deliverance.
- *2.28–3.21*: An apocalyptic description of the end-time in which Judah's enemies will be punished and its land restored to a paradisiacal abundance.

Scholars disagree on whether these two parts were originally a unity, or whether two separate compositions, Joel and Deutero-Joel as it were, have been combined; with a book as short as Joel (seventy-three verses in all) it is difficult to decide. Natural phenomena such as locust plagues were believed to be caused divinely, and so the two parts are linked by a sense of divine judgment that having been directed against God's people will be turned against their enemies.

In both parts of the book, Joel uses the phrase the "day of Yahweh" first introduced by Amos (see Box 18.2 on page 316). Both the locusts and the ultimate vindication of God's people are understood as a manifestation of the terrible power of God. In the second part of the book, in a style that anticipates later apocalyptic literature, on that day nature will be convulsed, the enemies of God's people will be defeated, and then Judah will be restored.

Neither the superscription (Joel 1.1) nor any historical references in the book provide explicit indications of its date. Indirect evidence, however, supports the scholarly consensus that the book is a product of the Persian period, in the fifth or fourth century BCE. There is mention of priests (1.9, 13; 2.17) and elders (1.2, 14), and the Temple is functioning (1.9, 14), but there is no mention of a king. Together with the reference to the exile in 3.1–3, these suggest a postexilic date, some time after the rebuilding of the Temple in the late sixth century. Moreover, Joel quotes or alludes to a number of other biblical books, and so must be later than they are. In addition to the quotations from Amos mentioned earlier, note especially the marked quotation in 2.32 ("for in Mount Zion and in Jerusalem there shall be those who escape, as the LORD has said"), apparently referring to Obadiah 17; the description of the day of Yahweh in 2.1–2, which borrows phrases from Zephaniah 1.14–15; and in 3.10 ("Beat your plowshares into swords, and your pruning hooks into spears") the reversal of Isaiah 2.4 (= Mic 4.3).

Later apocalyptic literature will make use of themes from Joel. The image of locusts is elaborated vividly in Revelation 9.3–11, and Christian tradition will see the promise of outpouring of the divine "spirit" to everyone in Joel 2.28–29 (see also Num 11.29) fulfilled in the new age by the coming of the "holy spirit" (Acts 2.16–21).

THE BOOK OF MALACHI

The short book of Malachi is one of the latest of the prophetic books, and the last of the twelve Minor Prophets (see further page 310). In the Jewish canon, it thus concludes the first two sections of the Bible, the Law and the Prophets, and appropriately ends with mention of Moses, the giver of the law, and Elijah the prophet (Mal 4.4–5). In the arrangement of the Christian canon it is the last of the books of the Old Testament, and the concluding reference to the return of Elijah before the "day of the LORD" (Mal 4.5) has traditionally been understood by Christians as referring to John the Baptist, who is explicitly identified as the messenger who prepares the way of the Lord (Mal 3.1, quoted in Mt 11.10 and Mk 1.2, although in Mark erroneously attributed to Isaiah; compare also Mal 4.6 and Lk 1.17). (See further the Appendix.)

The entire book seems to be essentially one unit, as the heading "an oracle" suggests. As we have seen, the latter part of the book of Zechariah, which immediately precedes Malachi, contains two units with the same heading (Zech 9.1; 12.1), suggesting a link between these two final books of the prophets. The opening verse also gives the prophet's name as Malachi, but no such individual is known from other sources. The name is probably not a person's name at all; rather, it means "My messenger" and was taken from 3.1: "I am sending my messenger to prepare the way before me, and the Lord whom you seek will suddenly come to his temple. The messenger of the covenant in whom you delight—indeed, he is coming." If this is the case, then we know nothing about the author of the book, not even his name.

The book contains no specific historical references, but a date in the fifth century BCE is likely. The Temple has been rebuilt and a sacrificial system is in place. We find no mention of a king, but the term "governor" (Mal 1.8) is the usual title of the administrator of the Persian province of Yehud (Judah). Finally, several of the issues addressed in the book, including marriages between Judeans and foreigners, divorce, and tithing, were concerns during the time of Ezra and Nehemiah during the mid-fifth century.

The structure of the book is understood best as a set of loosely connected divine accusations against the people in general and the priests in particular, with an introduction (Mal 1.1) and two brief concluding appendixes (4.4, 5). Throughout, the language is starkly antithetical. The Lord has loved Jacob, but hated Esau (1.2–3); the priests who give blessings will be cursed and the dung of the sacrificial animals smeared on their faces (2.2–3); anyone who has married "the daughter of a foreign god" (probably meaning a non-Israelite woman) shall be cut off from Jacob (2.11–12); all the evildoers will be burned like stubble, but for "those who revere my name the sun of righteousness shall rise, with healing in its wings" (4.1–2).

Within this general framework are many obscurities. What precisely is the relative status of the priests and the Levites (Mal 2.1–9; 3.3)? Who is "the messenger of the covenant" (3.1)? Although the second appendix (4.5) implicitly identifies him with Elijah, that may be a later editor's attempt at clarification; other possibilities are that it refers to the prophet himself, or to a divine messenger, as in Exodus 23.20. When does the writer expect the day of the Lord (3.2; 4.1) to occur? Is the book of remembrance (3.16) a reference to an actual document, as in Nehemiah 9.38–10.1, or to a future metaphorical "book of life," as in later apocalyptic literature (for example, Dan 12.1; Rev 20.12; 21.27)? Finally, while one of the central concerns of the writer, who may himself have been a priest or a Levite, is the careful carrying out of ritual prescriptions, at the same time we see a distancing from the Temple: "For from the rising of the sun to its setting my name is great among the nations, and in every place incense is offered to my name, and a pure offering; for my name is great among the nations, says the LORD of hosts" (1.11). Does this suggest that since Yahweh was worshiped throughout the Diaspora with incense rather than animal sacrifice, animal sacrifice was not essential (compare Ps 50.8)? Or does it, as in Second Isaiah (Isa 45.6; 49.6; 52.10), anticipate a time when Yahweh will be worshiped by all people? That a book of only fifty-five verses can raise so many questions is a salutary reminder of how incomplete our knowledge is and how difficult to interpret many biblical texts are.

The first of the concluding appendixes (Mal 4.4) stresses fidelity to the teaching (Hebr. *torah*) of Moses, using language that is derived from Deuteronomy. The second (Mal 4.5) promises the return of Elijah (see further Box 17.3 on page 305) before "the great and terrible day of the LORD." Like the books of Ezekiel and Zechariah, the book of Malachi concludes with a reference to the end-time, when the righteous will be rewarded and the wicked suffer a terrible punishment. This motif is also found in the book of Joel and in Zechariah 9–14.

Box 25.3 SECOND ESDRAS

Among several postbiblical works ascribed to or featuring Ezra (see also Box 24.2 on page 423) is the book of 2 Esdras, which is also known as the Apocalypse of Ezra and 4 Ezra. Although 2 Esdras was sometimes included in manuscripts of the Bible as a kind of appendix and is frequently included in modern study Bibles, it is generally not considered canonical. (See further the Appendix.)

The book contains three originally independent compositions in the apocalyptic genre; in the first two Esdras (the Greek form of Ezra's name) is the principal character. The three parts are as follows:

- *2 Esdras 1–2:* Also known as 5 Ezra, these chapters are a Christian apocalypse probably dating to the early second century CE.

- *2 Esdras 3–14:* Also known as 4 Ezra, this is a Jewish apocalypse originally written in Hebrew or Aramaic in the late first century BCE. In it Esdras receives revelations concerning the significance of the destruction of the Second Temple by the Romans in 70 CE and the eventual destruction of the Roman empire itself. Here is a characteristic sample:

> I got to my feet and listened; a voice was speaking, and its sound was like the sound of mighty waters. It said, "The days are coming when I draw near to visit the inhabitants of the earth, and when I require from the doers of iniquity the penalty of their iniquity, and when the humiliation of Zion is complete. When the seal is placed upon the age that is about to pass away, then I will show these signs: the books shall be opened before the face of the firmament, and all shall see my judgment together. Children a year old shall speak with their voices, and pregnant women shall give birth to premature children at three and four months, and these shall live and leap about. Sown places shall suddenly appear unsown, and full storehouses shall suddenly be found to be empty; the trumpet shall sound aloud, and when all hear it, they shall suddenly be terrified. At that time friends shall make war on friends like enemies, the earth and those who inhabit it shall be terrified, and the springs of the fountains shall stand still. (2 Esd 6.17–24)

- *2 Esdras 15–16:* Also known as 6 Ezra, this is another Christian apocalypse, probably dating to the third century CE.

Ezra is also a protagonist in other apocryphal works, such as the Greek Apocalypse of Ezra and the Vision of Ezra.

RETROSPECT AND PROSPECT

In the fifth century BCE, the restoration of the Jewish community in Judah continued. The reality of the restoration, however, failed to live up to the hopes of many, and so in apocalyptic literature the final restoration of the ideal community was deferred to a remote divine intervention.

Collection, revision, and quotation of earlier material is characteristic of much of biblical literature of the postexilic period. In part this is the result of the beginning of the process of the formation of what will become "sacred scripture," the identification of certain writings as authoritative. At the same time, it implicitly recognizes that those writings need to be adapted for new circumstances. In the following chapters we will see several further examples of such activity, beginning with the books of Chronicles.

IMPORTANT TERMS

apocalyptic   Isaiah Apocalypse   Second Zechariah

QUESTIONS FOR REVIEW

1. What were the principal issues that concerned Ezra and Nehemiah?
2. Discuss the tensions among various Jewish communities during the Persian period.
3. What are the characteristics of apocalyptic literature? Under what circumstances did it develop?

BIBLIOGRAPHY

For an overview of the history of the period, see the essay by Leith in the bibliography to Chapter 23.

A good commentary on Ezra-Nehemiah is H. G. M. Williamson, *Ezra/Nehemiah* (Waco: Word, 1985). For a shorter commentary, see Tamara Cohn Eskenazi, "Ezra-Nehemiah," pp. 123–30 in *The Women's Bible Commentary* (rev. ed.; ed. C. A. Newsom and S. H. Ringe; Louisville: Westminster John Knox, 1998).

A selection of the Elephantine texts has been translated by Bezalel Porten in *The Context of Scripture*, Vol. 3: *Archival Documents from the Ancient World*, (ed. W. W. Hallo; Leiden: Brill, 2003), pp. 116–32, 141–98.

For a brief introduction to apocalyptic literature, see D. S. Russell, "Apocalyptic Literature," pp. 34–36 in *The Oxford Companion to the Bible* (ed. B. M. Metzger and

M. D. Coogan; New York: Oxford University Press, 1993).

For commentaries on Isaiah, see the bibliography to Chapter 19.

For Zechariah 9–14, see David L. Petersen, *Zechariah 9–14 and Malachi* (Louisville: Westminster John Knox, 1995); and Carol L. Meyers and Eric M. Meyers, *Zechariah 9–14* (New York: Doubleday, 1993).

For an introduction to the book of Joel, see Theodore Hiebert, "Joel, The Book of," pp. 873–80 in *Anchor Bible Dictionary*, Vol. 5 (ed. D. N. Freedman; New York: Doubleday, 1992).

Two good short introductions to Malachi are Rex Mason, "Malachi," pp. 484–85 in *The Oxford Companion to the Bible* (ed. B. M. Metzger and M. D. Coogan;

New York: Oxford University Press, 1993); and David L. Petersen, "Malachi," pp. 209–11 in *The Prophetic Literature: An Introduction* (Louisville: Westminster John Knox, 2002).

For 2 Esdras, see Michael E. Stone and Theodore A. Bergren, "2 Esdras," pp. 705–18 in *The HarperCollins Bible Commentary* (ed. J. L. Mays; San Francisco: HarperSanFrancisco, 2000).

During the Hellenistic and Roman periods, Jewish writers produced many apocalyptic works, some of which have been translated and collected in James H. Charlesworth, ed., *The Old Testament Pseudepigrapha* (New York: Doubleday, 2 vols., 1983, 1985). For apocalyptic works among the Dead Sea Scrolls, see Geza Vermes, *The Complete Dead Sea Scrolls in English* (rev. ed.; London: Penguin, 2004).

HISTORY REWRITTEN

CHAPTER

26

1–2 Chronicles

The restoration of the Jewish community in Judah, beginning in the late sixth century BCE with the reconstruction of the Temple and continuing in the fifth century under Ezra and Nehemiah, was apparently complete by the fourth century BCE. Although our knowledge of Judah in that century is limited, one of the major works written during it is Chronicles. This work is an interpretive history of Israel with a vast chronological scope, extending from Adam to the Persian period. Because we have already discussed the history that is the subject of Chronicles throughout the earlier chapters of this book, we will focus in this chapter on the distinctive features of this late Persian period work.

THE BOOKS OF CHRONICLES

The books of Chronicles, like those of Samuel and Kings, originally were a single book. Its Hebrew title is "The (book of) the events of the days" ([*sepher*] *dibre hayyammim*), a generic term that also occurs repeatedly in the books of Kings as part of the title of sources used by the Deuteronomistic Historians (for example, 1 Kings 14.19, 29). In its ancient Greek translation Chronicles

was called "The things omitted" (*ta paraleipomena*), apparently meaning what had been left out in the books of Samuel and Kings. Neither title is especially descriptive. Since late antiquity the book has been called "Chronicles," also a somewhat vague name.

In Jewish tradition, the books of Chronicles are part of the Writings, the third division of the canon, and are often placed last in that section, after Ezra-Nehemiah; in this position they thus are the final book of the Hebrew Bible. In Christian canons, the books of Chronicles follow the books of Kings, and they are followed by Ezra-Nehemiah, which is in accord with the narrative chronology. (See further the Appendix.)

Contents

The contents of the books of Chronicles are as follows:

1 Chronicles 1–9	Genealogies, from Adam to the fifth century BCE
10	The death of Saul
11–29	The reign of David
2 Chronicles 1–9	The reign of Solomon

As this outline makes clear, the overall chronological framework of Chronicles is sweeping. Within this framework, however, the history is selective. The almost exclusive focus is the kingdom of Judah from David to the fall of Jerusalem in 586 BCE. Even though **the Chronicler**, a frequently used term for the author of Chronicles, was familiar with the traditions of Israel as they had been collected by his time into the Pentateuch and the Deuteronomistic History (see below), he omits, or barely mentions, the principal events described in the first five books of the Bible as well as in the books of Joshua, Judges, and 1 Samuel. Even the covenant at Horeb (Sinai) is mentioned just in passing, when the Chronicler explains the origins of the two tablets in the ark installed in the Temple (2 Chr 5.10). Only intermittent attention is given to the history of the northern kingdom of Israel, mainly when it relates to that of the southern kingdom of Judah; the Chronicler does not even mention the Assyrian capture of Samaria, the capital of the northern kingdom, in 722 BCE. Nor, despite the Chronicler's considerable interest in prophecy, does he mention the activity of Elijah and Elisha, whose activity was confined exclusively to the northern kingdom. He does include the story of Micaiah (2 Chr 18 = 1 Kings 22), but that is because the king of Judah, Jehoshaphat, is part of that story.

Sources

The principal source of the author of Chronicles is the Deuteronomistic History, especially the books of 2 Samuel and 1–2 Kings. Paragraph after paragraph, sometimes chapter after chapter, is taken from this earlier work, either verbatim or with slight alteration. This reflects a tendency we have already observed: that of one author to use freely the work of another. Ancient views on such issues as originality and plagiarism were clearly different from our own. Because of the Chronicler's extensive use of the earlier history of Israel in the Promised Land, we have examined already much of what the books of Chronicles relate. Rather, we will focus in this chapter on ways in which the Chronicler deviated from his principal source. As in the study of the Synoptic Gospels in the New Testament, it is by the study of such additions and omissions that we can learn what the author's intent was.

The Chronicler also uses other biblical sources. The Pentateuch, in relatively final form as compiled by P, was certainly familiar to him, and authoritative (see, for example, 1 Chr 16.40; 2 Chr 23.18; 31.3; 35.12). Details in the genealogies, although abbreviated, are clearly dependent upon the Pentateuch, along with Joshua and other books. There are frequent quotations from the book of Psalms, which had probably also been collected by this time (see further page 460), and occasional quotations from or allusions to the books of Isaiah, Jeremiah, and Ezekiel. Moreover, the ending verses of 2 Chronicles are the same as the opening verses of the book of Ezra (see further page 448).

In addition to biblical sources, like the Deuteronomistic Historians the Chronicler cites other works that we no longer have. Some of these are not named by the Deuteronomistic Historians and are principally writings attributed to various prophets, including Samuel (1 Chr 29.29), Nathan (1 Chr 29.29; 2 Chr 9.29), Gad (1 Chr 9.29), Isaiah (2 Chr 26.22; 32.32), and more than half a dozen other, less familiar prophets. Typical of such references is 2 Chronicles 9.29: "Now the rest of the acts of Solomon, from first to last, are they not written in the history of the prophet Nathan, and in the prophecy of Ahijah the Shilonite, and in the visions of the seer Iddo concerning Jeroboam son of Nebat?" (2 Chr 9.29). The citation of these prophetic sources is significant, because for the Chronicler, as for the Deuteronomistic Historians, the prophets functioned as primary transmitters of divine messages: "[T]he commandment was from the LORD through his prophets" (2 Chr 29.25).

In using these named and presumably other unnamed sources, the Chronicler often provides details that are not found elsewhere in the Bible. Some of these have been confirmed by ancient nonbiblical texts and archaeological data, such as the account of Shishak's campaign in the late tenth century BCE (2 Chr 12.2–4; see page 289) and the description of Hezekiah's protection of Jerusalem's water supply in preparation for the Assyrian attack in the late eighth century BCE (2 Chr 32.2–4, 30; see Box 19.5 on page 344). Chronicles is thus not just a revision of the already existing Deuteronomistic History, but a genuinely independent work, with its own perspective on Israel's past.

Date

No conclusive internal evidence enables us to set a precise date for the writing of Chronicles. It is clearly a product of the postexilic period, since it concludes with the decree of Cyrus in 538 BCE allowing the exiles to return. Other details support this. First Chronicles 29.7 mentions the "daric," a Persian coin named for Darius I (522–486 BCE) and first issued early in his reign, and 2 Chronicles 16.9 seems to contain an allusion to Zechariah 4.10, itself written no earlier than the late sixth century BCE. Moreover, the genealogy of David in 1 Chronicles 3 gives seven generations beyond Zerubbabel, the governor of Judah in the late sixth century BCE; this takes us at least well into the fifth century BCE. On the other hand, no evidence shows that the author was influenced by Greek thought, and so Chronicles must have been written before Hellenization made a significant impact on Judaism, beginning in the late fourth century BCE (see further pages 499–501). A majority of contemporary scholars date Chronicles to the late fifth or the fourth century BCE, during the latter part of the Persian period. Some prefer an earlier date, in the late sixth or early fifth century, or suggest a series of editions of the work, the earliest of which would have been in the late sixth century.

As we have observed in previous chapters, our knowledge of the history of Judah during the Persian period is spotty, and by the fourth century BCE, the preferred date for Chronicles, it becomes virtually nonexistent. Because Chronicles is concerned with events that occurred some time before it was written, little direct evidence in the book enables us to determine the social and historical context of its author, or of events that might have had an impact on him. In the broader region, we do know that in the late fifth and early fourth centuries a series of revolts against the Persians in Egypt and in the Phoenician cities on the Mediterranean coast occurred. The Persians lost control of Egypt in 405 BCE, and did not regain it until 334, but what effect this had on Judah is unclear.

The Relationship between Chronicles and Ezra-Nehemiah

From ancient times and until the late twentieth century, it was widely held that the books of Chronicles and the books of Ezra and Nehemiah had the same author. The close connection between the two works is shown by the overlap between them: The last verses of Chronicles (2 Chr 36.22–23), relating the decree of Cyrus the Great allowing the exiles to return to Judah, are repeated in the opening verses of Ezra (1.1–3). Both works thus clearly are written no earlier than the Persian period.

A further link is provided by the lists of Jews of the postexilic period in the genealogies in Chronicles (especially 1 Chr 3.19–24 and 9.2–34) and in the names of the returnees in Ezra-Nehemiah (Ezra 2; Neh 7, 11–12). There are also thematic links, including the importance of the "*torah* of Moses" (for example, Ezra 3.2; 2 Chr 23.18), the Temple, and the Temple's rituals and personnel.

Because of these connections, until the late twentieth century modern scholars generally assumed a common authorship for the books of Chronicles, Ezra, and Nehemiah and referred to the author of all of them as "the Chronicler." More recently, however, a consensus has developed among scholars that the books of Chronicles did not have the same author as those of Ezra and Nehemiah, and they use "the Chronicler" only for the author of Chronicles, as we do in this chapter. Among the reasons for this scholarly judgment are apparent differences in language and style and some significant differences in content. For example, the Chronicler is not as concerned with intermarriage between Jews and others as is the author of Ezra-Nehemiah. Also, the attitude of the Chronicler toward the former northern kingdom of Israel is much less antagonistic than that of Ezra-Nehemiah (see Box 26.1).

The Genealogies

The Chronicler begins his history by setting it in a universal context, drawing directly on the already formed Pentateuch sources. Thus, 1 Chronicles 1.1–4 condenses the P genealogy from Adam to Noah in Genesis 5, and 1 Chronicles 1.5–27 moves from Noah to Abraham, closely following Genesis 10.1–29 and 11.10–26. The Chronicler then summarizes the ancestral narratives, moving from Abraham to Isaac and Ishmael, from Isaac to Jacob and Esau, and from Jacob to his twelve sons (1 Chr 1.28–2.2). This material, then, is prologue, but it links the material to follow with Israel's past, a past apparently familiar to its audience, who do not need to be told who such individuals as Adam or Noah were.

Then the Chronicler slows the pace and focuses on the sons of Jacob, the ancestors of the tribes of Israel. The sons of Jacob are not given in birth order or by their various mothers (see Figure 5.5 on page 78), but rather by the importance to the Chronicler of the tribes named for them, in a roughly geographical order. In a careful arrangement, the genealogies of Judah and Benjamin, the most important tribes from the Chronicler's perspective, frame the genealogies of the others and are given in more detail, as the outline in Box 26.2 shows. Included in the genealogy of Judah is a lengthy genealogy of the descendants of David (see page 453).

In central place in the genealogies (1 Chr 6) is an extended list of the tribe of Levi, the priestly tribe whose responsibility was Israel's rituals. The Levites have a major role in Chronicles, with sev-eral lists of Levites and their sacred functions inserted by the Chronicler into his narrative (see 1 Chr 15.4–24; 23–26; 2 Chr 29.3–34). So important are the Levites in Chronicles that some scholars have conjectured that the Chronicler himself was a Levite. This is supported by the remarkable statement that in the time of Hezekiah "the Levites were more upright in heart than the priests in sanctifying themselves" (2 Chr 29.34). At the very least, and somewhat as in the book of Deuteronomy (see pages 178–79), the Chronicler seems to be offering a corrective to the subordinate position given to the Levites in P (see pages 157–58). But the Chronicler cannot change the assignment of the most sacred ritual functions to the priests, the branch of the tribe of Levi that had Aaron as their ancestor.

Chapter 9 updates the genealogies already presented, giving the names of those who returned from Babylon; it is closely related to Nehemiah 11.3–19 and 1 Chronicles 8.28–38. The postexilic community is thus directly linked with its past. Again, the Levites have the dominant position in this list (1 Chr 9.14–34). The genealogies conclude with a repetition of the lineage of Saul (1 Chr 9.35–44 = 1 Chr 8.29–38), providing a transition to the account of the death of Saul that follows in 1 Chronicles 10.

David

We get a good sample of the Chronicler's methods by comparing his presentation of David with that of the Deuteronomistic Historians (1 Sam 16–31; 2 Sam; 1 Kings 1–2). Omitting all of the material in 1 Samuel except for the account of Saul's death in battle against the Philistines in 1 Chronicles 10 (= 1 Sam 31), the Chronicler begins his narrative about David with the account of his anointing as king over all Israel (1 Chr 11.1–3). Although the Chronicler is aware that David ruled first at Hebron and then in Jerusalem (1 Chr 3.4), he does not mention that at Hebron David was king initially only of Judah and not of the ten northern tribes (see 2 Sam 2.1–7; 5.5). For the Chronicler, Israel was always a unified entity.

Box 26.1 SAMARIA AND THE SAMARITANS

Throughout the history of Israel in the preexilic period tensions existed between north and south, tensions retrojected into the narratives in Genesis about the rivalries among the twelve sons of Jacob. David and Solomon were able to unite the two regions during the tenth century BCE, but at Solomon's death they became separate entities, the northern kingdom of Israel with its capital for most of its history in Samaria and the southern kingdom of Judah with its capital in Jerusalem. From the perspective of the Deuteronomistic Historians, writing in Judah, the north was a sinful kingdom and was divinely punished for its idolatry by being conquered by the Assyrians in 722 BCE. Subsequently, we are told, the Assyrians colonized what had become the Assyrian province of Samaria with foreigners who worshiped other gods alongside Yahweh (2 Kings 17.24–34).

These tensions continued in the postexilic period. According to the books of Ezra and Nehemiah, antagonism existed between the northerners and the leaders of the restored community in Judah (see Ezra 4.1–3; Neh 2.10, 19; 4.1–8; 6.1–9). One of the major differences between the books of Chronicles and Ezra-Nehemiah is that while Ezra-Nehemiah is hostile toward its northern neighbors, as well as to others in the region except for the "true Israel," that is, the returned exiles, Chronicles seems to be much more inclusive. For the Chronicler, the ideal is of one Israel, all twelve tribes. Thus, according to the Chronicler, all Israel, north and south, participated in the national festivals inaugurated by David and reinstituted by Hezekiah and Josiah.

At the same time, the Chronicler seems to have been aware that there were tensions between the two regions. When Hezekiah invited all Israel "from Dan to Beersheba" to Jerusalem to celebrate the Passover, only a small number of northerners came; the others responded to Hezekiah's messengers with scorn (2 Chr 30.10–11). It is also reasonable to interpret the Chronicler's emphasis on Judah, and virtual ignoring of the northern kingdom of Israel, which had become the Persian province of Samaria, as evidence of continuing conflict and rivalry.

Over time the division became acute, although for reasons that are not entirely clear. Ben Sira, writing in Jerusalem in the early second century BCE, refers to the Samaritans as "the foolish nation of Shechem" who are "not even not a people" (Sir 50.25–26), linking them with Israel's ancient enemies, the Edomites and the Philistines. Eventually a complete break developed between the Samaritans and the Jerusalem establishment, each with its own Temple, and each claiming to be authentic Judaism and to possess the only authoritative version of the Torah. This schism probably had its roots in the history summarized here, but has left few traces in the Jewish scriptures; it is more prominent in the New Testament, in the first-century CE Jewish historian Josephus, and in some rabbinic writings.

Box 26.2 ARRANGEMENT OF THE GENEALOGIES OF THE SONS OF JACOB (THE TRIBES OF ISRAEL)

Judah	1 Chr 2.3–4.23
David	1 Chr 3.1–24
Simeon	1 Chr 4.24–43
Transjordanian tribes (Reuben, Gad,	
Eastern Manasseh)	1 Chr 5.1–26
Levi	1 Chr 6.1–81
Northern tribes (Issachar, Benjamin, Naphtali,	
Western Manasseh, Ephraim, Asher)	1 Chr 7.1–40
Benjamin	1 Chr 8.1–40

The Chronicler includes lists of David's heroes (1 Chr 11.10–47; compare 2 Sam 23.8–39), and adds to them another list of David's companions while he was on the run from Saul, along with a census of his army, drawn from all twelve tribes (1 Chr 12). Then, according to the Chronicler, having consulted with all Israel, David summoned the priests and Levites to Jerusalem and arranged for the ark to be brought there (1 Chr 13.1–4; 15.1–24). The actual discovery and transfer of the ark closely follow the version in 2 Samuel 6, but then in 1 Chronicles 16 the Chronicler describes David as ordering the singing of praises, and a collage of various psalms follows (1 Chr 16.4–42). David then arranges for the regular activities of the priests and the sacred singers and musicians. At this point the Chronicler returns to his source, closely following 2 Samuel 7–8 and 10, omitting only the material concerning Mephiboseth (2 Sam 9.1–13). The battle for Rabbah, the capital of the Ammonites, is taken from 2 Samuel 11.1, 12.26, and 12.30–31. But here is the Chronicler's most telling omission: None of the narrative in 2 Samuel concerning David and Bathsheba, the

arranged death of her husband Uriah, the rape of Tamar and the revolt of Absalom, and the machinations that led to Solomon becoming king is incorporated into the Chronicler's account. In other words, the Chronicler omits the Succession Narrative (2 Sam 9–20; 1 Kings 1–2; see page 249) almost in its entirety. The result is a one-dimensional portrayal of David very different from that with which we (and presumably the audience of Chronicles as well) are familiar. For the Chronicler, David is an ideal king, apparently without flaws.

The Chronicler then moves to an account of David's census, which leads to his purchase of the site of the future Temple (see further Box 26.3).

At this point the Chronicler abandons his source in 2 Samuel entirely and describes in detail how David made preparations for building "the house of the LORD God" (2 Chr 22.1), the Temple. David, of course, did not build the Temple himself, and the Chronicler knows this, but he makes David the virtual designer of the Temple and the founder of its worship because, we are told, Solomon was "young and inexperienced" (1

Box 26.3 COMPARISON OF 2 SAMUEL 24.1–9 AND 1 CHRONICLES 21.1–7

An example of the Chronicler's use of his sources is provided by comparing his version of David's census of Israel with that in the Deuteronomistic History:

2 Samuel 24.1–9

Again the anger of the LORD was kindled against Israel, and he incited David against them, saying, "Go, count the people of Israel and Judah."

So the king said to Joab and the commanders of the army, who were with him, "Go through all the tribes of Israel, from Dan to Beer-sheba, and take a census of the people, so that I may know how many there are."

But Joab said to the king, "May the LORD your God increase the number of the people a hundredfold, while the eyes of my lord the king can still see it! But why does my lord the king want to do this?"

But the king's word prevailed against Joab and the commanders of the army. So Joab and the commanders of the army went out from the presence of the king to take a census of the people of Israel. They crossed the Jordan, and began from Aroer and from the city that is in the middle of the valley, toward Gad and on to Jazer. Then they came to Gilead, and to Kadesh in the land of the Hittites; and they came to Dan, and from Dan they went around to Sidon, and came to the fortress of Tyre and to all the cities of the Hivites and Canaanites; and they went out to the Negeb of Judah at Beer-sheba. So when they had gone through all the land, they came back to Jerusalem at the end of nine months and twenty days.

Joab reported to the king the number of those who had been recorded: in Israel there were eight hundred thousand soldiers able to draw

1 Chronicles 21.1–7

A satan stood up against Israel, and incited David to count the people of Israel.

So David said to Joab and the commanders of the army, "Go, number Israel, from Beer-sheba to Dan, and bring me a report, so that I may know their number."

But Joab said, "May the LORD increase the number of his people a hundredfold! Are they not, my lord the king, all of them my lord's servants? Why then should my lord require this? Why should he bring guilt on Israel?"

But the king's word prevailed against Joab. So Joab departed and went throughout all Israel, and came back to Jerusalem.

Joab gave the total count of the people to David. In all Israel there were one million one hundred thousand men who drew the sword, the sword, and those of Judah were five hundred thousand.

and in Judah four hundred seventy thousand who drew the sword. But he did not include Levi and Benjamin in the numbering, for the king's command was abhorrent to Joab. But God was displeased with this thing, and he struck Israel.

In both texts, this episode serves as the prologue for the purchase of the site of the future Temple, the threshing floor of Ornan (called Araunah in 2 Sam 24.18) the Jebusite. The purpose of the census seems to have been military conscription, and it was apparently interpreted as a lack of confidence in Yahweh's ability to protect Israel (see further page 260). Because of the centrality of the Temple in the Chronicler's ideology, he cannot omit this episode, as he does so many others that cast David in a negative light. But by a number of changes, in the version in Chronicles neither David nor Yahweh seems to be ultimately responsible. The initiative for the census is transferred from Yahweh to "a satan," a rare word meaning "adversary." The word could also be understood as a proper name, "Satan," referring to the malevolent being already found in Zechariah 3.1 (see further Box 28.1 on page 483), although no evidence is found elsewhere in Chronicles of such a supernatural opponent of Yahweh. An alternative is to understand it as an unnamed human adversary (as in 2 Sam 19.22). In either case, David's responsibility for the census is also mitigated. An inconsistency remains, however, because elsewhere in Chronicles the taking of a census is a normal administrative practice (see 1 Chr 12.24; 23.3; 27.1–34). The Chronicler had to include this narrative from the Deuteronomistic History because of the location of the Temple, but he was not entirely successful in integrating it into his idealized portrayal of David.

Chr 22.5). Thus, all of 1 Chronicles 22–29 is the Chronicler's own material, much of it concerned with the duties of the various families of the priests and Levites. Finally, the Chronicler succinctly recounts David's death and the orderly succession of Solomon.

Like the Deuteronomistic Historians, the Chronicler devotes a disproportionate amount of space to David. For both, David was paradigmatic, the ideal king of Israel and a standard against which subsequent kings are judged. In the Chronicler's time, the Temple had been restored and was functioning, a powerful symbol of continuity between preexilic and postexilic Israel. This is also suggested in the genealogy of David (1 Chr 3), which lists the descendants of David several generations beyond Zerubbabel, that is, well into

the fifth century BCE at least. But the Davidic dynasty had not been reestablished, despite the hope of some that it would be. By giving such prominence to David, the Chronicler may also be hinting at support for the return of a Davidic king, if not in his own time, then at some future date.

Other Kings

The kings that the Chronicler treats positively in the rest of his history resemble David in a number of ways. Highest praise is given to those who were both pious and who ruled over all Israel. The first of these is Solomon.

In his account of Solomon's reign, the Chronicler reproduces much of the material in 1 Kings 1–11, including the actual construction of the Temple, the manufacture of its furnishings, and its dedication. He makes some telling changes and omissions, however. The Chronicler does not mention Solomon building the royal palace and associated structures (see 1 Kings 7.1–12). Also, according to 1 Kings 9.11, Solomon paid Hiram, the king of Tyre, with twenty cities in the Galilee for the raw materials used in the construction of the Temple and palace complex. According to the Chronicler, however, the cities were given by Huram (as Hiram is called) to Solomon (2 Chr 8.2); the territorial integrity of Israel was not only preserved, but increased. Finally, the Chronicler's summary of the end of Solomon's reign omits most of 1 Kings 11, the account of Solomon's foreign marriages and the apostasy that resulted from them.

Another king for whose reign the Chronicler gives considerable detail is Hezekiah, who ruled in the late eighth and early seventh centuries BCE. A lengthy addition to the material concerning Hezekiah found in 2 Kings narrates how Hezekiah restored the Temple and its worship according to the system established by David (2 Chr 29.3–36; 31.2–21) and invited the northern tribes to come to Jerusalem for the celebration of Passover (2 Chr 30). The same occurs in the reign of Josiah in the late seventh century BCE, with less attention being paid to the Deuteronomic reform than in 2 Kings (see pages 353–55). Typical of the Chronicler's approach is his treatment of the invasion of the Assyrian king Sennacherib in 701 BCE: He omits the account of Hezekiah paying tribute to Sennacherib perhaps because one source of that tribute was the treasury of the Temple and its ornamentation (2 Kings 18.14–16).

The treatment of Hezekiah's successor Manasseh is another example of the Chronicler at work. For the Deuteronomistic Historians, Manasseh was the worst of the kings of Judah. According to the Chronicler, however, Manasseh was taken to Babylon as a prisoner, and there he repented of his worship of other gods, returned to Jerusalem, and became a model ruler (2 Chr 33.11–16). The historicity of this episode is debated, and the mention of Babylon seems especially suspicious, anticipating the Judeans' exile to and return from there in the sixth century BCE. Perhaps for the Chronicler the length of Manasseh's reign, which implied divine protection and reward, needed some justification, so he constructed a story of Manasseh's repentance from his earlier apostasy.

In his accounts of these and other kings, the Chronicler can be tagged a revisionist historian, editing his sources and adding to them in support of his ideological program in which all Israel was best led by pious rulers who were faithful to the commandments given by God through Moses and united in worship at the Temple in Jerusalem. For the Chronicler, history provided a compelling model for the restored community of his day.

RETROSPECT AND PROSPECT

The books of Chronicles are, as the title of this chapter indicates, a rewritten history, highly selective and ideologically driven. We may also view it, however, as a daringly creative reinterpretation, in which familiar history and new details are combined to provide a model for a new generation of Israelites living in a new situation. The collection and reshaping of older traditions are also evident in several other books that belong to the Writings, and we will examine them in the next two chapters. Also, by the end of the fourth century BCE, the Greeks had replaced the Persians as rulers of the Near East, and the Hellenistic culture that the Greeks brought would pose further challenges to emergent Judaism; those challenges will be our focus in the last two chapters of this book.

IMPORTANT TERM

the Chronicler

QUESTIONS FOR REVIEW

1. What are the sources used by the author of the books of Chronicles, and how does he use them?

2. In what ways does the presentation of the history of Israel and Judah in Chronicles differ from that in the Deuteronomistic History? What do these differences indicate about the Chronicler's own views?

BIBLIOGRAPHY

For a brief introduction to Chronicles, see Gary N. Knoppers, "Chronicler's History" and "Chronicles, Books of," pp. 241–44 in *Eerdmans Dictionary of the Bible* (ed. D. N. Freedman; Grand Rapids: Eerdmans, 2000). An important commentary is Sara Japhet, *I & II Chronicles: A Commentary* (Louisville: Westminster/John Knox, 1993).

A complete side-by-side presentation of Chronicles and its biblical sources is provided in *Chronicles and Its Synoptic Parallels in Samuel, Kings, and Related Biblical Texts* (ed. J. C. Endres et al.; Collegeville: Liturgical, 1998).

For a summary of the evidence concerning the Samaritans, see James D. Purvis, "Samaritans," pp. 963–66 in *The HarperCollins Bible Dictionary* (ed. P. J. Achtemeier; San Francisco: HarperSanFrancisco, 1996).

THE CONSOLIDATION OF TRADITIONS

CHAPTER

27

Psalms and Proverbs

From the sixth to the fourth centuries BCE, especially during the Persian period (539–332 BCE), a wide variety of Israelite literary traditions were collected and edited; this process eventually would culminate in the formation of the Bible. In the arrangement of the books of the Bible in Jewish tradition, the third part is known as the "**Writings**," and it is a mixed bag containing a variety of genres. The books that comprise the Writings were either written or edited relatively later than the first two parts, the Law or Torah and the Prophets. (See further the Appendix.)

Among the books of the Writings are two major anthologies, the book of Psalms and the book of Proverbs. Perhaps neither was meant to be read as a single work; they are, rather, collections of hymns and sayings, respectively, and readers may be well advised to browse in the collections rather than to attempt to read them through. Because both books contain materials from a relatively broad chronological range, they give us a window into the personal and communal piety and values of ancient Israel over many centuries.

THE BOOK OF PSALMS

The book of Psalms is the longest in the Bible, with 150 chapters in the traditional numbering. (For variations and additions, see the Appendix). It is in effect an anthology of the hymns of ancient Israel, collected and edited into relatively final form probably in the fifth or fourth century BCE. Its title in Hebrew, *tehillim,* means "praises," a somewhat vague designation that does not take into account the various types of hymns found in the book. Praise is certainly an important element in the book, and the word *tehillim* is related to the phrase *hallelu-yah* ("Praise Yah[weh]"), which occurs more than twenty times at the beginning or end, or both, of psalms in the last part of the book, starting at Psalm 104.35. Another term used in the psalms themselves is the more generic "prayers" (Hebr. *tepillot,* Ps 72.20). The English title of the book, "Psalms," is derived from a Greek word for a stringed instrument (*psalterion*), reflecting the musical character of the book's contents.

The book of Psalms is divided into five parts, probably an intentional parallel to the Torah, the first five books of the Bible. This is also suggested by the content of Psalm 1, a wisdom psalm that describes divine reward for those who observe the Torah and punishment for those who fail to do so. The five parts are Psalms 1–41, 42–72, 73–89, 90–106, and 107–150. Each of the first four of these divisions ends with a doxology or blessing (Pss 41.13; 72.18–19; 89.52; 106.48), and the last psalm in the collection, Psalm 150, may be considered a conclusion to the fifth division, as well as to the book of Psalms as a whole.

This structure was the culmination of a long process of collecting and editing, and the book of Psalms contains much evidence of earlier stages in the process as well. Thus, Psalm 72 ends with the note "The prayers of David son of Jesse are ended"; apparently a collection of prayers attributed to David was incorporated into the book of Psalms at some earlier stage, although after Psalm 72 eighteen more psalms are attributed to David, indicating that "the prayers of David" was not a definitive edition. Within the book of Psalms there are other collections as well. For example, each of the psalms from 120 to 134 includes in its title the phrase "A Song of Ascents," probably because pilgrims used these psalms as they went up to Jerusalem; because of the city's geographical situation and elevation, traveling from almost any direction to Jerusalem, and especially to the Temple mount, meant going uphill. We should note, however, that these fifteen psalms include a number of different genres or forms, according to the form-critical analysis to be discussed later in this chapter.

Another collection is suggested by the title "of the sons of Korah," which is found in Psalms 42–49 and 84, 85, 87, and 88. Korah was the ancestor of one of the principal priestly families in the Temple in Jerusalem, which according to 2 Chronicles 20.19 led the people in song. Among the sons of Korah were Asaph and Heman. To Asaph are attributed Psalms 50 and 73–83, and to Heman Psalm 88. According to 1 Chronicles 6.31–43, Asaph and Heman were "in charge of the service of song" in the Temple. They also played cymbals (1 Chr 15.19), and their sons, along with those of Je-

duthun, to whom three psalms (39; 62; 77) are also attributed, prophesied "with lyres, harps, and cymbals" (1 Chr 25.1). We have already noted the connection between prophecy and music (see page 299), and it is possible that members of these priestly families also functioned as prophets, giving worshipers a divine oracle or response to prayer. (See Figure 27.1.)

Another indication of earlier collections that have been incorporated into the book is the close proximity of psalms that deal with divine kingship (93–99) and psalms that have the opening or closing "*hallelu-yah*" ("Praise Yah[weh]") (Pss 104–106; 111–113; 135; 146–150; these are sometimes called "Hallel" psalms).

In addition to these collections marked in the text itself, scholars also have identified another major collection, Psalms 42–83, called the "Elohistic Psalter" because in it the divine name *Elohim* ("God") is used about five times more frequently than *Yahweh* ("The LORD"), whereas in the rest of the book *Yahweh* is used about ninety-five percent of the time. This preference for *Elohim* has plausibly been suggested as evidence that some of these psalms originated in the northern kingdom of Israel, as did the Elohist (E) source in the Pentateuch, in which *Elohim* is also used in Genesis instead of Yahweh (see further page 26). It should be noted, however, that two of the hymns in this collection are hymns in praise of Zion (Jerusalem), which complicates the matter, since Jerusalem was the capital of Judah, the southern rival of the northern kingdom. This "Elohistic Psalter" also spans the second and third of the five divisions of the book of Psalms noted earlier, further indicating that the arrangement of the collection into five "books" took place at a later stage.

Additional evidence that the book of Psalms is an anthology, or perhaps more properly an anthology of anthologies, is the repetition that is found in the book. Thus, Psalms 14 and 53 are identical, except for the shift of the divine name from Yahweh to Elohim; Psalm 40.13–17 = Psalm 70; and Psalm 108 is a combination of Psalms 57.7–11 and 60.5–12.

FIGURE 27.1.   Musicians on a ceramic stand from Ashdod, dating to the early tenth century BCE. Each figure is about 2 in (5 cm) high. From the left, the instruments being played are a double flute, a lyre, and probably a hand drum. (For another depiction of a lyre player, see Figure 18.5 on p. 321.)

In recent years a number of scholars have attempted to discover more detailed principles of arrangement, in which various psalms are grouped together because of shared themes and vocabulary. These efforts, although instructive, have not yet won consensus.

The book of Psalms is therefore the result of a long process of compilation and editing. Each sanctuary or place or worship, preeminently but not exclusively Jerusalem, and perhaps each priestly family, would have had its own collection of hymns, and these different collections were gradually combined into the book we now know as Psalms.

Titles to the Psalms

We have already mentioned the "titles" that precede the text of most of the psalms; in fact, all but twenty-four of the psalms have these introductory notes, which were added by ancient editors. Sometimes the titles are brief—Psalm 98 is called simply "A Psalm," but occasionally they are lengthy, as in Psalm 18: "To the leader. A Psalm of David the servant of the LORD, who addressed the words of this song to the LORD on the day when the LORD delivered him from the hand of all his enemies, and from the hand of Saul. He said . . . ." The single most common title is "Of David," used in seventy-three psalms. An ambiguous Hebrew preposition is generally interpreted to mean that David was considered the author of the psalm in question; the same preposition is used, for example, in Proverbs 24.23: "These also are by the wise." Thirteen of these psalms, like Psalm 18 just quoted, do have historical notes connecting them with events in the life of David.

That David had a reputation as a poet and a musician is well attested (see Box 15.1 on page 250), and thus it is not surprising that many hymns are attributed to him, especially since in Chronicles he is presented as the originator of the Temple's elaborate system of worship (see, for example, 1 Chr 23–26). Thus, David becomes the presumed author of many of the psalms, just as Moses is presented as the human author of Israel's legal traditions and David's son Solomon as the author of writings about wisdom (see later in this chapter) and love (see page 496). It is unlikely, however, that David wrote most of the psalms attributed to him. Some, such as Psalms 68 and 122, refer to the Temple in Jerusalem, built by Solomon in the mid-tenth century BCE after David's death, and others, such as Psalms 69.35–36 and 137, mention the Babylonian destruction of Jerusalem in 586 BCE. This was apparently recognized in antiquity as well, for Psalm 72 is attributed to Solomon, although it concludes with the note discussed earlier that "the prayers of David . . . are ended."

Evidence of the increasing tendency to attribute psalms to David as time goes on is that while in the Masoretic Text (the traditional Hebrew text of the Bible) 73 are credited to David, in one of the manuscripts of Psalms from the Dead Sea Scrolls that number rises to 75, although not always the same psalms as in the Masoretic Text. Further, in the Septuagint (the ancient Greek translation of the Hebrew Bible) 84 are credited to David, and in rabbinic tradition all 150 psalms are said to be by David. In the New Testament we observe the same tendency, when Psalm 2 is attributed to David (in Acts 4.25), as is Psalm 95 (in Heb 4.7), although neither has that attribution in the Masoretic Text. Only two psalms are attributed to Solomon, Psalms 72 and 127. Psalm 72 is a royal psalm, which also mentions Sheba, whose queen is reported to have visited Solomon (1 Kings 10.1), and Psalm 127 refers to Yahweh building the house (v. 1) and to "his beloved" (v. 2; Hebr. *yedido*), which recall Solomon's construction of the Temple and the name Jedidiah (Hebr. *yedidyah*; 2 Sam 12.25) given him by the prophet Nathan. Others to whom psalms are attributed include Moses (Ps 90) and various priestly figures (see earlier in this chapter). Some psalms have more than one attribution (Pss 39; 62; 77; 88), making the accuracy of the ancient identification of authorship even less likely.

In addition to indicating authorship, some titles of the psalms include a number of mysterious rubrics, including "to the leader" (fifty-five times), and references to musical instruments and melodies (see further later in this chapter). What appear to be ancient categories of psalms, such as "miktam," "maskil," "mizmor, "song," "prayer," and others, also occur. In some cases two or more of these terms are applied to the same psalm, which makes their precise meaning elusive at best.

The Psalms in Israel's Worship

We get some understanding of how the psalms functioned in ancient Israel by observing the occurrence of hymnic prayers like them in other books of the Bible. Thus, we find prayers of individuals in the books of Jeremiah, Jonah, and Job and communal victory hymns in Exodus 15 and Judges 5. When King Hezekiah became ill, he composed a prayer for divine help (Isa 38.9–20; see also Hab 3). Hymns found in the book of Psalms are also found in other biblical books. Psalm 18 is inserted into 2 Samuel (chap. 22) as part of an appendix containing miscellaneous material concerning David. In the books of Chronicles a number of psalms are quoted, sometimes in different forms than in the book of Psalms. First Chronicles 16.8–36, presented as a hymn sung when David brought the ark to Jerusalem, is a pastiche composed of Psalm 105.1–15, Psalm 96, and Psalm 106.1 and 106.47–48. Moreover, the refrain "Give thanks to the LORD, for he is good, for his steadfast love endures forever" in Psalms 118 and 136 (see also Pss 100.5; 106.1; 107.1) is also used in accounts of ceremonies (2 Chr 5.13; 7.3; 20.21; Ezra 3.11; and Jer 33.11).

The adaptation of existing psalms and the composition of new ones continued throughout antiquity, as is evidenced in a number of hymnic prayers in the books of Tobit and Judith; in the Prayer of Azariah and the Song of the Three Jews (an addition to the book of Daniel); in many of the Dead Sea Scrolls; and in the New Testament (such as Lk 1.46–55, 68–79). Phrases and themes from the psalms have also been used in songs and hymns in ongoing Jewish and Christian traditions.

Dating the Psalms

The book of Psalms in more or less its present shape was probably formed before the end of the Persian period in the late fourth century BCE. We find no examples of Greek influence or vocabulary, as occur in writings from the succeeding Hellenistic period. Moreover, the Septuagint, the translation of the Hebrew Bible into Greek that dates from the third century BCE, includes an additional psalm after Psalm 150, known as Psalm 151 (and considered part of the Bible by some Orthodox Christian churches); the title to this psalm describes it as "outside the number" of the apparently already closed collection of 150.

Many of the psalms are clearly from the time of the monarchy, with their repeated references to the king and the Temple. Others seem to be from the exilic period, including Psalm 137 and some that describe a community without a Temple, either in Judah before the Temple was rebuilt or in exile without access to the restored Temple; an example is Psalm 51.18–19:

> Do good to Zion in your good pleasure;
>   rebuild the walls of Jerusalem,
> then you will delight in right sacrifices,
>   in burnt offerings and whole burnt offerings;
>   then bulls will be offered on your altar.

Many of the psalms also reflect already developed Pentateuchal traditions (see further pages 23–27), such as Psalm 78 with its echoes of Exodus 15 and Psalm 105's account of the ancestral period and the covenant between Yahweh and Abraham, Isaac, and Jacob, but such allusions provide only a relative chronology. The book of Psalms, then, as an anthology, contains poems from several periods in Israel's history, but most individual psalms are impossible to date precisely.

Ancient Near Eastern Parallels

Among the hundreds of thousands of texts recovered from the ancient Near East are personal and communal hymns and prayers similar to those found in the book of Psalms. Babylonian laments, for example, have a structure close to that of the biblical laments, and Psalm 104 is remarkably close even in precise details to the Egyptian Hymn to the Sun-disc (Aten) in its praise of the divine creator. While no direct links between the various texts can be proven or need even be assumed, these parallels are reminders that Israel did not exist in a vacuum, but was part of a cultural continuum, and that throughout the Near East similar genres and vocabulary were used in human communication with the divine.

As in the Bible, most of these ancient Near Eastern texts are poetic, and many also employ the poetic phenomenon of parallelism or thought rhyme (see Box 27.1). The texts include hymns and prayers to various deities in genres like those identified for the biblical psalms, such as laments and hymns of praise and thanksgiving.

Form Criticism of the Psalms

The most significant modern critical scholarship on the psalms is by the German scholar Herman Gunkel, who was also a pioneer in the study of the Pentateuch and prophets. Beginning with a study of selected psalms in 1904 and culminating in his commentary on the book of Psalms in 1926 and his introduction to the psalms published in 1933, shortly after his death, Gunkel applied the discipline of form criticism (see page 69) that he had developed to the psalms.

This method of analysis groups the psalms by genre, and sometimes by content. The main categories identified by Gunkel are individual and communal laments, songs of thanksgiving, royal psalms, and hymns, and, although subsequent scholars have refined his analysis, Gunkel's categorization of the psalms by form or genre has been followed widely. Categories often overlap, or rather, we see mixed types, as ancient repetitions also suggest. Box 27.2 is a list of the forms of the psalms and the psalms that are assigned to them. Box 27.3 gives an example of form-critical analysis.

The following is a summary, with examples, of the principal forms and subforms.

Box 27.1 PARALLELISM

Like most biblical poetry, the psalms have as their primary poetic device the use of **parallelism**. This technique, also found in Ugaritic and Mesopotamian poetry, is a kind of thought rhyme, in which an idea is developed by the use of repetition, synonyms, or opposites. In this example of synonymous parallelism, the two lines express essentially the same idea:

> The LORD is my light and my salvation;
>   whom shall I fear?
> The LORD is the stronghold of my life;
>   of whom shall I be afraid? (Ps 27.1)

In antithetic parallelism, opposites are used:

> The LORD watches over the way of the righteous,
>   but the way of the wicked will perish. (Ps 1.6)

Another type of parallelism is called climatic:

> Behold, your enemies, O Yahweh,
>   behold, your enemies shall perish;
>   all evildoers shall be scattered. (Ps 92.9)

In numerical parallelism, the corresponding parallel to any number ($\times$) is the next highest unit ($\times + 1$), in the patterns "three . . . four," "six . . . seven"; "a thousand . . . ten thousand"; and, in Ugaritic, "sixty-six . . . seventy-seven" and "seventy-seven . . . eighty-eight." Numerical parallelism occurs in proverbs (Prov 6.16–19; 30.15–16, 18–19, 21–31) and in other biblical and nonbiblical wisdom literature (for example, Job 5.19–22; 33.14–15; Eccl 11.2; Sir 25.7–10; Ahiqar), as well as in other genres (for example, Ugaritic myth and epic; Ps 62.11–12; Am 1.3–2.8; Mic 5.5).

Laments

Occurring both in the singular and in the plural, these appeals for divine help in distress could come either from an individual or from the community. The laments are subdivided into two principal categories:

- *Individual laments*: This is the most frequently occurring type in the book, with more than forty psalms belonging to this genre. The speaker of the psalm is an individual who speaks in the first person. Royal laments, in which the king is the speaker, overlap with this category (see page 465). The following elements are found in the laments, although the order in which they occur varies, and not all elements are always included:

Address to God.

Description of the suffering from which the
    individual wishes to be relieved. The lan-

Box 27.2 THE FORMS OF THE PSALMS*

Individual Laments

3	35	69
(4)	38	70 (= 40.13–17)
5	39	71
(6)	41	77
7	42–43†	86
(9–10)	51	88
13	53 (= 14)	102
14 (= 53)	54	109
17	55	120
22	56	130
25	57	(139)
26	59	140
(27)	61	141
28	(63)	142
31	64	143

Communal Laments

12	80	123
44	83	(125)
58	85	126
60	90	129
74	94	137
79		

Individual Songs of Trust

(4)	(27.1–6)	(63)
11	(52)	91
16	62	131
23		

Individual Songs of Thanksgiving

30	(40)	116
(32)	(66)	(118)
(34)	92	138

Communal Songs of Thanksgiving

65	75	136
(66)	107	145
67	117	146
69	(118)	150

Hymns of Divine Kingship

(24)	82	97
29	93	98
47	96	99

Creation Hymns

8	(33)	(147)
(19)	104	(148)

Hymns Celebrating Divine Actions in Israel's History

(66.1–12)	105	114
(78)	106	135
(100)	(111)	136
(103)	(113)	149

Hymns Concerning the Renewal of Israel's Covenant with God

50	81

Liturgies

15	81	121
(24)	115	134
50		

Royal Psalms

2	45	110
18	72	(132)
20	(89)	144.1–11
21	101	

Hymns Concerning the Davidic Covenant

(78)	(89)	(132)

Zion Hymns

46	76	87
48	(84)	(122)

Pilgrimage Hymns

(24)	95	(118)
(84)	(100)	(122)

Torah Psalms

1	19	119

Wisdom Psalms

(1)	49	112
(32)	(73)	(127)
(34)	(78)	128
37	(111)	(133)
		(139)

* Psalms in parentheses are mixed forms, or their classification is debated.

† This psalm, although separated as divided into two in some numbering systems, is actually one poem.

Box 27.3 FORM-CRITICAL ANALYSIS OF PSALM 3

The following is an example of form-critical analysis of the psalms, using Psalm 3, one of the shorter individual laments:

¹O LORD, how many are my foes! Many are rising against me;	*Address to God and description of suffering*
²many are saying to me, "There is no help for you in God."	
³But you, O LORD, are a shield around me, my glory, and the one who lifts up my head.	*Expression of confidence*
⁴I cry aloud to the LORD, and he answers me from his holy hill.	
⁵I lie down and sleep; I wake again, for the LORD sustains me.	*Expression of confidence*
⁶I am not afraid of ten thousands of people who have set themselves against me all around.	*Description of suffering*
⁷Rise up, O LORD! Deliver me, O my God!	*Petition for divine help*
For you strike all my enemies on the cheek; you break the teeth of the wicked.	
⁸Deliverance belongs to the LORD; may your blessing be on your people!	*Expression of confidence* *Thanksgiving*

guage used is often metaphorical and can be hyperbolic as well.

Petition for divine help and deliverance.

Cursing of the enemies the individual considers responsible for his situation.

Expression of confidence that God will hear the individual's prayer.

Protestation of innocence or confession of guilt.

A vow anticipating a positive divine response, in which the psalmist promises to thank God for it.

A song of thanksgiving, which follows naturally from the vow.

- *Communal laments:* These have the same elements as the individual laments, but the speakers are plural, presumably the entire community. The suffering is usually communal as well, such as famine, plague, or attack by enemies. In these laments the expression of confidence is often replaced by an appeal to God to continue to act on behalf of the community as he has in the past, and we see frequent references to the history of Israel.

Many of the other genres or forms used are expansions of one or more of the elements of the laments.

Songs of Trust

These psalms consist largely of the expression of confidence in divine assistance and may be either individual or communal.

Songs of Thanksgiving

These psalms consist largely of the expression of gratitude for divine assistance that has been granted and may be either individual or communal, in the latter case as for a military victory or a plentiful harvest.

Hymns

This category consists of songs of praise of Yahweh under various aspects:

- *Hymns of divine kingship*: In these hymns, Yahweh's rule over heaven and earth is celebrated, often in highly mythological language. Examples include Psalm 29, in which the entire assembly of the gods is called upon to praise Yahweh for his powers as the storm-god who defeated the primeval watery chaos.

  Three of the psalms in this category, which occur in close proximity, open with the phrase "Yahweh is king" (Pss 93.1; 97.1; 99.1; see also 47.8; 96.10). The Hebrew (*Yahweh malak*) can also be translated "Yahweh has become king" on the basis of passages such as 2 Samuel 15.10, 1 Kings 1.11 and 1.18, and 2 Kings 9.13 (see also Prov 30.22), in which a human king is acclaimed as he assumes the throne.

  Relying on these parallels, some scholars have posited that the Israelites held an annual celebration of the divine enthronement, similar to the Babylonian new year festival, in which Marduk's accession to rule over the gods was celebrated (see pages 5–7 and 412). In the ritual reenactment of myth, the primeval cosmic acts of the deity are in a sense repeated annually. Like Marduk and the Canaanite storm-god Baal, Yahweh became king when he defeated the forces of chaos, and

that event would have been celebrated in a festival of divine enthronement. A close parallel in Jewish tradition is the reenactment of the Exodus in the annual celebration of the Passover and in Christian tradition in the celebration of Easter, during which the congregation proclaims: "Christ is risen!"

As attractive as this theory is, however, apart from the psalms and similar hymns we find no evidence such a festival of divine enthronement in ancient Israel, and so it remains hypothetical.

- *Creation hymns*: Closely related to the hymns of divine kingship are hymns that describe divine activity in creation; these hymns also use mythological language.

- *Hymns celebrating divine actions in Israel's history*: These celebrate Yahweh's actions on behalf of Israel, from the time of the ancestors (Ps 105.7–22) through the Exodus and entry into the land (Pss 78.1–55; 106; 114), and to the choice both of the Davidic dynasty and of Jerusalem as his home (Ps 78.67–72). This last topic is developed at length in the songs of Zion (see page 465).

  Some of the hymns, notably Psalms 135 and 136, connect the themes of creation and Exodus, as indeed does the narrative of the Pentateuch. Yahweh's actions, in other words, are consistent; as Psalm 136 puts it, from the time when he "spread out the earth on the waters" (v. 6), to when he "divided the Reed Sea in two" (v. 13), "led his people through the wilderness" (v. 16), and "gave them their land as a heritage" (v. 21), Yahweh showed his covenant fidelity: For all of these actions, and others, the appropriate communal response is the refrain "for his steadfast love endures forever."

Liturgies

Some psalms have been identified as "liturgies" because their contents suggest that they were used during public worship. Some of them have internal indications of the ritual setting where they were used, including a procession (Ps 24) and a pilgrimage (for example, Ps 122; see further below and Figure 27.2).

Several of these psalms have a question-and-answer format:

> Who shall ascend the hill of the LORD?
>   and who shall stand in his holy place?
> Those who have clean hands and pure hearts,
>   who do not lift up their souls to what is false,
>   and do not swear deceitfully. (Ps 24.3–4; see also Ps 15)

Of interest here is the identity of the responder to the worshiper's question. One probability is that the response was given by the priest, or perhaps by a prophet.

Other psalms that include a liturgical element are responsorial psalms, like 136, in which a leader, perhaps a priest, would give the verse and the worshipers would reply with a repeated refrain; this alternation is known as antiphony. The ceremonies at which such psalms could have been used include the renewal of the covenant; such covenant renewal ceremonies are described in Deuteronomy 27, Joshua 24, and 2 Kings 23. Psalms 50 and 81, which are similar to the genre of the "covenant lawsuit" found in the prophets

(see page 323), could also have been used on such occasions.

Royal Psalms and Hymns Concerning the Davidic Covenant

Several psalms have the ruling king as their speaker, and others deal principally with the king. These include a royal wedding hymn (Ps 45), three that are probably coronation hymns (Pss 2; 72; 110), laments (Pss 89; 101; 144.1–11), and hymns of petition for victory (Ps 20) and thanksgiving for victory (Pss 18; 21). A related category is that called "hymns concerning the Davidic covenant" (Pss 78; 89; 132) in which the king is not the speaker, but the royal ideology (see further pages 277–84) is a principal subject. Although a specific king is not named in any of these psalms, they can be presumed to come from the time of the monarchy, except perhaps for Psalm 89 in its final form, which seems to speak of the fall of the dynasty.

Zion Hymns

Another small group of psalms, also overlapping in content with the royal psalms, is those that have as their subject Jerusalem and especially God's choice and protection of it and hence its invincibility. (See further Box 16.2 on page 279.)

Pilgrimage Hymns

A small number of psalms seem to have been written for use by pilgrims to a sacred place, specified as Jerusalem in Psalms 84 and 122; in the remaining psalms in this category, either Jerusalem or another sanctuary could have been the goal of the pilgrimage.

Wisdom Psalms

A few psalms belong to the category of "wisdom literature," to be discussed later in this chapter, because they deal with issues of human existence and use the same vocabulary as such books as Proverbs and Job. Other psalms also contain wisdom elements. An example is Psalm 37, which, since it is also an acrostic (see Box 22.1 on page 383), lacks a clear development, but seems almost

FIGURE 27.2. A drawing of five men in procession or in prayer. This is one of the graffiti from storage jars at Kuntillet Ajrud, dating to the eighth century BCE (see also Fig. 18.5 on p. 321).

to be a random assortment of proverbs expressing traditional views of divine justice.

Torah Psalms

Closely related to the wisdom psalms are three psalms that focus on the *torah* (see Box 11.3 on page 184), the divine law or teaching, observance of which guarantees divine reward. These are Psalms 1, 19 (especially vv. 7–14), and 119. These psalms are probably relatively late, in which case *torah* refers to the first five books of the Bible. That is suggested by the placement of Psalm 1 as the introduction to the entire collection of psalms, which, as we have seen, is also divided into five parts.

The form-critical analysis of the psalms has been extraordinarily productive; yet as the previous summary makes clear, the form-critical categories are not mutually exclusive, nor do they necessarily correspond to ancient understandings of genre. Moreover, some psalms, notably Psalm 68, do not seem to belong to any single category. The fluidity of the psalms, especially in the overlapping classifications noted here, cautions us against making these form-critical categories too rigid; rather, they should be taken as a starting point for interpretation.

The Psalms as Prayers

As we have seen, for the most part the psalms are lacking in specifics and thus difficult to date and to categorize. One reason for the preservation of these hymnic prayers, and not of others that must have existed in ancient Israel, may be this very lack of specificity, or, more positively, their universality. The absence of references in the psalms to the specific festivals and rituals of Israel is striking: We find no allusion to the Passover, the feast of Weeks, the feast of Tabernacles, or even the sabbath (except in the title of Ps 92), nor to the various types of rituals described in such detail in biblical legislation and narrative.

This generality explains, at least in part, the continuing appeal of the psalms, for they can be appropriated relatively easily in other times and circumstances. They are by and large concerned with fundamental aspects of the human condition, with individuals and communities who are, or feel, ill, threatened, and persecuted, or happy, grateful, and trusting. These prayers, through which ancient Israelites expressed and sustained their beliefs, are thus profound religious expressions. They have continued to be used by Jews and Christians in ceremonies of worship and have been sources of inspiration and expressions of piety for individuals throughout the ages.

EXCURSUS ON MUSIC IN ANCIENT ISRAEL

Readers of the Bible, especially the book of Psalms, encounter a bewildering array of references to music and dance. The frequency of these references makes it clear that these arts were a pervasive aspect of life in ancient Israel, as in the rest of the ancient world; but they are an aspect that we can barely recover. With the destruction of the Second Temple in 70 CE by the Romans, most of Israel's liturgical music was lost or deliberately abandoned. The reconstruction of Israel's musical traditions is thus a difficult task, and it relies on often obscure references in the Bible, occasional archaeological discoveries, and illustrations of musical instruments from the ancient Near East (see Figure 27.3).

The most frequently mentioned biblical form of music is the song, used to celebrate major events in the life cycle and the liturgical year. Laban complains that his son-in-law Jacob's hasty departure has prevented the typical farewell "with joy and songs, with tambourine and lyre" (Gen 31.27). We also find many references to funeral dirges, sung by both men and women—including David's laments for Saul and Jonathan (2 Sam 1.19–27) and for Abner (2 Sam 3.33–34) and Jeremiah's lament for the dead king Josiah (2 Chr 35.25)—and passing references to harvest songs (Isa 16.10; see also Judg 9.27; 21.21), wedding songs (Ps 45.8), and music at banquets (Isa 5.11–12; Am 6.4–6).

The prophets frequently made use of music in delivering their message. They adapted the fu-

FIGURE 27.3. A flute player. Detail of a relief from the palace of the Assyrian king Ashurbanipal at Nineveh, dating to the seventh century BCE.

and David with song and dance (1 Sam 18.6–7), as did Jephthah's daughter on her father's return in triumph from battle (Judg 11.34). Mixed choruses performed both the secular music of the court (2 Sam 19.35) and the hymnody of the Temple (1 Chr 25.5–6), and the tribute that King Hezekiah was required to pay to the Assyrian king Sennacherib included male and female singers (see Box 19.4 on pages 338–39).

Sacred music is most in evidence in the Bible, and it is in the detailed descriptions of the performers of sacred music (as, for example in 1 Chr 15.16–24) and in the psalms themselves that we find most references to music and dance. Many of the psalms are called "songs," and many more make use of the verb "to sing." The psalms also

neral dirge for satirical purposes in their oracles against foreign nations, such as Babylon (Isa 14.4–23), Tyre (Ezek 27), and Egypt (Ezek 32.2–16). In fact, music seems to have been a part of the prophetic repertoire: The "band of prophets" who meet Saul after his anointing by Samuel are accompanied by "harp, tambourine, flute, and lyre" as they prophesy (1 Sam 10.5); Elisha gives an oracle only after a musician begins to play (2 Kings 3.15); Isaiah sings a love song about a vineyard (Isa 5.1–7); and the Chronicler mentions those who "prophesy with lyres, harps, and cymbals" (1 Chr 25.1).

Many of the most famous biblical poems are in fact songs, including the textured love lyrics of the Song of Solomon (see pages 495–97) and the hymns celebrating the victories of God and Israel attributed to Miriam (Ex 15.21) and to Deborah and Barak (Judg 5.1). These and other references indicate that women were not just participants but on some occasions also leaders in music-making in ancient Israel (see Figure 27.4). The women of Israel celebrated the victories of Saul

FIGURE 27.4. Ceramic figurine of a woman playing a drum, about 8 in (20 cm) high, from the first half of the first millennium BCE.

refer to musical instruments, which fall into three groups: percussion, including tambourines, drums, cymbals, and bells; stringed instruments, such as the lyre and the harp; and winds, including the trumpet, the horn, the ram's horn, and the flute. The second-century BCE book of Daniel lists instruments found in a royal court: "horn, pipe, lyre, trigon, harp, drum, and entire musical ensemble" (Dan 3.5). The precise translation of the names of the more than twenty instruments named in the Bible is often a guess, based on related words in later languages, ancient interpretations and translations, representations of various instruments in Near Eastern art, and chance archaeological finds. Excavations in Jerusalem, for example, uncovered part of a flute made from a cow's hind leg bone, with six finger holes. Some of the titles to the psalms also seem to refer to musical directions, including well-known melodies, as in such evocative phrases as "The Doe of the Dawn" (Ps 22), "The Dove on Far-off Terebinths" (Ps 56), and "The Lily of the Covenant" (Ps 60), and perhaps even to musical notations, such as "the eighth" (Hebr. *sheminit*, Pss 6; 12), which may refer either to an eight-stringed instrument or perhaps to an octave.

Another mysterious term that may have musical significance is "selah," which occurs seventy-one times in the book of Psalms, and only three times elsewhere in the Bible, all in the "Psalm of Habakkuk" (Hab 3). It is placed either at the end of a psalm or at the end of what appears to be an ancient division into a stanza or strophe, but its precise function and meaning are unknown.

All of this detail is immensely frustrating. It is as if we had only the libretto and some of the orchestral instruments for a Verdi opera whose score was lost. We must therefore use our imagination in thinking about the poetry of ancient Israel, most of which as elsewhere in the ancient world was set to music, and in re-creating in our minds the sights and sounds of dancers and musicians, as in the final hymn of the book of Psalms (Ps 150.3–5), a virtual catalogue of ancient Israelite instruments, and in the liturgical procession mentioned in Psalm 68.25:

> the singers in front, the musicians last,
> between them girls playing tambourines.

WISDOM LITERATURE

Throughout the ancient Near East, from the third millennium BCE into the early Common Era, and from Egypt to southern Mesopotamia, existed a type of writing that has been called "**wisdom literature.**" This literature is concerned with the realities of human experience, from the mundane to the sublime, and with the relationship between that experience and the divine.

Wisdom literature is remarkably similar in different eras and different places, and so it can appropriately be called universal. In some ways it is analogous to philosophy, as developed by the Greeks, but it is not as abstract or as systematic. Rather, it is consistently rooted in the everyday, although from that perspective it also can deal with such profound questions as suffering, death, and divine justice.

The very word for "wisdom" (Hebr. *hokmah*, with related words in other Semitic languages) expresses the range of the literature. A "wise" man is one who has knowledge of some sort. Smiths, carpenters, and other craftsmen are therefore "wise" because they have technical expertise. Those who know how to succeed in life are also wise, as are, ultimately, those who know the ways of the divine.

Wisdom literature was an international phenomenon, with the same or similar genres, such as proverbs, instructions, dialogues, and fables, attested throughout the ancient Near East in most periods and places. Much of this literature consists of collections made by scribes, often under royal auspices, and since ancient Near Eastern literature in general is a literature of the elite, this is not surprising (see Figure 27.5). The precise degree of cross-fertilization among regions is unclear, although there is evidence that in centers of power such as royal courts scribes were familiar with the work of their colleagues elsewhere. We will examine in Chapter 28 considerations of the issue of divine justice in ancient Near East-

FIGURE 27.5. Detail of an Egyptian tomb painting from the fifteenth century BCE showing scribes recording a wheat harvest, probably for tax purposes. This illustrates the practical role of scribes in ancient Near Eastern societies. Because they were often the only members of society who could read and write, scribes were also responsible for the copying, editing, and preservation of ancient literatures.

ern texts that resemble the books of Job and Ecclesiastes. In this chapter we will focus on collections of proverbs.

The **proverb**, a short saying that pithily expresses insight into experience, is perhaps the most widely attested genre of wisdom literature. In Mesopotamia, collections of proverbs are known from as early as the third millennium BCE in Sumer, and the latest examples date to the third century BCE. Egyptian proverbs have a similar chronological span, continuing into the Common Era. From both regions, and from many other locales, thousands of proverbs have been found, similar in form and sometimes in content to those in the Bible. Because they often deal with ordinary life, borrowing is difficult to identify, but

in one notable case the compilers or authors of the biblical book of Proverbs seem to have been familiar with the Egyptian Instruction of Amenemope, which was compiled in the late second millennium BCE.

The preface to the Instruction of Amenemope provides a rationale for making an anthology of proverbs:

> The beginning of the instruction about life,
>   The guide for well-being,
> All the principles of official procedure,
>   The duties of the courtiers . . .
> Written by the superintendent of the land, experienced in his office,
>   The offspring of a scribe of the Beloved Land
>   . . .

For his son, the youngest of his children,
   The least of his family. (1.1–2.11)

It is likely that the frequent designation of the son as addressee of the maxims taught by his father ultimately came from a familial setting. Throughout the ancient Near East, proverbs often reflect what we may call a kind of folk wisdom, and thus, although they were ultimately collected and preserved in the royal courts, many probably come from a wider societal background. But the instruction of the son need not have been restricted to one who was to inherit his father's occupation and status, as was the case of Amenemope, or to any male offspring. The father-son metaphor could also be used of a teacher-student or master-apprentice relationship, as in the case of the "sons of the prophet" who addressed their leader as "father" (see page 300).

Learning and copying the proverbs was part of the curriculum of courtiers and of younger scribes in training for the civil service. Through the proverbs they learned about how to succeed—in the mundane sense (through proverbs about table manners and court protocol), in human relationships, and in a more profound way as well: how to live in a way pleasing to the gods. In a similar way, in American education in the nineteenth century, the copying of proverbs and maxims taught penmanship and needlework, as well as inculcating social and religious principles.

The Words of Ahiqar

A good example of the wisdom tradition is the text known as "The Words of Ahiqar." A composite work, it begins with the autobiographical narrative of Ahiqar, who identifies himself as a scribe and wise counselor of the Assyrian kings Sennacherib and Esarhaddon, in the late eighth and early seventh centuries BCE. In it Ahiqar relates how he was falsely accused of treason by his nephew, who was also his adopted son. His death sentence was avoided by the substitution of a slave, and when the king later required the assistance of a wise man, Ahiqar was reintroduced to the court and saved the day. The second part of the book consists of more than a hundred proverbs, fables, and other sayings attributed to the wise Ahiqar.

The story of the wronged courtier is a commonplace in ancient literature; biblical examples are found in the books of Esther and Daniel (see Chapter 30), and elements of the motif are found in the story of Joseph (Gen 37–50; see pages 75–76) and in the book of Job (see Chapter 28). The apocryphal book of Tobit refers to Ahiqar (Tob 1.21–22; 14.10; see further page 535). The story also apparently served as a basis for the *Life of Aesop*, a late classical Greek work.

The earliest surviving copy of the text is in Aramaic (see Box 24.1 on page 422), perhaps its original language. It was one of a group of papyri from the fifth-century BCE Jewish military colony at Elephantine, near modern Aswan in southern Egypt, which was probably originally founded by refugees from Judah in the early sixth century (see Box 25.2 on page 434). A number of translations into other languages are found beginning early in the Common Era, and it also occurs in some manuscripts of the Arabic anthology *A Thousand and One Nights*. The widespread appeal of the narrative, which may originally have been composed in the seventh century BCE, is one indication of the international character of wisdom literature.

Another is that many of the proverbs found in the second part of "The Words of Ahiqar" have close parallels in other ancient collections, including the biblical book of Proverbs. We find numerical sayings ("There are two things which are good, and a third which is pleasing to Shamash [the sun-god]"), as in the book of Proverbs and elsewhere in the Bible (see Box 27.1). As frequently in the book of Proverbs (for example, 1.8, 10, 15; 2.1; 3.1) and other wisdom texts, the reader is addressed as "my son" (which the NRSV usually translates as "my child"). In some cases there are even close similarities in wording (see Box 27.4).

Finally, like the book of Proverbs and other biblical and nonbiblical wisdom literature, the "Words of Ahiqar" combine sayings concerning ordinary human experience with sayings that

Box 27.4 AHIQAR AND PROVERBS

The following is an example of similarity between the "The Words of Ahiqar" and the biblical book of Proverbs:

Spare not your son from the rod;
   otherwise can you save him
   from wickedness?
If I beat you, my son,
   you will not die;
But if I leave you alone,
   you will not live. (Ahiqar 81–82)

Do not withhold discipline from a young
   man; if you beat him with the rod, he
   will not die.
You should beat him with the rod,
   and you will save his life from Sheol
   [the underworld].
(Prov 23.13–14)

These verses probably draw upon a common source rather than being directly related, but the similarity is striking and is further evidence of how wisdom traditions were interrelated throughout the ancient Near East.

---

have to do with the divine. The ancients held no sharp distinction between the sacred and the secular, and at all levels wisdom—the ability to live well in every sense—was ultimately a divine gift:

Wisdom is of the gods.
   Indeed, she is precious to the gods;
   her kingdom is eternal.
She has been established by heaven;
   the lord of the holy ones has exalted her.
   (Ahiqar 94–95; see further page 475)

Wisdom Literature in the Bible

In the canons, or arrangements, of the books of the Bible in both Jewish and Christian traditions, the distinctive material that scholars have called "wisdom literature" is for the most part clustered together. Although examples of wisdom literature occur throughout the Bible, it is mostly found in the third division of the Jewish canon, the Writings, in which the wisdom books of Proverbs, Job, and Ecclesiastes are found. The Roman Catholic and Orthodox canons, in the division that consists of poetical books, add to these other wisdom writings, notably the Wisdom of Solomon and Ben Sira ("The Wisdom of Jesus, Son of Sirach," or "Sirach" for short), which is also known as Ecclesiasticus (see further Chapter 29 and the Appendix).

The books of Proverbs, Job, and Ecclesiastes share a concern with the present and are largely focused on the human condition as it is actually experienced. These books are remarkable for their lack of explicit reference to the main events and personalities of Israel's history. We find no mention of Israel's ancestors, the Exodus, Moses, the covenant at Sinai, or Joshua and the conquest of the land of Israel. None of the prophets are mentioned. The kings David, Solomon, and Hezekiah are named only in occasional editorial notes. This literature, then, is essentially ahistorical, and this is consistent with the universal aspect of wisdom literature throughout the ancient Near East. Only in the later books of Sirach and the Wisdom of

Solomon, probably compiled in the second and first centuries BCE, respectively, are the familiar personalities and the events of Israel's history combined with the wisdom tradition.

Much of this literature, however, is attributed to Solomon. Just as his father David was credited with authorship of many of the psalms, Solomon became the favorite pseudonymous author of all sorts of wisdom literature, including not only the collections of proverbs (see later in this chapter), but also the book of Ecclesiastes and the Song of Solomon (see pages 489–90 and 496) and the later apocryphal book the Wisdom of Solomon (see page 518). In part this is because of Solomon's reputation as the quintessentially wise ruler, evidenced in a number of passages in 1 Kings, including the Solomonic judgment concerning the disputed child (1 Kings 3.16–28) and the visit of the queen of Sheba (1 Kings 10.1–10). A summary of Solomon's wisdom appears in 1 Kings 4.29–34:

> God gave Solomon very great wisdom, discernment, and breadth of understanding as vast as the sand on the seashore, so that Solomon's wisdom surpassed the wisdom of all the people of the east, and all the wisdom of Egypt. He was wiser than anyone else, wiser than Ethan the Ezrahite, and Heman, Calcol, and Darda, children of Mahol; his fame spread throughout all the surrounding nations. He composed three thousand proverbs, and his songs numbered a thousand and five. He would speak of trees, from the cedar that is in the Lebanon to the hyssop that grows in the wall; he would speak of animals, and birds, and reptiles, and fish. People came from all the nations to hear the wisdom of Solomon; they came from all the kings of the earth who had heard of his wisdom. (See also 1 Kings 10.23–25.)

Apart from the wisdom books themselves, elements of wisdom tradition are found throughout the Bible. As we saw earlier in this chapter, scholars have identified a number of the psalms as belonging to the category of wisdom literature. Popular proverbs are found in many biblical books, some apparently of considerable currency, as is shown by occurrence of the same proverb—"The fathers have eaten sour grapes, and the children's teeth are set on edge"—in both Jeremiah (31.29) and Ezekiel (18.2).

We find frequent references in biblical literature to wise women and wise men, such as the wise women of Tekoa and Abel Beth-maacah (2 Sam 14.2; 20.16) and the wise men of the Judean court (Isa 29.14; Jer 8.8–9; 9.23; 18.18), probably government officials who would have been involved in the editing and copying of various wisdom traditions. Scholars also have identified wisdom elements in the Joseph story (Gen 37–50), in the book of Deuteronomy, in some of the prophets, and, in fact, in almost every book of the Bible, although not all such identifications are equally compelling.

THE BOOK OF PROVERBS

Like the book of Psalms, which it follows in the Bible, the book of Proverbs is an anthology or, more accurately, an anthology of anthologies. This is clear from the headings provided in the book itself:

1.1	The proverbs of Solomon son of David, king of Israel.
10.1	The proverbs of Solomon.
22.17	The words of the wise.
24.23	These also are by the wise.
25.1	These are other proverbs of Solomon that the officials of King Hezekiah of Judah copied.
30.1	The words of Agur son of Jakeh, of Massa.
31.1	The words of Lemuel, king of Massa, which his mother taught him.

Although the attribution to Solomon of three of these collections is probably not accurate, taken together with the note that one collection of Solomon's proverbs was copied in the court of Hezekiah, the king of Judah in the late eighth and early seventh century BCE, and the attribution of other proverbs at the end of the book to King Lemuel, it is clear that in Israel as elsewhere in the ancient Near East one locale for the production of this type of literature was the royal court. The last two headings are more obscure. About Lemuel and Agur we know nothing, and about their presumed land of origin, Massa, only that is it in northern Arabia, as Genesis 25.14, which identifies Massa as one of the descendants of Ishmael, and a few nonbiblical sources attest. Wisdom is often associated with the regions east and southeast of Israel. The "people of the east" are considered among the wisest in the world (1 Kings 5.30). Jeremiah 49.7 refers to the wisdom of Teman, an area in northern Arabia, and the home of Job was in the same region.

Within the collections of proverbs the principle of arrangement is apparently random. Sometimes proverbs with a common theme or vocabulary are grouped together, and proverbs with a similar form, such as numerical sayings (Prov 30.15–31; see Box 27.1), also occur in proximity, but a deliberate arrangement for the book as a whole has eluded scholars.

As in the book of Psalms, which is also an anthology, we find repetitions. For example, the proverb

It is better to live in a corner of the roof
than in a house shared with a contentious wife

occurs in both 21.9 and 25.24. A variation on the same proverb also appears in 21.19:

It is better to live in a desert land
than with a contentious and fretful wife.

Other repetitions include 6.10–11 and 24.33–34; 10.1 and 15.20; 10.2 and 11.4; and 10.6 and 10.11.

Because the book of Proverbs is an anthology, and because the proverbs do not refer to specific historical events or circumstances, the individual proverbs are impossible to date with precision, although presumably those having to do with kings come from the time of the monarchy, which roughly corroborates the attribution of the collections to Solomon and the "men of Hezekiah." We find little evidence of Greek influence in vocabulary or thought, so that the consensus of scholars is that the collection itself was compiled before the Hellenistic period (which begins about 330 BCE), probably in the fifth or fourth century BCE.

The proverbs fall into two general categories: those that express, in memorable language, some insights about human experience—like Poor Richard's Almanac—and those that have a religious dimension. A close parallel is the Analects of Confucius, in which a successful life and a pious life are similar. Yet the two categories are not entirely separate. Proverbs having to do with Yah-weh are interspersed with those concerning ordinary life throughout the book, although those with a more explicitly religious dimension occur more frequently in its first nine chapters, perhaps to set a tone for the anthology as a whole.

The religious dimension is for the most part one of an absolute divine justice: Yahweh looks with favor on the righteous and punishes the wicked:

The LORD's curse is on the house of the wicked,
but he blesses the abode of the righteous. (3.33)
The way of the wicked is an abomination to the
LORD,
but he loves the one who pursues righteousness.
(15.9)

Just as the sacred and the secular cannot be separated, neither can the material and what we might call the spiritual. Attention to divine instructions was as important as to those of parents or rulers.

We must recall that the authors of the book of Proverbs, like the ancient Israelites in general, had no clearly developed belief in life after death, especially not in an afterlife where there was bliss for some and damnation for others (see further pages 493–95). The reward for "fear of Yahweh" was thus "riches and honor and [long] life" (Prov 22.4) in the present rather than in some postmortem future.

We also see a more spiritual dimension to the book of Proverbs. Since all facets of life were interconnected, true wisdom included what is called "fear of Yahweh," which was not just an attitude of dread, but rather one of total submission to the divine will. A repeated phrase in the book of Proverbs and elsewhere is that "fear of the LORD is the beginning of wisdom" (Prov 9.10; Ps 111.10; see also Prov 1.7; 15.33; Job 28.28), and the converse was also true: Foolishness, lack of wisdom, was in fact wickedness.

The Social Worlds of Proverbs

The proverbs contain simple insights into human life expressed in pithy aphorisms and metaphors. A probable origin for many of them is a kind of familial or clan lore. A family setting is the basis of the frequent address to the son, and explicit references to parental teaching are also found (1.8; 6.20). Some have retained currency in contemporary English, such as "Pride goes before destruction, and a haughty spirit before a fall" (Prov 16.18) and "A soft answer turns away wrath" (Prov 15.1), and also, unfortunately, "Those who spare the rod hate their children" (Prov 13.24), more familiar in its English adaptation, "Spare the rod and spoil the child."

Some proverbs may have originated in the life of agrarian towns and villages, as references to seasonal agricultural activities such as plowing, planting, and harvest suggest. Most of the proverbs, however, seem to reflect the lives of the wealthy elite, in an urban setting, and especially in the royal court. Many proverbs have as their general theme the way to advancement, from correct table manners (23.1–2) to a discreet tactfulness (25.6); this is unsurprising in view of the role of the royal bureaucracy in the collection and editing of the proverbs. We also find sly critiques of monarchic excesses, as in the numerical saying in 30.29–31 and elsewhere (for example, 29.4, 14; 30.24–28).

While generally conventional in its values, the book of Proverbs testifies to some of the ideals of ancient Israelite law and of the teachings of the prophets concerning social justice as well. Special attention is repeatedly given to the poor and the needy, whose rights are to be respected even though they are not described entirely sympathetically and can even be blamed for their own condition (10.4). The rights of widows and orphans are also to be protected, but resident aliens are less equitably treated than elsewhere in the Bible. Some proverbs are in fact xenophobic, expressing prejudice and hostility toward outsiders.

The social world of the book of Proverbs is essentially patriarchal, although as in the commandment to honor father and mother (Ex 20.12), the mother's status in the family is acknowledged (for example, Prov 1.8; 10.1). Somewhat remarkably, in fact, the book of Proverbs ends with an acrostic poem (see Box 22.1 on page 383) celebrating the qualities of an ideal Israelite woman (literally, "a woman of power" [Prov 31.10]; the ordinary translations, "a virtuous wife"

or "a capable wife," make the poem more patriarchal than it actually is). But the values of the authors of the book of Proverbs are for the most part conventional and male-dominated. The presumed addressee of the book is also a male, as is indicated by nearly two dozen explicit addresses to "my son" and by the advice to stay away from the "strange woman."

The Strange Woman

Over and over in the book of Proverbs the young man to whom the proverbs are addressed is warned about sexual relationships with a "foreign" or "strange" woman. For example, he is advised:

> Drink water from your own cistern,
>   flowing water from your own well (5.15),

rather than from the "narrow well" (23.27) of the foreign woman. In some passages she is described in detail, as a woman already married to someone else, who entices the young man to her house:

> I have decked my couch with coverings,
>   colored spreads of Egyptian linen;
> I have perfumed my bed with myrrh,
>   aloes, and cinnamon.
> Come, let us take our fill of love until morning;
>   let us delight ourselves with love.
> For my husband is not at home;
>   he has gone on a long journey.
> He took a bag of money with him;
>   he will not come home until full moon.
>   (7.16–20)

The young man is repeatedly warned that yielding to the seductive overtures of such a woman is a recipe for disaster. On one level this is practical advice; on another, the designation of the woman as "foreign" or "strange" (that is, a stranger, a non-Israelite) reflects the frequent biblical insistence on endogamy, marriage within the community.

Yet these passages advising against a relationship with such a woman (and she is always singular) are interspersed among the passages that advise the young man rather to seek after Woman Wisdom, and so on another, almost allegorical level, the "foreign" woman is a foil, a counterpart, to Wisdom and can be interpreted symbolically, as her alternate designation, "foolish woman" (9.13; 14.1), suggests. To understand this metaphorical meaning, we must look at the figure of Wisdom.

Woman Wisdom

In Proverbs 1–9, and implicitly elsewhere in the book, we find reference to Wisdom as a female figure who speaks to the young man and invites him into her house, and also who accompanies the deity. This "**Woman Wisdom**" speaks frequently in the first person (1.20–33; 8.1–36; 9.1–6) and identifies herself not just as the divine companion, but also as the source of order in society and success in life (8.15–21).

The same language is found in other wisdom literature, such as Ahiqar, Job 28, Wisdom of Solomon 7–9, and Sirach 24. In these texts, "Wisdom" is depicted as a divine being, but scholars are in disagreement about her exact status. For many, she is a hypostasis, a divinized personification of an abstract quality, like Victory or Justice. For others, she seems to have qualities that imply that she is depicted as a goddess. In support of this interpretation, we should note the remarkable hymn in Proverbs 8.22–30, in which Wisdom speaks of herself as having been created before anything else and as Yahweh's companion and even assistant at the creation of the ordered world. The language of this poem is highly mythological, and it also has some sexual overtones, a perhaps daring appropriation of the common ancient Near Eastern view that every male deity had a female consort.

That at least is one ancient strand of interpretation. In later writings Wisdom is described as a member of the divine council (Sir 24.2) and as Yahweh's lover (Wis 8.3), and the first-century CE writer Philo called God the "husband of wisdom." Textual evidence in other parts of the Bible and archaeological data also indicate that, despite the prohibition of the worship of other gods, the ancient Israelites were often not strictly monothe-

istic and that the deities they worshiped included not only the Canaanite goddess Asherah (as in 2 Kings 21.7; 23.7; see Figure 18.5 on page 321) but also the "queen of Heaven" (Jer 7.18; 44.17–19). Asherah in Canaanite myth is depicted as one who seduces young men, like Ishtar in the Gilgamesh epic (see page 15). Moreover, Egyptian mythology has a goddess called Maat, who represented truth and justice. Drawing, then, on ancient mythology, and perhaps on heterodox Israelite practice as well, the authors of the book of Proverbs may be offering an acceptable orthodox alternative in the figure of Woman Wisdom, a tree of life more valuable than silver, gold, or jewels (3.13–18).

The praise of the "woman of power" that ends the book has plausibly been interpreted as a continuation of the symbolic depiction of Wisdom, who, somewhat domesticated, is the perfect life companion for an Israelite male (a similar sentiment is expressed in Wis 8.2; Sir 15.2).

RETROSPECT AND PROSPECT

Taken together, the books of Psalms and Proverbs may be understood as dealing with the lives of individuals and communities in the present. Their shared perspective is of a God who is intimately involved with human beings, who answers the prayers of those in distress, and who rewards the good and punishes the wicked in this life. This perspective is essentially the same as that of the Deuteronomistic Historians and the prophets, who saw in the events of the past and of their own times the working out of the divine purpose.

The Bible, however, speaks with many voices, and not surprisingly they are not always in agreement. In the next chapter we will see radical questioning of the idea of divine justice, or theodicy, in the books of Job and Ecclesiastes. Those works challenge the dominant biblical view that a merciful and just God constantly guided the lives of individuals and of Israel and the Jewish people.

IMPORTANT TERMS

parallelism

wisdom literature

Writings

proverb

Woman Wisdom

QUESTIONS FOR REVIEW

1. How would you describe the book of Psalms, and what are its principal genres?

2. Discuss the various ways in which psalms were used in ancient Israel. How do these uses contribute to the preservation of the psalms?

3. What is wisdom literature? How do biblical examples of wisdom literature resemble others from the ancient Near East?

4. What functions would proverbs have had in ancient Israel?

BIBLIOGRAPHY

A good introduction to and commentary on the book of Psalms is C. S. Rodd, "Psalms," pp. 355–405 in *The Oxford Bible Commentary* (Oxford: Oxford University Press, 2001).

For an introduction to music and musical instruments in ancient Israel, see Philip J. King and Lawrence E. Stager, *Life in Biblical Israel* (Louisville: Westminster John Knox, 2001), pp. 285–300. A complete discussion is Joachim Braun, *Music in Ancient Israel/Palestine: Archaeological, Written, and Comparative Sources* (Grand Rapids, MI: Eerdmans, 2002).

For an introduction to wisdom literature, see Richard J. Clifford, *The Wisdom Literature* (Nashville: Abingdon, 1998). Samples of Mesopotamian and Egyptian wisdom literature are found in James B. Pritchard, ed., *Ancient Near Eastern Texts Relating to the Old Testament*, 2d ed. (Princeton, NJ: Princeton University Press, 1969); and

in William W. Hallo, *The Context of Scripture*, Vol. 1, *Canonical Inscriptions from the Biblical World* (Leiden: Brill, 1997).

The excerpts from "The Words of Ahiqar" are adapted from the translation by J. M. Lindenberger in *The Old Testament Pseudepigrapha*, Vol. 2 (ed. J. H. Charlesworth; New York: Doubleday, 1985), pp. 479–507.

The excerpt from "The Instruction of Amenemope" is taken from William Kelly Simpson, *The Literature of Ancient Egypt: An Anthology of Stories, Instructions, and Poetry* (New Haven: Yale University Press, 1972), pp. 242–43.

A good commentary on the book of Proverbs is Carole R. Fontaine, "Proverbs," pp. 447–65 in *The HarperCollins Bible Commentary* (ed. J. L. Mays; San Francisco: HarperSanFrancisco, 2000).

PART SIX

CONTROVERSY AND CHALLENGE

DISSIDENTS AND LOVERS

Job, Ecclesiastes, and the Song of Solomon

In this chapter we will consider three anomalous books of the Bible, books whose content and perspective differ greatly from most of the rest of biblical tradition. The remarkable breadth of wisdom literature is clear from the books of Job and Ecclesiastes. Both take positions opposed to the mainstream of the wisdom tradition in the Bible, as exemplified in the book of Proverbs, and indeed of biblical literature in general, especially the Deuteronomistic History and the prophets. That mainstream view is of a **theodicy,** a divine justice, which is operative in the history of nations and in the lives of individuals as well. But experience suggests otherwise, the authors of Job and Ecclesiastes argue. In their dissent, they join similar voices found in other ancient Near Eastern literatures. Finally, we will also look at the Song of Solomon, a series of love poems whose erotic language prompted debate about whether the book should be in the Bible at all.

THE BOOK OF JOB

"Ye have heard of the patience of Job" (Jas 5.11), says the author of the letter of James in the New Testament, in the famous phrasing of the King James Version's translators. In the book of Job, Job himself begins by demonstrating his proverbial "patience," but he soon becomes angry, passionately protesting his innocence and demanding to know why he has suffered unjustly at the hands of God. Was Job patient or not? Was God just or not? These questions lie at the heart of the interpretation of the book of Job, one of the most difficult and challenging books in the entire Bible.

The biblical book of Job is only one chapter in the history of the legend of Job, the innocent man who suffered. Although Job is not mentioned in any prebiblical ancient Near Eastern sources, Ezekiel refers to Job as a well-known character in folklore. Speaking of Jerusalem, which is so wicked that, in contrast to Sodom (see Gen 18.22–33), the presence of good people in the city could not save it, the prophet declares that "even if Noah, Danel, and Job, these three, were in it, they would save only their own lives by their righteousness" (Ezek 14.14; see also 14.20). (Danel is not the hero of the biblical book of Daniel, discussed in Chapter 30, but to the Canaanite hero known also from Ugaritic texts: See Box 5.4 on page 74.) As far as we can tell from this brief reference, the character of Job as a quintessentially good person was independent of the biblical book of Job, and the authors of that book made use of an earlier Job legend in confronting directly the problem of the suffering of the innocent.

Structure

The book of Job at first glance has a relatively simple structure, as the following summary shows:

Chapters 1–2	Prologue
3.1–42.6	Dialogues, between Job and his friends, and then between Yahweh and Job
42.7–14	Epilogue

The prologue and epilogue, which are in prose, frame the dialogues, which are in poetry. The dialogues are for the most part a pattern of alternating speeches between Job and his three friends, Eliphaz, Bildad, and Zophar, in what seems originally to have been three cycles:

I	Job	Chapters 3
	Eliphaz	4–5
	Job	6–7
	Bildad	8
	Job	9–10
	Zophar	11
II	Job	12–14
	Eliphaz	15
	Job	16–17
	Bildad	18
	Job	19
	Zophar	20
III	Job	21
	Eliphaz	22
	Job	23–24
	Bildad	25.1–5
	Job	26; 27–28; 29–31

As is clear from this outline, toward the end of the third cycle the pattern is apparently disrupted. Bildad's final speech is uncharacteristically short, only five verses long, and Zophar has no third speech. Moreover, rather than being continuous, the final speeches of Job to his friends are interrupted by repetitive introductions (27.1; 29.1; compare 26.1), and in these speeches Job sometimes expresses uncharacteristic views that would seem more appropriate in the mouth of one of his friends.

A majority of scholars conclude that the book has suffered some dislocation beginning in chapter 25. They differ, however, on the details. Many assign 26.13–23 to Zophar, and also consider chapter 28, a hymn to Wisdom (see page 475) that stresses her inaccessibility, to be a later addition.

Following the last words of Job (see 31.40), a new character appears on the scene, a young man named Elihu. For several chapters (32–37) he attempts to provide a better argument than Eliphaz, Zophar, and Bildad have. Elihu has little new to say, however, and many scholars consider these chapters to be another later addition, especially since Elihu is not named in either chapter 2 or chapter 42.

The conclusion that the present form of the book of Job shows evidence of additions by later hands is not supported by any independent textual data, and recently some scholars have attempted a more holistic reading of the book, in which the inner contradictions somehow make sense. But no consensus exists on these issues.

After Elihu's speeches comes a dialogue between Yahweh and Job. Yahweh answers Job out of the storm and speaks at some length (chaps. 38–39; 40.6–41.34); Job's replies are limited to a few verses (40.4–5; 42.2–6).

Authorship and Date

The author of Job is anonymous, although later rabbinic tradition attributed it to Moses. The narrative chronology of the book is Israel's ancestral period; although we find no mention of any specific figures from Genesis, there are many echoes of Genesis 12–50 in language and setting. Postbiblical Jewish tradition recognized this when it identified Job's unnamed wife as Jacob's daughter Dinah.

Since it belongs to the broader category of wisdom literature (see pages 468–72), the book of Job contains no references to specific historical events or persons that would help date it. As a result, it is not surprising that scholars disagree on when it was written; proposed dates range from the tenth to the third second centuries BCE, with many preferring a date sometime in the exilic period, perhaps as early as the sixth century.

In that context, the book of Job is a consideration not just of the general problem of theodicy, of divine justice, but of the issues raised by the destruction of Jerusalem in 586 BCE. This conjecture is supported by verbal connections between Job and the literature of the sixth century BCE, especially Jeremiah, Lamentations, and Isaiah 40–55.

Ancient Near Eastern Parallels

In the course of the dialogues, the author of the book of Job uses a wide variety of genres, including myth, hymn, lament, dialogue, proverb, parody, catalogue or list, and legal formulations. Many of these genres are also found in a number of ancient Near Eastern texts, which are often cited as antecedents and parallels to Job.

- "Man and His God": A fragmentary Sumerian text dating to the early second millennium BCE, sometimes also called "The Sumerian Job." In it, an individual laments to his god that he has become a social outcast and suffers from physical and psychological distress. He acknowledges that all humans are intrinsically sinful and asks that his own sins, even if inadvertent, be forgiven. At the end the deity restores the man's health.
- "I Will Praise the Lord of Wisdom" (*Ludlul bel nemeqi*): A Babylonian poem dating to the second half of the second millennium BCE, this is a thanksgiving hymn to the Babylonian god Marduk. In it, a man who has suffered social, physical, and emotional distress relates how

when he called to his gods for help, they did not respond, despite his life of piety:

> Prayer to me was the natural recourse, sacrifice my rule.
> The day for reverencing the god was a joy to my heart.

Puzzled by the discrepancy, the sufferer muses:

> Who can learn the will of the gods in heaven?
> Who understands the intentions of the gods of the underworld?
> Where have human beings learned the way of a god?

Finally, in a dream, a luminous young man sent by Marduk caused the man's health to return:

> The Lord took hold of me,
> The Lord set me on my feet,
> The Lord revived me . . . *

and all of Babylon praised Marduk.

- "The Babylonian Theodicy": A text dating to ca. 1000 BCE. Like the book of Job, this lengthy poem is in dialogue form. In it a sufferer, seeking an explanation of his anguish, consults with a friend, pointing out, as does Job, that those who lack piety often prosper and those who pray can become destitute. The friend replies that the intentions of the gods are inscrutable, but in the end the wicked will be punished. The poem ends with a prayer by the sufferer for pity from the gods. It is also an acrostic (see Box 22.1 on page 383).
- "The Protestation of Guiltlessness": From the Egyptian Book of the Dead (second and first millennia BCE). This lengthy collection of assertions of innocence formed part of the Egyptian burial traditions. In them individuals were provided with the formulaic catalogue of sins that they had not committed, to be recited as their souls were weighed and judged by the deity Osiris. Job's catalogue of

---

*   Translation adapted from B. R. Foster (trans.), *From Distant Days*, pp. 304–5, 311.

what he had not done (Job 31) is often compared to this text. It concludes with positive assertions of piety and goodness, for example:

> I have satisfied a god with that which he desires. I have given bread to the hungry, water to the thirsty, clothing to the naked, and a ferry-boat to the marooned. I have provided divine offerings for the gods and mortuary offerings for the dead. So rescue me, protect me.[*]

- "The Man Who Was Tired of Life": An Egyptian text from the First Intermediate Period toward the end of the third millennium BCE, a time of upheaval and social disorder. In this text, an individual engages in a conversation or dialogue with his soul. Despairing of the present, he longs for death, speaking of it in lyrical terms:

> Death is in my sight today
> as when a sick man becomes well,
> like going out of doors after imprisonment.
> Death is in my sight today
> like the smell of myrrh,
> like sitting under an awning on a windy day. . . .
> Death is in my sight today,
> as when a man desires to see home
> when he has spent many years in captivity.[*]

In the context of the elaborate Egyptian beliefs in the afterlife, the desire for death is not as shocking as it might seem to us. The man's soul, however, will have none of this, and urges the man to enjoy the present: "Follow the happy day and forget care," a sentiment also found in the book of Ecclesiastes (see pages 492–93).

Scholars have found no demonstrable direct connection between the book of Job and any of these texts. They do illustrate the use of similar genres, notably the dialogue form, and also how in pondering the problem of the suffering of the innocent, traditional views were often questioned and the nature of divine justice and of the human condition probed, as in the book of Job.

Interpretation

The interpretation of the book of Job begins not long after its composition. Since translation is one form of interpretation, the ancient translation of the Hebrew Bible into Greek, the Septuagint, dating from the third century BCE, is one of the earliest interpretations we have. Its book of Job, however, looks significantly different from that found in the traditional Hebrew text, the Masoretic Text. The Septuagint text of Job is about one-sixth shorter than the Hebrew, and missing verses are more frequent in later parts of the book. But we are see also additions, notably an expansion of the only speech of Job's wife (after 2.9; see Box 28.4 on page 489) and a supplement to the epilogue (after 42.17). There are also minor differences, which somewhat reduce divine responsibility for Job's misfortunes and which make Job less angry and more pious. It is possible that the Septuagint translators produced a thoroughgoing revision of Job rather than just a literal translation, but that seems less likely than that they were carefully translating the Hebrew text they had, a text significantly different from the Masoretic Text. Complicating the picture is another early but fragmentary text, a targum or translation into Aramaic, found among the Dead Sea Scrolls at Qumran (see Box 29.2 on page 508). In this version, the book ends at 42.11, six verses earlier than the Hebrew text.

Several factors may contribute to cause these variants. First, as is also the cases in Jeremiah and a few other books, the final form of the text was not fixed; rather, Job was something like a hypertext, a work in progress revised by writers and translators at different times. Second, Job traditions other than those found in the biblical book certainly existed, and these too may have influ-

---

[*]   J. A. Wilson (trans.), in Pritchard, *Ancient Near Eastern Texts*, p. 36.
[†]   W. K. Simpson (trans.), *Literature of Ancient Egypt*, p. 208.

enced some of the changes. Finally, some of the changes may have been motivated by theological concerns; in some of the translations verses that seem to attribute Job's problems directly to God are softened or omitted. It should also be noted that the Hebrew text of Job is probably the most difficult in the Bible. More than a hundred words occur in Job that occur nowhere else in the Bible, and many verses are simply unintelligible.

Even with these early variants and linguistic problems, however, the central issue of Job remains clear. As the folkloric prologue informs us, Job is a quintessentially good person "who feared God and turned away from evil" (1.1), and, following the retributive justice of biblical tradition, he has been amply rewarded, with prosperity and progeny. As the result of a challenge from Yahweh to one of the sons of God, "the *satan*" (see Box 28.1), Job suffers a series of disasters, culminating in the deaths of his seven sons and three daughters and in his being afflicted with a loathsome skin disease. Throughout these troubles, Job exhibits his proverbial "patience," and despite his wife's advice to the contrary continues to bless

Box 28.1 THE SATAN

In Job 1–2 appears a figure called "the *satan*," which probably means something like "the accuser," or, following the forensic metaphors that are employed throughout the book, "the prosecutor." He is a member of the divine council, "the sons of God," who appear periodically before Yahweh (see Box 3.3 on page 34). The word *satan* means an adversary, either military (1 Sam 29.4; 1 Kings 5.4) or legal (Ps 109.6). It occurs in four contexts in the Hebrew Bible of an adversary who is greater than human: Job 1–2; Numbers 22.22, 32, of the divine messenger sent to block the prophet Balaam's way; Zechariah 3.1, in a scene of the divine council resembling that in Job 1–2; and 1 Chronicles 21.1, explaining why David was motivated to conduct a census of Israel.

The last example is especially enlightening, for it points to the development of the figure of Satan. In 2 Samuel 24.1, the source for 1 Chronicles 21.1, it was Yahweh himself who incited David to take the census. In revising his source, apparently troubled by this attribution of temptation and sin to the deity, the author of Chronicles transferred the blame to "a satan" (see Box 26.3 on pages 452–53). Only in later Jewish and Christian tradition would this shadowy figure develop into the familiar devil, with attributes taken from other biblical narratives, such as the serpent in the garden of Eden (Gen 3) and the daystar who fell from heaven (Isa 14.12–15).

Although the *satan* is an important character in the folkloric prologue of the book of Job, he is absent in the conclusion to the folktale in the epilogue (42.7–17) as well as in the dialogues. For Job, for his friends, and for the narrator, it is ultimately Yahweh himself who is responsible for Job's suffering; as Yahweh himself says to the *satan*, "You incited me against him, to destroy him for no reason" (2.3). The later development of Satan as a theological explanation for the problem of evil in a monotheistic system is not the view of the book of Job.

Yahweh. His piety then, is not dependent on divine favor. To put the problem somewhat differently, Job is an innocent person who suffers at Yahweh's hands. This is the central issue of the book: Presuming divine causation for all aspects of life, why do the innocent suffer? This question, established in the prologue, is the subject of probing in the dialogues, first between Job and his friends, and then between Yahweh and Job.

The dialogues begin with an outburst by Job against God. In it, and throughout the dialogues with his friends, Job is anything but patient, as this vivid paraphrase by Stephen Mitchell shows:

> God damn the day I was born
>   and the night that forced me from the womb.
> On that day—let there be darkness;
>   let it never have been created;
>   let it sink back into the void. . . .
> My worst fears have happened;
>   my nightmares have come to life.
> Silence and peace have abandoned me,
>   and anguish camps in my heart. (Job 3.3–4, 25–26)

This passage, which seems to echo one of Jeremiah's confessions (Jer 20.14–18; see pages 371–72), begins the dialogues with high intensity, and it is difficult to see any development in Job's emotional state. So much does Job complain, in fact, that rabbinic tradition alleged that had he not done so, Jews would now pray to the god of Abraham, Isaac, Jacob, and Job, not just of the first three.

It is also difficult to ascertain any development in the arguments of his friends. These arguments are those of mainstream wisdom tradition (see page 473):

> Think now, who that was innocent ever perished?
>   Or where were the upright cut off?
> As I have seen, those who plow iniquity
>   and sow trouble reap the same.
> By the breath of God they perish,
>   and by the blast of his anger they are consumed. (Job 4.7–9)

> Do you not know this from of old,
>   ever since mortals were placed on earth,
> that the exulting of the wicked is short,

and the joy of the impious is but for a moment? (20.4–5)

The point of these arguments is clear: Since God always punishes the wicked, Job is suffering because he too has sinned. Job has only to confess his guilt, and Yahweh will look with favor upon him once again. Some early rabbinic commentators also, like Job's friends, while admitting Job's innocence in the beginning, maintained that by his complaints against God he did in fact sin.

In his replies, Job unequivocally rejects these arguments and challenges the wisdom of his interlocutors concerning divine justice. He observes that he can find no consistent correlation between goodness and the prosperity that indicates divine favor or between wickedness and the misfortunes that result from divine disfavor:

> Why do the wicked live on,
>   reach old age, and grow mighty in power?
> Their children are established in their presence,
>   and their offspring before their eyes.
> Their houses are safe from fear,
>   and no rod of God is upon them. . . .
> They sing with drum and lyre,
>   and rejoice to the sound of the pipe.
> They spend their days in prosperity,
>   and without lingering they go down to Sheol.
> They say to God, "Leave us alone!
>   We do not desire to know your ways.
> What is Shadday, that we should serve him?
>   And what do we gain if we pray to him?"
> Is not their prosperity indeed their own achievement?
>   The plans of the wicked are repugnant to me.
> How often is the lamp of the wicked put out?
>   How often does calamity come upon them?
>   How often does God distribute pains in his anger?
> How often are they like straw before the wind,
>   and like chaff that the storm carries away? . . .
> How then will you comfort me with empty nothings?
>   There is nothing left of your answers but falsehood. (21.7–9, 12–18, 34)

In expressing his views, Job even employs parody. The pious amazement of the author of Psalm 8,

> When I look at your heavens, the work of your fingers,

the moon and the stars that you have established;
what are human beings that you are mindful of
them,
mortals that you care for them? (Ps 8.3–4)

is turned by Job into a bitter complaint about excessive divine attention to mere mortals:

What are human beings, that you make so much of
them,
that you set your mind on them,
visit them every morning,
test them every moment?
Will you not look away from me for a while,
let me alone until I swallow my spittle? (Job
7.17–19)

Job rejects the trite clichés of his friends and
insists on a better explanation from God himself:

I would speak to Shadday,
and I insist on arguing my case with God.
(13.3)

Moreover, Job knows, as do we, the readers, that
he is in fact innocent (see also Box 28.2):

As long as my breath is in me
and the spirit of God is in my nostrils,
my lips will not speak falsehood,
and my tongue will not utter deceit.
Far be it from me to say that you are right;
until I die I will not renounce my integrity.
I hold fast my righteousness, and will not let it go;
my heart does not reproach me for any of my
days. (27.3–6)

And Job catalogues his innocence, stating the
highest values of Israelite ethics:

I delivered the poor who cried,
and the orphan who had no helper.
The blessing of the wretched came upon me,
and I caused the widow's heart to sing for joy.
I put on righteousness, and it clothed me;
my justice was like a robe and a turban.
I was eyes to the blind,
and feet to the lame.
I was a father to the needy,
and I championed the cause of the stranger.
I broke the jaws of the unrighteous,
and made them drop their prey from their teeth.
Then I thought, "I shall die in my nest,
and I shall multiply my days like the phoenix;

my roots spread out to the waters,
with the dew all night on my branches;
my glory was fresh with me,
and my bow ever new in my hand. (29.12–20)

Job concludes with a subpoena to God himself:

O that I had one to hear me!
Here is my signature! Let Shadday answer me!
(31.35)

Then, after the interpolation of the speeches
of Elihu, Yahweh does answer Job. For many interpreters, the very fact of the divine answer is
significant. God is neither absent nor silent. His
response, however, further complicates the issue.
It consists of a magnificent catalogue of the mar-
vels of the created cosmos, in some of the most
lyrical, and also highly mythological, poetry in
the Bible. Yet Yahweh does not give a direct answer to Job's passionate query about why he has
suffered. Moreover, the world so carefully designed by Yahweh is not entirely orderly: It includes the hungry raven chicks (38.41), the oddly
designed and foolish ostrich that abandons its
eggs in the open (39.13–18), and the terrifying
Behemoth and Leviathan (see Box 28.3).

The world described by the creator is one in
which nature is often violent and in which humans play a limited role. Most important, in his
speeches Yahweh completely ignores Job's cries
for justice, or at least for an explanation of the
divine purpose. Job had anticipated this reaction:

If I summoned him and he answered me,
I do not believe that he would listen to my
voice.
For he would crush me with a storm. (9.16–17)

Nevertheless, when Job is finally given the divine response, he apparently returns to the piety
and humility that he had shown at the beginning
of the book. In both of his replies to the divine
speeches (40.4–5; 42.2–6), he is docile and sub-
missive, more like the Job of the prologue than
the one who had argued so passionately with his
friends. His last response to Yahweh (42.1–6), and
his last speech in the book, is difficult to interpret, and it serves as a paradigm for the difficulties in understanding the book as a whole. He be-

Box 28.2 "I KNOW THAT MY REDEEMER LIVETH"

One of the most famous passages in the book of Job is 19.25–26. In the King James Version, made famous by its use in the libretto of Handel's *Messiah,* it is translated:

> For I know that my redeemer liveth,
>   and that he shall stand at the latter day upon the earth:
> And though after my skin worms destroy this body,
>   yet in my flesh shall I see God.

In Christian tradition this has been interpreted as an anticipation of the resurrection of Jesus (the "redeemer") and of the dead.

The verses are perhaps the most difficult in the book of Job. The Hebrew literally means:

> But as for me, I know that my vindicator lives,
>   and that he will at last stand for upon the dust.
> This will happen when my flesh has been stripped off,
>   but from my flesh I would see God.

The "vindicator" is the *goel,* in biblical law the next of kin who is obligated to avenge or to assume the duties of a person, usually someone who has died (see Num 35.19–21; Lev 25.47–49; Deut 19.11–13; Ruth 3.13). Job seems to be saying that he is confident that after he has died the truth of his case will be demonstrated by his *goel,* but he would rather it happen during his lifetime.

Nowhere else in the book does Job express any belief in a personal, bodily resurrection; in fact, that concept does not develop until near the end of the biblical era. Nor does he have a clearly developed view of the afterlife as a time when his innocence will be ultimately rewarded by God. In fact, throughout the book, he insists on an answer from God in his present life. (On the development of views concerning life after death, see pages 493–95.) Thus, only by ignoring the context and content of the rest of the book can the traditional Christian interpretation be accepted, as all but the most conservative commentators have recognized.

gins his brief statement with apparently total submission:

> I know that you can do all things, and
>   that no purpose of yours can be thwarted. (42.2)

He then repeats, although not verbatim, what Yahweh had said to him:

> "Who is this that hides counsel without knowledge?" (42.3; see 38.2)

and replies, again with submission:

> Therefore I have spoken, but did not understand;
>   things too wonderful for me, which I did not know. (42.3)

Box 28.3 BEHEMOTH AND LEVIATHAN

Yahweh concludes his poetic catalogue of the wonders of creation with lengthy descriptions of Behemoth (Job 40.15–24) and Leviathan (41.1–34). Since ancient times, commentators have often identified them as the hippopotamus and the crocodile, respectively, while recognizing that their descriptions have a fantastic quality, perhaps because of the unfamiliarity of an Israelite writer with these animals from the Nile valley in Egypt. More recently many scholars have understood both beasts as forms of the chaos deity destroyed by the storm-god in the battle that preceded creation (see pages 5–7).

"Leviathan" in particular is a term used for this adversary, in both Ugaritic and Hebrew. Leviathan is a seven-headed serpent (see Figure 28.1), a prototypical dragon, which is how the primeval sea-goddess Tiamat is depicted in Mesopotamian art. In the Bible, Leviathan is identified with the primeval sea (Job 3.8; Ps 74.13) and, in apocalyptic literature describing the end-time, as that adversary of the deity before creation will be finally defeated (Isa 27.1; see also Rev 12.3; 19.20; 21.1). In the Bible, Behemoth occurs only in Job 40, which describes it as "the first of God's creations." Ancient postbiblical tradition paired Behemoth with Leviathan, and it is likely that Behemoth is another form of the primeval sea-monster.

In the divine speeches in Job, Behemoth and Leviathan are composite mythical creatures with enormous strength, which humans like Job could not hope to control. But both are reduced to the status of divine pets, with rings through their noses and Leviathan on a leash (see also Ps 104.26).

FIGURE 28.1. Depiction of combat between a seven-headed dragon and a god, dating to the mid-third millennium BCE. Both in Canaanite myth and in the Bible, Leviathan is described as a seven-headed serpent who is defeated by the storm-god, either Baal or Yahweh respectively.

Then follows a second quotation of Yahweh's discourse:

"I will question you, and you inform me" (42.4; see 38.3; 40.7),

and then Job's final words in the book:

I had heard of you by the hearing of the ear;
  but now my eye sees you;
Therefore I despise myself,
  and repent in dust and ashes. (42.6)

The Hebrew of the last verse is especially difficult and has been understood in very different ways. One is to see this final verse as consistent with those immediately preceding and to understand Job as piously submitting to the divine revelation he has just received. His experience—his vision—was an almost mystical one, in which, enlightened by Yahweh, he no longer felt it necessary to question the divine purpose. Confronted with the wonders of creation as recited by Yahweh, and face to face with Yahweh himself, his perspective shifted dramatically. He recognized that he was insignificant in the divine scheme, being only "dust and ashes" (see Gen 18.27), yet, almost paradoxically, his vision of Yahweh had in a sense vindicated him. According to this interpretation, experience cannot be reduced to a simple formula, and human reason cannot comprehend the mysterious ways of God. All that is possible is for humans to submit in faith to God's providence, like Job.

A very different reading has been given by several modern scholars, beginning with the Swiss psychoanalyst Carl Jung. According to this view, Job's reasonable question about why he, an innocent man, has suffered, is not answered. Instead, Yahweh, speaking from the overwhelming power of the storm, recites for Job the wonders of creation but ignores Job's immediate concern. Job's response to this blustering tyrant is to say whatever it takes to make him stop talking, so he acquiesces, tongue in cheek.

Despite its presence in the Bible and its allusions to other biblical literature, Job is a book without explicit references to the great events and personalities of Israel's history. We find no promise to the ancestors here, no covenant with Abraham or with Israel, no explication of the divine guidance of the history of Israel and of all nations. The issue that is the focus of the book is a universal one, as other ancient Near Eastern texts sampled earlier in the chapter show. Neither Job nor his friends are Jewish, and they rarely if ever refer to the deity by his proper name Yahweh, using more often Elohim ("God"), and especially El and Shadday, the name of the god of the ancestors of Israel and of the Canaanites as well (see further pages 81–82). The author of Job, of course, is Jewish, and he uses the name Yahweh in narrative sections throughout the book. Thus, it is Yahweh who answers Job from the storm (38.1; 40.6), revealing himself not as one who acts in history but as the sovereign defeater of the forces of chaos and the establisher of order in the cosmos as whole. This deity is apparently neither loving nor just, but he is all-powerful, and the best mere humans can do is to accept him on his own terms.

Job's reply to Yahweh is not, however, the end of the book. The narrator resumes the old folktale, telling us how Job's fortune is restored, now doubled, and new children are born to him (see Box 28.4). Finally, having lived to a ripe old age, like Israel's ancestors, he dies, "sated and full of days" (Job 42.17; see Gen 25.8; 35.29).

So, the book of Job has an apparently happy ending, but many interpreters find it unsatisfactory. Job has indeed been rewarded for his endurance, and in the end, God has shown himself to be just. But why did all of Job's suffering have to happen, and why, in the service of theodicy, did his children have to die? Job had complained that his sufferings were "without cause" (9.17; see also 2.3); in the epilogue Yahweh affirms that it was Job, not his friends, who spoke the truth (42.7). Perhaps the ambiguity of Job's final reply to Yahweh, and of the book as a whole, is deliberate: No easy answer exists to the problem of suffering, no formula that can adequately explain the justice of God.

Box 28.4 JOB'S WIFE AND DAUGHTERS

Women in the book of Job occur only incidentally. Job's wife is typical: In the framework narrative she is mentioned only in 2.9–10 and not at all in the epilogue, and in the dialogues she is referred to in passing twice (19.17; 31.10). In the biblical book of Job, she is nameless. Postbiblical tradition gives her a name (Sitis in one version, Dinah, the daughter of Jacob, in a variant tradition) and also expands her speech, making her a more sympathetic character. In the ancient Greek translation of the Hebrew scriptures, the Septuagint, the brief speech of Job's wife in 2.9 is expanded poignantly as follows:

> How long will you endure, saying, "Behold, I will wait a little while, expecting the hope of my salvation"? For behold, your memorial has been abolished from the earth—sons and daughters, the labor pains of my uterus, for whom I toiled in distress for nothing. You yourself sit, spending the night outside in the corruption of worms, and I am a wanderer and a servant from place to place and from house to house, waiting until the sun sets, in order that I may rest from the distress and pain that have taken hold of me. But say some word against the Lord, and die.

As the story of Job is retold, his wife's role becomes more and more important; in the "Testament of Job" (see Box 28.5), she is a major character.

Most other women are given equally cursory treatment in the biblical book. Thus, Job refers in passing to his mother, and to his brothers and sisters, and in his protestation of innocence, he insists that he has never looked on a virgin with desire (31.1) or committed adultery (31.9).

Job's daughters, however, are given unusual attention. The epilogue tells us that Job had seven sons and three daughters, to replace those who had died. While the sons are anonymous, the three daughters are named: Jemimah (which means "dove"), Keziah ("cinnamon"), and Keren-happuch ("horn of eye-makeup") (42.14). As is typical in folklore, the daughters are the most beautiful women in the land (42.15). Moreover, contrary to the usual pattern of inheritance laws, the daughters are given a share of the inheritance. No precedent is found in biblical literature for this arrangement, although in Ugaritic the daughters of Kirta (see pages 73–74) are to be given the rights of a firstborn son.

Box 28.5 JOB IN LATER TRADITION

The story of Job has had a long life in postbiblical literature and art. By the first century CE, it was expanded into the often comical *Testament of Job*, in which Job tells his family gathered around his deathbed the story of his life. Many subsequent writers have taken up Job's case, with very different views. Among the most important modern interpretations are William Blake's *Illustrations of the Book of Job* (1825), C. G. Jung's *Answer to Job* (1952), and Archibald MacLeish's *J.B.: A Play in Verse* (1956). In the latter part of the twentieth century, writers pondering the Holocaust have also pondered Job, for the problem of the suffering of the innocent is raised in an especially acute way by that collective tragedy.

THE BOOK OF ECCLESIASTES

The short book of Ecclesiastes has been contro-versial since ancient times because of its un-orthodox views, and early in the Common Era rabbinical authorities disagreed about whether the book should be included in the Bible. The book of Ecclesiastes presents itself as the rumina-tions of David's successor Solomon, and this par-tially explains its acceptance as scripture. But Solomon did not write it, and the book's views on the meaning of life and especially on issues of divine justice are at odds with the mainstream of biblical tradition.

Authorship and Date

The author of the book identifies himself as "king of Israel in Jerusalem" (Eccl 1.12), an identifica-tion made more specific by the book's ancient ed-itor, who calls him "son of David" (1.1). The son of David who succeeded him on the throne was Solomon, whose reputation for wisdom is de-scribed in the account of his reign in 1 Kings. Solomon is credited with several collections of proverbs (Prov 1.1; 10.1; 25.1) and is also the pseudonym adopted by other ancient writers (see page 472). The author is further given the name, or more likely the title, "Qoheleth," both by the book's editor (1.1–2; 12.8–10) and by the author himself (1.12; 7.27). This Hebrew word is con-ventionally translated "the Preacher" but literally means something like "the assembler," although what precisely is being assembled—the commu-nity? random thoughts about life?—is unclear.

As an example of wisdom literature, which as we have seen is universal in tone, it is not sur-prising that there are no specific details by which the book might be dated. The oldest manuscript of Ecclesiastes is one of the Dead Sea Scrolls, dated to the mid-second century BCE, so the book must have been written earlier than that. It is un-likely to have been written much earlier than the fifth century, since it contains some loan words from Persian, reflecting the imperial control of the Near East by Persia that began in the late sixth century. There are also a number of Ara-maisms, reflecting the period when Aramaic (see Box 24.1 on page 422) had become the official language of the Persian empire. Most scholars therefore think that a date in the Hellenistic pe-riod, during the third or perhaps the fourth cen-tury BCE, is likely. A few, noting the absence of any specifically identifiable Greek words or con-cepts, prefer a date in the Persian period, perhaps as early as the fifth century. In any case, the lan-guage of the book is much later than that of the time of Solomon, who lived in the tenth century BCE.

Structure

Like most books of the Bible, Ecclesiastes was ed-ited after its completion. In the body of the book the author describes in the first person how, like the Greek philosophers Socrates and Diogenes, he went on a quest for the meaning of life. The book opens and closes, however, with notes in the third person, identifying the author at the begin-ning (1.1) and commenting on the book at the end (12.9–14; see page 493).

Despite attempts to discover a pattern in the book, it seems best to view it as essentially a col-lection of thoughts with no discernible structure, in which topics and phrases recur as variations on a theme. This random organization is suggested by the opening of the book's editorial postscript: "Besides being wise, the Teacher also taught the people knowledge, weighing and studying and correcting many proverbs" (12.9). Like collec-tions of proverbs, then, the book of Ecclesiastes is a collection of the author's ideas about the mean-ing of life. Pascal's *Pensées* is a close parallel.

One of the puzzling features of the short book of Ecclesiastes is the number of apparent contra-dictions in it. Often Qoheleth seems to be stat-ing a view that is at odds with the dominant per-spective of the book. One explanation for these inconsistencies is editorial activity; just as some later editor added the introductory verse and the epilogue, that same editor, or others, or perhaps the author himself later in his life, may have glossed Qoheleth's unorthodox views with more conventional statements. Another proposal is that these inconsistencies are a deliberate tactic by the author that reflects his view of the anomalies in life. Finally, a widely held suggestion is that Qoheleth frequently quotes or alludes to traditional views, only to refute them. Thus, in 8.12–13, the author says: "I know that 'it will be well with those who fear God, because they stand in fear before him, but it will not be well with the wicked, neither will they prolong their days like a shadow, because they do not stand in fear before God.'" This view, however, which corresponds to that found in Proverbs and other biblical wisdom literature, is contradicted both by what precedes (8.10–11a) and by what follows: "There are righteous people who are treated according to the conduct of the wicked, and there are wicked people who are treated according to the conduct of the righteous" (8.14). The most convincing explanation of this inner contradiction is to see the words in single quotation marks in the first excerpt, following "I know" (v. 12), as a traditional saying that the author then refutes on the basis of his own experience.

A similar explanation clarifies the apparently contradictory proverbs in 9.16–18: "So I said, 'Wisdom is better than might'; yet the poor man's wisdom is despised, and his words are not heeded. . . . 'Wisdom is better than weapons of war'; but one bungler destroys much good." In each case, Qoheleth seems to be quoting a proverb, and then refuting it with his own view. In ancient manuscripts, quotation marks (and other punctuation) were usually not indicated; they have been supplied here, as in most translations, and are themselves a form of interpretation. In the case of Ecclesiastes, the theory that the author used quotations resolves many of the contradictions in the book.

Interpretation

Qoheleth has been called a skeptic, a nihilist, an existentialist, a pessimist, and a realist. These and other labels show how difficult it is to categorize the content of the book. One thing is sure:

Qoheleth is not an atheist. A believer, at least a theist, he is not like the proverbial fool who says in his heart "There is no God" (Pss 10.4; 14.1 = 53.1). For Qoheleth, God exists, but human beings are unable to fathom the divine purpose, or in fact to detect any coherent pattern in human existence.

This perspective is not unique to Qoheleth, for it is found in the broader literature of the ancient Near East, as noted earlier. The following Babylonian proverb is a close parallel:

> The will of a god cannot be understood;
>   the way of a god cannot be known;
>   anything of a god is impossible to find out.[*]

Because it belongs to the larger category of wisdom literature, the book of Ecclesiastes is also concerned with the universal aspects of human existence, within a theistic context. The word theistic is appropriate, for the deity is consistently called God, never by his proper Israelite name Yahweh ("the LORD"). Moreover, as in the book of Job we find no reference to any of the major events and individuals of Israel's history. Rather, the book is concerned with the meaning of life, and especially with the issue of divine justice, or theodicy.

Near the beginning and end of the book is the motto "vanity of vanities, all is vanity" (1.2; 12.8). This traditional translation is an interpretation of the Hebrew *habel habalim*, which literally means "breath of breaths," expressing a superlative—approximately the most evanescent puff of air. The word *hebel* occurs more than thirty times in Ecclesiastes, and it expresses the essential point of view of the book: Human effort on any plane is insignificant and transitory. The same word is used elsewhere in the Bible of a woman's beauty, because it is fleeting (Prov 31.30), and of the statues of other gods, who are insubstantial and worthless (2 Kings 17.15; Jer 10.15; 16.19). The characterization of human existence as *hebel* is also found in the Bible outside Ecclesiastes (see Job 7.16; Pss 39.5, 11; 89.47).

---

[*] Translation adapted from B. R. Foster (trans.), *From Distant Days*, p. 387.

The inability of humans to understand and to control their existence is developed in 3.1–8. This famous poem is often misunderstood, especially in popular culture, which removes it from its context. "For everything there is a season," says Qoheleth, "and a time for every matter under heaven":

> a time to be born, and a time to die;
>> a time to plant, and a time to pluck up what is planted;
> a time to kill, and a time to heal;
>> a time to break down, and a time to build up;
> a time to weep, and a time to laugh;
>> a time to mourn, and a time to dance;
> a time to throw away stones, and a time to gather stones together;
>> a time to embrace, and a time to refrain from embracing;
> a time to seek, and a time to lose;
>> a time to keep, and a time to throw away;
> a time to tear, and a time to sew;
>> a time to keep silence, and a time to speak;
> a time to love, and a time to hate;
>> a time for war, and a time for peace.

These words, which are often invoked in support of both military action and pacifism, are in fact yet another statement of human inability to make sense of life, as the immediately following verses make clear:

> What gain have the workers from their toil? I have seen the business that God has given to everyone to be busy with. He has made everything suitable for its time; moreover he has put a sense of past and future into their minds, yet they cannot find out what God has done from the beginning to the end. (3.9–11)

There are—there must be—divinely decided times for various events in human existence, but humans are unable to know what those times are and hence are also unable to affect the course of events. The conclusion is that given their woeful ignorance of divine intentions the best that humans can do is to enjoy life—"to eat, and to drink, and to be merry," in the famous phrase of 8.15 as translated in the King James Version.

The author asks more questions than he provides answers, and his conclusion is that even wisdom itself is elusive. Human beings are unable to

fathom the divine purpose, and the standard view of the book of Proverbs concerning divine justice is unsatisfactory. Qoheleth repeatedly refers to his experience: Goodness is not always rewarded, and wickedness is not always punished. In fact, he finds no discernible pattern in life:

> Again I saw that under the sun the race is not to the swift, nor the battle to the strong, nor bread to the wise, nor riches to the intelligent, nor favor to the skillful; but time and chance happen to them all. For no one can anticipate the time of disaster. Like fish taken in a cruel net, and like birds caught in a snare, so mortals are snared at a time of calamity, when it suddenly falls upon them. (9.11–12)

The only certain thing in life is death, which is the same for all, regardless of how they have lived their lives:

> Everything that confronts them is vanity, since the same fate comes to all, to the righteous and the wicked, to the good and the evil, to the clean and the unclean, to those who sacrifice and those who do not sacrifice. As are the good, so are the sinners; those who swear are like those who shun an oath. This is an evil in all that happens under the sun, that the same fate comes to everyone. (9.1–3)

For Qoheleth, death was final: "[T]here is no work or thought or knowledge in Sheol" [the underworld; see below] (9.10).

The only conclusion to draw from this grim picture is to enjoy life while one has it. The book concludes with a lyrical and poignant admonition to the young to enjoy their vitality:

> Rejoice, young man, while you are young . . . before the days of trouble come, and the years draw near when you will say, "I have no pleasure in them" . . . before the silver cord is snapped, and the golden bowl is broken, and the pitcher is broken at the fountain, and the wheel broken at the cistern, and the dust returns to the earth as it was, and the breath returns to God who gave it. (11.9; 12.1, 6–7)

The subversive character of this remarkable book was evident to the ancients too. Only its presumed authorship by Solomon enabled it to be included into the canon of Scripture in the first century CE; even earlier, a pious scribe had added a cautionary epilogue:

The sayings of the wise are like goads, and like nails firmly fixed are the collected sayings that are given by one shepherd. Of anything beyond these, my child, beware. Of making many books there is no end, and much study is a weariness of the flesh. The end of the matter; all has been heard. Fear God, and keep his commandments; for that is the whole duty of everyone. For God will bring every deed into judgment, including every secret thing, whether good or evil. (12.11–14)

Whatever Qoheleth had written, this scribe seems to say, is only the idle speculation of intellectuals, those who write books. Rather, the tried and true wisdom of the ancients—as found in collections of proverbs—is sufficient. And the message of that proverbial wisdom is clear: In the end, all that matters is fear of God, because there is a divine justice. But Qoheleth had emphatically disagreed.

EXCURSUS ON THE DEVELOPMENT OF BELIEFS IN LIFE AFTER DEATH IN ANCIENT ISRAEL

The ancient Israelite view of life after death was complex, and it is perhaps more accurate to speak of differing views. In general, there does seem to have been a popular belief in some sort of survival for the dead. A standard idiom used for the death of individuals is that they "sleep with their fathers" (for example, Deut 31.16; 1 Kings 2.10; 11.43) or are "gathered to their kin" (Gen 49.29; Num 20.24; Judg 2.10); this can be interpreted both literally, as a reference to the deposit of a corpse in a family tomb, and symbolically, implying that the dead members of a family continued to have some existence (as in Gen 47.30, since burial will not take place for many months). When Jacob learned of his son Joseph's apparent death, his lament included the words: "I shall go down to Sheol to my son, mourning" (Gen 37.35), and David used similar language when his first son by Bathsheba died: "I shall go to him, but he will not return to me" (2 Sam 12.23).

The most common term for the underworld in the Bible is "Sheol." Like the grave itself, it is a dark, damp, and dirty place, and one descends to

it, as one is lowered into a grave, or pit; the latter is a frequent synonym for Sheol. It is the land of no return (see Job 7.9; 14.12), with gates and bars to keep its inhabitants from getting out. At the same time, like Hades in early Greek mythology, Sheol is a place where the dead do survive, although in a miserable and powerless state. Grave goods are found in many Israelite tombs from the Iron Age (ca. 1200–586 BCE), including jewelry, tools, weapons, combs, mirrors, and amulets, along with jars, bowls, and juglets that would have held food and perfumes for the use of the deceased after death (see Figure 28.2). It must be observed, however, that these funerary offerings are sparse compared to the much more elaborate contents of ancient Egyptian tombs of the wealthy. The Hebrew word *nephesh*, which is often erroneously translated "soul," usually refers to the whole person, or to the essence of the person, and it is the *nephesh* that goes down to Sheol.

Sheol is a place where all are equal, whether kings or slaves (Job 3.13–19), but there they cannot do anything. This is the view of Ecclesiastes, for whom death is irrevocable and life after death is devoid of content: "[T]he dead know nothing . . . for there is no work or thought or knowledge or wisdom in Sheol" (Eccl 9.5, 10). As the psalms repeatedly note, appealing to the divine self-interest, for God to allow a person to die, to go down to Sheol, would mean that that person would no longer be able to praise God (Pss 6.5; 30.9; 88.10–12; 115.17; Isa 38.18–19); an apparently contradictory view is also found (Ps 22.29). At the same time, as the supreme deity, Yahweh has control over Sheol, just as his Canaanite counterpart Baal was able to defeat Death.

Judging from the prohibitions and condemnations of necromancy, the consultation of the dead, in biblical law (for example, Lev 19.31; 20.6, 27; Deut 18.11) and in the prophets (Isa 8.19–20; 26.14; 65.4), the view that one could have contact with the dead was apparently widespread. The most detailed example is that of the raising of the spirit of the dead prophet Samuel by the woman of Endor (1 Sam 28); surprisingly, the narrative only implicitly condemns the practice. Saul, the king at whose request the medium

FIGURE 28.2.   Close-up of a bone repository in a rock-cut tomb in Jerusalem dating to the ninth to seventh centuries BCE. In family tombs like this, which could be used for many generations, the bodies of the deceased were placed on benches until the flesh had decayed. Then the bones, and often the grave goods, were collected and transferred into the repository below the bench. Tombs like this illustrate the biblical idiom that when individuals died, they were "gathered to their fathers" (Judg 2.10).

summoned Samuel, had forbidden it, but the medium is successful and Samuel, called a "god," does come up from the "earth," which here, as often elsewhere, means the underworld. There is also some evidence that in popular religion at least some form of ancestor worship was practiced in ancient Israel as it was elsewhere in the ancient Near East (see, for example, Deut 26.14; Ps 106.28).

These views parallel those of early Greek writers, who in general thought that all the dead were together in the underworld. Only in the fifth century BCE do we begin to hear of some souls surviving elsewhere, in "the upper regions," and slightly later there developed the notion that the spirit or "soul" (Grk. *psyche*) of the person was distinct from the body. In the dualism of the Greek philosopher Plato and his followers, while the

physical part of the person ceased to exist, the "soul" lived on.

Under the influence of Greek thought, this belief is found in Jewish writings of the Hellenistic period. The soul, some believed, survived after death and was either rewarded or punished at the moment of death for the life that the person had led. The book of the Wisdom of Solomon, probably written in the late first century BCE, contains a full statement of this view, which partially resolves the problem of theodicy (see pages 520–21).

The idea of bodily resurrection developed separately and was not universally held. According both to Josephus, the first-century CE Jewish historian, and to the New Testament, the Pharisees believed that the bodies of the dead would be raised and reunited with their souls, but the Sadducees did not. The earliest text that unequivocally affirms the bodily resurrection of at least some of the dead, and the rewards and punishments that will await them in the life to come, is in the book of Daniel, which was written in the second century BCE:

> Many of those who sleep in the dust of the earth shall awake, some to everlasting life, and some to shame and everlasting contempt. Those who are wise shall shine like the brightness of the sky, and those who lead many to righteousness, like the stars forever and ever. (Dan 12.2–3)

The same view is also found in 2 Maccabees, which was written in Greek in the late second century BCE (see page 511). In stirring speeches given by a mother and her seven sons before their execution for persisting in their Jewish faith and refusing to eat pork, they repeatedly express their beliefs in resurrection for those who observe God's law and eternal punishment for those who do not. Reflecting the same conviction is the author's comment on Judas Maccabeus arranging for offerings to atone for the failure of those who had died to observe the law fully:

> For if he were not expecting that those who had fallen would rise again, it would have been superfluous and foolish to pray for the dead. But if he was looking to the splendid reward that is laid up for those who fall asleep in godliness, it was a holy and pious thought. Therefore he made atonement for the dead, so that they might be delivered from their sin. (2 Macc 12.44–45)

It is significant that the idea of the bodily resurrection of the dead developed in the context of one of the darkest moments in early Jewish history, during the forced Hellenization and persecution by the successors of Alexander the Great in Palestine, especially the infamous Antiochus IV Epiphanes in the early second century BCE. It is also ironic that this development was possible in part because of the influx of Hellenistic ideas, many of which had been so strenuously opposed by those who resisted Antiochus. (See further pages 499–507.) In developing the idea of bodily resurrection, these writers were able to synthesize Greek views of body-soul dualism with earlier bib-

lical texts that speak of Yahweh's control over Sheol (see Job 26.6; Prov 15.11), as well as those that assert his ability to give life as well as to take it away (Deut 32.39; 1 Sam 2.6).

Later Jewish, Christian, and Muslim traditions would develop more elaborate mythologies about the rewards and punishments in the life to come, but these are largely undeveloped in the Hebrew Bible and the Apocrypha.

THE SONG OF SOLOMON

The short biblical book known as the "Song of Solomon" is also called "the Song of Songs," which is a superlative meaning "the best of all songs" (as in "king of kings" or "holy of holies"). In Jewish tradition it is one of the Writings and is generally placed as the first of the Five Scrolls, between the books of Job and Ruth. In Christian Bibles it usually follows Proverbs and Ecclesiastes, so that texts traditionally attributed to Solomon are grouped together. (See further the Appendix.)

The book consists of poetic speeches, mainly by two young lovers, with other occasional speakers, the woman's companions ("the daughters of Jerusalem," 5.9 and 6.1) and her brothers (8.8–9). As its title indicates, the book was traditionally attributed to King Solomon, in part because of his reputation as a writer of songs (see 1 Kings 4.32 and Box 16.1 on page 270), and also perhaps because of his sizeable harem, which consisted of "seven hundred princesses and three hundred concubines" (1 Kings 11.3). But although Solomon is mentioned half a dozen times in the Song, he is not its original author, as one passage, in which the male lover contrasts himself with the famous king, illustrates:

> Solomon had a vineyard at Baal-hamon . . .
> My vineyard, my very own, is for myself. (8.11–12;
>   see also 1.5; 3.9)

Furthermore, some of the vocabulary of the Song is much later than that of the tenth century BCE when Solomon lived.

In 6.4, the woman is compared to the cities of Jerusalem and Tirzah. The latter was for a brief time the capital of the northern kingdom of Israel in the late tenth and early ninth centuries BCE. Apart from the references to Solomon, no other details provide clues for the book's date. The general consensus of scholars, based on a few words of Persian and possibly Greek origin, is that in its present form at least it dates to the postexilic period.

The genre of the book is also unclear. Since late antiquity, many interpreters have viewed the Song as a dramatic dialogue consisting of speeches by the two protagonists accompanied by occasional choral interludes. But the dialogue is not very clearly structured or developed, and verses are often repeated either verbatim or with variation in no evident pattern. The closest ancient Near Eastern parallels are several collections of love poems of various lengths from Egypt, mostly dating to the late second millennium BCE. As in the Song of Solomon, these poems use lush imagery, and the apparently unmarried young lovers refer to each other as "brother" and "sister." Here is a sample:

> One alone is my sister, having no peer:
> more gracious than all other women . . .
> shining, precious, white of skin,
> lovely of eyes when gazing. . . .
> Long of neck, white of breast,
> her hair true lapis lazuli.
> Her arms surpass gold,
> her fingers are like lotuses.*

The Song of Solomon is often compared to these poems for its use of similar language and motifs. Like the collections in which the Egyptian love poems occur, the Song of Solomon is probably also an anthology of love poems, perhaps from several periods, finally collected in the fourth or third century BCE. It is possible that the poems may have functioned as wedding songs, but they were not necessarily written for that purpose.

Metaphors from nature pervade the book, with frequent references to gardens and vineyards, birds and animals, and fruits, flowers, and per-

fumes. We find detailed descriptions of the physical beauty of the two lovers, often using culturally distinctive images: The woman describes herself as "black and beautiful" (1.5, a more accurate translation than the older "black but beautiful"); her hair is "like a flock of goats, moving down the slopes of Gilead" (4.1); her nose is like "a tower of Lebanon, overlooking Damascus" (7.4); her teeth are "like a flock of shorn ewes that have come up from the washing" (4.2); her breasts are like "two fawns . . . feeding among the lilies" (4.5). The man's "eyes are like doves beside springs of water" (5.12); "his lips are lilies, distilling liquid myrrh" (5.13). The sensuous eroticism of the book is also striking, a characteristic sometimes obscured or softened in older translations. Here is a sample of a modern literal translation:

> I slept, but my heart was awake.
>   Listen, my lover is knocking.
> "Open to me, my sister, my love,
>   my dove, my perfect one,
> for my head is wet with dew. . . ."
> My lover thrust his hand into the hole,
>   and my insides yearned for him,
> I arose to open to my lover,
>   and my hands dripped with myrrh,
> my fingers with liquid myrrh,
>   upon the handles of the lock.
> I opened to my lover,
>   but he was gone.†

So erotic is the Song that from early in the Common Era Jewish and Christian commentators generally interpreted it allegorically, as a description of God's love for Israel or of Christ's love for the church, and this may have contributed to the book's retention in the canon of Scripture, along with the attribution to Solomon. The consensus of recent scholars, however, is that the book is originally secular, a conclusion supported by the absence of any reference in it to God and by a remark of Rabbi Akiba (late first–early second century CE) that it was sung in taverns.

In the end we can only marvel at the presence in the Bible of this lyrical celebration of a "love

---

*   M. V. Fox (trans.), in Hallo, *Contexts of Scripture*, Vol. 1, p. 128.
†   Adapted from C. E. Walsh, *Exquisite Desire*, pp. 111–12.

as strong as death" (8.6), set in the springtime when

> the flowers appear on the earth;
> the time of singing has come,
> and the voice of the turtledove
> is heard in our land. (2.12)

RETROSPECT AND PROSPECT

Both Job and Ecclesiastes leave the troubling issue of theodicy, of divine justice, unresolved. The author of Job lets God speak for himself, but in his speeches God has nothing to say about the problem of the suffering of the innocent Job. Ecclesiastes expresses a kind of agnosticism: God exists, but we can never fathom his intentions. It is a measure of the complexity and even the strength of biblical tradition that these books are included in the Bible, where the dominant view is emphatically that there is a divine justice, that God rewards goodness and punishes wickedness. Despite what the Deuteronomistic Historians and the prophets claim, Job and Ecclesiastes remind readers that there are no easy answers, only questions.

As the Jewish community in Palestine faced more and more difficulties under Greek and Roman rule, the issues raised by Job and Ecclesiastes would become as pressing as they had been in the aftermath of the destruction of Jerusalem in 586 BCE. In fact, questions about divine involvement in human affairs are also timeless, as the Holocaust and other modern catastrophes continue to remind us.

IMPORTANT TERM

theodicy

QUESTIONS FOR REVIEW

1. What is the central issue of the book of Job? How is the issue resolved?

2. What is the central issue of the book of Ecclesiastes? How is the issue resolved?

3. Discuss how both the book of Job and the book of Ecclesiastes differ from other biblical traditions.

BIBLIOGRAPHY

The best short commentary on Job is Carol A. Newsom, "The Book of Job," pp. 319–637 in *The New Interpreter's Bible*, Vol. 4 (ed. L. A. Keck et al.; Nashville: Abingdon, 1996). A starting point on the history of the interpretation of Job is the collection of essays edited by Leo G. Perdue and W. Clark Gilpin, *The Voice from the Whirlwind: Interpreting the Book of Job* (Nashville: Abingdon, 1992). The translation by Stephen Mitchell quoted in this chapter is from his work *The Book of Job* (San Francisco: North Point, 1987). For an imaginative modern reading, see Elie Wiesel, "Job Our Contemporary," pp. 211–35 in *Messengers of God: Biblical Portraits and Legends* (New York: Random House, 1976).

Translations of the ancient Near Eastern texts discussed in the chapter are available in B. T. Arnold and B. E. Beyer, eds., *Readings from the Ancient Near East: Primary Sources for Old Testament Study* (Grand Rapids: Baker Academic, 2002); Benjamin R. Foster, *From Distant Days: Myths, Tales, and Poetry of Ancient Mesopotamia* (Bethesda, MD: CDL, 1995); W. W. Hallo, ed., *The Context of Scripture*, Vol. 1: *Canonical Compositions from the Ancient World* (Leiden: Brill, 1997); Miriam Lichtheim, *Ancient Egyptian Literature: A Book of Readings* (Berkeley: University of California Press, 1973–80); James B. Pritchard, ed., *Ancient Near Eastern Texts Relating to the Old Testament* (3d ed.; Princeton, NJ: Princeton University Press, 1969); and William Kelly Simpson, *The Literature of Ancient Egypt* (New Haven: Yale University Press, 1972).

A good introduction to the book of Ecclesiastes is James L. Crenshaw, "Ecclesiastes, Book of," pp. 271–80 in *Anchor Bible Dictionary*, Vol. 2 (ed. D. N. Freedman; New York: Doubleday, 1992).

For a summary of the evidence concerning Satan, see pp. 974–75 in *The HarperCollins Bible Dictionary* (ed. P. J. Achtemeier; San Francisco: HarperSanFrancisco, 1996); for a fuller treatment, see pp. 726–32 in *Dictionary of Deities and Demons in the Bible* (2d ed; ed. K. van der Toorn et al.; Leiden: Brill, 1999).

A good summary of the evidence concerning life after death in ancient Israel is T. J. Lewis, "Dead, Abode of the," pp. 101–5 in *Anchor Bible Dictionary*, Vol. 2 (ed. D. N. Freedman; New York: Doubleday, 1992); see also "Death, Burial, and Afterlife," pp. 363–81 in P. J. King and L. E. Stager, *Life in Biblical Israel* (Louisville: Westminster John Knox, 2001).

For a good summary of scholarly views about the Song of Solomon, see Roland E. Murphy, "Song of Songs, Book of," pp. 150–55 in *Anchor Bible Dictionary*, Vol. 6 (ed. D. N. Freedman; New York: Doubleday, 1992). A fuller treatment that emphasizes the erotic dimension of the song is Carey Ellen Walsh, *Exquisite Desire: Religion, the Erotic, and the Song of Songs* (Minneapolis: Fortress, 2000). A selection of Egyptian love poems translated by Michael V. Fox is in *The Context of Scripture*, Vol. I (ed. W. W. Hallo; Leiden: Brill, 1997), pp. 125–30.

ENCOUNTERS WITH THE GREEKS

1–2 Maccabees, Baruch, Sirach, the Wisdom of Solomon, and 4 Maccabees

For most of the fifth and fourth centuries BCE, Persia and Greece were locked in a struggle of epic proportions for control of western Asia Minor and the Aegean. Under the leadership of Alexander the Great in late fourth century, the Greeks ultimately prevailed, and all of western Asia as far as the Indus River came under Greek control, as did Egypt. This conquest marks the beginning of what is called the Hellenistic period, which lasted until the Hellenistic empire was taken over by the Romans in the first century BCE. The struggle between the Persians and the Greeks had little direct impact on Jews, whether in Judah itself or in the Diaspora, and it is barely mentioned in the Bible. But the conquests of Alexander had a profound effect—the Greeks brought with them their language, their culture, and their philosophy, irrevocably transforming the entire Near East, a process known as **Hellenization**.

Judaism was changed inevitably by this veritable flood of Greek ideas, although many Jews fiercely resisted Hellenization both intellectually and even at times militarily, viewing it as a threat to Jewish identity and tradition. In this chapter and the next, we will consider the impact that the Greek military conquest and its cultural ramifications had on Jews both in their homeland and

in the Diaspora and will examine several books of the Bible that describe varied responses to Hellenization and that incorporate Greek ideas, sometimes to a surprising degree.

HISTORY

For the Hellenistic period in general we have a wide range of sources. Greek historians describe the major military and political events; in fact, the first important Greek historian, Herodotus, in the fifth century BCE wrote a history of the conflict between the Greeks and the Persians. Persian inscriptions and a considerable amount of archaeological data have also been found. For Judea (as Judah was now called), our primary source remains the Jewish scriptures, especially 1 and 2 Maccabees, which were written only a few decades after the events that they describe. From the first century CE we also have the writings of the Jewish historian Josephus, who made use of other sources in addition to such books as 1 and 2 Maccabees.

Under the leadership of Philip II (359–336 BCE), Macedonia, in northeastern Greece, assumed the dominant role among the Greeks, replacing Athens as the principal power in Greece. When Philip was assassinated in 336, he was succeeded by his twenty-year-old son Alexander, who had been groomed for rule by, among others, the philosopher Aristotle. By 330, Alexander had decisively defeated the Persians and had taken control of the Levant and Egypt. He continued to expand his control to the east, reaching the Indus River in 327.

Alexander was the single most important historical figure of the fourth century BCE, if not of the entire late first millennium. His conquest of the Near East profoundly altered the political, cultural, and linguistic scene, much as those of Genghis Khan and Napoleon would change their worlds in later times. Despite his enormous importance, however, Alexander is barely mentioned in the Bible, in part because his campaigns had no immediate effect on Judea. But after his death the process of Hellenization that he propelled profoundly affected Judaism, especially in the second century BCE.

It would be misleading to infer that contact between Greece and the Near East had not existed prior to Alexander. As early as the second millennium BCE evidence is found of frequent trade in both directions, and traders brought with them not just goods for sale, but their culture as well. For example, at many sites along the coast of the eastern Mediterranean from Ugarit to Palestine archaeologists have discovered tombs containing pottery in the style known as Mycenaean, from the city of Mycenae in Greece, over which, according to Homer, Agamemnon ruled. An example in the other direction is the borrowing of the Phoenician alphabet by the Greeks early in the first millennium BCE. As the first millennium continued, more and more trade between the two regions took place, Greek artifacts are found with increasing frequency throughout the coastal Levant, and several colonies of Greek traders were established. Some biblical evidence exists for this as well: In a catalogue of the lands that traded with the Phoenician city of Tyre, the sixth-century BCE book of Ezekiel mentions "Javan" (Ezek 27.13, 19), the Greek colonies in Ionia on the western coast of Asia Minor, as does

Zechariah (9.13; NRSV "Greece") in the fifth century. The very word "Bible" is from the Greek word for "book" (biblion), itself derived from the name of the Phoenician city of Byblos (modern Gebeil in Lebanon), where papyrus from Egypt used in the making of books was processed and then shipped to Greece. (See Figure 29.1.)

Alexander's conquests intensified contacts between Greece and the Levant. Throughout the eastern Mediterranean, Greek became the language of the elite, and, over time, that of ordinary people. The pervasiveness of Greek is illus-

FIGURE 29.1. Imported Greek vase from Tell Jemmeh in southern Israel, dating to the fifth century BCE. Such pottery is evidence of connections between Greece and the Levant before the Hellenistic period.

trated by the translation of the Hebrew Bible into Greek beginning in the third century BCE (the Septuagint); a wide variety of Jewish writings in Greek, many of which are discussed in this and the next chapter; and innumerable inscriptions, coins, and other texts in Greek from such centers as Jerusalem and among the Dead Sea Scrolls (see Box 29.2 on page 508). Every educated Roman could speak, read, and write Greek, and the entire New Testament, including Paul's letter to the Romans, was written in Greek. Greek remained the dominant language of the eastern Mediterranean until the Muslim conquest of the seventh century CE, when Arabic replaced Greek.

When Alexander died of a fever in 323 BCE, at the young age of thirty-three, the succession was by no means certain, and several of his subordinates fought it out, eventually dividing his empire into three principal parts: Greece itself, ruled by Antigonus; Egypt, ruled by the Ptolemies from their capital at Alexandria, with a relatively stable transfer of power from generation to generation; and Asia, ruled by the Seleucids, usually from their capital at Antioch on the northern Mediterranean coast of Syria, where in the second century BCE especially there were often rival claimants to the throne (see Box 29.1 and Figure 29.2). As had often been the case in the past, the Levant and especially Judea were caught between more powerful forces to their south and north. During most of the third century BCE, Judea was under the control of the Ptolemies, despite a series of campaigns by the Seleucids to dislodge them. Only in the Fifth Syrian War at the end of the third century was the Seleucid king Antiochus III ("the Great") able to defeat the Egyptians and confine them within their borders. During the period of Ptolemaic control, Judea had continued to enjoy a relative autonomy, especially of worship, as it had under the Persians. But that would soon change.

Greek domination of the eastern Mediterranean was challenged during the second century BCE by the rising power of Rome. After several decades of conflict with the Carthaginians, their principal rivals for control of the western Mediterranean, the Romans decisively defeated them at the end of the third century BCE (although Carthage itself did not fall until 146 BCE), and then turned their attention to the east. During much of the second century the Romans countered the expansionist tendencies of the Seleucids and Ptolemies. The treaty of Apamea in 188, in which Antiochus III ceded control of the Greek mainland and of western Asia Minor to the Romans, was only a step in the eventual Roman conquest of the entire eastern Mediterranean, which took place over the next century and culminated in the campaign of the Roman general Pompey, who captured Jerusalem in 63 BCE.

The growing importance of Rome in the second century BCE is evident in several references to it in the books of Maccabees. Thus, for example, Antiochus IV was himself raised in Rome, as a hostage according to the terms of the treaty of Apamea (1 Macc 1.10). On several occasions, rivals for the Seleucid throne tried to gain Roman support in their quest for power, as did Judean leaders, including, according to our sources, Judas Maccabeus (1 Macc 8), Jonathan (1 Macc 12.1), and Simon (1 Macc 14.24).

The Maccabean Revolt and Its Aftermath

In 175 BCE, Antiochus IV Epiphanes, a younger son of Antiochus the Great, succeeded Seleucus IV, his brother, who had been assassinated (see Figure 29.3). Early in his reign, Antiochus attempted to gain control over Egypt, but the Romans ordered him to withdraw. To finance his campaign, he imposed a tax on Judea and was paid by Jason, a brother of the high priest Onias III, to install him in that office. Jason seems to have been an avid Hellenizer as well, which suited Antiochus's goal of unifying his kingdom culturally as well as politically. A gymnasium and stadium were built in Jerusalem, and the Jews were prohibited from practicing their religion. Then, 1 Maccabees reports, Antiochus went further, installing in the Temple in 167, a statue of a deity, probably the Syrian god Baal Shamem who was identified with Zeus. This "abomination that makes desolate" (Dan 11.31; 12.11) was the breaking point for Jews who wished

Box 29.1 TABLES OF RULERS

Persia

Darius I (522–486 BCE)

Xerxes (**Ahasuerus**) (486–465)

Artaxerxes I (465–424)

Darius II (423–405)

Artaxerxes II (405–359)

Artaxerxes III (359–338)

Artaxerxes IV (338–336)

Darius III (336–330)

Greece

Philip II (359–336 BCE)

Alexander the Great (336–323)

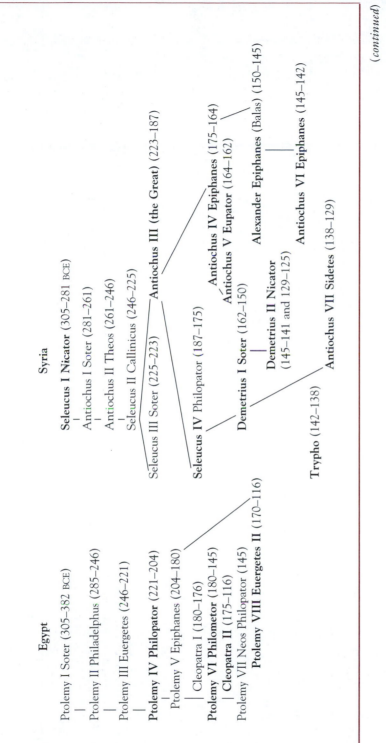

Egypt

Ptolemy I Soter (305–382 BCE)

Ptolemy II Philadelphus (285–246)

Ptolemy III Euergetes (246–221)

Ptolemy IV Philopator (221–204)

Ptolemy V Epiphanes (204–180)

Cleopatra I (180–176)

Ptolemy VI Philometor (180–145)

Cleopatra II (175–116)

Ptolemy VII Neos Philopator (145)

Ptolemy VIII Euergetes II (170–116)

Syria

Seleucus I Nicator (305–281 BCE)

Antiochus I Soter (281–261)

Antiochus II Theos (261–246)

Seleucus II Callinicus (246–225)

Seleucus III Soter (225–223)

Antiochus III (the Great) (223–187)

Seleucus IV Philopator (187–175)

Antiochus IV Epiphanes (175–164)

Antiochus V Eupator (164–162)

Demetrius I Soter (162–150)

Demetrius II Nicator (145–141 and 129–125)

Alexander Epiphanes (Balas) (150–145)

Antiochus VI Epiphanes (145–142)

Trypho (142–138)

Antiochus VII Sidetes (138–129)

(continued)

Box 29.1 TABLES OF RULERS (continued)

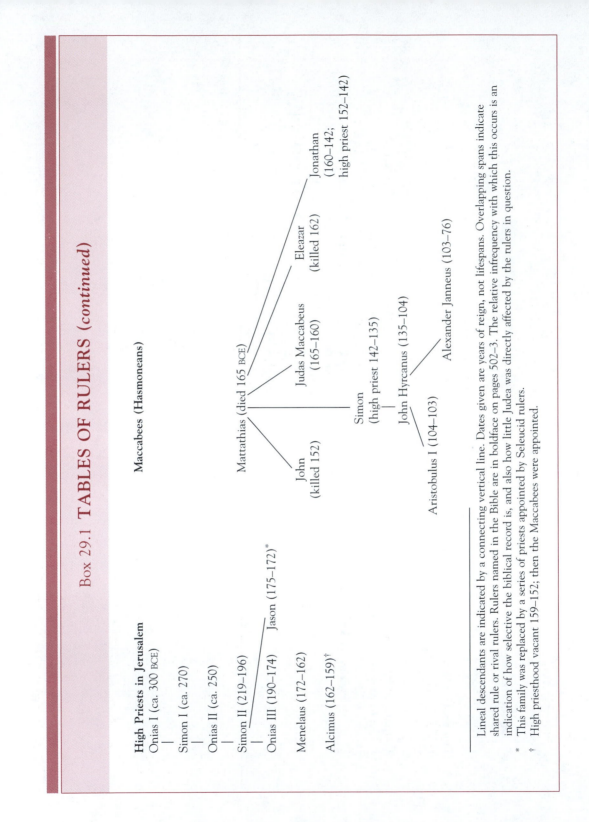

High Priests in Jerusalem

Onias I (ca. 300 BCE)

Simon I (ca. 270)

Onias II (ca. 250)

Simon II (219–196)

Onias III (190–174)   Jason (175–172)*

Menelaus (172–162)

Alcimus (162–159)†

Maccabees (Hasmoneans)

Mattathias (died 165 BCE)

John (killed 152)   Judas Maccabeus (165–160)   Eleazar (killed 162)   Jonathan (160–142; high priest 152–142)

Simon (high priest 142–135)

John Hyrcanus (135–104)

Aristobulus I (104–103)   Alexander Janneus (103–76)

Lineal descendants are indicated by a connecting vertical line. Dates given are years of reign, not lifespans. Overlapping spans indicate shared rule or rival rulers. Rulers named in the Bible are in boldface on pages 502–3. The relative infrequency with which this occurs is an indication of how selective the biblical record is, and also how little Judea was directly affected by the rulers in question.

* This family was replaced by a series of priests appointed by Seleucid rulers.

† High priesthood vacant 159–152; then the Maccabees were appointed.

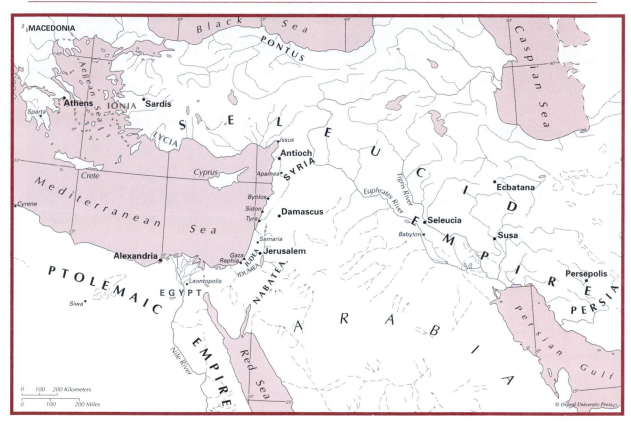

FIGURE 29.2. Map of the Near East during the Hellenistic period, showing the regions controlled by the Seleucid and Ptolemaic empires.

to remain faithful to their traditions, and under the leadership of Mattathias and his five sons, a revolt took place. It was a classic guerilla war, in which the outnumbered forces of the rebels, using to advantage their rugged home terrain, made surprise attacks against apparently more powerful enemies. After a series of victories, the rebels succeeded in gaining control of Jerusalem, and it was then, in 164, that they purified and rededicated the Temple, an event commemorated in the festival of Hanukkah (see Box 29.3 later in this chapter). Mattathias apparently died early in the revolt, and his son Judas assumed command. Judas was known as "the Maccabee" (or, more commonly, Judas Maccabeus), a nickname that probably means "the hammer." Following the successful takeover of Jerusalem, Judas Maccabeus was the de facto leader

of the Judeans for five years. This marked the beginning of the period of "Hasmonean" rule, a term, used only in nonbiblical sources, derived from the name of one of Mattathias's ancestors.

The struggle for autonomy continued, and when Judas died in battle in 160 BCE, leadership passed to his brother Jonathan, who completed the work of obtaining independence and assumed the position of high priest in 152. Jonathan himself was killed in battle in 142, and the last surviving Maccabee brother Simon took command and also became high priest, a position that passed to his son John Hyrcanus when Simon was killed in 135. (See Box 29.1.)

The books of 1 and 2 Maccabees give a detailed if inconsistent and one-sided account of the various military, diplomatic, and political events

FIGURE 29.3.   A coin issued by Antiochus IV Epiphanes (175–164 BCE), whose portrait is shown on the front (left). On the back (right) is a depiction of the god Zeus seated on a throne and holding in his right hand the goddess Nike (Victory). The inscription reads "King Antiochus, god manifest, bearing victory," suggesting that Antiochus considered himself to be divine.

of the mid-first century BCE. To describe them all would be simply to paraphrase what Maccabees and other sources provide. As a window into the period, we will examine two interrelated issues.

One of the precipitating factors in the Maccabean revolt was that the high priesthood, a hereditary office passed from father to son that since the time of David had belonged to the descendants of Zadok (see page 260), was first corrupted and then transferred by the Seleucid rulers to non-Zadokites. In 175 BCE, Jason, the brother of the high priest Onias III, bribed Antiochus IV to make him high priest, an office he held for three years, during which he apparently enthusiastically promoted Greek culture. In 172, another bribe resulted in the appointment as high priest of Menelaus, who was not from the traditional priestly family. Menelaus, also an avid Hellenizer, held the office for about a decade, but because he had advised an attack in which the Seleucid forces were defeated, he was executed, and Alcimus, from a different priestly family, was appointed to the office by Antiochus V. When after a few years Alcimus died, apparently peace-

fully, the office remained vacant until Jonathan, one of the Maccabees, who was already the military and political leader of Judea, was appointed high priest in 152. The Maccabees claimed descent from yet another priestly family (see 1 Macc 2.1), but what is noteworthy is that Jonathan, like Menelaus and Alcimus who had preceded him, did not inherit the office but was named to it by the Seleucid ruler. When Jonathan was killed, his brother Simon became high priest, and then the office was generally hereditary, passing from Simon's son John Hyrcanus to his sons Aristobulus and Alexander Janneus, although each had to be confirmed by the Seleucids.

On the one hand then, we have the establishment of a kind of theocracy, in which political power was vested in the high priest, the supreme religious authority. But it was a qualified autonomy at best, since these leaders from Jason on were appointed by the Seleucid rulers, who maintained their control through these clients, and the clients themselves often paid enormous sums to get and to keep their position. Thus, for example, as payment for his appointment Jason promised Antiochus a total of nearly six hundred talents of silver (2 Macc 4.8–9), about 45,000 lbs (26,400 kg), an enormous sum that even if exaggerated by the historians at least shows the order of magnitude, confirmed by other sources.

The second issue is factionalism with the Judean community. One group were avid Hellenizers, enthusiastically adopting Greek culture. On a mundane level this is evident in the names of the high priests Jason and Menelaus, familiar Greek names. A gymnasium, where following Greek custom athletes performed in the nude, was built in the shadow of the Temple, and some Jews underwent plastic surgery to remove "the marks of circumcision" (1 Macc 1.14–15; see also 2 Macc 4.12). Many Jews, we are told, adopted Greek dress and gave up their religious practices and worshiped other gods. On the other side were traditionalists, insistent on maintaining observance to the Law. Examples include those who when attacked on the sabbath refused to defend themselves (1 Macc 2.34–38), and the heroic martyrs who refused to eat pork and insisted on circumcising their sons (2 Macc 6–7).

Between these two groups stood the Maccabees, whose piety was tempered by an intense and pragmatic nationalism. For the sake of Judean independence, they were willing to fight on the sabbath. Their restoration of proper worship in the Temple can be understood both as demonstrating their commitment to Jewish tradition and at the same time as an assertion of political independence. Yet while the Maccabees were successful in restoring a measure of autonomy that allowed for the observance of the rituals and practices of Judaism, they could not escape the cultural effects of Hellenization; for example, eventually they too adopted Greek names, such as Alexander. They also were adept at seeking assistance from such powers as Sparta and Rome in their effort to weaken the grip of the Seleucids.

In addition to the Hasmonean establishment, which by the mid-second century BCE controlled both political and religious matters in Judea, although always under the watchful eyes of their patrons, the Seleucids and later the Romans, other groups emerged within the Jewish community at that time; these are the Essenes, the Sadducees, and the Pharisees. Unfortunately, our earliest documentation for these groups is from the first century CE, in the writings of the Jewish historian Josephus and in the New Testament. All seem to have been groups somewhat on the fringe of the religious establishment controlled by the Jerusalem Temple priesthood, with, as Josephus tells us, distinctive doctrines and, in the case of the Essenes, lifestyles as well.

The **Essenes** are the group that is most relevant to the second century BCE. They probably seceded from the Jerusalem establishment sometime after Jonathan assumed the priesthood in 152 BCE, and some of them seem to have founded a settlement at the site of Qumran, where the **Dead Sea Scrolls** were found (see Box 29.2).

1 MACCABEES

The principal account of the Judean revolt against the religiously offensive policies of Antiochus IV is found in the book known as 1 Maccabees, originally written in Hebrew in the late second or early first century BCE. Although it is a chronicle of resistance to Hellenization, it is preserved only in Greek, and probably for this reason was not included in the Jewish canon. It was, however, an important Jewish religious text and was part of the Christian Old Testament, until dropped from the Christian canon by Protestants during the Reformation. It is still part of the canon of Roman Catholic and Eastern Orthodox Christians (see further the Appendix). It is also a significant writing for Jews, containing among other things the account of the origins of the festival of **Hanukkah** (see Box 29.3 on page 509).

After a brief introduction concerning Alexander the Great and his successors, 1 Maccabees presents a partisan account of the period from 185 to 135 BCE. The detail is precise, especially of the geography and of the many military campaigns described. On first reading the book seems to be secular rather than sacred history. God never intervenes directly to save his people, and no

Box 29.2 THE DEAD SEA SCROLLS

In 1947, a Bedouin goatherd discovered jars containing scrolls in a cave near the Dead Sea, close to a site called Qumran. Subsequent discoveries by the Bedouin themselves, and later by archaeologists, uncovered several hundred mostly fragmentary documents, known as the Dead Sea Scrolls (see Figure 29.4).

The scrolls are written in Hebrew, Aramaic, and Greek and are of several different types. Many are biblical manuscripts, and their discovery provided Hebrew texts more than a thousand years earlier than the manuscripts of the traditional Jewish text of the Bible, the Masoretic Text. Every book of the Hebrew Bible except Esther is represented at least in fragmentary form in the scrolls, and by and large these texts do not differ significantly from the medieval Masoretic Text. Many minor differences are found, however, and the picture that emerges is of a somewhat fluid stage in the formation of the books of the Bible, for which a single canonical version had not yet been established. A second major category is works produced by the community for itself, including a text called the "Damascus Document," which describe the beginnings of the group, generally agreed to be the Essenes. Rejecting the leadership of the "wicked priest," probably one of the Maccabees, either Jonathan or Simon (see Box 29.1), they went into the wilderness under the guidance of an unnamed "teacher of righteousness." There they expected

an apocalyptic divine intervention on their behalf and the restoration of proper worship in Jerusalem. Other works include a "community rule," collections of hymns, and commentaries on various books of the Bible, many with a sectarian slant.

The group for whom these scrolls were a kind of library is generally identified as the Essenes mentioned in Josephus and other later sources. The community apparently hid the scrolls in caves during the First Jewish Revolt against the Romans in 66–73 CE, but the total victory of the Romans effectively wiped out the Essenes and the scrolls remained unknown until the twentieth century.

FIGURE 29.4. Caves near Qumran, where the Dead Sea Scrolls were found. To the left of the center of the photo is Cave 4, where fragments of many manuscripts of books of the Bible were found, some dating to the third century BCE.

Box 29.3 HANUKKAH

According to 1 Maccabees 4 (see also 2 Macc 10.1–10), after Judas and his brothers had defeated the forces of Antiochus IV in 164 BCE, they went to Jerusalem and restored the Temple to its proper purity, and for eight days celebrated its rededication. They then decreed that this should be an annual commemoration, known as the festival of Dedication (Hebr. *Hanukkah*) and, in some sources, as the festival of Lights, because of the relighting of the lamps on the sacred lampstand (the menorah; 1 Macc 4.50); the legend of the oil that miraculously was never used up is not found in the books of Maccabees. From a history-of-religions perspective, Hanukkah is a typical winter festival, emphasizing the presence of light at the darkest time of year; the Christian celebration of Christmas is a parallel.

---

prophets convey the divine perspective; in fact, God is not explicitly mentioned, although "heaven" occurs some dozen times. The author of 1 Maccabees wrote in Hebrew, but was familiar with the conventions of Hellenistic historiography. As in the works of Greek historians, the author quotes sources that are presented as archival, although some of them are probably his own compositions, and the principal characters often give speeches, also penned by the author.

On the other hand, throughout 1 Maccabees, parallels are drawn between the Maccabees, especially Judas, and earlier biblical heroes. These parallels are anticipated in the deathbed speech of Mattathias (1 Macc 2.49–68), itself reminiscent of blessings given by the dying Jacob to his sons (Gen 49.1–27; see 1 Macc 2.69). In the speech, Mattathias urges his son to follow the examples of those who, from Abraham to Daniel, were faithful and obedient to divine commands (1 Macc 2.51–60), some of whom, like Phinehas (Num 25.6–13; see also 1 Macc 2.23–26) and Elijah (1 Kings 18.40), killed those who had broken divinely given law. This speech in effect informs us that the presentation of the Maccabee broth-

ers is deliberately modeled on the earlier biblical narratives about the warrior heroes of Israel's past. Thus, when Judas died, the lament spoken is taken from David's lament over Saul:

> How is the mighty fallen,
> the savior of Israel! (1 Macc 9.21; compare 2 Sam 1.19)

Mattathias's speech also mentions Joshua, who "became a judge in Israel" (1 Macc 2.55); during Jonathan's tenure, we are told, "the sword ceased from Israel . . . and [he] began to judge the people" (9.73). Thus, like the judges of old, the Maccabees were divinely chosen leaders, "the family of those men through whom deliverance was given to Israel" (1 Macc 5.62; 1 Macc 3.6; 4.25; compare Judg 2.16; 3.9, 15, 31; 10.1; 15.18).

Furthermore, at the end of the book the author imitates the concluding formulation of the Deuteronomistic History for kings' reigns, when he writes concerning John Hyrcanus:

> The rest of the acts of John and his wars and the brave deeds that he did, and the building of the walls that he completed, and his achievements, are written in the annals of his high priesthood, from the

time that he became high priest after his father. (1 Macc 16.23–24; see also 9.22 and compare 1 Kings 11.41; 2 Kings 20.20)

First Maccabees is thus a kind of hybrid, combining both Hellenistic and biblical models. Throughout the book, not only do the principal characters give speeches, as in Greek historical writings, but the author also incorporates poetic laments and hymns reminiscent of biblical prototypes. While it certainly uses authentic sources in its pragmatic account of the victories of the Maccabees, it should also be understood as nationalistic propaganda, written to legitimate the rule of the Hasmoneans. With its many allusions to earlier biblical history, it presents the Hasmonean rulers descended from Mattathias as truly pious leaders chosen by God. Those who attempted to rid themselves of Hasmonean rule (1 Macc 10.61; 11.21), like those who abandoned the traditional practices of Judaism (1.11), are called "lawless men" (NRSV: "renegades" and "scoundrels"), the same phrase that is used in Deuteronomy 13.13 of those who would lead Israel into apostasy. Moreover, several times in the book, those who acted independently of the Maccabees were often defeated or died in battle, in biblical tradition an indication of divine displeasure. True believers, the author implies, "who are zealous for the law and who support the covenant" (1 Macc1.27), will support the Hasmoneans.

2 MACCABEES

The book of 2 Maccabees is another account of the Maccabean revolt, paralleling 1 Maccabees but covering a shorter period, from 175 to 161 BCE. The book is part of the canon of Roman Catholic and Eastern Orthodox Christians, but not of Jews and Protestants. (See the Appendix.) It was written in Greek, perhaps in Alexandria, in the late second or early first century BCE.

The book opens with two letters, both of which are probably additions to the original work. The first (2 Macc 1.1–9) is from the Jews of Judea and Jerusalem to those in Egypt and is dated to 124 BCE. It briefly recalls the origins of the festival of Hanukkah (here called the "festival of Booths," which elsewhere refers to the feast of Tabernacles, celebrated in September) and urges the recipients to celebrate it. The second letter (1.10–2.18), likewise presented as from those in Jerusalem and Judea, along with Judas Maccabeus, purports to have been written in 164, but it is probably not authentic. It also urges the Jews in Egypt to keep the newly prescribed festival and cites precedents from Israel's history for the establishment of festivals not found in the Torah.

The book then has a kind of introductory preface (2.19–32), in which its anonymous author explains both his source, a longer, five-volume work of an otherwise unknown writer, Jason of Cyrene, and the difficulties the author had in abridging it. The rest of the book is an independent account of the Maccabean revolt.

There are many differences between 1 and 2 Maccabees. Second Maccabees omits some details found in 1 Maccabees: It makes no mention of Mattathias, or of the death of Judah Maccabeus. Only Judas is given unalloyed praise among the five Maccabee brothers. We also find inconsistencies of chronology, most notably concerning the order of events: According to 1 Maccabees 6, Antiochus IV died in 163 BCE, some time after the rededication of the Temple, but according to 2 Maccabees 9, his death occurred in 164, before the holy city had been taken by Judas Maccabeus. The precise geography of 1 Maccabees is much vaguer and at points is confused, suggesting that the author (or his source) was not personally familiar with locations in Judea.

Second Maccabees is infused with the stylistic conventions of Greek historiography, such as addresses to the reader by the author, quotations of archival sources, and frequent speeches by the principal characters. Yet while 1 Maccabees has a decidedly secular character, 2 Maccabees is more explicitly religious. The author mentions God repeatedly, and we see several examples of direct divine intervention, some of which have an apocalyptic character. For example, in an encounter between the forces of Judas and those led by a southern adversary named Timothy,

When the battle became fierce, there appeared to the enemy from heaven five resplendent men on horses with golden bridles, and they were leading the Jews. Two of them took Maccabeus between them, and shielding him with their own armor and weapons, they kept him from being wounded. They showered arrows and thunderbolts on the enemy, so that, confused and blinded, they were thrown into disorder and cut to pieces. (2 Macc 10.29–30)

The principal characters are often described as praying, and the Temple has a central importance, being mentioned some two dozen times in the book. Second Maccabees also highlights the heroic piety of those who died rather than abandon their traditional religious practices, such as sabbath observance, circumcision, and diet, describing their sufferings in gory detail; this theme is elaborated in 3 and 4 Maccabees (see Box 29.6 later in this chapter and page 536).

Second Maccabees adopts the dominant biblical view of divine justice, in which God rewards the good and punishes the wicked. For the author, the persecution of Antiochus IV was a divinely sent punishment of the Jews for the Hellenizing tendencies of the high priest Jason (4.16–17). Antiochus's horrible death, described in gory detail, is also explained as the judgment of God, despite his purported repentance (9.5–28). In one of the battles, a few of Judas's men were killed; afterward, when the corpses were being gathered for burial, it was discovered that they had been wearing forbidden amulets, so their death was a punishment for their apparent idolatry. Judas ordered a collection to be taken for a sin offering because, our author tells us, he "expected that those who had fallen would rise again. . . . Therefore he made atonement for the dead so that they might be delivered from their sin" (12.44–45).

The concept of the resurrection of the dead is first clearly expressed in texts from the second century BCE, also being found in 2 Maccabees 7.10–11 and Daniel 12.2–3 (see pages 495 and 541). It is not directly related to the idea of the immortality of the soul, a concept derived from Greek philosophy. Bodily resurrection of the dead was believed to be granted only to the good; for

Antiochus "there will be no resurrection to life" (2 Macc 7.14). It represents another solution to the problem of divine justice: If death were the end, then the steadfast faith of martyrs would be unrewarded by God. Just as God had created the world out of nothing, so too would he restore the mutilated bodies of those who had lived righteously (7.23, 29). The author of 2 Maccabees also apparently believed that it was possible to assure an eternal reward for the dead by means of prayer and sacrifice.

Second Maccabees ends with the defeat of Nicanor, the general of Demetrius I, in 161 BCE (see 1 Macc 7.26–50). As with Hanukkah (see Box 29.3) and Purim (see Box 30.1 on page 529), the decisive victory over one of the persecutors of the Jews became a national holiday, the "Day of Nicanor" on the day before Purim, although one that is no longer observed. The book concludes with a personal note from its author, balancing the original preface in 2.19–32. Despite its very biblical flavor, 2 Maccabees also shows the effects of Hellenization, the most significant perhaps being that it was written in Greek.

BARUCH

The short book of Baruch is one of the Apocrypha, considered part of the Old Testament by the Roman Catholic and Eastern Orthodox churches but not by other Christians or by Jews. (See the Appendix.) Probably originally written in Hebrew, it survives in its Greek translation. Its purported author is Baruch, the scribe of the prophet Jeremiah, and the book dates itself to 582 BCE, the fifth year after the Babylonian conquest of Jerusalem. The actual author of the book, however, lived long after that event, probably in the second century BCE.

The book begins with a historical introduction (Bar 1.1–14), which contains a number of errors. For example, according to Jeremiah 43.6–7, Baruch and Jeremiah both were taken to Egypt, but Baruch 1.1–4 situates Baruch in Babylon. Like the book of Daniel (see page 538), the book of Baruch confuses the sequence of Babylonian rulers, making Belshazzar the son of Nebuchadnezzar instead of Nabonidus (Bar 1.11; Dan 5.2). And Baruch 1.8 attributes to Baruch himself the return of the sacred vessels looted from the Temple in Jerusalem, but that did not occur until several decades later, during the reign of Cyrus the Great (see Ezra 1.7–11).

Following the introduction, the book has three parts, each with a primary source in biblical literature. The first part (Bar 1.15–3.8) is a communal admission of guilt and plea for divine mercy, derived from Daniel 9.4–19 and supplemented by phrases taken from other biblical texts, including Leviticus, Deuteronomy, and Jeremiah. The second part (3.9–4.4) is a hymn to wisdom, based largely on Job 28; like Sirach 24.23 (see page 516), this hymn identifies wisdom with the Torah. The third part (4.5–5.9) is a poem of consolation, largely made up of phrases from Isaiah 40–66, in which Zion (Jerusalem) both speaks and is spoken to. The book thus appears to be a composite, in which three unrelated texts, each essentially a collage of biblical quotations, were combined under the supposed authorship of Baruch the scribe. (In the Roman Catholic canon, the Letter of Jeremiah forms chapter 6 of the book of Baruch; see Box 21.3 on page 369.)

The two works we will consider next are relatively late examples of wisdom literature (see pages 468–72). Unlike earlier wisdom literature of the Hebrew Bible, which tends to be universal, these works also include recapitulations of the history of Israel as a basis for comfort in the troubling contexts in which they were written. But ironically, despite the great resistance to Hellenization shown in the revolt of the Maccabees, Greek philosophical concepts and vocabulary began to permeate Jewish tradition.

THE WISDOM OF JESUS, SON OF SIRACH (ALSO KNOWN AS BEN SIRA AND ECCLESIASTICUS)

Although most wisdom literature is anonymous, the book of Ben Sira is named after its author,

"Jesus, son of Eleazar son of Sira of Jerusalem" (Sir 50.27). The author's name "Jesus" is a Greek rendering of Hebrew "Yeshua" (an alternate form of "Joshua"), a common name among Jews of the Hellenistic and Roman periods, as is Eleazar; the name "Sira" is obscure. The author is generally referred to as Ben Sira ("son of Sira") or as Sirach, a Greek form of the name, to distinguish him from Jesus of Nazareth. The Latin title of the book, "Ecclesiasticus" (not to be confused with Ecclesiates [Qoheleth]), meaning "the church book," is an alternate title often used.

Although originally written in Hebrew and known in its Hebrew form in the Roman period, Sirach was not included in the Jewish canon; in its Greek translation, however, it was widely used among Jews of the Diaspora and thus was included in the Christian Bible. As with the other apocryphal books, however, the Protestant Reformers excluded it from their Old Testament, and so it is considered canonical only by Roman Catholics and the Eastern Orthodox Churches. (See further the Appendix.)

The information given in the book itself enables us to date it relatively precisely. Ben Sira's grandson, who translated the book from Hebrew into Greek, says in the prologue that he began the translation after he came to Egypt in the thirty-eighth year of Euergetes, that is, in 132 BCE, during the long reign of Ptolemy VIII Euergetes (170–116), and implies that he completed it after that ruler's death. The book speaks in the past tense of the high priest Simon II, son of Onias II (50.1–24), who held that office from 219 to 196, but makes no mention of the events of the oppression under Antiochus IV and the revolt of the Maccabees, events that occurred in 167–164. The book was therefore written in the early second century BCE.

The informative prologue also tells us that the book was originally written in Hebrew, and Ben Sira's grandson sagely notes, "Not only this book, but even the Law itself, the Prophecies, and the rest of the books differ not a little when read in the original." The most complete form of the book is its Greek version, but several incomplete Hebrew manuscripts have also been found, including some among the Dead Sea Scrolls (see Figure 29.5). Thus, in various Jewish communities in the Hellenistic and Roman periods, Ben Sira's book circulated both in its original Hebrew form and also in Greek translation.

FIGURE 29.5. Fragment of a scroll of the book of Ben Sira (Sirach), found at Masada and dating to the first century BCE. The columns shown contain chapters 43 and 44.

Contents

Much of the book is a collection of wisdom sayings in the form of proverbs, like those in the book of Proverbs (see pages 469–70). In fact, many of the proverbs in Ben Sira repeat or modify those in the book of Proverbs. Like it, the book of Ben Sira deals with human existence on all levels, discussing such topics as table manners, the duties of children toward their parents, imprudent speech, dealing with social superiors, and relationships with women, especially wives and daughters (see pages 517–18), as well as issues of piety, including concern for the poor and the needy. The proverbs are often grouped together by topic or theme, but with no apparent logical order or clear structure. The difficulties in determining the structure of the book are ancient; the Hebrew and Greek manuscripts include several headings, but they are not placed consistently:

18.30	"Self-control" (in some Greek manuscripts, but not in Hebrew)
20.27	"Proverbial Sayings" (in some Greek manuscripts, but not in Hebrew; an almost random placement, perhaps suggesting the existence of an older collection)
23.7	"Instruction Concerning the Mouth" (in some Greek manuscripts, but not in Hebrew)
24.1	"Praise of Wisdom" (in some Greek manuscripts, but not in Hebrew)
30.1	"About Children" (in some Greek manuscripts, but not in Hebrew)
30.16	"About Foods" (in some Greek manuscripts, but not in Hebrew; other Greek manuscripts have "About Health")
44.1	"Hymn Concerning the Ancestors" (in some Hebrew and Greek manuscripts)
51.1	"Prayer of Jesus, Son of Sirach" (in some Greek manuscripts, but not in Hebrew)

The inconsistency of these headings underscores the loose structure of the collection.

In addition to proverbial sayings, the book also includes other genres, such as hymns of praise (for example, 39.12–35; 42.15–43.33), blessings (50.22–24), prayers (22.27–23.6; 36.1–22), and a lengthy catalogue of the major figures of biblical history (44.1–50.24; see pages 516–17). A number of appendixes were added to the book in different manuscript traditions, as is also the case with the book of Psalms. These additions, in chapter 51, consist of more hymns and, in one of the Dead Sea Scrolls, an acrostic poem (see Box 22.1 on page 383) about the author's love of Wisdom (printed as 51.13–30 in the NRSV).

Ben Sira, His Background and His Message

Taking the prologue by his grandson at face value (and not to do so seems unnecessarily skeptical), along with the autobiographical note in 50.27 and other details in the book, we can conclude that Ben Sira lived in Jerusalem during the late second and early first centuries BCE. He had devoted himself to studying the Jewish scriptures ("the Law, the Prophets, and the other books of our ancestors"; Prologue), and these were his primary source, although he was familiar with Greek literature. He was a pious individual, for whom religious observance was a primary concern. He was intellectually and emotionally attached to the Jerusalem Temple and to its rituals, and although he does not explicitly identify himself as a priest, he was apparently associated with the priestly establishment, perhaps as a scribe.

In chapters 38–39, Ben Sira discusses various professions, beginning with physicians (38.1–15). This is the most detailed discussion of medicine in the Bible, linking it, in accordance with his piety, to divine ordering of the world. After a brief hymnic digression, Ben Sira then turns to praise of the scribe, beginning by comparing that profession with others, especially those that involve physical labor (38.24–39.11). In these passages we have descriptions of ancient technology, which provide valuable details about farming (38.25–26), engraving (38.27), metallurgy (38.28), and ceramics (38.29–30). But, Ben Sira argues, while these professions are essential for society, that of the scribe surpasses them all. The scribe has the leisure that other professions lack, leisure that is essential for the investigation of all kinds of knowledge. In Ben Sira, a scribe is not just a professional writer or secretary (see Figure 27.5 on page 469), but an important official, who might preside over judicial hearings, advise rulers, and travel as an ambassador. Preeminently, however, the scribe is someone who, like Ezra in an earlier period, is "skilled in the law of Moses . . . a scholar of the text of the commandments of the LORD and his statutes for Israel" (Ezra 7.6, 11; surprisingly, Ezra is not included in the catalogue of Israel's "famous men" in chaps. 44–50, although Nehemiah is). These scribes also occur in other Jewish literature of the Hellenistic period, and in the Gospels of the New Testament, as recognized authorities on the interpretation of Jewish tradition and especially of the Torah.

In the hymn attributed to Ben Sira at the end of the book, mention is made of a "house of instruction," where the "uneducated" can acquire wisdom (51.23, 25). It is likely that, like other scribes, Ben Sira himself was a teacher in a formal school or academy, where both secular and sacred subjects were taught.

Ben Sira's Piety

As an educated person, Ben Sira was familiar with Greek literature and ideas. As one example, we may note the following passage:

> Give, and take, and indulge yourself,
>   for there is no seeking luxury in Hades;
> All flesh grows old like a garment,
>   for the covenant from of old is that all must die.
> Like abundant leaves on a flourishing tree,
>   some of which fall off, others grow,
> so are the generations of flesh and blood,
>   one dies, another is born. (14.16–18)

The comparison of the passage of generations to the life cycle of leaves on trees is strikingly parallel to a famous Homeric simile:

> Like the generation of leaves, so is that of men:
> the wind pours some leaves on the ground, but the
>   flourishing wood grows others, when springtime
>   arrives.
> So too is the generation of men: one grows, another ends. (*Iliad* 6.146–49)

Ben Sira seamlessly links this classical trope with biblical allusions. Like Ecclesiastes (for example, 9.7–10), Ben Sira recognizes that there is no pleasure after death, so the present life is to be enjoyed to the fullest. The comparison of human mortality to a worn-out garment is a biblical commonplace (see Isa 50.9; Ps 102.26; Job 13.28). Ben Sira thus combines both classical and scriptural sources in support of his argument.

Like Ecclesiastes, too, but unlike some other Jewish writers of the Hellenistic period, for Ben Sira there is apparently no reward or punishment after death. Ben Sira does not seem to have been troubled by the problem of divine justice, of theodicy, the focus of the books of Job and Ecclesiastes (see pages 482–92); rather, his view resembles that of Job's friends:

> Consider the generations of old and see:
>> has anyone trusted in the Lord and been disappointed?
> Or has anyone persevered in the fear of the Lord
>> and been forsaken?

> Or has anyone called upon him and been neglected?
> For the Lord is compassionate and merciful;
>> he forgives sins and saves in time of distress.
>> (Sir 2.10–11)

For Ben Sira, then, as for the authors of Job and Ecclesiastes, death was a universal end. The system of rewards and punishments by God was restricted to this life; people survive in their descendants, and in their "name," that is, their reputation (see 44.13–14). Only in the Greek translation of the original Hebrew of Ben Sira does an afterlife appear (see Box 29.4).

Ben Sira's piety thus is conventional, and although he was familiar with the book of Job (see 49.9), he does not address the issue of theodicy raised in it and in Ecclesiastes. That conventional piety is also evident in his attitude toward the Law. Unlike earlier wisdom literature, Ben Sira makes frequent and explicit mention of what for him are the essentials of Jewish tradition. Preeminent among these is the Law or Torah. "The Law" oc-

Box 29.4 DIFFERENT VIEWS OF IMMORTALITY IN THE HEBREW AND GREEK TEXTS OF BEN SIRA

The following examples show how the concept of an afterlife was added to the Greek translation of the original Hebrew of Ben Sira:

Passage	Hebrew	Greek
2.9	You who fear the Lord, hope for good things, for lasting joy and mercy.	You who fear the Lord, hope for good things, for lasting joy and mercy, for his reward is an everlasting gift with joy.
7.17	[T]he expectation of mortals is worms[.]	[T]he punishment of the ungodly is fire and worms[.]
19.19	———	[T]hose who do what is pleasing to him enjoy the fruit of the tree of immortality.

curs some two dozen times in the text of Ben Sira, and also several times in the prologue, always referring to the Torah, the first five books of the Bible, the Law or teaching of Moses (see Box 11.3 on page 184). For earlier biblical writers in the wisdom tradition, "the fear of the LORD" was "the beginning of wisdom" (see, for example, Job 28.28; Ps 111.10; Prov 1.7; 9.10). Ben Sira agrees, but specifies that fear of the Lord is shown by observance of the Law:

> The whole of wisdom is fear of the Lord,
>   and in all wisdom there is the fulfillment of the law. (19.20)

The centrality of the Law in Ben Sira's understanding is especially evident in his treatment of the figure of Woman Wisdom. In Proverbs 8.22–31, Job 28, and the Wisdom of Solomon, Wisdom is a divine figure (see page 475), and Ben Sira alludes to this view. As in the book of Proverbs, Wisdom was created before all else and was a member of the divine council, dwelling in heaven (Sir 24.2–4). Also as in the book of Proverbs, she is the appropriate object of a young man's affection:

> She will come to meet him like a mother,
>   and like a young bride she will welcome him.
>   (Sir 15.2; see also 4.12)

As we will see later in this chapter, the Wisdom of Solomon takes this depiction of Woman Wisdom even further, imaginatively appropriating both Egyptian mythology and Greek philosophy. Ben Sira, however, in effect demythologizes Woman Wisdom; for him, she is

> the book of the covenant of the Most High God,
>   the law that Moses commanded us
>   as an inheritance for the congregations of Jacob.
>   (Sir 24.23)

The same understanding is also found in the book of Baruch:

> She [Wisdom] is the book of the commandments of God,
>   the law that endures forever.
> All who hold her fast will live,
>   and those who forsake her will die. (Bar 4.1)

Wisdom, then, is to be found in the Law itself, the law given to the Israelites and whose primary location is Jerusalem. Although still personified, Wisdom is no longer to be found everywhere; rather, as she states

> I was established in Zion. . . .
> in the beloved city he gave me a resting place,
>   and in Jerusalem was my domain.
> I took root in an honored people,
>   in the portion of the Lord, his heritage. (Sir 24.10–12)

For Ben Sira, Jerusalem was the divinely chosen center of Judaism, where Wisdom was established and which the Lord chose as his home (36.18–19).

The centrality of Jerusalem and the rituals in the Temple is especially evident in the most unified section of the book, the "hymn in honor of our ancestors" in chapters 44–50. The passage begins, in the familiar translation of the King James Version, "Let us now praise famous men" (44.1). It constitutes a kind of poetic catalogue of the major personalities of the Bible, beginning with Enoch and Noah and continuing with Abraham, Isaac, Jacob, Moses, Aaron, Phinehas, Joshua, Caleb, the judges (none of whom are named), Samuel, Nathan, David, Solomon, Elijah, Elisha, Hezekiah, Isaiah, Josiah, Jeremiah, Ezekiel, Job, the Twelve ("Minor") Prophets, Zerubbabel, Jeshua, and Nehemiah. The conclusion of this section returns to Enoch, and then mentions in reverse chronological order Joseph, Shem, Seth, Enosh, and finally Adam. The author then moves to his own times and describes in an extravagant eulogy the high priest, Simon son of Onias.

The praise of earlier notables is not entirely unalloyed. Brief mention is made of David's "sins" (47.11) and Solomon's involvement with women, which brought divine anger on his offspring (47.20). Other "sinners" are also referred to, including most kings of Israel and Judah, as well as the rebels from the period of Israel's wandering in the wilderness, Dathan, Abiram, and Korah and his followers.

One theme that connects several of the encomiums is the role that various leaders played in the founding and carrying out of the rituals of the Temple. In a passage reminiscent of 1 Chronicles,

Ben Sira describes David's role in composing hymns and establishing the sacred calendar and the Temple's music (47.8–10) and gives special mention to Zerubbabel and Jeshua, who restored the Temple in the late sixth century BCE (49.11–12). The two longest passages highlight this theme. The first concerns Aaron (45.6–22), whose vestments are described in precise detail, as is his offering of sacrifices and his role as teacher of the Law. The second (50.1–21), a kind of reprise of the first, concerns the high priest Simon II, whose emergence out of the innermost room of the Temple, which he is credited with restoring, was

> Like the morning star among the clouds,
>> like the full moon at the festal season;
> like the sun shining on the temple of the Most
>> High,
>> like the rainbow gleaming in splendid clouds;
> like roses in the days of first fruits,
>> like lilies by a spring of water,
> like a green shoot on Lebanon on a summer day;
>> like fire and incense in the censer,
> like a vessel of hammered gold
>> studded with all kinds of precious stones;
> like an olive tree laden with fruit,
>> and like a cypress towering in the clouds.
> When he put on his glorious robe
>> and clothed himself in perfect splendor,
> when he went up to the holy altar,
>> he made the court of the sanctuary glorious.
>> (50.6–11)

It is tempting to see in the extravagant eulogy of Simon an admonition to his successors, but if that is Ben Sira's intent he is being extremely subtle. The praise of Simon in any case provides a fitting climax to Ben Sira's catalogue, with its emphasis on worship in Jerusalem.

Women in Ben Sira

Perhaps nowhere are Ben Sira's conventional views more evident, at least to modern readers, than in his treatment of women. Ben Sira provides a vivid example of the values of a patriarchal society, values that in many respects seem outrageous today. Moreover, the subject of women is one that he addresses repeatedly. Wives, daughters, mothers, prostitutes, singers, virgins, brides, widows, and servant girls all fall under his chauvinistic gaze, and the dominant attitude is one of fear of the female as dangerous, which leads to the need for strict control of women by men. Underlying this view is the innate superiority of men over women:

> Better is the wickedness of a man than a woman
>> who does good;
>> it is woman who brings shame and disgrace.
>> (42.14)

The ideal wife is a good cook and competent homemaker, physically beautiful and morally irreproachable, and quiet rather than talkative. A garrulous wife is as difficult for her taciturn husband as it is for the aged to climb a sand dune (25.20). A bad wife gets special attention:

> I would rather live with a lion and a dragon
>> than live with an evil woman. (25.16)

Ben Sira uses the garden of Eden story in Genesis 3 as a kind of proof-text: One of the reasons that women are evil is that

> From a woman sin had its beginning,
>> and because of her we all die. (25.24)

This negative attitude also applies to daughters. For Ben Sira, "the birth of a daughter is a loss" (22.3); he elaborates:

> A daughter is a secret anxiety to her father,
>> and worry over her robs him of sleep;
> when she is young, for fear she may not marry,
>> or if married, for fear she may be disliked;
> while a virgin, for fear she may be seduced
>> and become pregnant in her father's house;
> or having a husband, for fear she may go astray,
>> or, though married, for fear she may be barren.
>> (42.9–10)

Thus, an unmarried daughter is to be isolated not only from men, but even from married women, who could presumably inform her about her sexuality. Like much misogynistic literature, this has an almost prurient, not to say pornographic, tone; for example, the reader is advised to "keep a strict watch over a headstrong daughter" (26.10), because

> As a thirsty traveler opens his mouth
>> and drinks from any water near him,

so she will sit in front of every tent peg
and open her quiver to the arrow. (26.12)

For Ben Sira, women's sexuality was feared and needed to be controlled, and in his treatment of women throughout the book, only mothers (always parallel to fathers) are given an exclusively positive portrayal.

In summary, the Wisdom of Ben Sira is representative of one strand in Judaism as it encountered Greek ideas and culture. Although inevitably affected by Hellenism (something even more apparent in his grandson's Greek translation), Ben Sira was a conservative, maintaining a resolute attachment to Jewish tradition as found especially in the Scriptures, which he used with immense learning and profound, if conventional, piety.

THE WISDOM OF SOLOMON

The book called the Wisdom of Solomon (or sometimes just Wisdom) dates to the late first century BCE or the early first century CE. It was originally written in Greek, and so is not included in the Jewish and Protestant canons, but it is part of the Old Testament for Roman Catholic and Orthodox Christian Churches. (See further the Appendix.) Although it belongs to the category of wisdom literature, the book has a very different flavor from other books of that category. Not only was it written in elegant Greek, but it is permeated by Greek philosophical concepts. Scholars have suggested that the book was written in Alexandria in Egypt, a center of Hellenism in general and of Hellenistic Jewish learning as well. The city was the home of the first-century CE Jewish writer Philo of Alexandria (also known as Philo Judaeus), who used Greek philosophy in his commentaries on the Torah, and who, without any direct evidence, has been identified as the author of the book of Wisdom.

Like the author of the book of Ecclesiastes, the author of Wisdom identifies himself as David's son, King Solomon, who ruled over Israel in the tenth century BCE (see Wis 9.7–8). The ostensible form of the book is a speech given by Solomon to other kings. It is loosely based on the infor-

mation concerning Solomon found in 1 Kings 3–4, which tells how Solomon prayed for wisdom and was granted it by God. His wisdom was thus superior to that of everyone else, including the Egyptians, so that "people came from all nations to hear the wisdom of Solomon" (1 Kings 4.34). The historical Solomon was not the actual author of the book, since among other things he would not have known Greek; rather, the persona of Solomon is adopted by the author as a vehicle to present his own ideas. Those ideas are presented in a carefully structured meditative discourse, using a highly developed rhetorical style that imitates the parallelism of biblical poetry but with complex sentences and a sometimes striking lyricism.

The audience of the book must have been Jewish, for its negative portrayal of the Egyptians makes it unlikely to have been written to persuade non-Jews to become monotheists. Rather, it is a learned discourse combining earlier biblical traditions with Greek philosophy and other Hellenistic sources in order to demonstrate the superiority of Judaism and probably to persuade Jews who may have abandoned their religion to return to it.

The book consists of several interrelated sections, with the figure of Wisdom and God's protection of those who cultivate wisdom as unifying elements:

Chapters 1–6   A discussion of the fate of the righteous and the wicked, concluding with an appeal to the reader to cherish wisdom

7–10   An elaboration of Wisdom, including Solomon's prayer for her and her role in the history of the Jewish people

11–19   A retelling of the story of the Exodus from Egypt, contrasting the fates of the foolish idol-worshiping Egyptians and of God's people the Israelites.

As a Jewish work, the Wisdom of Solomon uses earlier biblical traditions, but without specifics.

Thus, even the references to Solomon himself are indirect, and unlike the books of Proverbs and Ecclesiastes, neither David nor Solomon is mentioned by name. In contrast to Sirach's repeated references to the major personalities and events of Israel's history, when the Wisdom of Solomon retells familiar biblical stories, it presents them in a generic, even vague way. A brief example is its summary of the narratives in the opening chapters of Genesis, which refers to Adam, Cain and Abel, and Noah without giving their names:

> Wisdom protected the first-formed father of the
>   world, when he alone had been created;
> she delivered him from his transgression,
> and gave him strength to rule all things.
> But when an unrighteous man departed from her in
>   his anger,
> he perished because in rage he killed his brother.
> When the earth was flooded because of him, wis-
>   dom again saved it,
> steering the righteous man by a paltry piece of
>   wood. (10.1–4)

Even in the extended retelling of the Exodus (Wis 11–19), neither Moses nor Egypt and the Egyptians are explicitly named. For the author, the story of the Exodus becomes an illustration of how true believers are rewarded and idolaters are punished, and the biblical sources are reshaped for the author's purposes.

In doing so, the Wisdom of Solomon also draws heavily on Greek philosophical vocabulary. Thus, for example, the Greek word *kosmos* (translated "world," "universe," and "creation" in the NRSV) occurs more than a dozen times. This cosmos is composed of "elements" (7.17) and was created from preexisting but formless matter (11.17). Wisdom, in the original Greek *sophia*, also an important philosophical concept, teaches her devotees self-control or temperance, prudence, justice, and courage (8.7), the four so-called "cardinal" virtues, as defined especially by the Stoic philosophers of the Hellenistic period, drawing on such earlier thinkers as Plato (see also 4 Macc 1.18). Finally, we may note that the catalogue of Wisdom's qualities in 7.22–23 contains twenty-one terms, probably a number symbolizing perfection (the product of seven times three); many of the terms also are technical philosophical vocabulary. In a similar way, Jewish and Christian thinkers in the Middle Ages adopted philosophical categories and vocabulary from Aristotle's writings.

The catalogue of Wisdom's qualities exhibits Hellenistic influence in another way. One of the most popular goddesses in the eastern Mediterranean world in the period when the book was written was the Egyptian goddess Isis. As the wife and sister of the dying and rising god Osiris and the mother of Horus, with whom the divine pharaoh was linked, Isis was an important deity in Egypt from early historic times (see Figure 29.6). In the Hellenistic and Roman periods her worship spread throughout the Mediterranean, and other Greco-Roman deities were often understood as her manifestations, as is illustrated in this excerpt from an Egyptian hymn to Isis, written in Greek in the early first century BCE:

> O greatly renowned Isis . . .
> because of you heaven and the whole earth have
>   their being,
> and the gusts of wind and the sun with its sweet
>   light. . . .
> All mortals who live on the boundless earth,
> Thracians, Greeks, and barbarians,
> express your fair name, a name greatly honored
>   among all,
> but each speaks in his own language, in his own
>   land. . . .
> Mighty one, I shall not cease to sing of your great
>   power . . .
> As many as are bound fast in prison, in the power
>   of death,
> as many as are in pain through long, anguished,
>   sleepless night,
> all who are wanderers in a foreign land . . .
> all these are saved if they pray that you be present
>   to help.[*]

At the same time, the figure of Wisdom was already a part of biblical tradition (see further page 475), and the depiction of Wisdom is an-

---

[*] Translation adapted from V. F. Vanderlip, *The Twelve Greek Hymns of Isidorus and the Cult of Isis* (Toronto: Hakkert, 1972), pp. 18–19.

FIGURE 29.6. Statue of the Egyptian goddess Isis suckling her son Horus. Statues like this were popular in the Hellenistic and Roman periods.

other illustration of how the author of the Wisdom of Solomon combines biblical traditions, Greek philosophy, and Hellenistic religion in a creative synthesis.

Eternal Reward for the Righteous

The first section of the Wisdom of Solomon deals with the issue of theodicy, of divine justice, es-

pecially the problem of the suffering of the innocent. In earlier biblical tradition this issue was addressed especially in the books of Job and Ecclesiastes but without an entirely satisfactory resolution, because death was inevitable, universal, and final (see, for example, Job 14.12; Eccl 9.2–3; and Chapter 28). In the Wisdom of Solomon the discussion has been altered profoundly because of the development of belief in the immortality of the soul, to which the author of Wisdom refers often. The Greek word for soul, *psyche,* is used some two dozen times in the book, and its author has adopted the Greek view that the soul survives death.

The wicked reason, in the manner of Ecclesiastes:

> Short and sorrowful is our life,
> and there is no remedy when a life comes to its
>   end,
> and no one has been known to return from
>   Hades. . . .
> Come, therefore, let us enjoy the good things that
>   exist,
> and make use of the creation to the full as in
>   youth. (2.1, 6; compare Eccl 9.6; 12.1–8)

They also do not hesitate to oppress the righteous, the poor, the widows, and the aged (2.10), arguing:

> Let our might be our law of right,
> for what is weak proves itself to be useless. (2.11)

Because the righteous man challenges their failure to observe the Law (the Torah), they determine to torture and kill him, unaware that

> God created us for incorruption,
> and made us in the image of his own eternity. . . .
> But the souls of the righteous are in the hand of
>   God,
> and no torment will ever touch them. . . .
> For though in the sight of others they were pun-
>   ished,
> their hope is full of immortality.
> Having been disciplined a little, they will receive
>   great good,
> because God tested them and found them worthy
>   of himself. (2.23–3.5)

The reasoning is based partly on biblical tradition and partly on Greek philosophy. Human beings are made in the image of God, who is eternal (2.23; see Gen 1.26; 21.33); but sin, prompted by the "devil's envy," brought death into the world; only the righteous, then, can escape the power of death. There thus seem to be two different ends for the good and the wicked. The souls of the wicked go down to Hades (the Greek term for the underworld, used in the Septuagint to translate the Hebrew Sheol), where they have a miserable existence; the souls of the righteous, however, achieve a true immortality, among the members of the divine assembly, "the sons of God . . . the holy ones" (5.5; NRSV: "children of God . . . the saints"). The eternal bliss that they enjoy, however, is completely spiritual; we see no hint of bodily resurrection (contrast Dan 12.2–3; 2 Macc 12.43–45).

The doctrine of the immortality of the soul solves the problem of theodicy, of divine justice in this life: God will reward the good in the life to come. The wicked have sided with death (who in 1.16 is almost a deity, like the Greek god Hades, the ruler of the underworld that has his name), but God has created life for the righteous, a life that is immortal. (See further pages 493–95.) The way to achieve this eternal life is through the pursuit of wisdom, to which the author next turns.

Wisdom

In 1 Kings 3, Solomon is described as requesting God not for long life or riches, but for wisdom to rule his people. This prayer is recalled in the Wisdom of Solomon (7.7; 9), and the speaker, according to the conceit of the book Solomon himself, describes at length his relationship with Wisdom. Wisdom, Greek *sophia*, is not, however, just an abstract quality; as in Proverbs 8, Job 28, and Sirach 24, she is presented as a woman, even a goddess. Solomon's attachment to her is romantic, even sexual:

> I loved her and sought her from my youth;
> I desired to take her for my bride,
> and became enamored of her beauty. . . .
> Therefore I determined to take her to live with me.
>   (8.2, 9)

The description of Wisdom elaborates those found earlier in the Bible, and also draws on Hellenistic philosophy and religion. Wisdom is "a breath of the power of God, and a pure emanation of the glory of the Almighty" (7.25); at the same time, she is described in mythological terms as one who, like Isis (see page 519), is more beautiful than the sun or any constellation (7.29), the partner of the male creator deity (8.4; 9.9) and his lover (8.3).

The pursuit of Wisdom is the way to achieve not only insight in this life, but also salvation and immortality in the next. As an image of the invisible and transcendent deity, Wisdom was directly involved in human history, and especially in the history of Israel. This is illustrated by a summary retelling of how Wisdom rescued the principal heroes of Israel's history, from Adam to Joseph, and then Israel itself under the leadership of Moses, the "servant of the Lord" (10.16). This leads to an extended elaboration of the Exodus, the third section of the book.

The Exodus

The final section of the book is an interpretive retelling of the narrative of the Exodus from Egypt, contrasting the idolatrous Egyptians and the faithful Israelites and God's appropriate treatment of both. There are a series of developed ironic contrasts, anticipated in 11.5: "For through the very things by which their enemies were punished, they themselves received benefit in their need." Thus, for example, because the Egyptians, according to the author, worshiped animals, God punished them with appropriate irony by sending plagues of small animals (16.1, specified as the familiar frogs of biblical tradition in 19.10); to his people, however, he sent quail, showing his control of the animal kingdom. Likewise, the Egyptians were killed by locusts and flies, but the poisonous snakes in the wilderness were unable to kill those whom God protected (16.9–10). (See Box 29.5.)

The series of contrasts are interrupted from 11.15 to 15.19 by a lengthy digression on idol worship, which includes other ironies. Thus, because the Egyptians worshiped animals, they were plagued by "irrational creatures" so that they "might learn that one is punished by the very things by which one sins" (11.15–16). The rest of the digression is a polemic against the worship of nature and of idols,

Box 29.5 CONTRASTS IN THE DIVINE TREATMENT OF THE EGYPTIANS AND THE ISRAELITES DURING THE EXODUS

The following list outlines the parallel contrasts between God's treatment of the Egyptians and of the Israelites according to the Wisdom of Solomon:

Egyptians	Israelites	Passage
Nile turned to blood	Water from rock	Wisdom 11.1–14
Noxious frogs	Quails for food	16.1–4
Locusts and flies	Bronze serpent	16.5–14
Rain and hailstorms	Manna from heaven	16.15–29
Darkness	Pillar of fire	17.1–18.4
Death of firstborn	Deliverance of Israel, God's son	18.5–25
Death at the sea	Salvation at the sea	19.1–21

developing a motif found most prominently in Isaiah 44, but also in much Jewish Hellenistic literature, such as the Letter of Jeremiah and Bel and the Dragon (see further Box 21.3 on page 369 and pages 412 and 540).

The book ends with an account of the killing of the firstborn of the Egyptians and the escape of the Israelites, described in lyrical terms:

> For while gentle silence enveloped all things,
> and night in its swift course was now half gone,
> your all-powerful word leaped from heaven, from
>   the royal throne,
> into the midst of the land that was doomed,
> a stern warrior
> carrying the sharp sword of your authentic command. (18.14–16)

During the escape, the "raging waves" of the Reed Sea became a "grassy plain" (19.7), and in a kind of new creation, nature was transformed:

> For the elements changed places with one another,
> as on a harp the notes vary the nature of the rhythm,
> while each note remains the same. (19.18)

In the end, the author of the Wisdom of Solomon is offering to Hellenized Jews in Egypt an exhortation to remain faithful, because everything that the larger Hellenistic world offers, especially its philosophy and mythology, is found in a superior way in Jewish tradition itself. True wisdom, the author suggests, is not derived from philosophy nor from the worship of Isis, but from God. To prove these assertions, the author reinterprets biblical sources, providing a striking example of the creativity of biblical interpretation of the Hellenistic and Roman periods.

RETROSPECT AND PROSPECT

The Greek takeover of the Near East had a major impact on Judaism and produced a spate of writings in various genres. For some, the arrival of the Greeks was an opportunity; for others it was a threat to the existence of their beliefs and practices. In the next chapter we will examine some fictional works that illustrate diverse reactions to the impact of Hellenism both for Jews in Judea and for those in the Diaspora.

Box 29.6 4 MACCABEES

The book called 4 Maccabees is not part of the canon of any religious community, although since ancient times it has often been included in editions of the Bible because it includes a retelling of events described in 2 Maccabees. It was probably written, in Greek, during the same general period as the Wisdom of Solomon (first century BCE to first century CE) and shares with it a philosophical tone and a belief in the immortality of the soul (4 Macc 7.19; 9.18). Like the Stoic philosophers, its author argues that "reason is dominant over the emotions" (4 Macc 1.7), especially those opposed to the other "cardinal" virtues of justice, courage, and self-control.

In the introductory chapters the author, whose identity and place of origin are unknown, gives examples from Jewish history and practice, including observance of dietary regulations (1.34), Joseph's resistance to seduction (2.2–3; see Gen 39.6–21), and David's control of his thirst (3.6–18; see 2 Sam 23.13–17). The book then moves to a summary of the crisis that led to the revolt of the Maccabees, beginning with the raid on the Temple treasury during the late second century BCE that was thwarted by divine intervention (see 2 Macc 3). Most of the book, however, is devoted to an elaboration of the stories of Eleazar (4 Macc 5–7; see 2 Macc 6.18–31) and the seven brothers (4 Macc 8–14; see 2 Macc 7).

Eleazar, an aged priest, challenged by Antiochus IV to eat pork because not to do so is irrational, replies with a lengthy philosophical discourse in which he argues that observing the dietary laws in fact inculcates self-control, and by extension courage and justice as well. His argument does not persuade the king, and Eleazar suffers a horrible death, during which he demonstrates his courage and offers his life as a purification offering for the apostasy of his fellow Jews.

The book concludes with an account of the seven young brothers, an appropriate parallel to the aged Eleazar. They too preferred death to eating unclean food because they knew that if they stayed faithful to the Law they would be with God after death. In gruesome detail, the torture and death of each of the seven is described successively, and each remained true to the religion of his ancestors. These examples prove, the author concludes, that reason is sovereign, as does the example of the mother of the seven, who also urged them to remain faithful, like Abraham when he was ordered to sacrifice Isaac and like Daniel in the lions' den. As a result, "the sons of Abraham with their victorious mother are gathered together into the chorus of the fathers, and have received pure and immortal souls from God" (4 Macc 18.23).

IMPORTANT TERMS

Dead Sea Scrolls   Hanukkah   Hellenization
Essenes

QUESTIONS FOR REVIEW

1. Discuss the effects of Hellenization on Judaism during the second and first centuries BCE.
2. What were the causes of the Maccabean revolt? To what extent did it succeed?
3. Compare the distinctive themes and interpretations of biblical history in Ben Sira and the Wisdom of Solomon.

BIBLIOGRAPHY

For the history of the period, see Leonard J. Greenspoon, "Between Alexandria and Antioch: Jews and Judaism in the Hellenistic Period," chap. 9 in *The Oxford History of the Biblical World* (ed. M. D. Coogan; New York: Oxford University Press, 1998).

A convenient recent translation of the Dead Sea Scrolls is Geza Vermes, *The Complete Dead Sea Scrolls in English* (rev ed.; London: Penguin, 2004).

A good short commentary on 1 and 2 Maccabees is Robert Doran, "I and II Maccabees," pp. 93–114 in *The Books of the Bible*, Vol. II: *The Apocrypha and the New Testament* (ed. B. W. Anderson; New York: Scribner's, 1989).

A good commentary on the book of Baruch is Daniel J. Harrington, "Baruch," pp. 781–86 in *The HarperCollins Bible Commentary* (ed. J. L. Mays; San Francisco: HarperSanFrancisco, 2000).

A good short commentary on Ben Sira is John J. Collins, "Ecclesiasticus, or The Wisdom of Jesus Son of Sirach," pp. 667–98 in *The Oxford Bible Commentary* (ed. J. Barton and J. Muddiman; Oxford: Oxford University Press, 2001).

Two good short commentaries on the Wisdom of Solomon are James M. Reese, "Wisdom of Solomon," pp. 749–63 in *The HarperCollins Bible Commentary* (ed. J. L. Mays; San Francisco: HarperSanFrancisco, 2000); and Sarah J. Tanzer, "The Wisdom of Solomon," pp. 293–97 in *Women's Bible Commentary* (rev. ed.; ed. C. A. Newsom and S. H. Ringe; Louisville: Westminster John Knox, 1998).

A good short commentary on 4 Maccabees is Robin Darling Young, "4 Maccabees," pp. 330–34 in *Women's Bible Commentary* (rev. ed.; ed. C. A. Newsom and S. H. Ringe; Louisville: Westminster John Knox, rev. ed., 1998).

HEROES UNDER FOREIGN RULERS

Jonah, Esther, Additions to Esther, Judith, Tobit, 3 Maccabees, Daniel, and Additions to Daniel

After the Babylonian conquest of Judah in 586 BCE, Jews both in exile and those who remained in the Promised Land found themselves under foreign rule. Babylonian imperial control of the Near East passed to the Persians in the mid-sixth century BCE, and then to the Greeks in the late fourth. Greek rule by the successors of Alexander the Great was at times especially harsh, as we have seen in the previous chapter. One of the genres of literature that developed during the Persian and Hellenistic periods was a kind of romance, which featured a Jewish hero demonstrating loyalty to his or her fellow Jews and to the religion of their ancestors in the often difficult circumstances of foreign rule. In this chapter we will consider several such romances and will conclude with the book of Daniel, which is part historical romance and part apocalyptic.

Like the Joseph story in Genesis that is their ultimate model, these romances, which have also been called "Jewish novellas," are short works of fiction. Each has a historical setting, although many of the details are inaccurate. Some scholars have suggested that these inaccuracies are deliberate, signaling to readers that these works are to be understood as fiction. The characters usually are drawn broadly, and women are often major protagonists. Recurring motifs in these novellas are threats to the protagonists because they are Jewish, ironic reversals of plot in which their persecutors are punished with the same means they had planned to use on the Jews, and satisfying resolutions and happy endings. They seem to have been written both to entertain and to instruct Jews on how to remain faithful to their traditions and to each other under foreign rule. Many also would have provided comfort for those experiencing severe persecution, as Jews did under the Seleucids (see further pages 501–5). Perhaps because it was too dangerous to criticize the ruling powers directly, these narratives of resistance and fidelity were deliberately set in earlier periods.

We will begin by looking at the book of Jonah, also a short work of fiction, although somewhat different in character.

THE BOOK OF JONAH

In the mid-eighth century BCE, according to the Deuteronomistic History, Jeroboam II, the ruler of the northern kingdom of Israel, "restored the border of Israel . . . according to the word of the

LORD, the God of Israel, which he spoke by his servant Jonah son of Amittai, the prophet, who was from Gath-hepher" (2 Kings 14.25). This obscure prophet is the protagonist of the short book that bears his name, and because he was a prophet, that book is included in the collection of the twelve Minor Prophets (see page 310). But unlike the books that surround it in the Bible, it contains few of the prophet's own words. Rather, it is a fictional narrative about the prophet, probably written in the early postexilic period, between the sixth and the fourth centuries BCE, which uses satire and irony to convey a number of messages.

The four chapters of the book of Jonah present four successive scenes. In the first, the prophet receives the divine call, a remarkable mission to proclaim divine judgment directly to the wicked city of Nineveh, the capital of Assyria, the primary enemy of Israel and Judah from the ninth through the seventh centuries BCE. Jonah's reluctance to undertake this task is understandable, perhaps, but is far greater than the hesitation shown by Moses (see Ex 4.1–17) or Jeremiah (see Jer 1.6): He boards a ship headed in the opposite direction from Nineveh. Yahweh will have none of this, and sends a storm that threatens to sink the ship. More pious than the prophet, who is snoring in the ship's hold, the non-Israelite sailors pray to their gods for help. When Jonah reveals that the storm is a divinely imposed punishment on him, they refuse to throw him overboard until they have no choice, another indication of their righteousness.

The chapter ends with Jonah being swallowed by a "great fish" (not a whale), a widespread folkloric motif, and from the belly of the fish he finally prays. Chapter 2 is presented as Jonah's prayer for divine aid, but in fact it is an individual song of thanksgiving (see page 464), probably an independent composition not entirely appropriate to Jonah's specific setting but incorporated into the narrative secondarily. Finally, after three days, the fish vomits Jonah on shore, and he heads for Nineveh.

In the third scene, Jonah is in Nineveh. There his message—"Forty days and Nineveh will be destroyed"—is heeded, and all the city's inhabitants fast and repent, starting with the king himself, and its animals too: Again, the pagans are models of piety. In response God also repents of the evil he had planned to bring on Nineveh.

Finally, in chapter 4, we see Jonah outside the city, waiting for his prophetic word to be fulfilled. The divine mercy infuriates him, and, referring to an ancient formula, he complains: "That is why I fled to Tarshish at the beginning; for I knew that you are a gracious God and merciful, slow to anger, and abounding in steadfast love, and ready to relent from punishing" (Jon 4.2; see Ex 34.6). Using a quick-growing plant as a parable, Yahweh reminds Jonah that he has concern for all, even the cattle of Nineveh.

The book has a comical side, but it is also puzzling. It can be understood as a statement of divine freedom, an elaboration, as it were, of Jeremiah: "At one moment I may declare concerning a nation or a kingdom, that I will pluck up and break down and destroy it, but if that nation, concerning which I have spoken, turns from its evil, I will change my mind about the disaster that I intended to bring on it" (Jer 18.7–8). The prophets repeatedly pronounced divine judgment on the Assyrians, for their destruction of the northern kingdom of Israel in the eighth century BCE and their attack on Jerusalem in 701 BCE, and the book of Nahum is entirely devoted to an oracle against the Assyrian capital of Nineveh (see page 357). Is the book of Jonah rejecting the intense nationalism of such attacks, suggesting, like Second Isaiah (see Isa 45.12–14; 51.4–5), that Yahweh controls history for good and not just for woe, that Yahweh has a message for all, and that it is the obligation of the Israelites—typified in their prophet Jonah—to proclaim him to the entire world? Or is the central message of the book one of divine forgiveness as a response to repentance, of divine mercy trumping divine justice? With the Promised Land under foreign control and Jews dispersed all over the Near East, the book of Jonah seems to be a creative attempt to understand what this new context means for Jewish identity and the understanding of God's purposes for the entire world. The book ends with a question, a rhetorical question perhaps, but one that also suggests that various levels of interpretation are possible.

THE BOOK OF ESTHER

The book of Esther is one of the Five Scrolls, which form part of the Writings, the third division of the canon in Jewish tradition; in Christian Bibles it is usually included among the historical books. (See further the Appendix.) It is a gripping tale of palace intrigue, in which the Jewish queen of Persia, Esther, for whom the book is named, saves her people from destruction. It is also a puzzling book, for although it shares some plot elements with other short fictions of the postexilic period, it is essentially a secular book, in which God is not mentioned and in which Jewish identity is a matter of ethnicity rather than of religious observance.

Although the book of Esther is set in the early fifth century BCE during the reign of the Persian king Ahasuerus (Xerxes; 486–465 BCE), it was probably written in the following century, in the late Persian or early Hellenistic period. Many details in the book concerning the Persian court and the workings of the imperial bureaucracy appear to be accurate, but there is no independent evidence that Esther, Mordecai, Haman, or Vashti ever existed. The book also has a major chronological error: Mordecai is described as one of the exiles deported from Jerusalem in 597 (Esth 2.6; the NRSV gratuitously emends the text here), which would have made him well over a hundred years old when the events described in the book took place. It is thus the consensus of modern scholars that the book is fictional, a kind of historical novella written to provide an etiology, a narrative explanation, for the Jewish festival of **Purim**.

The story begins with the refusal by the chief wife of Ahasuerus, Queen Vashti, to obey a royal summons to attend a banquet where her beauty would be paraded before the guests, and with her being banished for her rebelliousness (see Figure 30.1). She was replaced by the beautiful Esther, the cousin of Mordecai, a Jewish exile from Ju-

FIGURE 30.1. An ornate Persian drinking cup on a ram, from the fifth century BCE. Made of silver, it is about 8 in (20 cm) high and is the kind of vessel that might have been used at a banquet like that described in Esther 1.5–8.

dah. Esther's Jewish identity, however, had not been revealed to the king. After Esther had become queen, Mordecai uncovered a plot to assassinate the king, which Esther passed on to her royal husband.

The king had appointed a man named Haman as the second highest person in the kingdom, and all except Mordecai acknowledged his status by bowing in his presence. Infuriated, Haman plotted to kill Mordecai and all the Jews in the kingdom and informed the king that they refused to obey his edicts. The day for their execution, the thirteenth day of the month of Adar, the twelfth month, was chosen by lot.

Mordecai instructed Esther to intervene with the king to save her people. Violating court protocol, she approached the king and invited him and Haman to dinner in her quarters. Meanwhile, Haman prepared a gallows for Mordecai. That night, suffering from insomnia, the king read reports of how Mordecai had saved his life and asked Haman: "What shall be done for the man whom the king wishes to honor?" (Esth 6.6). Thinking that the king was speaking of him, Haman suggested lavish public acclaim, and the king instructed him to arrange it for Mordecai. Then, at the banquet, Esther revealed Haman's intentions. The king ordered him executed on the gallows he had prepared for Mordecai and gave Mordecai royal authority. Mordecai issued edicts in the king's name protecting the Jews, and on the same day that the Jews were to be killed, they attacked and massacred their enemies. The next day, the fourteenth of Adar, was declared an annual holiday for feasting and rejoicing, called Purim. (See Figure 30.2.)

In the story of Mordecai, we have a variant of that of Joseph (Gen 39–41), the Jew who although falsely accused becomes the most powerful royal functionary in a Gentile land; the same plot is also found in the book of Daniel (see pages 537–38). Ironically, Mordecai received the honors that his persecutor Haman had desired, and Haman suffers the punishment that he had planned for Mordecai. We also see other ironic reversals. Ahasuerus, "who ruled over one hundred twenty-seven provinces from India to Ethiopia" (Esth 1.1), is easily manipulated by his wives and courtiers. Esther is installed in the royal harem at Mordecai's initiative and initially follows his instructions, but as the plot develops she takes matters into her own hands and even in-

FIGURE 30.2. Detail of a fresco from the third-century CE synagogue at Dura Europos in northern Syria, showing an imaginative representation of a scene from the book of Esther. Mordecai, on horseback, is approaching Ahasuerus, the king of Persia, who is seated on his throne. Esther is on the far right.

structs Mordecai. The ultimate reversal is the victory of the Jews over their enemies and their being granted "peace and security" in all the provinces of the Persian empire (9.30).

The secular nature of the book of Esther has been observed since ancient times. It never refers to such primary components of Jewish tradition as Abraham, Moses, torah, covenant, or Jerusalem. For the author of the book, being Jewish has to do with ethnic identity rather than piety. Unlike the heroes of the books of Maccabees, for whom religious observance was more important than life itself, Esther has fully assimilated to her Gentile environment. She is married to a non-Jew and does not seem to be concerned about dietary purity. She uses her sex, as does Judith (see page 531), to secure safety for her people, but unlike Judith, she is not depicted as praying. The book of Esther never even makes reference to God, except perhaps implicitly in one speech of Mordecai: "For if you keep silence at such a time as this, relief and deliverance will rise for the Jews from another quarter, but you and your father's family will perish. Who knows? Perhaps you have come to royal dignity for just such a time as this" (Esth 4.14). This secular character will be altered in the version of Esther preserved in the ancient Greek translation (see below). The primary purpose of the book of Esther, then, seems to be entertainment rather than religious edification, like the holiday of Purim for which the book provides a narrative explanation (see Box 30.1).

The Additions to Esther

In antiquity the concept of a literary work was more fluid than it is today, and later writers often modified or added to earlier compositions. We have seen this in the books of Jeremiah, Job, and Ezra, and the same is also true of the book of Daniel, discussed later in this chapter. Another such case is the book of Esther, for which the ancient Greek translation of the Hebrew Bible, the Septuagint, has an altered and expanded version of the traditional Hebrew text. One motivation for many of the changes was to make an apparently secular book more explicitly religious.

The "Additions to the Book of Esther" are among the Apocrypha, those Jewish religious writings that are not part of the traditional Jewish canon (the Hebrew Bible) but which were part

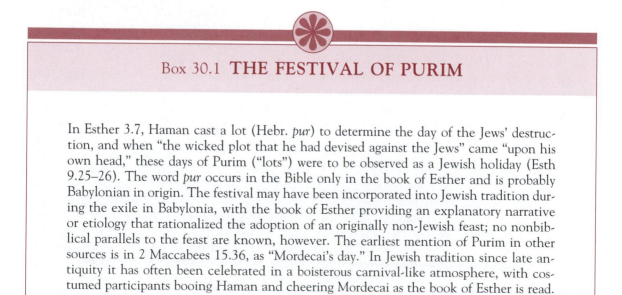

Box 30.1   THE FESTIVAL OF PURIM

In Esther 3.7, Haman cast a lot (Hebr. *pur*) to determine the day of the Jews' destruction, and when "the wicked plot that he had devised against the Jews" came "upon his own head," these days of Purim ("lots") were to be observed as a Jewish holiday (Esth 9.25–26). The word *pur* occurs in the Bible only in the book of Esther and is probably Babylonian in origin. The festival may have been incorporated into Jewish tradition during the exile in Babylonia, with the book of Esther providing an explanatory narrative or etiology that rationalized the adoption of an originally non-Jewish feast; no nonbiblical parallels to the feast are known, however. The earliest mention of Purim in other sources is in 2 Maccabees 15.36, as "Mordecai's day." In Jewish tradition since late antiquity it has often been celebrated in a boisterous carnival-like atmosphere, with costumed participants booing Haman and cheering Mordecai as the book of Esther is read.

of Christian Bibles until the Reformation, when they were excluded by the Protestant churches (see further the Appendix). In some modern Bibles the entire Greek text of Esther is presented with the additions inserted where they occur; reading this version in comparison to the shorter Hebrew text shows the differences between the two books.

The Greek version of the book of Esther adds repeated references to God guiding events and includes lengthy prayers by Mordecai (13.8–17) and Esther (14.3–19), making them both more pious than they are in the Hebrew version. Esther is now an observant Jew, who fears God and keeps his commandments (2.20), hates that she sleeps with one who is uncircumcised (14.15), and apparently observes the dietary laws (14.17). The Greek writers also corrected some details and introduced some errors. An example of the latter is the misidentification of Ahasuerus as Artaxerxes (I; 465–424 BCE) rather than his predecessor Xerxes, which makes Mordecai even more improbably older when the story begins.

These additions were incorporated at different times, probably before the end of the second century BCE.

THE BOOK OF JUDITH

Like the book of Esther, the book of Judith is named for its heroine, a fictional character who uses sexual wiles to save her people. The name Judith literally means "the woman of Judah" or "the Jewess," suggesting that Judith is a personification, perhaps even a prototype or model, of the ideal Jewish woman and of Judaism itself. Not surprisingly, therefore, the book is more explicitly religious than the book of Esther. Unlike the other novellas considered in this chapter, the book's setting is not the Diaspora but Judea, as Judah came to be called in the Hellenistic and subsequent periods.

The book of Judith was probably written during the second century BCE, not long after the Maccabean revolt. It is known only in Greek, although it may have been translated from a He-

brew or Aramaic original, and it is thus not included in the Jewish canon, which contains only books written in Hebrew or Aramaic, or at least surviving in those languages when the canon was determined. But as an authentic Jewish religious writing in Greek, it was used by Jews in the Greek-speaking Diaspora, and so, like other books in the Apocrypha, it was included in the Christian canon, until excluded from it by Protestants during the Reformation. (See further the Appendix.)

As in the other novellas considered in this chapter, some historical details in the book of Judith are inaccurate. The opening verse introduces Nebuchadnezzar (also known as Nebuchadrezzar; see pages 359–60) as king of the Assyrians in Nineveh. But Nebuchadnezzar was a Babylonian, not an Assyrian, and the Assyrian capital of Nineveh was destroyed eight years before he assumed the throne in 604 BCE. Later in the book Nebuchadnezzar is described as ruling after the return of the Judeans from exile and the rebuilding of the Temple (Jdt 4.3), events that took place several decades after Nebuchadnezzar's reign ended in 562. Much of the geography of the book is also confused, especially the account of the progress of the Assyrian army under Nebuchadnezzar's general Holofernes (Jdt 2.21–27). Moreover, Bethulia, the city from which Judith comes, is not known in any other source and may be a fictional location.

The book has two parts. The first (chaps. 1–7) sets the stage for the rest. It describes how Nebuchadnezzar, preparing to wage war on the king of the Medes, summoned military support from the western provinces of his empire. They refused, and, after his defeat of the Medean king, Nebuchadnezzar sent his general Holofernes to punish them. With an army of 120,000, Holofernes proceeded to devastate Asia Minor, northern Syria, and apparently Transjordan as well. Fearing the worst, the coastal cities from Sidon to Ashkelon sued for peace. Holofernes accepted their offer, but destroyed the shrines of their deities and forced them to worship Nebuchadnezzar. Concerned about what would happen to the Temple in Jerusalem, which had just been rebuilt, the Israelites under the leadership of the high priest seized and fortified the strategic passes that led from the coast to the Judean heartland and prayed for divine assistance.

Enraged at these rebels, Holofernes learned about their history from the leader of the Ammonites, Achior, who further informed him that this was a special people, who could only be defeated if their God allowed it because they had sinned; if they had not, Holofernes should leave them alone. Holofernes's response was to accuse Achior of disloyalty and to hand him over to the Israelites. The next day, Bethulia was placed under siege, cut off from water and food, and soon the Israelites were ready to surrender.

At this point the second part of the book (chaps. 8–16) begins, and Judith is introduced as a pious and beautiful widow. Exhorting her fellow citizens to trust in divine deliverance, she herself prayed, reminding God how he had protected the Israelites in the past, and asking for his help to defeat the Assyrian foe herself. She then removed her widow's garb, adorned herself in finery, and talked her way into the Assyrian camp and into the tent of Holofernes, who was captivated by her beauty and her wisdom. Holofernes invited Judith to join him at dinner, but she requested that she be permitted to eat the food she had brought with her, and also to leave the Assyrian camp for prayers.

After several days, she was invited to a private dinner with Holofernes, at which he planned to have sex with her. At the dinner Holofernes became intoxicated and passed out, and Judith cut off his head, which she then placed in her food sack and with it left the Assyrian camp and returned to Bethulia. There she showed her compatriots Holofernes' severed head, and they praised both God and Judith. At her suggestion, they attached the head to the wall of the city and left the city to do battle. In the morning the Assyrians mustered to attack them, but when they discovered Holofernes's headless corpse they panicked and were easy prey for the Israelites, who routed them and looted their camp. The book ends with a victory celebration led by the women of Israel, a lengthy hymn sung by Judith, and an epilogue that tells how Judith returned to her life of pious widowhood until her death at the age of 105.

What appears at first to be a dramatic adventure story of the defeat of a powerful enemy by a woman, on closer reading is a kind of pastiche of biblical and ancient Near Eastern motifs. Judith and her actions recall a number of biblical characters. Like Judah's daughter-in-law Tamar (Gen 38.14), she puts aside her widow's garb and dresses herself in finery; the same action is also reported of Jezebel (2 Kings 9.30) and in a very close parallel in the Ugaritic epic of Danel, in which the sister of Danel's murdered son Aqhat dresses herself up and visits the tent of his killer, where she plies him with wine and presumably (the text is broken here) kills him. Like the judge Ehud (Judg 3.19–23), Judith is left alone in the private quarters of her people's enemy and kills him. Like Delilah (Judg 16.4–21) she uses feminine ploys to overcome a powerful man. Like Jael (Judg 4.17–22; 5.24–27) she kills the general of her people's enemy in a tent. Like David (1 Sam 17.51) she decapitates her foe with his own sword. Like Miriam (Exod 15.20–21) and Deborah (Judg 5.1) she leads the people in a victory hymn. And after the victory, as was the case with several of the judges, "no one ever again spread terror among the Israelites during the lifetime of Judith, or for a long time after her death" (Jdt 16.25; compare Judg 3.30; 5.31; 8.28).

Other details also have antecedents. Like Rahab, the Canaanite woman of Jericho (Josh 2.9–11), and Naaman, the commander of the army of the king of Aram (2 Kings 5.15), Achior, the Ammonite officer of Holofernes, professed his faith in the god of Israel, "was circumcised, and joined the house of Israel, remaining so to this day" (Jdt 14.10; see Josh 6.25). Like Sisera (Judg 4.9) and Abimelech (Judg 9.54), Holofernes is killed "by the hand of a woman" (Jdt 13.15).

We also find echoes of later history. The Selucid ruler Antiochus IV (175–164 BCE), whose persecutions led to the revolt of the Maccabees (see further pages 501–5), was known as "Epiphanes," which means "(God) manifest," and it may be that in decreeing that the Greek god Zeus be worshiped in the Jerusalem Temple (2 Macc 6.2) he was promoting a kind of emperor-worship, or at least was thought to be doing so; this is what is claimed, improbably, for Nebuchadnezzar in Judith 3.8. An even closer parallel is that after the defeat of Antiochus's general Nicanor by Judas Maccabeus and his forces, "they cut off Nicanor's head and the right hand that he had so arrogantly stretched out, and brought them and displayed them just outside Jerusalem. The people rejoiced greatly and celebrated that day as a day of great gladness" (1 Macc 7.47–48). This parallel is one of the principal reasons for dating the book of Judith not long after the Maccabean revolt against Antiochus IV.

In that context Judith is a model of both piety and resistance. Even in the Assyrian camp, she eats only permitted food, having brought her own supplies and dishes with her (Jdt 10.5; 12.2; compare Add Esth 14.17), and wherever she is, she prays repeatedly. She trusts in the God of Israel, for it is he, not Nebuchadnezzar, who is the only true God; in its emphasis on monotheism the book of Judith echoes other literature of the postexilic period. With God's help Judith defeats the Jews' enemy single-handedly and against the odds. Here, as elsewhere in the Bible, the reversal of expectations and the support of the underdog is a demonstration of divine power: He is "God of the lowly, helper of the oppressed, upholder of the weak, protector of the forsaken, savior of those without hope" (Jdt 9.11; compare 1 Sam 2.4–9). The vulnerable widow (see Box 30.2) turns out to be the strong one because of her trust in God.

Box 30.2 WIDOWS

In the ancient Near East, women were controlled and protected by men—their fathers, brothers, husbands, and sons. Widows were vulnerable because they had no male protector. They were thus linked with the poor, aliens, and orphans (a term that in the Bible means one whose father has died) as those most needing protection and assistance. In the epilogue to the Code that has his name (see further pages 120–22), Hammurapi asserts that he erected the monument on which the laws were written "so that the strong might not oppress the weak, and justice might be provided to the orphan and the widow." Throughout ancient Near Eastern and biblical literature, kings claimed to have done just that and were often attacked for not having done so. One reason for this is that a ruler demonstrated his power by his ability to protect the powerless.

In the Bible, this same concern for the powerless in general, and for widows and orphans in particular, is attributed to God, who shows his kingly powers by being "father of orphans and protector of widows" (Ps 68.5), the one who "executes justice for the orphan and the widow, and who loves the strangers, providing them food and clothing" (Deut 10.18). In keeping with the principle of imitation of God, as in the rest on the sabbath (see Ex 20.11; Deut 5.14–15) and in the injunction to be holy (Lev 19.2), the Israelites are to "seek justice, rescue the oppressed, defend the orphan, plead for the widow" (Isa 1.17), and for their failure to do so they are frequently condemned by the prophets. The same concern is echoed in the New Testament: "Religion that is pure and undefiled before God, the Father, is this: to care for orphans and widows in their distress" (Jas 1.27).

The oppressed, weak, and lowly, however, are only implicitly Judith's compatriots. Like the book of Esther, the book of Judith is intensely nationalistic. The survival of the Jews is paramount, and whatever means Judith uses to achieve that goal are acceptable. She joins other biblical women who lied for a greater good, including the midwives in Egypt (Ex 1.19); Rahab, the prostitute of Jericho (Josh 2.4–5); and David's wife Michal (1 Sam 19.14). Deception and violence can also hurt the innocent, but like the account of the killing of the firstborn in Egypt (Ex 11.5; 12.30) the book of Judith is not concerned with such ethical nuances. Thus, in her prayer before undertaking her mission, Judith recalls how when Simeon avenged his sister's rape, which also involved deception (Gen 34.13–29), God allowed him to capture the wives and daughters of the enemy (Jdt 9.4). So Judith, like the God she serves so faithfully, is primarily concerned for her people. The stirring tale of Judith is intended as an inspiration for Jews in the most trying times, and Judith herself personifies the ideal Jew, pious but not passive.

THE BOOK OF TOBIT

The book of Tobit is another tale illustrating how Jews are to live under foreign rule, emphasizing individual piety. The book was probably originally written in Aramaic, or perhaps in Hebrew; the Dead Sea Scrolls (see Box 29.2 on page 508) include several fragmentary manuscripts of Tobit in Aramaic and one in Hebrew. The book is best preserved in its Greek translation, however, and in that version it was included in the Christian canon until the Reformation. But it is not in the Hebrew Bible, and so was not included in the Protestant Old Testament. (See further the Appendix). It probably dates to the early Hellenistic period, in the fourth or third century BCE, before the persecutions of the early second century BCE.

The narrative setting of the book is the Diaspora, among the exiles deported by the Assyrians from the northern kingdom of Israel in the late eighth century BCE. As is the case with other fictional works discussed in this chapter, the book is considerably confused concerning Assyrian history, chronology, and geography. There are two interlocking plots. The first concerns the hero for whom the book is named, Tobit, a pious Jew living in the Assyrian capital of Nineveh. According to the first-person narrative with which the book begins, he had entrusted some of his fortune to a distant relative, Gabael, in Media, to the east of Mesopotamia. In Nineveh, although originally a favored courtier of the Assyrian king Shalmaneser, Tobit fell into disfavor with Shalmaneser's successor Sennacherib for burying the corpses of dead Judeans killed by that king. (For the historical background, see 2 Kings 18–19 and pages 339–44.) Tobit's property was confiscated and he was forced to flee, but when the evil king Sennacherib died, he was reinstated because his nephew Ahiqar (see pages 470–71) was a court official. His troubles continued, however, for while he was continuing his pious custom of burying the dead, a sparrow dropped its dung on him and he was blinded. Tobit's wife Anna was forced to work, and she reproached him for his piety. In a prayer reminiscent of those of Elijah (1 Kings 19.4), Job (Job 7.15–16), and Jonah (Jon 4.3), Tobit asked that God take away his life: "For it is better for me to die than to see so much distress in my life and to listen to insults" (Tob 3.6).

At this point the scene shifts far to the east at Ecbatana in Media, and the narrative is in the third person for the rest of the book. In the second plot, a distant relative of Tobit, Sarah, was also praying that she be allowed to die, for she had been afflicted by a demon named Asmodeus who had killed in succession seven of her husbands before their marriages had been consummated. In response to both Tobit's and Sarah's prayers, the angel Raphael (see Box 30.3), whose name appropriately means "God has healed," was sent to rectify their situations. Tobit sent his son Tobias on a journey to Media to recover the money he had left with Gabael, and before he departed gave him lengthy moral instructions, including the command to marry a woman from his own extended family.

As the plot unfolds, Tobias and Raphael, disguised as a man named Azariah, made their way

Box 30.3 **ANGELS AND DEMONS**

In the book of Tobit an angel, Raphael, is a major character, and a demon, Asmodeus (whose originally Persian name means "wrathful demon"), also figures in the plot. Both angels and demons appear frequently in the literature of the later postexilic period.

The English word "**angel**" comes from the Greek *aggelos,* which means "messenger" (as does the Hebrew word *mal'ak,* for which *aggelos* is the ordinary translation) and refers to both human and divine messengers. Although most English translations use the term "angel" for this word in the Hebrew Bible, only in its latest books does it come to mean the benevolent semidivine beings familiar from later mythology and art. In earlier biblical literature, the term simply means a messenger sent by God, probably to be understood as one of the lesser members of the divine council presided over by Yahweh, much as in Greek mythology Hermes and Iris were the messengers of the Olympian gods. Thus, Jacob dreams of a staircase between heaven and earth, on which messengers are going up and down (Gen 28.12), and these divine messengers often appear to human beings to announce divine protection and assistance. In the Elohist source of the Pentateuch (see page 26), these messengers often function as an indirect means of divine revelation, in contrast to the more direct and anthropomorphic language of the Yahwist source (J).

In the postexilic period, with the development of explicit monotheism (see Box 23.2 on page 413), these divine beings—the "sons of God" who were members of the divine council (see further Box 3.3 on page 34)—were in effect demoted to what are now known as "angels," understood as beings created by God, but immortal and thus superior to humans. Corresponding to the angels are malevolent entities, or demons, understood as "fallen" angels.

In addition to Raphael, the Hebrew Bible also names the angels Gabriel, the principal messenger of God who appropriately flies swiftly (Dan 9.21), and Michael, the warrior angel (Dan 10.13; both also appear in the New Testament. Later Jewish and Christian traditions will develop elaborate systems of angelology and demonology, often based on reinterpretations of earlier biblical passages. There are various ranks or "choirs" of angels, among which are included the cherubim and seraphim of biblical tradition. The demons are headed by Satan, identified in postbiblical Jewish and Christian writings as the snake in the garden of Eden (Gen 3.1). He is also called Lucifer (Isa 14.12; see also Lk 10.18), Belial, and Beelzebul, and his lineage can be traced back to the sea-monster of ancient Near Eastern myth. In Christian apocalyptic he is identified as "the great dragon . . . that ancient serpent, who is called the Devil and Satan, the deceiver of the whole world" (Rev 12.9); see further Box 28.1 on page 483.

The dualism implicit in the conception of angels and demons is heavily influenced by the ancient Persian religious tradition of Zoroastrianism, which viewed the world as a battleground between forces of good and forces of evil, between light and darkness, language that pervades many subsequent Jewish and Christian writings, especially apocalyptic literature (see further pages 436–38).

to Media. On the journey, a large fish jumped out of the Tigris River as if to devour Tobias, but following Raphael's directive he killed it, kept its inner organs as medicine, and roasted and salted the rest. When they reached their destination Raphael arranged a marriage between Tobias and the hapless Sarah, his distant cousin. Following Raphael's instructions, on the wedding night Tobias put the liver and heart of the fish on the incense that was burning in the bridal chamber, and the stench forced the demon to flee all the way to Egypt. The successful nuptials were celebrated for another two weeks, during which time Raphael went to Gabael and retrieved Tobit's money. Finally Tobias and Sarah went back to Nineveh, where his parents Tobit and Anna feared the worst because of the delay. When they arrived, Tobias smeared the bile of the fish on Tobit's eyes, and his blindness was healed. After another seven days of feasting, Raphael revealed his true identity as "one of the seven angels who stand ready and enter before the glory of the Lord" (Tob 12.15). Tobit blessed God in a lengthy hymn and died in peace. Before his death at the age of 112, Tobit had advised Tobias his son to leave Nineveh, for the prophet Nahum (see page 357) had predicted that it would be destroyed. So Tobias moved to Media, where his in-laws lived, and died a wealthy man at the age of 117.

Many of the plot elements in the book of Tobit are found in other biblical and nonbiblical literatures and folklore. We see close parallels between Tobit and Job: Both are pious individuals who lose their property and their health and are reproached by their wives (compare Job 2.9 and Tob 2.14), but their piety is rewarded in the end. The story of Ahiqar, the wronged courtier (see further pages 470–71) is incorporated into Tobit (1.21; 2.10; 11.18; 14.10), with Ahiqar identified as a relative of Tobit, although in other sources he is Assyrian; Tobit himself is also identified as a wronged courtier. One of Tobit's manifestations of piety is his concern for burying the dead, like that of Rizpah, the wife of Saul whose sons had been killed at David's order (2 Sam 21.7–14), and Antigone in Greek myth. In many variants of this

motif in world literature, the "grateful dead" reward the person who buried them, often by undoing a spell or banishing a demon. The motif was modified in the book of Tobit, probably to avoid attributing powers to the dead, with the angel Raphael replacing the appreciative ghost. One of the problems that Raphael solves is another widespread folkloric element, that of the demon in the bridal chamber, also known as the motif of the dangerous bride. There is a biblical variant of this motif in the story of Tamar, the daughter-in-law of Judah, two of whose husbands died before she was able to produce offspring (Gen 38.6–11). The fish that attempts to eat Tobias is probably an allusion to Jonah 1.17 (see page 526), and in the use of the organs of a fish both to exorcise a demon and to heal blindness there is an element of folk medicine. All of these elements are combined in the book of Tobit, but they are modified as appropriate to preserve the religious orthodoxy of its protagonists.

Tobit in particular is a model Jew, who followed the "law of Moses" (1.8). Before his exile from the northern kingdom of Israel, he used to worship in Jerusalem, as the book of Deuteronomy implicitly commands (Deut 14.23), rather than at the idolatrous shine at Dan, close to his own home, where the golden calf was located. In exile too he was generous to the needy, especially to orphans and widows, practiced tithing, observed the dietary laws, and celebrated the prescribed festivals. He also urged his son to marry a woman from his own kinsfolk, rather than a foreigner. Other Jewish exiles were equally observant, especially Raguel, Sarah's father, who carefully followed the "book of Moses" in allowing Tobias to marry her (6.13; 7.11–13).

As in the other books considered in this chapter, prayers are frequently inserted into the narrative, including a lengthy address to Jerusalem (Tob 13.8–17), which Tobit understands to have been punished for its sins, but to be restored to magnificence by God. Another typical genre found in the book of Tobit is the deathbed speech or farewell address, which occurs twice in the book (chaps. 4 and 13). Both contain various moral admonitions in the style of wisdom literature (see pages 468–72), as does Raphael's speech in which he reveals his true identity (12.6–15).

With its intricate plot and well-developed characters, the book of Tobit is one of the most entertaining of the novellas considered in this chapter, but like the others it is also a religious text, providing instruction for Jews about how to survive in the Diaspora as a community of believers.

3 MACCABEES

The book of 3 Maccabees has a misleading title, since it is not about the second-century BCE fighters with that name who are the subject of 1 and 2 Maccabees. Rather, it is set in the preceding century, during the reign of Ptolemy IV Philopator (221–204 BCE). Like the other books considered in this chapter, however, it is a short historical fiction and has several similarities with them. Written in Greek, probably during the first century BCE, the book is included in the canon of many Eastern Orthodox Christian churches. (See the Appendix.)

The plot of 3 Maccabees is straightforward, although the book opens abruptly and the beginning may have been lost. After a victory over his rival Antiochus III at Raphia northeast of Egypt, Ptolemy wished to visit his subjects and thank them and their gods. In Jerusalem, however, he was informed that he was not permitted to enter the innermost room of the Temple, the holy of holies. When the king expressed his determination to do so, the high priest Simon prayed for divine assistance, and Ptolemy was paralyzed as if by a stroke. When he had recovered and returned to Egypt, he began a persecution of his Jewish subjects there, decreeing that they be subject to a special tax and branded as slaves, unless they gave up the worship of God and became devotees of the Greek god Dionysus. When most refused to do so, Ptolemy decreed that all the Jews in Egypt be arrested and put to death, along with any non-Jews who protected them. The Jews were rounded up and confined in a hippodrome, a stadium for

horse races. Ptolemy ordered that five hundred elephants be drugged and made drunk and let loose on the Jews. After several divinely caused delays, the elephants were finally brought to the stadium, but in response to a prayer by one of the priests, Eleazar, God sent two angels who directed the frenzied elephants against the Jews' persecutors. The king repented and decreed a festival, like Purim, during which the Jews executed those of their number who had given up their faith.

In its account of royal persecution thwarted by Jewish solidarity and divine intervention, 3 Maccabees is similar to several of the books already considered in this chapter. Like them, it also features lengthy prayers in the course of the narrative, and it especially resembles the book of Esther in its narrative explanation of a festival celebrating deliverance. Such a festival in Egypt is also mentioned by the first-century CE Jewish historian Josephus.

Apart from the battle of Raphia, none of the details of the book seem to be historical. Rather, like the other books we have examined, 3 Maccabees uses historical fiction to exemplify how steadfast piety in the face of persecution is rewarded by God, who, as Ptolemy proclaims, "surely defends the Jews, always taking their part as a father does for his children" (3 Macc 7.6).

THE BOOK OF DANIEL

The book of Daniel has had a significance disproportionate to its relatively short length since it was written in the second century BCE. On a mundane level, images from the book such as Daniel in the lions' den (6.16–24) are well known, and phrases such as "feet of clay" (see 2.42) and "the writing on the wall" (see 5.1–9) have become proverbial in English. Moreover, Daniel's fantastic visions have been taken as detailed predictions of the end of the world since antiquity, and early Christian writers made use of them in their interpretations of Jesus, especially the account of the "son of man" in Daniel 7. But the nature of the book of Daniel is far from agreed upon. In Jewish tradition, it is placed among the Writings, the third part of the Hebrew Bible, in part at least because of its relatively late date. In the Christian arrangement of the books of the Bible, it is placed among the prophets, after Ezekiel, because the second half of the book appears to consist of predictions. (See further the Appendix.) But the book of Daniel is unlike other prophetic books, such as Amos, Isaiah, and Jeremiah, and Daniel is never called a prophet in the book itself, although he was identified as such within little more than a century after the book's composition (as, for example, in one of the Dead Sea Scrolls and, a century later, in Mt 24.15).

In fact the book of Daniel is not prophecy, but comprises two distinct genres. Chapters 1–6 are tales of heroic fiction in which Daniel is the protagonist, containing many plot motifs like those we have seen, especially in the books of Esther and Tobit; chapters 7–12 are apocalyptic literature, giving detailed if somewhat encrypted interpretations of history and somewhat vaguer predictions of the future. Despite their different content, however, the two parts of the book are linked not just by the figure of Daniel himself, but also by a shared view both of the ultimate supremacy of God and of the progression of various empires.

The book of Daniel has another unusual feature: Like the book of Ezra (see page 431), part of it is not in Hebrew but in Aramaic (see Box 24.1 on page 422). The shift to Aramaic begins in the middle of a conversation between the Babylonian king Nebuchadnezzar (as Nebuchadrezzar is called in this book) and his dream interpreters in Daniel 2.4b and continues to the end of chapter 7; from chapter 8 to the end of the book the language is Hebrew. The Aramaic sections thus do not correspond to the two-part structure of the book, and the shifts from Hebrew to Aramaic and back to Hebrew are difficult to explain, except that in general the book itself is a composite, drawn from different sources, some of which may have been preserved in Aramaic. In this connection we should also note the additions made to the book in its Greek version (see pages 539–40).

Daniel 1–6

The first six chapters are a collection of interrelated tales concerning a legendary hero named Daniel. He is probably not the same "Daniel" (more correctly "Danel") mentioned in the book of Ezekiel (14.14, 20; 28.3), who is to be identified with the Danel known from Ugaritic epic (see Box 5.4 on page 74); Ezekiel links this Danel with Noah and Job as legendary ancient righteous individuals, who also happen to be non-Jewish.

The main character of the book of Daniel is a Jew in exile under foreign rule, in the Diaspora. Like Judith and Tobit, he remains faithful to Jewish beliefs and practices. He refuses to worship any god other than Yahweh, the God of Israel; observes the dietary laws; and prays frequently. Like Joseph, he is a divinely endowed interpreter of dreams, and like Joseph and Mordecai, although falsely accused, he eventually rises to a position of prominence in the court of a foreign ruler. The tales in these chapters include numerous miraculous elements, like those that are especially prominent in the book of Tobit. Daniel thus serves both as a model of how Jews are to act under foreign rule and as an example of how God will protect his faithful followers.

In Daniel 1, Daniel and his companions, Hananiah, Mishael, and Azariah, are in training in the court of Nebuchadnezzar and are given Babylonian names, Belteshazzar, Shadrach, Meshach, and Abednego, respectively. At Daniel's initiative they refuse to eat the food provided for them because it is impure, but after ten days on a diet of only vegetables and water, they are healthier than those who had eaten the assigned rations. When their training is complete, they are recognized as superior to their fellow trainees because God had endowed them with wisdom. They are better than all the other magicians and enchanters in Nebuchadnezzar's kingdom; the Hebrew word for magicians used here occurs elsewhere in the Bible only in the stories of Joseph and Moses, both of whom were superior to the magicians of the Egyptian kings of their times. Daniel in particular was also a skilled dream interpreter.

Daniel 2 is devoted to a dream that troubled Nebuchadnezzar; he summoned his interpreters, ordering them not only to interpret the dream, but first to tell what he had dreamt. When they were unable to do so, Daniel received a revelation, and after praying to God went to the king and told him the dream. In it, there was a statue made of four different materials, a head of gold, torso and arms of silver, abdomen and thighs of bronze, legs of iron, and feet of iron and clay. A stone smashed the statue and was transformed into a great mountain. The four materials are, Daniel explained, four kingdoms, that of Nebuchadnezzar and three successive kingdoms, each weaker than the previous. The stone is a new kingdom established by God and therefore one that will endure forever.

In Daniel 3, Nebuchadnezzar erects a huge gold statue and orders all to worship it on pain of death by being thrown into a blazing furnace. Shadrach, Meshach, and Abednego, being pious Jews, refuse to do so and are thrown into the furnace. The flames are so hot that they kill those who throw them in, but the young men are protected by an angel. The king is so impressed that he issues a decree protecting them and acknowledging the power of their God.

Daniel 4 contains another royal dream, of a great tree that was cut down by divine command. The tree, Daniel explains, is the king, who will be cast out from his kingdom and become like an animal. As we have seen (on pages 401–2) this probably refers to the mysterious absence from Babylon of Nabonidus, Nebuchadnezzar's successor, rather than to Nebuchadnezzar. The prediction proves true, and when the king recovers, he again recognizes the greatness of God.

In Daniel 5, during a banquet given by King Belshazzar (misidentified as Nebuchadnezzar's son and successor) at which the guests drank from goblets looted from the Temple in Jerusalem in 586 BCE, disembodied fingers mysteriously appear and write on the wall the words "Mene, mene, tekel upharsin." No one at the banquet is able to decipher the words, except of course Daniel. He decodes the words, which literally refer to units of weight (a mina, a mina, a shekel, and two paras [half-shekels]), in terms of their etymology: God has numbered (Aramaic *mena*) the days of Belshazzar's kingdom, he has weighed it out (*teqal* [Hebr. *shaqal*]), and it will be divided (*perisat*) between the Medes and the Persians. And that night the king is murdered, and his kingdom given to an otherwise unknown ruler, Darius the Mede.

Daniel 6 is a variation on chapter 3. Darius is about to appoint Daniel as head of his governors, when they plot against him "in connection with the law of his God" (6.5). They persuade Darius to decree that only he is to be worshiped, and anyone who refuses to do so will be thrown into a lions' den. Daniel, a pious Jew who prays only to God, and facing Jerusalem, is accordingly thrown to the lions, to the king's regret, but an angel saves him. The next day, the king is relieved to discover that Daniel is unharmed, orders his accusers to be thrown to the lions themselves along with their wives and children, and recognizes the power of the God of Daniel, as "the living God, enduring forever" (6.26).

These narratives are relatively free-standing, set in the reigns of three different kings, and probably formed part of a cycle of tales about Daniel that circulated widely in the Hellenistic period but originated as early as the Persian period. These tales were collected and modified by the author of the book of Daniel in the second century BCE. As in the other narrative fictions that are the focus of this chapter, the history and chronology are confused. Thus, Nebuchadnezzar assumed the throne in 605 BCE, and the first exile from Judah took place in 597, the seventh year of his reign (see Jer 52.28), but his dream, interpreted by Daniel, one of the exiles, is dated to the second year of his reign (Dan 2.1). The successors of Nebuchadnezzar were Amel-Marduk (Evilmerodach, 2 Kings 25.27) and Nabonidus, not Belshazzar, as Daniel 5.2 states; Belshazzar was Nabonidus's son and coregent (see further page 401). Darius the Mede is unknown and is probably a confusion with the Persian king Darius, who succeeded Cyrus in 522. These errors suggest that the book was written a considerable time after the events described, or they may be deliberate indications that it is not to be understood as historical.

Additions to the Book of Daniel

As is the case with the book of Esther (see pages 529–30), the Septuagint includes several additions to the book of Daniel. But unlike those to Esther, which amount to a rewriting of the book, each of the three Additions to Daniel is relatively self-contained, elaborating on or providing additional narratives in the folkloric style as Daniel 1–6. They are preserved only in Greek, but evidence shows that at least some of them were originally written in Hebrew or Aramaic, probably in the late Persian or Hellenistic period. Together with very fragmentary Aramaic manuscripts of other episodes concerning Daniel in the Dead Sea Scrolls, these additions provide further evidence for a cycle of tales concerning Daniel. They are not included in the Jewish or Protestant canons, but are part of the Roman Catholic and Eastern Orthodox Old Testament. (See further the Appendix.)

The Prayer of Azariah and the Song of the Three Jews

The first addition occurs between Daniel 3.23 and 3.24, right after Shadrach, Meshach, and Abednego have been thrown into the fiery furnace. The addition states that they sang hymns and prayed, and two prayers follow. The first (vv. 3–22), attributed to Abednego (called by his Hebrew name Azariah), is not entirely appropriate to its context, like psalms found in other narratives (for example, 1 Sam 2.1–10; 2 Sam 22; Jon 2); also like them, it was an independent work only secondarily inserted into the narrative. It belongs to the genre of communal laments (see page 463) and is a penitential acknowledgment of the community's failure to obey divine commandments and a prayer for divine deliverance. Since the three have been thrown into the fire precisely because they refused to bow down to the golden statue that Nebuchadnezzar had made, the psalm scarcely fits their situation.

The addition continues with a prose interlude (vv. 23–27), in which the Chaldeans make the fire so hot that they themselves are burned, but inside the furnace it is cool because of the presence of an angel of the Lord. A lengthy hymn follows (vv. 29–68), in which a varying responsive refrain is repeated (as in Ps 135). The hymn is a communal praise of God, especially for the wonders of creation, and, except for the final verses, which refer to the three in the furnace, seems also to have been an originally independent composition.

Susanna

The second addition is usually added to the book as an appendix, although it takes place early in Daniel's life in Babylon. It is a classic tale of false witnesses exposed by a clever interlocutor and has been called the first detective story.

Two lecherous old judges attempt to rape the beautiful and virtuous wife of a wealthy man in whose house they are hearing cases, surprising her while she is bathing; the scene is reminiscent of David's observing Bathsheba (2 Sam 11.2). If she refuses to sleep with them, they say, they will accuse her of adultery with a young man. She prefers to suffer death, the punishment for adultery, than to sin, and when she screams for help, they accuse her of having committed adultery with a young man; this scene is reminiscent of the false accusation of adultery brought against Joseph (Gen 39.11–18).

In a formal legal proceeding, the two judges give their false testimony. Because of their standing in the community they are believed and Susanna is sentenced to death, presumably by stoning (as in Deut 22.24; Jn 8.5). Susanna prays to God, professing her innocence, and just before she is to be executed, "a young man named Daniel," not previously introduced, states that he will not participate in the communal execution, for the trial has been improperly conducted. The execution is postponed, and Daniel interrogates the witnesses separately. When details of their testimony are inconsistent, he accuses them of perjury and perversion of justice, and they are executed instead of Susanna. The story concludes with a note that this was the beginning of Daniel's reputation, presumably for wisdom.

Although set in the Diaspora, the tale is entirely an intra-Jewish narrative; the villains are Jews, as are the heroes, Susanna and Daniel. The somewhat simplistic moral of the story is that obedience to the "law of Moses" (v. 3; the Torah) will be rewarded by God, and the innocent will be vindicated.

Bel and the Dragon

The third addition is a two-part narrative based on the postexilic motif of a satire against the worshipers of false gods. In the Bible versions of this motif are found in Second Isaiah (Isa 44.9–20) and Psalm 115.3–8 and in the Apocrypha especially in the Letter of Jeremiah (see Box 21.3 on page 369) and Wisdom of Solomon 13–15 (see pages 521–22). The closest parallel in biblical narrative is the account in 1 Samuel 5.1–5 of how the ark of Yahweh caused the statue of the Philistine god Dagon to fall and break.

The tale is set in the mid-sixth century BCE, in the time of Cyrus, the king of Persia who captured Babylon. In the first part (vv. 1–22), Cyrus questions Daniel about his failure to worship the Babylonian deity Bel (another name of Marduk), who consumes large quantities of food every day. Daniel proves that it is Bel's priests and their families who are eating the food rather than Bel himself, and Bel's temple is destroyed and the priests killed.

In the second part (vv. 23–42), Daniel poisons a great dragon or serpent also worshiped by the Babylonians, proving that the serpent is not divine. Pressure from the Babylonians forces the king to throw Daniel into the lions' den (a variation on Dan 6.16–24). But the lions, despite having been starved, leave Daniel unharmed, and Daniel himself is miraculously fed by the prophet Habakkuk (see page 365), who is transported by the hair of his head from Judea to Babylon. Once again, the king recognizes that Daniel's god is the true God, and his accusers are thrown to the lions and immediately devoured.

The moral of this composite narrative is clear: Jews in the Diaspora should recognize that the

gods of other nations are "idols made with hands" (v. 5), and only God, the creator of all, is to be worshiped. As in the tales in Daniel 1–6, Daniel is able to outwit the pagans, and the truth of monotheism is affirmed.

Daniel 7–12

In their context in the book, the tales in Daniel 1–6 are not just folklore, but also include a kind of code that must be deciphered. This is clearest in the interpretation of the composite statue of Nebuchadnezzar's dream. This interpretation was revealed to Daniel, which explained that the four parts of the statue are four kingdoms, of which only the first is identified, that of the Babylonians. But the book later identifies them all (Dan 8.20–22): They are those of the Babylonians, the Medes, the Persians, and the Greeks—the latter a composite, both iron and clay, and unable to hold together, just as the kingdom of Alexander the Great was disrupted after his death in 323 BCE. The successor kingdom, the stone that destroys the others, is later identified as a restored Israel.

The two parts of the book are thus linked not just by the person of Daniel but also by a kind of subtext: a divinely revealed interpretation of the past, present, and future. The second half of the book is a series of related visions that interpret the past in detail and more generally predict the future.

In contrast to the first half of the book, which is a third-person narrative about Daniel, beginning in chapter 7 almost all of the rest of the book is a first-person account supposedly by Daniel himself. But the character of Daniel is very different. Whereas in the first half of the book Daniel was the consummate interpreter of the dreams of others, in the second half he himself has dreams and visions and can only interpret them with the assistance of the angel Gabriel. These chapters also exhibit a developed angelology (see Box 30.3), with Michael the commander of the armies of God in their battle with the forces of evil (10.13, 21; compare Jude 9; Rev 12.7), and Gabriel the principal messenger of the deity (Dan 8.16; 9.21; compare Lk 1.19, 26). The presence of the messenger from heaven is an important characteristic of apocalyptic literature, a genre for which Daniel 7–12 provides the most developed example in the Hebrew Bible. (For a fuller discussion of apocalyptic literature, see pages 436–38.)

Like other apocalyptic literature, these chapters are highly mythological in tone and draw heavily on earlier biblical material, as the vision in Daniel 7 illustrates. The four creatures come from "the great sea," which as we have often seen is the primeval force of chaos needing to be controlled by a storm-god. The deity appears as the "Ancient of Days," a title reminiscent of epithets of the god El, "the father of years" in Ugaritic texts and "the eternal one" in Genesis. This white-robed and white-haired "Ancient of Days" is seated on a fiery wheeled throne (compare Ezek

Box 30.4 "SON OF MAN"

Mainly because of its use in the New Testament, the term "**son of man**" has been the subject of considerable discussion. It is used in a general sense in the Bible to mean "human being," often in contrast to a divine being. Thus, for example, in one of the oracles of Balaam, the prophet states: "God is not a man, that he should lie, or a son of man that he should change his mind" (Num 23.19), and the same contrast is found elsewhere (for example, Pss 8.4; 144.3; Isa 51.12; Mk 3.28). The prophet Ezekiel is repeatedly addressed as "son of man" (Ezek 2.1; etc.), as is Daniel himself (Dan 8.17), in both cases emphasizing their status as mere mortals, inferior to the one making a revelation to them. (In all of the occurrences of the term in the Hebrew Bible, the NRSV paraphrases it with "human being," "mortal," and the like.) "Son of man" is also frequently used by Jesus in the Gospels as a way of referring to himself.

In Daniel the term is used once of one "like a son of man coming with the clouds of heaven" who was presented to the Ancient of Days and given universal rule (Dan 7.13). The apparent sense of the term here is of a figure who looks human but is clearly more than human. The precise identification of the figure is debated. In the context of the book of Daniel, one possibility is that it refers to the angel Michael, who elsewhere in the book is a leader, together with Gabriel, of divine forces against Persia and Greece (10.13, 21), and who is also the protector of the Jewish people (12.1). If Michael is the "one like a son of man," then he is given supreme power on earth. A second possibility is that the figure "like a son of man" is the faithful people of Israel personified, "the holy ones of the Most High" to whom are also given an "everlasting kingdom" (7.27). A third identification, made in Jewish writings as early as the first century CE, is as a Messianic figure. This is also found in the New Testament, which, as part of its designation of Jesus as the Messiah, speaks of his return "in clouds with great power and glory" (Mk 13.26) to gather the elect and to punish the wicked. It is disputed, however, whether or not Jesus ever referred to himself as the son of man in this eschatological sense, or whether this derives from early Christian belief rather than from Jesus himself.

1.13–28) and surrounded by innumerable attendants (as in Deut 33.2; Ps 68.17). A meeting of the divine council is taking place, at which Daniel is an observer, like the prophets of old (see 1 Kings 22.19; Isa 6.1; Jer 23.18; see further page 302). At the meeting "the court sat in judgment, and the books were opened" (Dan 7.10). The last most terrifying of the four beasts was destroyed, and then Daniel saw a figure "like a son of man," coming with the clouds of heaven and given supreme power (see Box 30.4).

The interlocking visions of Daniel 2 and 7–12 describe in symbolic language the succession of imperial powers in the ancient Near East from the sixth to the second century BCE; see Box 30.5. The four empires are those of Babylonia (609–539 BCE), Media (originally independent, but united with Persia in the mid-sixth BCE century by Cyrus the Great), Persia (539–332), and Greece under Alexander the Great (336–323). After Alexander's death his empire was divided and there was a succession of rulers, whose reigns are presented in the narrative chronology of context of the book as revelations to Daniel concerning the future. The later the ruler, the more detailed is the description in Daniel, and the last ruler referred to in the book is Antiochus IV Epiphanes, whose edicts provoked the revolt of the Maccabees in 167 BCE (see further pages 501–5.)

The prominent position given to Antiochus IV is obvious and also important. In the visions, he will replace the prescribed offerings in the Temple in Jerusalem with an "abomination that makes desolate" (Dan 11.31; 12.11) and will persecute the "people who are loyal to their God" (11.32). At this point the revelation becomes more general: "[H]e shall come to his end, with no one to help him" (11.45), and the people will be delivered (12.1).

This shift from vagueness to precision is the principal reason for the scholarly consensus that the book was written during the difficult years immediately preceding the revolt of the Maccabees in 167 BCE. The book is thus a work of propaganda, arguing in often symbolic and extravagant language that God will ultimately prevail for his people over the forces of evil, of which Antiochus is the latest manifestation.

That deliverance has not yet happened at the end of the book, but is only promised. When will it happen? Here the book is again vague: In "a time, two times, and half a time" (12.7; see also 7.25), perhaps meaning that the persecution will end after three and a half years (the 1,290 days of 12.11). The book concludes with a message of hope for Daniel himself, who according to the book's narrative chronology lived centuries before the events that are presented as prediction: "But you, go your way, and rest; you shall rise for your reward at the end of the days" (12.13). Daniel himself, as one of the wise, shall be raised from the dead, and with them "shine like the brightness of the sky . . . like the stars forever" (12.2–3); the concept of the resurrection of the dead (see further page 495) is first mentioned in the Hebrew Bible here.

RETROSPECT AND PROSPECT

The book of Daniel is the latest of the books of the Hebrew Bible, the canon of Judaism; in some Christian canons there are slightly later works, including those discussed in this chapter, as well as Sirach and the Wisdom of Solomon (see Chapter 29). In both cases the ending of the canon is somewhat arbitrary, for the history of Judaism has continued, as have the religions derived from it, Christianity and Islam. The last books of the Hebrew Bible (and of the Old Testament) to be written are thus not a conclusion, but simply a stage in an ongoing process. That process continues in other Jewish writings of the Hellenistic and Roman periods and, after the fall of Jerusalem to the Romans in 70 CE, ultimately in rabbinic literature. It also continues in a different line in the New Testament, and somewhat later in the Quran.

All of these writings exhibit not just the creativity but also the diversity that characterize the books of the Hebrew Bible. This diversity creates a tension that is not negative, but rather productive; each generation in effect rethinks the fundamentals of tradition for itself, or, to put it somewhat differently, the process of interpreting scriptural texts begins in those texts themselves and continues beyond them. We have seen this process at work, for example, in Deuteronomy's alternate collection of laws, in the revision of the history of the monarchy found in 1 and 2 Chronicles, and in innumerable smaller ways in almost every book of the Old Testament. The process of interpretation does not end with the close of the canon of texts regarded as Scripture, but has continued to the present, as each community of faith for which the texts are in some sense authoritative reconsiders how they are relevant to its changing circumstances. In that sense, the Bible is an open-ended book, inviting, even authorizing, its readers to continue the task of interpretation. Moreover, interpretation is found not only in explicitly religious texts and commentaries but also in literature, art, and music that use biblical themes. For all of these reasons, the Bible is one of the most important, most challenging, and most rewarding books to study.

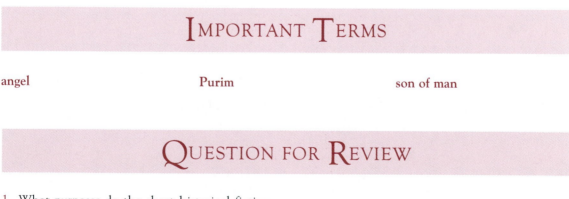

IMPORTANT TERMS

angel   Purim   son of man

QUESTION FOR REVIEW

1. What purposes do the short historical fictions in the Bible serve for their audiences?

BIBLIOGRAPHY

A good short commentary on the book of Jonah is Sidnie White Crawford, "Jonah," pp. 656–59 in *The Harper-Collins Bible Commentary* (rev. ed.; ed. J. L. Mays; San Francisco: HarperSanFrancisco, 2000). The same scholar also has a good short commentary on Esther on pp. 131–31 in *Women's Bible Commentary* (rev. ed.; ed. C. A. Newsom and S. H. Ringe; Louisville: Westminster John Knox, 1998). Adele Reinhartz has a good commentary on the Greek book of Esther on pp. 286–92 in *Women's Bible Commentary* (rev. ed.; ed. C. A. Newsom and S. H. Ringe; Louisville: Westminster John Knox, 1998). A fuller recent commentary on Esther is Jon D. Levenson, *Esther: A Commentary* (Louisville: Westminster John Knox, 1997).

For Tobit, see George W. E. Nickelsburg, "Tobit," pp. 719–31 in *The HarperCollins Bible Commentary* (ed. J. L. Mays; San Francisco: HarperSanFrancisco, 2000).

For Daniel, an excellent introduction is John J. Collins, "Daniel, Book of," pp. 29–37 in *Anchor Bible Dictionary*, Vol. 2 (ed. D. N. Freedman; New York: Doubleday, 1992). For the Additions to Daniel, see George

J. Brooke, "Additions to Daniel," in pp. 704–11 *The Oxford Bible Commentary* (ed. J. Barton and J. Muddiman; Oxford: Oxford University Press, 2002).

For 3 Maccabees, see Sarah Pearce, "3 Maccabees," pp. 773–75 in *The Oxford Bible Commentary* (ed. J. Barton and J. Muddiman; Oxford: Oxford University Press, 2002).

For Judith, see Amy-Jill Levine, "Judith," pp. 632–41 in *The Oxford Bible Commentary* (ed. J. Barton and J. Muddiman; Oxford: Oxford University Press, 2001).

During the Hellenistic and Roman periods, Jewish writers produced many other fictional expansions of biblical narrative; many are conveniently translated and collected in James H. Charlesworth, ed., *The Old Testament Pseudepigrapha* (New York: Doubleday, 2 vols., 1983, 1985), and also in Lawrence E. Wills, *Ancient Jewish Novels: An Anthology* (New York: Oxford University Press, 2002). These collections do not include material from the Dead Sea Scrolls; see the bibliography to Chapter 29.

THE CANONS OF THE HEBREW BIBLE/OLD TESTAMENT

The word "Bible" means "book"; the Bible, however, is not one book but many, a collection of separate books that is an anthology, as it were, of the religious literature of ancient Israel and early Judaism, and, for Christians, of earliest Christianity as well. Religious communities differ regarding which books are included in that anthology and in what order. The technical term for the list of books that a particular community considers sacred and authoritative is "canon," a word meaning "rule" or "measure." The processes by which Jewish and Christian communities formed their respective canons were complicated, and we can only highlight some of them here. The end results for the books of the Hebrew Bible/Old Testament are shown schematically in Box A.1.

JUDAISM

In Jewish tradition, the Bible (often called the "Hebrew Bible" in preference to the "Old Testament") has three principal parts: the Torah, the Neviim ("Prophets"), and the Ketubim ("Writings"). This division into three parts was in place before the Common Era, as is clear from references to "the Law, the Prophets, and the other books" in the Prologue to Sirach. From the initial letters of the names of each of these parts comes the term "Tanak" (or "Tanakh"), which also means "the Bible."

The Torah (see Box 11.3 on page 184) consists of the first five books of the Bible, from Genesis through Deuteronomy. It is a historical narrative from creation, at the beginning of Genesis, to the death of Moses, at the end of Deuteronomy. Within its narrative framework are included a large number of divinely given laws (613, according to medieval authorities), so that the word "torah" comes to mean "law." The Torah had a long process of formation (see Chapter 2), but it seems to have been substantially complete at least in substance by the fifth century BCE (see further page 406).

The second part of the Hebrew Bible is the Prophets. It contains several internal divisions. First are the "Former Prophets" ("Neviim Rishonim"), the books of Joshua, Judges, 1 and 2 Samuel, and 1 and 2 Kings; in some manuscripts the book of Ruth is also included here. The Former Prophets continues the narrative history of the Torah, dealing with the history of Israel in the Promised Land, beginning with the account

Box A.1 THE CANONS OF THE HEBREW BIBLE/ OLD TESTAMENT

JUDAISM	CHRISTIANITY		
Hebrew Bible (Tanak)	*Old Testament*		
	PROTESTANT	ROMAN CATHOLIC	EASTERN ORTHODOX
Torah	**[Pentateuch]**		
Genesis	Genesis	Genesis	Genesis
Exodus	Exodus	Exodus	Exodus
Leviticus	Leviticus	Leviticus	Leviticus
Numbers	Numbers	Numbers	Numbers
Deuteronomy	Deuteronomy	Deuteronomy	Deuteronomy
Prophets (Neviim)			
Former Prophets	**[Historical Books]**		
Joshua	Joshua	Joshua	Joshua
Judges	Judges	Judges	Judges
1 & 2 Samuel	Ruth	Ruth	Ruth
1 & 2 Kings	1 & 2 Samuel	1 & 2 Samuel	1 & 2 Samuel
Latter Prophets	1 & 2 Kings	1 & 2 Kings	1 & 2 Kings
Isaiah	1 & 2 Chronicles	1 & 2 Chronicles	1 & 2 Chronicles
Jeremiah	Ezra	Ezra	Ezra
Ezekiel	Nehemiah	Nehemiah	1 Esdras
The Twelve	Esther	Tobit	2 Esdras
Hosea		Judith	Nehemiah
Joel		Esther	Tobit
Amos		1 Maccabees	Judith
Obadiah		2 Maccabees	Esther
Jonah			1 Maccabees
Micah			2 Maccabees
Nahum			3 Maccabees
Habakkuk	**[Poetical Books]**		
Zephaniah	Job	Job	Job
Haggai	Psalms	Psalms	Psalms
Zechariah			Psalm 151
Malachi			Prayer of Manasseh
Writings (Ketuvim)	Proverbs	Proverbs	Proverbs
Psalms	Ecclesiastes	Ecclesiastes	Ecclesiastes
Proverbs	Song of Solomon	Song of Solomon	Song of Solomon
Job		Wisdom of Solomon	Wisdom of Solomon
		Sirach (Ecclesiasticus)	Sirach (Ecclesiasticus)

Five Scrolls	[Prophets]		
Song of Solomon	Isaiah	Isaiah	Isaiah
Ruth	Jeremiah	Jeremiah	Jeremiah
Lamentations	Lamentations	Lamentations	Lamentations
Ecclesiastes		Baruch	Baruch
Esther			Letter of Jeremiah
Daniel			
Ezra-Nehemiah	Ezekiel	Ezekiel	Ezekiel
1 & 2 Chronicles	Daniel	Daniel	Daniel
		Additions to Daniel	Additions to Daniel
	Hosea	Hosea	Hosea
	Joel	Joel	Joel
	Amos	Amos	Amos
	Obadiah	Obadiah	Obadiah
	Jonah	Jonah	Jonah
	Micah	Micah	Micah
	Nahum	Nahum	Nahum
	Habakkuk	Habakkuk	Habakkuk
	Zephaniah	Zephaniah	Zephaniah
	Haggai	Haggai	Haggai
	Zechariah	Zechariah	Zechariah
	Malachi	Malachi	Malachi
			(4 Maccabees)

of the conquest of the land in Joshua and concluding with the Babylonian destruction of Jerusalem in 586 BCE. The "Latter Prophets" ("Neviim Aharonim") are those books to which the names of individual prophets are attached. First come the "Major Prophets," so called because of their length, the books of Isaiah, Jeremiah, and Ezekiel, usually in that order, which is chronological. Then follows the "Book of the Twelve," or the Twelve Minor (that is, short) Prophets, from Hosea through Malachi. For the Minor Prophets we find considerable variation in the order of the books. In the arrangement used today, they are roughly in chronological order, with the eighth-century BCE prophets Hosea and Amos near the beginning of the collection, and those from the Persian period—Haggai, Zechariah, and Malachi—at its end.

The third part of the Hebrew Bible, the Writings, is the most fluid in terms of the order of the books. In general, it contains the books written latest and comprises a wide variety of genres. There are historical narratives, such as 1 and 2 Chronicles, Ezra-Nehemiah, Esther, and Ruth; wisdom literature, including Job, Proverbs, and Ecclesiastes; the books of Psalms, Song of Solomon, and Lamentations, three collections of poems in different genres; and the latest book in the Hebrew Bible, the book of Daniel.

The Writings also has one major division, the "Five Scrolls" (Megillot), selected or at least attached to the major festivals, as follows: The Song of Solomon is traditionally read at Passover; Ruth at the festival of Weeks (Pentecost), the time of the barley harvest (see pages 134–36), because of the chronology given in the book itself (see Ruth 3.2); Lamentations at the holy day of Tisha B'Ab, commemorating the destruction of the Temple on the ninth day of the month of Ab (see 2 Kings 25.8); Ecclesiastes at the festival of Booths

(Tabernacles), the fall harvest festival, at the end of the year, perhaps because it was thought to have been written by King Solomon at the end of his life; and at Purim, the book of Esther, which provides a narrative explanation of the origins of that festival. An alternate arrangement, found in some medieval manuscripts, is apparently based on the supposed dates of the books: First Ruth, traditionally ascribed to the prophet Samuel; then Song of Solomon and Ecclesiastes, both ascribed to King Solomon; then Lamentations, traditionally ascribed to the prophet Jeremiah; and finally Esther. The five scrolls were probably originally on one scroll, since they are the five shortest books of the Writings.

The Christian Canons of the Old Testament

Organization

The traditional Jewish order of the Law, the Prophets and the Writings, also found in the New Testament (see Lk 24.44), was altered in early Christian tradition to reflect the Christian belief that the prophets were primarily predicting the details of the life of Jesus of Nazareth. The resulting order has its own rationale. First come the books that are concerned with the past, the "historical" books, including—in addition to the Torah and the Former Prophets of Jewish tradition—the books of Ruth, Chronicles, Ezra, Nehemiah, and Esther, all in roughly chronological order. Then follow several poetical books that can be understood as dealing with the present: Psalms, for worship; and Job, Proverbs, Ecclesiastes, and Song of Solomon, having to do generally with the human condition. Finally, at the end of the Christian Old Testament, come the Prophets, in the same order as in the Hebrew Bible, so that the books of the prophets immediately precede the New Testament, whose events they were understood to predict. In fact, the last prophetic book, Malachi, refers to the coming of a "messenger to prepare the way (Mal 3.1) and of the return of

the prophet Elijah (4.5), both of which are referred to in the Gospels (see, for example, Mt 11.10–14). To the prophets in the Christian canon is added the book of Daniel because of his designation as a prophet in the New Testament (Mt 24.15; Mk 13.14), as is also the case in some first-century CE Jewish sources. (In the Hebrew Bible, however, the book of Daniel is among the Writings, principally because it was written after the contents of the second division of the canon, the Prophets, had already been determined.)

Thus, in Christian canons, some books are shifted from the Writings of the Jewish canon to the historical books (Ruth, 1 and 2 Chronicles, Ezra, Nehemiah, and Esther). Others occur in a different order; for example, the books of Proverbs, Ecclesiastes, and Song of Solomon are grouped together, presumably because they all identify King Solomon as their author.

Contents

Christianity arose in the Hellenized world of the eastern Mediterranean at the beginning of the Common Era, and all of the early Christian writers seem to have written in Greek. The sacred scriptures of Judaism that they quoted and adopted as their "Old Testament" (a term first used in the late second century CE) were thus the scriptures of the Greek-speaking Jewish community of the Diaspora, which included a number of books that had either been translated into or originally written in Greek. These books are Tobit, Judith, 1 and 2 Maccabees, the Wisdom of Solomon, Sirach, and Baruch (to which the Letter of Jeremiah is usually attached), as well as expanded versions of the books of Esther and Daniel.

All of these are authentic Jewish religious texts, but for a variety of reasons they were not included in the Hebrew Bible, and their status as canonical scripture for Christians was debated. The fifth-century CE biblical scholar Jerome, recognizing that they were not part of the Hebrew Bible, referred to these books as "apocrypha," a word that misleadingly means "hidden (books)";

the term "deuterocanonical," that is, belonging to a second canon, is also used.

With some minor variants (for example, the inclusion by most Orthodox churches of Psalm 151, the Prayer of Manasseh, 1 and 2 Esdras, and 3 Maccabees), this was the Old Testament of Christianity until the Reformation. In the sixteenth century, Martin Luther decided that only books in Hebrew (the "Hebrew truth") should be included in the Old Testament, and following his lead most Protestant churches no longer consider the apocryphal/deuterocanonical books as scripture. Modern study Bibles frequently include these books, however, often in a special section between the Old and New Testaments or after the New Testament.

BIBLIOGRAPHY

For an introduction to the development of the canon, see Marc Zvi Brettler, "The Canonization of the Bible," pp. 2072–77 in The Jewish Study Bible (ed. A. Berlin and M. Z. Brettler; New York: Oxford University Press, 2003); for a fuller treatment see D. N. Freedman, "Canon of the OT," pp. 130–36 in The Interpreter's Dictionary of the Bible: Supplementary Volume (ed. K. Crim; Nashville: Abingdon, 1976). On the order of the books, see Nahum Sarna, "Order of Books in the Hebrew Bible," pp. 98–100 in The Oxford Companion to the Bible (ed. B. M. Metzger and M. D. Coogan; New York: Oxford University Press, 1993).

CHRONOLOGY

DATES	PERIOD	CANAAN	SYRIA
ca. 3300–2000 BCE	**Early Bronze Age**	Under Egyptian influence and control	Under Mesopotamian influence and control
ca. 2300–2000			
ca. 2000–1550 ca. 1650–1550	**Middle Bronze Age**		
			Rise of Hittites
ca. 1550–1200	**Late Bronze Age**		Under Hittite influence and control
		Israelite Exodus from Egypt (?)	
ca. 1200–586	**Iron Age**	*Arrival of the Philistines in Canaan*	
		The Israelite judges (ca. 1150–1025)	

————Emergence of independent states————

ISRAEL

Saul (1025–1005)

David (1005–965)

Solomon (968–928)

ISRAEL	JUDAH
Jeroboam I (928–907)	Rehoboam (928–911)
Nadab (907–906)	Abijam (Abijah) (911–908)
Baasha (906–883)	Asa (908–867)
Elah (883–882)	
Zimri (882)	

Date ranges for rulers are for reigns, not life spans. Overlapping dates indicate coregencies. Vertical lines show genealogical connections. Important events are in italics.

EGYPT	MESOPOTAMIA	PERSIA	GREECE
Early Dynastic Period and Old Kingdom	Sumerian city-states		
First Intermediate Period			
Middle Kingdom Second Intermediate (Hyksos) Period	Rise of Babylon Hammurapi (1792–1750)		
New Kingdom Seti I (1294–1279)			
Rameses II (1279–1213)			
Merneptah (1213–1203)			

Invasion of Shishak (924)

DATES	PERIOD	ISRAEL	JUDAH	SYRIA
ca. 1200–586	**Iron Age**	Omri (882–871)		
		Ahab (871–852)	Jehoshaphat (870–846)	*Battle of Qarqar (853)*
		Ahaziah (852–851)		
		Jehoram (Joram) (851–842)	Jehoram (Joram) (851–843)	
		Jehu (842–814)	Ahaziah (Jehoahaz) (843–842)	
			Queen Athaliah (842–836)	
			Jehoash (Joash) (836–798)	
		Jehoahaz (817–800)		
		Jehoash (Joash) (800–784)	Amaziah (798–769)	
		Jeroboam II (788–747)	Azariah (Uzziah) (785–733)	
			Jotham (759–743)	
		Zechariah (747)		
		Shallum (747)		
		Menahem (747–737)	Ahaz (745/735–727/715)[*]	
		Pekahiah (737–735)		
		Pekah (735–732)		
		Hoshea (732–722)		
		Fall of Samaria (722)		
			Hezekiah (727/715–698/687)[*]	
			———*Invasion of Sennacherib (701)*———	
			Manasseh (698/687–642)[*]	
			Amon (641–640)	

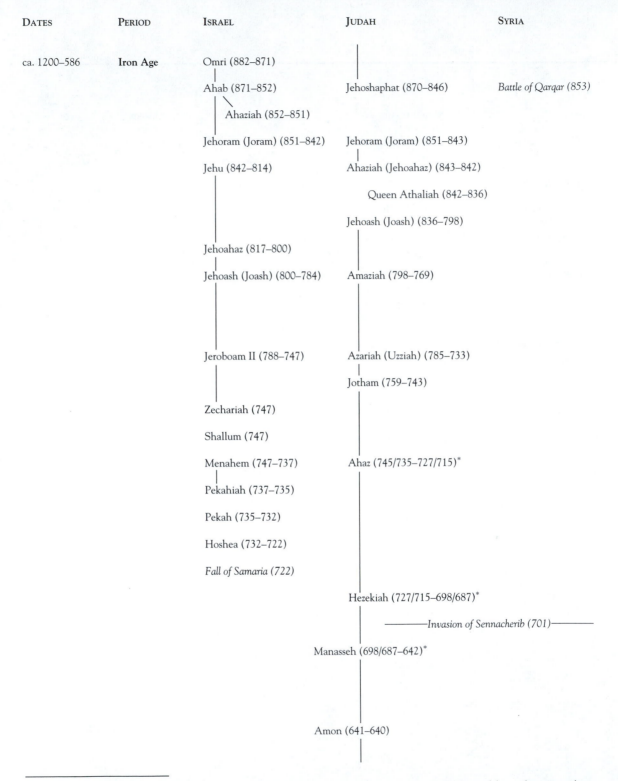

Date ranges for rulers are for reigns, not life spans. Overlapping dates indicate coregencies. Vertical lines show genealogical connections. Important events are in italics.

[*] The data are inconsistent for the reigns of Ahaz, Hezekiah, and Manasseh.

Kings of Assyria

Adad-nirari III (810–783)

Shalmaneser IV (783–773)

Ashur-dan III (773–755)

Ashur-nirari V (775–745)

Tiglath-pileser III (Pul) (745–727)

Shalmaneser V (727–722)

Sargon II (722–705)

Sennacherib (705–681)

Esarhaddon (681–669)

Ashurbanipal (669–627)

Psammetichus I (664–610)

DATES	PERIOD	JUDAH	SYRIA
ca. 1200–586	**Iron Age**	Josiah (640–609)	
ca. 600–539	**Neo-Babylonian Period**	Jehoahaz (Shallum) (609)	
		Jehoiachin (also called Jeconiah, Coniah, etc.) (597)	
		First Babylonian Siege of Jerusalem (597)	
		Zedekiah (Mattaniah) (597–586)	
		Babylonian Capture of Jerusalem (586)	
ca. 539–332	**Persian Period**		
		Jews return from Babylon (538)	
		Reconstruction of the Temple (520–515)	
		Mission of Ezra (458)	
		Governorship of Nehemiah (445–433)	
ca. 332–63 BCE	**Hellenistic Period**		

Date ranges for rulers are for reigns, not life spans. Overlapping dates indicate coregencies. Vertical lines show genealogical connections. Important events are in italics.

EGYPT	MESOPOTAMIA	PERSIA	GREECE

Kings of Babylon

Nabo-polassar (625–605)

Sack of Nineveh (612)

Neco II (610–595) Nebuchadrezzar II (605–562)

Amel-Marduk (Evil-merodach) (562–560)

Nergal-sharezer (Neriglissar) (560–556)

Labashi-Marduk (556) Cyrus II (the Great) 559–530

Nabonidus (556–539)

Psammetichus II (595–589) Belshazzar (Bel-shar-usur) (coregent 555–543)

Hophra (Apries) (589–570)

Persians capture Babylon (539)

Persians capture Egypt (525)

Cambyses (530–522)

Darius I (522–486)

Xerxes (Ahasuerus) (486–465)

Artaxerxes I (465–424)

Darius II (424–405)

Artaxerxes II (405–359)

Artaxerxes III (359–338)

Philip II (359–336)

Artaxerxes IV (338–336) Alexander the Great (336–323)

Darius III (336–330)

DATES	PERIOD	JUDEA
ca. 332–63 BCE	**Hellenistic Period**	<u>High Priests in Jerusalem</u>

Onias I (ca. 300 BCE)
|
Simon I (ca. 270)
|
Onias II (ca. 250)
|
Simon II (219–196)
|
Onias III (190–174)   Jason (175–172)

This family was replaced by a series of priests appointed by Seleucid rulers:

Menelaus (172–162)

Alcimus (162–159)

High priesthood vacant 159–152; then the Maccabees were appointed:

<u>The Maccabees and Their Successors</u>
<u>(the Hasmoneans)</u>

Mattathias (died 165 BCE)

John (killed 152)   Judas Maccabeus (165–160)   Eleazar
(killed 162)

Jonathan (160–142;
high priest 152–142)

Simon (high priest 142–135)
|
John Hyrcanus (135–104)

Aristobulus I (104–103)

Alexander Janneus (103–76)

ca. 63 BCE–330 CE	**Roman Period**	

Fall of Jerusalem and destruction of the Second Temple (70 CE)

Date ranges for rulers are for reigns, not life spans. Overlapping dates indicate coregencies. Vertical lines show genealogical connections. Important events are in italics.

SYRIA

Seleucus I Nicator (305–281)

Antiochus I Soter (281–261)

Antiochus II Theos (261–246)

Seleucus II Callinicus (246–225)

Seleucus III Soter (225–223)   Antiochus III ("the Great")
(223–187)

Seleucus IV Philopator (187–175)

Antiochus IV Epiphanes
(175–164)

Antiochus V Eupator (164–162)

Demetrius I Soter (162–150)

Alexander Epiphanes
(Balas) (150–145)

Demetrius II Nicator
(145–141 and 129–125)

Antiochus VI Epiphanes
(145–142)

Trypho (142–138)

Antiochus VII Sidetes (138–129)

EGYPT

Ptolemy I Soter (305–382)

Ptolemy II Philadelphus (285–246)

Ptolemy III Euergetes (246–221)

Ptolemy IV Philopator (221–204)

Ptolemy V Epiphanes (204–180)

Cleopatra I (180–176)

Ptolemy VI Philometor (180–145)

Cleopatra II (175–116)

Ptolemy VII Neos Philopator (145)

Ptolemy VIII Euergetes II (170–116)

GENERAL BIBLIOGRAPHY

Suggestions have been made for further reading at the end of each chapter. This bibliography consists of more general works. Many are reference books and are not intended to be read from cover to cover; others provide essential background for discerning the meanings of a text for its earlier and later audiences; still others are syntheses that have proven of lasting importance. Many of the items listed here include fuller bibliographies.

Annotated Bibles

A variety of translations and study Bibles exist. Some of the most recent are:

The HarperCollins Study Bible (ed. W. A. Meeks). New York: HarperCollins, 1993. (Uses the NRSV.)

The Jewish Study Bible (ed. A. Berlin and M. Z. Brettler). New York: Oxford University Press, 2004. (Uses the Jewish Publication Society translation.)

The New Interpreter's Study Bible (ed. Walter J. Harrelson). Nashville: Abingdon, 2003. (Uses the NRSV.)

The New Oxford Annotated Bible with the Apocryphal/ Deuterocanonical Books, 3d ed. (ed. M. D. Coogan). New York: Oxford University Press, 2001. (Uses the NRSV.)

Commentaries on the Bible

A number of valuable commentaries in series, in which one or more volumes are devoted to a single book of the Bible, include those in:

Abingdon Old Testament Commentaries (Abingdon)
Anchor Bible (Doubleday)
Berit Olam (Liturgical)
Continental Commentaries (Fortress)
Hermeneia (Fortress)
International Critical Commentary (T. & T. Clark)
Interpretation (Westminster John Knox)
JPS Bible Commentary (Jewish Publication Society)

JPS Torah Commentary (Jewish Publication Society)
New Cambridge Bible Commentary (Cambridge University Press)
Old Testament Library (Westminster John Knox)
Westminster Bible Companion (Westminster John Knox)
Word Biblical Commentary (Word)

Many works also cover all of the books of the Bible in one or a few volumes. Among the best are:

Anderson, B. W., ed. *The Books of the Bible*. 2 vols. New York: Scribner's, 1989.

Barton, J., and J. Muddiman, eds. *The Oxford Bible Commentary*. Oxford: Oxford University Press, 2001.

Brown, R. E., et al., eds. *The New Jerome Biblical Commentary*. Englewood Cliffs: Prentice-Hall, 1990.

Dunn, J. D. G., and J. W. Rogerson, eds. *Eerdmans Commentary on the Bible*. Grand Rapids: Eerdmans, 2003.

Keck, L. A., et al., eds. *The New Interpreter's Bible*. 12 vols. and index. Nashville: Abingdon, 1994–2004.

Mays, J. L., ed. *The HarperCollins Bible Commentary*. San Francisco: HarperSanFrancisco, 2000.

Newsom, C. A., and S. H. Ringe, eds. *The Women's Bible Commentary*, expanded ed. Louisville: Westminster John Knox, 1998.

History of Ancient Israel

Coogan, M. D., ed. *The Oxford History of the Biblical World*. New York: Oxford University Press, 1998 (pb ed. 2001).

Isserlin, B. S. J. *The Israelites*. Minneapolis: Fortress, 2001.

Soggin, J. A. *An Introduction to the History of Israel and Judah*. Philadelphia: Trinity, 1993.

Vaux, R. de *The Early History of Israel*. Philadelphia: Westminster, 1978.

Ancient Near Eastern and Other Nonbiblical Texts

Charlesworth, J. H., ed. *The Old Testament Pseudepigrapha*. 2 vols. New York: Doubleday, 1983, 1985.

Coogan, M. D., ed. and trans. *Stories from Ancient Canaan*. Philadelphia: Westminster, 1978.

Hallo, W. W., and K. L. Younger, eds. *The Context of Scripture*. 3 vols. Leiden: Brill, 1997–2002.

Parker, S. B., ed. *Ugaritic Narrative Poetry*. Atlanta: Scholars Press, 1997.

Pritchard, J. B., ed. *Ancient Near Eastern Texts Relating to the Old Testament*, 3d ed. Princeton, NJ: Princeton University Press, 1969.

Archaeology of Ancient Israel and the Near East

Ben-Tor, A., ed. *The Archaeology of Ancient Israel*. New Haven, CT: Yale University Press, 1991.

King, P. J., and L. E. Stager. *Life in Biblical Israel*. Louisville: Westminster John Knox, 2001.

Mazar, A. *Archaeology of the Land of the Bible: 10,000–586 B.C.E.* New York: Doubleday, 1990.

Meyers, E. M., ed. *The Oxford Encyclopedia of Archaeology in the Near East*. 5 vols. New York: Oxford University Press, 1997.

Stern, E. *Archaeology of the Land of the Bible, Vol. 2: The Assyrian, Babylonian, and Persian Periods (732–332 B.C.E.)*. New York: Doubleday, 2001.

———, ed. *The New Encyclopedia of Archaeological Excavations in the Holy Land*. 4 vols. New York: Simon and Schuster, 1993.

Theology of the Old Testament

Birch, B. C., et al. *A Theological Introduction to the Old Testament*. Nashville: Abingdon, 1999.

Childs, B. S. *Biblical Theology of the Old and New Testaments: Theological Reflection on the Christian Bible*. Minneapolis: Fortress, 1993.

Hanson, P. D. *The People Called: The Growth of Community in the Bible*. San Francisco: Harper & Row, 1986.

Levenson, J. D. *The Hebrew Bible, the Old Testament, and Historical Criticism: Jews and Christians in Biblical Studies*. Louisville: Westminster John Knox, 1993.

Rad, G. von *Old Testament Theology*. 2 vols. New York: Harper & Row, 1962–65.

History of the Religion of Ancient Israel

Albertz, R. *A History of Israelite Religion in the Old Testament Period*. 2 vols. Louisville: Westminster/John Knox, 1994.

Cross, F. M. *Canaanite Myth and Hebrew Epic: Essays in the History of the Religion of Israel*. Cambridge, MA: Harvard University Press, 1972.

———. *From Epic to Canon: History and Literature in Ancient Israel*. Baltimore: The Johns Hopkins University Press, 1998.

Eilberg-Schwartz, H. *The Savage in Judaism: An Anthropology of Israelite Religion and Ancient Judaism*. Bloomington: Indiana University Press, 1990.

Kaufmann, Y. *The Religion of Israel from Its Beginnings to the Babylonian Exile*. Trans. and abridged by M. Greenberg. University of Chicago, 1960.

Miller, P. D. *The Religion of Ancient Israel*. Louisville: Westminster John Knox, 2000.

Niditch, S. *Ancient Israelite Religion*. New York: Oxford University Press, 1997.

Smith, M. S. *The Memoirs of God: History, Memory, and the Experience of the Divine in Ancient Israel*. Minneapolis: Fortress, 2004.

Vaux, R. de. *Ancient Israel: Its Life and Institutions*. New York: McGraw-Hill, 1965.

Weber, M. *Ancient Judaism*. New York: Free Press, 1952.

Dictionaries and Encyclopedias

Achtemeier, P. J., ed. *The HarperCollins Bible Dictionary*. San Francisco: HarperSanFrancisco, 1996.

Coggins, R. J., and J. L. Houlden, eds. *A Dictionary of Biblical Interpretation*. Philadelphia: Trinity, 1990.

Freedman, D.N., ed. *The Anchor Bible Dictionary*. 6 vols. New York: Doubleday, 1992.

———. *Eerdmans Dictionary of the Bible*. Grand Rapids, MI: Eerdmans, 2000.

Hayes, J. H., ed. *Dictionary of Biblical Interpretation*. 2 vols. Nashville: Abingdon, 1999.

Metzger, B. M., and M. D. Coogan, eds. *The Oxford Companion to the Bible*. New York: Oxford University Press, 1993.

Meyers, C., ed. *Women in Scripture: A Dictionary of Named and Unnamed Women in the Hebrew Bible, the Apocryphal/Deuterocanonical Books, and the New Testament*. Boston: Houghton Mifflin, 2000.

Toorn, K. van der, et al., eds. *Dictionary of Deities and Demons in the Bible*, 2d ed. Leiden: Brill, 1999.

GLOSSARY

This glossary provides brief definitions of the "Important Terms" printed in boldface in the text and listed at the end of each chapter. In the glossary itself cross-references are also in bold. For information about other people, places, events, institutions, realities, and concepts in the Bible, students should consult a concordance and one of the dictionaries or encyclopedias listed in the Bibliography on page 559.

acrostic: A text in which the opening letters of successive lines form a word, phrase, or pattern. The acrostics in the Bible are poems in which the first letters of successive lines or stanzas are the letters of the Hebrew alphabet in order.

Ammonites: **Israel**'s neighbors east of the Jordan River. The Ammonites are the "sons of Ammon," who according to Genesis 19 was the offspring of Lot by one of his daughters. Their name is preserved in the modern city of Amman, Jordan.

angel: A word of Greek origin originally meaning messenger. In the Bible, these are supernatural beings sent by God to humans.

anthropomorphic (anthropomorphism): The attribution of human characteristics to a nonhuman being, usually a deity.

apocalyptic: A genre of literature in which details concerning the end-time are revealed by a heavenly messenger or **angel**.

Apocrypha: Jewish religious writings of the Hellenistic and Roman periods that are not considered part of the Bible by Jews and Protestants, but are part of the canons of Roman Catholic and Orthodox churches, who also call them the deuterocanonical books.

apodictic law: A type of law characterized by absolute or general commands or prohibitions, as in the **Ten Commandments.** It is often contrasted with **casuistic law.**

Aramaic: A language originating in ancient Syria that in the second half of the first millennium BCE became used widely throughout the Near East. Parts of the books of Daniel and Ezra are written in Aramaic.

ark of the covenant: The religious symbol of the premonarchic confederation of the twelve tribes of **Israel**, later installed in the **Temple** in Jerusalem by Solomon in the tenth century BCE. It formed the footstool for the **cherubim** throne on which **Yahweh** was thought to be invisibly seated.

avenger of blood: In Hebrew the *goel*, the closest male relative who is legally responsible for his kin, usually in matters relating to death or property. The word is often translated "redeemer."

Baal: The Canaanite storm-god, who in **Ugaritic myth** defeats Sea and Death. In the Bible, worship of Baal is condemned.

ban (Hebr. *herem*): Something dedicated to a deity and restricted for the deity's use, such as the spoils of war, including captured people.

Canaan: The name of the **Promised Land** before the Israelite conquest. In second-millennium BCE Egyptian sources, Canaan refers to the entire southern **Levant**. According to Genesis 9, the Canaanites, the inhabitants of the land of Canaan, were descendants of Noah's grandson Canaan.

casuistic law: Case law, often in the form of a conditional sentence, in which specific situations are addressed. It is often contrasted with **apodictic law.**

cherubim: Composite supernatural beings who function as guardians of the entrance to the garden of Eden in Genesis 3.24 and whose outstretched wings over the **ark of the covenant** supported the throne of **Yahweh.**

Chronicler: In modern scholarship, the term used for the author(s) of the books of Chronicles and, according to some scholars, of the books of Ezra and Nehemiah.

circumcision: The ceremonial removal of the foreskin of the penis. According to Genesis 17.9–14, it is the sign of the **covenant** between God and Abraham and is to be performed on all of Abraham's male descendants on the eighth day after birth.

cities of refuge: In the Bible, six cities set aside as places where someone accused of murder could find asylum until the case was decided.

city of David: Another name for Jerusalem, especially the ancient pre-Israelite city that King David captured and made his capital in the early tenth century BCE. In later tradition it is also used of Bethlehem, David's birthplace.

Code of Hammurapi: An ancient collection of laws issued by the Babylonian king Hammurapi (also spelled Hammurabi) in the mid-eighteenth century BCE.

confessions of Jeremiah: In modern scholarship, those parts of the book of Jeremiah in which he laments to God the difficulties he experienced as a **prophet.** The confessions are in Jeremiah 11.18–12.6, 15.10–21, 17.14–18, 18.18–23, and 20.7–18.

cosmology: An account of the origins of the world; in the ancient Near East cosmologies are usually creation **myth**s.

covenant (Hebr. *berît*): A term originally meaning "contract," used in the Bible of marriage, slavery, and international treaties and used metaphorically to characterize the relationship between God and the Israelites and between God and individuals such as Abraham, Aaron, and David.

Covenant Code: In modern scholarship, the collection of laws found in Exodus 20.22–23.19, identified as "the book of the covenant" (Ex 24.7). It is generally thought to be the oldest collection of laws in the Bible.

covenant lawsuit: A genre used by the **prophet**s in which **Israel** is put on trial by **Yahweh** for having violated its **covenant** with him.

D: The Deuteronomic source according to the **Documentary Hypothesis,** which is found almost exclusively in the book of Deuteronomy.

Davidic covenant: The **covenant** between **Yahweh** and David, which guaranteed the divine protection of the dynasty that David founded and of Jerusalem, its capital city.

Day of Atonement: A fall ritual of purification, described in Leviticus 16, later known as Yom Kippur. *See also* **scapegoat.**

day of the LORD: A genre used by the **prophet**s, describing **Yahweh**'s fighting against his enemies. In **apocalyptic** literature it is used of the final battle between good and evil.

Dead Sea: A large body of water in the Rift Valley into which the Jordan River flows. Due to evaporation it has a high mineral content and no life is found in it, hence its name.

Dead Sea Scrolls: Ancient manuscripts found in caves on the western side of the Dead Sea beginning in 1948; some are the oldest surviving manuscripts of the books of the Bible, dating as early as the third century BCE.

Decalogue: A word of Greek origin that means "ten words"; another name for the **Ten Commandments.**

deuterocanonical books: *See* **Apocrypha**.

Deuteronomic Code: According to modern scholars, the core of the book of Deuteronomy in chapters 12–26, consisting of ancient laws that differ in many details from those found in the books of Exodus and Leviticus.

Deuteronomistic History: According to modern scholars, the books of Joshua, Judges, 1 and 2 Samuel, and 1 and 2 Kings, which form a narrative history of **Israel** in the **Promised Land.** It was produced in several editions from the late eighth to the sixth centuries BCE by the Deuteronomistic Historians, who were informed by the principles of the book of Deuteronomy.

Diaspora: Literally, scattering or dispersion, used to refer to exiles from **Judah** to Babylonia in the early sixth century BCE, and subsequently for any Jews living outside of **Israel.**

divination: The practice of interpreting ordinary phenomena, such as the flight of birds and the inner organs of animals, as divine revelation.

divine council: The assembly of gods, over which the high god presides. In the Bible **Yahweh** is described as the head of the divine council, and **prophet**s claim to have witnessed or participated in its meetings.

Documentary Hypothesis: The theory classically formulated by Julius **Wellhausen** in 1878, which explains the repetitions and inconsistencies in the first five books of the Bible, the **Pentateuch,** as the result of originally independent sources or documents having been combined over several centuries. The principal hypothetical sources are **J, E, D,** and **P.**

E: The Elohist source according to the **Documentary Hypothesis,** found in the books of Genesis through Numbers.

El: The name of the creator deity in **Ugaritic** texts, who presides over the divine council. It is also used of **Yahweh.**

elohim: The Hebrew word for god or gods, which, although plural in form, is often used as a title for **Yahweh** and is translated "God."

endogamy: The custom of marrying within one's ethic or religious group.

Enkidu: In the epic of *Gilgamesh*, the wild man created by the gods to distract Gilgamesh from his antisocial activities. Gilgamesh and Enkidu became friends, and Enkidu's death motivated Gilgamesh to seek immortality.

Enuma elish: Also called the "Babylonian Creation Epic," this is a work on seven tablets in praise of the patron god of Babylon, **Marduk**. It describes how **Marduk** defeated the primeval sea-goddess **Tiamat** and then created the world and humans. Its title is its opening words, which mean "when above."

Essenes: A Jewish sect of the second and first centuries BCE and the first century CE that produced the **Dead Sea Scrolls.**

etiology: A narrative that explains the origin of a custom, ritual, geographical feature, name, or other phenomenon.

Fertile Crescent: The arable area of land from southern **Mesopotamia** northward and then westward and southward through the **Levant.**

First Isaiah: In modern scholarship, the parts of Isaiah 1–39 that are associated with the eighth-century BCE **prophet** Isaiah.

First Zechariah: In modern scholarship, chapters 1–8 of the book of Zechariah, dated in substance to the late sixth century BCE.

form criticism: The study of relatively short literary units in literature and in folklore with regard to their forms or genres, their original settings (German *Sitz im Leben*), and their social, religious, and political functions. It was developed by Herman **Gunkel.**

Former Prophets: In Jewish tradition, the first division of the **Prophets,** comprising the books of Joshua, Judges, 1 and 2 Samuel, and 1 and 2 Kings.

genealogy: A family history in the form of a list of descendants.

Gilgamesh/*Gilgamesh*: The hero of the Mesopotamian epic named for him, who with **Enkidu** travels widely and ultimately meets **Utnapishtim.**

golden calf: The statue of a calf that the Israelites worshiped at Mount **Sinai** according to Exodus 32, and also similar statues worshiped at the shrines of Bethel and Dan in the **northern kingdom of Israel.**

Gunkel, Hermann (1862–1932): The German scholar whose commentaries on Genesis and Psalms applied **form criticism** to the Bible.

Hanukkah: The festival commemorating the rededication of the Temple in Jerusalem in 164 BCE, which had been profaned by the Seleucid king Antiochus IV Epiphanes.

Hebrew: The language of ancient and modern Israel. In the Bible the term is usually used of individuals or groups living outside their homeland.

Hellenization: The transformation of Near Eastern culture and society by Greek ideas, especially after the conquest of the Near East by Alexander the Great in the late fourth century BCE.

Hezekiah's Tunnel: A 1700-ft (500-m) long tunnel under the **city of David,** constructed during the reign of King Hezekiah of **Judah** in the late eighth century BCE. Its function was to divert the waters flowing from the Gihon Spring to a location within the city wall.

Holiness Code: In modern scholarship, chapters 17–26 of the book of Leviticus, generally recognized as an originally independent source whose principal theme is the holiness of **Yahweh** and of his people.

Horeb: The name used in **E** and **D** for Mount **Sinai.**

Immanuel: The child whose birth and early life were signs from God to Ahaz, king of **Judah,** during the Syro-Ephraimite War (Isa 7.14). He was probably the child of the **prophet** Isaiah and his wife, who was also a **prophet.**

Isaiah: *See* **First Isaiah; Second Isaiah; Third Isaiah.**

Isaiah Apocalypse: In modern scholarship, chapters 24–27 of the book of Isaiah, an early example of **apocalyptic** literature perhaps dating to the fifth century BCE.

Israel: This name is used in several senses. First, it is the new name given to the patriarch Jacob in Genesis 32.28; Jacob's twelve sons then become the ancestors of the tribes of **Israel.** Second, it designates the people and later the geopolitical entity formed from the twelve tribes. Third, it is used as the name of the **northern kingdom of Israel**, as opposed to the **southern kingdom of Judah.**

J: The Yahwist (or Jahwist) source according to the **Documentary Hypothesis**, found in the books of Genesis through Numbers.

Judah: The name of one of Jacob's sons, the ancestor of the tribe of Judah. This tribe dominated southern **Israel** and became the **southern kingdom of Judah.** Later the same region was called Judea.

judge: A ruler or a military leader, as well as someone who presided over legal hearings.

Kirta: The hero of the **Ugaritic** epic that is named for him; the epic has many connections with biblical literature. Also called "Keret."

Latter Prophets: In Jewish tradition, the second part of the **Prophets,** comprising the books of Isaiah, Jeremiah, and Ezekiel and the book of the Twelve (**Minor Prophets**).

Levant: A term used for the western part of the Near East, comprising the modern countries of Syria, Lebanon, Israel, Palestine, and Jordan.

Levites: The priestly tribe, named for Jacob's son Levi, whose primary responsibility was ritual.

Major Prophets: In modern scholarship, the books of Isaiah, Jeremiah, and Ezekiel, so called because of their relative length compared to the shorter books of the **Minor Prophets**. In Christian tradition, the books of Lamentations and Daniel have often been included under this heading.

manna: The divinely given "bread from heaven" (Ex 16.4) that fed the Israelites in the wilderness after their escape from Egypt.

Marduk: The chief god of Babylon, the storm-god who defeated **Tiamat**, as recounted in *Enuma elish*.

Masoretic Text: The traditional medieval text of the Hebrew Bible.

Megiddo: A major city in northern **Israel** that because of its strategic location was the site of many battles. In **apocalyptic** literature it can be called Armageddon and is the site of the final battle between the forces of good and evil.

Mesha Stela: An inscribed monument erected by the **Moabite** king Mesha in the mid-ninth century BCE celebrating his victory over the Israelites.

Mesopotamia: A word of Greek origin meaning "(the land) in the middle of the rivers." It refers to the fertile floodplain between the Tigris and the Euphrates rivers and comprises much of modern Iraq and northern Syria.

messiah: Derived from the Hebrew word *mashiah*, meaning "anointed one," this term is used in the Hebrew Bible to refer to past and present kings and priests who had been anointed. In later Jewish and Christian traditions it is used of a future leader to be sent by God.

Midian: A region in northwestern Arabia where Mount **Sinai** may be located.

Minor Prophets: In modern scholarship, the twelve shorter prophetic books, from Hosea through Malachi.

Moabites: Israel's neighbors east of the Dead Sea. The Moabites are the "sons of Moab," who according to Genesis 19 was the offspring of Lot by one of his daughters.

myth: A traditional narrative concerning the remote past in which gods and goddess are often principal characters.

northern kingdom of Israel: The territory that split from **Judah** after the death of Solomon in the late tenth century BCE and was an independent kingdom with its capital in **Samaria** until the Assyrians conquered it in 722 BCE.

oracle against the nations: A genre used by the **prophets** and in **apocalyptic** literature to describe **Yahweh**'s judgment on foreign nations.

P: The Priestly source according to the **Documentary Hypothesis**, found in the books of Genesis through Numbers and at the end of the book of Deuteronomy.

parallelism: A feature of biblical and other ancient Near Eastern poetry, in which one phrase or line is followed by another that is synonymous, contrasting, or climactic.

Passover: The spring festival commemorating the Exodus from Egypt.

Pentateuch: A word of Greek origin, meaning "five books," used by modern scholars to refer to the first five books of the Bible. *See also* **Torah.**

Philistines: One group of the **Sea Peoples**. In the late second millennium BCE, having failed to conquer the Egyptians, they settled on the southeast coast of the Mediterranean where they vied with **Israel** for the control of **Canaan**. The term "Palestine" is derived from their name.

Promised Land: The land promised by God to Abraham and his descendants. Its boundaries vary, but it corresponds roughly to the territory comprising modern Israel and Palestine.

prophet: A word of Greek origin meaning "spokesperson." The prophets were believed to be recipients of direct communications from God. Sayings of and stories about many of the prophets are found in the part of the Bible known as the **Prophets**.

prophetic gesture: The use or interpretation by a **prophet** of an ordinary phenomenon as having symbolic meaning.

Prophets: In Jewish tradition the second of three parts of the Hebrew Bible, comprising the books of Joshua to 2 Kings and Isaiah to Malachi. *See also* **Former Prophets; Latter Prophets; Major Prophets; Minor Prophets; Torah; Writings.**

proverb: A short pithy saying, often in poetry.

Purim: The festival commemorating the deliverance of the Jews by Esther and Mordecai from the plot of the Persian official Haman.

redaction criticism: In modern scholarship, the study of the processes of redacting or editing, by which such larger works as the Pentateuch and the book of Isaiah were given their final forms.

Reed Sea: The body of water that the Israelites crossed in their Exodus from Egypt. Although later identified as the Red Sea, it is more likely one of several smaller bodies of water or wetlands east of the Nile Delta.

Ritual Decalogue: In modern scholarship, the replacement copy of the **Ten Commandments** that Moses received from God after he had broken the first set because of his anger at the golden calf incident. Found in Exodus 34.10–26, it is exclusively concerned with worship, hence its name.

royal ideology: In modern scholarship, the term for the complex of ideas associated with the Davidic monarchy, including the **Davidic covenant.**

sabbath: The day of rest, the seventh day of the week. The term can also be used for longer periods of time, as in a "sabbatical year."

sacrifice: The ritual offering of food or incense to a deity.

Samaria: The capital of the **northern kingdom of Israel** from the early ninth century to 722 BCE, when it fell to the Assyrians. Subsequently Samaria was used as the name of the region in which the city was located.

scapegoat: A goat "for Azazel" (Lev 16.10), probably originally a desert demon, to which the sins of the community are symbolically transferred on the **Day of Atonement.**

Sea Peoples: A coalition of peoples who in the late second millennium BCE moved from their homeland in the Aegean Sea through the eastern Mediterranean. One of the Sea Peoples was the **Philistines.**

Second Isaiah: In modern scholarship, chapters 40–55 of the book of Isaiah, dated to the mid-sixth century BCE. Also called Deutero-Isaiah.

Second Temple: The Temple completed in 515 BCE to replace the **Temple of Solomon**, which had been destroyed by the Babylonians in 586.

Second Zechariah: In modern scholarship, chapters 9–14 of the book of Zechariah, probably dated to the fifth century BCE. Also called Deutero-Zechariah.

Septuagint: The ancient Greek translation of the Hebrew scriptures, made beginning in the third century BCE.

servant songs: In **Second Isaiah**, a group of four poems that speak of a servant of **Yahweh**. They are Isaiah 42.1–4, 49.1–6, 50.4–11, and 52.13–53.12.

Sheol: The Hebrew term for the underworld, where persons go at death.

Shema: In Jewish tradition, three excerpts from the books of Deuteronomy and Numbers that are recited daily and, written on small scrolls, attached to the body during prayer and to the door of a house. The term means "Hear," from the opening word of Deuteronomy 6.4.

Siloam Tunnel: *See* **Hezekiah's Tunnel.**

Sinai: The mountain on which God revealed himself to Moses and made the **covenant** with **Israel.** Its location is disputed.

son of man: A phrase that in the Hebrew Bible means human being. In Daniel 7.13 it is used of someone who is given universal rule; the identity of this person is disputed.

southern kingdom of Judah: The kingdom that after the death of Solomon in the late tenth century BCE continued to be ruled by the Davidic dynasty with its capital in Jerusalem, until it was captured by the Babylonians in 586 BCE. *See also* **Judah.**

succession narrative: In modern scholarship, the originally independent source incorporated into the **Deuteronomistic History** that relates how Solomon eventually succeeded David on the throne. It is found in 2 Samuel 9–20 and 1 Kings 1–2. Also called the "Court History of David."

suzerainty treaty: In modern scholarship, a binding agreement between a king or suzerain and a lesser king, the suzerain's vassal. Elements of suzerainty treaties are used by the biblical writers in their presentation of the **covenant** between God and **Israel.**

synagogue: A word of Greek origin meaning "gathering together," used of religious assemblies of Jews and the buildings in which such assemblies took place.

Syro-Ephraimite War: The attack on **Judah** and Jerusalem by the **northern kingdom of Israel** and Aram in 734 BCE, in an attempt to force the king of **Judah**, Ahaz, to join an anti-Assyrian alliance.

tabernacle: The movable shrine that served as the Israelites' place of worship after the Exodus from Egypt, described in detail in Exodus 26. Also called the "tent of meeting."

tell: An artificial mound formed from the stratified accumulated debris of successive human occupations.

Temple of Solomon: The Temple in Jerusalem built by King Solomon in the mid-tenth century and destroyed by the Babylonians in 586 BCE. It is also known as the First Temple.

Ten Commandments: The text of the contract or **covenant** between God and **Israel** made on Mount **Sinai.** *See also* **Decalogue.**

Tetragrammaton: A word of Greek origin meaning "four letters," referring to the four consonants (*yhwh*) of the name of the God of **Israel, Yahweh.**

theodicy: A word of Greek origin meaning "divine justice," used with reference to literature that deals with the problem of human suffering, especially the suffering of the innocent.

theophany: A word of Greek origin meaning the appearance of a god, used by modern scholars to refer to the appearance of a deity to humans, usually with appropriate manifestations of divine power.

Third Isaiah: In modern scholarship, chapters 56–66 of the book of Isaiah, dating to the late sixth or early fifth century BCE. Also called Trito-Isaiah.

Tiamat: The goddess of the primeval salt water who in *Enuma elish* is defeated by the storm-god **Marduk.**

Torah/*torah*: In Jewish tradition, the Torah is the first of three parts of the Hebrew Bible, comprising the five books of Moses from Genesis to Deuteronomy. The word *torah* literally means "teaching" or "instruction" and is often translated "law." *See also* **Prophets; Writings.**

tradition history: In modern scholarship, the study of the stages in the development of a genre, theme, or concept prior to its incorporation into the biblical text.

tree of life: The tree in the **garden of Eden** whose fruit provided immortality.

tree of the knowledge of good and evil: The tree in the **garden of Eden** whose fruit was forbidden.

Ugaritic: A Semitic language closely related to Hebrew used in second-millennium BCE texts from the site of Ugarit on the Mediterranean coast of Syria. The Ugaritic texts include a number of **myth**s and epics that shed light on Canaanite religion.

United Monarchy: During the tenth century BCE, the ten northern tribes of **Israel** and the southern tribe of **Judah** were united under the rule of David and his son Solomon, both of whom are called "king of **Israel.**"

When Solomon died in 928 BCE, the united kingdom of **Israel** was split into the **northern kingdom of Israel** and the **southern kingdom of Judah**.

Utnapishtim: In the *Gilgamesh* epic, the hero of the story of the Flood.

Wellhausen, Julius (1844–1918): A German scholar who wrote A *History of Israel* (1878), which is the classic formulation of the **Documentary Hypothesis.**

wisdom literature: A type of writing whose focus is human existence and often its relationship to the divine. It employs a wide variety of forms, such as proverbs, dialogues, and fables. Wisdom literature was used widely in the ancient Near East and is found throughout the Bible, especially in the books of Job, Proverbs, Ecclesiastes, Sirach, and the Wisdom of Solomon.

Woman Wisdom: The depiction of the quality of wisdom as a goddess who is the companion of **Yahweh.**

Writings: In Jewish tradition, the third of three parts of the Hebrew Bible, comprising the books of Psalms, Proverbs, Job, Song of Solomon, Ruth, Lamentations, Ecclesiastes, Esther, Daniel, Ezra, Nehemiah, and 1 and 2 Chronicles. *See also* **Prophets; Torah.**

Yahweh: The personal name of the God of **Israel.** *See also* **Tetragrammaton.**

Zion: A name of Jerusalem, used especially in poetic texts.

INDEX

Slavery, in covenant code, 124
Slingers, 238
Snakes, 16, 17, 165
Social justice
    covenant lawsuit and, 323, 335
    demand for, 315, 318
    in law codes, 151
    in Proverbs, 474
    vs ritual observance, 319, 428
Socrates, 368
Soil, 31–33
Solomon
    in Chronicles, 453–54
    dating of reign of, 270
    in later tradition, 270
    two names of, 254
    wealth of, 268–69
Son of man, 541
Song of Deborah, 216
Song of Hannah, 232
Song of Miriam (Song of the Sea), 87, 96
Song of Solomon, 270, 320, 495–97, 546–47, 548
Song of the Three Jews, 459, 539
Song of the Vineyard, 335
Songs of Ascent, 375, 457
Songs of Thanksgiving, 464, 526
Songs of Trust, 464
Sons of God, 34
Soul, 495, 520–21
Southern kingdom. See Judah
Spies, episode of in Numbers, 161–64
Stoning, 149
Strangers. See Outsiders
Succession, 243, 292
Succession Narrative, 249–51
    in Chronicles, 451
    conclusion of, 267
    Susanna, 539–40
Suzerainty treaty, 107–9
    Assyrian, 181–83
    form of, in biblical covenants, 110, 111–13
    Hittite, 110, 111–12
Synagogues, 386
Synonymous parallelism, 324
Syria, kings of, 503
Syro-Ephraimite War, 309, 336

Tabernacle, 128–29
Table of Nations, 36–37
Taboos, 143
Tattenai, 420–21
Taxation, 140, 290
Tell, 64
Tell Tayinat, 281
Temple of Jerusalem, 257, 271, 273
    dedication of, 268
    destruction of, by Babylonians, 365
    details of, 276–77
    rebuilding of, by Cyrus, 404
    rivalries concerning, 420–21
Temple Sermon, 373
Ten Commandments. See also Decalogue
    different versions of, 114–15
    status and numbering of, 118
    values expressed in, 116–17

Terah, 78
Teraphim, 80, 239
Tetragrammaton, 13, 89
Theodicy
    problem of, in Ecclesiastes, 492–93
    problem of, in Job, 479, 484–88
    resurrection as solution to, 511
    theological perspective of, 336, 367, 407
Theophany, 86, 388
Throne names, 362
Tiamat, 5, 9, 101, 412, 487
Tiglath-pileser III, 307, 309, 336–37
Time, sacred, 146, 147
Timeline, of ancient world, 55, 550–57
Tithes, 140
Tobit, Book of, 533, 535–36, 546, 548
Tombs, 494, 495
Torah, 545. See also Pentateuch
    doublets in, 21
    formation of, in exile, 406
    meanings of, 184
Torah psalms, 466
Tower of Babel, 35, 283
Trade, 271, 500
Tradition history, 64
Treaties
    blessings and curses in, 110, 181, 182, 313
    in Decalogue, 115–16
    father-son metaphor in, 113
    form of, 109–13
    with Hiram of Tyre, 254–55
    imitative rituals in, 114
    parity, 107–9
    suzerainty, 107–13, 181
Tree of knowledge, 14, 16–17
Tree of life, 14, 475
Trial by ordeal, 155
Tribal structure, 222
Tricksters, 214
Tyre
    oracles against, 313, 394–95
    treaties with, 254–55

Ugaritic texts, 74, 221
United Monarchy, 248, 256
Ur of the Chaldeans, 79–80
Urim and Thummim, 129–30, 244, 298
Utnapishtim, 16, 40–41

Vanity of vanities, 492
Vestments, 129–30, 298
Virginity, 124, 337
Visions
    of Amos, 311
    in apocalyptic literature, 437
    of Ezekiel, 388–90, 393–94, 397–99
    of Jeremiah, 368–69
    of Zechariah, 425–27
Vows, 156

Wailing Wall, 257
War
    ark of the covenant role in, 128, 207
    as holy war, 177, 206–7
Waters of Meribah, 164–65

Wellhausen, Julius, 23
Wette, Wilhelm de, 353
Widows, 532
Wisdom literature
    in the Bible, 471–72, 547
    as international phenomenon, 468–69
Wisdom of Solomon, 270, 471–72, 518–20, 546, 548
Wisdom psalms, 465–66
Woman Wisdom, 475, 516, 521
Women
    barren, who conceive, 77, 232, 239
    the dangerous bride, 535
    in Deuteronomic Code, 180
    in Exodus narrative, 95–96
    familial role of, 241, 243
    foreign, 202, 219, 268, 269, 474–75
    independent action by, 239
    influential, 259
    and inheritance, 156, 489
    as judges, 216–17
    as matriarchs, 77
    and menstruation, 143, 144, 150
    and music, 467
    negative image of, 517–18
    as property, 150, 241
    as prophets, 301–2
    as queens and queen mothers, 295–97
    royal, 254, 258–59
    subordinate status of, 149–50
    and virginity, 124
    as widows, 532
Word, creative power of, 9
Words of Ahiqar, 470–71
Worship
    centralization of, 140, 260, 274, 283
    in covenant code, 123
    exclusive, of Yahweh, 175
    overview of, 244–46
    use of psalms in, 459–60
Wrestling with God, 72–73
Writings, 456, 471, 545–48

Yahweh, 13. See also God
    "glory of," 393–94
    as "lord of history," 305, 335–36, 342
    as parent, 322
    sacredness of name, 89
    servant of, 411–12
    as violent spouse, 391
    wife of, 321, 475
Yom Kippur, 144–45

Zechariah, 420, 423, 424
Zechariah, Book of, 310, 424, 546–47
    and apocalyptic literature, 437
    First, 424–27
    Second, 439–40
Zephaniah, Book of, 355–57, 546–47
Zerubbabel, 415, 420–21
Zion
    Jerusalem as, 263
    psalms of, 279
    in royal ideology, 278
Zion hymns, 465